PROPORTIONALITY AND THE RULE OF LAW

Rights, Justification, Reasoning

To speak of human rights in the twenty-first century is to speak of proportionality. Proportionality has been received into the constitutional doctrine of courts in continental Europe, the United Kingdom, Canada, New Zealand, Israel, South Africa, and the United States, as well as the jurisprudence of treaty-based legal systems such as the European Convention on Human Rights.

Proportionality provides a common analytical framework for resolving the great moral and political questions confronting political communities. But behind the singular appeal to proportionality lurks a range of different understandings. This volume brings together many of the world's leading constitutional theorists – proponents and critics of proportionality – to debate the merits of proportionality, the nature of rights, the practice of judicial review, and moral and legal reasoning. Their essays provide important new perspectives on this leading doctrine in human rights law.

Grant Huscroft is Professor in the Faculty of Law at Western University in London, Canada, where he is a founding member of the Public Law and Legal Philosophy Research Group. His research focuses on constitutional rights and judicial review and has been published in Canada, the United States, the United Kingdom, New Zealand, and Australia. He is a coauthor of the treatise *The New Zealand Bill of Rights* (2003) and has edited and coedited seven collections of essays.

Bradley W. Miller is Associate Professor in the Faculty of Law at Western University in London, Canada, where he is a founding member of the Public Law and Legal Philosophy Research Group. His research focuses on theories of constitutional interpretation and the place of moral reasoning in legal reasoning. He has been published in the *American Journal of Jurisprudence*, the *Canadian Journal of Law and Jurisprudence*, and *Constitutional Commentary*.

Grégoire Webber is Associate Professor of Law at the London School of Economics and Political Science. His research focuses on rights, public law, and the philosophy of law and has been published in the *Oxford Journal of Legal Studies*, the *Law Quarterly Review*, and the *Modern Law Review*. He is the author of *The Negotiable Constitution: On the Limitation of Rights* (2009), published by Cambridge University Press.

Proportionality and the Rule of Law

Rights, Justification, Reasoning

Edited by

GRANT HUSCROFT
Western University, Canada

BRADLEY W. MILLER
Western University, Canada

GRÉGOIRE WEBBER
London School of Economics

CAMBRIDGE
UNIVERSITY PRESS

CAMBRIDGE
UNIVERSITY PRESS

32 Avenue of the Americas, New York NY 10013-2473, USA

Cambridge University Press is part of the University of Cambridge.

It furthers the University's mission by disseminating knowledge in the pursuit of
education, learning and research at the highest international levels of excellence.

www.cambridge.org
Information on this title: www.cambridge.org/9781107647954

© Cambridge University Press 2014

First published 2014
First paperback edition 2015

A catalogue record for this publication is available from the British Library

Library of Congress Cataloguing in Publication data
Proportionality and the rule of law : Rights, Justification, Reasoning / [edited by] Grant Huscroft,
Bradley W. Miller, Grégoire Webber.
    pages cm
Includes bibliographical references and index.
ISBN 978-1-107-06407-2 (hardback)
1. Proportionality in law.   2. Human rights.   3. Rule of law.   I. Huscroft, Grant, editor
of compilation.   II. Miller, Bradley W. (Bradley Wayne), 1968– editor of compilation.
III. Webber, Grégoire C. N. (Grégoire Charles N.) editor of compilation.
K247.P79   2014
340′.11–dc23   2013044707

ISBN 978-1-107-06407-2 Hardback
ISBN 978-1-107-64795-4 Paperback

Contents

Contributors

T.R.S. Allan, Professor of Jurisprudence and Public Law, University of Cambridge

Mark Antaki, Associate Professor of Law, McGill University

David Dyzenhaus, Professor of Law and Philosophy and Albert Abel Chair, University of Toronto

Richard Ekins, Tutorial Fellow in Law, St John's College, University of Oxford

Timothy Endicott, Professor of Legal Philosophy and Dean of the Faculty of Law, University of Oxford

Stephen Gardbaum, MacArthur Foundation Professor of International Justice and Human Rights, UCLA School of Law

Grant Huscroft, Professor of Law, Western University

Mattias Kumm, Inge Rennert Professor of Law, New York University; Managing Head, Rule of Law Center, WZB, Berlin

Martin Luterán, Rector, Collegium of Anton Neuwirth

Bradley W. Miller, Associate Professor of Law, Western University

Kai Möller, Associate Professor of Law, London School of Economics and Political Science

George Pavlakos, Professor of Globalization and Legal Theory, University of Antwerp and University of Glasgow

Iddo Porat, Senior Lecturer, Academic Center of Law and Business

Frederick Schauer, David and Mary Harrison Distinguished Professor of Law, University of Virginia

Alec D. Walen, Associate Professor of Law and Philosophy and Criminal Justice, Rutgers University

Grégoire Webber, Associate Professor of Law, London School of Economics and Political Science

Alison L. Young, Senior Law Tutor, Hertford College, University of Oxford

Preface

This volume originates from a colloquium on proportionality hosted by the Public Law and Legal Philosophy Research Group at the Faculty of Law at the University of Western Ontario. The colloquium's participants were drawn from legal jurisdictions throughout the common law and civil law worlds, reflecting proportionality's international reach. Following the colloquium, the papers were revised for publication and additional papers were commissioned to fill in some topical and jurisdictional gaps. The resulting collection provides a comprehensive analysis and critique of proportionality from the perspectives of philosophy, constitutional theory, and law.

We are grateful to the University of Western Ontario, which provided the financial support required to stage the colloquium, and to all of the contributors. It is a privilege to work and learn together with scholars of such distinction.

Bradley W. Miller was the Ann and Herbert W. Vaughan Visiting Fellow in the James Madison Program in American Ideals and Institutions at Princeton University during the 2012–2013 academic year. He acknowledges the outstanding support provided by the Madison Program and its Fellows.

We want to thank Western Law JD students Jeff Claydon, Brandon Duewel, and Danilo Popadic (JD 2013) and Tori Crawford (JD 2014) for the research and editorial assistance that helped us complete the volume.

This is the third collection of essays on constitutional law and legal theory that the Public Law and Legal Philosophy group has published with Cambridge University Press, the first two being *Expounding the Constitution: Essays in Constitutional Theory* (2008) and *The Challenge of Originalism: Theories of Interpretation* (2011). We thank Adrian Pereira and his editorial team for their work on this volume, and our publisher John Berger, who has been an enthusiastic supporter of all three books.

Grant Huscroft
Bradley W. Miller
Grégoire Webber

1 Introduction

Grant Huscroft, Bradley W. Miller, and Grégoire Webber

I. THE RISE OF PROPORTIONALITY

To speak of human rights is to speak of proportionality. It is no exaggeration to claim that proportionality has overtaken rights as the orienting idea in contemporary human rights law and scholarship. Proportionality has been received into the constitutional doctrine of courts in continental Europe, the United Kingdom, Canada, New Zealand, Israel, and South Africa, as well as the jurisprudence of treaty-based legal systems such as the European Court of Human Rights, giving rise to claims of a global model,[1] a received approach,[2] or simply the best-practice standard of rights adjudication.[3] Even in the United States, which is widely understood to have formally rejected proportionality, some argue that the various levels of scrutiny adopted by the U.S. Supreme Court are analogous to the standard questions posed by proportionality.[4] As proportionality scholars are well aware, some of the early literature on balancing and rights is American, with special reference to the First Amendment.[5]

---

[1] See Kai Möller, *The Global Model of Constitutional Rights* (2012).
[2] See Grégoire Webber, *The Negotiable Constitution: On the Limitation of Rights* (2009).
[3] See Jud Mathews and Alec Stone Sweet, "All Things in Proportion? American Rights Review and the Problem of Balancing," 60 Emory L.J. 797 at 808 (2011). See further Mattias Klatt and Moritz Meister *The Constitutional Structure of Proportionality* (2012) 1: "there is a firm consensus that the proportionality test plays an indispensable role in constitutional rights reasoning" (footnote omitted).
[4] See, e.g., Paul Yowell, "Proportionality in United States Constitutional Law" in Liora Lazarus, Christopher McCrudden, and Nigel Bowles (eds.), *Reasoning Rights: Comparative Judicial Engagement* (2013).
[5] See, e.g., Alexander Meiklejohn, "The First Amendment Is an Absolute," [1961] Supreme Court Rev. 245; Laurent B. Frantz, "The First Amendment in the Balance," 71 Yale L.J. 1424 (1962); and T. Alexander Aleinikoff, "Constitutional Law in the Age of Balancing," 96 Yale L.J. 943 (1987) [Aleinikoff, "Age of Balancing"].

Notwithstanding proportionality's popularity, there is no consensus on its methodology. Neither does the use of a proportionality doctrine guarantee consensus on substantive rights questions. What the principle of proportionality does promise is a common analytical framework, the significance of which is not in its ubiquity, but in how its structure influences (some would say controls) how courts reason to conclusions in many of the great moral and political controversies confronting political communities. As a framework, proportionality analysis is superficially straightforward, setting out four questions in evaluating whether the limitation of a right is justifiable. A serviceable – but by no means canonical – formulation follows:

1. Does the legislation (or other government action) establishing the right's limitation pursue a legitimate objective of sufficient importance to warrant limiting a right?
2. Are the means in service of the objective rationally connected (suitable) to the objective?
3. Are the means in service of the objective necessary, that is, minimally impairing of the limited right, taking into account alternative means of achieving the same objective?
4. Do the beneficial effects of the limitation on the right outweigh the deleterious effects of the limitation; in short, is there a fair balance between the public interest and the private right?

There are other formulations. For example, some courts formulate the last question as a comparison of the deleterious effects on a right against the importance of the objective, rather than against the beneficial effects of the limitation.[6] Other courts employ the proportionality framework without explicit reference to the final question.[7] Still others insist that the question of "fair balance" is "inherent in the whole" of a bill of rights, which, on its best reading, is concerned both with "the demands of the general interest of the community and the requirements of the protection of the individual's human rights."[8] Although some courts insist on a systematic review of each of the

---

[6] See, e.g., *R. v. Oakes*, [1986] 1 S.C.R. 103, at para. 71; *cf. Dagenais v. Canadian Broadcasting Corp.*, [1994] 3 S.C.R. 835 at 839.

[7] See *de Freitas v. Permanent Secretary of Ministry of Agriculture, Fisheries, Lands and Housing*, [1999] 1 A.C. 6 (Judicial Committee, Privy Council), adopted by the Appellate Committee of the House of Lords in *R (Daly) v. Secretary of State for the Home Department*, [2001] UKHL 26; [2001] 2 A.C. 532 and *Huang v. Secretary of State for the Home Department*, [2007] UKHL 11; [2007] 2 A.C. 167.

[8] *Soering v. United Kingdom*, [1989] 11 E.H.R.R. 439 at para. 89. See also *Wilson v. First County Trust Ltd*, [2003] UKHL 40; [2004] 1 A.C. 816 at para. 181 (Lord Rodger).

questions of proportionality, others maintain that the role of the judge is to "arrive at a global judgment on proportionality and not [to] adhere mechanically to a sequential check-list."[9] Others commit themselves to the formality of proportionality's framework, only to entertain arguments relevant to one question in their answers to another.[10]

Now, these differences in formulation and practice need not detract from the claim that proportionality is the *jus cogens* of human rights law, any more than the existence of different theories of rights poses an obstacle to the ascendance of rights discourse. Despite variations in the full articulation of the proportionality doctrine, some or all of the four proportionality questions commonly feature in the assessment of rights claims. Few moral-political debates implicating rights escape proportionality analysis. Are limits on freedom of expression justified by the public interest in promoting tolerance and redressing the harms caused by racist speech? Is a prohibition on assisted suicide justified given its impact on the rights of those who wish to choose the timing and circumstances of their death? Does the provision of national security justify the establishment of limits on the due process rights of alleged terrorists? In each case, and countless others, the answer is to be determined by asking and answering some or all of the questions that are common to proportionality analysis.

That said, it would be too quick to conclude that proportionality is a uniform doctrine. Even putting aside the difference in formulations of the doctrine and the disagreement on the importance of the framework questions – differences and disagreements that obtain not only between jurisdictions but also within any one jurisdiction – it is not clear that the different uses are mere variations on a common concept.[11] In short, there may be different conceptions of proportionality in play.[12]

We surmise that behind the singular appeal to proportionality lurks a range of different understandings of proportionality – a range of *proportionalities*. Does this apparent diversity pose a challenge to proportionality as the global engine of human rights law? To what extent does the ascendance of

[9] *S v. Manamela and Another (Director-General of Justice Intervening)* (CCT 25/99) 2000 (3) SA 1 at para. 32.

[10] The Supreme Court of Canada sometimes reviews the "balance of interests" in its evaluation of "minimal impairment". See, e.g., *Eldridge v. British Columbia*, [1997] 3 S.C.R. 624 at para. 93 and discussion in Webber, *Negotiable Constitution, supra* note 2 at 77.

[11] For example, consider Julian River's thesis that there is a British "state-limiting" conception of proportionality and a European "optimizing" conception of proportionality: "Proportionality and Variable Intensity of Review," (2006) 65 Cambridge L.J. 174.

[12] See Alec Stone Sweet and Jud Mathews, "Proportionality Balancing and Global Constitutionalism," 47 Columbia J. Trans. L. 72 (2008).

proportionality demonstrate how, to borrow Alexander Aleinik's memorable phrase, "familiarity breeds consent"?[13] As with Aleinikoff's pathbreaking work on the debate over balancing in U.S. constitutional law, our intention is to provoke a debate about the nature and future of the principle of proportionality more generally by inviting proponents and opponents of proportionality to engage with each other and to offer their evaluations of the impact of proportionality on the nature of rights, the practice of judicial review, and legal reasoning generally. Accordingly, this collection not only has proponents engaging with critics on the merits of proportionality, but also has proponents engaging each other on their differing conceptions of proportionality. Throughout, proportionality is challenged and defended in ways that, we hope, provide new perspectives on this leading doctrine in human rights law.

II. CONCEPTIONS OF PROPORTIONALITY

The opening chapters explore different conceptions of proportionality observable in scholarship and judicial writing. Martin Luterán (Chapter 2) advances the argument that the proliferation of proportionalities stems from confusion between two conceptions, both of which are observable within academic and judicial writing and reasoning: "proportionality as balancing" and "proportionality between means and ends." Luterán argues that present-day doctrinal confusion can be traced to a disconnect between contemporary practice and proportionality's life prior to its reception into public law. This earlier and, he argues, truer account of proportionality lies within a particular ethical tradition. Luterán argues that proportionality as balancing is such a departure from the focal meaning of proportionality that it should not be a surprise that critics complain of its rational deficiency. Proportionality between means and ends is more conducive to a principled practice of judicial review, while proportionality as balancing is an invitation to more or less arbitrary judicial decision making.

Luterán locates the "lost meaning" of the doctrine of proportionality in the philosophical principle of "double-effect" reasoning that draws a distinction between: (1) consequences that are intended and (2) consequences that are not intended, but perhaps foreseen, and nevertheless accepted as side effects. The purpose of double-effect reasoning in ethics is to identify requirements that must be cumulatively fulfilled in order for human action with both positive and negative effects (that is, *double* effect) to be morally permissible. Proportionality between ends and means was traditionally the fourth and final requirement

---

[13]   Aleinikoff, "Age of Balancing," *supra* note 5 at 945.

of double-effect reasoning. These requirements can be formulated as: the chosen act must not (apart from its negative side effect) be wrongful on another ground; the actor may not intend the bad effect of the chosen act as an end; the actor may not intend the bad effect as a means to a further good effect; and there must be a proportionate reason for choosing an act that has negative side effects.

Luterán proposes a reconstructed proportionality test, one that focuses on ends and means rather than balancing, and argues that it provides resources for resolving several qualitatively different kinds of constitutional conflict that are not identifiable in the standard fare of balancing conflicts of rights, interests, or values. Furthermore, where balancing ultimately leaves a court without a rational basis for choosing one option over another, the reconstructed proportionality test provides determinate rules capable of resolving at least some classes of disputes.

Alison Young in Chapter 3 shares Luterán's view that there is more than one conception of proportionality, but appeals to a different axis. Drawing on conceptions of proportionality articulated by Julian Rivers,[14] Young argues that proportionality can be understood as "state-limiting" or as "optimizing" and, in her view, the two conceptions are complementary, each corresponding to a different role. The state-limiting conception attempts to determine the proper bounds of state action and is focused primarily on the question of lawfulness; in turn, the optimizing conception seeks to determine the nature and scope of the right in question. Young argues that the state-limiting conception works with a conception of rights that affords rights priority, allowing legislatures to develop policy in pursuit of the public interest while ensuring that there is a judicial check on legislative action. In contrast, the optimizing conception of proportionality, as favored by Robert Alexy and others sympathetic to his theory of constitutional rights,[15] corresponds to an interest-based theory of rights: it does not automatically favor the right, but may allow public interest gains to prevail.

Young suggests that we need to assess the purpose of constitutional adjudication before we can assess proportionality. She argues that where there is a common culture defining a right, a state-limiting conception of proportionality can be adopted together with a corresponding immunity theory of rights. But in the absence of such a common culture, an optimizing theory is required to help establish a right as part of the common culture.

[14] Julian Rivers, "Proportionality and Variable Intensity of Review," (2006) 65 Cambridge L.J. 174.
[15] Although Mattias Kumm and Kai Möller both draw inspiration from Alexy's theory of constitutional rights, it is Matthias Klatt and Moritz Meister who have carried on Alexy's theory most faithfully: see *The Constitutional Structure of Proportionality* (2012).

Mattias Kumm and Alec Walen (Chapter 4) take up the question of whether the concept of proportionality is sufficient for the protection of human dignity or if, as some critics have argued, engaging in proportionality reasoning risks balancing away human rights. Although Kumm once conceded that there might be a class of cases in which government action violated human rights while nevertheless satisfying the proportionality test, Kumm and Walen now reject that proposition. Instead, they argue deontology is ubiquitous in proportionality analysis, in all stages, and that there is nothing in the concept of balancing that precludes taking it into account. Balancing, as conceived by Kumm and Walen, is a residual category within rights analysis that says nothing about what kinds of things are relevant to balancing or what weights to assign to them.

The mistake in the conception of proportionality that allowed for human dignity exceptionalism, they argue, was in denying that (or underappreciating how) balancing requires moral reasoning. They argue that deontology covers a range of reasons for giving some interests more or less priority over others, and that proportionality reasoning must include constraints that arise from what is required to respect human dignity. In developing an example from proportionality-based challenges to different criminal punishments and procedures, Kumm and Walen demonstrate how balancing requires attending to moral foundations; that is, attending to a morally thick account of the institutions and concepts related to the government's purpose (such as, in this example, the concept of punishment) in order to evaluate that purpose when balancing.

Like Kumm and Walen, George Pavlakos in Chapter 5 is concerned with proportionality's normativity. He argues that the current theory and practice of proportionality supports a "filter conception of proportionality." On this conception, law is primarily about means-ends or instrumental rationality and engages in categorical or absolute moral prohibitions only in exceptional cases. When such exceptional cases arise, proportionality functions like a moral filter or litmus test designed to double-check the legitimacy of authoritative law. But the moral-filter conception of proportionality gives rise to a paradox: in discharging its controlling function, proportionality drives a wedge between authoritative directives and the moral grounds that can legitimize them in the first place. Along these lines, proportionality seems to assume that authoritative legal directives obligate irrespective of their substantive legitimacy. The result is that categorical prohibitions are not internal to law but need to be imported from some other realm.

Pavlakos argues that the paradox arises from a positivist understanding of legal obligation that works in tandem with a conception of autonomy as negative freedom. Autonomy *qua* negative freedom assumes that the function of autonomy is to create a sphere that is free of intervention with respect to very important interests of individuals. All else that remains outside this sphere is a question not of freedom but of unprincipled politics. In this picture, authoritative legal directives operate as standards of instrumental rationality, by aligning the relevant means with whatever ends legislators have put into place. When those ends appear extremely unjust, they need to be "corrected" by ad hoc appeal to categorical constraints that are external to law.

In questioning the philosophical assumptions of the filter conception of proportionality, Pavlakos advances a conception of autonomy that supports a non-positivist understanding of legal authority. On the one hand, he argues that legal obligation is grounded on deontological (moral) reasons. On the other hand, he argues that legal rights are better understood not in their traditional "defensive" role as negative constraints but as opening up spaces of freedom that need to be fleshed out by publicly authorized norms. He concludes that proportionality ought to function not as a moral filter for authoritative norms but instead as an interpretative principle that organizes a legal system as a system of publicly authorized norms, which aim at the realization of the autonomy of those living under it.

These four chapters outline some of the competing conceptions of proportionality. Significantly, these chapters rely on very different criteria to identify and assess plausible conceptions of proportionality. Luterán's focus is both ethical and historical, whereas Young engages heavily with current legal practice. Kumm and Walen, together with Pavlakos, draw on legal theory, and Young and Pavlakos insist on a correlation between conceptions of proportionality and conceptions of rights. The relationship between proportionality and rights is also front and center in the contributions to Part II.

III. PROPORTIONALITY AND RIGHTS

The relationship between rights and proportionality analysis is examined from a variety of different perspectives in Part II. Grégoire Webber (Chapter 6) defends the view that rights are conceptually interrelated to justice and, like justice, are peremptory and directive of what is to be. His argument tracks the etymology of "rights" from the Latin *ius*, exploring the conceptual relationship of objective right (justice) and subjective right (rights). Within this framework, he argues that the received approach to human rights together with the appeal to proportionality divorces rights from what *is right* and, in so doing, fails to capture the moral priority of rights. In short, human rights law-in-action suffers from a loss of rights.

In an effort to reclaim rights from this position of inconsequence, Webber draws attention to the equivocation in the use of the term "right" in catch-phrases such as "Everyone has a right to. . . ." In reasoning toward the states of affairs and sets of interpersonal actions, forbearances, and omissions that realize rights in community, one merely begs the question, by affirming as conclusive, that one has a *right* to life, liberty, and so forth. The practical question is what, specifically, is to be established and brought into being in order to realize one's rights. The complex process of practical reasoning required to answer that question situates the would-be right-holder in a community of other actual and potential right-holders. It is a process of reasoning under-taken by the lawmakers who bear a special responsibility for their community to settle, justly and authoritatively, right relationships between persons.

That special responsibility, argues Webber, invites a different understanding of the relationship of rights to law: rather than understanding the legislature as the author of the infringement of rights (as Möller [Chapter 7] and Schauer [Chapter 8] and many others presuppose in their accounts of rights under proportionality), the legislature sets out to realize rights in community. Albeit with many failings, many legal directives stand as true specifications of right relationships, giving proper effect to the subject matters of justice outlined in bills of rights.

Kai Möller in Chapter 7 exemplifies the conception of rights rejected by Webber. For him, proportionality implies "rights inflation," which is to say that it implies an expansion of the range of interests protected by rights. Noting the trend toward the inclusion of a variety of interests within the scope of human rights in the jurisprudence of the European Court of Human Rights and, especially, in the jurisprudence of the German Federal Constitutional Court, Möller argues that this tendency is not only encouraged but required by the logic of proportionality analysis. Furthermore, he argues, it is the best means of ensuring that state action is justified.

Rejecting what he terms the "threshold model" of rights, Möller challenges attempts to articulate a standard according to which an interest would be of sufficient importance to qualify as a right. Arguing that any such threshold would risk arbitrariness, Möller introduces and defends a "comprehensive model" of rights according to which all autonomy interests qualify as rights. He acknowledges that such a model incorporates a range of interests, from the inconsequential (e.g., feeding pigeons in the park) to the grossly immoral (e.g., the right to murder), but argues that this does not trivialize or undermine the idea of rights.

Recognizing that the implications of the "comprehensive model" will give many reason to hesitate, Möller reiterates that recognizing an interest as a right is not conclusive: the right to murder, for example, is justifiably infringed, and proportionality analysis would allow for this justification. This conclusion is, for him, more secure and agreeable than the conclusion, suggested by the "threshold model," that some interests could be unjustifiably interfered with and yet, because they fail to meet a minimum threshold to qualify as rights, would not be subject to proportionality review. The lesson of Möller's argument concludes in the affirmation that proportionality analysis invites us to revisit our assumptions that rights have special importance and special normative force. Rather, rights are better understood as endowing us with the right to be treated with a special attitude: an attitude that takes each and every individual seriously as a person with a life to live and that allows government to interfere with our activities only if there are sufficient, and proportionate, reasons to do so.

Frederick Schauer (Chapter 8) shares with Möller the premise that rights and proportionality are in a special relationship, but disagrees on the nature of that relationship. For Schauer, only when rights enter the picture does the language of proportionality come onto the scene. The language of proportionality contrasts with the language of balancing, which captures the policy-making process, according to which competing but non-rights-protected goals are weighed. The special relationship of rights to proportionality, then, is a function of the special weight of rights. Attending to the "question of weight" in proportionality analysis, Schauer reviews how the special weight of rights frames proportionality analysis.

In Schauer's argument, all non-absolute rights are subject to limitation, and proportionality arbitrates between justified and unjustified limitations. But while non-rights-protected goals or interests can be balanced, stronger arguments are necessary to limit a right because each right is weightier than non-rights-protected interests. There is thus a presumption in favor of rights, which places the burden of proof on those who would limit the right. That burden is absent in the normal cost-benefit policy analysis.

Schauer introduces the idea of a "rule of weight" to capture proportionality analysis: a second-order rule prescribes the weight of first-order considerations about what should be done. Proportionality thus frames decision-making processes: the presumption is against limiting a right, but the presumption can be rebutted. The question put forth by proportionality analysis is whether the extent to which a limitation on a right is justified by the increase in public order or other end that the limitation on the right is expected to bring.

Grant Huscroft in Chapter 9 argues that we must be concerned with not only what it means to have a right, as Webber argues, but also with the meaning of the particular rights that we have. This, he argues, means that we must attend to the foundational significance of the decision of a political community to enact a bill of rights. Political communities choose whether or not to enact a bill of rights and choose which rights are to receive the special protection that a bill of rights affords. In Huscroft's account, bills of rights are finite in nature; they protect some, but not all, possible rights and set out particular conceptions of some of the rights they include. In short, bills of rights reflect a "constitutional settlement" on rights questions, and this settlement must be respected before proportionality analysis can occur.

Huscroft argues that the "rights inflation" advocated by Möller is unjustified, and so too are approaches to proportionality such as Mattias Kumm's[16] that render the process of rights interpretation all but irrelevant. By expanding the scope of rights and hence judicial review, some conceptions of proportionality effect radical changes to the constitutional order and should be rejected on this account, however desirable an expanded requirement of justification for state action may be.

The contributors to Part II all insist on a relationship between rights and proportionality and, despite important disagreements, there is common ground among both the proponents and critics of proportionality. All four chapters share the view that proportionality and absolute rights are difficult, if not impossible, to reconcile. For some authors, the very idea of rights presupposes that they are absolute and so not subject to proportionality (at least as conceived within the frame of "balancing"); for others, proportionality engages only with non-absolute rights. Möller and Webber share the view that proportionality and rights inflation are conceptually interrelated, but disagree on the merits of this relationship: for Möller, the gains in subjecting government authority to justification review is important; for Webber, the loss of rights and the decision to divorce rights from what is right is morally burdened. Schauer and Huscroft insist on the importance of attending to what rights mean: for Schauer, that question is related to the special role of weight in undertaking proportionality analysis; for Huscroft, that question is a precondition to justifying the decision to undertake proportionality analysis. In both cases, rights matter in a way that Möller would reject.

IV. PROPORTIONALITY AND JUSTIFICATION

The chapters in Part III of the collection explore proportionality as justification, with special reference to the "culture of justification." T.R.S. Allan

---

[16] Mattias Kumm, "The Idea of Socratic Contestation and the Right to Justification: The Point of Rights-Based Proportionality Review," (2010) 4 Law & Ethics of Human Rights 141.

(Chapter 10) defends a common law approach to democratic constitutionalism. Legislation, he argues, is best understood as providing "influential guidance to the requirements of reason," such that its application to particular cases requires judicial judgment and, at times, modification in order to respects rights. That common law requirement derives its authority from the concept of human dignity and not from a bill of rights. Bills of rights are important but they are, contra the position advocated by Huscroft, only "inessential, approximations."

On Allan's account, justice involves the resolution of disputes according to moral principle and this, in turn, requires proportionality. A law is proportionate whenever an alternative law, less restrictive of rights, would be significantly less effective. Allan considers the last step in proportionality analysis – the fair balance test – to be the most difficult, but even allowing for the problem of incommensurability he argues that comparability remains possible: it is rational to prefer a trivial interference with one right or interest to a greater interference with another. To the extent that a range of answers is possible, deference to the legislative choices from within that range is appropriate.

Allan outlines an approach to statutory interpretation that renders it unlikely that courts will be called upon to strike down legislation or otherwise declare it incompatible with rights. The correct construction of a statute is, in his view, the one that best reconciles general statutory aims with respect for citizens' autonomy and dignity.

David Dyzenhaus (Chapter 11) argues that the culture of justification echoes Lon Fuller's commitment to "reasoned argument in human affairs." His focus is on the justifiability of the reasons for which political authority acts. Confronting the view that proportionality would invite too much judicial interference in the administrative state, Dyzenhaus argues that a focus on a decision maker's reasons for a decision, rather than a review of the correctness of that decision, strengthens the administrative state by keeping all decisions within its province. The role of the court is to challenge the reasons why decisions are reached, not to make those decisions itself.

Proportionality is therefore at the core of the culture of justification. It asks of decision makers to take seriously the claims of rights made by individuals and acknowledge their duty to justify the exercise of authority that affects them. Like Allan, Dyzenhaus argues that this idea is not bounded to the context of constitutional rights; it is, he argues, central to public law as a whole.

In contrast to these two proponents of proportionality, Stephen Gardbaum (Chapter 12) is agnostic as to proportionality's virtues. His purpose is to consider the normative justification for adopting proportionality by exploring an alternative conception to the culture of justification. Proportionality is better understood, Gardbaum argues, as promoting a "culture of democracy." In the culture of democracy, proportionality is important because it acknowledges the democratic weight that attaches to claims that compete with rights, and so establishes a middle ground between absolute rights and majoritarianism. Gardbaum argues that the culture of democracy is best reflected by Schauer's conception of rights: rights are important, but there is a limited ability to override them in some circumstances. This ability reduces the concern that would otherwise arise from the decision of past majorities to protect rights so as to limit the law-making authority of future majorities. It also mitigates the problem of judicial supremacy in interpreting underdeterminate rights.

Gardbaum acknowledges that the culture of democracy reaches the same point as the culture of justification, but insists that it does so in a manner that emphasises the democratic function of proportionality review over its constraining and justificatory function. In order to give effect to the democratic purposes of proportionality review, Gardbaum argues that judicial review should be deferential: courts should ask whether a legislative rights judgment is reasonable.

Mark Antaki's contribution in Chapter 13 challenges the claims – explicit and assumed – of proportionality-talk by both proponents and critics of its place in human rights law. He highlights the obviousness, inevitability, inescapability, and universality of reasoning and rights contemplated by proportionality's culture of justification. Exploring the forms of thought that give proportionality its appeal, he argues that the culture of proportionality is rationalism, rooted in the technical and calculative and which purports to demystify the human experience.

Antaki traces the appeal to objectivity and escape from tradition contemplated by the calculation and policy assessment of balancing. In this "worldlessness," proportionality is taken to promise unsituated reason and an Archimedean point of view. So successful is this promise that we may forget just how recent the rise of proportionality has been and how significant its lexicon has become. Drawing on Hannah Arendt, Antaki invites us to explore worldly judgment, where one's articulation of the "facts" relevant to proportionality analysis cannot proceed without contemplating the weight one attaches to them or the interests they implicate. Antaki outlines how an understanding of judgment as worldly can lead to a rehabilitation of authority and analogy. In this way, Antaki's chapter invites us to appreciate the connection between proportionality and analogy. Despite its claims to escape context, proportionality, like analogy, assumes a world for comparison and understanding. In this frame, one cannot separate the aesthetic from the mathematical, perception from cognition, the poetic from the propositional, world from reason.

Although differing in many respects, the four chapters in Part III all share the view that proportionality invites a judicial role that is different than the one sometimes assumed by the rule of law's commitment to the administration of legal rules. For Allan and Dyzenhaus, the judicial role is to examine and evaluate the reasons for government action: Allan's focus on legislation and Dyzenhaus's focus on administrative action share a commitment to justification as central to the relationship of law and rights. Gardbaum shares this appeal to justification, but suggests that it empowers legislative action by denying to the court categorical conclusions: the government may act where its reasons for action are good. Allan's, Dyzenhaus's, and Gardbaum's shared commitment to justification – a commitment shared by many other authors in this collection – is critically examined by Antaki, who questions the assumptions inherent in talk of justification. In this way, the contributors to Part III provide the reader with different accounts of proportionality's relationship to justification, accounts that cannot be reduced to a simplifying assumption that proponents and critics of proportionality share one or another view.

V. PROPORTIONALITY AND REASONING

The contributions in Part IV explore the mode of reasoning presupposed and promoted by the doctrine of proportionality. If the constitutional validity of legislation turns on its proportionality, does it follow that the legislature should use the doctrine of proportionality to frame how it reasons and chooses when legislating? In answering this question, Richard Ekins cautions in Chapter 14 against an affirmative reply.

Exploring what it means to "legislate well," Ekins argues that law-making is a moral choice made in response to reasons. The legislator's reasoning is informed by moral truths and the duty to specify those truths into forms appropriate to the needs of the community. The legislator forms, refines, and scrutinizes proposals for legislation by identifying goals and means to realize those goals. Throughout this process, the legislator seeks to specify the rights of persons having in view an image of what is conducive to human well-being.

Ekins cautions that the proportionality doctrine does not do justice to the complexity of sound legislative reasoning. There are some valuable aspects of legislating that are not recognized by proportionality, and some corrupting mistakes. Such a mode of reasoning will stultify legislative reasoning, which should aim to specify that to which each is entitled, consistent with the disposition to be open to the flourishing of all persons.

Timothy Endicott explores the commensurability assumption in proportionality's claim to balance in Chapter 15. The resolution of the incommensurability problem lies in accepting that in some instances, leaving matters to the discretion of judges is less arbitrary than trying to remove that discretion through the imposition of rules that are themselves arbitrary. That resolution rests on what Endicott terms the "institutional premise"; namely, the premise that "the respect that all public authorities must have for certain human interests can best be secured by a power in an independent tribunal . . . to pass judgment on the justice of pursuing public purposes in ways that affect those interests." Proportionality reasoning is not generally pathological if the institutional premise holds. Rather, given the institutional premise, the pathologies of proportionality ("structured tendencies towards misconceived decisions") are particular and depend on judges making particular mistakes.

Those pathologies come in pairs, because they are either in favor of the claimant or in favor of the public authority. They relate to (1) spillover, such as including on the balancing scales interests that do not warrant consideration; (2) uncertainty, including uncertainties resulting from judicial consideration of complex social facts, future contingencies, and unpredictable social responses to policy choices; and (3) deference, both in respect of jeopardizing the judicial protection of human rights and in respect of failing to award public authorities their rightful place under the constitution.

These three pairs of pathologies under proportionality all relate to incommensurability. According to Endicott, incommensurability undermines attempts to achieve objectivity, transparency, and judicial legitimacy such that, even if incommensurability as a *general* pathology can be answered by the institutional premise, it resurfaces at the particular level in the form of one or more of these three more specific and contingent pairs of pathologies.

Bradley Miller in Chapter 16 follows on from Endicott's exploration of proportionality's pathologies and, developing a theme suggested in Richard Ekins' chapter, proposes one more. What Miller perceives in proportionality reasoning (particularly as conducted by judges) is a propensity to discount, or exclude a priori, many aspects of the public good that are commonly the concern of the legislator. Miller argues that proportionality reasoning, although intended to promote objectivity and transparency, serves as ready cover for the judicial adoption of undefended (and sometimes unarticulated) commitments of political philosophy. As it happens, chief among these commitments are the assumptions of political liberalism, and particularly the thesis that the political community must remain neutral about what constitutes a good life. Such an assumption has an obvious impact on the justification of legislation found to restrict autonomy interests. Miller's concern is not only – or even primarily – with the decisions that result from such a practice. This practice of a priori exclusion ought to be judged as pathological by anyone who believes that legitimacy of judicial review requires that controversial principles of political philosophy not be pressed into law either covertly or accidentally.

Iddo Porat brings together a review of contested accounts of reasoning under proportionality with a review of institutional responsibility in Chapter 17. By tracing these debates over the U.S. Supreme Court's case law exploring the merits of balancing under the Bill of Rights, Porat argues that the American case law and literature suggests that constitutional rights lend themselves to two readings: either they are first-order considerations to be balanced against other first-order considerations, or they are second-order rights that prevent government from acting for some first-order considerations. The first reading lends itself to balancing rights, but contrary to present day assumptions, the history of U.S. Supreme Court decisions reveals that this conclusion was regularly accompanied with the assumption that the legislature, not the court, was to do the balancing. In turn, the second reading of constitutional rights, although not inviting balancing, nonetheless regularly appeals to balancing to "smoke out" whether the government, purporting to act on a permissible first-order consideration, in truth was motivated by an excluded first-order consideration. Here balancing is transparently the duty of the court, albeit for the limited purpose of identifying the motivating first-order consideration of government action.

By contrasting the different possible answers to the two separable questions, Porat identifies one strong and three weak positions on rights and balancing: the strong position reads rights as first-order considerations and assigns to courts the responsibility to balance; the weak positions trade on opposite answers to one or the other or both positions on rights and judicial review. Although the strong position dominates in much of Europe, it is not embraced in the United States, where one or the other of the three weak positions finds expression in the case law.

The question of proportionality's relationship to reasoning is examined from different angles in these four chapters, each of which challenges common assumptions in proportionality judgments and scholarship. Ekins resituates proportionality from the judicial forum to the legislative forum to test the assumption, shared by many proportionality proponents, that proportionality is the only way to reason. Endicott challenges a different assumption: namely, the commensurability thesis, and situates the institutional question at the heart of that assumption. Miller demonstrates and challenges how political liberalism is assumed, but not defended to be the default moral-political philosophy in undertaking proportionality analysis. Finally, Porat, drawing primarily on

U.S. case law, challenges both the assumption that the U.S. Supreme Court has rejected proportionality, but also the assumption that proportionality can make claim to a singular view of the place of rights and institutional responsibility.

VI. CONCLUSION

Proportionality's current status as an orthodoxy has become something of an impediment to scholarly debate. This collection's aim is to open up lines of debate beyond simplistic "for" and "against" positions, demonstrating the complexity of rival positions.

Where there is a range of proportionalities, it is important for critics to attend to relevant differences. Defenders of proportionality quite reasonably insist that critiques of one theorist's articulation of proportionality should not be understood as necessarily applying to all articulations. By supplying detailed accounts of competing proportionalities in conversation with others, this collection helps identify similarities and differences. It thus provides an important antidote to the easy rebuff that because there is no standard account of proportionality, critiques of proportionality simpliciter are off target. In turn, it enables critics to better understand their subject matter. Similarly, this collection moves some distance toward answering the criticisms that challenges to proportionality are either unpalatable[17] or, alternatively, reducible to proportionality.[18]

The contributions to this collection instead demonstrate that debate can be more fruitfully focused elsewhere. Differing conceptions of proportionality can be drawn from the history of ideas, from different readings of judicial practice, from theoretical understandings of deontic and consequentialist reasoning, and from different conceptions of rights, law, and legislating. Does proportionality signal the special priority of rights or deny rights special importance and special normative force? Is proportionality consistent with a conception of absolute rights? Would the invitation to look to reasons as part of a culture of justification produce a different account of the judicial role, including a transformation of the relationship of judicial authority to legislative authority? What role, if any, should proportionality play as a guide to legislative

[17] E.g., "not taking human rights seriously"; Barak, *Proportionality* (2011) 495, or presenting a "seriously degraded" account of rights; Tom Hickman, "Negotiable Rights, What Rights?" (2012) 75 Modern L. Rev. 437 at 446, 454.
[18] E.g., the Judge Sir Gerald Fitzmaurice of the European Court on Human Rights in *Marckx v. Belgium* (1979), application no. 6833/74 (June 13, 1979), para. 5, insisted that proportionality includes a set of "elementary, standard propositions which should not need stating because they are such as everyone would assent to in principle."

reasoning? Is the moral reasoning that takes place within proportionality open to all sound moral theories or does it privilege some? Does the commensurability objection hold, and if so, what are the consequences for the moral choice?

The sheer ubiquity of proportionality analysis will suggest to some, perhaps to many, that the time to debate these questions is long over and it does not much matter whether proportionality is adopted for its rational appeal or for its sheer familiarity. This collection is offered, by both proponents of critics of proportionality alike, as a corrective to this complacency.

PART I

CONCEPTIONS OF PROPORTIONALITY

2   The Lost Meaning of Proportionality

Martin Luterán

I. INTRODUCTION

What is the meaning of the principle of proportionality in human rights law? Although many agree that proportionality is an important concept in constitutional law and judicial review,[1] agreement as to what proportionality means is either elusive or acquired through abstraction and superficiality. Most proportionality theorists would define proportionality as a test comprised of four inquiries addressing: (1) the legitimacy of governmental aims, (2) the suitability of the means chosen to achieve those aims, (3) the necessity of the means chosen to achieve the aims, and (4) the overall balance of a state action (sometimes referred to as "proportionality in the narrow sense" or "proportionality stricto sensu" or the "law of balancing"). However, the meaning of these four inquiries, especially the requirement of the overall balance, is controversial. Different authors and judges emphasize different inquiries and conceptualize the inquiries differently. Not to mention that such a neat ordering of questions is not followed by all courts: the European Court of Human Rights often deploys the concept of proportionality without following this order.[2]

A skeptic may well ask why these questions are united under the label of proportionality. This chapter suggests that the present chaos in the use of proportionality by judges and academics has partly resulted from a loss of connection

---

[1]   See Alec Stone Sweet and Jud Mathews, "Proportionality, Balancing and Global Constitutionalism," 47 *Colum. J. Transant'l. L.* 72 (2008).

[2]   P. van Dijk, G.J.H. van Hoof and A.W. Heringa, *Theory and Practice of the European Convention on Human Rights* (3rd ed., 1998) 81; Richard Clayton, "Regaining a Sense of Proportion: The Human Rights Act and the Proportionality Principle," (2001) *Eur. H.R.L. Rev.* 504, at 510; Aileen McHarg, "Reconciling Human Rights and the Public Interest: Conceptual Problems and Doctrinal Uncertainty in the Jurisprudence of the European Court of Human Rights," (1999) 62 *M.L.R.* 671, at 686; Yutaka Arai-Takahashi, *The Margin of Appreciation Doctrine and the Principle of Proportionality in the Jurisprudence of the ECHR* (2002) 193.

with proportionality's historical roots in a particular ethical tradition. I would like to elucidate the lost meaning of proportionality and argue for the advantages to its recovery. The lost meaning of proportionality that I articulate here is simple and attractive, neither overly ambitious nor modest. It cannot magically resolve all of the challenges of judicial review, but it can provide some improvements and save proportionality from some valid critiques.[3]

This chapter sets out the lost (and focal)[4] meaning of proportionality. The principal contribution of the lost conception of proportionality is to indicate those criteria that bear on the evaluation of side effects of the actions of persons and states. It can provide nothing more. It provides no measure to evaluate the ends that are pursued, or the goodness or badness of the means chosen to achieve those ends. In its lost context, proportionality was simply meant to bring one's attention to the problem of evaluating the acceptability of side effects. Of course, to conduct an analysis of state action using the lost conception of proportionality requires a sound understanding of the crucial elements of an action, such as means, ends, and side effects. Contemporary proportionality doctrine, now separated from the historical context of the lost meaning, is understood by its proponents as a genie let loose from the bottle – meant to fulfill any wish. It is striking how much work some believe that proportionality can do.[5] However, as many have argued in this volume, proportionality cannot meet the many expectations lavished on it;[6] the genie is an illusion.

II. CONTEMPORARY CONCEPTIONS OF LEGAL PROPORTIONALITY

This section will present an overview of the diverse conceptions of proportionality currently at play in scholarship, particularly with respect to (1) the link between balancing and proportionality, and (2) the concepts of "means" and "ends."

---

[3] The proposed meaning of proportionality should escape the important criticisms offered by Grant Huscroft in Chapter 9 of this volume.

[4] For an explanation of the central case and focal meaning methodology in social sciences, see John Finnis, *Natural Law and Natural Rights* (2nd ed., 2011) ch. 1.

[5] David Beatty's work has become infamous for its almost unconditional praise of proportionality as a "universal criterion of constitutionality": David M. Beatty, *The Ultimate Rule of Law* (2004) 162.

[6] See the contributions of Timothy Endicott in Chapter 14 and Richard Ekins in Chapter 15 of this volume. For an argument showing the failures of proportionality in English administrative law, see Paul Daly, "Blown Out of Proportion: The Case against Proportionality as an Independent Ground of Judicial Review" in Cian C. Murphy and Penny Green (eds.), *Law and Outsiders: Norms, Processes and "Othering" in the 21st Century* (2011).

Proportionality as Balancing

Although many of the proponents and opponents of proportionality share the conception of proportionality as balancing,[7] an increasing number recognize a conception of proportionality that is not equivalent to balancing.[8] Julian Rivers recognizes such a non-balancing conception of proportionality, although he ultimately disagrees with it. He rejects the proposition that "there is essentially one doctrine of proportionality offering a range of tests directed towards the same end, with minor variations in formulation".[9] Instead, Rivers argues that there are two different conceptions at work in judicial reasoning, the optimising conception of proportionality and the state-limiting conception: "[t]he optimising conception sees proportionality as a structured approach to balancing fundamental rights with other rights and interests in the best possible way. The state-limiting conception sees proportionality as a set of tests warranting judicial interference to protect rights".[10] Rivers applauds the optimizing conception at work in decisions of the European Court of Human Rights and criticizes "the inadequate 'state-limiting' alternative which has predominated in British courts".[11] The state-limiting conception of proportionality, in Rivers's view, is not "about optimising costs and benefits but about the efficient pursuit of pre-determined goals. . . . [I]t imposes a judicially-generated criterion of correctness in respect of necessity, or efficiency".[12] In other words, the courts that accept the state-limiting conception of proportionality ask only whether the means adopted by a state are suitable and necessary to achieve a legitimate aim. They do not ask whether the suitable and necessary means also strike a fair balance. That is why Rivers finds this conception of proportionality inadequate.

---

[7] Those who praise proportionality precisely because it brought balancing to the center stage of human rights review include Robert Alexy, *A Theory of Constitutional Rights* (2002); and Carlos Bernal Pulido, "The Rationality of Balancing," (2006) 92 A.R.S.P. 195. Those rejecting proportionality because of the various problems they associate with balancing include Basak Cali, "Balancing Human Rights? Methodological Problems with Weights, Scales and Proportions," (2007) 29 *Hum. Rts. Q.* 251; Stavros Tsakyrakis, "Proportionality: An Assault on Human Rights?" (2009) 7 *Int'l. J. Const. L.* 468 (hereinafter Tsakyrakis, "Proportionality"); Grégoire C.N. Webber, *The Negotiable Constitution: On the Limitation of Rights* (2009) [hereinafter Webber, *Negotiable Constitution*].

[8] Julian Rivers, "Proportionality and Variable Intensity of Review," (2006) 65 *C.L.J.* 174 (hereinafter Rivers, "Proportionality"); Martin Lutéran, "Towards Proportionality as a Proportion Between Means and Ends" in Cian C. Murphy and Penny Green (eds.), *Law and Outsiders: Norms, Processes and "Othering" in the 21st Century* (2011) (hereinafter Lutéran, "Towards Proportionality"); see also the contribution of Alison L. Young in Chapter 3 of this volume.

[9] Rivers, "Proportionality," 178.　　　　[10] Ibid., 176.

[11] Ibid.　　　　[12] Ibid., 178–179.

Benjamin Goold, Liora Lazarus, and Gabriel Swiney also make a sharp distinction between proportionality and balancing in their comprehensive analysis of the case law on national security in several jurisdictions, including Strasbourg: "Proportionality as a legal concept must be distinguished from the concept of balancing. Balancing, as identified in this report, involves a broad brush, and sometimes opaque, analysis aimed at a resolution of the interests and rights involved".[13]

Alison Young provides an interesting attempt to bridge the two different conceptions. She accepts Rivers's distinction between optimizing and state-limiting conceptions of proportionality, but argues that one does not have to choose one or the other. Instead, both have a place in constitutional adjudication. The difference is that they should be applied at different levels of abstraction:

> [D]iscourse surrounding the application of different conceptions of proportionality take place at two different levels of abstraction, connected to different understandings of the purpose of a constitution. . . . An optimizing conception of proportionality does not recognise clearly delineated agreements as to the content of a particular right, or its application in particular circumstances. Consequently, balancing is used to refine this process. State-limiting conceptions of proportionality apply in a less abstract manner, occurring within a legal system that has accepted particular, more refined definitions of rights. As such, a focus on the definition of the right is more able to determine the outcome in particular circumstances.[14]

In other words, at the most abstract level of interests, where rights are not yet properly specified, it is appropriate to balance interests in order to determine the more precise contours of rights. Once this is done and the more refined definition of a right is available, there is no more space for balancing. Instead, a state-limiting conception of proportionality should be applied to determine the outcome of the case.

Divisions go further. There are many different meanings of balancing. These can be categorized into two main groups: those that subscribe to the claim that balancing is a special kind of legal reasoning and those that do not. The leading proponent of the first view is Robert Alexy.[15] His conception

---

[13] Benjamin Goold, Liora Lazarus, and Gabriel Swiney, "Public Protection, Proportionality, and the Search for Balance," (2007) 10 UK *Ministry of Justice Research Paper* i.

[14] Alison L. Young, "Proportionality Is Dead: Long Live Proportionality!" Chapter 3 in this volume at 58.

[15] Robert Alexy, "On Balancing and Subsumption: A Structural Comparison," (2003) 16 *Ratio Juris* 433.

of balancing is meant to capture a special way of reasoning about conflicting considerations that involves establishing their respective degrees of importance and non-satisfaction, and the subsequent weighing of them. As such, it is supposed to be different from the reasoning process of subsumption, in which one categorizes a situation under a general rule. Those in agreement with this view think that balancing is capable of generating, in a unique way, conclusions from premises, and can thus equip courts with an important tool for deciding cases.[16]

On the other hand, there is a diverse group of scholars who use the language of balancing, but do not subscribe to the "special legal reasoning" thesis. Their use of the term does not denote anything more specific than general practical reasoning or a need for prudential consideration of all the relevant factors. The authors exhibiting the second approach are not concerned with elucidating the process of establishing degrees of importance or of the actual weighing. Rather, they focus on the balancing arguments commonly used by courts. Jeremy Gunn's analysis can be seen as an illustration of this approach. He proposes forms of proportionality arguments that favor complainants (overbreadth, less-restrictive alternative, speculative, discriminatory, discounting, overly punitive) or the state (minimal infringement, compelling community need). These "ideal-type" proportionality problems are the result of weighing various relevant components against each other.[17] However, Gunn never explains what he means by "weighing" and one could reasonably conclude from the context of the article that weighing is nothing other than reasonable and prudential judgment about the relevant factors. The examples of proportionality analysis he then offers seem nothing other than systematic descriptions of the most common types of judgments. Steven Greer makes a similar argument when he says that "in some sense 'balancing' amounts to no more than an exercise in interpretation, common in some form or other to the proper understanding of any legal standard, including Convention norms and even to apparently crystal clear legal rules".[18]

---

[16] For a recent defence of this view, see Virgílio Afonso da Silva, "Comparing the Incommensurable: Constitutional Principles, Balancing and Rational Decision," (2011) 31 O.J.L.S. 273; and Kai Möller, "Proportionality and Rights Inflation," Chapter 7 in this volume.

[17] T. Jeremy Gunn, "Deconstructing Proportionality in Limitations Analysis," (2005) 19 *Emory Int'l. L. Rev.* 465 at 494–498. For a study of proportionality under the European Convention, which pursues questions similar to those asked by Gunn, see Jeremy McBride, "Proportionality and the European Convention on Human Rights" in Evelyn Ellis (ed.), *The Principle of Proportionality in the Laws of Europe* (1999).

[18] Steven C. Greer, *The European Convention on Human Rights: Achievements, Problems and Prospects* (2006) 211.

T.R.S. Allan's use of the concept of balancing in this volume also comes close to this understanding: "[t]he need for judgment, maintaining a fair balance between statutory objective and claims of individual right, is inherent in any effort of rational interpretation".[19] Endicott's reflection on the nature of such "balancing" is revealing: "The proportionality doctrine requires the judges to reconcile incommensurable interests. The judges and many commentators call the reconciliation 'balancing', but the interests at stake cannot actually be weighed with each other on any sort of scales. . . . To make these decisions, they [the judges] have to throw the scales out the window, and just *choose*."[20] Alexy's and Endicott's views on balancing are almost exact opposites. One conceives of balancing as a special kind of reasoning that can yield true (or at least rationally defensible) conclusions. The other sees balancing as a mere label to describe the act of choosing from among several incommensurable options. One's conception of balancing of course influences one's take on proportionality. The proportionality test proposed and defended in this chapter includes Endicott's balancing in the evaluation of side effects of state action, but it is not reduceable to such balancing.

Proportionality between Means and Ends

It is noteworthy that the concept of proportionality first arose on the Convention scene as a criterion for assessing the relationship between the means and ends of state action. The Court held that it is not sufficient for a state merely to pursue a legitimate aim. There has to be a "reasonable relationship of proportionality between the means employed and the aim sought to be realised".[21] Proportionality became equated with balancing in the Convention system of human rights protection only twenty years later.[22] As a matter of legal history alone, there is therefore good reason to consider a conception of proportionality as distinct from balancing. It is through the idea of proportion between means and ends that the word "proportionality" entered European human rights law in 1968.[23]

---

[19] T.R.S. Allan, "Democracy, Legality, and Proportionality," Chapter 10 in this volume, at 223.

[20] Timothy Endicott, "Proportionality and Incommensurability," Chapter 14 in this volume, at 311, 315.

[21] *Case Relating to Certain Aspects of the Laws on the Use of Languages In Education In Belgium* (1968), Part I B para 10.

[22] *Lithgow and others v. United Kingdom* (App nos 9006/80; 9262/81; 9263/81;9265/81; 9266/81; 9313/81; 9405/81) (1986) 8 E.H.R.R. 329 at para. 120. A similar, explicit identification of proportionality and balancing can be found in *AGOSI v. United Kingdom* (1987) E.H.R.R. 1 at para. 52.

[23] It is arguable that the European Court was inspired by the use of the concept by the German Federal Constitutional Court, which first explicitly mentioned the principle of proportionality

Despite the priority (at least historical) of the conception of proportionality as a relationship between means and ends, not much attention has been paid by European human rights legal scholars to the concepts of means and ends. They may seem so basic and self-evident that they do not require further elaboration. Nevertheless, a closer look at some of the uses of these concepts by courts and scholars alike reveals some confusion. What follows is the outline of some of the inconsistencies and confusions surrounding means and ends in the proportionality literature.

Michael Fordham and Thomas de la Mare see proportionality as a four-question template. The first question asks about the legitimacy of the aim of the measure, the second and the third about the measure's suitability and necessity for achieving the aim, and the fourth about the "means/ends fit": "viewed overall, do the ends justify the means?"[24] The relationship between the fourth sub-principle and the rest is illustrated by an example given in a footnote: "So, if prevention of rape is a permissible aim (*legitimacy*), which can (*suitability*) and can only (*necessity*) be furthered by forced castration, the question is then one of overall cost and benefit (*means/ends fit*)".[25] Here, means/ends fit is given as just one of the criteria to establish that a measure is proportionate; a criterion that is distinct from both the suitability and the necessity of the measure. But there is reason to question whether proportionality can, logically, be broken down in the way described by Fordham and de la Mare. After all, what are suitability and necessity assessing if not the relationship between the means and ends of a particular measure? The fact that the means chosen are incapable of achieving the desired end is a reason to conclude that the means are unsuitable. Similarly, the fact that there are other less-restrictive ways of achieving the same end suggests that the more restrictive means is not necessary. These are quintessential features of any means-ends relationships and there does not seem to be any good reason to avoid the language of means and ends when discussing the sub-principles of suitability and necessity.

More importantly, it is not clear which feature of the means-ends relationship is expressed by Fordham and de la Mare's phrasing of the fourth question. What do they mean by "viewed overall"? The example cited goes some way to providing an explanation, through the reference to "overall cost and benefit". The example suggests that even if the means were suitable and

---

(der Grundsatz der Verhältnismäßigkeit) in one of its judgments on June 3, 1954 (BVerfGE E 3, S 383 (1954) 399).
[24] Michael Fordham and Thomas de la Mare, "Identifying the Principles of Proportionality" in Jeffrey L. Jowell and others (eds.), *Understanding Human Rights Principles* (2001) 28.
[25] Ibid., 28.

necessary, they could still be unjustified if, viewed overall, the costs that they impose outweighed the benefits provided. Although the conclusion suggested by Fordham and de la Mare's example – that forced castration would be unjustified – is uncontroversial, the reasons suggested by the example are very interesting. Forced castration is unjustified not because such an intentional mutilation of men would be a violation of several human rights (e.g., right to respect for private life, right to found a family), but rather because it would cause more harm than good. Thus, theoretically, if one could conceive of a situation where the benefits of forced castration outweighed the costs (using whatever metric is at hand), one would have to conclude that forced castration would be justified according to the methodology of proportionality employed by Fordham and de la Mare. This highlights the essential difference between cost-benefit analysis and means-ends analysis.

What do the costs and benefits of any measure consist of? Are they in any way determined by the relationship between means and ends? It does not seem to be the case. Costs and benefits are a matter of desirable or undesirable effects of a measure. Ignoring for the moment the question of whether a cost-benefit analysis is even possible or appropriate in the context of human rights, determining the costs or benefits of a measure would in any case be a completely different procedure from assessing the means and ends of a measure. All that we need to know to assess the costs and benefits of a measure are ex ante predictions and/or ex post facts about the effects of the measure and a metric for their comparison. Such assessment could be done without knowing what other means were available or which means were chosen. Although it will often be the case that choosing some means rather than others will affect the overall effects, an inquiry about costs and benefits is nevertheless a different kind of inquiry than one about means and ends.

Nevertheless, Fordham and de la Mare appear to equate benefits with ends, and costs with means. Thus, in their formulation, the question "Do the ends justify the means?" is equated with the overall cost-benefit analysis. However, that identification is a mistake. First of all, no particular chosen means can be wholly explained by its costs. The essence of means is a contribution to the achievement of an end. Means themselves are in this sense beneficial only to the extent to which they contribute to the benefit of the accomplished end. Understanding means as purely "costs" is misunderstanding their role in practical reasoning, and leads to absurd results. If means were properly identified with the costs of a measure, the degree of harm/costs caused by means could always, at least theoretically, be "outweighed" by a sufficient degree of benefit. This conception would not allow for a priori rejection of any available means; even forced castration, torture, or fake trials could be amenable to justification under special (but not inconceivable) circumstances, provided that there be an overall positive outcome of the cost/benefit analysis. Fordham and de la Mare's conception of means/ends fit turns out to have nothing to do with the actual relationship between means and ends, a relationship I explore below as part of the lost meaning of proportionality. It is rather identical with a cost-benefit analysis, which is a radically different operation than means-ends analysis.

The above analysis documents several different conceptions of proportionality that are live in the academic debates. The divergence in conceptions is surprising, yet understandable. It is surprising because "proportionality" is such an ascendant term in constitutional law that one would expect its meaning to be both stable and sound. On the other hand, proportionality is not the first (and probably not the last) concept to run such a course. The story of the legal principle of proportionality is similar in some sense to the story of the principles of subsidiarity or solidarity in EU law.[26] All of these principles originated in Catholic moral and political philosophy and were later transposed into legal contexts. A truth well recognized among comparative lawyers – transplantation of legal concepts can be a dangerous business – has its bite in the stories of subsidiarity and solidarity as well as proportionality. If a concept is removed from its natural environment, stripped of its foundational principles, and applied in a new context, it should be expected that the concept will lose some of its original appeal, become unclear in terms of its content as well as its application, and develop a new life barely reminiscent of its original form. In other words, such transplantations are sure recipes for confusion.

The rest of this chapter is devoted to presenting, explaining, and partially defending the lost meaning of proportionality. Were this meaning to be restored by academics and judges, it would alter the course of much of the present debate on judicial review, adjudication, and human rights, enriching them with sound principles of action theory that could help both judges and academics focus on the questions that really matter.

III. THE LOST MEANING

Proportionality in Ethics

To understand the original meaning of proportionality and its intellectual appeal, we have to explore briefly its original context – the doctrine of double

---

[26] On the roots of subsidiarity, see P.D. Marquardt, "Subsidiarity and Sovereignty in the European Union," 18 *Fordham Int'l. L. J.* 616 (1994–1995); Romano Prodi, *Europe as I See It* (trans. Allan Cameron, 2000). For an argument suggesting differences between Catholic and European subsidiarity, see N.W. Barber, "The Limited Modesty of Subsidiarity," (2005) 11 *Eur. L. J.* 308.

effect (henceforth DDE),[27] also known as the "principle of double effect" or more recently as "double-effect reasoning".[28] The purpose of DDE is to articulate requirements that have to be cumulatively fulfilled in order for a human action with both positive and negative effects (hence "double" effect) to be morally good. The requirement of proportionality was usually articulated as the fourth and last requirement of DDE. The four requirements of DDE can be well explained in the context of the classic problem: killing in self-defense.[29] When is a self-defensive action that results in the death of the attacker morally justified? First, apart from the death of the attacker, the action must not be evil on another ground. Second, the attacked person must intend his own self-defense (not revenge, proving his strength to others, and so forth). Third, the death of the attacker must not be an intended means used to achieve the end of self-defense. In other words, the death of the attacker has to be a side effect of using the necessary means for stopping the attack. Fourth, the negative side effect must not be disproportionate in the given circumstances. Since no one has a moral duty to refrain from saving one's life from an unjustified attack, the death of the attacker is not disproportionate if brought about by the only available means for stopping the attack.[30] To find negative side effects disproportionate, one has to make a prudential judgment that brings into play requirements of all the different virtues.[31] Proportionality here serves a fairly limited role. It is a label for various requirements bearing on the problem of evaluating the negative side effects of a human action. This evaluation of side effects comes as a last step. One first has to determine the content of the actor's

---

[27] For a historical overview of the development of the DDE, see J.T. Mangan, "An Historical Analysis of the Principle of Double Effect," (1949) 10 *Theological Stud.* 41.

[28] Thomas Cavanaugh, "The Intended/Foreseen Distinction's Ethical Relevance," (1996) 25 *Philosophical Papers* 179.

[29] The famous passage in Aquinas that inspired later authors to formulate DDE deals with the case of self-defense: "And yet, though proceeding from a good intention, an act may be rendered unlawful, if it be *out of proportion* to the end [*si non sit proportionatus fini*]. Wherefore if a man, in self-defence, uses more than necessary violence, it will be unlawful: whereas if he repel force with moderation his defense will be lawful": Thomas Aquinas, *The Summa Theologica* (Kevin Knight [ed.], 2nd ed., 2008) II-II Q 64 a 7 (emphasis added).

[30] Notice that this conclusion does not follow from any kind of measuring/balancing of the values of the lives concerned. The attacker's life is not less valuable than the life of the attacked. Also, a truly self-defensive action against many attackers would not be less justified because it would result in more deaths.

[31] This is my application of a relatively traditional formulation of DDE's requirements, which is found in G.G. Grisez, "Toward a Consistent Natural-Law Ethics of Killing," 15 *Am. J. Juris.* 64 at 78 (1970). For two other formulations of DDE, see Alison McIntyre, "Doctrine of Double Effect" in Edward N. Zalta (ed.), *The Stanford Encyclopedia of Philosophy* (Fall 2008 ed.) retrieved from http://plato.stanford.edu/archives/fall2008/entries/double-effect/.

intention – his ends and means chosen in deliberation from the available alternatives. If the means or ends chosen are flawed for some reason, there is no need/reason to evaluate side effects.

It is noteworthy that the problem faced by human rights courts has a very similar structure. State actions of the kind considered by such courts usually have or are claimed (by the governing authorities, legislative or executive) to have legitimate aims – that is, they seek desirable effects – while also causing those undesirable effects that motivated the applicants to challenge the state actions in court. Thus, the usual matter for the court's consideration is some state action with two effects: one good/desired or desirable/legitimate, and one bad/undesired or undesirable/illegitimate. It is precisely this problem that provides the intellectual bridge between the idea of proportionality in ethics and in law.

Drawing on the tradition of double-effect reasoning, I articulate four main principles that a court should take into account in its review of state action.[32] A brief explanation of the meaning and importance of the first three follows:[33]

1.   There is an essential difference between what the state is intending and what the state is causing and accepting as a foreseeable side effect.
2.   The state intends both its ends and the means. There is no fundamental difference between means and ends for the purposes of evaluation.
3.   The evaluation of the state's responsibility for those effects brought about intentionally requires different standards than the evaluation of the state's responsibility for side effects, which are not intended.

---

[32] I will assume that human and state actions have similar structure. This assumption is shared and argued for by many authors from different schools of thought: see e.g., John Finnis, "Persons and Their Associations" in John Finnis, *Intention and Identity: Collected Essays, vol. II* (2011) (hereinafter Finnis, "Intention and Identity") 92; Michael E. Bratman, "Shared Cooperative Activity," (1992) 101 *The Philosophical Rev.* 327; E.S. Anderson and R.H. Pildes, "Expressive Theories of Law: A General Restatement," 148 *U. Pa. L. Rev.* 1503 (2000). For a partial argument against this assumption, see David Enoch, "Intending, Foreseeing, and the State," 13 *Legal Theory* 69 (2007).

[33] My analysis here is inspired mainly by the following works: G.E.M. Anscombe, *Intention* (1957); John Finnis, "Object and Intention in Moral Judgments According to Aquinas" in Finnis, *Intention and Identity, supra* note 32, 152; John Finnis, "Intention and Side-Effects" in Finnis, *Intention and Identity,* ibid. 173; John Finnis, Germain Grisez, and Joseph Boyle, " 'Direct' and 'Indirect': A Reply to Critics of Our Action Theory," (2001) 65 *The Thomist* 1; Ralph McInerny, *Aquinas on Human Action: A Theory of Practice* (1992); David S. Oderberg, *Moral Theory: A Non-Consequentialist Approach* (2000); Stephen L. Brock, *Action and Conduct: Thomas Aquinas and the Theory of Action* (1998); Christian E. Brugger, "Action, Intention and Self-Determination" (2005) 6 *Vera Lex: J. Internat'l Natural L. Society* 79.

4. There are certain effects that should never be intended by the state, either as means or as an end.[34]

Intention and Foresight

The most fundamental principle of action is the recognition of the distinction between what is intended and what is foreseen and caused as an unintended side effect. This difference is crucial for identifying as clearly as possible what exactly is under review, i.e., what the state has done, what state action is called to question. Notwithstanding the substantial controversy surrounding these concepts in ethical discussions, they are fundamental to many legal categories.[35]

What is the difference between what is intended and what is caused and accepted solely as a side effect? At the most fundamental level, it is the difference in a state's attitudes toward certain states of affairs. When a state pursues something by intentional action, the character of the thing pursued throws light on the character of the state.[36] A state that adopts a course of extermination of some of its citizens is different in character from a state that equally defends all of its citizens from attack. A state that administers justice by collecting evidence through torture, or even the threat of torture, is different from a state that administers justice by giving the accused a fair trial and an opportunity for legal counsel. What the state chooses to do as an ends or means determines most profoundly what kind of state it is. This is not necessarily so with other effects that the state foreseeably causes and accepts but does not

[34] This is a claim that is perhaps much more controversial in ethics than in the context of human rights law. Who would deny that states should never intend mass murders, organized rapes, false convictions, genocide, and so forth? The European Court of Human Rights regularly admits the existence of absolute/exceptionless rights: e.g., *Chahal v. United Kingdom*, (1997), (App no 22414/93), 23 E.H.R.R. 413 at para. 79.

[35] The intention/foresight distinction is essential in some legal systems for some distinctions made in criminal law, tort law, law of negligence, law of war, as well as constitutional law. This is demonstrated in the following works: A. Duff, *Intention, Agency and Criminal Liability: Philosophy of Action and the Criminal Law* (1990); John Finnis, "Intention and Side-Effects" in Finnis, *Intention and Identity, supra* note 32, 173; John Finnis, "Intention in Tort Law" in Finnis, *Intention and Identity*, ibid. 198; E.C. Lyons, "In Incognition – The Principle of Double Effect in American Constitutional Law," 57 *Fla. L. Rev.* 469 (2005); E.C. Lyons, "Balancing Acts: Intending Good and Foreseeing Harm – The Principle of Double Effect in the Law of Negligence," 3 *Geo. J. L. & Pub. Pol'y.* 453 (2005).

[36] For a discussion of character-constituting nature of human actions, see J. Gardner, "Wrongs and Faults" in A.P. Simester (ed.) *Appraising Strict Liability* (2005) 61–67. It is not clear to what extent Gardner would be willing to extend his analysis of individual action to state action. However, one of the examples he uses in the course of the argument is an example of a state action – a preemptive strike on Iraq. See also N.W. Barber, *The Constitutional State* (2010).

intend. Such negative side effects are regretted, undesired, and minimized.[37] For example, a state intending to build a highway knows that such a project will have a negative impact on those of its citizens whose homes happen to be located on the land designated for the projected highway, or who live nearby. Nevertheless, those negative effects are not intended; if they could have been reasonably avoided, they would have been. Such a situation is very different from one where a state wants to "punish" a certain minority of its citizens and uses the highway building project as a pretext or an opportunity for destroying their homes and causing them to disperse. In both cases, some of the citizens will lose their homes; the result of the state action is thus the same. However, the situation of the latter citizens is fundamentally different because the state action is fundamentally different. The negative impact caused by the destruction of their homes was part of the state's means or proposal for action (and therefore intended). They were thus treated differently by the state than the former citizens. The difference is not illusory: it is as real as being intentionally kicked or just accidently tripped over – a person is treated differently even though the bruise is the same. To summarize the meaning of the intention-foresight distinction: there are certain states of affairs, which, when intended, are the product of a state failing to deal with its citizens in the way that is due to them; that is, they constitute a failure of commutative justice. This is the case even though the same states of affairs would not constitute the same failure if they were just side effects of a legitimate action.

Responsibility for Side Effects

Nevertheless, the state carries responsibility for the side effects of its intended actions, and there are circumstances in which certain side effects should not be accepted. In other words, foreseeing negative side effects of an action (in some circumstances) would be a reason not to undertake that action. States can be blamed for causing negative effects even if they are unintended. However, it is crucial to realize that the responsibility for side effects is different than the responsibility for intended means and ends, and it should be evaluated by different criteria.[38]

---

[37] This is not to say that the state cannot be culpable for side effects. The state's responsibility for side effects will be discussed below.

[38] For an example of working out some of these criteria in respect to negative side effects relevant in the law of negligence, see Edward C. Lyons, "Balancing Acts: Intending Good and Foreseeing Harm – The Principle of Double Effect in the Law of Negligence," 3 *Geo. J. L. & Pub. Pol'y.* 453 at 482–489 (2005).

The criteria include all available moral and legal standards, except for those that bear only on what is intended. A driving principle in judging the acceptability of side effects is the requirement to prevent harm/evil if possible. In fact, the principle's bite may be much stronger in cases of state action than individual action. Perhaps states are required to take more care in preventing foreseeable negative side effects of their actions since their actions would usually have much greater impact on many people than an individual action. However, it would be absurd to expect that such side effects could be wholly eliminated. Moreover, requiring such elimination might lead to a different kind of injustice.[39]

The first obvious criterion in considering side effects is the question of whether due care was paid to prevent the side effects.[40] There could be numerous ways in which the state fails to pay due care and many of them can be discerned in the Convention case law: not taking the side effects into consideration in the deliberation leading to action, treating them very lightly and diminishing their importance, not trying to find ways to avoid them, and so forth. Imagine a state building a highway without due consideration being given to the number and type of landowners and property affected. Let us say that a decision is made to destroy several historical villages in order to build a small part of an international highway system although there are alternative (albeit more expensive) plausible routes. It would be outrageous, but the fault of such action would not stem from the intention of the highway planners (the ends and means chosen are good or neutral by themselves), or from the strict financial cost-benefit analysis (the chosen route is cheaper even if all the landowners are paid market prices for their property), but rather from the glaring disregard for the value of people's homes and historical sites.

There are other criteria for evaluating the willingness to accept certain negative side effects, which are less objective. Which side effects are acceptable and which are not will often partly depend on who carries the responsibility for considering them, and their prior commitments, roles, and relationships.

---

[39] This point is well illustrated in *Saadi v. Italy* (App no 37201/06) (2008) European Court of Human Rights (hereinafter *Saadi*). The Court found a rights violation when the state sought to deport a dangerous person to a country where he could face torture. The state was forbidden to be a partial cause of torturing someone, while being forced potentially to be a partial cause of torturing someone else (if the person concerned continued with his criminal activity). The Court completely disregarded the distinction between intention and side effect. For further analysis of the case, see Lutéran, "Towards Proportionality," *supra* note 8, at 17.

[40] There is undoubtedly a relevant difference between foreseen and unforeseen side effects, although a further question can always be asked whether the unforeseen side effects could and/or should have been foreseen.

There may be many unique features of a particular state or government that would either justify accepting certain side effects or make such acceptance a scandal.[41] For example, a right-wing government might have greater moral difficulty in accepting the side effect of diminishing personal wealth of the rich sections of a society through a progressive tax scheme than a left-wing government, which might even welcome (but not intend) such a side effect. The customs, traditions, or conventions may all play a role in deciding which side effects are too negative to allow.

This poses clear problems for the human rights review. Once a court gets to the stage of evaluating side effects of state action, it should proceed with great caution. There will be cases of glaring state negligence and ignorance of important interests protected by rights, which a court can pinpoint. However, there will be many more cases where the justifiability of accepting the negative side effects will depend on many subjective features of particular states and societies, of which a reviewing court (especially an international court) will have no significant knowledge. Different societies may be justified in accepting and rejecting different side effects.[42] The fact that a certain negative impact on someone's interests was a side effect of a state action is a reason (although not conclusive) to defer to the state's practical deliberation unless causing such side effects is grossly unacceptable. Ultimately, there can be no clear-cut a priori rules for judging which side effects are grossly unacceptable: this requires the well-informed prudential judgment of virtuous persons. This is what some people[43] understand "balancing" to mean, and there is no harm in admitting that in this limited sense, the proportionality test requires balancing. It is noteworthy, however, that once a reviewing court gets to this stage there is no point invoking proportionality (or balancing) anymore. A reviewing court's only role at this point is to signal that it has approached an issue where prudential/reasonable judgment and choice are required.

---

[41] For an example from Canada, see *Lalonde v. Ontario* (*Commission de restructuration des services de sante*), (2001) 56 O.R. (3d) 577 (Ont. C.A.), where the Court of Appeal quashed a decision of the Ontario government to close a hospital. The reason for closing the hospital (which was the only French-language hospital in Ontario) was to achieve fiscal savings, but the unintended side effect was to restrict the access to health care by Ontario Francophones. Because of the prior constitutional and legal commitments to the French linguistic minority in Ontario, the Court was able to judge the side effect to be unacceptable.

[42] For example, a more risk-averse society might lower the speed limits in order to decrease deaths on roads while foreseeing and accepting resulting economic burden. A different society may be more inclined to accept higher risk of traffic accidents as a side effect of higher speed limits and faster transportation.

[43] See Endicott, "Proportionality and Incommensurability," Chapter 14 in this volume.

IV. THE RECONSTRUCTED PROPORTIONALITY TEST

Although the principle of proportionality was traditionally associated only with the problem of evaluating side effects, contemporary common usage (and want of a better term) justify labeling the four principles of state action articulated above as a proportionality test. It should be clear, however, that strictly speaking, the requirement of proportionate side effects is just one (and not the most essential) of the conditions of this reconstructed proportionality test.[44] This section will argue that this reconstructed proportionality test should be preferred to the balancing test that is commonly used by the European Court of Human Rights.

The standard balancing test reduces all constitutional conflicts to a conflict between two values/interests/rights. The proportionality test identifies at least three different kinds of constitutional conflicts, each requiring a slightly different approach from a court. These distinctions stem from a realistic understanding of the nature of constitutional rights and of state action. They equip a court with a meaningful structure for reviewing state action. These claims will be substantiated in the following paragraphs.

An increasing number of legal scholars warn of the destructive power of the language of balancing over the capacity of rights to guide judicial decision making. Many think that "the language of balance begs more questions than it solves",[45] that it is "a very difficult and, in a way, arbitrary reasoning",[46] that it "camouflages much of the scholar's and the court's thinking underlying rights",[47] and that the "balancing approach fails spectacularly to deliver what it promises" because it "does not lend itself to a rational reconstruction of the argumentative path that has led to a particular decision".[48] Many agree that balancing can be nothing more than a pleasant-sounding rationalization for beliefs of the balancers, beliefs held in some sense a priori. Where balancing is a juridical tool, it embeds arbitrariness into the structure of judicial reasoning. Such arbitrariness leads to outcomes greatly dependent on individual factual

---

[44] The reconstructed proportionality test, here defended, is analogous to the double-effect test traditionally formulated as a doctrine of double effect, in which proportionality is just one of the requirements.

[45] Lorenzo Zucca, *Constitutional Dilemmas: Conflicts of Fundamental Legal Rights in Europe and the USA* (2007) 86 (hereinafter Zucca, *Constitutional Dilemmas*).

[46] Albert Bleckmann and Michael Bothe, "General Report on the Theory of Limitations on Human Rights" in Armand L.C. De Mestral and others (eds.), *The Limitation of Human Rights in Comparative Constitutional Law = La Limitation des Droits de l'Homme en Droit Constitutionnel Comparé* (1986) at 109.

[47] Webber, *Negotiable Constitution, supra* note 7 at 86–89.

[48] Tsakyrakis, "Proportionality," *supra* note 7 at 18.

circumstances and prior judicial beliefs. An ability to be governed by law decreases as a result.[49]

In a typical balancing approach, a court presents itself with two broad rights and/or interests, discusses several considerations, and reaches a result that does not obviously follow from the explicit premises. For example, the main issue in *Evans v. United Kingdom*, in the view of the European Court of Human Rights, was a conflict between the Article 8 rights of two private individuals.[50] The core issue in *Dickson v. United Kingdom* was formulated in terms of a balance between the competing public and private interests involved.[51] The issue before the Court in *Otto Preminger Institut v. Austria* was the weighing up of two conflicting fundamental freedoms – freedom of expression and freedom of thought, conscience, and religion.[52] Such vague formulations of the core/fundamental issue for the Court to decide are typical of the balancing approach. However, they are obviously unhelpful for reaching a solution.

The reconstructed proportionality test can help the Court structure its inquiry in a more helpful way. Instead of presenting it with two conflicting values, it invites the Court to search the legal and possibly moral terrain in order to find a rule that could solve the issue and prevent the "constitutional dilemma" of having to choose between two conflicting values. Thus, the resolution of the three above-mentioned cases would depend on such fundamental questions as the following: Does Article 8 prohibit state actions that cause the unintended side effect that a person will be prevented from becoming a genetic parent? Is such an action prohibited by Article 8 even if the alternative course of action would cause as its side effect someone being forced to become a

---

[49] For a classic exposition of the requirements of the rule of law, see Lon L. Fuller, *The Morality of Law* (1964). Also see Endicott, "Proportionality and Incommensurability" and T.R.S. Allan, "Democracy, Legality, and Proportionality," Chapters 14 and 10, respectively, in this volume.

[50] [2006] ECHR 200, (2006) 43 E.H.R.R. 21, at para. 73 (hereinafter *Evans*). The applicant sought an order to preserve embryos which had been conceived using IVF treatment with her eggs and her (then) partner's sperm. After their relationship ended, Ms Evans's partner withdrew his consent to the continuation of the IVF treatment (that is, the implantation of one or more embryos in Ms Evans's uterus), which then required, under UK law, that the embryos be destroyed. Ms Evans complained that her former partner's right under UK law to withdraw his consent to continuation of the IVF treatment violated her Convention right to respect for her private and family life.

[51] (App no 44362/04), 46 E.H.R.R. 41, at para. 71 (hereinafter *Dickson*). The applicants complained that the UK decision to refuse one of them, a prisoner, access to artificial insemination of the second applicant, his wife, violated their Convention right to respect for private and family life. For a deeper analysis of the *Dickson* case, see Lutéran, "Towards Proportionality," *supra* note 8, at 18–22.

[52] (App no 13470/87), 19 E.H.R.R. 34 at para. 55 (hereinafter *Otto Preminger*). The applicant association complained that a seizure and forfeiture of its blasphemous film violated its Convention right to freedom of expression.

parent against his will (the *Evans* case), or decreased trust in the penal system
and changes to the punitive character of imprisonment (the *Dickson* case)?
Does Article 10 prohibit states from intentionally limiting expression on the
ground that it offends certain religious groups? The balancing approach would
have us believe that there is only one kind of constitutional conflict – conflict
of two rights/interests/values. A reformed proportionality test would recognize
and bring to the fore several qualitatively different kinds of conflict. The chart
illustrates the difference between these conflicts.[53]

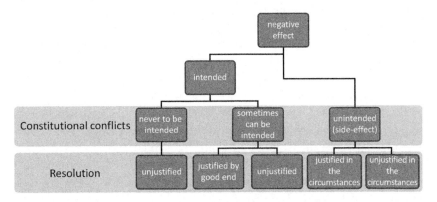

There are essentially three different kinds of constitutional conflicts. The
first kind involves a state action intending a negative effect that can never be
intended. For example, after the *Dudgeon* case[54] determined that one's interest
in engaging in private homosexual practices is an interest that cannot be intentionally harmed,[55] any state criminalizing homosexual acts of adult individuals
in private would be violating a right to respect for private life.[56] The balancing
approach sees such cases as conflicts of two considerations – the reasons for
the criminalizing law and the negative effects on the private life of individuals.
The proportionality test, however, sees it as a relatively simple subsumption
of a state action under the norm entailed by a right. Much of human rights
adjudication deals with this kind of conflict. Some authors conceptualize this
aspect of adjudication in terms of applying "exclusionary reasons" for action

---

[53] Proportionality assessment today usually takes place when the Court asks whether a particular
interference was necessary in a democratic society, having established that the interference
was prescribed by law and pursued a legitimate aim. The reconstructed proportionality test
has nothing to say about the "prescribed by law" requirement. The remaining two steps are
integrated and somewhat transformed in the proposed structure.

[54] *Dudgeon v. United Kingdom* (1982), (App. no. 7525/76).

[55] That is arguably why *Dudgeon* is considered a landmark case for the interpretation of the
Article 8 right to respect for private life.

[56] *Norris v. Ireland* (1988), (App. no. 10581/83); *Modinos v. Cyprus* (1993), (App. No. 15070/89).

entailed by rights.[57] For example, R.H. Pildes argues that this is precisely what much of American constitutional adjudication consists of: "An exclusionary reason identifies particular reasons as inappropriate justifications for government action. When certain reasons are ruled out as permissible bases for action, they are simply excluded from being given any potential weight in a decision making calculus".[58] This is the first kind of constitutional conflict.[59] Balancing has no role to play in reaching its solution; all that is needed is to determine the correct description of the state action,[60] the interest harmed, and then judge whether the interest belongs to the category of interests that can never be intentionally harmed. This should be the most difficult hurdle for a state to overcome. For example, it is hardly controversial to say that states may never torture, stage fake trials, quiet political opponents by imprisonment, eradicate unwelcome minorities, and so forth. This idea is expressed in the Convention case law by the idea of an "absolute right"[61] and, arguably, by the idea of an "essence" of a right.[62] Thus, if the Court finds that a negative effect was intended and that it is the kind of effect that cannot be intended, it has to find the state action unjustified.

The second kind of conflict involves a state action pursuing a good end by means that harm an interest that, although in some way constitutionally protected, is nonetheless a kind of interest that can at times be constitutionally – that is, permissibly – harmed. These are, for example, cases where states prohibit certain kinds of expression or assembly with a view of promoting some public interest.[63] Here the Court can examine whether the means chosen truly promote the proclaimed public interest and it was open to the state to use means that, although similarly effective, would not harm the protected interest (or other protected interests). If these requirements are satisfied, the Court should be very slow to find the state action unjustified. If the action is found

---

[57] For the development of the concept of "exclusionary reason," see Joseph Raz, *Practical Reason and Norms* (2nd ed. 1990).

[58] Richard H. Pildes, "The Structural Conception of Rights and Judicial Balancing," (2002) 6 *Rev. Const. Stud.* 179, at 189.

[59] For another argument that at least some constitutional conflicts involve "the problem of identifying which considerations are being altogether excluded and in what way," see Iddo Porat, "The Dual Model of Balancing: A Model for the Proper Scope of Balancing in Constitutional Law," 27 *Cardozo L. Rev.* 1393 at 1448 (2005–2006). For a similar argument suggesting that rights should be treated as second-order reasons, see Denise Meyerson, "Why Courts Should Not Balance Rights against the Public Interest," (2007) 31 *Melbourne U. L. Rev.* 801.

[60] It will be the description picking out the intention of the state.

[61] *Chahal, supra* note 34 at para. 80; *Saadi, supra* note 39 at para. 127.

[62] *Rees v. United Kingdom* (1987), (App. no. 9532/81) at para. 50; *F v. Switzerland* (1987), (App. no. 11329/85) at para. 32.

[63] See, e.g., *Ezelin v. France* (1992), 14 E.H.R.R. 362; *Otto Preminger, supra* note 52; *Wingrove v. United Kingdom* (1996), (App. no. 17419/90).

unjustified, the Court should give reasons that would specify the subjects or circumstances of the action that made it unjustified. In so doing, the Court would formulate a rule that would serve to specify a given right in the present case and in the future. For example, an ability to vote in parliamentary elections is certainly an interest protected by the European Convention.[64] However, it is undeniable that it is permissible for states to "harm" this interest intentionally under certain conditions and circumstances. Can states disenfranchise all convicted prisoners? Such was the question asked by the European Court of Human Rights in *Hirst v. United Kingdom*.[65] The Convention does not provide an answer to this question. One has to engage in full-blooded moral and political analysis. The arguments given by the Court in this case can be criticized at different points. However, the result is clear. The Court specified a Convention right to vote by articulating a rule prohibiting states from disenfranchising all convicted prisoners in custody. This is a rule that can be applied in similar cases in the future.[66] One should be reminded that a proportionality test alone cannot resolve such a case; a substantive legal and/or moral argument is also needed. The only thing that a proportionality test can do is alert the Court to the type of conflict involved and structure the inquiry.

The third kind of conflict involves a state action pursuing the common good both in its means and ends, but nevertheless causes negative side effects. This is perhaps the situation most reminiscent of the case of two values standing against each other. Whatever the state does, it will cause some negative side effects. Sometimes the side effects will not touch an interest protected by a right. At other times, there will be obvious reasons why states should not allow certain side effects. However, there will be cases when both choosing X and non-X would result in side effects damaging a protected interest and there will be no reason why the state should refrain from acting one way or the other. The *Evans* case is a good illustration. So are *Odievre v. France* or *Saadi v. Italy* and many others.[67] If the Court is asked to review such a situation, it has no rational criteria to adjudicate between the two values. All it can do is to choose one or the other value. This choice is not guided by reason, but instead by feelings and preferences. To decide such a case is "to prioritize certain values over others under certain circumstances. By so doing, we may reshape the whole identity of our communities. We have to think carefully before

---

[64] Article 3 of Protocol no 1.

[65] *Hirst v. United Kingdom* (no. 2) (2005), (App. no. 74025/01), [2005] E.C.H.R. 681.

[66] It is of course open to question whether this is a good rule and whether the European Court is the legitimate authority for creating it.

[67] *Odievre v. France* (2003), (App. no. 42326/98); *Saadi, supra* note 39.

suggesting outcomes that are potentially disruptive".[68] There is no reason to think that such judicial decisions are going to be "more just than any other institution's decision. In this case, it may be desirable to consider a greater degree of deference".[69]

Each constitutional conflict identified above requires a different approach from the Court. This realization itself is a useful insight provided by the principles of state action underlying the reconstructed proportionality test. This insight provides a much more structured and principled approach to human rights review. The balancing approach reduces all cases to the problem of weighing two rights/principles/values/interests – a problem that is unsolvable almost by definition. There is a qualitative difference between the balancing approach and the proportionality test, one of which leads systematically to rational stalemate and the second of which leads systematically away from it, although both of them sometimes end at the same spot.

V. CONCLUSION

I have outlined the lost meaning of the principle of proportionality and suggested the usefulness of its rediscovery for human rights adjudication. The idea of proportionality in ethics served as a label for prudential considerations of the acceptability of negative side effects of a human action. It played a part in a realistic and sophisticated structure for evaluating human action. The intellectual appeal of this structure for the problems faced by human rights review courts arguably brought proportionality to the center stage of constitutional legal debates. However, the interconnected web of principles of action from which proportionality sprang has largely been forgotten. As a result, more and more human rights cases are reduced to a conflict between two values/interests/rights, and the language of balancing is presented as an arbiter of these conflicts.

This chapter has not provided a conclusive critique of the language of balancing. Instead, it offered an alternative to balancing – a reconstructed proportionality test. This test invites the Court to identify as precisely as possible the intentional state action and the negative effect complained of. The Court is then faced with potentially three different kinds of constitutional conflicts, all of which require slightly different approaches. If the Court were to follow this test, it could not reach a result without answering several important questions. As a result, it would have to make transparent many moral positions that,

---

[68] Zucca, *Constitutional Dilemmas, supra* note 45 at 24 (citations omitted).
[69] Ibid., at 84.

in contemporary practice, remain largely hidden. This could arguably lead to more principled and predictable decision making. Without doubt, the proportionality test here defended needs further elaboration. The present argument has succeeded, however, if it has shown that such elaboration is worth the effort.

3   Proportionality Is Dead: Long Live Proportionality!

Alison L. Young

I. INTRODUCTION

Debates about proportionality take place in different arenas. Barristers and scholars of English public law debate the suitability of the legal test of proportionality. Public law theorists, however, are more concerned with the concept of proportionality. When understood as a legal test, the groundswell of opinion in English public law is that proportionality is very much alive, its influence growing as it is applied to more and more areas. English courts use proportionality when determining aspects of European Union law[1] and for evaluating whether actions of public authorities are unlawful for having transgressed Convention rights or legislation is compatible with Convention rights, particularly the non-absolute rights of Articles 8–11.[2] Proportionality is emerging as the main test to determine whether there are sufficiently strong arguments of public policy to override a substantive legitimate expectation.[3] In addition, arguments abound that proportionality should be accepted as the main test for the substantive review of discretionary powers, replacing the test of *Wednesbury*[4] unreasonableness.[5] However, when understood as a concept,

---

[1] For example, when determining whether restrictions placed on the free movement of goods or services are justifiable in European Union law, as in *R v. Chief Constable of Sussex ex parte International Traders' Ferry Ltd* [1999] 2 A.C. 418; [1999] 1 All E.R. 129 and *R (Countryside Alliance) v. Attorney General* [2008] 1 A.C. 719, and most recently, in *Sinclair Collis v. Secretary of State for Health* [2012] 2 W.L.R. 304 (hereinafter *Sinclair Collis*).

[2] *R (Daly) v. Secretary of State for the Home Department* [2001] 2 A.C. 532.

[3] *R v. North and East Devon Health Authority ex parte Coughlan* [2001] Q.B. 213; *R (Niazi) v. Secretary of State for the Home Department* [2008] E.W.C.A. Civ. 755; *R (Abdi) v. Secretary of State for the Home Department* [2005] E.W.C.A. Civ. 1363; and *Paponette v. Attorney General for Trinidad and Tobago* [2011] 3 W.L.R. 219.

[4] *Associated Provincial Picture Houses v. Wednesbury Corporation* [1948] 1 K.B. 223.

[5] *R (Association of British Civilian Internees: Far Eastern Division) v. Secretary of State for Defence* [2003] Q.B. 1397, where the Court of Appeal seemed sympathetic to this argument, but held

a different picture emerges. Far from being seen as an emerging legal test, proportionality as a concept is more dead than alive, given that it fails to understand the nature of rights. To apply a test of proportionality to human rights is to reduce rights to mere interests, requiring them to be balanced against other "rights" and interests. But the precise nature of a right means that it cannot be balanced in this manner: rights override other interests. To apply a test of proportionality, therefore, is to undermine the very purpose of possessing a right in the first place.

This chapter examines the disparity between the growing acceptance of proportionality as a legal test in English law, particularly as regards its role in human rights adjudication, and the growing level of criticism of proportionality as a concept that may undermine as opposed to protect human rights. It will argue that the best means of explaining this disparity is through recognizing that debates as to the legal test of proportionality and debates as to its utility as a concept take place at different levels of abstraction. Once this is recognized, it will be argued that there are consequences not just as to whether proportionality is a suitable test for human rights adjudication, but also whether proportionality should only be applied by courts.

This chapter proposes a dual role for proportionality, applying different conceptions of proportionality to contestable, watershed issues of rights and non-contestable, non-watershed issues of rights. In the context of English law, this would also apply differently depending on whether courts were reading and giving effect to legislation so as to ensure its compatibility with Convention rights, for the purposes of sections 3 and 4 of the Human Rights Act 1998, or determining whether the action of a public authority was compatible with Convention rights for the purposes of section 6. I will argue that proportionality and deference are suitable for the latter, but not for the former, where deference is not needed given the design of the Human Rights Act 1998, which provides for a democratic dialogue model of rights protections, which could be undermined were proportionality and deference to be applied in the applications of sections 3 and 4.[6]

---

that it would take a decision of the then-House of Lords to achieve this objective. Recently, in *Quila v. Secretary of State for the Home Department*, Lord Justice Sedley appeared to suggest that proportionality would be applied in cases of common law rights as well as Convention rights: [2011] 3 All E.R. 81 at paras. 34–40; however, on appeal to the Supreme Court, their Lordships did not discuss this aspect of the case: [2011] 3 W.L.R. 836.

[6] For a more detailed discussion of the application of proportionality in "dialogue" models of human rights protections, see Stephen Gardbaum, "Proportionality and Democratic Constitutionalism," Chapter 12 in this volume.

In order to make this argument, this chapter will first explore two further possible explanations for the disparity between the growing acceptance of proportionality as a legal test for human rights adjudication and growing criticisms of the conceptual disparity between proportionality and human rights. The first section explains how the disparity between proportionality and rights is best understood as a disparity between particular conceptions of proportionality and particular conceptions of human rights. The second section explores the relationship between the legal test of proportionality and deference, exploring the extent to which the legal test of proportionality is suited to exclusive application by the courts. Both of these sections provide a partial insight into competing conceptions of proportionality and rights and the application of these conceptions by courts when applying the legal test of proportionality. What is missing from these accounts is a focus on how debates concerning rights occur at different levels of abstraction. This will be explored in the third section of this chapter, which proposes a dual role for proportionality with different conceptions of proportionality being applied by the legislature and the courts.

II. PROPORTIONALITY AND CONCEPTIONS OF RIGHTS

One of the main criticisms of proportionality is that it is incompatible with rights. Proportionality requires balancing. However, rights are not about balancing; rights override other interests. This section will explore this criticism, focusing in particular on the work of Robert Alexy – who provides one of the strongest defenses of the principle of proportionality – and criticisms of his theory of constitutional rights and constitutional adjudication.[7] The purpose of this examination is two-fold. First, I hope to demonstrate that it is not the case that proportionality is incompatible with rights, but that a *particular conception* of proportionality is incompatible with a *particular conception* of rights. As such, it is possible for proportionality to be reconciled with theories of rights, provided that specific conceptions of rights and proportionality are paired together to ensure this compatibility. Second, this section will provide part of the groundwork for a reorientation in our analysis of proportionality. It will suggest that our choice as to possible reconciliations between proportionality and rights need not depend on

---

[7] Robert Alexy, *A Theory of Constitutional Rights* (Julian Rivers translation, 2002) (hereinafter Alexy, *A Theory of Constitutional Rights*); and Robert Alexy, "Balancing, Constitutional Review and Representation," 3 *Int'l. J. Con. Law* 572 (2005) (hereinafter Alexy, "Balancing, Constitutional Review").

our theory of rights, but on the nature of constitutional adjudication, in particular on the level of abstraction at which constitutional adjudication takes place. This will be explained more clearly in the third section of this chapter.

The Contradiction between Proportionality and Rights

Alexy's support of proportionality stems not only from his analysis of the way in which proportionality is applied in decisions of the Federal Constitutional Court in Germany, but also from his analysis of the nature of rights and of constitutional rights in particular. First, Alexy regards rights not as rules, but as principles. Principles, in turn, are optimization concepts, or "ideal-oughts". Therefore, they are distinguished from rules. To understand the implications for Alexy's conception of rights, and therefore his defense of proportionality, requires further investigation of the distinction between rules and principles.

First, it is important to recognize that Alexy draws this distinction differently from Ronald Dworkin. In particular, it is not the case for Alexy that principles apply on a prima facie basis and rules apply on an all-or-nothing basis. Alexy accepts that exceptions to rules can be made, and concludes from this that both rules and principles apply on a prima facie basis. The difference between the two stems from the way in which exceptions or restrictions can be placed on principles and rules. The manner in which a principle is applied in a particular situation is not predetermined. The value of the principle is balanced against the value of a competing principle, through the use of an analysis of suitability, necessity, and proportionality. If the value of a competing principle outweighs the value of the original principle, then the original principle is defeated. When determining an exception to a rule, the reason for the restriction does not only need to outweigh the reason for the rule; it also needs to outweigh reasons for forming the rule and fixing the judgment in the first place – for example, it would also need to override the reasons for obeying the rules established by a legitimate law-making authority in that particular legal or political order.[8]

To regard rights as principles draws the necessary connection between rights and balancing. Principles, like values, need to be refined if we are to determine how they are to be applied in particular situations. However, balancing need

[8] See Alexy, ibid.; Kai Möller, "Balancing and the Structure of Constitutional Rights," 5 *Int'l. J. Con. Law* 453 (2007) (hereinafter Möller, "Balancing"); and Mattias Kumm, "Constitutional Rights as Principles: On the Structure and Domain of Constitutional Justice," 2 *Int'l. J. Con. Law* 574 (2004) (hereinafter Kumm, "Constitutional Rights as Principles").

not dictate that proportionality be employed as the means through which to balance one right against other rights and interests. The test of proportionality is required because Alexy views constitutional rights as a hybrid between rules and principles. Like principles, constitutional rights express ideal-oughts – values that require optimization. They are not rules as the delineation of their content requires balancing. To classify constitutional rights as rules would require either that all constitutional rights be applied on an all-or-nothing basis, or that any element of a conflict between a right and other interests be resolved through modifying the definition of rights, refining its true meaning so as to apply or not apply in a particular situation.

For example, were constitutional rights to be regarded as rules, it would not be the case that the constitutional right to privacy and the constitutional right to freedom of expression conflicted. Rather, it would be the case that the very definition of the right to freedom of expression and the right to privacy would determine how this apparent conflict should be resolved. If the right to freedom of expression requires the local council to print stories about how I spend my weekends, then this is because my right to privacy does not extend to the protection from detailed exposure of my weekend pursuits, even if I find this harmful. For Alexy, it is hard to see how this refinement of the definition of rights is anything other than balancing in disguise.

Constitutional rights, however, share some aspects of rules. In particular, constitutional rights contain an element of judgment as to how the right is applied in certain circumstances, ruling out some methods of balancing and giving an element of additional weight to constitutional rights in the balancing process. To determine otherwise would be to fail to recognize the importance of the constitutions containing these rights. To return to our example of the local council's publication of my weekend pursuits, captured by their many CCTV cameras and camera-equipped traffic-control helicopters, if all that was revealed were details of activities I performed in public over the weekend, then publication would not interfere with my right to privacy. I may have an interest in ensuring that my activities are not made known to a wider audience, but this interest would not be sufficient to outweigh the right to freedom of expression precisely because this is a constitutional right. Consequently, it requires more than a mere balancing of interests to be outweighed. A constitutional right can only be outweighed by a narrower set of rights and interests. Proportionality is the best means of achieving this balancing because the test of proportionality is capable of assigning greater weight to constitutional rights in the balancing exercise, and of restricting the range of justifications that can be used to restrict a constitutional right, through its account of suitability, necessity, and proportionality *stricto sensu*.

However, the idea that rights may be balanced appears to contradict the nature of constitutional rights, if not of rights themselves. Arguably, the concept of a right requires that rights are capable of overriding particular interests – in particular, arguments based on the common good. It makes no sense to talk of a right that has to be balanced against other interests if the nature of a right is that it overrides other interests. The classic exposition of this argument is found in the work of Dworkin, particularly as concerns his classification of "rights as trumps".[9] Dworkin's theory advocates that the concept of a right implies its ability to trump arguments from social policy. Even if the legislature or the executive were to believe that acting in a particular manner would promote the public good, it is prevented from doing so if this would require the restriction of a right. Even if it were the case that the world would be a better place were stories of my weekend activities to be published, or cameras used to follow my every move and broadcast this to a waiting world, my right to privacy would trump such arguments. It does not matter that protecting my right to privacy would render the population less happy; the purpose of a right is to ensure that such decisions are not made. Rights trump the public good.

In addition, the insistence on a connection between rights and balancing may undermine the aim of constitutional rights. Constitutions are designed, at least in part, to place restrictions on the activities of those in power. Constitutional rights limit the actions of the state, ensuring that states do not transgress the proper bounds of their power.[10] As Grégoire Webber points out, to interpret rights as optimizing principles requiring the application of proportionality could undermine this function in two ways. First, it is hard to see how rights place any distinct restriction on the state other than the requirement to act according to the principle of proportionality. Consequently, it is difficult to determine the restrictions placed on the state and to determine the range of rights possessed by individuals. To return to our example, although I may possess a right to privacy, I would not know beforehand what the right entailed, it being, in essence, part of a general right that the state not act in a disproportionate manner. Does the state act in a disproportionate manner if the council publishes its CCTV recordings of my weekend antics? The situation is more complicated if the publication is made not by the council, but by my neighbor exercising his right to freedom of expression. If neither of us have the certainty as to the content of our rights, we may not act to protect our rights from potentially

---

9 Ronald Dworkin, "Rights as Trumps" in Jeremy Waldron (ed.), *Theories of Rights* (1984) 153 (hereinafter Dworkin, "Rights as Trumps").
10 No claim is made at this stage as to whether this should be understood in deontological or instrumental terms.

unjustifiable infringement by the state, potentially defeating rights in practice.[11] Second, to draw a logical connection between constitutional rights and proportionality makes it impossible to provide a constitutional protection of categorical or absolute rights, as every right can be balanced against other rights and interests.[12]

A Tale of Two Complementary Conceptions

The previous section appears to provide conclusive evidence for the assertion that proportionality is incompatible with the nature of rights and purpose of constitutional rights. However, it would be wrong to conclude that proportionality is incompatible with constitutional rights and, therefore, should be abandoned. A more accurate understanding is to recognize that one particular conception of proportionality is incompatible with one particular conception of constitutional rights.

An insight into this possible reconciliation can be found in Mattias Kumm's analysis of Alexy's theory of constitutional rights. Kumm argues that Alexy's account of constitutional rights is incomplete and that, if supplemented, it can accord lexical priority to constitutional rights.[13] The most persuasive interpretation of Dworkin's theory of constitutional rights, for example, affords lexical priority to rights over social policy issues not because rights necessarily have more value than social policy issues, but because protecting rights is necessary to ensure the protection of equal concern and respect that underpins utilitarianism. To allow a conclusion as to the greater good that overrides a right would be to undermine the justification for deciding issues in order to maximize the greater good in the first place.[14] Although Alexy's theory of proportionality would appear to undermine Dworkin's conception of rights, it can be modified to accommodate these concerns through excluding social policy goals from the list of legitimate aims for which a right can be restricted. To return to our privacy/free speech example, if the council were publishing CCTV

---

[11] Grégoire C.N. Webber, "Proportionality, Balancing and the Cult of Constitutional Rights Scholarship," (2010) 23 *Can. J. L. & Jur.* 179 at 198–199. See also Webber's contribution to this volume in Chapter 6.

[12] Ibid., at 199–200. See also Stavros Tsakyrakis, "Proportionality: An Assault on Human Rights?" 7 *Int'l. J. Con. Law* 468 (2009).

[13] Kumm, "Constitutional Rights as Principles," *supra* note 8; see also Möller, "Balancing" *supra* note 8.

[14] Dworkin, "Rights as Trumps," *supra* note 9. See also, Richard H. Pildes, "Why Rights Are Not Trumps: Social Meanings, Expressive Harm and Constitutionalism," (1998) 27 *J. Legal Studies* 725; Jeremy Waldron, "Pildes on Dworkin's Theory of Rights," (2000) 29 *J. Legal Studies* 301; and Richard H. Pildes "Dworkin's Two Conceptions of Rights," (2000) 29 *J. Legal Studies* 309.

footage of my weekend antics merely because the population found it enter-
taining, then when applying proportionality, my right to privacy could not be
restricted merely because others enjoyed watching my private life unfold. My
right to privacy would trump the social goal of entertainment. The application
of proportionality in this way would appear to replicate the application of rights
as trumps.

A similar conclusion could be reached if lexical priority were granted to
rights merely because rights always were more important. Alexy's application
of proportionality relies on an analysis of the importance of the rights and
interests being balanced, as well as an assessment of the degree to which these
rights are infringed. If there are sufficiently strong reasons for giving greater
weight to the right in this calculation, then these reasons would also operate
when proportionality was applied, to accord enough weight to the right in
question that it would nearly always override the restriction placed on the
right. The right would operate in practice as though it were a trump over other
rights and interests by virtue of its importance.

Second, proportionality and theories of rights as trumps may be incompatible if the concept of a right requires that rights always apply in a categorical
manner. However, it is not clear that an acceptance of a conception of rights
as entailing lexical priority need always lead to the conclusion that rights can
only apply on a categorical basis. Schauer, for example, grants rights lexical priority not through regarding them as trumps, but through reclassifying rights as
shields. Non-rights can be defeated when there is a rational basis for defeating
them. However, stronger justifications are required if rights are to be defeated.
To possess a right is to require a stronger justification for the limitation of
that right.[15] This does not mean that rights are inevitably connected to balancing and proportionality; but it is to recognize that affording lexical priority to
rights need not entail that rights are always protected in an absolute manner.
Proportionality may be an effective means through which the strength of a
justification for the limitation of a right can be assessed, ensuring that rights
are only defeated by sufficiently strong rights and interests.

However, it is also important to recognize that, despite this apparent reconciliation between proportionality and conceptions of rights that afford lexical
priority to rights, there are still important differences between the two theories. A better understanding of the possible ways in which proportionality
can be reconciled with rights becomes apparent when we turn to analyses of
different conceptions of proportionality. In doing so, we begin to recognize

[15] Frederick Schauer, "A Comment on the Structure of Rights," 27 *Ga. L. Rev.* 415 (1992).

that different theories of rights are more suitable for a possible reconciliation with different conceptions of proportionality. Julian Rivers draws a distinction between "state-limiting" and "optimising" conceptions of proportionality. A state-limiting conception of proportionality, as its name suggests, uses proportionality as the means by which to determine the proper limits of state action. An optimizing conception of proportionality does not focus predominantly on determining whether the action of the state is unlawful; instead, an optimizing conception of proportionality uses proportionality as a means of balancing different interests, so as to correctly define the right in question.[16]

State-limiting theories of proportionality lend themselves to conceptions of rights that grant strong, lexical priority to rights. Rights are regarded as suitable for resolution by the judiciary, having lexical priority over policy decisions that are, in turn, regarded as suitable to be taken by more democratically accountable bodies such as the legislature and, indirectly, the executive.[17] Proportionality plays a role in resolving conflicts between rights and restrictions placed on rights to serve the public interest. As rights are afforded lexical priority to the public interest, any restriction placed on a right must be as small as possible in order to satisfy the test of proportionality. When applying a state-limiting conception of proportionality, the court aims to define the right, looking in particular at delineating the core elements of the right. This is frequently achieved by examining the values underpinning the right in question. Any restriction that harms the core of the right is deemed disproportionate, with those restricting marginal elements of the right being more likely to be proportionate restrictions.[18]

Optimizing conceptions of proportionality lend themselves to interest-based theories of rights. Interest-based theories of rights also examine the values behind the right, as well as the value in the public interest used to justify the restriction placed on the right when applying proportionality. However, optimizing conceptions of proportionality use the concept of proportionality as a means of weighing the importance of both the right and the public interest, without automatically tipping the scales in favor of the right. Balancing is used to weigh up the relative weight of the public interest and the right to determine whether the public interest gain is sufficient when compared to the restriction

---

[16] Julian Rivers, "Proportionality and Variable Intensity of Review," [2006] *C.L.J.* 174 at 177–182 (hereinafter Rivers, "Proportionality and Variable Intensity").

[17] Ibid., at 179.

[18] See Aileen McHarg, "Reconciling Human Rights and the Public Interest: Conceptual Problems and Doctrinal Uncertainty in the Jurisprudence of the European Court of Human Rights," (1999) 62 *M.L.R.* 671 at 680–681.

placed on the right.[19] Consequently, the optimizing theory of proportionality is more suited to Alexy's theory of constitutional rights.

It is not the case that proportionality is incompatible with the, or indeed even a, conception of constitutional rights. It is more accurate to conclude that a particular conception of rights – one that allocates lexical priority to constitutional rights – is incompatible with a particular conception of proportionality – an optimizing conception of proportionality. The choice between conceptions of proportionality may well be dictated by one's commitment to a particular theory of rights. Moreover, the connection is much deeper than the above analysis suggests. Optimizing theories of proportionality lend themselves to interest theories of rights and state-limiting theories of proportionality are connected to immunity-based theories of rights.[20]

Having recognized this possible refinement in the relationship between proportionality and rights, it is not the purpose of this chapter to weigh up the arguments for and against different theories of rights so as to determine which theory of rights – and of proportionality – should be adopted. Moreover, it is not the aim of this chapter to argue that this is the best means through which to resolve whether constitutional adjudication should employ proportionality. Instead, I wish to argue that this possible reconciliation is only partial. A better explanation is found through the realization that principles and rules operate at different levels of the reasoning process. This will be developed further in the third section of this chapter. First, we need to investigate a further criticism of proportionality.

III. PROPORTIONALITY, RIGHT ANSWERS, AND THE ROLE OF THE COURT

A second criticism of proportionality stems not from its incompatibility with particular conceptions of rights but from the justification of its application by the courts, both in terms of whether proportionality places a legitimate restriction on the actions of a democratically accountable legislature and also whether it is justifiable for the court to determine the precise scope of these restrictions. In particular, it is argued that an application by the courts of the principle of proportionality, particularly when used to balance

---

[19] Rivers, "Proportionality and Variable Intensity," *supra* note 16 at 181; and McHarg, ibid., at 678.

[20] See George Letsas, "The Truth in Autonomous Concepts: How to Interpret the ECHR," (2004) 15 *European J. Int'l. Law* 279, and "Two Concepts of the Margin of Appreciation," (2006) 26 *O.J.L.S.* 705; and Jeremy Waldron, "Rights in Conflict," (1989) 99 *Ethics* 503.

competing interests, is not able to provide objectively justifiable conclusions. Consequently, proportionality should not be applied as a means of restricting the democratically justifiable conclusions of the legislature. This section of the chapter will investigate this criticism. It will use the distinction drawn above between different conceptions of proportionality and different conceptions of rights to show that, as argued above, the criticism is specifically leveled at optimizing conceptions of proportionality and interest theories of rights. In addition, it will suggest that this potential contradiction can also be explained through regarding these debates as taking place at different levels of abstraction.

The example of an optimizing theory of proportionality combined with an interest theory of rights used by this chapter is Alexy's theory of constitutional rights. Alexy argues that balancing and proportionality are capable of providing an objectively justifiable answer to the issue of whether a particular action transgresses constitutional rights. His theory of proportionality requires courts to address three considerations:

1. The degree to which there is detriment to, or non-satisfaction of, principle A;
2. The importance of satisfying a competing principle, B, which has led to the detriment or non-satisfaction of principle A; and
3. An examination of the justification for limiting principle A in order to justify the achievement of principle B.

Alexy uses measurements of light, moderate, or serious in assessing these considerations. We can understand this formulation more clearly by applying it to the example referred to throughout this chapter – that of the local council using its CCTV footage to compile an account of my weekend pursuits, which it broadcasts more generally on the Internet. As Kumm recognizes,[21] the definition of a constitutional right used by Alexy is broad, meaning that constitutional rights are easily engaged. So, in identifying whether a right is engaged, the court would determine whether the broadcasting of details of my weekend pursuits is broadly consistent with the constitutional right to privacy, as well as whether this material was broadly within the constitutional right to freedom of expression, with both privacy and freedom of expression being understood as interests. An argument could be made that both privacy and freedom of expression are engaged – requiring the assessment of the balance of these interests. To allow anyone to have access to information about my weekend activities does appear to engage my right to privacy. Moreover, even

---

[21] Kumm, "Constitutional Rights as Principles," *supra* note 8.

though my weekend activities may appear to be dull, they may fall within a broadly construed right to freedom of expression for the general public to know what an Oxford academic gets up to in her "spare" time on the weekend.

Once these interests are triggered, the court determines the extent to which privacy has been infringed by freedom of expression before examining the justification for the restriction on privacy. The importance of my right to privacy, arguably, depends on the circumstances. It is only a slight interference if the council merely broadcasts my activities that take place in public – for example, visits to museums, parks, and libraries. The interference to privacy would be greater if information from CCTV cameras that recorded activities in my home were broadcast to the wider public. The value to the interest of freedom of expression would, for the most part, appear to be slight. There is very little value in knowing of the weekend antics of academics! We could, however, imagine situations in which this could be greater – for example if I had publically claimed that, as an academic, I worked a seventy-hour week, including spending my weekends marking essays, but in fact I spent my weekends on shopping expeditions. The value of the interests of freedom of expression and privacy become more apparent when we examine the justification provided for publishing my weekend activities. Was the council trying to show how effective their CCTV surveillance was for the purposes of dissuading potential criminals, trying to expose fraud, or merely trying to entertain?

If the council had published details of activities taking place in the privacy of my own home just to demonstrate how effective their CCTV cameras were, then the interference with privacy would be more serious and the value of freedom of expression in those circumstances would be light, justifying a decision that my right to privacy should be protected in this instance. In contrast, if I had claimed to spend my weekends working, demanding higher pay from the public purse, but actually spent them shopping, as seen from CCTV footage of my activities carried out in a public shopping area, then the restriction of my privacy would be light and the interest in freedom of expression would be moderate or serious, justifying restricting my right to privacy in order to promote the right to freedom of expression.

Applying proportionality in this manner may provide a means through which an application of the proportionality test furnishes objectively reasoned conclusions. However, the judiciary may not always be the best institution to make these assessments. What if, for example, the council was instructed to provide CCTV surveillance of my weekend activities to the secret service because the secret service suspected that I was not an academic but really a spy? The court may not be in a position to perform this balancing exercise, given that it would not have the necessary knowledge or expertise to determine whether the threat I presented to the nation was light, moderate, or severe. Consequently, it may be better for the court to defer in such circumstances, giving weight to the opinion of the executive as to whether such surveillance was compatible with privacy. A similar concern may arise if the CCTV surveillance equipment used to broadcast my public activities were new. It may be that the judiciary alone is not able to determine the relative weights of privacy and freedom of expression in these circumstances, where more democratic input into their relative weights is required. This is not to argue that proportionality is not applicable in these circumstances. Rather, it is to argue that proportionality may be better applied by a different institution – by the legislature or executive as opposed to the judiciary.

This approach is contrasted with the analysis provided by an immunities-based theory of rights, coupled with a state-limiting theory of proportionality. The difference is two-fold. First, when analyzing the examples given above, the first stage would not be to merely identify whether the actions were within the range of the rights to privacy and freedom of expression when broadly defined, but rather would require a more detailed analysis of the precise definition of these rights. This analysis may, for example, examine the values underpinning these rights, and the way in which these rights had been interpreted by previous court decisions. The aim would be to determine the core and more marginal elements of the right. Greater immunity from restriction is granted to the core as opposed to the peripheral elements of the right. Second, as the determination of the question depends on an interpretation of a right, the court is regarded as the primary, if not the sole institution to determine the correct answer to whether a particular constitutional right can be and has been lawfully restricted. This is for two reasons: either we recognize that the determination of the right answer requires an analysis of precedents and legal reasoning that is more suited to the court given their expertise,[22] or we recognize that the court, as an independent arbiter with skills in determining long-standing rights, is better able to determine those long-standing rights that restrict the legitimate activities of the executive or the legislature.[23]

To return to our examples of balancing freedom of expression and privacy, the court would first examine the content of the right to privacy. If previous case law demonstrated that the right to privacy normally extended only to

---

[22] Ronald Dworkin, *Taking Rights Seriously* (1977); *Law's Empire* (1986); and *Freedom's Law: The Moral Reading of the American Constitution* (2nd ed., 1997).
[23] T.R.S. Allan, *Constitutional Justice: A Liberal Theory of the Rule of law* (2001).

private and not public situations, or if the values underpinning the right to
privacy made it clear that privacy extended to acts performed in private and
not in public, then the court would conclude that my right to privacy had not
been breached were the council merely to broadcast footage of my shopping
trips to public shopping centers. There would be no need to balance privacy
and freedom of expression to reach this conclusion. If, on the other hand,
the council had broadcast footage of the activities in my house, the right to
privacy would be breached. The question would then be whether the right to
freedom of expression entitled publication of my weekend antics. Again, this
would be examined by determining whether the broadcast of this information
would be within the scope of the right to freedom of expression. It may
well be the case, for example, that broadcasting specific information to the
security services for the purposes of confirming or denying their suspicions
that I was a spy, or in order to inform my employer whether I was really
working when claiming to on weekends, was within the core of the right
to freedom of expression. However, publishing the antics of an academic
merely for the very minimal entertainment value that they could provide
is much more likely to be a peripheral element of the right to freedom of
expression. Consequently, if the council were broadcasting footage of my
activities taking place in my private home merely to amuse a certain section of
the population, then not only would my right to privacy be breached, but the
right to freedom of expression would not extend to this situation. The solution
to these issues is not reached by balancing interests, but by defining the rights
engaged more clearly. Proportionality would only be required where both
rights are engaged – for example, when the council communicates footage of
the activities taking place in my private home on the weekend to the security
services for the purposes of determining whether I am a spy. Here, it could
be argued that the right to privacy does not provide immunity from this type
of invasion, being outweighed by the right to freedom of expression in these
circumstances.

The differences between the two approaches may be hard to delineate in
practice. They would appear to reach similar, if not the same, conclusions in
the examples discussed above. Indeed, as noted above, Alexy regards the second approach as a form of "balancing in disguise". However, the approaches
use different mechanisms to justify the outcomes reached and entail different roles for the court. This difference in the reasoning process gives rise to
the criticism that optimizing conceptions of proportionality fail to provide
objectively correct answers to questions concerning the application of constitutional rights. This criticism takes two main forms. First, it is argued that
balancing is not possible in practice because of issues of incommensurability.

Second, it is argued that the concept of balancing is unable to provide objective justifications, providing instead only explanations for why a particular outcome was reached in particular circumstances. These arguments are used to justify the superiority of the second approach, combining state-limiting conceptions of proportionality and immunity theories of rights. Here, courts are not merely balancing different interests, but are inquiring into the nature of the right, using these criteria to determine whether a right has been restricted or not. This process does not raise issues of incommensurability, as there is no requirement to afford weight to competing interests. Rights and interests are not weighed against each other; instead, the scope and application of a right is refined through a more detailed process of definition. In addition, the process of defining a right is conceptually distinct from balancing and optimization, thus enabling an objective, right answer to be reached.

Alexy responds to these criticisms in two ways. First, he rejects the problem raised by incommensurability by explaining that there is no need for a precise scale of measurement – setting out the delineation between light, moderate, and serious infringements of rights. A precise scale of measurement against which to weigh competing interests is not required for the court to provide objective assessments of the relative interests. It does not matter that the factors that determine that an infringement or promotion of interest A is light, moderate, or serious are different from the factors that determine the same issue as regards interest B. Moreover, as constitutional rights incorporate some elements of principles and some elements of rules, constitutional documents may exist that delineate the relative importance of interests A and B. Consequently, a constitutional court is in a position to determine the extent to which light, moderate, and serious infringements of interests relate to one another.[24]

Alexy rejects the second criticism by drawing a connection between constitutional review and deliberative democracy. He argues that constitutional review can be understood as a different means of representation of the interests of the people from that found in democratic debate. By bringing a constitutional review case, an individual is represented by those skilled in making legal arguments, with the decision being determined, in turn, by those skilled in this field. Consequently, it provides a means through which rational arguments can be provided to those skilled in accepting arguments on the grounds of their rationality. Constitutional review, therefore, is "an enterprise of institutionalising reason and correctness".[25] As such, it provides for more

---

[24] Alexy, "Balancing, Constitutional Review," *supra* note 7.
[25] Ibid., at 581.

sound, rational arguments than would perhaps emerge through the democratic process, where there is greater, broader representation, but where there are fewer rules to facilitate rational discourse. The extent to which courts are a better means of facilitating rational discourse not only justifies the role of the court in performing judicial review, but also in justifying judicial review itself. A rational, correct answer to how to balance rights is preferable to a more broadly representative answer, which is less likely to be either a rational or a correct answer to this question. Deference is relevant when, for institutional reasons, the legislature is more able to determine the right answer to the question than the court.

As with the previous section, the purpose of this section is not to enter into the debate as to the relative merits of these different conceptions of proportionality when analyzed from the perspective of the promotion of objectivity and the requisite role of the court. The difference between the two in practice may be small indeed, albeit based on different reasoning processes. It is hard to think of circumstances in which an application of optimizing or state-limiting conceptions of proportionality would produce different results. This is particularly the case as the values and interests used to determine the definition of a right are similar to the values and interests balanced when applying the optimizing conception of proportionality. In a similar manner, a court which referred to previous case law as a means through which to discern whether infringements were light, moderate, or serious would be likely to reach a similar conclusion to a court that examined previous case law to determine the more precise definition of a particular right.

However, as with our analysis of the extent to which conceptions of proportionality may contradict conceptions of rights, a better explanation for why a particular conception of proportionality is adopted can be found from recognizing that discourse surrounding the application of different conceptions of proportionality take place at two different levels of abstraction, connected to different understandings of the purpose of a constitution. Alexy's approach, using optimizing conceptions of proportionality, occurs at a higher level of abstraction than theories that use state-limiting conceptions of proportionality. An optimizing conception of proportionality does not recognize clearly delineated agreements as to the content of a particular right, or its application in particular circumstances. Consequently, balancing is used to refine this process. State-limiting conceptions of proportionality apply in a less abstract manner, occurring within a legal system that has accepted particular, more refined definitions of rights. As such, a focus on the definition of the right is more able to determine the outcome in particular circumstances. This difference will be explained more clearly in the next section.

IV. RIGHTS, INTERESTS, AND THE PURPOSE OF CONSTITUTIONAL DISCOURSE

The two previous sections suggested that there is a common theme running through the debates concerning whether proportionality is compatible with theories of rights and whether proportionality is capable of providing objective/legitimate justifications for empowering the judiciary to restrict the democratic will of the people and overturn legislative measures that contravene human rights. Differences occur not merely because of diverging conceptions of rights, or because of different reasoning processes when determining whether a restriction of a right is justified. Competing conclusions also arise because the application of optimizing and state-limiting conceptions of proportionality takes place at different stages of the reasoning process. This section aims to explain and justify this assertion, focusing on drawing out its implications for the purposes of constitutional discourse and the relative roles of the legislature and the judiciary.

A helpful means of understanding how discourse can take place at different stages of the reasoning process can be found in the theory of rights advocated by Joseph Raz.[26] Raz argues for an interest theory of rights, arguing that X has a right if "other things being equal, an aspect of x's well-being (his interest) is a sufficient reason for holding some other person(s) to be under a duty."[27] Of particular importance is Raz's explanation of the relationship between interests, rights, and duties. Interests are used to justify the existence of rights. In turn, rights justify the creation of duties. Consequently, rights represent "intermediate conclusions in arguments from ultimate values to duties".[28] Despite being intermediate conclusions, rights are referred to as if they are complete reasons for the establishment of duties. There are advantages to referring to rights in this manner. A weak argument is the practical utility of rights, understood as intermediate conclusions. To refer to a right as opposed to ultimate values to justify the imposition of a duty is quicker and more practical, saving time as well as the tediousness that may ensue from continual debate over the same issue. Second, rights "enable a common culture to be formed round [sic] shared intermediate conclusions, in spite of a great degree of haziness and disagreement concerning ultimate values."[29]

---

[26] This is not to argue that this is a better theory of rights; nor is an acceptance of Raz's theory of rights necessary for an acceptance of the arguments in this section. The example is used for the purposes of illustration only.
[27] Joseph Raz, "On the Nature of Rights," (1984) 93 *Mind* 194 at 195.
[28] Ibid., at 208.   [29] Ibid.

Raz's delineation between interests, rights, and duties helps to illustrate the different levels of abstraction at which the debate between conceptions of proportionality and rights takes place. Optimizing theories of proportionality apply principles of proportionality at the interest level, using proportionality to optimize values and interests in order to form intermediate conclusions that are transformed into rights. State optimizing theories of proportionality are applied at the rights level, determining the extent to which rights are immune from being overridden from other interests and competing rights. The delineation between rights and interests also explains the different ways in which courts are encouraged to reason about rights, as well as their different roles in constitutional rights adjudication. When arguing at the level of interests, there are no intermediate conclusions to apply, either to a more refined definition of a right or its more precise application to the circumstances before the court. Consequently, theories of constitutional adjudication that rely on an optimizing conception of proportionality regard rights as easily engaged, the main work being performed by the balancing exercise of proportionality to determine the resolution of the case before the court. There are no intermediate conclusions giving rise to definitions of rights that can be relied on by the court to determine the issues before it. When arguing at the interest level, a case can be made of the need for the involvement of democratic law-making institutions, as well as the courts. Although their reasoning processes may be different and complimentary, both may be needed to grant legitimacy to the resolution of the issue before the court.

In contrast, state-limiting conceptions of proportionality rely on the intermediate conclusions that form constitutional rights. These intermediate conclusions help to provide a firmer definition of the right. As such, it is harder for the court to reach the conclusion that a particular right is engaged. Moreover, reasoning as to rights focuses predominantly on the definition of the right, ascertaining how it should be applied to the more precise situation before the court. As rights can be understood as intermediate conclusions, there is less of a need for balancing. Rights are granted priority over other interests because the reasoning process at the level of interests, where competing interests were balanced in order to justify the creation of a right, determines why the right is granted lexical priority over other interests. Proportionality is used not as a means of refining the right, but as a means of determining the outcome of conflicts between rights. In turn, given that rights reflect intermediate conclusions, which help to establish a common culture, it is easier to justify the predominant role of the court in defining rights and determining their application to the situation before the court.

Evidence in support of this alternative underlying explanation for the difference between optimizing and state-limiting conceptions of proportionality can be found in Alexy's writing. As discussed previously, Alexy's theory of constitutional adjudication relies on his distinction between rules and principles. Rules differ from principles, as they are "fixed points".[30] As Kumm remarks,

> Rules ... are norms that express judgments on the way that values, interests and principles play out once they engage the world. Rules can be derived from balancing the relevant competing concerns. They reflect judgements on how all the relevant factors operate in the circumstances defined by the conditions of the rule. This is what Alexy means when he says that rules contain fixed points in the field of the factually and legally possible.[31]

Alexy's classification of rights as principles of optimization places constitutional rights, and reasoning about these rights, more firmly in the sphere of debate at the interest level, a higher level of abstraction than debates that take place at the rights level, where intermediate conclusions have been derived to give rise to rules as to how the right is to apply. This also explains why, for Alexy, it is more difficult to grant an exception to a rule than it is to grant an exception to a principle. When balancing principles, exceptions or permissible restrictions arise through the balancing exercise designed to refine the definition of a constitutional right, in the sense of pinpointing its precise application to the situation before the court. To grant an exception to a rule would require overturning the precise pinpointing of the application of the right to the situation before the court. Consequently, there is a need to justify overriding the advantages derived from the rule – as representing an intermediate conclusion at the rights level of reasoning, to employ Raz's terminology, it requires a justification to remove the advantages of speed and the formation of a common culture. In addition, the rule may reflect the outcome of a prior balancing process at the level of interests and this process may be a more legitimate means of refining the right than that of the court alone.

In a similar manner, evidence can be adduced to support the claim that state-limiting conceptions of proportionality and immunity theories of rights operate at the rights level as opposed to the interest level. When explaining why rights should operate as trumps over social policy issues, Dworkin places his argument against a background principle of utilitarianism. Utilitarianism requires that people be treated as equals, weighing the preferences of each individual in order to determine public policy. Consequently, any assessment that would count the choices of anyone twice over, or ensure that the choices of others were not counted, would undermine the aims of utilitarianism. Therefore, Dworkin argues that a right to moral independence is needed in

---

[30] Alexy, *A Theory of Constitutional Rights, supra* note 7 at 44.
[31] Kumm, "Constitutional Rights as Principles," *supra* note 8 at 578.

order to ensure that preferences that would undermine utilitarianism are not allowed to count in the social policy balancing. When providing examples to support his argument, Dworkin explains that the preferences of a Nazi, which would require that Aryans have more and Jews have less, should not be counted precisely because it would undermine utilitarianism: "Political preferences, like the Nazi's preference, are on the same level — purport to occupy the same space – as utilitarian theory itself. Therefore, though the utilitarian theory must be neutral between personal preferences like the preferences for push-pin and poetry, as a matter of the theory of justice, it cannot, without contradiction, be neutral between itself and Nazism."[32]

Dworkin's defense of rights as trumps is made within a particular political theory as to the distribution of goods – utilitarianism – that would be contradicted by an alternative political theory as to the distribution of goods – Nazism. His theory of rights operates at a different level of abstraction, deriving from conclusions reached at a higher level of abstraction concerning choices as to a particular political theory. In addition, the right to moral independence determines the definition of those rights required to operate as trumps. To use Raz's terminology, the argument is focused at the rights level as opposed to the interest level, giving rise to intermediate conclusions determining the legitimate and illegitimate exercise of state power within a theory of utilitarianism.

When the distinction is understood in this manner, it casts a different light on the debates discussed in the previous sections. I argued above that the debate as to the potential conflict between proportionality and rights was perhaps better understood as a conflict between a particular conception of proportionality and a particular conception of rights. When understood as a debate taking place at different levels of abstraction, we can see that the delineation need not turn on whether we adopt a state-limiting or an optimizing principle of proportionality or on whether we adopt an immunities- or an interest-based theory of rights. Instead, it depends on the level of abstraction at which the debate takes place. An optimizing conception of proportionality is best suited to debates at the interest level, used to help determine an intermediate conclusion that becomes a right. It may be that the right, once established, operates as a trump over other rights and interests. However, as its relative weight has still not been determined, there is no justification, at that stage of the reasoning process, for the right to operate as a trump over other rights and interests. A state-limiting conception of proportionality is suited to arguments taking place at the rights

---

[32] Dworkin "Rights as Trumps," *supra* note 9 at 157.

level, when rights represent intermediate conclusions that have lexical priority over conclusions of the public good.

The analysis in terms of different levels of debate also illuminates the conclusion reached on the connection between proportionality, rationality, and the role of the court. When applying a state-limiting conception of proportionality, the court is engaged in reasoning at the rights stage, examining the intermediate conclusions reached as to the legitimate restraints on the actions of the legislature. These intermediate conclusions are easier to rationalize and justify. This is because, as intermediate conclusions, certain types of debates on the value or justification of these rights are excluded from the reasoning process. The intermediate conclusions are accepted as true, for the purposes of the culture that such intermediate conclusions are used to establish. The role of the court is to determine these intermediate conclusions. The court is better placed to do so, as an institution that is better equipped than the legislature to ascertain the long-standing principles that make up the rights that place restrictions on the actions of the legislature. As well as these institutional reasons, the court also has constitutional reasons for taking such decisions. The purpose of constitutional adjudication is to determine that the actions of the legislature are legitimate, taking place within the limits established by rights. As an independent arbiter, the court has greater authority to determine these limits than the legislature.

In contrast, when courts apply an optimizing conception of proportionality, reasoning at the level of interests, the connection between the rights defined in this manner and the limits of legitimate action of the legislature are not so clear-cut. In addition, the purpose of constitutional adjudication is more expansive. Constitutional adjudication is not merely a means of ensuring that the legislature acts within the legitimate confines of its powers. In addition, constitutional adjudication is a means through which a series of intermediate conclusions, at the rights level, are reached. These intermediate conclusions serve to create a common culture that can be used to aid the reasoning process and determine the legitimate actions of the legislature. When understood in this manner, it is no longer clear that the court alone is the best institution to adjudicate on the content of constitutional rights. Legitimacy may also require the input of the legislature. As such, we begin to understand the reason why optimizing conceptions of proportionality lend themselves to arguments from deference in a way that state-limiting conceptions of proportionality do not.

The analysis in terms of different levels of abstraction and the role of the court also helps to clarify how proportionality is used by different academic commentators, particularly illustrating the different uses of this concept by T.R.S. Allan, David Dyzenhaus, and Stephen Gardbaum in this volume.

Allan argues that, when applying proportionality, courts determine the definition of a right, as opposed to balancing between a particular right and other
rights and interests. Consequently, his theory resembles a state-limiting theory
coupled with an immunities-based theory of rights. However, his theory also
appears to advocate a more general application of proportionality, regarding
proportionality as a general principle of optimizing decisions in society. It can
be difficult, therefore, to classify the conception of proportionality used by
Allan were we to merely focus on the connection between proportionality and
different conceptions of rights. This is because Allan's theory is more abstract
than one relying merely on a protection of human or constitutional rights. The
state is limited more generally, in that its actions are only legitimate when they
are compatible with underlying principles that contain both human rights
and proportionality when understood as a general principle through which
to ensure that the legislature (and executive) takes rational, reasonable, and
reasoned decisions in line with the requirements of the rule of law. The court,
as an independent arbiter, is best placed to determine these principles and
to ensure the legislature only acts with the proper bounds of its powers. His
approach to precedent helps to delineate between those instances in which
the courts apply these principles in a more abstract or precise level.

Dyzenhaus has a different approach to proportionality because he views the
role of the court as different from that of Allan. Dyzenhaus does not regard
the role of the court as that of ensuring that the legislature takes decisions
that are legitimate, as they match a series of substantive principles. Rather, the
court is required to scrutinize the reasoning of the legislature and executive.
Proportionality aids this checking function through helping to structure the
reasoning process, ensuring that public authorities justify their actions and
conclusions, aiding the courts, in turn, to check this reasoning process. Gardbaum regards proportionality as justified partly because of its ability to facilitate
a culture of justification, but also because it provides a means of balancing
the respective roles of the legislature and the judiciary in the determination of
rights, recognizing the way in which proportionality and due deference ensure
a better distribution of authority between these two institutions in the field of
human rights adjudication.

V. CONCLUSION – A DUAL ROLE FOR PROPORTIONALITY

If we understand proportionality in this manner, then a new series of issues
becomes relevant when determining whether proportionality is a necessary
component of human rights adjudication and, if so, the conception of proportionality that should be adopted. Instead of focusing on the relative merits

of different conceptions of rights and their connections to different conceptions of proportionality, there is a need to assess the purposes of constitutional
adjudication, particularly as regards the level of abstraction at which such
debates should take place. Raz argues that the use of rights as intermediate
conclusions avoids time wasting and tedium and also helps to create and rein-
force a common culture. Applying the latter reason for using rights provides a
different perspective from which to determine whether proportionality serves
a useful purpose and, if so, the conception of proportionality that should be
adopted. When a common culture exists as to the definition of a right, then
constitutional adjudication is more suited to the adoption of a state-limiting
conception of proportionality coupled with an immunities theory of rights.
When there is no common culture surrounding the right in question, then,
in these circumstances, proportionality is not being used as a means through
which to restrict the actions of the legislature. Rather, proportionality is used
as a means of weighing up competing interests to help determine a right that
can become part of the common culture. As such, an optimizing conception of proportionality, used to weigh up these competing interests, should be
adopted.

The implications for constitutional adjudication may depend on the nature
of the right before the court, as well as the constitutional background found
in a particular legal system. I have argued elsewhere, for example, that, for
the purposes of English law, the Human Rights Act 1998 is best understood as
providing a democratic dialogue model of rights protections. Constitutional
adjudication is not used to determine the legal limits on legislation, although
declarations of incompatibility do place considerable political pressure on the
legislature to amend or overturn legislation to ensure its compatibility with
Convention rights. As such, different tools are required in English law. The
above analysis suggests a use of optimizing conceptions of proportionality,
coupled with deference, when arguing at the interest level, where there is
no common culture or consensus surrounding the definition of a right. In a
similar manner, such issues are best resolved through the use of section 4 declarations of incompatibility. I have referred to such situations in earlier work as
those giving rise to watershed/contestable rights issues – that is, where the issue
before the court is novel, raises important issues, and has not been previously
determined by the court.[33] The application of an optimizing conception of proportionality, accompanied by the appropriate degree of deference as respect

[33] Alison L. Young, *Parliamentary Sovereignty and the Human Rights Act* (2009), and "The
Practicalities of Dialogue: Is Dialogue working under the Human Rights Act 1998?," [2011]
Public Law 273.

based on constitutional and institutional grounds, would be more suited to
section 6 applications of the Act, determining whether the actions of a public
authority are contrary to Convention rights. In contrast, where there is a clear
consensus, such that a right represents an intermediate conclusion, human
rights adjudication requires an application of a state-limiting conception of
proportionality, where deference as respect should only be based on institutional features. For the purposes of the Act, this would require the application,
prima facie, of section 3 as opposed to section 4. In addition, given that section
3 only empowers the court to interpret legislation, retaining the possible power
of the legislature to legislate so as to overturn this interpretation, deference is
not required. However a state-limiting conception of proportionality and an
appropriate level of deference as respect on institutional grounds would be
applicable to section 6 in these circumstances.

4 Human Dignity and Proportionality: Deontic Pluralism in Balancing

Mattias Kumm and Alec D. Walen

The proportionality test is at the heart of much of contemporary human and constitutional rights adjudication.[1] It is the central structural feature of a rights-based practice of justification.[2] Notwithstanding its widespread acceptance, a number of challenges have been brought forward against it.[3] Perhaps one of the most serious is the claim that an understanding of rights that makes the existence of a definitive right dependant on applying a proportionality test undermines the very idea of rights.[4] In the liberal tradition, rights are

---

[1] For the spread of the proportionality test, see Aharon Barak, *Proportionality: Constitutional Rights and their Limitations* (2012) at 175–210; see also, Alec Stone Sweet and Jud Matthews, "Proportionality Balancing and Global Constitutionalism," 47 *Columbia J. Trans. L.* 72 (2008–2009). A reconstructive structure-focused theory of rights that places the proportionality test at the heart of rights practice was first provided by Robert Alexy for the German constitutional context in *Theorie der Grundrechte* (1985), translated into English by Julian Rivers: *A Theory of Constitutional Rights* (2002). For a normatively richer reconstructive claim and argument that proportionality is at the heart of a global model of constitutional rights, see Kai Möller, *The Global Model of Constitutional Rights* (2012).

[2] For the turn from interpretation to public reason-oriented justification see Mattias Kumm, "Socratic Contestation and the Right to Justification: The Point of Rights-Based Proportionality Review," (2010) 4 *Law & Ethics of Human Rights* 141. On the idea that a right to justification grounds human rights, see Rainer Forst, *The Right to Justification: A Constructivist Theory of Justice* (2011). For the connection between rights, proportionality, and a culture of justification, see the contribution by David Dyzenhaus in Chapter 11 in this volume; see also Moshe Cohen-Eliya and Iddo Porrat, "Proportionality and the Culture of Justification," 59 *Am. J. Comp. L.* 463 (2011).

[3] See, e.g., Matthias Klatt and Moritz Meister, *The Constitutional Structure of Proportionality* (2012) at 45–71, who distinguish between eight types of criticisms of balancing: that balancing tends to go together with a broad definition of rights, its indeterminacy undermines the rule of law, morality is not about balancing, balancing gives a false impression of calculability, the idea of balancing is incompatible with a core of inviolable rights, balancing gives up the standard of correctness in favor of a weaker standard of appropriateness or adequacy, and balancing tends to swallow up other prongs of the proportionality test.

[4] See Grégoire Webber's contribution, "On the Loss of Rights," Chapter 6 in this volume.

widely imagined as "trumps" over competing considerations of policy.[5] They
are claimed to have priority over "the good" in some strong sense.[6] They are
described as "firewalls" providing strong protections against demands made
by the political community.[7] And they are thought to be grounded in human
dignity,[8] which in turn is held to be inviolable.[9] Even though there are interesting and significant differences between conceptions of rights in the liberal
tradition, they generally[10] share the idea that something protected as a matter of
right may not be overridden by ordinary considerations of policy. Circumstan-
tial all-things-considered judgments regarding what serves the general welfare
are generally thought to present insufficient grounds to justify infringements
of rights. If human dignity is inviolable, and rights are grounded in human dignity, must they not provide for very strong, perhaps even absolute, constraints
on what governments may impose? Can a human and constitutional rights
practice that puts proportionality analysis front and centre capture this core
deontological feature of rights grounded in human dignity? Is not the proportionality test a misguided and dangerous invitation to balance away human
dignity?

In an earlier article[11] one of us argued that any plausible structure of
rights must be able to accommodate core anti-perfectionist, anti-collectivist,
and anti-consequentialist ideas underlying the liberal democratic rights tradition. Whereas proportionality analysis could adequately accommodate anti-
perfectionist commitments (by screening out, as illegitimate ends, perfectionist

---

[5] Ronald Dworkin, "What Rights Do We Have?" in *Taking Rights Seriously* (1977) at 266; see
also Ronald Dworkin, "Principle, Policy, Procedure" in *A Matter of Principle* (1985) at 72.
[6] John Rawls, *Political Liberalism* (1993) at 173–211.
[7] Jürgen Habermas, *Faktizität und Geltung* (1992) at 315. English translation: *Between Facts and
Norms* (1992).
[8] See Art. 1 of the Universal Declaration of Human Rights: "All men are born free and equal in
dignity and rights"; Art. 1 of the German Basic Law declares: "Human Dignity is inviolable.
To respect and protect it is the duty of all public authority"; Art. 1 of the European Charter of
Fundamental Rights states: "Human dignity is inviolable. It must be respected and protected";
Art. 1 of the Constitution of South Africa states: "The Republic of South Africa is one, sovereign,
democratic state founded on the following values: a. Human dignity, the achievement of
equality and the advancement of human rights and freedoms."
[9] Kant, for example, insisted that although everything that has a value has a price, that which
has dignity is above all price and thus, presumably, above competing values. See *Grundlegung
zur Metaphysik der Sitten*, in Immanuel Kant, *Werke*, Wilhelm Weischedel (ed.), vol. IV,
Wiesbaden 1956, 51 (BA 68).
[10] Exceptions include Joseph Raz, *The Morality of Freedom* (1986), and Robert Alexy, *A Theory
of Constitutional Rights* (2002).
[11] Mattias Kumm, "Political Liberalism and the Structure of Rights: On the Place and Limits of
the Proportionality Requirement" in George Pavlakos (ed.), *Law, Rights and Discourse: The
Legal Philosophy of Robert Alexy* (2007) 133.

purposes in the first prong of the proportionality test) and anti-collectivist commitments (by weighing correctly the relevant considerations when conducting the balancing test), there were certain structural features of political morality that could not be adequately captured by the proportionality framework. More specifically, there existed a distinct class of cases, characteristically involving the protection of human dignity, where even measures meeting the proportionality test could still constitute a violation of rights. The idea of human dignity, it was argued, was connected to deontological constraints in a way that the proportionality test could not adequately take into account. The task was to distinguish those types of cases from ordinary cases to which proportionality analysis properly applied. If that distinction was not made, there was indeed a danger that human dignity would be balanced away. Because this is a position that embraces the proportionality test generally, but insists on carving out a distinct category of cases involving human dignity in which rights provide stronger, more categorical protection, this position might be called *human dignity exceptionalism*.

Others have since then either endorsed[12] or criticized[13] this position. We argue here that human dignity exceptionalism is false. Whereas it was right to insist that the structure of political morality is not automatically captured by the four prongs of the proportionality test – at least not if the balancing prong is used in a fundamentally consequentialist way – the proportionality test and the idea of balancing in particular is flexible enough to allow for the structural complexities of political morality to be taken into account. The article was misguided in carving out a relatively narrow set of issues and limiting the idea of deontological constraints to them. Here we will illustrate how constraints that are not merely consequentialist operate in very different ways and inform the reasoning that takes place within the balancing test across a much wider range of cases. Deontology is ubiquitous, and there is nothing in the idea of balancing that precludes taking it into account. Indeed, balancing properly understood requires it to be taken into account.

This chapter seeks to establish two core points about balancing. The first is negative. Balancing is not a mechanical exercise: it is a metaphor we use to describe a residual category within rights analysis that registers the importance of the various concerns at stake. But the idea of balancing itself says nothing about what kind of things are relevant or what weight to assign the relevant concerns. When balancing is misunderstood as a technique that somehow

---

[12] Barak, *Proportionality, supra* note 1 at 471.
[13] Robert Alexy, "Thirteen Replies" in George Pavlakos (ed.), *Law, Rights, Discourse: The Legal Philosophy of Robert Alexy* (2007) at 344.

allows lawyers and courts to avoid substantive moral reasoning or engagement
with policy, it is likely to lead to bad results.[14]

The second point is positive. This chapter shows that balancing ought to
be understood as thoroughly deontological. But deontology, if taken seriously,
is not captured by a single, simple concept, such as the restriction against
using people simply as a means. Rather, it covers a range of reasons for giving
some interests more or less priority over others. In that sense, we argue for
an understanding of deontology as itself structurally pluralist (call this "deontic pluralism"). Although we believe it is true that in some contexts simple
interest-based balancing is the correct way to proceed, there are a variety of
contexts in which special weight is accorded to one side because of structural features of the situation. We offer no complete typology of structures,
let alone a comprehensive conception of balancing that determines what the
right balance will be in all cases. We argue only that the balance will have
to make appropriate reference to constraints that arise out of what is required
to respect dignity and illustrate what that means across the range of chosen
cases.

In order to establish these points, we discuss three clusters of cases, raising
distinct structural issues. We focus on these three sets of cases because of the
diversity of deontological reasons that they raise. All the reasons are grounded
in respect for human dignity, but none can be reduced to the others. The first
set of cases concerns *instrumentalizing* individuals against their will, making
them means for public ends in a way that is incompatible with their dignity.
The second addresses the question of how to make sense of the relatively
strict, but not maximally strict, standards of proof in criminal proceedings.
And the third addresses questions of long-term detention and the conditions
under which it can be legitimately authorized. In each of the cases our point is
not to enter controversial substantive debates, even though that will in part be
inevitable, but to highlight some structural features that any balancing exercise
must take into account if it is to be plausible.

I. HUMAN DIGNITY AND NONINSTRUMENTALIZATION

It might seem that balancing is a consequentialist form of reasoning that does
not fit the deontological nature of at least some rights. The rights in question
capture the idea that people are inviolable in a way that imposes constraints
on actors even if they are seeking to bring about desirable consequences. To

---

[14] For a similar emphasis, see Möller, *Global Model, supra* note 3 at 134–177, in particular at 177;
see also Klatt and Meister, *supra* note 3 at 51–56.

give some non-contentious examples: Individuals may not be used for the purposes of medical experiments without their free and informed consent, even if using them in such a way would save very many lives. The death of a terminally ill patient may not be actively hastened by a doctor seeking to save the lives of three or four others by way of transplanting the organs of the terminally ill person to those others. Accidental witnesses to the crimes of a dangerous killer who refuse to cooperate with the police for fear of retaliation may not be forced to reveal what they saw by way of torture or threat of torture by the authorities, even if such coerced cooperation would save the lives of many future crime victims. Given that in each of these cases the rights of one person not to be killed, seriously harmed, or endangered stand against policies seeking to avert similar harm to a greater number of others, would balancing not inevitably lead to the result that such actions would, at least sometimes, be permitted, if necessary to avert greater harm? Our answer is no. There is a way to frame even such uncompromising rights within the proportionality framework.

In order to gain a better understanding of the relationship between proportionality analysis and these sorts of deontological constraints, the trolley problem may provide a helpful, if not particularly original,[15] point of entry. Consider the following two scenarios:

1. A runaway trolley will kill five people if a bystander does not divert it onto another track, where, she foresees, it will kill one person.
2. A runaway trolley will kill five people if a bystander does not topple a massive man standing close by onto the track to stop the trolley. The massive man will foreseeably die in the process.

In both cases, the intervention by the bystander foreseeably leads to the death of one person in order to save five. Yet it is a widely shared view that in the first case the bystander may divert the trolley, thereby killing one person (let us call him "V" for victim), whereas in the second case she may not.[16] There is something puzzling about this result – hence the name the trolley *problem*. Why is it that the only thing that matters morally is not the fact that in both

---

[15] The problem was first introduced by Philippa Foot in "The Problem of Abortion and the Doctrine of Double Effect" in *Virtues and Vices* (1978). For further illuminating discussions of the issue, see Judith Jarvis Thompson, "The Trolley Problem," 94 *Yale L. J.* 1395 (1985); and Frances M. Kamm, *Morality, Mortality*, vol. II (1996) at 143–171. See also Thomas Nagel, *The View from Nowhere* (1986).

[16] For just one example of the vast empirical literature supporting this claim, see Fiery Cushman, Liane Young, and Marc Hauser, "The Role of Reasoning and Intuition in Moral Judgments: Testing Three Principles of Harm," (2006) 17 *Psychological Science* 1082.

scenarios V dies and five are saved? Would it not be more consistent either to allow the bystander to save the five in both cases if you are a consequentialist, or to insist that the life of V cannot be traded off against another life, whatever the circumstances, if you believe in the existence of deontological constraints? There is considerable debate on what justifies making a distinction between these cases. The following can do no more than briefly present one central idea, without doing justice to the various facets and permutations of the debate.

A significant difference between the cases is that in the first, the death of the one person is a contingent side effect of the bystander's choice to turn the trolley away from the five. In the second example, the massive man is being used as a means – he is being instrumentalized to bring about the end of saving the five. His being toppled onto the tracks in front of the trolley is the means by which the five would be saved. Without V's involvement there would be no rescue action to describe in the second case, whereas the five can be saved just as well without V's involvement in the first case.

But why should there be such a strong justificatory hurdle for using people as a means, as opposed to harming people as a side effect of pursuing a good end, as in the case of turning a trolley from five onto one? There are two ways to conceive of what it means to "use another as a means," and once they are distinguished it becomes quite puzzling that the relationship of "using as means" should carry any moral weight.

The two interpretations of what it means to use another as a means are a subjective, intention-focused interpretation and an objective, causal role-focused interpretation, and both face potent objections.[17] The objection to the subjective interpretation is that although of course it matters morally what intentions an agent has with respect to others, intentions have only derivative or secondary significance.[18] What fundamentally matters is what is done to a rights-holder, not what intentions an agent has. The claim that intentions are fundamentally significant misdirects agents to focus inwardly on how they think about others as they act, rather than outwardly on how to act in ways consistent with the respect that others deserve.[19] The objection to the objective interpretation is that it is not obvious why causal role should matter morally.

---

[17] This paragraph is substantially drawn from Alec Walen, "Transcending the Means Principle," *Law and Philosophy* (forthcoming).

[18] See Thomas Scanlon, *Moral Dimensions* (2008) at 29.

[19] See Judith Jarvis Thomson, "Self-Defense," (1991) 20 *Philosophy and Public Affairs* 283 at 293. For a fuller discussion of this, see also Alec Walen, "Intentions and Permissibility," retrieved from http://peasoup.typepad.com/peasoup/2012/04/intentions-and-permissibility.html#more.

As Thomas Scanlon puts it: "being a means in this sense – being causally necessary – has no intrinsic moral significance".[20]

It is our view that the causal interpretation is descriptively accurate, but that to see why a victim's causal role in an agent's actions matter, one must examine the structural role played by the claims of the rights claimant. The key is in the distinction between restricting and non-restricting claims. A restricting claim has the normative effect of "pressing" to restrict an agent from doing what she could otherwise permissibly do to achieve some good end, given competing property or property-like claims over the means she would need to achieve it. What she has a right to use, taking into account all competing property and property-like claims over the possible means to her end, establishes her baseline freedom to pursue that end. A restricting claim presses to restrict an agent relative to this baseline freedom. It has the potential, if respected as a right, to make other people, who would benefit by her pursuing that end, worse off against this baseline. This potential impact of restricting claims on the welfare of others explains why they are weaker than non-restricting claims.[21]

Illustrating again with the trolley problem, the role of V's claim in the first hypothetical is potentially to make the others, the five who might be saved by the agent, worse off than they would be if his claim did not restrict the bystander. For if his claim did not restrict the bystander, the latter would not only be permitted to use the switch to save the five, she would likely be obliged to do so. Even if we assume that the switch is owned by someone else, the owner, if not harmed himself, can have no complaint if the bystander uses the switch to save a net four lives. Against that baseline, V's claim not to be killed presses to restrict the bystander so that she may not do what she otherwise could permissibly do, if his claim were not an obstacle, namely to divert the trolley and save the five. In other words, they press to disable her, making those who have such claims potential disablers.[22]

On the other hand, non-restricting claims, if respected as rights, would not restrict an agent relative to her baseline freedom to pursue an end. This is for

---

[20] Scanlon, *supra* note 18 at 118; see also H.L.A. Hart, "Intention and Punishment" in *Punishment and Responsibility: Essays in the Philosophy of Law* (1968) at 124; and Victor Tadros, *The Ends of Harm* (2011) at 152–155.

[21] This formulation of the "restricting claims principle" departs from that used in "Transcending the Means Principle". We now view that appeal to what the agent could do if the claimant were absent as flawed.

[22] This terminology was first introduced by Alec Walen in "Doing, Allowing, and Disabling: Some Principles Governing Deontological Restrictions," (1995) 80 *Philosophical Studies* 183.

the straightforward reason that non-restricting claims are property or property-like claims over the means she could use. The underlying normative idea is that there is a limited range of things agents are normally free to use: things they own or have rented, unowned things, things in the public domain, things that others own but the use at issue would do little harm to the owner's interests. Agents do not normally have a right to use the property or bodies of others if the cost to the owner or person whose body is being used is substantial. A claimant's claim over his own body, to withhold that from the range of things than an agent is free to use, does not press to restrict the agent from making use of the things he has a baseline right to use.

Again, illustrating with the trolley problem, in the second hypothetical, V's rights claim not to be used to stop the trolley does not press to restrict the agent from doing anything she could permissibly do using the means she has a baseline right to use. She does not have the right to use the body of another without that person's consent, and maybe not even then. The massive man and those who would likewise be used as a means without their consent are not potential disablers; they are potential enablers.

This account does not simply invoke the difference between using people as a means and harming them as a side effect; it tries to explain why those who are harmed as a side effect have weaker claims not to be harmed in the context of a world in which agents are normally free to use some things and not others. Claims not to be harmed as a side effect press to restrict agents even further than the baseline restriction on what they are free to use. That puts the competing restricting claims on a kind of par, in a kind of competitive balance, which explains why those with restricting claims can permissibly be harmed for the sake of others even when those with non-restricting claims cannot.

Another way to put it is to say that a rights-bearer with a restricting claim cannot lay claim to the fundamental claim to be left alone to lead his own life – an idea closely connected to human dignity – in the way that a rights-bearer with a non-restricting claim can. The rights-bearer with the restricting claim does not do anything to make others worse off, but he has a claim that presses to make others worse off. Accordingly, his claim has to be treated as substantially weaker than an otherwise identical non-restricting claim. Or, looking at it from the other side, because non-restricting claims can be respected without making anyone else worse off against the relevant baseline, they should, when life or serious bodily harm are involved, give rise to rights that are absolute, or nearly absolute.[23]

---

[23] It is disputed whether these kinds of deontological constraints are absolute or not. Can you push the massive man to save 1,000 people, a million, the world? According to Kant, even the

This is not the place to probe more deeply into questions concerning the use of persons as a means. But if an account along these lines can make sense of the trolley problem, and of the (often) categorical rights-based constraints relating to instrumentalization more generally, then it justifies constraints that cannot be captured by consequentialist accounts of morality. But what follows from this for balancing? In an earlier article one of us argued, on the basis of an analysis similar to the one above that:

> [t]he idea of deontological constraints cannot be appropriately captured within the proportionality structure. The reasons why proportionality analysis and the balancing test in particular is insufficient to capture these concerns is that it systematically filters out means-ends relationships that are central to the understanding of deontological constraints. When balancing, the decision-maker first loads up the scales on one side, focusing on the intensity of the infringement. Then he loads up the other side of the scales by focusing on the consequences of the act and assessing the benefits realised by it. Balancing systematically filters out questions concerning means-ends relationships. Yet the nature of the means-ends relationship can be key. Whether the claims made by the rights-bearer against the acting authority are made as an enabler or a disabler, whether public authorities are making use of a person as a means, or whether they are merely disregarding the claim to take into account his interests as a constraining factor in an otherwise permissible endeavour, are often decisive. These questions only come into view once the structure of the means-ends relationship becomes the focus of a separate inquiry.[24]

What is correct about the analysis is that there is nothing in the idea of balancing itself that helps create awareness for the way means-ends relationships matter. What was misguided, however, was the claim that questions concerning the moral significance of the means-ends relationship cannot be taken into account when balancing. It can be. But to see how, one must recognize that whether the infringed person is an enabler or a disabler is not only relevant in the weak sense that it provides additional reasons to be put on the scale when balancing. The distinction between enablers and disablers completely changes the way the balancing should take the competing interests into account. The relevant baseline for comparing or weighing the competing

---

existence of the world would not provide a good reason to overcome these kinds of deontological restrictions (*fiat iustitia pereat mundus!*). According to Nozick, deontological constraints are overcome in exceptional circumstances to prevent "catastrophic moral horrors": Robert Nozick, *Anarchy, State and Utopia* (1974) at 29.

[24] Kumm, "Political Liberalism", *supra* note 11 at 162.

interests depends on whether the interests are represented in the balance by restricting or non-restricting claims.

Note that this does not mean that there is a categorical prohibition against using people as a means – as enablers – to further a desirable purpose. We generally use people as a means to further our purposes all the time. For the most part, however, we do so with their consent.[25] Even absent consent, there is no categorical prohibition on using people as a means. Provisions of tort law and criminal law that require a passer-by to suffer minor inconveniences to come to the aid of another person in serious distress, for example, raise no serious moral concerns. There is no general categorical prohibition on requiring people to make themselves available as a means to serve the needs of other people or the larger community. Nor is there a general categorical prohibition on treating them as they may be required to treat themselves. The point is merely that the baseline used to discuss these issues is very different from the baseline used in cases where individual citizens are not the instruments used to realize political purposes. It still makes perfect sense to require that when individuals are drafted into the service of the community these impositions have to meet proportionality requirements. The individual may be used as a means by public authorities only if it is necessary to further a legitimate public purpose and is not disproportionate. The different moral baseline merely means that, on balance, what counts as proportionate is very different from what counts as proportionate in situations where the individual person is not used as an enabler invoking a non-restricting rights claim, but as a disabler invoking a restricting rights claim.

It is central to the assessment of a government act whether it uses individuals as a means; that is, whether the individual is an enabler or a disabler. Once this feature of the situation is included in the description of the infringing act, proportionality analysis applies. But the substantive evaluation of the competing concerns changes radically. More specifically, on application it suggests that the ultimate sacrifice of a citizen's life or physical integrity, when the person is used as a means of achieving some good without his consent, is never, or nearly never, justifiable.[26]

---

[25] Think of ordinary contractual relationships. When I buy apples in the market, I use the seller as a means to satisfy my craving for apples, but I do so by paying the agreed upon sum of money, as part of a consensual exchange.

[26] The German Constitutional Court endorsed a version of this principle in striking down §14(3) of the Federal Air-transport Security Act of 2005: 59 NEUE JURISTICHE WOCHENSCHRIFT 751 (2006). This section of the Act "empowered the minister of defense to order that a passenger plane be shot down, if it could be assumed that the aircraft would be used against the life of others and if the downing is the only means of preventing this present danger." But the

One may object that we have described one way of conceiving of deontological restrictions, but that we have not shown that one must proceed this way. One might suggest that the position that one of us took before, that they work as "side-constraints"[27] on balancing is still an option. Indeed, one might argue it is a better option because the right not to be used as a means, without one's consent, when the harm to one would be large, is rarely if ever justifiable. But this model of side constraints is appealing only if one thinks of deontological restrictions as operating essentially in an all-or-nothing fashion. If they change the way interests are taken into consideration, but do not rule out certain kinds of actions categorically, then balancing is a better model. We noted above that the restriction on harming an enabler with non-restricting claims is not, in fact, categorical. To further demonstrate that this is a core point about deontology, and not some marginal phenomenon, we turn now to two other categories of action in which deontological considerations are clearly relevant and yet cannot be represented as side constraints. Instead, the only plausible way to represent them is as affecting the balance of interests, so that it is not a mere impartial weighing up of consequences.

II. CRIMINAL LAW'S STANDARD OF PROOF BEYOND A REASONABLE DOUBT

The constitutionally required standard of proof in criminal cases in liberal democracies is generally proof "beyond a reasonable doubt" (BARD).[28] This standard strikes a balance between competing interests that is neither absolutely tipped in the direction of protecting innocents from being wrongly punished, nor equally concerned with the interests of all involved. If the balance were absolutely tipped in favor of protecting the innocent from wrongful punishment, there could be no institutionalized practice of punishment: The only way never to convict the innocent is not to convict at all.[29] Most would

Court mistakenly asserted that shooting down a weaponized plane treated the persons aboard it merely as a means. In truth, the passengers on the plane have restricting claims, and the Act is consistent with their dignity.

[27] This is the terminology Robert Nozick introduced in *Anarchy, State, and Utopia, supra* note 23.

[28] See *In re Winship*, 397 U.S. 358 (1970).

[29] There are some who interpret the BARD standard to be maximally strict while still allowing for criminal convictions in those cases in which the jury can find no reasonable doubt about the defendant's guilt. See, e.g., Laurence Tribe, "A Further Critique of Mathematical Proof," 84 *Harv. L. Rev.* 1810 (1971). Authors of this ilk take a position that would nonetheless make it much harder to incapacitate dangerous criminals than any existing court does. See Larry Laudan, "The Rules of Trial, Political Morality, and the Costs of Error: Or, Is Proof Beyond

insist, however, that this would impose unacceptable costs. There is value in criminal punishment both to deter potential criminals and to incapacitate, at least for a period of time, those who have committed serious crimes, thereby preventing them from striking again.[30] If one is a retributivist, as most criminal law theorists today are,[31] then one also wants to add that criminals *deserve* punishment. That provides *some* reason to punish the guilty, even if it is a reason that is relatively easily outweighed by other concerns, such as the costs of providing prosecutorial and penal resources.[32] Yet if we accept that the interests served by deterrence and incapacitation, not to mention those served by retributive desert, justify convicting people with less than proof to a moral certainty, we need to know *how much less certain* the finder of fact may be. Why is BARD the right way of striking a balance between competing concerns? Why not a lower standard, perhaps "clear and convincing evidence", "preponderance of the evidence", or even "plausible evidence"? Should anything less than BARD be held to violate a defendant's right to a fair criminal trial or the right to liberty?

To feel the force of the problem, consider an instance in which the state is prosecuting someone for a heinous crime that bears all the marks of a serial murder with a high probability that if the murderer is released, more murders will be committed. Does the insistence on BARD not violate the protective duties of the state vis-à-vis potential future victims, if there is a preponderance of the evidence suggesting the defendant is guilty? How should we think about striking the balance in these kinds of cases? On what grounds is it plausible to insist on BARD as the correct standard?

A wide range of views on the correct trade-off between false positives (convicting innocent defendants) and false negatives (letting a guilty defendant go free) has been offered over the years.[33] Voltaire held: "Tis much more Prudence to acquit two persons, tho' actually guilty, than to pass Sentence of Condemnation on one that is virtuous and innocent."[34] Matthew Hale

---

a Reasonable Doubt Doing More Harm than Good" in Leslie Green and Brian Leiter (eds.), *Oxford Studies in Philosophy of Law*, vol. 1 (2011) 195–227.

[30] Of course, most prisons do not incapacitate them from harming fellow prisoners.

[31] See David Dolinko, "Three Mistakes of Retributivism," 39 *U.C.L.A. L. Rev.* 1623 at 1623 (1992).

[32] Kant famously wrote, "woe to him who crawls through the windings of eudaimonism in order to discover something that releases the criminal from punishment": *The Doctrine of Right*, Academy, at 331 (*Metaphysical First Principles of the Doctrine of Right: Part I of the Metaphysics of Morals*, trans. Mary Gregor 1991). But even the most hard-core retributivists today accept that point. See, e.g., Michael Moore, *Placing Blame* (1997) at 151.

[33] The following have all been taken from Larry Lauden, *Truth, Error, and Criminal Law: An Essay in Legal Epistemology* (2006) at 63. A similar range is discussed in Frederick Schauer, "Proportionality and the Question of Weight," Chapter 8 in this volume.

[34] *Zadig* (photo. reprint 1974) at 53.

wrote: "It is better that five guilty persons should escape punishment than one innocent person should die."[35] William Blackstone got the better of these two in the popular imagination by writing: "It is better that ten guilty persons escape [punishment] than that one innocent suffer."[36] But the numbers go up from there. John Fortesque opined that he would "prefer twenty guilty men to escape death through mercy, than one innocent to be condemned unjustly."[37] Benjamin Franklin upped the ante, writing: "It is better a hundred guilty persons should escape than one innocent person should suffer."[38] But highest honors belong to Moses Maimonides, who wrote: "It is better . . . to acquit a thousand guilty persons than to put a single innocent man to death."[39]

What can one say in the face of such a range? On the one hand, it is unclear that we are comparing apples to apples, because it is unclear if all of these writers were concerned about the future crimes that the guilty who are allowed to go free would likely commit, crimes that would otherwise be prevented by punishment. It is also unclear what they would say if so many of them were not focused on capital punishment as the relevant form of punishment, and considered instead lesser, alternative punishments. On the other hand, we might notice an interesting signal in the norms implicitly used by the lower and higher ends of the range. Voltaire spoke of prudence, which suggests a utilitarian calculus, whereas Maimonides wrote from a religious point of view, one presumably far removed from the utilitarian calculus.

Let us start, then, with Voltaire's end of the spectrum. One way to get his ratio is to suppose that, on average, an offender who is not punished will go on to commit one more comparable offense. If we suppose that the harm of being punished for a particular crime (whether murder or theft or anything in between) when one is innocent is on a par with the harm the victims of unpunished criminals who commit such a crime would suffer, and if we suppose that these are the only relevant consequences, then the ratio is a straightforward consequence of the assumptions. For if we convict an innocent person, then he suffers a serious harm, and a guilty person is presumably left free to victimize another – giving us two victims. But if we let a guilty person go free, then we can expect him to victimize another – giving us one victim. Hence the ratio is two-to-one.[40] If we adopt the retributive premise that there

---

[35] 2 Hale PC 290 (1678).

[36] *Commentaries on the Laws of England*, c. 27, at 358 (margin).

[37] *De Laudibus Legum Angliae* 65 [1471] (S. Chimes ed. and trans. 1942).

[38] Letter from Benjamin Franklin to Benjamin Vaughn (March 14, 1785), in *The Works of Benjamin Franklin* vol. 11, 11 at 13 (John Bigelow, ed., fed. edn., 1904).

[39] Moses Maimonides, *The Commandments*, vol. 2 (Charles Chavel, trans., 1967) at 270.

[40] See Richard Lippke, "Punishing the Guilty, Not Punishing the Innocent," (2010) 7 *Journal of Moral Philosophy* 462 at 468.

is some additional value in punishing the guilty, we do not really change the ratio, because the guilty go unpunished if either error is committed – although one could argue that the ratio moves in the direction of one-to-one. The ratio would move further in that direction if we suppose that if we let the guilty go free then they will victimize many. Then the number of victims caused by the unpunished criminals would tend to swamp the harm to the innocent who are punished. On the other hand, if we suppose either that being wrongfully punished is worse than being a victim of crime, or that unpunished criminals will commit, on average, less than one other similar act, then the ratio would climb toward Maimonides's.

The problem with this sort of utilitarian thinking is that it could easily, at least in certain categories of cases, suggest that the state should use preponderance of the evidence as the relevant evidential standard. And if we were to be truly utilitarian about punishment, we would realize that the evidence of guilt has to rise to more than 50 percent likelihood only if we remain committed to punishing only one person for a given crime (discounting extra punishments for complicity). If we free ourselves of that fundamentally retributive assumption, and allow ourselves to think of the criminal law as fundamentally a tool for incapacitation and deterrence, then we could punish more than one person for a given crime or set of crimes, as long as there is sufficient evidence for each person that he did it. What would constitute sufficient evidence? Evidence such that we are confident we will protect more innocent people overall. Given that we are trying to incapacitate someone such as a serial killer or serial rapist, we might want to prosecute every suspect who does not have a conclusive rebuttal of the evidence against him. Accordingly, we might want to instruct the jury that it can convict more than one of them, to ensure that the true criminal does not escape justice, as long as it believes that a particular defendant *might* have committed the crimes at issue.

This pure utilitarian position is shocking to contemplate. But even if we add the premise that only one person may be convicted for a given crime, the utilitarian approach would allow juries to convict on mere preponderance of the evidence. This is not a shocking position, but it is one so at odds with our current practices, that it strongly suggests that we should look for another way of balancing the competing concerns.[41] So we are back to the question: How can we find a weighting factor owed the innocent, protecting them from a false

---

[41] Lippke offers pragmatic reasons to use proof beyond a reasonable doubt as a hedge against the state's potential to abuse its power. But that argument seems wrongly to allow lesser standards of proof to be used if other ways of ensuring that the state does not abuse its power can be found.

conviction, which strikes the right middle note between preponderance of the evidence and conviction only on proof that leaves *no* rationally defensible doubt?

The answer, we believe, is connected to what it means to *punish* people; it requires something pretty much along the lines of a BARD standard. Punishment is not just the act of harming a person. It is an act with a distinctive significance for both the person who is punished and for the rest of the community. In part, it is a communicative act, communicating censure for the commission of a crime.[42] This presupposes that the basis for the censure, the conviction, is reliable. In addition, punishment is in part the intentional infliction of suffering, justified in a retributive framework by the idea that the defendant *deserves* it. Again, to justify doing that the presupposition is that the fact finder must positively believe that the person *deserves* such punishment. It would be jarringly disconcerting if the state were willing to do that even though the fact finder thought the defendant simply *might* deserve it, or even asserted that he *probably* deserved it.

It might be thought that what is at work here is an appeal to the agent-centered distinction between doing and allowing, or the parallel patient-centered distinction between the claim not to be harmed and the claim to be helped. Focusing on the agent-centered distinction first, one might suggest that the state has special reasons to avoid dirty hands, and that it should therefore be more willing to *allow* criminals to go free, allowing *them* to cause unjust harm, than to cause harm directly by punishing the innocent. But agent-centered deontology, as noted above, seems to get the very idea of deontology backward. Agents should not be obsessively concerned with how dirty their hands are; they should be concerned with respecting the rights of those with whom they interact. This is at least as true when the state acts as the agent of us all as it is for any private agent. Instead, we should shift the focus to the patient-centered distinction between positive and negative claims. Those who would be harmed by criminals unless they are convicted and incapacitated have a positive claim on the state to be saved from those private harms; those innocents who would be unjustly harmed by the state itself if they are wrongfully punished have a negative claim on the state not to harm them. Arguably, negative claims are stronger, all else equal, than positive claims. This could be offered as *the* explanation of the priority the state should show for not convicting the innocent over not allowing the guilty to go free.

---

[42] For the leading statement of this view, see Anthony Duff, *Punishment, Communication, and Community* (2003).

We think this is *part* of the story – and notice, it, too, appeals to a deonto-logical tipping of the scales. But it would be a mistake to take it as all of the story. The priority negative claims have over positive claims, at least when all the claims are restricting, seems fairly weak. The principle of necessity or less evil in criminal and international law seems to allow negative claims to be outweighed by even slightly greater interests protected by positive claims. In the context of criminal trials, that might allow the use of a standard of proof not much higher than preponderance of the evidence if that would predictably reduce the overall incidence of innocent people being harmed – whether by criminals or the state.

Our position, then, builds on the significance of the distinction between positive and negative claims. It adds the thought that the claim not to be wrongfully punished is particularly strong not just because it is a claim not to be harmed, but because it is a claim not to be treated in a particular way without high level of confidence, on the basis of empirically sound reasons, that the treatment is warranted. The expressive content of punishment, the dimension of censure, the claim that the sanction is deserved, these all require a high level of confidence that the punishment *is* deserved. That high level of confidence is captured by the BARD standard.

Many defenders of BARD seem to think that they are defending the highest possible standard of proof, one which requires that there be no practical pos-sibility that the innocent will be convicted.[43] We are not taking that position. We acknowledge that BARD does and should give some weight to the impor-tance of obtaining convictions, and thus tolerates a certain amount of error. The point is that the finder of fact should feel highly confident, beyond the level of confidence derived from mere "clear and convincing" evidence, that the defendant is guilty before agreeing to say that he *deserves* punishment.

Bringing this back to the balance in proportionality analysis, our point is that BARD should be required as the correct constitutional standard for a criminal conviction because that level of proof is required to respect the dignity of criminal defendants. This is not merely because of their welfare interests. It is not because it is, in some objective sense, worse to be an innocent person convicted than to be an innocent person victimized by crime. It is because of the moral import of a criminal conviction, which presupposes that the finder of fact *believe*, on the basis of proof that leaves no reasonable doubt, that the defendant committed the crime for which he is to be punished. The

---

[43] See, e.g., Tribe, *supra* note 29. See also Alex Stein, *Foundations of Evidence Law* (2005), at 175; Rinat Kitai, "Protecting the Guilty," 6 *Buffalo Crim. L. Rev.* 1163 (2003). For a stinging critique of this position, see Lauden, "The Rules of Trial," *supra* note 29.

right standard gives substantial priority to the claims of the innocent not to be punished, while tolerating some accidental false convictions in order to obtain many true ones, because that is required to act on a concept of punishment that takes seriously the need to make punishment consistent with respect for the dignity of persons.

III. LIMITS ON PREVENTIVE DETENTION

Preventive detention is a policy that, like criminal punishment, can incapacitate the dangerous. But unlike criminal punishment, it is not premised on a claim that the detainee *deserves* to lose his freedom. Instead, it is premised simply on the thought that some people are *too dangerous* to be allowed to move about in society, and therefore must be detained. Given that it lacks the moral import of punishment, one might think that the implication of the previous section would be that the right balance to strike when considering a detainee's claim not to be detained is simply a neutral, utilitarian balance of competing interests.[44] But in liberal constitutional democracies, it is rightly considered fundamentally unjust to subject mentally sane persons to long-term preventive detention (hereinafter LTPD) on grounds that are no stronger than a simple utilitarian balance of competing interests.[45] The question is why that is so.

Our answer runs as follows. For a state to respect the dignity of people with autonomous or free wills, at least if it is obliged to act on the assumption that they have a right to be in the state's territory, it must not subject them to LTPD if it can hold them accountable for wrongful choices after the fact. Using LTPD instead of the criminal law would deny them the presumption to which they are entitled, namely that they will use their free will to choose to act only in lawful ways. We call the account of detention that justifies this position on LTPD the Autonomy Respecting (AR) model of detention.[46]

It might seem that the AR model implies an absolute tipping of the balance against LTPD of autonomous and accountable individuals. But of course, as in the criminal justice area, there is a range of difficult issues. First, there is the question of the standard of proof. If someone can be shown not to possess some threshold level of autonomous capacity, and then subjected to LTPD

---

[44] Some writers do seem to think this is the right position to take. See, for example, Benjamin Wittes, *Law and the Long War* (2008), at 35.

[45] See, e.g., European Convention on Human Rights, Art. 5 (limiting the use of preventive detention).

[46] One of us spelled out this position most fully in Alec Walen, "A Unified Theory of Detention, with Application to Preventive Detention for Suspected Terrorists," 70 *Maryland L. Rev.* 871 (2011).

if the danger she poses to herself or others outweighs her liberty interest, one needs to know both what the threshold level is and what the standard of proof is. Is it preponderance of the evidence? Proof beyond a reasonable doubt? Some standard in between?[47] But we do not want to focus on the standard of proof issue in this section. We want, instead, to focus on the question of what it means for someone not to be accountable, not because of their intrinsic incapacity as a moral agent, but because of the extrinsic fact that adequate policing capacity is not available to hold her accountable. This is a central prong in our AR model of detention, but it leaves an important substantive issue to be settled: How much security must the police be able to provide in order to say that a person can be held accountable? The answer to *that* question, we argue, requires an intermediate weighting factor, somewhere between neutral and the (nearly) absolute weighting due to those with non-restricting claims.

Before we can try to explain why the minimal amount of security for accountability should be set using an intermediate weighting factor, we need to explain a bit more about how the AR model is supposed to work.[48] At its most basic, the AR model holds that individuals who can be adequately policed and held criminally liable for their illegal choices, as normal autonomous actors, and who can choose whether their interactions with others will be impermissibly harmful or not, can be subjected to long-term detention *only if* they have been convicted of a crime for which (a) long-term punitive detention, and/or (b) the loss of the right not to be subject to long-term preventive detention is a fitting punishment.

This can be broken down into its constituent parts as follows: Punitive detention, as long as it is in response to the violation of a just criminal law and proportional to the convicted criminal's culpability for her crimes, respects a person's dignity because it is on the basis of the convicted criminal's autonomous choice to commit a crime. Preventive detention, as noted above, is not in that way based on desert, but instead only on dangerousness.

As far as we can see, LTDP is justifiable in only four conditions, namely when:

1. People lack the normal autonomous capacity to govern their own choices;

2. They have, in virtue of one or more criminal convictions, lost their right to be treated as autonomous and accountable;[49]

3. They have an independent duty to avoid contact with others, because such contact would be impermissibly harmful (e.g., those with contagious and deadly diseases), and LTPD simply reinforces this duty; or

4. They are incapable of being adequately policed and held accountable for their choices by any country obliged or willing to police them like any other free resident of the territory.

It is only the fourth of these possibilities that concerns us here.

The paradigmatic type of person to fall into the fourth category is the captured enemy combatant or prisoner of war (POW).[50] A combatant under the traditional law of war is, and will remain until the war is over or he is released from military service, privileged to engage in combat with the detaining power.[51] If he is released or escapes from detention, he has the right to take up arms again.[52] This means that not only can the detaining power not hold him criminally responsible for his past violent actions – at least as long as those acts do not violate the laws of war – but also that the detaining power may not hold him criminally responsible for any *future* acts of violence that conform to the law of war. The state is not required to allow itself to be attacked. Therefore, it can subject POWs to LTPD to prevent them from attacking. And it can do so without disrespecting them as autonomous people because their legal status makes them unaccountable.[53]

More normative difficulty arises when dealing with what lawyers in the administration of George W. Bush more broadly called "enemy combatants," (i.e., suspected terrorists [STs]) who have no right to use military force. We divide these into two categories: alien STs who come from countries where

---

[49] This is certainly the most controversial of the four prongs. It matches the practice in the United States and elsewhere, but many theorists consider it clearly unjustifiable for a person to be subject to LTPD as a result of a past criminal action. One of us argues, however, that we can see loss of the normal right not to be subject to LTPD as an element of punishment that can complement the more standard use of prison terms and fines. See Alec Walen, "A Punitive Precondition for Preventive Detention: Lost Status as an Element of a Just Punishment," 63 *San Diego L. Rev.* 1229 (2011).

[50] This paragraph is taken, with minor modifications, from Walen, "Unified Theory of Detention", *supra* note 46 at 922.

[51] Dieter Fleck, *The Handbook of Humanitarian Law in Armed Conflict* (2008) at 361.

[52] Ibid.

[53] There are complications that concern the possibility of a combatant giving up his combatant status, but these need not worry us here.

the police power is largely dysfunctional, such as Yemen,[54] and those that come from countries with normally functioning police powers, such as those of Western Europe and the United States. We believe that no country has an obligation to release into its territory, and police, those who are not its citizens (with the rare and limited exception of cases in which a country has special responsibilities for certain noncitizens who it would otherwise wrong if it does not admit them).[55] Thus, we think that if the United States has captured Yemeni STs, and no country with a normally functioning police force volunteers to take them in and police them, then the United States can treat them as unaccountable, because they will not be adequately policed in the country that has a duty to take them in and police them: their home country. This licenses LTPD of STs from such countries, provided there is sufficient evidence that they are indeed dangerous – a separate and difficult question, but analogous to the idea that in times of invasion or rebellion, when the normal policing capacity of a state is overwhelmed, rights connected to ending LTPD, paradigmatically habeas rights, can be suspended. What is not permitted according to the AR model is LTPD of STs from countries that do have adequately functioning police forces. But this now gets us to the heart of the matter for present purposes. What does it mean for a state to lack the ability to provide adequate policing of STs?

One way of asking that question is to ask when a state's ability to provide police protection has been so degraded that it shifts from the kind of state where the policing capacity is adequate to one where it is inadequate – the habeas point mentioned immediately above. We want to focus on another way of asking the question, however: How does adequacy of policing capacity relate to the threat posed by a particular individual? Are there individuals who are so dangerous that they may be subject to LTPD even though others who pose more mundane threats may not, because the policing capacity is adequate with respect to the latter but not the former?

It is a little hard to imagine how a government could have sufficient evidence that it had captured someone who was dangerous to a degree far exceeding that seen among normal criminals and yet not have evidence of crimes that should be sufficient for a conviction of a serious felony. This is especially true in this age of expanded counterterrorism crimes, such as providing material

---

[54] See Department of Justice et al., *Final Report: Guantanamo Review Task Force* 23 (January 22, 2010) at 18 (explaining that the "security situation in Yemen had deteriorated" in such a way that the release of the Yemeni detainees at Guantánamo Bay represented a "unique challenge"), retrieved from http://www.justice.gov/ag/guantanamo-review-final-report.pdf.

[55] We think the Uighurs held in Guantanamo fit this description, pace the holdings of U.S. courts.

support to terrorist groups.[56] But it is not completely beyond imagining how such a situation could come about. Perhaps the government feels it cannot put on a trial without risking too much sensitive information,[57] perhaps the relevant law was not on the books when the person committed the acts for which the state would like to prosecute,[58] or perhaps, like many a mafia boss, there are lots of reasons to suspect a particular individual, but all on the basis of hearsay or the testimony of uncooperative witnesses that will not yield a conviction.

Whatever the reason, imagine that the government has a person that it takes itself to have very good reason to believe is a charismatic terrorist mastermind, the kind who, if allowed to move about outside of a maximum-security prison, would likely conspire with others to kill thousands of innocents, or maybe orders of magnitude more than that. How are we to weigh the lives of thousands or more innocent victims against his liberty? Is normal policing "adequate" when it would be so much less effective at ensuring that he does no harm than LTPD in a maximum-security facility?[59]

This is a point at which we think the sane person admits that there may be cases in which normally adequate policing is not adequate. But that then opens up the key question: How do we get a measure for that? The neutral, utilitarian answer would be: policing is adequate if we expect that it will do more harm to a supposedly dangerous person to subject him to LTPD than would likely result to others if the state were to rely on the police's ability to deter him or intercept him before any plans to commit violent acts reach fruition – modulo, of course, the dangers that accompany allowing LTPD ever to be used on autonomous and accountable individuals who have a right to be in a given country. This measure, however, undermines almost the whole point of the AR model of detention. It's not clear why we don't end up simply doing a full utilitarian analysis, which would fully undermine the point of the AR model.

---

[56] See 18 U.S. §2339B.

[57] See Michael Mukasey, "Jose Padilla Makes Bad Law," *Wall St. Journal*, August 27, 2007 (p. A15).

[58] A situation such as this recently arose with respect to Yasim Hamdan, whose conviction in a military tribunal for providing material support to al Qaeda was overturned because that was not a crime under the law of war at the time he was a driver for Osama bin Laden. See *Hamdan v. U.S.*, 696 F.3d. 1238 (DC Cir. 2012).

[59] Even British "control orders," which put those subject to them under something close to house arrest, have limitations as security measures. See Alec Walen, "Criminalizing Statements of Terrorist Intent: How to Understand the Law Governing Terrorist Threats, and Why It Should Be Used Instead of Long-Term Preventive Detention," (2011) 101 *The Journal of Crim. L. and Criminology* 803 at 823–824.

A better answer goes back to the basis of the AR model and says that what is crucial is that once the state accepts that it has an obligation to police someone, it must seek to respect that person as an autonomous and accountable agent if he has at least a threshold level of autonomy and if the state can in fact hold him accountable for any wrongful choices he might make. Doing otherwise is inconsistent with respecting his dignity. In practice, that has to mean providing as much police surveillance – including perhaps limits on his freedom and intrusions into his privacy that are normally not permissible in a liberal society, but that are far easier to justify than LTPD – as can be afforded, consistent with other priorities for the state. Those efforts would be judged inadequate only if the state could prove to a properly constituted neutral body, by a sufficiently high degree of proof – another issue we leave to the side here – that the person of concern is likely to try to commit a major terrorist act, and that the danger to his fellow citizens of *not* subjecting him to LTPD *far outweighs* the harm to him of being subjected to LTPD. This last balance term, "far outweighs", is still vague, but we think it captures the relevant middle space in approximately the right way. It captures the idea that the state is committed to respecting the dignity of autonomous individuals by not simply predicting what they will do and then acting on a utilitarian calculus.

IV. CONCLUSION

The previous three sections illustrate that balancing is not mechanical but requires the decision maker to appropriately take into account everything relevant that is not already addressed in the first three prongs of the proportionality test. But the fundamental lessons to draw from these discussions go significantly beyond that. First, deontology is not in tension with balancing. It is a mistake to believe that human rights are bifurcated: mostly subject to balancing, but deontological with regard to some aspects, in particular with regard to human dignity. Instead, the kind of moral reasoning that balancing requires is thoroughly deontological and always grounded in human dignity. Second, human dignity-related deontology, if taken seriously, is not limited to a simple structure (persons being used as a means for others' ends) covering only a relatively small part of rights practice, as one of us had previously argued. Human dignity-based deontology is structurally diverse and considerably more ubiquitous.

In the classic cases typically associated with human dignity, cases such as those involving the use of persons for medical experiments, organ harvesting, the torture of innocents, or targeting of non combatants, and so forth, the rights claimant invokes not only fundamental interests, but makes non-restricting claims: He insists on a nearly absolute right not to be required to make himself an instrument for the use of others (a means to another's end), if that involves the sacrifice of his life, his physical integrity, or other fundamental interests. It is the non-restricting nature of these claims that justifies assigning to them a weight so great that it is never (or nearly never) outweighed by countervailing concerns. But human dignity-based deontology is not only relevant in cases that involve non-restricting claims; it comes into play in a far wider range of cases. In these cases claims are not absolute, but still considerably stronger than neutral interest balancing would suggest. We discussed two main examples. An appropriate standard of proof in criminal law strikes a balance between the right of the accused not to be convicted erroneously and the interest of the community to ensure a sufficient number of criminals get convicted. However, the right-bearer's interest in not being falsely convicted and baselessly punished may not be neutrally balanced against the interests of those who would benefit from more criminal punishments being doled out. The defendant's interests should be treated as substantially more weighty, because that is the only way to respect the moral preconditions of punishment. Furthermore, if the rights-bearer's claim is the claim not to be subject to LTPD as a resident in a liberal democracy, then his interest in not be subject to LTPD should not be neutrally balanced against the interests of those who could expect to benefit from his LTPD. Taking the rights-bearer seriously as an autonomous and accountable agent requires the state to subject him to less harmful treatment unless the threatened harm to others far outweighed the harm to him of being subjected to long-term preventive detention.

We provided neither a moral theory of human dignity as it relates to balancing nor a comprehensive typology of structures as they relate to balancing. The types of cases we focused on served merely to highlight some of the structural complexity involved in balancing. In all cases, the correct way to balance depends on standards that only substantive reasoning can establish. There are two conclusions to be drawn from the argument presented. The first is negative: Human dignity is not primarily about rule-like absolutes and balancing is not primarily about simple interest balancing. The second is positive: Once the potentially complex nature of the balancing exercise is understood, there is no tension between human dignity and balancing. Indeed, respect for human dignity requires balancing.

5 Between Reason and Strategy: Some Reflections on the Normativity of Proportionality

George Pavlakos*

I. SOME PRELIMINARIES

Proportionality is considered by lawyers and non-lawyers alike to be the ubiquitous guardian of legitimacy of our public life.[1] Be it as a judge-made principle or as an instituted legal rule, its ability to guarantee the supervisory function of the courts within the state and, notably, to extend it over supra- and international sources of authority, has made it particularly adept for the age of globalization, where the sources of authority and the grounds of legitimacy are often assumed to be disparate.

Yet, it would seem that despite its legitimacy-driven interest, proportionality, or rather its current practice, is entangled in an odd paradox. In a nutshell: in discharging its controlling function, with an eye to enhancing legitimacy, it drives a disquieting wedge between authoritative directives and the moral grounds that are supposed to legitimize them. It is, in particular, the practice of courts to use proportionality as a moral filter – that is, an ex post imposition of moral value on morally unoriented authoritative facts – which is conducive to the paradox. Along these lines, proportionality seems to have two faces: on a normal day it operates as a mere means-ends test, purporting to secure the consistent alignment of legal precepts with the ends pursued by the law.

* For comments and discussion, I am very grateful to Grant Huscroft, Bradley Miller, Grégoire Webber, and the other participants of the Proportionality Colloquium at Western University in October 2010, where I presented an early draft of this chapter. The writing of the chapter was supported by the generous funding of an Odysseus Grant of the Research Foundation Flanders (FWO) and the long-term strategic development financing of the Institute of State and Law of the Academy of Sciences of the Czech Republic (RVO: 68378122).

[1] See Robert Alexy, *Theorie der Grundrechte* (1985) (English translation by Julian Rivers, *A Theory of Constitutional Rights* [2002]) (hereinafter Alexy, *Constitutional Rights*); David M. Beatty, *The Ultimate Rule of Law* (2004); Mattias Kumm, "Political Liberalism and the Structure of Rights" in G. Pavlakos (ed.), *Law, Rights and Discourse* (2007) at 131–166.

But when duty calls, its role is to intervene where the ends pursued by the law become morally questionable, usually in the form of an infringement on categorical prohibitions.[2]

A Janus-faced proportionality cannot survive independently of a specific picture of the law. If my suspicion is correct, then what underpins the current practice of proportionality (or at least a significant part of it) is a positivist understanding of legal obligation, one that locates its grounds in the institutional facts that present it to the world. Consider, however, that *that* picture of the law is precisely what resists the cure of any moral filter, for it can always claim that legal obligations exist antecedently of their moral impact on persons. It follows that whatever the function of a moral filter, it would come too late to define what we are obligated to do "under the law". This is, then, the paradox stated in full: the practice of proportionality is in danger of rendering proportionality ineffective on the exact grounds that its practitioners judge it to be effective. Letting the paradox survive commits us to the disquieting claim that legal authority is to remain morally arbitrary *until* a judgment to the contrary is passed.

What is at stake here is more than some eccentric jurisprudential dispute over law's nature. If legal obligation is trapped within the cage of positivism, then it is very hard to understand what obligates us outside the confines of nation-states or the institutions they have authorized. And yet, the unique challenge of globalization is precisely about the obligations we bear beyond and across states, a challenge that often becomes difficult to identify when looking at it through the looking glass of domestic law. For within the institutional framework of the state, questions of moral legitimacy and institutional fact are interwoven into a seamless "lore that is black with fact and white with value and yet at no point appears as quite white or black".[3] By contrast, once we broaden our perspective beyond the state there is no easy shortcut from institutions to obligations or vice-versa. Thus, even though national judges rarely need to address fundamental questions of normativity before they deliver (morally) grounded judgments, the supra- and international levels pose fundamental questions requiring a clear stance on the force and the grounds of legal obligation. To cut the long story short, we need to get things right as to what

---

[2] I shall assume that this becomes the case when the law interferes with the autonomy of its subjects. Although there seems to be agreement at this general level of formulation, once one starts digging deeper, deep disagreements on the precise meaning of autonomy surface. For the moment, it suffices to focus on the general formulation. For a more detailed formulation of the content of autonomy, see section III of this chapter.

[3] To paraphrase a famous expression of W.V.O. Quine in "Carnap and Logical Truth," *The Ways of Paradox, and Other Essays* (2nd ed., 1976) 132.

obligates at home before we can tackle the complex questions of obligation at the global level. Yet the global level is far more adept for setting the agenda of our enquiry. In this endeavor, a reformed notion of proportionality can play a crucial role, given its potential at both the national and supra-national levels.

In what follows, I organize the discussion in two parts. In the second part of the chapter I shall propose a more detailed explanation of the paradox. I will juxtapose two types of normativity in order to model the two conflicting understandings of the law that the practice of proportionality reveals: on the one hand, the normativity of means-ends rationality; and on the other, the normativity of morality (or the normativity of reasons). Whereas the former corresponds to a positivistic understanding of rights and broadly legal obligation, the latter is more in line with a non-positivist, if not necessarily anti-positivist, view that takes rights and legal obligation to be grounded on the moral ideal of autonomy. The combination of the two leads to the filter conception of proportionality, as identified previously, and the resulting inability to offer a convincing explanation of the normativity of legal authority.

In the third part, I shall attempt to show that the filter conception and the attendant paradox of proportionality are rooted in a particular conception of autonomy that needs to be revisited. As attested by the theory and practice of proportionality, most lawyers agree that legal rights are institutional expressions of a moral ideal of autonomy. Why is it then that they allow the normativity of means-ends rationality to infiltrate the structure of legal obligation and, predictably, to compete with the moral grounds of the law (those enshrined in rights)? I propose to answer this question by pointing to a particular understanding of autonomy that, if taken on board, not only fails to exclude but rather invites, as complementary to it, the positivistic understanding of authority. This is the understanding commonly associated with autonomy qua negative freedom. Autonomy qua negative freedom assumes that the function of autonomy is to create a sphere that is free of intervention with respect to very important interests of individuals. All else that remains outside this sphere is not a question of freedom but of unprincipled politics.

But what if, in a Kantian spirit, we show that autonomy does not merely exclude interventions into very important interests but also includes positive public action that enables the realization of its various facets for the simple reason that autonomy requires for its own realization that such enabling actions take place? On the proposed picture, political authority is already embedded within the purview of autonomy. In fact, it operates as an enabler of autonomy, which otherwise would be condemning persons to a state of practical stagnation (as no one agent would be able to act, on pain of infringing the autonomy of others). Of course, a lot of detail is required in order to fill in the picture appropriately, which for now must be left in the background. However, even at this general level, the consequences for the nature and workings of proportionality become clear: its role is not to bridge what would otherwise be incompatible normative requirements, but instead to work out a seamless normative web by focusing on the normative grounds shared by the entirety of legal obligations.

Finally, in positioning the chapter philosophically within the rest of this volume, I should like to point out that ultimately it undertakes a defense of rationalism with respect to practical and legal philosophy.[4] In casting a critical eye on the current practice and concept of proportionality, I am merely rejecting a particular conception (or rather misconception) of the role of reason in our (practical) lives – that is, the common view that takes reason and rationality to embody means-ends normativity or even a "technical" understanding of our lives within the world, which reduces them to chains of causes and effects. However, on the account I am offering, reason and rationality are about a lot more than strategic or instrumental relations; they are primarily capacities

---

[4] Contributions to this volume appear to be divided on their stance on the significance of reason and rationality. A prominent instance of antirationalism is Mark Antaki, "The Rationalism of Proportionality's Culture of Justification," Chapter 13 in this volume. Antaki, however, operates with a very narrow conception of rationalism: one that takes reason to consist in logical-deductive reasoning, which merely aims to reduce normative relations to quantifiable sizes, which, subsequently, can be pursued or avoided by aligning the right means to those ends that have come out as most "weighty". If that were all there is to reason, then few rationalists would disagree with Antaki. However, there are at least two more foundational operations of reason: a) its constitutive role for judgment; and b) its constitutive role for normativity. Allow me a few thoughts on each: rationalists argue that judging is a rule-governed activity that organizes the brute facts of the environment – as those "hit" us through our perceptual apparatus – into the familiar categories of "facts", "objects", "events", "properties" and the relations between them. To that extent, reason sets up the matrix or "grammar" of judging about anything. Short of giving up those fundamental categories or the possibility of knowledge, reason must remain indispensable. The second foundational operation of reason is its constitutive role for normativity. Even conceding that reason is not constitutive to judgment in general, it is difficult to grasp normativity as a modality that is different from actuality and possibility (both of the latter falling within the mode of presentation "what is the case"), without the help of reason. Nothing in the environment can, on its own, answer the normative question "Why ought I/we to do X?" Christine Korsgaard in her *The Sources of Normativity* (1996) (hereinafter Korsgaard, *Sources*) beautifully illustrates how the dimension of normativity emerges from the human capacity to reflect, and subsequently, how reflection generates, internally to it, criteria for what may count as appropriate normative items (rules, values, etc.) that satisfy the normative question. It is telling that in either of its foundational operations reason is much richer than instrumentalism, quantification, or deductive reasoning. Characteristically, when arguing for those foundational operations, proponents of reason do not even consider deductive argument but, instead, avail themselves of so-called transcendental arguments. Critics of rationalism, such as Antaki, should consider rationalism from within this perspective, sharing – even if just as an instance of interpretive charity – rationalism's own aspirations prior to critique.

for regarding ourselves as normative beings who can register and respond to anything that has a normative pull on them (be it a norm, some value, an interest, or other). What is more, it is within reason and rationality alone that any such normative item makes sense qua normative. What we need to discard is the erroneous idea that reason and rationality embody a detached, theoretical perspective, which cannot capture the richness of our lives as practical beings. On the contrary, reason's primary task is to articulate this richness in ways that concern us in our capacity as normative beings. As soon as we begin to regard reason in its entirety, the naïve reductions of reason begin to come under serious pressure and lose their persuasive force.[5]

II. LAW'S NORMATIVITY

Courts and other adjudicative bodies around the globe appeal to proportionality in ways that often conceal diverse understandings of how law obligates. In particular, two such understandings seem to resurface time and again in constitutional rights reasoning: one takes law to "obligate" in a manner similar to the requirements of instrumental rationality; another takes law to generate reasons for action which are – or can be traced back to – all-things-considered (or moral) reasons. These two conceptions of normativity are not mutually compatible, and may lead to confusions and paradoxes when they are combined, as is often the case in most systems of constitutional adjudication. In particular, the normativity of instrumental rationality, when applied to law, leads to a conception of authority that is not subject to any other substantive constraints beyond those it itself has pronounced. Its only constraint consists in aligning the relevant means with whatever ends it has decreed in the first place. By contrast, if law's normative force is underpinned by the normativity of morality, then there exist *obligations simpliciter* antecedently to the pronouncements of any authority; obligations that apply over and above the requirements of means-ends rationality.

Is Law Like Instrumental Rationality?

The question wherein rests the normative force of rational requirements has been the object of a deep and long-lasting controversy. For the purposes of the

---

[5] Christine Korsgaard in her classic "The Normativity of Instrumental Reason" (hereinafter Korsgaard "Instrumental Reason") (repr. in Korsgaard, *The Constitution of Agency* [2008] 27–68) has persuasively argued that the normativity of instrumental reasons derives from substantive reasons of morality. It is worth pointing out that the latter cannot be grounded via deductive reasoning, but requires the test of the categorical imperative.

present discussion, it is sufficient to conceive of the "ought" of rationality as proscribing conflicts between the mental states of either a sole deliberator or those who are involved in a common process of deliberation.[6] Such proscriptions include, for example, the rational requirement not to hold inconsistent intentions or beliefs, as in the case of someone who simultaneously believes that he ought to act so as to alleviate poverty but intends not to do it. Another case – that of a requirement of instrumental rationality – is where someone does not intend to do what he believes to be the necessary means to achieve his intended ends.[7] In these cases (as well as in various others), rationality requires a certain kind of consistency among one's mental states. Some of our acquired attitudes will not fit the current shape of our mental states, and thus need to be properly adjusted or even abandoned if one is to avoid conflict.[8]

To capture this aspect of the "ought" of rationality, some have suggested to model it as a wide-scope "ought"; that is, one that does not aim at identifying the all-things-considered reasons for adopting an attitude, but rather aims at retaining an equilibrium among one's mental states.[9] To put it in plain language, a wide-scope ought is not looking into what is happening outside the "heads" of agents, but mainly focuses on keeping the heads' contents tidy and in good order. It should be mentioned, in passing, that the move toward interpreting rational requirements as incorporating a wide-scope ought was devised in response to the so-called problem of bootstrapping, which more or less stands for the danger of taking the rabbit of normativity out of the hat of means-ends coherence.[10] An example might help: Notoriously, Rudolf Höß, the commandant of Auschwitz, intended to exterminate his prisoners. Did he also have a reason to intend to undertake the most efficient means to their extermination? Well, it would appear that if rationality were to enjoy any normative force, then Höß "ought", in some sense, to intend what

---

[6] Rather than implying the existence of collective mental states, I am simply suggesting that each of the agents involved retain a coherent set of mental states *relationally to* the common process of deliberation.

[7] In what follows, I shall use "rationality" to denote more specifically "instrumental rationality"; for a similar restriction, see Michael Bratman, "Intention, Practical Rationality and Self-Governance," (2009) 119 *Ethics* 411 (hereinafter Bratman, "Intention").

[8] Ibid.; Triantafyllos Gkouvas and George Pavlakos, "Preliminary Remarks on a Theory of Legal Normativity" in Jerzy Stelmach and Bartosz Brozek (eds.), *The Normativity of Law* (2011) at 33–43.

[9] I have come to realize the possibility of modeling the legal ought as a wide-scope ought, owing to innumerable discussions with Triantafyllos Gkouvas. Some of these discussions culminated in Gkouvas and Pavlakos, ibid.

[10] Again, as indicated earlier, I am focusing only on requirements of instrumental rationality.

he believed to be the most efficient means to his intended end. However, prescribing the extermination of human beings, undesirability aside, would be like bootstrapping a "novel" reason alongside the set of all other moral reasons we have (what is worse, one that would even contradict all those reasons).

To avoid bootstrapping, while at the same time salvaging a minimum of normative content for rational requirements, some philosophers suggest blocking the attachment of the "ought" of rationality to the conclusion of any conditional that links means to intended ends: "You ought rationally, if you intend E, to intend M" (where E stands for "End" and M for "Means", respectively).

Thus, instead of saying, "If you intend E, you ought to intend M", which would lead to the familiar problem of bootstrapping, we should be saying, "You ought (if you intend E, then you intend M)". In becoming wide-scoped, the ought is being detached from either of the constituents of the conditional: "If E...then M". To put it in more figurative language, courtesy of the detachment, the wide-scope ought does not "freeze" intended means into a new normative reason, but merely says that one ought to be consistent amongst one's own mental states. Notably, in order to abide by the requirement of a wide-scope ought, one can do either of two things: align one's intended means to one's intended ends, or stop intending E in the first place (if one discovers that one's intended ends run, say, against the moral self-understanding of the entire human species!).

Leaving aside the philosophical controversy[11] surrounding the success of this move, I shall rest on its intuitive appeal, and transcribe some of its lessons for the practice of proportionality. The rationale of the wide-scope "ought" is compatible with at least the first two stages of proportionality control; that is, the tests of suitability and necessity.[12] These two tests range over the condition of factual possibility[13] in inquiring into the internal relationship between the intended end and the means for its realization. As such, they control whether the means that were aligned with the intended end were intrinsically suitable to lead to its realization (this includes the requirement that there exist no less intrusive means to the realization of the same end). So far, proportionality treats legal norms as hypothetical imperatives whose normative force is exhausted

[11] See Bratman, "Intention," *supra* note 7; Niko Kolodny, "Why Be Rational?," (2005) 114 *Mind* 509; John Broom, "Normative requirements," (1999) 12 *Ratio* 398 and "Wide or Narrow Scope?," (2007) 116 *Mind* 359; Kieran Setiya, *Reasons without Rationalism* (2010).
[12] I use here Alexy's analysis of proportionality, which I take to be the most sophisticated discussion hitherto; see Alexy, *Constitutional Rights*, *supra* note 1.
[13] Ibid. at 66–69.

by a wide-scope "ought" as outlined earlier: they recommend that one adjust one's means with one's intended ends.[14] Recall that a wide-scope ought can be complied with in one of two ways: either by lining up the appropriate means with the intended ends or giving up the ends altogether. The first two prongs of the proportionality test (suitability and necessity) address the first modus of compliance: they check whether the means taken have been appropriately aligned to the intended ends.

The third prong of proportionality purports to go a step further by addressing the second mode of compliance within the wide-scope "ought": it tests whether the intended ends are proportional *stricto sensu*, with an eye to disqualifying them altogether, in case they are not. This test, to recall Alexy, controls the legal possibility of the intended ends. In the language of the wide-scope ought, the third prong of proportionality asks whether there are good reasons to give up or revise the ends pursued by a particular legal provision in the light of the fundamental norms/values of a legal system.

Yet, it would seem that even that third stage is not capable of escaping the rationale of means-ends instrumentalism that is implied in the first mode of compliance of the wide-scope "ought".[15] That mode submits that the normative meaning of any requirement of rationality is to command an agent to intend the means that correspond to their intended ends. By contrast, the second mode of compliance commands that one stop intending the intended ends (in the light of some other, overriding reason).[16] In effect, this mode of compliance opens up, as it were, the possibility of stepping out of the self-sufficiency of means-ends relations and, instead, substituting in instrumental requirements that are non-conditional or categorical reasons.

Is, however, *stricto sensu* proportionality up to the task? Rather not. For when courts apply it, they merely consider what is "legally possible" by taking on board just another layer of legal norms; that is, those norms that institute important legal values (frequently depicted as principles).[17] Now, assuming

---

[14] For a more detailed discussion of the view that legal norms are like the requirements of rationality, see Gkouvas and Pavlakos, "Preliminary Remarks," *supra* note 8 at 33.

[15] See Grégoire Webber, "Proportionality, Balancing, and the Cult of Constitutional Rights Scholarship," (2010) 23 *Can. J.L. & Jur.* 179 (hereinafter Webber, "Cult of Constitutional Rights").

[16] Of course, one could stop intending an end simply out of whim. I shall not consider such cases because I want to retain a connection between the normativity of instrumental reason and noninstrumental or categorical reason; see Korsgaard, "Instrumental Reason," *supra* note 5.

[17] Alexy, *Constitutional Rights, supra* note 1 at 47. In Alexy, principles are optimization standards. This contrasts with Ronald Dworkin's conception of principles, which views them as categorical norms that "trump" all other considerations. *Cf.* Ronald Dworkin, "Rights as Trumps" in Jeremy Waldron (ed.), *Theories of Rights* (1984) 153.

that those norms (i.e., principles) themselves incorporate a wide-scope ought, they, too, would merely be prescribing that agents intend the right means to their intended ends, without claiming for those ends any special status, on pain of leading to the phenomenon of bootstrapping.[18] It would then follow that the proportionality test in its third prong as well merely controls means-ends relationships and would rarely lead to reconsideration, or even discarding, of legal ends in the light of categorical (moral) reasons.[19]

But why assume that the normativity of principles is of the wide-scoped kind, just like the normativity of all other legal rules? Why not say, instead, that principles or at least a subset of them, contain categorical constraints that can determine what one ought to intend antecedently to anyone's intentions? One reason is that there is ample evidence from the judicial practice and scholarship on proportionality to suggest that the latter is not the case. There appears to be a widespread consensus that when it comes to inquiring into the legitimacy of the ends of legislation, the appropriate deliberative schema to apply is that of balancing. What is being balanced is the principle that supports the legal precept under scrutiny against any competing principles that are to be found in the constitutional order. This requirement of balancing is telling about the wide-scoped structure of principles. Let me unpack this a little bit.

Robert Alexy, the most prominent proponent of balancing, argues that the requirement of balancing is intrinsically linked with the nature of principles as optimization requirements.[20] The latter is taken to mean that principles are norms "which require that something be realized to the greatest extent possible given the legal and factual possibilities . . . The scope of the legally possible is determined by opposing principles and rules".[21] Owing to their structure as optimization requirements, when principles meet with other principles, it follows that each of the competing principles claims its realization to the greatest extent possible. As a consequence, a form of argument is called for with an eye to resolving the competition in a rational manner. Alexy puts forward a "law of competing principles", which pronounces: "The circumstances under which one principle takes precedence over another constitute the conditions of a rule which has the same legal consequences as the principle taking precedence".[22] This "law" is an implicit expression of the requirement to balance. For in

[18] One might want to think of such principles as the notorious "Führerprinzip" to want to agree why bootstrapping is undesirable!
[19] I think this is a general accusation for the wide-scope construction, as the possibility to discard or revise intended ends is granted only to the extent that the agent's mental world can appreciate reasons that lie beyond it.
[20] Alexy, *Constitutional Rights, supra* note 1 at 67.
[21] Ibid. at 47–48.   [22] Ibid. at 54.

order to determine those circumstances "under which a principle takes precedence", Alexy argues, an act of balancing needs to be undertaken. The latter is
explicitly regulated by the so-called law of balancing: "The greater the degree
of non-satisfaction of, or detriment to, one principle, the greater must be the
importance of satisfying the other".[23]

Notwithstanding other criticisms that have been advanced recently in the
literature,[24] the law of balancing and the optimization structure of principles
suggest the wide-scoped character of the normativity of principles in the following sense: there is nothing that is antecedent to the legislative intention
that is required to ground legal principles.[25] What is more, once something
is awarded the status of a principle on the grounds of legislative intentions,
it is automatically equipped with a claim to full optimization, a claim whose
intensity is symmetrically distributed amongst all other principles. To that
extent the requirement for balancing serves the purpose of resolving a certain
aporia that emerges from the inability to specify any independent criterion
for the resolution of the conflict amongst what appears to be equally potent
normative positions.[26] Alas, no sooner have principles been deprived of any
normative content (other than the intention of the legislator), than balancing
turns anew into an exercise of aligning means with intended ends. It should
not come as a surprise then that no principle is rendered immune to balancing.[27]

However, this is precisely the rationale of the wide-scoped ought that is
enlisted by rational requirements. For any "ought" that is rendered wide-
scoped declines to take a stance with respect to what it is that renders something valuable, good, right, and so on, independently of the attitudes of agents.
Alasdair MacIntyre, in his celebrated monograph *After Virtue*,[28] identifies this

---

[23] Ibid. at 102.
[24] See more recently, Kai Möller, "Balancing and the Structure of Constitutional Rights," (2007)
   5 *Int'l. J. Const. L.* 453; Grégoire Webber, "Cult of Constitutional Rights," *supra* note 15;
   also the contributions of Mark Antaki (Chapter 13) and Grégoire Webber (Chapter 6) in this
   volume.
[25] I am not suggesting that Alexy's theory of balancing ought to lead to an understanding of legal
   normativity as instrumental normativity. In fact, Alexy's theory of principles is articulated within
   a much richer theory of law (the so-called discourse theory of law) that, in my view, avoids the
   pitfalls which here I associate with crude instrumentalism (see G. Pavlakos, "Constitutional
   Rights, Balancing, and the Structure of Autonomy," (2011) 24 *Can. J.L. & Jur.* 129. All that I
   am arguing in this chapter is that if the theory of principles is adopted selectively, it cannot
   preclude the instrumental interpretation.
[26] See Alexy about the parity of principles· *Constitutional Rights, supra* note 1 at 195–196; and
   Webber, "Cult of Constitutional Rights," *supra* note 15, who offers an incisive critique of this
   point at 199 ff.
[27] See Alexy, *Constitutional Rights, supra* note 1 at 196, as quoted in Webber, ibid. at 200.
[28] Alasdair MacIntyre, *After Virtue* (1981).

detached stance toward value as the malaise of enlightenment. He characteristically attributes this malaise to a cluster of philosophical positions that
have come to be known as *emotivism*; that is, the thesis that there exists no
vantage point for making normative judgements other than the point of view
of each individual agent. Emotivism is the inescapable conclusion of the conjunction, on one side, of the proposition that moral questions are saddled by
pervasive disagreement and, on the other, the diagnosis that ultimately the
semantic status of normative judgments is not to depict facts but to express
the speaker's attitudes. Even if one does not want to follow MacIntyre all the
way into his doomsday scenario (and he soon abandoned his early diagnosis in
later work),[29] there is a kernel of truth in his concerns. There is something, in
speaking of the normativity of law or morality, that goes amiss if the normative
"ought" is being reduced to the attitudes of speakers.

The Model of Authority

In the case of the law, those attitudes that ground the content of legal obligations are not just anyone's attitudes; rather, they are the attitudes of whoever
counts as an official within the relevant legal system. In having substituted
a wide-scope "ought" in any substantive considerations, it is left up to the
attitudes of officials to determine what is normatively required. Yet, recall that
one mode of compliance with a wide-scoped ought is to simply discard the
relevant attitude that lies in its core. True enough, the reconstruction of legal
principles as optimization requirements and the resulting structure of balancing, which logically follows from it, seem to undermine that mode of
compliance. However the theory of balancing does not offer on its own any
knockdown argument against the recourse to substantive moral arguments,
with an eye to scrutinizing and, if need be, rejecting the attitudes of legal
officials.[30] Were such scrutiny to remain a live option, any early bad effects
of wide-scoping would be mitigated. What shuts down any remaining hope of
mitigation is a theory of legal normativity that purports to offer a normative
justification of why substantive moral considerations ought to be ruled out by
the legal "ought". I shall refer to the theory that justifies the wide-scoping of
the legal "ought", while blocking any direct recourse to moral reasons, as the
model of authority (MoA). Although it draws on a body of ideas that have been

---

[29] See especially, Alasdair MacIntyre *Dependent Rational Animals* (1999).
[30] I believe that this is a live option for Alexy's theory of constitutional rights provided it is not
read in isolation but in the context of his wider theory of legal argumentation (see Pavlakos,
supra note 25 at 129).

advanced by Joseph Raz, my main aim here is not exegetical; my development of MoA casts its net wider than Raz's own theory.[31]

MoA takes a very narrow view on what constitutes the directing force of the law. It takes the view that law's directive capacity is exhausted by the content of the edicts that are uttered by officials within a legal practice. This view stems from the more general claim, itself almost a stipulation, that for something to be capable of directing action it must be self-contained in its directing powers; which is to say, it must make a practical difference to the reasons of an agent directly, that is without any reference to its impact on any of the other normative circumstances of agents.[32] The claim rests on a very sophisticated conceptual edifice, whose main tenets I will attempt to summarize.[33]

MoA sets out from the premise that authority generates a special type of reason for action, which mediates between right reasons and agents, and is known as the service conception of authority. In that respect, reasons of authority are peremptory, for they aim to replace dependent reasons; that is, reasons that would apply anyway to the addressees of the authoritative directives, and which apply anyway to the authority that decides. This is summed up by Raz as the "dependence thesis": "All authoritative directives should be based, among other factors, on reasons which apply to the subjects of those directives and which bear on the circumstances covered by the directives. Such reasons I shall call dependent reasons".[34]

However, even though authoritative directives rest on dependent reasons, the latter must recede into the background. This condition is spelled out through the idea that authoritative directives are, practically speaking, superior

---

[31] Assuming that the model of authority or something close to it is paradigmatically instantiated in the theory of Joseph Raz, an objection looms that any notion of balancing that presupposes a common standard for appraising different values is incompatible with the model of authority (given Raz's prominent endorsement of a version of incommensurability of value). However, I hope to have shown that the theory of principles does not reduce principles to any objective values, but merely to authoritative intentions. To that extent it is perfectly compatible with the model of authority and vice-versa. That said, I am not arguing that Alexy, in putting forward his theory of principles, intended to argue for that conclusion (see *supra* notes 21 and 24). My discussion of the model of authority is indebted to Nicos Stavropoulos, "The Relevance of Coercion: Some Preliminaries," (2009) 22 *Ratio Juris* 334 (hereinafter Stavropoulos, "Relevance of Coercion").

[32] See M. Greenberg, "The Standard Picture and its Discontents" in Leslie Green and Brian Leiter (eds.), *Oxford Studies in Philosophy of Law* (2011); and Stavropoulos, ibid.

[33] My summary shall rely on two key texts of Joseph Raz, which in my view sum up accurately the philosophical background of his ideas as well as their relevance to law: see Joseph Raz, "Reasons for Action, Decisions and Norms," (1975) 84 *Mind* 481; Joseph Raz, "Authority, Law and Morality" in Joseph Raz, *Ethics in the Public Domain* (rev'd. ed., 1994) at 210.

[34] Ibid. at 214.

to the agent's own compliance with the reasons that he has. This is Raz's venerable "normal justification thesis":

> The normal and primary way to establish that a person should be acknowledged to have authority over another person involves showing that the alleged subject is likely better to comply with reasons which apply to him (other than the alleged authoritative directives) if he accepts the directives of the alleged authority as authoritatively binding, and tries to follow them, than if he tries to follow the reasons which apply to him directly.[35]

The combination of the above two theses lead to what Raz has coined the "service conception of authority", which claims that authorities mediate between agents and the right reasons that apply to agents anyway (independently of authority): "[the two theses] regard authorities as *mediating* between people and the right reasons which apply to them, so that the authority judges and pronounces what they ought to do according to right reason".[36] It follows that authoritative reasons preempt dependent reasons, in the sense that agents are required to set aside their reasons and replace them with those of the authority. This is the preemption thesis: "The fact that an authority requires performance of an action is a reason for its performance which is not to be added to all other relevant reasons when assessing what to do, but should replace some of them".[37] The preemption thesis does not imply that dependent reasons have no role to play when it comes to the justification of authority; it merely says that they have no role to play at the level of action:

> This brings into play the dependent reasons, for only if the authority's compliance with them is likely to be better than that of its subjects is its claim to legitimacy justified. At the level of general justification the pre-empted reasons have an important role to play. But once that level has been passed and we are concerned with particular action, dependent reasons are replaced by authoritative directives. To count both as independent reasons is to be guilty of double counting.[38]

Owing to its peremptory force, authority can be of two kinds: legitimate, when it succeeds to realize the reasons that it replaces; and de facto, which merely mirrors the structure of legitimate authority in the sense that it still possesses the capacity to be the kind of thing that can possess legitimate authority. Although only legitimate authority generates genuine obligations, in the sense that it realizes the normal reasons that agents already have (normal justification

---

[35] Ibid.
[37] Ibid. at 214.
[36] Ibid.
[38] Ibid. at 215.

thesis), even de facto authority raises a claim to legitimacy. It follows that all kinds of authority – be they legitimate or de facto – raise a claim to legitimacy.

It follows that, necessarily, every legal system has de facto authority: that is, the law as a minimum claims that it possesses legitimate authority irrespective of whether it actually possesses it:

> A legal system may lack legitimate authority. If it lacks the moral attributes required to endow it with legitimate authority then it has none. But it must possess all the other features of authority, or else it would be odd to say that it claims authority. To claim authority it must be capable of having it, it must be a system of a kind which is capable in principle of possessing the requisite moral properties of authority.[39]

Even though it is possible that some legal system may lack legitimate authority, it is necessary that every legal system possess all characteristics such as pertaining to the possibility of legitimate authority. Consequently the argument turns on which are the characteristics that make law capable of having legitimate authority, even when it fails to do so. Raz submits that these are normatively neutral characteristics that exist at a level that is "thinner" than the one of substantive (dependent) reasons that control the actual success of any authority to serve right reason:

> The two features are as follows. First, a directive can be authoritatively binding only if it is, or is at least presented as, someone's view of how its subjects ought to behave. Second, it must be possible to identify the directive as being issued by the alleged authority without relying on reasons or considerations on which [the] directive purports to adjudicate.[40]

These non-normative characteristics, which are necessary conditions for the possibility of legitimate authority, are possessed by every legal system, whether it be legitimate or not. What is more, they are adduced to support the conclusion that all it takes to identify the content of a legal obligation within any legal system is reference to the social facts that lead to the creation of the relevant norm (this is the so-called sources thesis). The edict or the say-so of some official under such conditions that the system identifies as appropriate for the creation of a norm is sufficient for individuating the content and grounds of the relevant obligation. Of course it is a further question whether the obligation that has been identified will finally succeed in obligating its

---

[39] Ibid.   [40] Ibid. at 218.

addressees.[41] However, it remains crucial that the content and grounds of any legal obligation not only *can* but also *must* be identified with reference to the say-so of officials without any recourse to other dependent substantive reasons, on pain of depriving legal norms of their authoritative character.[42]

Despite its conceptual elegance and subtlety, MoA, assuming that it is the best justification of the instrumental explication of the legal "ought", seems intuitively implausible to a large number of academic lawyers, and in particular human rights theorists, who think that at least some legal norms exist that are not merely expressions of attitude but rather introduce obligations that are categorical or *simpliciter*.[43] Even though their arguments are formulated with respect to the scope and nature of constitutional rights, it is quite clear that what is at stake here is the deep picture of law's normativity as advanced by MoA and the model of rights that it encourages. What do these scholars propose instead?

Narrow-Scope "Ought" and Model of Reasons

The alternative model of normativity attempts precisely to correct the picture about law's normativity: even though on weekdays law obligates like the requirements of instrumental rationality, on a Sunday, when wisdom descends on lawyers, law works in tandem with morality; that is, enforcing or safeguarding categorical reasons/values. Even though, to take but a trivial example, traffic regulation or road safety can become subject to balancing and the logic of instrumental rationality, surely such important matters as freedom of speech or human dignity cannot be placed on the same scale with considerations of policy, the common good, or some consequentialist understanding of what is normatively required.

Several contemporary authors,[44] taking their cue from the work of Ronald Dworkin and other liberal thinkers, argue that constitutional rights obligate

---

[41] Thus, the model of authority needs to introduce an artificial distinction between the content and grounds of legal obligation on one side, and the conditions of success thereof on the other. For a similar distinction, see Stavropoulos, "Relevance of Coercion," *supra* note 31 at 341–342.

[42] For a detailed discussion, see Stavropoulos, ibid.; George Pavlakos, "Law, Normativity and the Model of Norms" in Stefano Bertea and George Pavlakos (eds.), *New Essays on the Normativity of Law* (2011).

[43] See in this volume especially, the contributions of Mattias Kumm and Alec Walen (Chapter 4); T.R.S. Allan (Chapter 10); and Kai Möller (Chapter 7).

[44] See George Letsas, *A Theory of Interpretation of the European Convention on Human Rights* (2007), chapters 1, 5, and 6; and "Two Concepts of the Margin of Appreciation," (2006) 26 O.J.L.S. 705; Kai Möller, "Balancing and the Structure of Constitutional Rights," (2007) 5 *Int'l. J. Const. L.* 453, and "Two Conceptions of Positive Liberty: Towards an Autonomy-Based Theory of Constitutional Rights" (2009) 29 O.J.L.S. 757; and Mattias Kumm, "Political Liberalism

as categorical reasons or reasons *simpliciter*, rather than express, in one form or another, an instrumental ought that is conditioned by what someone said or intended. True enough, these scholars do not discuss directly the nature of legal normativity, nor are they primarily interested in how to model the legal "ought" more accurately. That said, their position is sufficiently clear to allow one to bring out some sharp differences from the normativity of instrumental rationality, after which the first picture of legal normativity was modeled.

Recall that the idea of a wide-scoped "ought" was used to bracket off substantive normative reasons and, in their place, to insert a requirement of coherence between one's intended means and one's intended ends. At that juncture of the discussion, I argued that there are two ways to comply with the wide-scope "ought": either to intend what one believes to be the necessary means to one's intended ends, or to stop intending those ends. However, neither of the disjuncts enjoy priority in virtue of the normativity of the rational requirement: that is, there exists – internally to the wide-scope "ought" – no reason to prefer to comply with one or the other. It would follow that if I chose to stop intending the extermination of the entire Jewish population of Europe, then that would only be a matter of choice. For, from the point of view of the "ought" of rationality, nothing compels me to do so, even if I knew that there existed a different category of reasons (i.e., moral reasons) that commands me to stop intending that end. Now, if law were modeled after the normativity of rationality, it would follow that there would be no normative reason to take into account categorical moral reasons when determining the scope and content of legal obligations.

By contrast, the view that admits categorical normative reasons into the realm of legal obligation regards legal "ought" as narrow-scoped. This means roughly that whatever one intends, says, or does as a matter of social fact with an eye to obligating others can only succeed if it is in line with the normative reasons we all have, independently of what we think or undertake as a matter of social fact.[45] The term "narrow-scope" applies with an eye to declaring that it is not possible to detach the ought from our attitudes, precisely because we are required to intend anything only if we actually have a reason to do so!

An important part of this argument is its capacity to ground legal normativity on reasons of agent autonomy, independently of what agents think, desire, intend, or, for that matter, do. (I will postpone to section 3 a discussion of the

and the Structure of Rights: On the Place and Limits of the Proportionality Requirement" in George Pavlakos (ed.) *Law, Rights and Discourse* (2007) 131.

[45] What these reasons are, how they are instantiated (ontologically speaking), and to what extent they can prescribe concrete tokens of action are very complicated matters, which cannot be discussed at present. For an attempt to tackle some of these questions, see Pavlakos, "Law, Normativity and the Model of Norms," *supra* note 42.

content of autonomy that is envisaged by the model of reasons.) Autonomy is always on the cards when we talk about legal obligation. The reason is that any deed or say-so that purports to direct the action of others is coercive because, if unjustified, it interferes with their autonomy. Thus, coercion is the link between events that purport to obligate and the grounds of obligation, which reside with autonomy.

Central to my argument is the idea that no account of the grounds of legal obligation can be given independently of the concept of coercion (and, hence, autonomy).[46] Not merely institutions, but anything that has the capacity to exert (coercive) impact on the autonomy of persons will be relevant to the grounding of obligation, not because coercive acts themselves can ground obligation, but because coercive acts are appropriately configured to "tease out" what in fact grounds obligation: namely, the moral status of autonomous persons. However, and this is the rub, what actually constitutes coercion also depends on the moral status of persons, for precisely the reason that coercion derives its grounding capacity from its affinity to autonomy. This conception of coercion that is appropriately configured to generate normative results is the Normative Conception of Coercion (NCC). In what follows, I shall offer an outline of NCC while attempting to ground it on some ideas from Kant's moral and political philosophy.

One immediate objection comes from the realm of MoA, discussed previously. MoA submits that the law consists of a set of authoritative edicts, which need not be supplemented by the use of force. Availing itself of the thought experiment of an angelical society, this view argues that even in such a society, even if there is no need for coercion, there remains a need to direct action through authoritative edicts. Absent the need for coercion, the argument continues, there is no necessary link between law's authority and any conditions for the legitimacy of coercion. The upshot of this reasoning is that authority is not conceptually entwined with coercion; hence, moral reasons need not feature among the grounds of law. Were this true, it would sever the link between the moral status of persons and the content of legal obligation. NCC, in advancing a more fine-grained understanding of the workings of coercion, aims (among other things) precisely to block that kind of objection. It argues instead that institutional interaction is coercive for reasons that are institution independent.

---

[46] This view has in modern years gained prominence through the work of Dworkin and Nagel. See Ronald Dworkin, *Law's Empire*, (1986) at 190–191; Thomas Nagel, "The Problem of Global Justice," (2005) 33 *Philosophy & Public Affairs* 113, who appeals to state coercion to justify principles of egalitarian justice.

Coercion is always on the cards when it comes to law, not because of some property exclusive to law, but because institutional facts related to law possess a deeper structure, which is not unique to them; they are action-directing in an inherent or intrinsic manner. Roughly put, this means that they interfere with the reasons agents have antecedently to institutions by rearranging those reasons in one way or another. Normatively speaking, however, this rearrangement is not indifferent – at least not to the extent that we take action-directing acts to be directing the action of autonomous agents that respond to reasons and who are likely to be already embedded in a network of reasons at the moment when an institutional act impacts on their lives. Hence, action-direction is not morally neutral; in fact, it acquires the morality of those reasons (principles) that already apply to agents who are capable of handling reasons for action. But if so, then the morality of action-directing acts points the way forward in establishing the content of legal obligation: action-directing acts amount to legal obligations to the extent and in the manner that they fit into the overall scheme of reasons on which they impact.[47] Coercion, therefore, is always on the cards whenever agents interact, irrespective of the institutional form of their interaction: proper action-directing action entails legitimate coercion while flawed action gives rise to illegitimate coercion and constitutes an instance of injustice that ought to be blocked.[48]

A few more remarks on the logic (and morality) of action-direction are due. Action-directing reasons are reasons that purport to get other agents to act in ways that converge with one's purposes, usually against the background of joint projects or activities. To that extent, action-direction is a special mode of normativity that usually pertains to the contexts of joint endeavors. Given that such contexts require coordination, action-directing reasons, if successful, can underpin the task of coordination. Thus, if A is engaged in a joint project with B, and R is a valid action-directing reason, then A is entitled to appeal to R for guiding B's behavior. More specifically, if the joint project is one that encapsulates elements that are typical of a basic structure of a political community, then action-directing reasons can be legally enforced with an eye to coordination.

An action-directing reason becomes a valid source of obligation when it meets the negative constraint of not amounting to illegitimate coercion.

---

[47] See Stavropoulos, "Relevance of Coercion," *supra* note 31 at 343–344, where he builds on ideas of T.M. Scanlon on the grounding of promissory obligations, see T.M. Scanlon, "Reasons: a Puzzling Duality" in R.J. Wallace (ed.), *Reasons and Value: Themes from the Philosophy of Joseph Raz* (2006) 231.

[48] A.J. Julius, "Getting People to Do Things," MS version April 20, 2009, on file with the author, at 7–9.

Although this negative constraint does not point directly at any grounds that positively shape the content of action-directing reasons, it does so indirectly. Before elaborating further on this point, let me spell out the negative constraint for action-directing action:

> (1) A should not (do y, believe that her y'ing will lead B to x and that this fact is a reason to y and fail to believe with justification that A's y'ing will facilitate B's coming to x on the basis of her recognition of reasons to x that she has independently of A's y'ing.)[49]

(1) says that leading B to x on grounds that B does not share as leading to x independently of A's action-directing act would constitute an instance of (illegitimate) coercion.[50] Clearly, this stipulation does not directly spell out which among such independent grounds are involved; it does so indirectly, however. In recognizing the authority of any agent as a negative constraint for coercion, it implicitly takes the same authority to be capable of specifying positively the content of such grounds that would constitute appropriate action-directing reasons. Thus, (1) tells us that action-directing reasons may be only such items that can be authorized by the reason-giving or deliberative capacities of agents and do not violate (1). But notice this: (1) is not an extra filter or sieve that comes later to contain or purify items that have been designated as reasons for action antecedently of (1). Rather, (1) is the starting point for grounding action-directing precepts in a manner that is agent-relative, if not relativistic (in fact, I would argue that [1] assumes something like a unified normative point of view, one that can ground reasons for action *simpliciter*).[51]

In explaining coercion as action-directing action, NCC underpins a full-blooded account of coercion that fully satisfies the constraint that nothing

---

[49] I adapt from Julius, ibid., at 1. I am aware that at the time of writing Julius was further elaborating his thoughts on the matter. To that extent, I am not claiming that the quoted formulation exhaustively captures the content that Julius confers to action-directing action. That said, it suffices for my purposes here.

[50] Further intricacies of action-direction amounting from (1) include: a) The thesis that an independent reason that applies to my doing X, should also apply to all antecedent actions that lead me to X; b) In the absence of any reason to the contrary, the same structure should be expanded to interpersonal relations: I ought not to lead you to do X without considering the reasons you have for X-ing as applying also to my own acts that purport to lead you to X; c) Finally, a and b yield the thesis that coercion, when it serves to coordinate joint action, is justified under the condition that it is legitimate from the first-person point of view before it is addressed to others. For, if coercion facilitates someone's response to a joint requirement, then this person can rely on the fact that the threat of coercion will facilitate everyone else to pursue the same joint requirement, without wronging them in any way (A.J. Julius, ibid.).

[51] See George Pavlakos, "Practice, Reasons and the Agent's Point of View," (2009) 22 *Ratio Juris* 79; and, "Law, Normativity and the Model of Norms," *supra* note 42 at 246.

is a genuine obligation unless it constitutes a reason for the agent. The full-blooded account of NCC moves well beyond traditional accounts of coercion that mainly focus on brute force, the harm caused to agents, or some other fact about the agent's psychology. In such *outcome-oriented* accounts, coercion comes too late to point to the morally or normatively significant elements that contribute to the genesis of legal obligation. There, coercion assumes the role of an additional incentive for compliance to a norm, but fails to explain what it is in virtue of which a fact that takes place in the external environment acquires normative significance (that is, becomes obligatory) for the agent. Instead, NCC understands coercion as constituting a constraint on agent autonomy that is antecedent[52] to any loss of welfare (i.e., harm), the application of brute force to the agent, any claims to legitimacy raised by the coercer or, finally, the acceptance or consent of the coercee.[53]

Proportionality as a Moral Filter[54]

Surprisingly, neither the theory nor the practice of constitutional rights law is prepared to make a choice between the two conceptions of normativity, despite the prima facie incompatibility that they demonstrate. This leads to an unprincipled borrowing of elements from both of those. Most commonly, courts employ proportionality with an eye to upholding means-ends rationality, although in a few sensitive cases they resort to categorical reasons in order to contain the bad effects that pertain to a strategic understanding of legal obligation. Likewise, constitutional law scholars propose to mix and match elements from both conceptions with an eye to achieving a division of labor between the two conceptions of normativity.[55]

---

[52] It is antecedent in the sense that it determines the normative significance of any loss of welfare or causing of harm as wrongdoing rather than vice-versa.

[53] On the distinction between harm and wrongdoing, see Arthur Ripstein, *Force and Freedom: Kant's Legal and Political Philosophy* (2009) at 42–47 and 81–85 (hereinafter Ripstein, *Force and Freedom*). Other "full-blooded" accounts of coercion are to be found in Julius, "Getting People to Do Things," *supra* note 48; and N. Stavropoulos, "The Relevance of Coercion: Some Preliminaries," (2009) 22 *Ratio Juris* 339. The term "Normative Conception of Coercion" is coined by George Pavlakos and Joost Pauwelyn, "Principled Monism and the Normative Conception of Coercion under International Law" in Malcolm Evans and Panos Koutrakos (eds.), *Beyond the Established Legal Orders: Policy Interconnections between the EU and the Rest of the World* (2011) 317.

[54] For a thorough analysis of a moral filter in legal theory, see Nicos Stavropoulos, "Why Principles?", *Oxford Legal Studies Research Paper* No. 55/2011.

[55] Mattias Kumm in earlier work succumbs to this strategy when he proposes a mixed model of proportionality. See Mattias Kumm, "Political Liberalism and the Structure of Rights," *supra* note 44. However, in his contribution (with Alec Walen, Chapter 4) to the present volume, Kumm rejects the "filter conception of proportionality" in arguing that deontological

In all of these cases, proportionality assumes the role of a moral filter that operates outside the standard rationale of law, as soon as "things get out of hand". And yet, reconciling the two models of normativity would require a lot more than imposing some ex post facto filter on instrumental imperatives. For, to the extent to which legal obligation is grounded on autonomy, as the normative conception of coercion has demonstrated and probably most lawyers would concede, autonomy ought to determine from the outset the existence and content of legal obligations. Imposing a deontological filter at a later stage in order to recover law's moral core simply comes too late. Hence, the main problem with taking proportionality to be a moral filter is that it creates a presumption against the legitimacy of authoritative legal norms.

If lawyers agree that autonomy is the ultimate ground of legal obligation, why then defer its day-to-day workings to instrumental normativity? Why allow a gap to open up between two types of normativity that sit uncomfortably together; a gap that, moreover, portrays the legal system with a Janus face? The third part of this chapter aims to tackle this question by, first, diagnosing a stereotype and, second, proposing an alternative. The stereotype is symptomatic of an understanding of autonomy, which considers it as a negative constraint on political authority (and politics more generally). Whereas politics sets out to realize the various projects of a political community, rights guard against a trespassing on the autonomy of its members. On this standard picture it is assumed that authority is irrelevant or ungrounded from the point of view of autonomy *until* it is pronounced legitimate (or not pronounced illegitimate) by the courts. The paradox amounting from this construction is striking: on the one hand, it is claimed that obligation flows out from autonomy; on the other, it is conceded that no authoritative act is obligatory at the point of its creation (but only becomes so in hindsight). Driving so grave a split into the core of legal obligation is rather disquieting, not to say conceptually incoherent. For it seems profoundly absurd to claim that authoritative statements can be understood as being authoritative independently of their being obligatory. One wonders what kind of thing would instantiate the property "being authoritative" over and above the property "being obligatory".

or categorical prohibitions must be viewed as internal to proportionality control. Whether categorical constraints can be coherently combined with balancing within the structure of proportionality control is a question that merits deeper reflection. That aside, with his recent move Kumm comes closer to an understanding of law's normativity that is akin to the model of reasons (see section 2.2 of this chapter).

III. THE PLACE OF AUTONOMY

One may wonder why, despite having demonstrated the necessary relevance of autonomy with respect to authoritative directives, a mixed picture of legal normativity should continue to survive. Why, in other words, should it be the case that legal norms are treated on some occasions as encompassing a wide-scoped, instrumental "ought" and on others a narrow-scoped "ought" that is responsive to categorical reasons. It is precisely the coexistence of these two conflicting conceptions of normativity that compels one to resort to a moral filter in the practice of proportionality. Yet, no sooner a filter conception enters the picture than the paradox of authority emerges: authoritative directives are constructed as having authority independently of their power to obligate. How is it possible to claim authority independently of the power to obligate, given that any institutional utterance or, more generally, institutional fact already constitutes a token of coercion that calls for justification?

Autonomy qua Negative Freedom

I wish to suggest that the reason for the "split" notion of authority, which we encountered earlier, is the standard picture of autonomy that lawyers associate with the law. This standard picture, which is shared by most liberal thinkers, is that of autonomy as negative freedom. I shall discuss the pitfalls of the standard picture by focusing on the influential contemporary view that understands constitutional rights as reason-blocking norms.[56] On this view, rights render a class of reasons (that is, reasons referring to hostile external preferences about a person's way of life) impermissible as grounds for government intervention. Any public authority acting on such impermissible reasons will be deprived of a valid justificatory basis for its actions and, instead, engage in illegitimate coercion.[57] This is a powerfully articulated view, which, however, begins to appear less appealing once one takes a closer view.

---

[56] See Ronald Dworkin who, in *Taking Rights Seriously* (1978), famously labeled his version of the view I am discussing as "Rights as Trumps"; for more recent instantiations and/or discussions of the same ideas, see George Letsas, *A Theory of Interpretation*, *supra* note 44, chapters 1, 5, and 6; and "Two Concepts of the Margin of Appreciation," *supra* note 44; Kai Möller, "Balancing and Structure of Constitutional Rights," *supra* note 44, and "Two Concepts of Positive Liberty," *supra* note 44.

[57] Although initially Dworkin attempted to ground his theory on egalitarian considerations, he eventually conceded – in the light of a critique by H.L.A. Hart – that it is a concern for autonomy that is actually blocking hostile external preferences. See George Letsas, "Two Concepts of the Margin of Appreciation," *supra* note 44.

The standard picture assumes that the function of autonomy is to create a sphere that is free of intervention with respect to very important interests of individuals. All else that remains outside this sphere is not a question of freedom but of unprincipled politics. It follows that legal precepts amounting from the activity of politics are obligatory merely as hypothetical imperatives: that is, to the extent that they can successfully pursue those interests that have prevailed in the political arena. There is nothing principled or categorical at this level of legal obligation. By contrast, (constitutional) rights embody deontological or non-conditional reasons that protect very important interests of individuals and block any authoritative act that purports to infringe on them. Such constraints are called on rigorously whenever politics has the nerve to enter the realm of autonomy.

The key problem arises with the dichotomy that the standard picture allows to open up between the realm of political authority and the sphere of legitimate action-directing action.[58] It is as if political authority as human activity did not possess any inherent normative value, other than satisfying the moral test set by rights as trumps. However, this is extremely impoverishing: it would mean that there existed nothing in the dimension of our public coexistence that can be the source of distinct, self-standing obligations; instead, all obligations must be grounded on the limits that are (reciprocally) set by our private selves. In this rather depressing picture of public life, authoritative public acts of government remain normatively unorientated until they meet with the approval of individual normative positions. What is worse, we are led to the paradox that calls on proportionality to function as a moral filter: even though all legal obligation is grounded in autonomy, there is nothing in the public character of an authoritative act that can contribute to its being obligatory. Obligation, in other words, is a quality posterior to authority and can only be earned where there is a match with the demands of negative freedom. We are witnessing here a complete disengagement of authority from obligation.

To the extent to which this is an accurate depiction of the standard picture of autonomy, it should not come as a surprise that the survival of autonomy depends on this impoverished picture of political authority that it has set up. The reason is that autonomy as negative freedom cannot enable on its own any publicly authorized action, which makes it dependent on politics as a means for realizing joint projects. The reverse is also the case, as already submitted: the impoverished conception of public authority requires the standard picture of autonomy with an eye to avoiding serious moral blunders.

---

[58] For the content of action-directing action, see section 2.2 of this chapter, especially notes 48, 49, and 50.

But why should one accept the dualism that is forced on us by the choice between a picture of legal authority along the lines of the model of authority,[59] and a picture that corresponds to the standard picture of autonomy? Is the dilemma of choosing between authority without obligation and obligation without authority a real or a false one? With an eye to rejecting the dilemma as false, I shall turn next to discuss a different way for conceptualizing legal obligation, one that aims to bring out the internal normative connection between individual autonomy and public authority in order to offer a more coherent view of the normativity of law, which avoids the paradox we began with.

Autonomy qua Public Authorization: An Argument along Kantian Lines

I want to propose that autonomy encompasses the entire domain of authoritative practices and institutions, and not only the domain of private normative positions. Taking my cue from a broadly Kantian account of autonomy, I shall argue that owing to its character as negative constraint, autonomy requires *conceptually* that it be "fleshed out" or "realized" through public acts of authority.[60] Here is the argument in a nutshell:

> P1: Autonomy as a negative constraint says that one ought not to substitute one's ends for the ends of another. Were this to occur, the latter person would be employed as a means to the first person's ends; that is, the second person would be (illegitimately) coerced.
> P2: Any act of unilateral interference with the agency of another constitutes coercion in the aforementioned sense.
> C1: No unilateral act can obligate.
> C2: Only acts that are publicly authorized amount to genuine obligation; that is, can change the normative situation of persons.

Kant's writings on legal and political philosophy offer a rich understanding of legal obligation that helps overcome the undesirable dualism between political authority and individual autonomy. The question that sets the agenda of the analysis is: "In virtue of what is interference with anyone's capacity for choice covered by genuine obligation?" Famously, for Kant, the capacity of each individual to set their own ends, free from interference by any extraneous factor, lies in the core of his understanding of moral autonomy. In asking

---

[59] See section 2.3 of this chapter.
[60] My analysis borrows heavily from Ripstein, *Force and Freedom*, *supra* note 53.

this question in the context of a political community, Kant is looking into conditions of legitimacy for obligations that hold between persons, as opposed to those obligations that agents set for themselves.

This account of autonomy focuses on the concept of interference, which it renders crucial for identifying under what conditions an act originating in another may amount to a valid obligation from the point of view of the agent. Here, interference is the property that divides all acts that originate outside the agent into those that ground obligation and those that constitute wrongdoing. Up to this point, the structure – if not the content – of interference can be fully determined from within the resources of the agent's rational capacities: anything that has not been authorized by the agent's own reflective endorsement would count as interference.[61] However, and this is the rub, a complete account of interference in Kant's legal philosophy requires the inclusion of a further dimension, a collective dimension as it were, which extends beyond the confines of the agent's reflective endorsement. It is the aspect of omnilateral authorization, which is exclusively rooted in the public institutions of a legal system (the rightful condition).[62] True enough, the structure of interference can be determined through the elements of autonomous agency that render it ill-suited for obligation in the first place. Yet a fully fledged account of interference and the requirements for legitimate obligation that originates in others' actions calls for some institutional arrangements that ensure omnilateral authorization; otherwise, any interference that remains unilateral would constitute coercion. Let me try to shed some light on the need and added value of omnilateral authorization and the institutional edifice that grounds it.

Agents, in being rational legislators of their own reasons for acting, are, as a consequence, exposed to coercion by others whenever they act together with them (which, naturally, is de facto unavoidable).[63] Thus, the puzzle arising is how to explain the fact that often the deeds and words of others give rise to genuine obligations (call these relational obligations) as opposed to being acts of coercion, even though they originate in someone other than the agent herself. Given that law is the paradigmatic source of such obligations, the puzzle hits

---

[61] For this interpretation, see C. Korsgaard, *Sources, supra* note 4 at 90–130.

[62] Ripstein, *Force and Freedom, supra* note 53, at 190ff. As one would assume, such institutions cannot take any possible form but need to be in conformity with the outer limits set by individual autonomy; no omnilateral authorization could validate obligations that would have been rejected by the reflective authority of the agent (*Force and Freedom*, ibid. at 202).

[63] For the unavoidable character of interaction between agents as a result of the spacio-temporal limitations of the environment, see ibid.

directly at the heart of legal obligation, its nature and possibility. Arthur Ripstein argues, with Kant, that what grounds legal obligation is a set of publicly authorized legal institutions (rightful condition), which render the exercise of the capacity for freedom of each agent compossible against the background of positive laws that enjoy omnilateral authorization: "Rather than trying to reduce the public to the private, Kant's argument shows that the private is rightful only in the context of the public."[64] It would seem then that legal institutions are constitutive, in some sense of the word, of legal obligations. Moreover, this line of reasoning would offer the most complete explanation of Kant's claim that the possibility of coercive enforcement exhausts the content of legal obligation (whereas moral obligation requires in addition that one make the duty the content of one's own motivation).

Thus, the answer to the question "what obligates" has two prongs: for one part, what determines whether something constitutes interference with someone's ability to set one's own ends is derived from Kant's account of the Moral Law. However, on the other hand, what renders such interference legitimate seems to hinge on the institutional structure of the law. We need, Ripstein argues, public institutions of law such that are omnilaterally authorized in order to render interferences with autonomy legitimate.[65] In Ripstein's own words:

Legal institutions can generate novel obligations, and necessarily have moral powers that no private person could have, including the power to resolve disputes, enforce acquired rights, tax, and punish. Those distinctive moral powers reflect the fact that the concept of a legal institution is already morally infused . . . Officials acting within institutional roles are subject to moral obligations that follow from the nature of the institutions in which they act, but those obligations reflect the moral nature of the institutions, the fact that they are the precondition of the coexistence of free human beings.[66]

And elsewhere:

Kant proposes: rights are merely provisional in a state of nature. Procedures are required in order to make those rights conclusive and binding by making them omnilateral rather than merely unilateral. The rights do not themselves make procedures valid; the rights make procedures necessary. The procedures make the rights valid, but only because procedures are the only solution

---

[64] Ibid., 156. See more generally, ibid., chapter 2.
[65] Ibid., ch. 7.
[66] Arthur Ripstein, "Reply to Flikschuh and Pavlakos," (2010) 1 *Jurisprudence* 317 at 322.

to a moral problem. . . . Kant argues that there is a duty to 'exit' a state of
nature and enter into a rightful condition, so that everyone can enjoy their
rights.[67]

That said, an important qualification on the need for institutions of omnilateral
authorization needs to be introduced. The account of individual autonomy can
by itself ground an obligation on everyone not to interfere with my body. This
obligation corresponds to what Kant labels innate right and which is grounded
irrespective of institutional arrangements or the existence of other agents.[68]
However, everything else I do (from appropriating objects for my purposes, to
putting others at my service through contract, or exercising relations of status)
can only obligate others "to play along" if there is a legal system in place.[69]
Finally, all those laws that structure the public space with a view to realizing
autonomy (e.g., traffic laws, or the power to tax, and the obligation to provide
public education) also require public institutions in order to be generated.
With respect to all obligations that do not correspond to innate right, public
institutions are not mere enablers, but exert a constitutive function:

> It's not that there is an obligation, which then needs to be instantiated; instead,
> there are obligations between human beings, which require that they enter
> a rightful condition together which has authority that they as individuals
> lack; the setting of the speed limit instantiates the obligation on the part of
> a rightful condition to give laws omnilaterally. The same is true of all the
> other requirements of public right; they constitute a system of equal external
> freedom, but they matter because freedom does.[70]

It would seem then that the Kantian account of legal obligation offers a way out
of the paradox of proportionality, by way of replacing a "shallow" conception
of autonomy as negative freedom with one that authorizes public institutions
to fill in the space opened up by autonomy. Here, legal obligation is not
grounded ex post facto via a moral test, but already resides in the public
character of authority, whose normative relevance is in turn grounded in
individual autonomy as freedom from interference under conditions of acting
in concert with others.

---

[67] Ibid. at 322.
[68] Ripstein, *Force and Freedom, supra* note 53, ch. 2.
[69] Ibid., chs. 3–5. Interestingly, Kant views the grounding of property rights, albeit not their
enforcement, as independent of institutions: "the form of interaction in which property rights
constrain the conduct of others does not depend on positive law," ibid. at 87.
[70] Ripstein, "Reply to Flikschuh and Pavlakos," *supra* note 66 at 13.

The Role of Proportionality Reconsidered

Of course, there remains a lot of detail to be added before the Kantian conception of legal obligation can be made workable in the context of the theory and practice of constitutional rights. Having said that, the account just sketched suffices as a basis for drawing a number of important conclusions with respect to the theory and practice of proportionality.

To begin with, the function of proportionality as a moral filter is to be abandoned. There is no need to reconcile instrumental or strategic normativity with the normativity of categorical reasons, precisely because law's normativity is grounded in a notion of individual autonomy that requires, normatively speaking, legislation via public institutions. Consequently, the kind of discontinuity between authority and obligation, which is characteristic of some portions of liberal political philosophy, need not arise in the Kantian account. Rights, which arguably carry the normative force of law, do not stand in opposition to other legal precepts, because both they and the latter derive their normative content from the same grounds; that is, the space of reasons that pertain to the autonomy of individuals, which in turn demands that it be realized by publicly authorized norms.

Notably, this understanding of autonomy implies that whatever does not pertain to a person as a matter of innate right is not as yet "crystallized" as part of the content of a persons' autonomy. Rather, it can become part of the content of autonomy only if it is regulated or "instituted" by a publicly authorized act of legislation. To give a somewhat simplistic example: traffic regulations cannot be regarded as infringing on an unrestricted freedom of movement against which they would need to be balanced appropriately. It is rather the case that prior to their being instituted no particular freedom exists, but merely a very abstract freedom that persons move freely. Even though the domain of traffic is somewhat trivial, the same conclusion can be expanded to apply to any other area that lies beyond the scope of innate right.[71]

So how should the role of proportionality be understood? Here a distinction between innate right and the remaining space of legal obligations can meaningfully be drawn. With respect to innate right, when different aspects of it collide, then what proportionality can do is offer a coherent interpretation with a view to securing the harmonious coexistence of any aspects that are in tension with one another:

> If freedom of expression appears to come into conflict with the fundamental entitlements of equal citizenship – as is sometimes argued in the context of

---

[71] For a contrary view, see the contribution of Kai Möller in Chapter 7 in this volume.

hate speech – any restriction of the former must be justified as an expression
of the underlying and more basic innate right of humanity that gives rise to
both . . . reconciling different aspects of innate right does not weigh one thing
against the other, but rather adjusts each so as to work the various aspects of
innate right into a coherent doctrinal whole.[72]

With respect to ordinary legal precepts, proportionality has a double function:
on the one hand, it ensures that no legal precept institutes anything that would
run against innate right. Even though this requirement may sound too close
to the logic of a moral filter, it is not, for it has a radically different direction
of fit than the former; it is not the case that the requirements of innate right
are imposed externally on the ends pursued by ordinary legal precepts. Rather,
legal precepts are responsive to the limits of innate right because the latter is
the justificatory basis for public legislation. On the other hand, proportionality
control gains a much less pronounced function when it comes to controlling
legal statutes that flesh out the space of autonomy, in tandem with innate right.
In this case, proportionality control is about ensuring that legal precepts realize
their role as particular instantiations of individual autonomy in conditions of
acting in concert with others. It would follow that authoritative precepts and
individual autonomy do not stand in opposition, but complement one another
mutually.

However, the two aspects just mentioned do not demarcate distinct conceptual (or, for that part, temporal) sequences: publicly authorized legislation
exists with an eye to realizing autonomy, on the condition that it does not
infringe on innate right. This existence condition of legal norms is complex
and cannot be put into a succinct canonical proposition, but instead needs
to be elaborated through detailed normative argument that may shift when
factual conditions change. Proportionality, in this context, undertakes the task
of articulating those arguments. While doing so, it might appear as engaging
in acts of balancing between competing interests. One should not let appear-
ances deceive, however, for the picture of competing interests that are equally
endowed with normative force does not hold good in the Kantian conception
of legal obligation: no (private) interests may enjoy normative force over and
above the legal norms that flesh out the space of persons' autonomy, in accordance with innate right.[73] It would follow that there is no (normative) need to

---

[72] Ripstein, *Force and Freedom, supra* note 53 at 214.
[73] To make the same point differently: for Kant, even though any activity we engage in raises a
question of freedom, there is no right or entitlement vis-à-vis others until there is a rule of law
to enable or activate it. This is so because any one claim directed at others that is not backed
by omnilateral authorization (that is, a rule of law) would constitute illegitimate coercion on
those others. See section 2.3 of this chapter.

balance such private interests, but only a need to ascertain which legal obligations can be born equally by the addressees of the law, without infringing on their innate right.

All in all, proportionality, on the Kantian conception of legal obligation, tends to produce a coherentist account of the different aspects and various enablers of one and the same realm of autonomy, rather than reconciling competing individual interests or acting as a moral filter between antithetical normative sizes.

PART II

PROPORTIONALITY
AND RIGHTS

6 On the Loss of Rights

Grégoire Webber*

I. INTRODUCTION

Two questions can now be asked that in times past would not have been asked: Do rights matter? Can one reason about rights otherwise than by appealing to the proportionality of means to ends and balancing all relevant considerations? The difference between past and present is marked not only by the sudden relevance of these questions, but also by the answers that many will give: to the first, a qualified no; to the second, a near unqualified no.[1] What may be called the received approach to human rights law[2] – or, more or less synonymously, the "global model of constitutional rights",[3] the "'best-practice standard' of global constitutional law",[4] the "conventional view",[5] the "near-universal" or "very widely adopted"[6] judicial practice – reduces rights to defeasible interests, values, or principles and evaluates the justification for interferences with rights

---

* For comments on a draft of this essay, I thank my fellow editors, Grant Huscroft and Bradley W. Miller, David Dyzenhaus, Stephen Gardbaum, Mattias Kumm, Kai Möller, Luc Tremblay, Samuel Tschorne, Francisco Urbina, and Paul Yowell.
1   These questions and answers relate to human rights law interpreting and applying human rights documents of international, constitutional, and legislative rank. As will be seen below, legal rights (in contract, tort, property, and so forth) are not so afflicted.
2   This is the expression employed in Grégoire Webber, *The Negotiable Constitution: On the Limitation of Rights* (2009).
3   See Kai Möller, *The Global Model of Constitutional Rights* (2012). See also Alec Stone Sweet and Jud Mathews, "Proportionality Balancing and Global Constitutionalism" 47 *Columbia J. Trans. Law* 72 at 74 (2008) (a "defining feature[] of global constitutionalism"), 79 (a "global constitutional standard"), 76 (a "taken-for-granted feature of constitutionalism").
4   Jud Mathews and Alec Stone Sweet, "All Things in Proportion? American Rights Review and the Problem of Balancing" 60 *Emory L.J.* 797 at 808 (2011).
5   Aharon Barak, "Proportionality (2)" in Michael Rosenfeld and András Sajo (eds.), *Oxford Handbook on Comparative Constitutional Law* (2012) 740.
6   Stephen Gardbaum, "Proportionality and Democratic Constitutionalism," Chapter 12 of this volume, 260, 267.

so defined against the principle of proportionality and its insistence that one "balance".

The defenders of this approach (model, view, practice) dissent from moral-political understandings that award rights special status and from the range of other modes of reasoning employed in philosophical, legal, and everyday argument. In so doing, their strongest argument lies in tracking the judicial practice of human rights law. That practice is not unanimous in all respects and there is reason to doubt the claims that there is but one global model.[7] Nonetheless, descriptions of a "received", "near-universal", and "taken-for-granted" approach to human rights law are not misplaced. Allowing for the reconstruction of varying judicial practices within and ranging from Canada, the United States,[8] Israel, South Africa, and the many countries within the jurisdiction of the European Court of Human Rights, that approach may be said to encompass the following: (a) evaluating whether legislation (or other government action) violates a right proceeds by way of a two-stage inquiry: the first stage evaluates whether a right has been infringed, the second whether the infringement can be justified; (b) the distinction between the two stages draws on the understanding that the limitation of a right is synonymous with its infringement, which may or may not be justified – if justified, the infringement stands; if unjustified, the infringement constitutes a violation; (c) by divorcing the question of the scope and content of the right from the question of what the right conclusively requires, the received approach favors a generous reading of rights, with the consequence that rights encompass many activities that are regularly and justifiably infringed by legislation; (d) the justification analysis at the second stage proceeds by way of a proportionality evaluation, with its all-important balancing stage; and (e) it is only at this stage that the right and the right-holder are socially situated and that "all the relevant circumstances" may be taken into account; at the first stage, the rights of others and the other requirements of a free and democratic society are not controlling – indeed, their consideration is discouraged.

There are many other features of judicial practices under the received approach and the scholarly interpretation and defense of those practices, some

---

[7] Among those reasons: careful comparative analysis suggests that notwithstanding its superficial commonality, "the language of balancing might well mean very different things at different times and in different places": Jacco Bomhoff, "Genealogies of Balancing as Discourse" (2010) 4 *Law & Ethics of Human Rights* 107 at 113 (emphasis in original removed).

[8] On the United States and the received approach, see Iddo Porat, "Mapping the American Debate over Balancing," Chapter 17 in this volume; Stephen Gardbaum, "The Myth and the Reality of American Constitutional Exceptionalism" 107 *Mich. L. Rev.* 391 (2008); Mathews and Stone Sweet, "All Things in Proportion?" *supra* note 4.

of which will be reviewed below. At present, it is sufficient to note that these five features are endorsed by those who share a basic commitment to the negative answers to the two questions posed above: rights more or less do not matter and proportionality analysis is, quite simply, unavoidable. For Robert Alexy, rights are not "definitive" requirements but only "optimisation" requirements and balancing is "unavoidable, since there is no other rational way in which the reason for the limitation can be put in relation to the constitutional right";[9] for David Beatty, rights hold "no special status" and "[i]t is all and only about proportionality";[10] for Aharon Barak, rights "cannot be realized to [their] fullest extent" and a "limitation on a constitutional right by law ... will be constitutionally permissible if, and only if, it is proportional";[11] for Mattias Kumm, "comparatively little is decided by acknowledging that a measure infringes a right" and, he asks rhetorically, "what could justify protecting an interest beyond what proportionality requires?";[12] and for Kai Möller, rights have neither "special importance" nor "special normative force" and "proportionality analysis must be employed at the justification stage in order to assess whether a policy pays adequate respect to the right-holder's autonomy interest".[13]

This chapter defends a simple proposition: rights matter. It is a troubling reflection of the current state of juridical thought that it is in relation to human rights law that the proposition is defended. I argue that rights are conceptually interrelated to justice and, in this frame, argue that rights acknowledge the foundational equality of persons by delimiting what is due to each member of a political community. After introducing the relationship of objective right to subjective right (section II), the chapter reviews how human rights law-in-action reduces rights to defeasible interests and fails to capture the moral priority of rights (section III). Notwithstanding this approach to rights, the practice and discourse of human rights law-in-action at times appeals to the priority of rights, leading to a confusion of thought and discourse by many defenders of

---

[9] Robert Alexy, *A Theory of Constitutional Rights* (2002) at 48–49, 57, 74.
[10] David Beatty, *The Ultimate Rule of Law* (2004) at 171, 170.
[11] Aharon Barak, *Proportionality: Constitutional Rights and Their Limitations* (2012) at 40 (the point is made with respect to freedom of expression, but can be generalized), 3.
[12] Mattias Kumm, "Institutionalising Socratic Contestation: The Rationalist Human Rights Paradigm, Legitimate Authority and the Point of Judicial Review," (2007) 1 *E.J.L.S.* 1 at 11; and Mattias Kumm, "Political Liberalism and the Structure of Rights: On the Place and Limits of the Proportionality Requirement" in George Pavlakos (ed.), *Law, Rights, and Discourse: The Legal Philosophy of Robert Alexy* (2007) 151. A similar rhetorical question is put by Matthias Klatt and Moritz Meister, "Proportionality – a benefit for human rights?" 10 *Int'l. J. Con. L.* 687 at 701 (2012): "How, after all, could one arrive at a specific narrow definition without using balancing for delineating the scope of the right?"
[13] Kai Möller, "Proportionality and Rights Inflation," Chapter 7 in this volume, 156, 172.

the received approach (section IV). A conceptual re-ordering of human rights law is proposed so as to reclaim rights from the position of inconsequence to which they have been relegated, with the most important re-ordering being a reaffirmation of the need for law to realize rights in community (sections V and VI).

II. RIGHTS AND *IUS*, JUSTICE AND JUSTIFICATION

The conception of rights contemplated by the received approach is not in keeping with moral-political understandings that, albeit with many discordant voices, affirm the conclusive, peremptory, and decisive quality of rights. This much is readily acknowledged by defenders of the received approach, who recognize the "sharp contrast to the conceptions of rights proposed by most if not all moral and political philosophers"[14] and how the "special priority of rights sits uneasily with a prominent feature of constitutional and human rights adjudication"[15] – namely, that under the received approach, rights are awarded no special priority.

To understand how much is lost with the conception of rights promoted by the received approach, let us begin with the understanding of rights that is lost. To this end, one need not appeal to Ronald Dworkin's theory of rights as trumps,[16] Robert Nozick's theory of rights as side-constraints,[17] or other competing and compelling understandings of rights, all of which share a commitment to the special status of rights. My present aim is to recall how the concept of right has special significance, a significance that these and other understandings of rights explore but that the received approach abandons. By tracing the history of our language's appeal to the term "right(s)", I aim to suggest that there lies a deep conceptual (not merely etymological) relationship between rights and another concept, one with an undeniable claim to conclusiveness and peremptory status: justice.

The English word "right" translates the Latin *ius* (*jus*), being the root of the words "justice" and "justification", as well as "jurist", "juridical", and "jurisprudence". In exploring the relationship of "right" to "justice", we could

[14] Möller, *Global Model, supra* note 3 at 1.
[15] Kumm, "Political Liberalism," *supra* note 12 at 131. For an attempt to overcome this bifurcation, see Mattias Kumm and Alec Walen, "Human Dignity and Proportionality: Deontic Pluralism in Balancing," Chapter 4 in this volume.
[16] For a summary account, see Ronald Dworkin, "Rights as Trumps" in Jeremy Waldron (ed.), *Theories of Rights* (1984). On close inspection, "trump" for Dworkin means either (a) to award rights special weighting, with a consequential recourse to balancing or (b) to exclude certain reasons. A careful analysis of Dworkin on rights is provided in Paul Yowell, "A Critical Examination of Dworkin's Theory of Rights," 52 *Am. J. Juris.* 93 (2007).
[17] See Robert Nozick, *Anarchy, State and Utopia* (1974) chapter 3.

follow H.L.A. Hart in tracing "right" back to Plato and Aristotle, not in the sense of "a right", but rather in the sense of "the 'right action' or 'the right thing to do'".[18] Hart's invitation to focus on "acting" and "doing" is welcome and is captured, albeit less transparently, in the comparatively more recent uses to which "right" (*ius*) was put by Aquinas and other contemporaries.[19] In this frame, the historically primary meaning of *ius* was understood as "the just thing itself", where "thing" signals acts, objects, and states of affairs, all "subject-matters of relationships of justice".[20] In this usage, *ius* looks to states of affairs and evaluates them as just, in the right. One may term this the "objective" sense of *ius*, meaning that the acts and arrangements, with all of their contemplated and actualized interpersonal actions, forbearances, omissions, and relationships, are "themselves" right, as signalled by our modern language's expressions: "this is the right decision", "it is right that this be done".

The Latin word *ius* developed a second, now prevailing meaning: in alleged contrast to the "objective" sense, a second "subjective" sense refers to a right that someone (the subject) has. Here, *ius* is possessed by a person rather than attributed to a state of affairs (an object), as captured by our modern language's frequent recourse to the formulation: "Everyone has the right to . . . ". Notwithstanding the different grammatical and syntactic uses to which this second meaning can be put, one would be mistaken to assume any sharp conceptual break between the primary and second meanings. A "subjective" right does not take the right-holder outside of the domain of what is "objectively" right; instead, it situates evaluations of justice explicitly "in the hands" of a person and provides a perspective (that of the right-holder) for evaluating states of affairs. It relates the primary meaning "exclusively to the beneficiary of the just relationship",[21] the person whose right the relationship respects. It translates the impersonal ("objective") third-person perspective of justice into the first-person ("subjective") point of view and provides a complimentary and ultimately synonymous way of speaking about giving to each his due. In so doing, the second meaning of *ius* captures how providing "persons with that which they are justly owed" can be equivalently stated as "respecting the rights of persons".[22]

---

[18] H.L.A. Hart, "Legal Rights" in *Essays on Bentham* (1982) at 163.

[19] This account draws on John Finnis, *Natural Law and Natural Rights* (2nd ed., 2011) at 206–210, 423–424, 465–466; John Finnis, *Aquinas: Moral, Political, and Legal Theory* (1998) at 132–138; John Finnis, "Aquinas on *ius* and Hart on Rights" (2002) 64 *Review of Politics* at 407

[20] Finnis, *Natural Law and Natural Rights*, ibid. at 206.

[21] Ibid. at 207 (emphasis omitted).

[22] Bradley W. Miller, "Justification and Rights Limitations" in Grant Huscroft (ed.), *Expounding the Constitution* (2008) at 115.

The academic career of *ius* allows the substitution of claims of right for claims of justice and vice-versa: what one formulation affirms from the "subjective" point of view, the other affirms from the "objective" point of view. Rights, like justice, are relational: they concern the domain of the interpersonal. In affirming that one has a right, one affirms one's right relationship with another; synonymously, one affirms that this relationship is a requirement of justice. On this understanding, I may not affirm my right *before* having considered the rights and freedoms of others, for all of these others are members of my community and justice requires that they, like me, be given what is their due (that is: their rights). The appeals to the indivisibility and interdependence of human rights common to international human rights instruments and institutions capture, even if with some exaggeration, the view that one's rights cannot be in conflict with another's or with the other requirements of justice in a free and democratic society. Stated otherwise: justice does not demand and deny the same action.

By appealing to the conceptual relationship between rights and justice, my intention is not to favor one or another of the moral-political philosophies awarding rights special status. Rather, the highlighted conceptual interdefinability seeks to bring that special status to light, a status that affirms the conclusiveness of rights in evaluating what is to be done. In his insightful account of moral rights, John Oberdiek is, I think, similarly motivated when he appeals not to "justice" but to "justification",[23] a word (and idea) also indebted to the Latin *ius*. On Oberdiek's account, rights relate to one's (or another's) justified acts and deeds, such that one cannot be said to be acting contrary to rights when one acts justifiably. What is permitted by one's rights is what is justified: justified conduct delimits the content of rights, such that the scope and significance of rights are in unison. Now, much will turn on one's view of what is justified conduct, just as much will turn on one's understanding of what justice requires, but in both accounts rights matter precisely

---

[23] Unfortunately, Oberdiek repeatedly suggests that the justifiability of acts and deeds animating his account of rights is limited to "necessity", a term which frames "justification" as responding to something akin to an "emergency". Consider, in addition to the title of the essay "Specifying Rights Out of Necessity," (2008) 28 O.J.L.S. 127, the following passages: ibid. at 136 ("it is necessity that triggers the qualification . . . and circumstances of necessity are quite rare"); ibid. at 146 "([c]ases of necessity, in particular, highlight the way in which justifiable behaviour specifies property rights"); and John Oberdiek, "Lost in Moral Space: On the Infringing/Violating Distinction and its Place in the Theory of Rights" (2004) 23 *Law and Philosophy* 325 at 329 ("one could maintain that the right is specified precisely so that it does not to stand in the way of 'necessary' conduct"). Notwithstanding these passages, I understand Oberdiek's argument as promoting an understanding of "justification" in a more encompassing way than "necessity".

because they are the product of reasoning about what justice or justification requires. Along similar lines, one could appeal generally to "conclusions of practical reasoning" to capture this emphasis on the practical point of rights: to be determinative of what it is right (just, justified) to do.[24] In what follows, I appeal interchangeably to justice and justification to capture this conclusive quality about rights, a quality that signals the peremptory and decisive status of rights as providing undefeated reasons for action.

But what of appeals to rights that are at some distance from justified and just conduct, appeals that take rights (as does the received approach) as premises in argument about what is justified and just? Is this not how bills of rights employ the idea of rights? Yes and no. Bills of rights appeal to subject matters of relationships of justice – life, liberty, security, expression, association, peaceful assembly, and so forth – which persons ("Everyone", "Every citizen", "Every accused person") are identified as having a *right to*. Yet, this mode of appeal to "subjective" rights is liable to omit from view the "objective" relationships between persons necessary to realize one's own and everyone's rights. Under the generality of *one* subject matter of justice (life, liberty, equality, expression, association) that "everyone" is declared to have a "right to" lies a *multiplicity* of possible acts and arrangements that, if just, will respect, protect, and comply with everyone's rights. The journey from the open-ended appeal to "life", "liberty", and so forth to the specific relationships between persons that realize a just state of affairs is, needless to say, complex. It is a journey guided by the understanding that to neglect or to fail to realize these subject matters of justice in our community truly is *unjust* and *unjustified*, and that justice requires that one determine the claim-rights, duties, liberties, powers, and so forth of each and every member of the community in a manner that is in harmony with every other member's. Relationships between persons must be arranged so that I can respect and comply with your rights as you respect and comply with mine. Such harmony is a requirement of reason in community.

In reasoning toward the states of affairs and sets of interpersonal actions, forbearances, and omissions, one merely begs the question by affirming as conclusive that one has a *right to* life, liberty, and so forth, for the practical question is what, specifically, is to be established and brought into being in order to realize one's rights. Awareness of the equivocation in the use of the term "right" in the catch-phrase "Everyone has a right to . . . " is necessary to resist the hazards of overreach in formulating claims of rights. This equivocal use of the term "right" has guiding force only insofar as it identifies the end

---

[24] That is the approach adopted in Webber, *The Negotiable Constitution*, *supra* note 2, chapter 4 ("Constituting Rights by Limitation").

(life, liberty, and so forth) that is to be secured, an end that can only be secured by "a process of rational decision-making which cannot reasonably be concluded simply by appealing to any one of these rights (notwithstanding that all are 'fundamental' and 'inalienable' and part of 'everyone's' *entitlement*)".[25] That process of rational decision-making is a process of practical reasoning that requires one to situate the would-be right-holder in a community of other actual and potential right-holders. As we will see in section VI, the lawmakers responsible for a community bear a special responsibility to settle, justly and authoritatively, the right relationships between persons that establish rights in law.

The willingness to reformulate one's ("subjective") claims of rights into ("objective") claims of justice can serve as a ready corrective to overreach. For justice, unlike the now common currency of rights, sits less easily as a premise in evaluating what to do: it directs one to what, conclusively, is to be done. So, when the question is: "Should racist propaganda be permitted in our community?", the answer cannot be: "Yes *because* I have right to free expression." For the question is equivalent to asking: "What are the requirements of justice in relation to racist propaganda in our community?", and one cannot, true to reason, claim as premise what is a conclusion. The conclusion to practical reasoning about the place of this "speech" in our community will be that one is either at liberty to engage in racist propaganda *or* has a duty not to, a conclusion evaluated in contemplation of the potential victims of racist propaganda and their correlative no-right against another's racist propaganda *or* correlative claim-right not to be subject to such expression.[26] The conclusion may be more complex as we contemplate differences in civil and criminal duties and allow for criminal liberties in combination with civil duties. Nevertheless, the central idea is straightforward: many claims of right must be subject to a process of specification so as to warrant the peremptory and conclusionary status that is the true normative force of rights. In this way, whilst open-ended claims of right may play a "helpful heuristic role in normative argument", it must be recalled that they are a "kind of normative shortcut" to what is one's true

---

[25] Finnis, *Natural Law and Natural Rights*, *supra* note 19 at 212 (footnote omitted, emphasis in original).

[26] I accept that the correlatives here are not as straightforward as the paradigmatic examples in Hohfeld's scheme. I appeal to the idea of correlatives to signal how one's conclusion on the question of hate propaganda establishes a relationship between persons, even if it is one that is not as immediate or direct as contemplated by Hohfeld. I here bracket the question of the directionality of duties and associated debates surrounding the "interest" and "will" theories of rights.

right:[27] the conclusion of practical reasoning about what ought to be done, what is justified, what is just and in the right.

The peremptory and decisive status of rights is warranted when and because rights are conclusions of practical reasoning about what ought to be done. Whilst it is possible to speak of rights as intermediary conclusions about those requirements (as with expressions like: "Everyone has a right to life"), those conclusions are not determinative; they do not warrant peremptory or conclusionary status.[28] To achieve that status, the intermediate conclusion must be carried through to a final conclusion. Here, genuine rights are "designated only after the *final* interaction of *all* of the reasons bearing upon the justifiability of a given action" and enter the stage "as conclusions about, and not as potential explanations of, the justifiability of certain actions".[29] On this understanding, in evaluating what justice requires in communities of persons, one cannot "start with rights" or reason "from rights"; in truth, one reasons – and, taking the focal meaning of rights, can only reason – "towards rights".[30]

As we will now turn to see, the question of rights under the received approach is burdened by the assumption that rights are much simpler than philosophers have long understood them to be. One's thinking enters muddied waters when one denies the relational character of rights, brackets questions of justice and justification, and equates rights with defeasible interests, values, or principles understood only from the perspective of the "right-holder". The hazards of this understanding of rights are not to be discounted as mere semantics. The hazards are philosophical and, rights being a part of practical philosophy, practical too: a conception of rights grounded in a theory of justice can be expected to provide for different duties and obligations than one grounded in a theory of defeasible interests.[31]

---

[27] John Oberdiek, "Specifying Constitutional Rights," 27 *Const. Comm.* 231 at 240 (2010).

[28] In *The Morality of Freedom* (1988), Joseph Raz explores the claims that "[a]ssertions of rights are typically intermediate conclusions in arguments from ultimate values to duties".

[29] Oberdiek, "Specifying Rights Out of Necessity," *supra* note 23 at 135 (emphasis in original). Miller echoes this point in concluding that "rights" at this preliminary stage "can only generate a tentative, intermediate conclusion that some *claim* of constitutional right is a candidate for qualification as a genuine right on further analysis": "Justification and Rights Limitations," *supra* note 22 at 95.

[30] Oberdiek, "Lost in Moral Space," *supra* note 23 at 340, 339; Oberdiek, "Specifying Rights Out of Necessity," *supra* note 23 at 141.

[31] In his reply to this chapter, Möller summarizes my argument as claiming that he and others engage in "semantic sloppiness" and misunderstand the concept of rights: "Proportionality and Rights Inflation", *supra* note 13, part V. The two are related: semantic sloppiness being the consequence of, not ground for, conceptual confusion. Consider, for example, Möller's paradigmatic duty correlative to rights: the duty of government to take everyone's autonomy

III. ON THE LOSS OF RIGHTS

The received approach to human rights law does not maintain the inter-definability of justice and rights. It does not situate rights as conclusions of what is justifiable according to practical reason. It does not award peremptory or conclusionary force to rights. It does not understand rights as relations between persons. Instead, rights are equated with interests (or values or principles, terms employed more or less interchangeably),[32] are divorced from the moral-political context in which they are claimed, are regularly infringed once situated in that moral-political context, and are reduced to defeasible premises in reasoning about proportionality. The consequence is straightforward: the received approach reifies rights and regularly divorces rights from *what is right*.

This animating conception of rights turns on a distinction between a right and its limitation, corresponding to the two stages of human rights law-in-action: at the first stage, the right is *defined* and its scope and content *determined*; at the second stage, any limitation on (equivalently: interference with, infringement of)[33] the right is evaluated as justified or not because the relation of interests and burdens is proportionate or not. By conceiving of rights as belonging exclusively to the "right-holder", the received approach omits from view the relationships between persons that are a defining mark of rights. The other whom, with the right-holder, constitutes the right relationship is either discounted or omitted, and so, too, is the essential inter-definability of one's rights and another's duty, to recall but one of Wesley Hohfeld's correlatives.[34] For the reason that evaluations of what is right ("in the right") look both ways along a relationship between persons, the interests of one person are insufficient in and of themselves to conclude that another has a duty to (or other Hohfeldian correlative with) that person. This willingness to hold others in view in thinking through one's rights is lost under the received approach: one person's interests are now the mark of rights.[35]

---

interests adequately taken into account. A concept of rights grounded in a theory of justice would not identify this as a paradigmatic claim-right.

[32] See e.g., Alexy, *Theory of Constitutional Rights*, *supra* note 9 at 86: "statements of the Federal Constitutional Court about values can be reformulated in terms of principles and vice versa without loss of meaning." For a critical review, see Mark Antaki "The Turn to 'Values' in Canadian Constitutional Law" in Luc Tremblay and Grégoire Webber (eds.), *The Limitation of Charter Rights: Critical Essays on R. v. Oakes* (2009).

[33] See e.g., Barak, *Proportionality*, *supra* note 11 at 101: "A limitation of a constitutional right by law also means its infringement".

[34] See W.N. Hohfeld, *Fundamental Legal Conceptions As Applied in Judicial Reasoning* (1919).

[35] It bears noting that even on Raz's influential interest theory of rights, "[i]f conflicting considerations show that the basis of the would-be right is not enough to justify subjecting anyone to

Why does the received approach assume rights to be far simpler than philosophical analysis has long assumed them to be? At one level, it would seem that the account of rights under the received approach is explicable by a somewhat exceptional understanding of the interpretation of legal text. A generous reading is given to the legal guarantee of a right so as to include within its scope and content all that fits within the semantic reach of the words "Everyone has a right to *x*", where *x* stands for life, liberty, free association, free expression, and so forth. Matthias Klatt and Moritz Meister tell us that a "broad definition" of rights "interprets the constitutional text without taking conflicting considerations into account";[36] Barak argues that the "scope of a constitutional right is determined in accord with the principles of constitutional interpretation" but that "[i]n determining scope, one should not take account of any opposing constitutional right or conflicting public interest";[37] Alexy advocates for a "broad and comprehensive" reading of rights;[38] Kumm maintains that the definition of "the scope of the interests to be protected" includes "all those interests that relate [for example] to 'freedom of expression' or 'the free development of the personality'"[39]; and Möller argues that "the scope of freedom protected by rights must extend to everything which is in the interest of a person's autonomy".[40]

This is an unconventional understanding of the art and technique of legal interpretation. In other contexts, one would reject as unreasonable readings of legal text that lead to the inevitable inconsistency of two or more directives of a single legal instrument or of that instrument's directives with the family of standing legal directives within the legal system. To do so would frustrate the rule of law's commitment to coherence (non-contradiction) and the related requirements that law not be impossible to comply with.[41] Yet, it seems not

---

any duty, then *the right does not exist*": *The Morality of Freedom, supra* note 28 at 183 (emphasis added).

[36] Matthias Klatt and Moritz Meister, *The Constitutional Structure of Proportionality* (2012) 47.

[37] Barak, "Proportionality (2)," *supra* note 5 at 740. See also Barak, *Proportionality, supra* note 11 at 71: "interpretation should reflect the spectrum of reasons underlying the right's creation."

[38] Robert Alexy, "Constitutional Rights, Balancing, and Rationality" (2003) 16 *Ratio Juris* 131 at 131–132.

[39] Kumm, "Institutionalising Socratic Contestation," *supra* note 12 at 7.

[40] Möller, *Global Model, supra* note 3 at 76. At 88, Möller argues in favour of simplifying the interpretive task, claiming that "[n]othing would be lost in theory by simply acknowledging one comprehensive prima facie right to personal autonomy". See also Möller, "Proportionality and Rights Inflation," *supra* note 12 at 163.

[41] In his contribution to this volume (Chapter 11), David Dyzenhaus focuses on the rule of law desideratum of "congruence", being the congruence between the administration of rules and the rules as announced: "Proportionality and Deference in a Culture of Justification". Missing from Dyzenhaus's analysis is concern for the other desiderata of the rule of law and an

to trouble those who insist on a generous reading of rights that it is inevitable
that rights so defined will conflict with each other and will stand opposed
to many settled instances of legal regulation. On this reading, rights are not,
without more, controlling; they are not promoted on the expectation that
one ought to comply with them. In short, the resulting *legal* interpretation
of *legal* rights takes them some distance from what is a defining mark of
the central case of *law*: that it outlines what is to be done, identifying some
action or omission as mandatory, non-optional. On the interpretation of rights
promoted by the received approach, not only do rights fail to provide one with
reasons for action, one may have conclusive reasons for acting *contrary* to the
right.

Now, without doubt the semantic reach of key terms like "liberty", "association", and "expression" should *inform* one's evaluation of the scope and
meaning of rights. But the assumption that everything within the semantic
reach of such key terms should be included within the scope and content of
rights is unsound. The key word "expression" might semantically extend to
"political criticism", "sports commentary", and "murder and rape",[42] but it
would be an elementary mistake to assume that the phrase "freedom of expression" extends to all such activities. As Meiklejohn would argue in relation to
the First Amendment, an individual may not rely on the freedom of speech
"to advocate some public policy . . . by interrupting a church service, or a classroom, or a sickroom, or a session of Congress or of the Supreme Court, or by
ringing a doorbell and demanding to be heard".[43] It simply does not follow
that all "expression" is the concern of "freedom of expression", just as it does
not follow that more "talk" signals a freer community. It is simply "unsound to
maximize every instance of a right as if one were maximizing a single value",[44]
as though each and every instance of regulation of "expression" wrongs or
upsets "freedom". But what is more, even if one were tempted to *inform* one's
understanding of rights by appealing to everything within the semantic reach
of key terms like "expression", why should one accept that this should *exhaust*

---

interrogation whether, under the received approach, there are any "rules" to be administered.
This question is examined in Grégoire Webber, "Rights and the Rule of Law in the Balance,"
(2013) 129 *L.Q.R.* 399.

[42] See *Irwin Toy v. Quebec*, [1989] 1 S.C.R. 927 at 970 where the Supreme Court of Canada,
after ruling that "the guarantee of free expression protects all content of expression", added: "a
murderer or rapist cannot invoke freedom of expression in justification of the form of expression
he has chosen".

[43] Alexander Meiklejohn, "The First Amendment is an Absolute" [1961] *S. Ct. Rev.* 245 at 261.
He adds: "The Amendment, I repeat, does not establish 'an unlimited right to talk' ".

[44] Francisco J. Urbina, "A Critique of Proportionality," 57 *Am. J. Juris.*, 49, 65, and more generally,
63–65 (2012).

one's understanding of rights? Why deny that other considerations are relevant to one's understanding of rights?

The answer: within the logic of the received approach, these considerations are for the second stage of analysis. They constitute the "external" limitation of a right, as opposed to what is sometimes termed the right's "internal" limitation as framed by legal interpretation (see section VI). At the second stage, all that has been omitted from the first is considered, including the rights and freedoms of others and the other requirements of a free and democratic society. However, and this bears emphasis: one engages with this second stage only if one concludes (or assumes *arguendo*, as courts sometimes do) that the right as defined at the first stage has been *infringed* (interfered with, "externally" limited), that the putative right-holder has been *wronged* in some way. A limitation is thus understood to frustrate a right, to render it "less than fully realized".[45] The limitation is "external" to the right and not, in any sense, constitutive of the right. Stated otherwise: the relationships between persons that are a defining mark of rights become, under the received approach, a restriction on rights, circumventing their scope and restricting their otherwise "limitless" reach.

Now, the conclusion that a right has been infringed is itself inconclusive; it does not create a presumption that the infringing act (or omission) should cease. Indeed, under the received approach, rights are regularly and, in many instances, continuously infringed. After all, the infringement of a right is not an exceptional conclusion; many infringements are not only justified, but anticipated because necessary – the inevitable conflicts between rights will, after all, have to be resolved, leaving one or the other right infringed. Recall how little informs the scope and content of a right: there is no concern to resolve potential conflicts between rights or between rights and the other requirements of a free and democratic society; there is no concern to situate the right-holder in a series of relationships; there is no concern to situate the right in community. *These* are the very considerations that are liable to infringe the very many interests equated with rights at the first stage. In some, perhaps many instances, the infringement of a right will be justified, with the consequence that, under the received approach, it is not uncommon to conclude that what rights require is not what justified action requires; that reasoning "within the right" provides one answer, whereas reasoning "within practical reasonableness" provides another. Not only is it the case that to

---

[45] Barak, "Proportionality (2)," *supra* note 5 at 739. See also Barak, "Proportionality and Principled Balancing," (2010) 4 *Law & Ethics of Human Rights* 1, 5: "the limitations imposed on [a right] by law that prevent its full realization".

comply with rights one may have to do more than act justly or justifiably, it is also the case that in complying with rights one may be acting *unjustly* or *unjustifiably*; stated otherwise, *not* to infringe a right may be unjust and without justification.

What picture of rights emerges from all this? At one level, the picture is remarkably simple: one has many rights, but no right is controlling *as a right*. In the words of proponents of the received approach, the "fact that a person has a right thus does not imply that he holds a position that gives him *any kind of priority* over competing considerations".[46] Animated by similar reflections, Beatty writes that the concept of rights is rendered "almost irrelevant" and is liable to "disappear" except as "rhetorical flourish";[47] for Kumm, "a rights-holder does not have very much in virtue of his having a right",[48] a conclusion endorsed by Alec Stone Sweet and Jud Mathews;[49] and for Möller, "rights operate on the same plane as . . . policy considerations".[50] Everything is ultimately decided at the second (justification) stage, which sets out "the conditions under which infringements of these interests [i.e., rights] can be justified".[51]

This second stage gives ready cover to the willingness to include more within the scope and content of a right. When in doubt, acknowledge that a right is in play; exaggerated claims of right will be infringed and the justification analysis will discriminate between the true and the false. But what is more, because the first stage is the gateway to justification, and because we are told that "all acts by public authorities affecting individuals [should] meet the proportionality requirement",[52] all that "affects" an individual should be acknowledged to be an infringement of that individual's right(s): there are, Kumm insists, "no obvious reasons for defining narrowly the scope of interests

---

[46] Klatt and Meister, *Constitutional Structure of Proportionality*, *supra* note 36 at 16 (emphasis added, footnote omitted).

[47] Beatty, *Ultimate Rule of Law*, *supra* note 10 at 160, 171, 171.

[48] Kumm, "Political Liberalism," *supra* note 12 at 139; Mattias Kumm, "The Idea of Socratic Contestation and the Right to Justification: The Point of Rights-Based Proportionality Review," (2010) 4 *Law & Ethics of Human Rights* 140 at 150.

[49] Matthews and Stone Sweet, "All Things in Proportion?" *supra* note 4 at 809: "a right gives a right-bearer an entitlement to have her claim evaluated under the proportionality framework, and nothing more."

[50] Möller, "Proportionality and Rights Inflation," *supra* note 13 at 156.

[51] Kumm, "Institutionalising Socratic Contestation," *supra* note 12 at 7. For this reason, it can be claimed that human rights law-in-action can be reduced to one right: "a right to proportionality": see Webber, *Negotiable Constitution*, *supra* note 2 at 4; and Möller, *Global Model*, *supra* note 3 at 178.

[52] Kumm, "Political Liberalism," *supra* note 12 at 140.

protected as a right".[53] So, when Beatty affirms that it is "all and only about proportionality",[54] he is not far off the mark. Notwithstanding the familiar refrain that judicial practice proceeds according to a two-stage inquiry, the second stage seems to overpower the first, more or less collapsing analysis into a single inquiry into justification. However, unlike the inquiry into the requirements of justice and justification that concludes in the *identification* of a right, this inquiry is into the justification of the *infringement* of a right. Rights matter, on this account, as weak gatekeepers to the second stage, where they are considered only because infringed. The framework question is no longer "What is the right?", but rather: "Is the right's infringement justified?"

IV. CONFUSING RIGHTS

Two understandings of rights are on offer: one, controlling in political morality, according to which rights matter; another, controlling in human rights law, according to which they do not.[55] Given that the gulf between them is so great, one might be forgiven for thinking that it is but an accident of language that both accounts appeal to the word "right". Consequently, the potential for confusion might be thought to be a standing concern; one might conclude that overzealous definitions of rights to everything would be liable to trade on "the higher prestige and greater strength of a moral right that provides an undefeated reason for action",[56] with the perils of mistakenly concluding that there is true loss whenever one concludes that a right has been infringed. In turn, one might express concern that the ready, regular, expected, and unavoidable infringement of rights will numb one's reaction to the infringement of true, genuine rights, taking it as granted that rights are less than philosophical

[53] Kumm, "Idea of Socratic Contestation", *supra* note 48 at 151. See also Klatt and Meister, "Proportionality – a benefit for human rights?" *supra* note 12 at 702: "[t]his avoids 'black holes' of non-protection". Notwithstanding Kumm's widely shared assertion, Gardbaum is correct to note that "[t]here appears to be nothing inherent in the framework itself to prevent a more stringent approach to the first step": "Proportionality and Democratic Constitutionalism", *supra* note 6 at 281.

[54] Beatty, *Ultimate Rule of Law*, *supra* note 10 at 170. See also Möller, *Global Model*, *supra* note 3 at 178: "It is therefore partly correct to say that human and constitutional rights law is all about proportionality".

[55] Frederick Schauer's contribution to this volume (Chapter 8) can be taken to argue for a middle ground, according to which rights protect not all, but only *special* interests. That middle ground collapses into the position defended by Kumm, Möller, and others insofar as it also frames rights unilaterally and not relationally. It commits fewer errors than the "all interests" account of rights, but it nonetheless fails to relate rights to justice and to others in community.

[56] Miller, "Justification and Rights Limitations," *supra* note 22 at 96.

argument has long assumed them to be and, so, never provide conclusive reasons for action. The dangers of the juxtaposed accounts of rights are therefore two-fold: one may erroneously conclude that the infringement of a right is conclusive of the *unjustifiability* (the *injustice*) of infringing legislation or one may conclude that there really are no rights that are controlling and conclusive of what is right, just, justified.[57]

We are told that these concerns are misplaced, as we are assured that these dangers are unlikely to manifest themselves: all depends on how the word "right" is used and, in any event, the suggestion that anyone would be misled is "unsubstantiated".[58] There is reason to question the assurance. Consider how Beatty, in the same breath that he affirms the "irrelevance" of rights, insists that his fact-focused approach to proportionality will "maximise the rights of those who ask for their protection".[59] The intelligible force of the claim presupposes that one put to one side Beatty's assertions, elsewhere, that rights hold "no special status". Consider, in turn, how for Kumm the "point of rights-based proportionality review" is explained by the "idea of Socratic contestation and the *right to justification*", where "right" is appealed to first in the sense of a weak, defeasible, non-controlling interest subject to proportionality review and second as conclusive and determinative of what is to be done.[60] To distinguish the weak from the strong senses of right, Kumm sometimes substitutes the weak version of "right" for the language of "burden", reserving the word "right" for what is conclusively required, as when he speaks of "the burdened parties' right to justification".[61] The "right to justification" is elsewhere reformulated as the "right to contest",[62] both of which trade on an understanding that, contrary

---

[57] Although Panaccio does not endorse this concern, he documents it well: Charles-Maxime Panaccio, "In Defence of Two-Step Balancing and Proportionality in Rights Adjudication" (2011) 24 *Can. J.L. & Jur.* 109 at 114, 116.

[58] Möller, *Global Model*, *supra* note 3 at 5 n16. See also Charles-Maxime Panaccio, "Book Review" 8 *Int'l. J. Con. Law* 988 at 990 (2010): "Rights could be both premises and conclusions, as long as one is clear about the context in which one speaks of them. And I doubt, seriously, that variable uses of the same word ('right') leads to confused communication or moral decay." But compare Möller in Chapter 7 of this volume, where he acknowledges the problem that "ordinary citizens without legal training could occasionally get confused about rights" and "accept[s] that this is a problem": "Proportionality and Rights Inflation", *supra* note 13 at 171.

[59] Beatty, *Ultimate Rule of Law*, *supra* note 10 at 73. At 92, he speaks of "how seriously a law adversely affects the constitutional rights of those who fall within its terms".

[60] Both uses of right are employed in Kumm's title: "The Idea of Socratic Contestation and the Right to Justification: The Point of Rights-Based Proportionality Review," *supra* note 48.

[61] Kumm, "Idea of Socratic Contestation," ibid. at 168. See also Mattias Kumm, "Alexy's Theory of Constitutional Rights and the Problem of Judicial Review," in Matthias Klatt (ed.), *Institutionalised Reason: The Jurisprudence of Robert Alexy* (2012) 168.

[62] Kumm, "Alexy's Theory of Constitutional Rights," ibid. at 213.

to what Kumm otherwise insists upon, rights *do* "imply that [the right-holder] holds a position that gives him . . . priority over countervailing considerations of policy".[63] Along similar lines, Möller affirms that every person has a "right to challenge acts of public authorities before courts", a "right" he elsewhere terms a "right to justification" correlative to a "duty of justification" on the legislature, all of which assumes, notwithstanding what is elsewhere affirmed, that rights *do have* "special importance" and "special normative force".[64] It would seem that the pull toward the philosophical understanding of rights is great, even for those who insist that it plays no part under the received approach. The confusion is liable to misrepresent the requirements of justice in community.

These illustrations may not be enough to "substantiate" the concern that the juxtaposed account of rights is liable to confuse, but they highlight the potential to do so. Perhaps in an effort to demarcate weak from strong understandings of rights, Möller and to an uncertain extent Kumm have introduced a distinction between "prima facie rights" and "definite rights", corresponding to the two stages of analysis under the received approach.[65] In doing so, they take their distance from the vocabulary of courts, which otherwise grounds their account of rights. On this reconstructive account, the first stage of analysis interrogates not rights *simpliciter*, but rather "prima facie rights"; the label "definite rights" is reserved for the end of the inquiry into justification. In this way, Möller and Kumm seek to reframe their and others' discussions dismissing rights as "irrelevant" and without "priority", "special importance", or "special normative force" as pertaining *only* to prima facie rights, thus paving the way for reinstituting the priority and special importance and force of (definite) rights.

The willingness to rescue the concept of rights from the position of inconsequence to which the received approach has relegated it is welcome. The qualification "prima facie" signals that the speaker is hedging the claim of right, acknowledging that what is now being claimed as a right might, *with justification,* be defeated, not be a right. Yet, despite this promise, Kumm's and Möller's own usage of the qualifiers "prima facie" and "definite" is not

[63] Kumm, "Idea of Socratic Contestation," *supra* note 48 at 150.
[64] Möller, *Global Model, supra* note 3 at 208, 87.
[65] The distinction draws on Alexy, *Theory of Constitutional Rights, supra* note 9 at 60: "Decisions about rights presuppose the identification of definitive rights. The route from the principle, that is, the prima facie right, to the definitive right runs by way of the relation of preference." But compare Barak, "Proportionality (2)," *supra* note 5 at 739: "That a constitutional right is relative does not mean, however, that it is a prima facie right. A relative right is still a definite right." See further Barak, *Proportionality, supra* note 11 at 39–42.

always consistent, such that it is not always clear what the qualifier qualifies. For example, Kumm speaks of (a) "a *prima facie* violation of a right",[66] (b) the "domain of interests that enjoy *prima facie* protection as a right",[67] and (c) "a violation of a *prima facie* right",[68] oscillating between qualifying the protection afforded by a right, the right itself, and its violation. In turn, however, Kumm speaks only of (a) the "*definitive* violation of the right",[69] omitting to speak of (b) the "definitive protection" of interests or of (c) a "definitive right". The focus for Kumm remains on the *violation* of a right, something the received approach already captures by distinguishing between the "infringement" and "violation" of a right.

Möller's usage is more regularly fixed on "prima facie right" and "definite right", although he sometimes appeals, more or less equivalently, to the "prima facie scope of constitutional rights"[70] and to the "prima facie stage of rights and the justification stage";[71] at other times, Möller omits to draw any distinction, as when he affirms that "to defend the claim of a *right* to autonomy, one must abandon the idea that rights hold a special normative force",[72] that "[p]roportionality is simply a structure that guides judges through the reasoning process as to whether a policy does or does not respect rights",[73] that "the point of rights is to enable people to live their lives autonomously",[74] and that a murderer "should be punished because he violates the rights of others".[75]

---

[66] Kumm, "Institutionalising Socratic Contestation," *supra* note 12 at 7; Kumm, "Idea of Socratic Contestation," *supra* note 48 at 146; Kumm, "Political Liberalism," *supra* note 12 at 135. See also Stone Sweet and Mathews, "Proportionality Balancing and Global Constitutionalism," *supra* note 3 at 75: "In the paradigmatic situation, PA [proportionality analysis] is triggered once a *prima facie* case has been made to the effect that a right has been infringed by a government measure" (footnote omitted).

[67] Kumm, "Institutionalising Socratic Contestation," *supra* note 12 at 12; Kumm "Political Liberalism," *supra* note 12 at 140. This idea is echoed in Klatt and Meister, "Proportionality – a benefit for human rights?", *supra* note 12 at 702: "The state faces a duty to give reasons for not protecting rights only if certain behavior is protected prima facie."

[68] Kumm, "Institutionalising Socratic Contestation," *supra* note 12 at 9; Kumm "Idea of Socratic Contestation," *supra* note 48 at 148.

[69] Kumm, "Institutionalising Socratic Contestation," ibid. at 7; Kumm, "Idea of Socratic Contestation," ibid. at 146.

[70] Möller, *Global Model, supra* note 3 at 134.   [71] Ibid. at 23.

[72] Ibid. at 73 (emphasis in original).

[73] Kai Möller, "Proportionality: Challenging the Critics" 10 *Int'l. J. Con. Law* 709 at 726 (2012) (emphasis omitted).

[74] Möller, *Global Model, supra* note 3 at 23.

[75] Ibid. at 78. A similar ambiguity is to be found in Klatt and Meister, *Constitutional Structure of Proportionality, supra* note 36 at 48: "the state faces a duty to give reasons for not protecting rights when certain behaviour is protected prima facie."

Notwithstanding these ambiguities in exposition, the point Möller and Kumm seek to make is communicated clearly enough: true, genuine rights are identified only as the conclusion of what is justified. With this in mind, Möller's claim that there is a "right to murder" is less sensational than it might otherwise appear. He insists that "nobody can possibly have a *definite* right" to murder,[76] such that his claim is only that one has a "prime facie right to murder". Now, the tragedy of Möller's argument lies less in the claim itself than in how he arrives at it following a plausible reconstruction of the received approach. This is not to suggest that courts are likely, as a predictive manner, to make the jump from a "right to feed pigeons in public squares" and a "right to smoke marijuana for recreational purposes" to a right to kill.[77] However, Möller's reconstruction makes clear how, true to the conception of rights they have developed, they could.[78] The weakness awarded to prima facie rights allows for the ready inclusion within the category of "rights" of many activities that are definitely not *in the right*, precisely because what is in the right is determined only after the infringement of a right has been concluded and evaluated. On Möller's reconstructive account, a prima facie right is simply synonymous with "interest". And whilst there is reason to question the claim that one can have an "interest" in murdering (where murder is understood, as Möller invites us to understand it, as intentionally taking the life of an innocent person), it is clear that the headline "an interest to murder" has far less traction than "the right to murder". For "interest", on Möller's reading of the received approach, approximates one's wants or preferences; in its radical subjectivity, it makes no room for the possibility that one may be simply wrong or misguided.[79] What is more, this radical subjectivity implies that the upright

---

[76] Möller, "Proportionality and Rights Inflation", *supra* note 13 at 163. See also Möller, *Global Model*, *supra* note 3 at 77.

[77] "Kill" better captures what Möller attempts to communicate with "murder". On pigeon-feeding: see, e.g., BVerfGE 54, 143; on smoking marijuana: see, e.g., *R. v. Malmo-Levine* [2003] 3 S.C.R. 571 Although the majority of the Supreme Court of Canada affirms that "[t]here is no free-standing constitutional right to smoke 'pot' for recreational purposes", it proceeds to the justification stage of analysis on the grounds that the threat of imprisonment triggers a "liberty interest", thereby muting much of the force of its previous assertion. For present purposes, nothing turns on whether the justification for the infringement of the right to liberty is undertaken within s. 7 or s. 1 of the Canadian Charter of Rights and Freedoms.

[78] Barak's labored efforts to deny a "constitutional right to steal" seem to support Möller's argument: *Proportionality*, *supra* note 11 at 42–43.

[79] Although Möller states that his account of the "self-conception of the agent" is "different from one focussing exclusively on what people *want*" and is "equally different from one focussing on a person's *preferences*", he allows that any activity will qualify as an "interest" if "it affects or reflects something which the agent considers to be giving meaning and value to his or her life": *Global Model*, *supra* note 3 at 61.

community member, concerned to play his part and to give to each his due, will have fewer "interests" than the corrupt community member, who is self-ish, without care for others, and intent on willing and doing evil and seeking more than his fair share. Of course, Möller can reply that both the upright and the corrupt community members will be more or less aligned in their claims to *definite* rights, but it remains an open question why one should dignify raping, torturing for pleasure, trafficking children, and enslaving a population – all of which Möller would admit as consistent with his account of "interests" – as cognizable "rights", even if qualified by "prima facie". To do so is to give up on the notion that one bears a special responsibility when making claims of right.

V. RECLAIMING RIGHTS

The distinctions between the infringement and the violation of a right, between what "reasoning within the right" requires and what "reasoning within practical reason" requires, between a prima facie right and a definite right, and between the premise that one "wrongs" a right-holder by infringing his right and the conclusion that one's wrongful action is right because justified all trade on a simplified understanding of rights that, in turn, "makes the moral universe more complicated".[80] The moral universe is complicated by the availability of two potentially incompatible answers to the same practical question: What ought to be done? The potential for the incompatibility is the result of how little informs the answer to this question from the perspective of the right and of how much informs the answer from the perspective of what one is justified to do. The "subjective" and "objective" meanings of "right" are now wholly divorced. And yet, under the received approach, the two perspectives on this question must be considered, for one is never justified in acting only in the name of one's or another's ("subjective") rights; one is only ever truly justified in acting in the light of what is truly ("objectively") right. Rights, on this view, both resist their limitations (infringements, impairments) and cannot fully be understood without them: all the while insisting that a right is informed only by its "internal" limitation and without engaging at all with its "external" limitation, the received approach acknowledges that the "external" limitation of a right is an inevitable part of understanding rights.

On this understanding, rights are both aspects of our moral universe yet inde-pendent of what morality requires; they require as intermediate conclusions

---

[80] Oberdiek, "Lost in Moral Space," *supra* note 23 at 327.

what need not obtain as final conclusions all the while insisting that we hold on to the defeated intermediate conclusion. We should not. Rights, like justice, are situated in a community of persons and should be understood in such a way as to be in harmony with the moral universe that gives them sense. Because the received approach promotes a definition of rights exhausted by one's interests, a definition that is uninterested in context, others, relationships, and what is ultimately just and justified, there seems to be no reason to award the label "right" when another English word would seem more suitable: interest. The word "interest" captures the controlling idea in the account of rights under the received approach: all that is advantageous for, beneficial to, or the concern of an individual. An individual's interests, we might say, are fixed, stable, and unchanging *insofar as* they are the individual's and do not depend on others or on context (though their satisfaction may well). They are regularly frustrated in the circumstances of community life, as one's relationships with others and the need to take others into account demarcate whether, when, and how one's interests will be realized. *But such is life in community.* If under the received approach "rights" are only another way of talking about what is already covered by "interests" – and the received approach's frequent appeal to the discourse of "conflicts of interests" suggests this to be the case – then little is gained and much is lost. For rights – true, genuine rights – acknowledge the foundational equality of persons by delimiting what is due to each in the light of one's being in community with others who also have "interests" and rights. Interests are defeasible premises in evaluations of what is just, but rights, properly under-stood, are not: they are conclusive, determinative, and worthy of the status awarded to them when contemplated as right relationships between persons. They give expression by specifying what is due to each in community as a matter of justice. This concern for persons is at risk of being lost if rights are equated with interests.

How might the received approach reorient itself so as to reclaim rights, their priority and conclusiveness? A conceptual reordering of human rights law is proposed, one that rejects the analysis of the received approach, but makes sense of the two stages commonly appealed to by court and scholar. In so doing, I seek to demonstrate how rights can be conceived as conclusions of practical reasoning about what justice requires all the while being claimed by persons against legislation (or other government action).

A claim of right should not be confused for a right. The first stage of analysis under the received approach should be reoriented away from the assumption that it evaluates one's rights for, in truth, the only matter evaluated at the first stage is a claimant's defeasible claim of right. Without doubt, the claimant aspires to be a right-holder and, so, aspires that the claim of right be recognized *as a right*. Gardbaum sees this more clearly than many others in affirming that "what an individual has by virtue of being able to claim protection of a constitutional right . . . is an important prima facie legal claim".[81] There may be good reasons to set the threshold low for allowing an individual to make a claim of right, and different reasons are on offer.[82] They are not my present focus. I aim to highlight how, no matter the strength of those reasons, they do not translate a defeasible claim of right into a defeasible right.

By understanding the first stage of analysis in the frame of a claim of right, the conclusions arrived at the second stage of analysis are also reframed. So: rather than concluding that the "infringement" of a "right" is *justified*, one should affirm the *defeat* of a claim of right.[83] If it is concluded that what is just or justified according to practical reasoning is not what the claimant seeks, then the conclusion is that the claimant has *no right*. This is not to suggest that the claimant's claim of right was spurious or ill-intentioned (though some will be). Rather, because there lies a multiplicity of possible just acts and arrangements that will give effect to one's rights, authority will be required to choose between them so as to give to each and all their rights. (Consider, for example, the range of reasonable alternative schemes for realizing fair trial rights, fair election procedures and the right to vote, the provision of healthcare and the right to life, and so forth.) One's claim of right may be defeated because another scheme of acts and arrangements was selected, one that falls within a range of reasonable alternatives. The authority responsible for making that choice may be the legislature or the court or the legislature subject to override by the court, depending on the community's constitution and practice. Whoever is identified as having responsibility for the community in such matters will exercise authority in identifying the rights of each and all and, so, will reject some claims of right in part because *this* scheme rather than *that* scheme of acts and arrangements was adopted for the community.

What of the conclusion, under the received approach, that the "infringement" of a "right" is *unjustified*? In the straightforward case, that conclusion

[81] Stephen Gardbaum, "The Comparative Structure and Scope of Constitutional Rights" in Rosalind Dixon and Tom Ginsburg (eds.), *The Research Handbook in Comparative Constitutional Law* (2011) 388; Stephen Gardbaum, "A Democratic Defense of Constitutional Balancing," (2010) 4 *Law & Ethics of Human Rights* 77 at 79.

[82] Among them: Kumm seeks to subject *all* acts (and omissions) of public authorities to "Socratic contestation"; Panaccio defends shifting the burden of proof from the claimant to public authorities ("In Defence of Two-Step Balancing," *supra* note 57).

[83] See Miller, "Justification and Rights Limitations," *supra* note 22 at 96: "[t]o contend that state action limiting a person's claim to a benefit or liberty of action is *justified* is precisely to make the claim that there are competing demands or reasons that defeat the *claim* of constitutional right" (emphasis in original).

should be reframed thus: the claimant's claim of right is recognized *as a right*. The impugned act is unjustified as contrary to the claimant's right. The conclusive, peremptory, and decisive reason for action that is the right has been disrespected and, so, the author of the impugned act committed a wrong. The legislation is to be denied its status of law (either by judicial declaration or by legislative repeal): it fails to provide members of the community with reasons for action because it violates the reasons for action that constitute the right.[84]

These corrections to the errors of human rights law-in-action go some way: they reorient the frame of analysis from premature ascriptions of "rights" to "claims of rights" and allow for the conclusion that claims of rights may be defeated or recognized *as rights*. But this conceptual re-ordering does not go far enough, for it conceives of only two possible conclusions following judicial evaluations of a claim of right: either the claimant has no right (the claim of right is defeated) or the claimant's right has been violated (the claim of right is successful). This discloses a most curious and unfortunate feature of the received approach: *we come to know what rights truly, justifiably require only through their violation*. Altogether missing from the received approach is a third alternative: the affirmation of one's rights together with the affirmation that they are respected. To grasp this alternative requires further re-ordering: acknowledging that the "external limitation" of rights – what is otherwise termed the infringement of a right – can be enabling and constitutive of rights.

Gardbaum articulates the distinction between the "internal" and "external" limitation of rights with welcome clarity. Tracking the case law of the received approach, he explains that internal limits are about the "scope and definition" of rights as determined by legal interpretation of text and that external limits are "constitutionally permissible restrictions on rights" – in short, "infringements" of rights.[85] External limitations are "inconsistent" with the right and constitute a legislative power to "override" a right. The distinction turns primarily on "an essentially interpretive function", such that whatever

---

[84] In the less straightforward case, the conclusion that the "infringement" of a "right" is unjustified cannot be reframed as the affirmation of the claimant's right. For sometimes, the unjustifiability of the "infringement" is the result not of the act or deed required or prohibited by legislation, but of the *reasons* animating the choice of the impugned scheme intended to realize the rights of each and all. Here, the affirmation of "unjustifiability" does not necessarily signal that the claimant's right was violated: alternative reasons or schemes may be available that would defeat the claimant's claim of right.

[85] Stephen Gardbaum, "Limiting Constitutional Rights," 54 *U.C.L.A L. Rev.* 789 at 795, 801 (2007). For similar usage of the "internal" and "external" distinction, see Barak, *Proportionality*, *supra* note 11 at 36.

limits cannot find an "internal" textual anchor are "external" to the right-as-guaranteed.[86] Breaking stride with other proponents of the received approach, Gardbaum recognizes that "there is nothing obvious or self-evident. . . about the proposition that legislatures should be empowered to act inconsistently with entrenched rights".[87]

I agree and add that there is no reason to conclude that any legislature is so empowered. Thankfully, the error in Gardbaum's faithful reporting of the received approach is quickly diagnosed (and does not impugn his otherwise compelling account of how rights can promote a "culture of democracy"[88]). The analysis confuses the distinction between what is settled and unsettled in a bill of rights with what is and is not a right. Bills of rights are inchoate legal instruments: for many of the reasons recognized by the received approach, two-term rights ("Everyone has a right to *x*") provide one with no conclusive or determinative reason for action. They do not conclude the scope and content of rights and to think otherwise is to mistake an open-ended formulation of a right for an open-ended right. Bills of rights follow a regular pattern of settling little, minimizing what Gardbaum labels "internal" limits and channelling the resolution of what rights require to "external" limits. But properly understood, these "external" limits, *when justified*, perform a task no different than "internal" limits: they define the right. The opened-ended formulations of rights in bills of rights are inchoate as law; a bill of rights stands not as a statement of law, but as a promise of law.

To conceive of justified external limits as infringing, derogating from, breaching, contravening, encroaching upon, impairing, or overriding a right is to commit oneself to a "formalist" understanding of legal rights. If a bill of rights guarantees "freedom of expression" without specifying further the definition of the right, Gardbaum and others[89] would label all such further specification an "external" limit that "infringes" or "overrides" the right. So: the legislative determination that freedom of expression *does not* extend to (a) propaganda for war, (b) incitement of imminent violence, or (c) advocacy of hatred that is based on race, ethnicity, gender or religion, and that constitutes incitement to cause harm is to be conceived as "wronging" the

---

[86] Gardbaum, "Limiting Constitutional Rights," ibid. at 811.

[87] Ibid. at 794.

[88] See Gardbaum, "Proportionality and Democratic Constitutionalism," *supra* note 6.

[89] This same misguided formalist afflicts Barak's insistence on a distinction between the "constitutional level" (which defines "the scope of the right") and the "sub-constitutional level" (which accounts for "the extent of the right's protection"): *Proportionality*, *supra* note 11 at 23–24 *et passim*. See also 34, where Barak examines the very provision of the South African Bill of Rights reviewed in this paragraph.

"right-holder" in some way, as frustrating the right's realization. However, if this same determination is incorporated into the bill of rights, as is the case with the South African Bill of Rights,[90] then it constitutes an "internal" limitation that defines the scope and content of the right. The difference between the definition and the infringement of a right turns, it would seem, on whether the determination of what is just and justified is in legislation or the bill of rights.

Now, there is reason to attend to the difference between the interpretation of text in a bill of rights and such further specification of rights as provided for in legislation, but that difference is not one of *defining* or *overriding* right. Only a misguided formalism would lead to the conclusion that the deprivation of life resulting from "the use of force which is no more than absolutely necessary" is a *definition* of Article 2's right to life *because* stipulated in the European Convention rather than a justified *infringement* of the right *because* in legislation. The same could be said of the Article 4 right not to be "required to perform forced or compulsory labour", which is specified in the Convention "*not [to] include . . .* any service of a military character [or] any work or service which forms part of normal civic obligations". So too with the familiar references to the rights against "*unreasonable* search and seizure" and "*arbitrary* detention" and to "*peaceful* assembly": they define the rights no less and no more than legislation with the same content. If these various specifications are justified, they define the right; if they are unjustified, they do not. That is the only controlling distinction.

There is no denying that this aspect of the intellectual disorder of human rights law-in-action takes its cue from the grammar and structure of bills of rights. That cue is three-fold: first, rights are drafted as two-term relations between a right-holder and a subject matter of justice, omitting from view the third term that is the other who is in a relationship to the right-holder in order *to realize* the right-holder's right; second, the focus on subject matters of justice (life, liberty, security, association, and so forth) overshadows the need to focus on persons acting and doing, such as what the "third term" (the other) must *do* or refraining from *doing* to satisfy his duty to the claim-right-holder; and third, the attempt to acknowledge the "other" and "acting and doing" is undertaken in limitation clauses that employ the "uncraftsmanlike language" of "interference" and "restriction" to signal the relationship of the "third term" to rights and right-holders.[91]

---

[90] South African Bill of Rights, s. 16(1).
[91] See John Finnis, "Human Rights and Their Enforcement" in *Collected Essays of John Finnis, vol. III: Human Rights and Common Good* (2011) 19 at 45.

Consider this uncraftsmanlike language. Notwithstanding its powerful contributions to our understandings of rights in many other respects, the Universal
Declaration on Human Rights is liable to readings that misconceive of the
"other" and "acting and doing". At its Article 29(1), the Declaration recognizes
that "[e]veryone has duties to the community in which alone the free and full
development of his personality is possible". Now, whilst the emphasis on *duty*
and its *necessity* for each and every person in community is rightly highlighted,
the affirmation that duties are owed to "the community" may obfuscate the
more exact point that one owes those duties to each and every *member* of
the community in satisfaction of their rights, just as each and every member
of the community owes duties to oneself in satisfaction of one's rights. The
missed opportunity here pales in comparison with the misguided conception
of "others" in Article 29(2): "In the exercise of his rights and freedoms, everyone shall be subject only to such limitations as are determined by law solely
for the purpose of securing due recognition and respect for the rights and
freedoms of others and of meeting the just requirements of morality, public
order and the general welfare in a democratic society". Albeit acknowledging
the importance of acting and doing by appealing to the idea that rights are to
be "exercised", this limitation clause frames the mind of the reader around
the idea that such limitations are restrictive of an otherwise limitless right, as
limitations are said to be "subject only" to select "purposes". Even the invitation to look to "acting" and "doing" misfires by focusing on the *right-holder's*
exercise of his rights when, for so many of our rights, the right's "exercise" is to
be undertaken *by others* who owe duties to us to act or to refrain from acting
in satisfaction of our rights.

These errors are magnified by the European Convention on Human Rights.
Here, "duty" makes only an exceptional appearance[92] and the relationship
of others in community to right-holders is framed in even more suspicious
terms. The limitation clauses found in the second paragraphs of Articles 8,
9, 10, and 11 speak variously of "*interference* by a public authority with the
exercise of this right", of "*subjecting*" the "exercise of these freedoms . . . to such
formalities, conditions, *restrictions* or *penalties*", and of how "*restrictions* shall
be placed on the exercise of these rights". Gardbaum is correct to highlight
that these terms carry the mind of the reader away from the specification and
delimitation of rights to the interference with and infringement of *already
specified and delimited* rights.[93] Human rights law-in-action is all the worse
for it.

---

[92] And without signaling anything close to a duty's relationship to another's right: Article 10(2):
    "The exercise of these freedoms, since it carries with it duties and responsibilities . . . ".
[93] Gardbaum, "Proportionality and Democratic Constitutionalism", *supra* note 6 at 269.

That the drafting process of the European Convention and many other bills of rights "mangled into an ungrammatical shambles" the relationship of limitations and rights is a truth of human history.[94] It bears partial responsibility for guiding courts under the received approach to the mistaken two-stage analysis reviewed above. But in no way should such errors be controlling of our understanding of rights, for the mistake is obvious: assertions of "infringement", "impairment", "interference", and so forth all assume the very point in dispute – *the definition of the right.* Unless one commits the errors reviewed above (among them, assumes that the semantic reach of two-term rights sets out the definition of a right), there is no reason to conclude that limitation clauses, properly understood, direct one to evaluate *interferences* with rights. Whilst Gardbaum is correct to highlight that the key term "limitation" does not, for many, lend itself on its "most compelling or plausible reading" to the synonyms "specification", "delimitation", "boundary", and "definition",[95] *that* is what limitation clauses concern themselves with. The force of this claim does not depend on the fact that the received approach's appeals to the vocabulary of "violate", "derogate from", "contravene", "impair", "deny", "override", and so forth are themselves not in keeping with the actual key terms used by the limitation clauses of the European Convention, Canadian Charter, the New Zealand Bill of Rights Act, or South African Bill of Rights. Rather, the full force of the claim rests on the straightforward mistake that limitations are "external" and "restrictive" if omitted from text of the bill of rights but "internal" and "constitutive" if stipulated within the text and on how, by rejecting such formalist commitments, one can align what is in the right (just, justified) with the definition of rights.

The journey to reclaim rights under the received approach begins by reordering defeasible rights as defeasible *claims* of rights and by reframing the conclusion on justification as either the defeat or the recognition of such claims. It includes acknowledging that what is labeled the "limitation" or "infringement" or "impairment" of rights under the received approach can be and when justified is the constitutive "definition" of a right. But this is not enough: the relationship of rights to law must be rehabilitated.

---

94 Timothy Endicott, "Proportionality and Incommensurability," Chapter 14 in this volume at 332. Endicott makes the point with respect to Article 8 of the European Convention and draws special attention to the Article's reference to "respect for". Notwithstanding this, his point can be generalized, as disclosed by the conceptual truth of his conclusion: "Legitimate [I would say: justified, just, right] actions taken in the interests listed in [Article] 8(2) are not 'interferences' with the 'exercise' of the right to respect, but actions that are compatible with respect for privacy and family life and the home." The words "to respect" can be removed from Endicott's conclusion without detracting from its force.

95 Gardbaum, "Proportionality and Democratic Constitutionalism," *supra* note 6 at 281.

VI. LEGISLATING RIGHTS

It is telling that Richard Ekins, in his contribution to this volume (Chapter 15), is compelled to insist that the reasonable legislature does not set out to infringe rights, but to determine what rights citizens have, including by giving effect to the rights of each and all in legislative acts.[96] Having primary responsibility for the community, the legislature is tasked with settling, decisively, what each and every member is to do in those matters of concern to the community as a whole. Among those matters are the subject matters of justice regularly affirmed in bills of right, matters that each and all have a "right to". To legislate reasonably is to settle upon one among a range of reasonable schemes of acts and arrangements according to which all members of the community get what is theirs by right; stated otherwise, legislating is the "function of judging just".[97] That function is not exhausted by outlining various subject matters of justice – life, liberty, security, association – and declaring that each and every member of the community has rights. For the community members will ask: What are we to do in the name of our rights? What are we to do so as to respect the rights of each other? To answer these questions in law, the legislature must translate the open-ended references to the subject matters of justice into rights – that is, the legislature must provide the jural structure that characterizes law: the determination of right relations between persons oriented around acting and doing. That structure and determination are to be pursued in keeping with the principles of legality, principles that highlight law's guiding and facilitative function to give to each his rights; stated otherwise: to provide for justice according to law.

Law, on this understanding, is the act of judging and implementing the requirements of justice in community. As outlined in section II, the Latin *ius* (*jus*) is the root not only of "right" and "justice", but also of the legal terms "jurist", "juridical", and "jurisprudence". This linguistic relationship of right(s) and law is perhaps more evident in the French, Spanish, Italian, and German vocabularies, where what in English is encompassed by the single term "law" is therein expressed as both *droit, derecho, diritto, Recht* ("right", "just") and as *loi, ley, legge, Gesetz* ("a law", "a statute"). These vocabularies signal how legal directives, albeit with many failings, aspire to respect and comply with, *by authoritatively establishing*, that which is right. And that which is right concerns not only giving to each and all their *rights*, but also establishing *duties* for others.

---

[96] Richard Ekins, "Legislating Proportionately," Chapter 15 in this volume at 359–360.
[97] Jeremy Waldron, *The Dignity of Legislation* (1999) at 86.

In this frame, John Finnis rightly insists that "laws and decisions declaring and giving effect to human rights have the complexity characteristic of positive law".[98] The appeal to "human rights" here is not to bills of rights – which have none of the complexity of positive law – but to the particulars of legislation and other instances of positive law that establish right relations between persons. That legislation and positive law will settle, inter alia, (a) the description of the class of persons who have a claim-right, liberty, power, or immunity; (b) the description of the class of persons who are under a correlative duty, no-right, liability, or disability; (c) the content of the relationship in terms of the act-description to be performed (or not) by one or the other class of persons; and (d) an account of the circumstances and conditions (time, place, and manner) for the performance of the act-description. To these principal specifications outlining the relationships between persons and act-descriptions that *are* the right relationship must be added: (e) the circumstances and conditions (if any) under which the right-holder may waive or forfeit or otherwise lose his right; (f) the secondary relationships that will obtain between the two classes of persons (or some such third parties, such as a prosecutor or judge) if duties are not performed; and, *at each and every stage*, (g) an evaluation whether the relationships and act-descriptions just specified cohere and are consistent with the family of relationships and act-descriptions *already* existing in the community so that each and every one can *have* rights and can *respect* the rights of others.[99] By resolving these various instances of specification defining rights and by doing so in compliance with the rule of law, law shares the appeal to conclusiveness and decisive and peremptory status that is the mark of rights. To achieve this, the law seeks to identify, with sufficient specificity, what each is to do in satisfaction of the rights of others, ensuring that one's duties to one's fellow community member are in harmony with one's duties to another as well as in harmony with one's own rights.

Now, none of this assumes that the legislature – even the reasonable legislature – will not err.[100] The legislature will err straightforwardly when it

---

[98] John Finnis, "Introduction," in *Collected Essays of John Finnis, vol. III: Human Rights and Common Good* (2011) 1 at 3.

[99] This paragraph draws on Finnis, *Natural Law and Natural Rights, supra* note 19 at 218–219.

[100] On this point, misreadings of the argument developed in *The Negotiable Constitution, supra* note 2 are to be found in Tom Hickman, "Negotiable Rights, What Rights?" (2012) 75 M.L.R. 437 at 440 "[Webber argues that] the legislature should *never* be regarded as infringing constitutional rights . . . legislation that gravely restricted the rights of the defence would have to be regarded as necessarily compatible with and indeed *defining* what our rights to a fair trial are" (emphasis in original) at 449 "on Webber's view [a legislative specification] will be a proper limitation simply by dint of being embodied in primary legislation"; and Barak, *Proportionality, supra* note 11 at 494: "Webber . . . views the scope of constitutional rights as determined by

mistranslates a determinate moral right into legal form, for example by failing to "outlaw" murder, rape, torture, or slavery or by outlawing such moral
wrongs selectively, leaving some members of community outside the scope of
legal protection. (This does not deny that the process of translating a determinate moral right into legal form will require the exercise of judgment when
appealing to legal language, concepts, and categories, none of which are, in
all of their detail, wholly determined by reason.) The legislature will err less
straightforwardly when morality underdetermines what is required to secure
one's rights, such as when the legislature must choose from among a range of
reasonable schemes any one of which would be reasonable even if it could
reasonably be different in many respects. Here, the legislature errs in selecting
from outside this range, for example by failing to attend to all participants in
determining a fair trial process or by failing to review a previously enacted
reasonable scheme now that circumstances have changed. Even if it mischar-
acterizes this process in almost every other respect, the received approach's
invitation to examine the *reasons* supporting legislative action is one welcome
aspect of human rights law-in-action, for it correctly points to the process of
practical reasoning leading to the legislatively established rights as the focus
of analysis (even if it distorts that process by insisting on proportionality as the
only mode of reasoning).[101]

Against the standard and measure of reason, many legislative directives
in community will "stand to the right they purport to enforce as more or less
unsatisfactory would-be specifications which, on a better understanding of that
or other rights, would be reversed or amended more or less extensively".[102] Of
this there can be no doubt. But this truth need not be understood to cast
a shadow so long and dark as to hide from view another truth: many legal
directives in community stand to the right they purport to enforce as true,
just, justified, genuine specifications of right relationships giving effect to the
subject matters of justice outlined in bills of rights. When the law does so, it
unites *droit* and *loi*, *derecho* and *ley*, *diritto* and *legge*, *Recht* and *Gesetz*, right
and law.

---

the legislator – the very same body that expresses that type of tyranny of the majority . . . [the
legislature is] permitted to act as it pleases." The argument defended in *The Negotiable Constitution* is that legislation, *when justified*, defines the open-ended rights in bills of rights. When
unjustified, it does not, which is not to deny that it is best read as having attempted to do so
justifiably.

[101] The distortions of proportionality reasoning are well documented in the contributions to this
volume by Timothy Endicott (Chapter 14), Richard Ekins (Chapter 15), and Bradley Miller
(Chapter 16).

[102] Finnis, "Introduction," *supra* note 98 at 3.

Now, there is no doubt that the specification of right relations between persons, because it draws on evaluations of what is just and justified according to time, place, person, circumstance, and community, is liable to change: the reasonable legislator must keep under ready evaluation every legal settlement of schemes of acts and arrangements that seek to give effect to the rights of each and all. This "dynamic" or "negotiable" quality of rights in no way undermines the promise of uniting right and law.[103] It is in this way that, albeit with many failings, law can achieve what morality cannot: the settlement, for this community, of determinate right relations between persons across the range of subject matters of relationships of justice.

VII. CONCLUSION

In uniting right and law, legislation may realize absolute rights. It is a defining feature of the received approach that no right is absolute,[104] but that understanding rests on an account of rights that divorces the definition of rights from what is just and justified. When the definition of ("subjective") rights is realigned with what is ("objectively") right, the claim that rights are absolute is within reach and not only for the rights that make regular claim to being absolute (such as the rights to be free from torture and rape). I will not here say enough about this claim to sustain it, but hope – by recalling some of the arguments charted in this chapter – to set the stage for a subsequent development of the claim.

Those arguments include: (a) the received approach reifies rights and regularly divorces rights from what is right; (b) when rights are united with what is right, they stand as conclusions of practical reasoning about what ought to be done; (c) rights, like justice, are relational and concern the domain of the interpersonal; (d) a conception of rights grounded in a theory of justice can be expected to provide for different duties and obligations than one grounded in a theory of defeasible interests; (e) some of those duties will be unchanging (e.g., the duty not to torture) and, so, will be correlative to unchanging rights;

---

[103] Both Raz, *The Morality of Freedom, supra* note 28 at 171 and Oberdiek, "Specifying Rights Out of Necessity," *supra* note 23 at 153, appeal to the "dynamic aspect of rights". The expression "negotiable" is similarly inspired and draws on the discussion in Webber, *Negotiable Constitution, supra* note 2 at 27–30.

[104] I do not mean to deny that judicial practice affirms that the injunctions against torture and rape are absolute, meaning "not subject to proportionality analysis". But that is the point: insofar as proportionality is a defining feature of the received approach and insofar as proportionality is excluded when it comes to absolute rights, so it is a defining feature of the received approach that no right is absolute.

(f) other duties will change as the circumstances of the community change and, so, will be correlative to changing rights. Now, if the thought that rights can be absolute and yet subject to change troubles some, consider this near equivalent way of putting the idea: justice is always to be done, but what justice in community requires will change as the community's circumstances and membership changes. In this way as with many others explored in this chapter, understanding rights in the frame of justice resists the loss of rights.

7   Proportionality and Rights Inflation

Kai Möller

Proportionality is the most important principle of constitutional rights law around the world, but our theoretical grasp of both the principle itself and the conception of rights of which it is the crucial part is still emerging. The goal of this chapter is to contribute to the scholarly discussion on proportionality by exposing and exploring an important link between proportionality and rights inflation; that is, the phenomenon that increasingly relatively trivial interests are protected as rights. My claim is that proportionality is not only compatible with rights inflation, but that it necessitates it: under a theory of rights that endorses proportionality, there is no coherent way to avoid the conclusion that all autonomy interests should be protected as rights, and this includes interests in engaging in trivial and even immoral activities. Although this intuitively implausible result may strengthen some in their doubts about or rejection of proportionality, this chapter will proceed by showing that even if my argument, if correct, necessitates the revision of some widely held views about the nature and justification of human and constitutional rights, there is nothing incoherent or unattractive about such a view. On the contrary, rights inflation and proportionality are part and parcel of an attractive conception of constitutional rights.

I. THE PRINCIPLE OF PROPORTIONALITY

Proportionality is a doctrinal tool used to establish whether an interference with a prima facie right is justified, and this justification succeeds if the interference is proportionate (or alternatively and probably more precisely, if it is not disproportionate). The test consists of four stages:[1] first, the interference must

[1] There exist slightly different versions of the test in different jurisdictions. For the purposes of this chapter, those differences do not matter as long as balancing features as part of the test. The

serve a legitimate goal; second, it must be suitable for the achievement of that goal (suitability, rational connection); third, there must not be a less restrictive but equally effective alternative (necessity); and fourth and most importantly, the interference must not be disproportionate to the achievement of the goal (balancing, proportionality in the strict sense).

The principle is best understood as providing guidance in the structured resolution of a *conflict* between a (prima facie) right and another right or a public interest. The legitimate goal stage identifies the conflicting value. The suitability stage determines the extent to which there is a genuine conflict between the two in the sense that one can only be realized at the cost of the other: when a policy which interferes with a right does not contribute to the achievement of the legitimate goal, then there is no conflict between the right and the goal. The necessity stage requires that the conflict be resolved in a way that is as respectful of the right as possible; thus, the less restrictive but equally effective alternative must be chosen. Although the suitability and necessity stages are important for the overall test, in most cases the decisive stage is the balancing stage where the two values are balanced against each other. The challenge that proportionality in general and balancing in particular present to traditional philosophical theories of rights is that they do not recognize any *special normative force* of rights, for example by regarding them as trumps or side constraints.[2] Rather, rights operate on the same plane as (conflicting) policy considerations, and it is precisely for this reason that it is appropriate to balance them against conflicting public interests. Robert Alexy's influential theory of rights as principles (which have to be balanced against competing principles) captures this feature of contemporary rights jurisprudence nicely.[3]

Canadian understanding often tries to avoid explicit reliance on balancing and resolves at the least restrictive means stage issues that, in other jurisdictions, are considered at the balancing stage. Denise Réaume criticizes this, arguing that "this question [the question of which of the values is more important], which has so often been disguised and hidden elsewhere in the steps of the *Oakes* test, or simply not been addressed, properly belongs at the end of the process, with the other steps serving simply to disqualify bad justificatory arguments and refine the ultimate contest." See Denise Réaume, "Limitations on Constitutional Rights: The Logic of Proportionality," (2009) *University of Oxford Legal Research Paper Series*, Paper No. 26/2009 at 26. Dieter Grimm makes essentially the same point in his "Proportionality in Canadian and German Constitutional Jurisprudence," (2007) 57 *U.T.L.J.* 383.

[2]   On rights as trumps, see inter alia Ronald Dworkin, "Rights as Trumps" in Jeremy Waldron (ed.), *Theories of Rights* (1984); on rights as side constraints, see Robert Nozick, *Anarchy, State, and Utopia* (1974), ch 3.

[3]   Robert Alexy, *A Theory of Constitutional Rights* (2002).

II. CONSTITUTIONAL RIGHTS AND THE TREND TOWARD RIGHTS INFLATION

Constitutional rights protect autonomy interests such as a person's interests in life and physical integrity, freedom of expression, private life, or freedom of religion. I refer to these interests as autonomy interests in order to stress that what is protected by constitutional rights is not an entitlement to live one's life in accordance with some objectively valuable way of life, but rather to live it in accordance with the agent's (subjective) self-conception: the agent is prima facie entitled to live his life in accordance with his views on who he is and who he would like to be, for the determination of which considerations relating to his personal history and circumstances and his position within his social environment will be crucial.[4] This understanding of the freedom protected by constitutional rights helps explain the set of traditionally acknowledged rights, such as the right to freedom of religion (religion is often an important part of a person's self-conception), private life (which is partly about protecting certain important choices, for example relating to sexual relationships and procreation), freedom of expression, and others.[5] Furthermore, it explains those rights that are not about activities, but about what one might call a person's resources, such as his life, property, and personal data: autonomy is not, under the conception endorsed here, primarily about actions; rather, it is about being able to live one's life, and the protection of life, property, and personal data is, for different reasons, important for this.[6]

The interests and rights mentioned in the previous paragraph have in common that they are all relatively important for the purpose of living one's life. What about interests in engaging in activities that are of less importance? Especially in Europe, the protection offered by constitutional rights extends to relatively trivial interests. The European Court of Human Rights routinely reads such interests into the right to private life (Article 8 of the European Convention on Human Rights). For example, in the famous *Hatton* case concerning a policy scheme that permitted night flights at Heathrow airport, thus leading to noise pollution that disturbed the sleep of some of the residents living in the area, the Court discovered as part of Article 8 the right not to be "directly and seriously affected by noise or other pollution",[7] dismissively

---

[4] I develop this point in greater length in my "Two Conceptions of Positive Liberty: Towards an Autonomy-based Theory of Constitutional Rights," (2009) 29 O.J.L.S. 757 at 772–776.

[5] Ibid. at 776–783.   [6] Ibid.

[7] *Hatton v. United Kingdom*, (2003) 37 E.H.R.R. 28 at para. 96.

dubbed "the right to sleep well" by George Letsas.[8] The broad understanding the Court takes toward the right to private life becomes clear in one of its more recent attempts to circumscribe it:

> The Court recalls that the concept of "private life" is a broad term not susceptible to exhaustive definition. It covers the physical and psychological integrity of a person. It can therefore embrace multiple aspects of the person's physical and social identity. Elements such as, for example, gender identification, name and sexual orientation and sexual life fall within the personal sphere protected by Article 8. Beyond a person's name, his or her private and family life may include other means of personal identification and of linking to a family. Information about the person's health is an important element of private life. The Court furthermore considers that an individual's ethnic identity must be regarded as another such element. Article 8 protects in addition a right to personal development, and the right to establish and develop relationships with other human beings and the outside world. The concept of private life moreover includes elements relating to a person's right to their image.[9]

Thus, the Court has considered the storing of fingerprints and DNA samples by the state[10] and the publication of photographs of a person in her daily life by a magazine[11] as falling within the scope of "private life". Article 8 also protects a right of access to the information relating to a person's birth and her origin.[12] With regard to sexual autonomy, the Court held not only that consensual homosexual sex was part of private life,[13] but also that homosexual sadomasochistic group sex orgies involving considerable violence were included within the scope of Article 8.[14]

Although the European Court of Human Rights has not provided a comprehensive definition of the meaning of "private life", it requires that the interest in question be part of "private life", whatever that term exactly means; thus, the Court will not accept *any* interest as falling within the scope of Article 8. In other words, there is a threshold to be crossed for an interest to become

[8] George Letsas, *A Theory of Interpretation of the European Convention on Human Rights* (2007) at 126.
[9] *S v. United Kingdom*, (2009) 48 E.H.R.R. 50 at para. 66 (references omitted).
[10] Ibid. at para. 67.
[11] *Von Hannover v. Germany*, (2005) 40 E.H.R.R. 1 at para. 53.
[12] *Odievre v. France*, (2004) 38 E.H.R.R. 43 at para. 29.
[13] *Dudgeon v. United Kingdom*, (1982) 4 E.H.R.R. 149 at paras. 40–41.
[14] *Laskey, Jaggard and Brown v. United Kingdom*, (1997) 24 E.H.R.R. 39 at para. 36. The Court left the question open whether the activities in question fell within the scope of Article 8 in their entirety, but proceeded on the assumption that they did.

a right. By way of contrast, the German Federal Constitutional Court has explicitly given up any threshold requirement to distinguish a mere interest from a constitutional right. As early as 1957, it held that Article 2(1) of the Basic Law, which protects everyone's right to freely develop his or her personality, is to be interpreted as a right to freedom of action.[15] The Court provided various doctrinal reasons for this result, its main argument being that an earlier draft of Article 2(1) had read "Everyone can do as he pleases" (*"Jeder kann tun und lassen was er will"*), and that this version had been dropped only for linguistic reasons.[16] The Court reaffirmed this ruling in various later decisions; most famously, it declared that Article 2(1) included the right to feed pigeons in a park[17] and the right to go riding in the woods.[18]

The explanation of this trend toward rights inflation must be found either in the unwillingness or inability of the courts to identify a threshold that separates important interests that attract the protection of human or constitutional rights from those that are relatively trivial. The following section will examine the issue of the threshold by identifying a link between the appropriate scope of prima facie rights and the principle of proportionality.

III. THE RELATIONSHIP BETWEEN PROPORTIONALITY AND RIGHTS INFLATION

The argument of this section is that there is a connection between proportionality and rights inflation. It is widely accepted that proportionality analysis is *compatible* with rights inflation: for example, it is perfectly possible to accept, as the German Federal Constitutional Court does, a right to feed birds, and then to apply proportionality analysis in order to establish whether an interference with this right is justifiable. My argument in this chapter goes further than this: I claim that proportionality is not only compatible with rights inflation, but that it *necessitates* it. Proportionality and rights inflation are two sides of the same coin, or two features of the same conception of rights.

The Inevitability of Rights Inflation

One of the features of proportionality analysis in general and its balancing stage in particular is that rights are not seen as different in structure from mere interests or policy considerations: this is why they can and must be balanced against them, as opposed to being awarded some special normative force

---

[15] BVerfGE 6 at 32 (*Elfes*).
[16] Ibid. at 36–37.
[17] BVerfGE 54 at 143 (*Pigeon-Feeding*).
[18] BVerfGE 80 at 137 (*Riding in the Woods*).

(for example, as trumps or side constraints on action), making them wholly or partly immune to trade-offs.[19] This section will demonstrate that if rights do not hold special normative force, then any attempt to limit their scope would be arbitrary; thus, coherence requires that rights inflation be embraced.

What would be wrong with accepting that, although rights do not hold special normative force, the scope of rights should be limited to certain important interests? Consider the example of hobbies: collecting stamps, playing tennis, or riding in the woods. Although these hobbies may be reasonably important activities for the people engaging in them, they do not display crucial life decisions such as whether to procreate, whom to choose as a partner, or which profession to take up. Would it not be possible to say that although hobbies have some importance for autonomy, this importance is simply not great enough to attract the protection of constitutional rights? The idea would be to introduce a *threshold of importance*, and only autonomy interests that reach a certain level of importance would be protected as constitutional rights. If protected, any limitation of those rights would be permissible only if proportionate; in turn, an autonomy interest that did not reach the threshold would not be protected and could therefore be limited unrestrictedly. This model, the *threshold model*, can be contrasted with the *comprehensive model*, according to which any autonomy interest, however trivial, is sufficient to attract the protection of constitutional rights.

An autonomy-based conception of constitutional rights must favor the comprehensive model for two reasons. First, under the logic of an autonomy-based approach, the relevant question must be whether the interest in question has some, however small, importance: as long as it has *some* importance, as is certainly the case with the pursuit of hobbies, *something would be lost* for autonomy if it were not protected at all. This leads to the second point: the threshold model would have to draw a line somewhere, stipulating that anything below that line falls foul of the necessary threshold and is therefore not protected. However, it is hard to see how such a threshold could be set in a non-arbitrary way. Would the interest have to be of reasonable, average, high, or fundamental importance? What should be the criteria here? The consequence of accepting a threshold at any specific level of importance would be that an interest that is just below the threshold receives no protection whatsoever, whereas an interest that is just above the threshold can only be interfered with in a proportionate manner. This difference in protection cannot be justified if all that separates the two interests is a tiny margin of importance; it is simply incoherent to attach such morally significant consequences to such a small difference in importance. To be sure, we might just draw the line somewhere in a pragmatic way and declare that from now on, only interests that are at least, say, "very" important are protected. But the defining feature of pragmatic approaches to moral questions is the absence of principle, and we are looking for a principled approach to limit the domain of constitutional rights; therefore, a pragmatic solution is not acceptable.

To this conclusion, one might object that it is simplistic to assume that the threshold must be set at some level of importance, such as "reasonable" or "high" importance. Perhaps the threshold points to a qualitative difference? The most promising attempt in this direction has been made by James Griffin in his book *On Human Rights*, and his discussion is of particular interest in the present context because Griffin's conception of human rights relies heavily on the value of personal autonomy (albeit under a slightly different terminology). He argues that the threshold can be derived from the idea of personhood:

> Human life is different from the life of other animals. We human beings have a conception of ourselves and of our past and future. We reflect and assess. We form pictures of what a good life would be . . . And we try to realise these pictures. This is what we mean by a distinctively *human* existence . . . And we value our status as human beings especially highly, often more highly than even our happiness. This status centres on our being agents – deliberating, assessing, choosing, and acting to make what we see as a good life for ourselves.

> Human rights can then be seen as protections of our human standing or, as I shall put it, our personhood. And one can break down the notion of personhood into clearer components by breaking down the notion of agency. To be an agent, in the fullest sense of which we are capable, one must (first) choose one's own path through life – that is, not be dominated or controlled by someone or something else (call it "autonomy"). . . . [And] (third) others must not forcibly stop one from pursuing what one sees as a worthwhile life (call this "liberty").[20]

Griffin tells us more about how demanding the right to liberty is:

> [L]iberty applies to the final stage of agency, namely to the pursuit of one's conception of a worthwhile life. By no means everything we aim at matters to that. Therefore, society will accept a person's claim to the protection of

---

[20] James Griffin, *On Human Rights* (2008) at 32–33 (hereinafter Griffin, *Human Rights*). Griffin's second point, omitted in the quote, is about "minimum provision" of resources and capabilities that it takes to be an agent.

liberty only if the claim meets the material constraint that what is at stake is indeed conceivable as mattering to whether or not we function as normative agents.[21]

Griffin's idea is that "personhood" functions both as the basis of human rights and a limitation on their scope: only those interests that are important for personhood are protected as human rights. So we might argue that constitutional rights ought to protect only interests that are important for personhood, and that constitutional rights protecting personhood can then only be limited when this limitation is proportionate. In light of the importance of the value of personhood, limitations of rights will normally be disproportionate at least when they are pursued for the protection of values that are not grounded in personhood. On this account, we might endorse proportionality and reject rights inflation.

However, this account does not work. Its failure is that the personhood approach does not offer a coherent way to delineate interests relevant for personhood from other interests. For Griffin, personhood requires autonomy and liberty (in my terminology, personal autonomy); basically, control over one's life. But it requires only that kind of control over one's life that is required by the value of personhood. This leaves open the question of what the test is for determining whether some instance of liberty (autonomy) is required for personhood. My suspicion is that it is simply "importance". For example, Griffin explains that "the domain of liberty is limited to what is *major enough* to count as part of the pursuit of a worthwhile life".[22] At another point, he defends a human right to gay marriage on the ground "of its *centrality* to characteristic human conceptions of a worthwhile life".[23] Thus, it seems that the threshold of personhood simply refers back to a sliding scale of importance; an interest that is "major enough" or "central" will acquire the status of a human right. But such a sliding scale cannot, as explained above, do the moral work. The threshold would have to be between "not quite major enough" and "barely major enough" or "not quite central" and "barely central". But then, under Griffin's model, all that separates an interest that is just below from one that is just above the threshold is a small difference in terms of importance or centrality, and this small difference cannot justify the great normative significance that for proponents of threshold models comes with one of them being a simple interest and the other a human right. I believe that this is a general problem of threshold theories that is not limited to Griffin's

[21] Ibid. at 167.
[22] Ibid. at 234 (emphasis added).
[23] Ibid. at 163 (emphasis added).

account.[24] If that is true, then the only possible conclusion is that the threshold requirement should be dropped and it should be acknowledged that the scope of freedom protected by rights must extend to *everything that is in the interest of a person's autonomy.*

This conclusion sits well with the practice of constitutional rights law and its trend toward rights inflation; and herein lies a further indicator of its correctness. Someone might object that although such a trend exists, it would still be an overstatement to say that constitutional rights law generally protects *all* autonomy interests as rights. This is true insofar as the German account of freedom of action as including the rights to go riding in the woods and feed pigeons in the park remains an outlier in constitutional rights law around the world. But it must be acknowledged that once we agree that the point of constitutional rights is to enable people to follow their projects, the inclusion of hobbies loses any flavor of absurdity. In fact, on this understanding, the only difference between the German approach and other, less generous approaches is that the German approach sets the threshold lower, or even sets aside any threshold, whereas other jurisdictions continue to follow a threshold model. But the most likely explanation for this threshold lies not in a morally different conception of rights, but in a simple institutional consideration, namely a sense that constitutional courts should, because of their limited resources, only deal with matters of a certain importance. This presents only a minor variation in the scope of rights adopted in different jurisdictions and leaves intact their moral core as being about protected autonomy interests comprehensively understood.

The Inclusion of "Evil Activities"

The question whether both liberty and rights, properly understood, include immoral or even "evil"[25] activities such as murdering is a recurrent one in political theory.[26] The dispute is not about whether such activities can be prohibited – of course they can; in fact, taking into account the widely acknowledged doctrine of positive obligations, they usually must be prohibited.

---

[24] For a similar view, *cf.* Joseph Raz, "Human Rights without Foundations" in Samantha Besson and John Tasioulas (eds.), *The Philosophy of International Law* (2010) at 326 (hereinafter Raz, "Human Rights").

[25] The point of labeling the activities in question somewhat vaguely as "evil" is to indicate that they are the sorts of activities that, because of their extremely harmful and immoral nature, nobody can possibly have a *definite* right to engage in.

[26] See Isaiah Berlin, "Two Concepts of Liberty" in *Liberty* (2002) 166 at 169; Ronald Dworkin, *Justice in Robes* (2006) at 112.

Proponents of a wide understanding of rights include murdering at the prima facie stage, but there is no doubt that there are reasons of sufficient weight (in particular, the rights of the possible victims) in favor of a prohibition, which are to be taken into account at the justification stage. In fact, proportionality seems to be ideally suited to conduct this inquiry, an approach that acknowledges, first, that there is a right to murder and then, at the justification stage, deals with the permissible limitations of this right, addresses all morally relevant considerations, and reaches the right conclusion. So what is the problem with a right to murder?

I believe that many will be hesitant about accepting that there is a genuine (autonomy) interest in engaging in immoral or evil activities. One might argue that a person can only have an interest in an activity if that activity carries some value, and that, because in the case of murdering there is no such value, no interest in murdering should be acknowledged. Consequently, a prohibition of murder does not engage a person's interests, properly understood, and is therefore not in need of justification.

However, we must be careful not to confuse two distinct issues. It does not follow from the fact that murdering is worthless that we ought to deny the existence of an autonomy interest in murdering. If that logic were correct, then a person could not possibly have interests, protected by rights, in engaging in worthless activities, and that seems wrong. An attractive understanding of the freedom protected by constitutional rights cannot protect only those exercises of freedom that are valuable. Rather, a commitment to personal freedom includes a commitment to moral agency, and this means that it must in principle be left to the agent to decide for himself whether a particular activity is morally valuable. For example, in the old debates about the decriminalization of homosexual sex, one of the two important arguments was that the question whether homosexual sex is valuable is not the business of the state; rather, it is for each agent to decide this for himself. (The second argument is that there is nothing morally wrong with homosexuality or homosexual sex, but this is an independent point and even if it were not true, homosexual sex should be protected by rights.) But this point can be generalized, and it can be concluded that judging the value of an agent's project is not the business of the state. Thus, the question cannot be whether it is objectively the case that murdering (or any other activity) is valuable or not, but the crucial question must be whether the activity is valuable *from the perspective of the agent*. If it is, then the agent has an autonomy interest in the activity that must be protected by a right.

This of course does not mean that "anything goes": if someone chooses murdering as his project, he should be punished because he violates the rights of others. But he should not be punished on the ground that he has chosen a worthless project. The same point is captured by Ronald Dworkin's distinction between ethics and morality: ethical questions are about how to live a good life, whereas moral questions concern the duties we owe to each other.[27] The prima facie stage of rights is solely concerned with ethics in the Dworkinian sense: the murderer, as a moral agent, is entitled to decide for himself whether murdering promotes or ruins the value of his life. In a community committed to personal freedom, judging the value of his projects is the agent's responsibility and not that of the state.

Under a proportionality-based approach to rights, there must be a right to engage in evil activities; this can be explained in the following way. There are two possible reasons why the state might want to prohibit such activities. The first is their ethical worthlessness; but as explained above, judging ethical value is not the rightful concern of the state. The second is their immorality. This issue is indeed the concern of the state, but under proportionality, it is addressed at the justification stage, where the rights of others and relevant public interests are considered, and those rights reflect precisely the domain of morality in the Dworkinian sense. Adding a morality filter for evil activities at the prima facie stage would lead to conducting the same inquiry at two different stages of the test and would thus point to incoherence and structural confusion.

IV. IMPLICATIONS FOR A PROPORTIONALITY-BASED THEORY OF RIGHTS

The conclusion of the previous section may embolden some in their skepticism about proportionality-based judicial review. It is certainly true that, intuitively, many will find the phenomenon of rights inflation troubling and would prefer to see it limited rather than comprehensively embraced; and things seem to get even worse when immoral and evil activities are regarded as falling within the scope of rights. My argument in this section will not be that because of those arguably counterintuitive conclusions, proportionality-based judicial review should be abandoned or modified. On the contrary, I will argue that both proportionality and rights inflation are part of an attractive conception of rights. To grasp its appeal, one must dispense with some traditionally held views about human and constitutional rights.

Why do many perceive rights inflation as a troubling development? Rights inflation calls into question two related and deeply held views about human

[27] Ronald Dworkin, *Is Democracy Possible Here? Principles for a New Political Debate* (2006) at 21.

and constitutional rights: (1) that they protect only interests of a *special importance*, and (2) that it is this special importance that lends rights their *special
normative force*. Rights inflation denies both premises: rights do not have a
special importance, and precisely because of the lack of special importance
they do not have special normative force. Proportionality affirms this because
proportionality, just like rights inflation, denies the special normative force of
rights, and as shown in the previous section, properly understood, it must also
deny their special importance.

Thus, the conception of rights that rights inflation and proportionality are
features of challenges some views about rights that many are strongly committed to. Is it possible to preserve a special role for rights while denying that
they have special importance and special normative force? I want to propose
the following account of the point and purpose of human and constitutional
rights. Human rights are commonly referred to as the rights to which a person
is entitled simply by virtue of his or her humanity. Most would agree that the
best interpretation of this very abstract idea has something to do with personal
autonomy (Griffin would say, autonomy and liberty). But it does not follow
that we should think about the point of autonomy as being provided with
certain goods (in particular, freedoms), such as the freedoms to speak one's
mind, choose one's partner, and follow one's religion. Under proportionality-
based judicial review, the main entitlement that a human being has simply
by virtue of being human *and* with regard to how she lives her life is being
treated with a certain *attitude*: an attitude that *takes her seriously as a person
with a life to live*, and that will therefore deny her the ability to live her life in
a certain way only when there are *sufficiently strong reasons* for this. Applied
to the case of hobbies such as feeding the birds, this means that we should not
ask whether the freedom to feed birds is indispensable for making a person
a person. Rather, we should ask whether the state treats a person subject to
its authority in a way that is in line with that person's status flowing from her
humanity when the state prohibits, for example, her participation in the activity
of feeding birds; and this will be the case only when there are sufficiently strong
reasons supporting the prohibition. Thus, the point of rights is not to single
out certain especially important interests for heightened protection. Rather,
it is to show a particular form of respect for persons by insisting that each
and every state measure that affects a person's ability to live her life according to her self-conception must take her autonomy interests adequately into
account.

Rights inflation and proportionality are the two crucial features of a conception of rights that embodies this basic idea. Rights inflation is required
because showing the right attitude toward a person requires taking all of his

projects seriously, including those of trivial importance and even immoral or evil ones. Proportionality is required because, properly understood, it assesses precisely the question of whether a person's autonomy interests have been adequately taken into account by the policy that interferes with his autonomy. For this to be the case, (1) the policy must pursue a legitimate goal; (2) it must be a suitable means of achieving that goal; (3) there must not exist a less restrictive but equally effective alternative means; and (4) it must not impose a disproportionate burden on the right-holder. Where one of these conditions is not met, the reasons for the limitation are not sufficiently strong; where all four conditions are met, they are and the policy is therefore constitutionally legitimate.[28] This approach makes sense of the powerful idea of "simply in virtue of being human" without taking the misguided step from that idea to an entitlement to certain especially important freedoms.

Furthermore, this approach helps to rebut an objection that might be raised against a conception of rights that endorses rights inflation, namely that it succumbs to a conceptual confusion by acknowledging the existence of a right without giving an account of its corresponding duties. One might argue that something does not become a right simply by virtue of the fact that it is important for my autonomy. For example, if it is the case that I enjoy feeding birds in my local park, it may follow that I have an autonomy interest in feeding the birds, but it may be an entirely different question of whether I do indeed have a *right* to feed the birds. Consider Raz's famous account of rights: "*Definition*: 'X has a right' if and only if X can have rights, and, other things being equal, an aspect of X's well-being (his interest) is a sufficient reason for holding some other person(s) to be under a duty".[29] This is sometimes taken to mean that all one needs for a right to come into existence is an interest; but this is a misunderstanding. Rather, it must be the kind of interest that grounds duties in others. Thus, as Raz explains elsewhere, just because the love of my children is the most important thing to me, it does not follow that I have a right to it.[30] To get back to the example of feeding birds, just by virtue of the fact that feeding the birds is of some importance to me, it does not follow that I have a right to it unless this interest can be shown to ground a duty of noninterference in the state.

[28] *Cf.* Mattias Kumm, "The Idea of Socratic Contestation and the Right to Justification: The Point of Rights-Based Proportionality Review," (2010) 4 *Law & Ethics of Human Rights* 141 at 144: "[The proportionality test] provides little more than a check-list of individually necessary and collectively sufficient criteria that need to be met for behaviour by public authorities to be justified in terms of reasons that are appropriate in a liberal democracy. In that sense it provides a structure for the assessment of public reasons."
[29] Raz, *The Morality of Freedom* (1986) at 166.　[30] Raz, "Human Rights," *supra* note 24 at 325.

The straightforward solution to this problem lies in the distinction between prima facie rights and definite rights. A definite right to engage in a particular activity indeed grounds a duty of non-interference on the side of the state. The prima facie right, by way of contrast, grounds a different duty: the duty of the state to take the respective autonomy interest adequately into account. For example, the prima facie right to feed birds grounds the state's duty to take the autonomy interest in bird feeding adequately into account in its policy making; this means that feeding birds can only be regulated or prohibited if there exist sufficiently strong reasons for such interference (for example, the prevention of pollution) that are such that they justify the prohibition or regulation in spite of the fact that thereby the would-be bird feeder is denied the pursuit of this activity. This understanding of rights and their corresponding duties resolves the conceptual puzzle and explains why it is indeed coherent to accept a right to everything that is in the interest of a person's autonomy.

V. WEBBER'S CRITIQUE

In his contribution to this volume (Chapter 6), Grégoire Webber objects to splitting up reasoning with rights into the prima facie stage, which is concerned with the question of whether there has been an interference with the right, and the justification stage, where the justification of the interference is examined.[31] He believes that invoking the concept of a right for something to which a person has no definite but only an (often quite weak) prima facie entitlement is inappropriate because the prima facie right does not exhibit what for him is a crucial component of the concept of a right, namely its connection with justice. Webber's objection is not to the substance of my theory of rights (it is rather best understood as accusing me of semantic sloppiness), and therefore it is possible to reformulate my approach in a terminology to which Webber would not object. This will enable me to assess whether that terminology is superior to the one that, following an emerging global practice, I have adopted in this contribution as well as in previous work.

We could abandon the language of, for example, "the right to freedom of expression" and "the right to life" because, as Webber argues, those "rights" cannot really be rights, given that they are not absolute: the "right" to freedom of expression can be limited, for example in the case of hate speech; and the right to life can be limited, for example, in the case of self-defense. Under the approach advocated above, I can easily fix this assumed problem by

---

[31] Grégoire Webber, "On the Loss of Rights," Chapter 6 in this volume.

distinguishing sharply between the prima facie right and the definite right, and using the term "right" only for the latter. The definite right that every person has is the right to have his or her autonomy interests adequately taken into account. Thus, Webber would have no objection if instead of a "right to life" I spoke of a "right to have one's autonomy interest in life adequately taken into account", or instead of a "right to freedom of expression" I spoke of a "right to have one's autonomy interest in freedom of expression adequately taken into account". Alternatively, one could speak, following Kumm, of a "right to a justification in the case of a limitation of a person's life, expression, . . . ", and so on. Webber would not even object to applying this approach to the right to feed birds or the right to murder: properly understood, we would have to speak of a "right to have one's autonomy interest in bird feeding / murder adequately taken into account", or, alternatively, a "right to a justification of the prohibition of bird feeding / murder". At the level of an accurate use of the concept of a right, there is nothing suspicious about this; or in any case, to the extent to which it may still be problematic, it is not Webber's concern in his contribution to this volume.

Thus, achieving the conceptual precision and accuracy Webber insists on is possible, but it comes at a cost: any talk of rights would become semantically awkward and complicated. For example, when designing a new constitution or human rights treaty, or when discussing issues of rights with fellow citizens, we would have to give up including or referring to the right to freedom of religion, property, and all other commonly acknowledged rights, except of course those that even under the global model are absolute (such as the rights to freedom from torture and inhuman and degrading treatment and freedom from slavery). Instead, to avoid the semantic sloppiness that is at the heart of Webber's concern, we could only use the longer and more awkward formulations that I have proposed above.

I am not convinced that this change would be worthwhile. Judges, academics, lawyers, politicians, and ordinary citizens around the world have come to use the phrase "A has a right to X" (where X could represent, for example, life, freedom of expression, freedom of religion, privacy, property, health care, housing, and so forth) in a way that, as I argue, is best reconstructed as invoking not a definite entitlement to X, but rather a prima facie claim that, when interfered with, requires a justification that shows that A's (autonomy) interests in X have been adequately taken into account. On purely pragmatic grounds, I would object to Webber's proposed change of the usage of the term "right" because, first, the transactional costs of changing a globally dominant semantic practice would be very high; and, second and more importantly, because I find Webber's alternative – to replace the language of a right to life, freedom of expression, and so forth with a right to have one's interest in life/expression/and so forth adequately taken into account – semantically impossibly awkward.

Those pragmatic considerations are sufficient to reject Webber's proposal even on the assumption that he is right in his diagnosis that the world has come to use the word "right" in a conceptually mistaken way. But there is also reason to doubt the correctness of Webber's diagnosis, because it is based on the misguided assumption that the concept of a right has a meaning that is fixed independently of the particular conception of political morality within which it has a role to play. Thus, he insists that to say "A has a right to X" necessarily implies that "it is just that A enjoy X". The reason for this, for Webber, is that as a matter of history of ideas, there is an intimate connection between rights and justice. But if for the sake of the argument I grant that this connection is as intimate as Webber claims it is, that still leaves open the possibility that we may have made progress in our understanding of the concept of a right, much in the same way in which we have made or are in the process of making progress with our understanding of other concepts, such as the concept of marriage (as being also available to same-sex couples). Under the new, refined understanding of rights, there continues to be a connection between definite rights and justice (although I think this connection is less straightforward than Webber assumes, but that is not the topic here); and there is also a connection between prima facie rights and justice, but it operates in a different way, namely via the duty of justification – which is itself a requirement of justice – that is triggered by an interference with the prima facie right. Therefore, I see no reason to insist that as a matter of semantics or conceptual necessity the phrase "right to X" must refer only to a definite entitlement to X and cannot possibly refer to an entitlement to have X adequately taken into account. Of course, whether it is indeed attractive to use the word "right" in the way that is now globally dominant is a different question and will depend on whether this usage illuminates the structure of the moral-political issues at stake. But this is a substantive question that is not Webber's concern in his contribution to this volume.

Webber has a valid point, however, that followers of what he labels "the received approach" use the word "right" sometimes with regard to the prima facie right and sometimes with regard to the definite right. He is certainly right to insist that any usage of the word "right" should be consistent. But again, I doubt that the stakes are high: once one understands that we have to distinguish between prima facie and definite rights, it is in almost all cases entirely clear which of the two we are referring to; thus, the potential for a good faith misunderstanding is very low. Webber quotes me as arguing that "proportionality is simply a structure that guides judges through the reasoning process as to whether a policy does or does not respect rights", and takes this as an example of the confusion that may be caused by invoking the concept of a right without making it clear whether one means the prima facie or the definite right. But I doubt that anyone familiar with contemporary human rights discourse would take my statement to mean that proportionality is about determining whether a law *interferes with* (prima facie) rights; rather, it is obvious that proportionality is a tool used to determine whether a policy *violates* (definite) rights. The reason I did not specify in the above statement whether it is about prima facie or definite rights is precisely that I considered there to be no potential for misunderstanding. I do not deny the possibility of there being instances in my writing or the writings of other authors where it would have been prudent to add "prima facie" or "definite" to the word "right"; and to the extent that this is so, all of us should pay greater attention to avoid misunderstandings in the future. Furthermore, I accept that ordinary citizens without legal training could occasionally get confused about rights; for example, a would-be bird feeder could respond to the prohibition of bird feeding in her local park by exclaiming, "But I have a *right* to feed the birds here!" and a racist could respond to the banning of hate speech by insisting, "But I have a *right* to freedom of expression!". Thus, the general point is that people could mistakenly confuse their prima facie rights with their definite rights. But again, although I accept that this is a problem, Webber's alternative, which involves the flat denial of the existence of, for example, a right to freedom of expression (because of its lack of absoluteness) would have far more confusing and misleading consequences.

In sum, I do not believe that Webber's strategy of attacking what he calls the received approach and what I have called the global model of constitutional rights on the grounds of its using language in a conceptually inaccurate way is promising. I could, for the sake of the argument, reformulate my approach in a language to which he would not object; but that reformulation would make any discussion of rights semantically impossibly awkward and complicated. As I mentioned in the introduction to this chapter, scholars are only beginning to develop theories of the global model, including its moral defensibility, and a lot of work remains to be done. The most promising engagement with the global model, however, will be one that focuses squarely on its moral attractiveness. Thus, it is of course possible that my argument in this chapter is wrong as a matter of substance, that both rights inflation and proportionality ought to be rejected, and that there exists no general right to have one's autonomy interests adequately taken into account. But those points would have to be argued as a matter of substantive engagement with my or others' theories, not as a matter of the conceptually accurate use of language.

VI. CONCLUSION

Although the principle of proportionality is widely endorsed in human rights law today, the phenomenon of rights inflation is often viewed with suspicion, as something that ought to be controlled and pushed back rather than embraced. This chapter has argued that the two belong together: we cannot coherently endorse proportionality and reject rights inflation. Rather, endorsing proportionality implies acknowledging a right to feed birds and even a right to murder. But far from concluding that this result shows the absurd consequences of a misguided doctrine, this chapter has defended the conception of constitutional rights that emerges from the endorsement of rights inflation and proportionality; its point is to show a specific kind of respect for persons that requires that every person's autonomy interests are adequately taken into account at all times. To implement this basic idea in a theory of rights, one must accept, first, a comprehensive (prima facie) right to autonomy whose function it is to ensure that every policy that affects a person's ability to live his life according to his self-conception will interfere with a right and therefore trigger the duty of justification. Second, proportionality analysis must be employed at the justification stage in order to assess whether a policy pays adequate respect to the right-holder's autonomy interests. Thus, rights inflation and proportionality belong together as two building blocks of a globally successful and theoretically attractive conception of rights.

8 Proportionality and the Question of Weight

Frederick Schauer

I.

William Blackstone famously observed that it is "better that ten guilty persons escape, than that one innocent suffer."[1] The basic idea has an even more ancient, and possibly Biblical, lineage,[2] but more important is the fact that the numerical values inserted into the basic idea have varied considerably, including, for example, Benjamin Franklin's 100,[3] Thomas Starkie's 99,[4] and, earlier, Sir John Fortescue's 20.[5]

The choice among 10, 20, 99, and 100 is far from inconsequential. These varying numerical ratios express, with undoubtedly more precision than can be defended, the relative tolerance for the mistakes of acquitting the guilty and those of convicting the innocent. And thus the varying ratios used by different commentators reflect the relative value that they or a society might place on personal liberty compared to the value that they or the society place on security, retribution, deterrence, or any of the other goals that are served by convicting the guilty.

Once we recognize that the value of liberty can vary across societies and commentators and legal regimes, from something less than infinity (were the value of liberty infinite we would not attempt to convict even the guilty, given the inevitable errors that any decision-making process will produce) to

---

[1] William Blackstone, *Commentaries on the Laws of England*, vol. 1, p. 352 (1768).
[2] See Alexander Volokh, "Guilty Men," 146 *U. Penn. L. Rev.* 146 at 173 (1997).
[3] Benjamin Franklin, Letter to Benjamin Vaughan, March 14, 1785, in John Bigelow, ed., *The Works of Benjamin Franklin* (1904), vol. 11, 11 at 13.
[4] Thomas Starkie, *A Practical Treatise on the Law of Evidence, and Digest of Proofs, in Civil and Criminal Proceedings* (1824) at 751.
[5] Sir John Fortescue, *De Laudibus Legum Angliae*, John Selden trans. (1775) ch. 27.

something more than one,[6] we can understand how it might be useful to be able to specify that ratio. Indeed, to put it more strongly, some designation, even if not a precise numerical specification, of the ratio between the errors of false conviction and those of mistaken acquittal is implicit in valuing liberty as a right and not just another value or interest. And thus, attempting to specify the ratio in numerical terms is a way of recognizing just how strong the right is. Franklin's 100-to-1 ratio embodies a stronger value for the right to liberty than does Blackstone's 10 to 1, and recognizing this comparative strength shows that even the rights that operate as side constraints on welfare maximization can vary in their degree of stringency. Ronald Dworkin has provided us with the possibly useful metaphor of rights as trumps,[7] but in life and in law, and indeed as in bridge, some trumps are stronger than others.

II.

Recognition of the way in which rights vary in strength is a useful window into the increasingly ubiquitous topic of proportionality in rights adjudication. And I say "rights adjudication" rather than "constitutional adjudication" or "judicial decision making" for an important reason. Although it is commonplace to equate proportionality adjudication with balancing,[8] doing so creates a false equivalence. Consider first the policy process by which policy-makers weigh competing but non-rights-protected goals.[9] If we raise the speed limit, traffic deaths and injuries and property damage will increase. But so, too, in the normal course of things, will personal and business efficiency. We would certainly have fewer deaths were the speed limit on interstate highways (in the United States) to be set at forty miles per hour, but doing so would impose a cost in terms of efficiency that people appear generally unwilling to pay. But

---

[6] The value of liberty could of course be one, or less than one, but I say "more than one" to preserve the idea that liberty is a right, and that implicit in the very idea of a right is that, at the margin, a certain amount of deprivation of liberty is, loosely put, more harmful than the same amount of loss of security. Expressing the nature of a right in this way assumes a rough commensurability, but I presuppose, without much argument here, that we can compare different kinds of errors (or gains) even when we cannot reduce them to exactly the same units on exactly the same scale. That I would be willing to lose my little toe in exchange for $10 million (which I would) is, more or less, the kind of crude comparability that I presuppose here.

[7] Ronald Dworkin, *Taking Rights Seriously* (1977) at 157; Ronald Dworkin, "Rights as Trumps," in Jeremy Waldron, ed., *Theories of Rights* (1984) at 153–167.

[8] See, for example, Charles-Maxime Panaccio, "In Defence of Two-Step Balancing and Proportionality in Rights Adjudication," (2011) 24 *Can. J. L. & Jur.* 109.

[9] On cost-benefit policy analysis generally, see Edith Stokey and Richard Zeckhauser, *A Primer for Policy Analysis* (1978).

because there is neither a right to economic efficiency nor a right to be free
from the risks of driving, the determination of the optimal speed limit, even
assuming the absence of purely political considerations, is a matter of weighing
the relative net efficiencies of various different limits. The cost-benefit analysis
involved here, whether it be done mathematically or intuitively, is a process
or methodology that can certainly be plausibly understood as one involving
balancing.

But now suppose, counterfactually, that there is a *right* to drive at sixty miles
per hour, and suppose as well that the right is something less than absolute
(or infinitely stringent, which is the same thing). Under such circumstances,
the right to drive at sixty miles per hour would because of its non-absolute
nature be subject to limitation or override, but the strength of the evidence or
arguments necessary for override would have to be stronger than the evidence
or arguments sufficient to outweigh the *interest* in driving at sixty miles per hour
were that interest not understood as, or protected by, a right.[10] Thus, if there
is a right to drive at sixty miles per hour, that right can be limited in order to
reduce deaths or injuries, but it would be understood that the process would
take into account, by requiring stronger evidence or more powerful arguments
than in the absence of a right, the fact that there was a right to drive at a
certain speed but no right to be free from injuries. Indeed, the example and
the relationship it is designed to demonstrate becomes even more plausible if
we put the right on the other side. If there were a non-absolute right to be free
from traffic risks, but no right to drive at a certain speed, then the calculation
of the appropriate speed limit would need to take into account that a given
amount of increased risk was more harmful than a given amount of decreased
efficiency, and thus that the arguments and evidence necessary to impose this
risk would need to be stronger than the arguments and evidence sufficient to
impose the risk in the absence of a right to be free of that risk.

The same analysis holds true when we are thinking of the real rights protected by real constitutions and by real human rights laws and documents.[11]
All of the jurisdictions that recognize a right to freedom of expression, for

[10] For a more extended analysis of this idea, see Frederick Schauer, "Can Rights be Abused?"
(1981) 31 *The Philosophical Quarterly* 225.
[11] I mention human rights documents, for example the Universal Declaration of Human Rights
(1948), in order to emphasize that the analysis here is independent of the existence of institutions
of enforcement. The question I address is about the nature of rights-based reasoning and
argumentation, a question that is logically distinct from the question of which arguments are
actually likely to prevail in actual decision-making settings (including the domain of public
opinion), and that is also logically distinct from the question of what consequences follow from
the success of one side or another in a rights-based argument.

example, recognize as well that freedom of expression can be restricted so
as to preserve public order, among other limitations,[12] but where freedom of
expression is a genuine right a given degree of restriction on freedom of expression is understood to be a more serious deprivation than the same degree of
decrease in public order.[13] Similarly, there is widely understood in all modern
democracies a right to equality, but commonly, even if not universally, such a
right can be restricted even for the inequalities covered by the right when the
reason for imposing or using the inequality is a reason of special strength.[14]

It is thus not merely a historical quirk that the language and the idea of
proportionality arose in parallel with the rise of recognition, entrenchment,
and enforcement of rights through legal and constitutional means.[15] Of course,
even in a rights-free environment it remains incumbent on policy-makers to
balance costs and benefits, gains and losses, advantages and disadvantages,
and the utility increments or decrements that any policy will produce for all
affected interests and individuals. But where rights are absent, we rarely see the
word "proportionality," nor do we see even the idea that the word represents.
Only when rights enter the picture does the language of proportionality come

[12] See, for example, European Convention on Human Rights, Article 10. Such limitations are
implicit or elaborated by case law even when they are not explicitly designated in the constitutional document. See, for example, *Feiner v. New York*, 340 U.S. 315 (1951); *Ward v. Rock
Against Racism*, 491 U.S. 781 (1989).

[13] Thus, in the United States the famous idea of a "clear and present danger," *Schenck v.
United States*, 249 U.S. 47 (1919), since somewhat modified by *Brandenburg v. Ohio*, 395
U.S. 444 (1969), is not merely an empty slogan. Rather, it embodies the idea that the dangers
necessary to restrict freedom of speech must be especially clear and imminent, as should be
apparent from the vast number of speculative and remote dangers with which governments
routinely and properly deal. Many environmental and product risks, for example, are neither
clear nor present, but remain legitimately subject to regulation in ways that equivalently risky
consequences of speech are not. For an elaboration on this very comparison, see Frederick
Schauer, "Is It Better to Be Safe than Sorry?: Free Speech and the Precautionary Principle,"
36 *Pepperdine L. Rev.* 301 (2009).

[14] Thus, we see the basic idea in U.S. constitutional law that some classifications or distinctions
(those on the basis of race, ethnicity, and nationality, most prominently) are treated as "suspect."
Suspect classifications may be used, but only if there is a "compelling interest" in doing so.
Loving v. Virginia, 388 U.S. 1 (1967); *Palmore v. Sidoti*, 466 U.S. 429 (1984); *Grutter v. Bollinger*,
539 U.S. 306 (2003). The basic conceptual apparatus was created in the Japanese internment
case, *Korematsu v. United States*, 323 U.S. 214 (1944), a case whose profoundly mistaken
outcome needs to be distinguished from the important and valuable principle first developed
there.

[15] On the debate, centered in New Zealand but relevant elsewhere, about whether proportionality
analysis is applicable only to rights adjudication (the bifurcation thesis) or instead is a general
principle of constitutional review, see Paul Craig, "Proportionality, Deference, *Wednesbury*:
Taking Up Michael Taggart's Challenge: Proportionality, Rationality, and Review," [2010]
N.Z. L. Rev. 265.

onto the scene. Proportionality adjudication and decision making with respect
to rights does recognize that rights are typically, even if not necessarily, non-
absolute. But it also recognizes that rights are worth more than non-rights-
protected interests,[16] in just the way that Blackstone recognized with respect
to the right to liberty. As a result, equating proportionality with balancing,[17]
unfortunately common these days, is misleading precisely because it collapses
this important difference. It is true that rights can typically be overridden
not only by other rights, but also by a sufficient quantity of non-rights-based
interests.[18] And it is also true that determining when and how the override
actually occurs involves a process that involves some weighing of, let us say,
comparable incommensurables. But there are sufficient differences among
three different relationships – rights versus rights, rights versus interests, and
interests versus interests – that the use of the term "balancing," most appropriate
for the last member of this triad, for all three of these relationships loses far
more than it gains. It is of course useful to recognize that rights can be rights

---

[16] This conclusion does not depend on rights having Kantian or other deontological origins
or status. Even in a purely consequentialist world, it might be valuable to create legal or
constitutional rights under circumstances in which recognizing those rights would have the best
long-term consequences, or, put differently, better long-term consequences than empowering
individual decision makers (including courts) to make case-by-case determinations of the best
consequence. In such circumstances, rights would be created for consequentialist reasons, and
they might well have the same status as the rights that are recognized for non-consequentialist
reasons. Thus, to use Ronald Dworkin's example, Ronald Dworkin, *A Matter of Principle*
(1987), the right to freedom of the press might be understood entirely in instrumental and
consequentialist policy terms even as other rights (freedom of belief, for example, or freedom
from torture or, for Dworkin, individual freedom of expression).

[17] For commentary on the common conjunction of the two, see Vicki Jackson, "Being Proportional about Proportionality," 21 *Const. Comm.* 803 (2004). Examples of the ubiquitous
conjunction include *R. v. Oakes*, [1986] 1 S.C.R. 103; Aharon Barak, "Proportionality and Principled Balancing," (2010) 4 *Law & Ethics of Human Rights* 1; Walter van Gerven, "The Effect
of Proportionality on the Actions of Member States: National Viewpoints from Continental
Europe," in Evelyn Ellis (ed.), *The Principle of Proportionality in the Laws of Europe* (1999)
37; Gerald V. La Forest, "The Balancing of Interests under the Charter," (1992) 2 N.J.C.L. 113;
Iddo Porat, "Mapping the American Debate over Balancing," (Chapter 17 in this volume).

[18] The language of rights as trumps blinds us to this possibility, as does thinking of rights as
exclusionary reasons in Joseph Raz's sense of exclusionary reasons. See Joseph Raz, *Practical
Reason and Norms* (1975; 2nd ed., 1990). Rights do not necessarily win against non-rights
considerations, and thus the trumping metaphor is inapt. And rights do not exclude non-rights
considerations. Rather, rights devalue non-rights considerations, such that there need to be
more of such considerations in order to prevail than would be the case were rights not part of
the picture. The interplay between rights and non-rights interests is analyzed carefully in Alan
Gewirth, "Are There Any Absolute Rights?" (1981) 31 *The Philosophical Quarterly* 1; Robert
Nozick, "Moral Complications and Moral Structures," 13 *Natural Law Forum* 1 (1968); Judith
Thomson, "Some Ruminations on Rights," 19 *Arizona L. Rev.* 45 (1977). See also Frederick
Schauer, "A Comment on the Structure of Rights," 27 *Georgia L. Rev.* 415 (1993).

while not being absolute. And perhaps it is useful to recognize as well that making rights override determinations does involve some form of comparing competing values. But when rights are on one side of the equation, there is a presumption in favor of the right, or, which is more or less the same thing, a burden of proof imposed on those who would restrict the right in ways that are not present in the normal cost-benefit policy analysis. To the extent that using the word "balancing" ignores these important issues of presumptions and burdens of proof, it is far more misleading than helpful.

III.

One way of understanding proportionality analysis in the narrower sense I have just described is thus as imposing a "rule of weight" on the process of evaluating competing interests. Of course, we evaluate competing obligations, duties, goals, interests, factors, and facts in numerous aspects of our decision-making lives. And typically we do so by giving each relevant obligation, duty, goal, interest, factor, and fact the weight we think it deserves under the circumstances. But in some decision-making environments, various second-order rules prescribe the weight that these and other first-order considerations should receive. These are "rules of weight" and their use is relatively common, and even more so in the past, in the law of evidence in common law jurisdictions.[19] A rule specifying that the evidence from one type of witness should be credited more than from another type, for example, is a rule of weight, as would be a rule specifying that more weight should be given to an original document than to a copy, or to oral testimony about the contents of that document.

Once we understand that rights-based adjudication is importantly different from non-rights-based interest balancing, and once we understand as well that rights can still be rights even without being absolute, the relevance of rules of weight becomes apparent. We need some way to conceptualize not only the way in which rights may at times compete with other rights, but also, and more

---

[19] See Charles L. Barzun, "Rules of Weight," 83 *Notre Dame L. Rev.* 1957 (2008); Mirjan Damaška, "Evidentiary Barriers to Conviction and Two Models of Criminal Procedure: A Comparative Study," 121 *U. Penn. L. Rev.* 506 at 515 note 10 (1973); Mirjan Damaška, "Free Proof and Its Detractors," 43 *Am. J. Comp. L.* 343 at 344, 347–348 (1995); Sean Doran, John D. Jackson, and Michael L. Seigel, "Rethinking Adversariness in Nonjury Criminal Trials," 23 *Am. J. Crim L.* 1 at 17–18 (1995); George Fisher, "The Jury's Rise as Lie Detector," 107 *Yale L. J.* 575 at 629 note 231 (1997); Jennifer L. Mnookin, "Bifurcation and the Law of Evidence," 155 *U. Penn. L. Rev PENNumbra* 134 at 138, 142–143 (2007); David J. Sharpe, "Judges Evaluate Seafarers as Witnesses," 34 *Journal of Maritime Law and Commerce*, 87 at 92 (2003). On rules of weight to assign weights to different types of precedents, see Owen Fiss, "Objectivity and Interpretation," 34 *Stanford L. Rev.* 739 at 761 (1982).

importantly, the way in which rights are superior to but neither trumping nor excluding of non-rights-based interests and other considerations. And it is just at this point that the idea of a rule of weight is most useful. Just as a rule of weight can specify that an original document would carry more evidentiary weight than a copy even while not excluding copies (including copies inclining in the opposite direction from the original, or, more plausibly, oral testimony about the contents of the document that goes against what the document appears to say), so, too, can a rule of weight specify the way in which a right can be more heavily weighted than a potentially competing interest while not excluding interests from the ensuing calculation.

Seen through the lens of rules of weight, we can understand proportionality analysis, as commonly practiced in the jurisdictions in which it predominates, as itself a rule of weight. As applied to freedom of expression, for example, a proportionality analysis (and especially in the final step of the analysis in those regimes in which the proportionality analysis is subdivided into multiple steps[20]) will ask whether the restriction on freedom of expression is proportionate to the policy goal that supports the restriction, for example the goal of preserving public order. In some cases the restriction on freedom of expression will simply be superfluous, in the sense that a lesser degree of restriction on freedom of expression will produce no less of an ability at all to preserve public order. In such cases, however, the very term "proportionality" seems inapt, because it is not that the restriction on freedom of expression is disproportionate; it is simply that it is entirely superfluous and thus irrational. If the same goal can be served to the same extent without restricting the right, then the problem is not that the restriction is disproportionate. Rather, it is that the restriction is unnecessary, or, to put it more directly, pointless.

More commonly, however, and consistent with the very emergence of the term "proportionality" in the first place, it is commonly (and correctly) understood that, to continue with the same example, fully serving the goal of preserving the public order will entail some restriction on freedom of expression, and, conversely, curtailing the ability to restrict freedom of expression will come at the price of at least some restriction of the state's ability to preserve public order.[21] The question then, the genuine question of proportionality, is

---

[20] See Jeremy Kirk, "Constitutional Guarantees, Characterisation and the Concept of Proportionality," (1997) 21 *Melb. U. L. Rev.* 1.

[21] There is an interesting and important psychological question here, one traveling roughly in the neighborhood of the idea of cognitive dissonance, about the common phenomenon of attempting to reach factual conclusions that will eliminate the conflict between policies and rights. Those who (rightly) oppose torture in any form for any reason seem to find it necessary to claim as well that torture does not work. More plausibly, torture might be effective

whether the amount of restriction on freedom of expression is justified in light of the amount of the increase in public order that the restriction on freedom of expression is expected to bring.

Framing the issue in this way not only explains why "proportionality" is the proper term in cases such as this, but also exposes the fact that engaging in the appropriate proportionality analysis requires that we assign weights to the gains and losses on each side of the equation. But the very fact that the analysis is run in one direction and not the other reveals the weighting process. The courts do not typically say that the loss in public order can be no more than necessary in light of the goal of pursuing freedom of expression, but they do say that the restriction on freedom of expression can be no more than necessary in light of the goal of pursuing public order. The asymmetry reveals that there is a presumption at work, that the burden of proof is on those who would restrict freedom of expression and not on those who would jeopardize public order, and that lurking beneath the presumption and the allocation of the burden of proof is a rule of weight giving more weight to the right to freedom of expression than to the goal of public order that the right to freedom of expression will arguably threaten. And this is as it should be, not as a matter of high moral or political principle, but simply because this rule of weight is implicit in the very idea of a right, and in the very structure of the way in which non-absolute rights intersect with non-rights interests. If it were otherwise, if there were a right to live in a safe environment but no right to freedom of expression, for example, the rule of weight would be just the opposite, placing the burden of proof on any action that would jeopardize a safe environment merely to further the non-rights interest in increased expression. But it would still be a rule of weight.

Thus, the idea of a rule of weight is implicit in the common structure of proportionality analysis, and, indeed, the rule of weight that is implicit in any rights-based proportionality analysis is a rule of disproportionate weight. But the existence of a rule of disproportionate weight is a structural and not a substantive matter. It is a structure that is entailed by the what it means for

---

often, but nevertheless morally and legally impermissible. So, too, with freedom of expression; that it is properly impermissible in most liberal democracies to restrict expression that might simply offend others does not make the offense less real and harmful. And that it is properly impermissible in most liberal constitutional democracies for the policy to use force to coerce suspects to confess does not mean that the coerced confessions are necessarily unreliable, or even that the benefits of the aggregate number of accurate coerced confessions might not outweigh the costs of the aggregate number of coerced inaccurate confessions. But again, the fact that coerced confessions might often be reliable is, at least for me, insufficient to justify their use.

there to be a right, and what it means for a non-absolute right to conflict with an interest, but it is a structure that exists across the full panoply of actual or possible rights, and also across the range of actual or possible interests that might conflict with those rights. The rule of (disproportionate) weight that structures the proportionality analysis thus emerges from the idea of a right, and explains much of the difference between proportionality analysis and the more routine but typically non-weighted first-order balancing methodology that pervades the policy process.

IV.

Although the typical proportionality analysis is thus itself a rule of weight, it may also be that the idea of disproportion that infuses proportionality review itself could be the foundation for any number of more specific rules of weight. The common "least restrictive alternative" analysis that one sees in some form or another in numerous contexts of rights review[22] could be understood as one such more specific rule, but in important ways it may fail to be up to the task required of it. The least restrictive alternative idea is perfectly serviceable as a way of identifying entirely superfluous restrictions on a right, because such restrictions are more restrictive than necessary to achieve some non-right goal to the level desired by the state. And thus, the least restrictive alternative rule is also a way of exposing illegitimate governmental motivations. When the government imposes a restriction on a right that is more than necessary to serve the goal identified by the government to the extent desired, one possibility is that the government is simply being clumsy. But another possibility is that the government has other and less legitimate goals in mind.[23] If it turns out, for example, that a curfew in a particular neighborhood is totally unnecessary to restrict crime to exactly the extent to which the authorities want

---

[22] It is often said that proportionality is the dominant approach in European law, and in the constitutional law of, for example, Canada, South Africa, Germany, and New Zealand, but that the U.S. approach is different. In some respects this may be true: see Frederick Schauer, "Freedom of Expression Adjudication in Europe and America: A Case Study in Comparative Constitutional Architecture," in Georg Nolte (ed.), *European and U.S. Constitutionalism* (2005) 47; but the widespread (and, it should be chauvinistically noted, temporally prior) use in the United States of "least-restrictive alternative" approaches to a wide variety of rights (see, among many examples, *Williams v. Illinois*, 399 U.S. 235 (1970); *California v. La Rue*, 409 U.S. 109 (1972); *Sosna v. Iowa*, 419 U.S. 393 (1975), *Boos v. Barry*, 485 U.S. 312 (1988)), suggests that something very similar to proportionality analysis has long been a central feature of American rights adjudication.

[23] See Elena Kagan, "Private Speech, Public Purpose: The Role of Governmental Motive in First Amendment Doctrine," 63 *U. Chi. L. Rev.* 413 (1996).

to restrict it, we might suspect that the underlying and less legitimate goal of the curfew is to place restrictions on people of certain races, ethnicities, or religions just because of those characteristics. We might be wrong, of course, and it may well be that reflexive reactions to certain problems, reactions excessively driven by past practice or inapt examples or path dependence or blind obeisance, are simply stupid but not invidious. Nevertheless, a least restrictive alternative methodology may provide a valuable evidentiary window into genuinely impermissible motivations and consequently impermissible practices.[24]

But although a least restrictive alternative approach might well be a valuable way of invalidating genuinely irrational or genuinely invidious rights-restricting actions, it may not serve the purpose we desire from a genuine rule of weight. Suppose, as is the more common scenario, the genuinely least restrictive alternative would impede to some extent the government's pursuit of a legitimate goal. If there is a right to physical liberty and freedom of movement, for example, then the least restrictive alternative in the curfew context would simply be not to have a curfew. But if a curfew may also increase security in some contexts, the question is then whether having no curfew, the least restrictive alternative, is worth the loss of security that will come from the absence of a curfew. Or the question might then be whether a limited curfew, limited to some people or hours or neighborhoods, would be permissible under circumstances in which the limited curfew produces some gains in security but fewer gains than would be produced by a less-limited curfew. At this point, it would be good to know just how much of a gain in security would be worth how much of a loss of the right to freedom of movement, and for this task the general idea of the least restrictive alternative would be of little assistance.

Or consider the question of defamation and freedom of expression. Assume we are in a jurisdiction, the United States or Canada or the United Kingdom, but not Germany or France, in which there is an interest in but not a constitutional (or other) right to reputation, but in which there is a genuine constitutional right to freedom of expression and/or freedom of the press. And assume as well that it is well understood that the rights to freedom of expression and freedom of the press are not absolute. At that point the question is one of how much of a loss of the genuine rights would be worth incurring in order to

---

[24] There is an interesting question whether an impermissible governmental motivation will invalidate an otherwise (or facially) permissible regulation. In the United States it will; see, for example, *Wallace v. Jaffree*, 472 U.S. 38 (1985), but there is no reason to believe that such an approach is either universal or necessary for robust rights enforcement.

secure some gain in reputation preservation, or some gain in the interest (but not the right) in having people enter the public arena. Most of the common law jurisdictions that have confronted the issue in recent (and, in the case of the United States, not so recent) years[25] have recognized that we are no longer in the realm of non-weighted balancing, but they have recognized as well that, with the appropriate thumb on the scales, the relevant rights can be limited to secure the relevant gains in interests. But just how many damaged reputations are worth how much restriction of press freedom? How many qualified people unwilling to enter public life are worth how many examples of public misdeeds exposed? Even recognizing that the components of this calculation are, as a practical matter, both incommensurable and immeasurable, and even recognizing that the losses on one side of the equation (or, if you must, balance) must be treated as more serious than the losses on the other, it may be useful to recognize, as a conceptual matter, the need for a rule (or, perhaps, principle) of weight to structure the inquiry.

And thus we return to Blackstone. And also to his "friends" Starkie, Franklin, and Fortescue. There is no one who seriously believes, of course, that we can actually calculate the number of mistaken convictions and acquittals under any of the different maxims expressed by these and other luminaries. But the numbers they used express a relationship, and the different numbers express different relationships. We may not be able to calculate the number of Type I and Type II errors, to use the statistician's terminology,[26] under any of these rules, but we do know that the idea expressed by Franklin is more defendant protective than the idea expressed by Blackstone, and thus we know that the idea expressed by Blackstone is more law protective or authority protective or order protective than the idea expressed by any of the others.

When we return to proportionality, the number of possible relations becomes more complex. That is, not only might we have numerous variations in how different courts or commentators view the right, but also multiple variations in how different courts or commentators view the different countervailing interests. Moreover, and perhaps most importantly, even the same courts and commentators might also perceive variations in the weights they would attach to different rights. Just as, in American law, the right to be free from discrimination on the basis of race is stronger than the right to be free

---

[25] See, for example, *Lange v. Australian Broadcasting Corp.*, [1997] 189 C.L.R. 520 (Australia); *Theophanous v. Herald & Weekly Times, Ltd.*, [1994] 182 C.L.R. 104 (Australia); *Lange v. Atkinson*, [1998] 3 N.Z.L.R. 424 (New Zealand); *Hill v. Church of Scientology of Toronto*, [1995] 2 S.C.R. 1130; *Grant v. Torstar Corp.*, [2009] 3 S.C.R. 640 (Canada); *Reynolds v. The Times*, [2001] 2 A.C. 127 (Great Britain); *New York Times Co. v. Sullivan*, 376 U.S. 254 (1964).

[26] Or, depending on how we characterize the goals, false positives and false negatives.

from discrimination on the basis of gender,[27] so, too, might there be variations
in the strengths accorded to various rights. This might be a function of the
source of the rights – are the rights that are understood as deontological or
natural or something of that order to be considered stronger (or weaker) than
the rights that are understood as rule-consequentialist side-constraints on act-
consequentialist maximization? – but might also be a function of the fact that
different rights having the same type of moral or metaphysical foundations
might still vary with strength, as a long literature on moral dilemmas makes
clear.[28]

That we can conceive of so many variations is no cause for abandoning the
enterprise of trying to understand proportionality review in terms of second-
order rules of weight. On the contrary, the wide array of variations makes it
clear that simple talk of proportionality and the coarse rules that are currently
employed to implement proportionality review are insufficient to the task. Of
course, if proportionality review is little more than the assertion of judicial pre-
rogative, as some critics believe,[29] or essentially irrational, as others maintain,[30]
then the absence of structuring and disciplining rules is not a problem, and
indeed is an impediment. But if proportionality review is, like the common
law itself, to become more refined, detailed, and rule-based as time progresses,
then the development of those structuring and disciplining rules is only to be
expected. Not all of those rules will be rules of weight, but rules of weight,
with their compatriots burdens of proof and presumptions, can be expected to
occupy pride of place.

Finally, it is worth noting that all of this depends on a host of psychological
and thus empirical assumptions about the ability of actual legal decision
makers to follow various rules structuring and disciplining their own decision-
making processes. The American Legal Realists, most prominently, questioned
the extent to which the formal rules to be found in law books were actually
causal of judicial decisions. To the extent that they were right, then it would be
surprising to find that rules of weight were any different, and thus surprising to

---

[27] See *Mississippi University for Women v. Hogan*, 458 U.S. 718 (1982), applying so-called intermediate scrutiny to discrimination on the basis of gender, and recognizing that this was a lower
hurdle for state or federal legislation than the strict scrutiny applicable to discrimination or
classifications on the basis of race, ethnicity, or nationality.

[28] See, for example, Walter Sinnott-Armstrong, *Moral Dilemmas* (1984).

[29] See, for example, Grégoire C.N. Webber, "Proportionality, Balancing, and the Cult of Constitutional Rights Scholarship," (2010) 23 *Can. J. L. & Jur.* 179.

[30] For my discussion of this largely German debate, see Frederick Schauer, "Balancing, Subsumption, and the Constraining Role of Legal Text" in Mathias Klatt (ed.), *Institutional Reason:
The Jurisprudence of Robert Alexy* (2012) 307.

discover that proportionality methodology could in fact constrain or structure or discipline a judge's first-order political or ideological or policy preferences. But to the extent that the Realist claims were mistaken or exaggerated, then we might actually expect the structure of proportionality adjudication, especially as refined by various second-order rules including but not limited to rules of weight, to have a genuine impact on the substance of rights decisions. But as the Realists argued – indeed, insisted – their claims were irreducibly empirical. We can structure proportionality review by the use of logical and decision-theoretic and legal doctrinal devices in order to make proportionality decisions, in theory, as rational as the abstract idea of proportionality suggests. But whether those structures will make a difference, and indeed whether proportionality review as now structured makes a difference, is an empirical agenda that must wait for another day – and a cohort of empirically trained researchers – to investigate.

9   Proportionality and the Relevance of Interpretation

Grant Huscroft*

I. INTRODUCTION

Although the basic questions posed in proportionality analysis seem clear,[1] they can be very difficult to answer. Information is likely to be imperfect or incomplete and there are bound to be difficulties in establishing cause and effect, especially in matters of social policy. For example, in order to determine whether a particular limit is necessary – minimally impairing of the right – courts engage in counterfactual analysis: they consider whether an approach not chosen by the legislature would be equally effective in achieving the legislature's objective while limiting rights to a lesser extent. Given that the effectiveness of one approach or another will often be a matter of conjecture, we should expect to find reasonable disagreement about necessity, and so we do. The ultimate question in proportionality analysis – whether a limit is proportional *stricto sensu* – poses the greatest difficulties, for it assumes that conflicting rights and interests can be weighed, but weighing is beset by the problem of incommensurability.[2] In sum, judges applying proportionality analysis may disagree about everything from the characterization of the dispute to the nature of the considerations and the weights that should be ascribed to them, and their disagreement will likely be reasonable.

Doctrinal differences may be an additional cause of disagreement, even where basic common law values are shared. Judges may be more or less

---

* Thanks to Grégoire Webber and Bradley Miller for their comments and suggestions and to Jeffrey Claydon, JD 2013, for research assistance.
[1] The basic approach is set out in the Introduction to this volume at 2.
[2] On incommensurability see, e.g., John Finnis, "Legal Reasoning as Practical Reason" in *The Collected Essays of John Finnis Vol. I: Reason in Action* (2011) at 224 (incommensurability understood in the sense of "the absence of any *rationally* identified metric for measuring, or scale for 'weighing', the goods and bads in issue"); Timothy Endicott, "Proportionality and Incommensurability," Chapter 14 in this volume.

committed to *stare decisis*; more or less influenced by comparative law; more or less deferential to legislative choices. More fundamentally, they may disagree about the nature of rights, the separation of powers, and the legitimacy of judicial review itself. Disagreement over the answers reached in proportionality analysis may also reflect disagreement at the level of political or philosophical commitment.[3] It should come as no surprise, then, that cases that yield "obvious" proportionality outcomes in one jurisdiction may yield different outcomes in another.[4]

No approach to rights delivers answers that cannot reasonably be denied,[5] but the reasons to be wary of proportionality analysis go beyond methodological concerns. A more profound objection to proportionality analysis is that it denies the moral priority of rights in the constitutional order. As Grégoire Webber argues, proportionality analysis diminishes rights by equating them with mere defeasible interests. The "received approach", as he describes it, "reifies rights and regularly divorces rights from *what is right*."[6]

I share Webber's concern but want to consider a related problem. In order to respect the community's decision to adopt a bill of rights, courts employing

---

[3] See Bradley W. Miller, "Proportionality's Blind Spot: 'Neutrality' and Political Philosophy," Chapter 16 in this volume.

[4] Robert Alexy's standard example of a limitation that is obviously justified includes the requirement that health warnings be placed on cigarette labels. Alexy states: "In light of the minor intensity of the interference and the great weight of the reason for the interference, it can well be described, along with the Federal Constitutional Court, as 'obvious'." (Robert Alexy, *A Theory of Constitutional Rights* (Julian Rivers translation, 2002) at 402, citing BVerfGE 95, 173 [187]). In contrast, the Supreme Court of Canada rejected compulsory warnings as an unjustifiable infringement of freedom of expression under the Canadian Charter of Rights and Freedoms in *RJR MacDonald v. Canada* [1995] 3 S.C.R.199. Although the majority of the Supreme Court of Canada considered that the state was "clearly justified" in requiring health warnings on tobacco packaging, it held that the state had not established that it was necessary for the warning to be unattributed to the state, accepting that an unattributed warning was, in essence, an example of compelled expression by the tobacco companies of an "opinion" with which they did not want to be associated.

[5] As Jeremy Waldron has written, "The assumption of disagreement has nothing to do with moral relativism or non-cognitivism. It is perfectly compatible with there being a truth of the matter about rights and the principles of constitutionalism – only, it assumes that our condition is not one in which the truth of the matter discloses itself in ways that are not reasonably deniable" ("Some Models of Dialogue" in Grant Huscoft and Ian Brodie (eds.), *Constitutionalism in the Charter Era* (2004) 11–12).

[6] See Grégoire Webber, "On the Loss of Rights" (Chapter 6 in this volume) and reply remarks by Kai Möller (Chapter 7 in this volume), "Proportionality and Rights Inflation," both in this volume. See generally, Stavros Tsakyrakis, "Proportionality: An Assault on Human Rights?" (2009) 7 Int'l. J. Const. L. 468; and Grégoire Webber, *The Negotiable Constitution: On the Limitation of Rights* (2009) at 112–113: "The reduction of all constitutional rights to evaluations of proportionality and balancing is the substitution of a standard for any rule, the transformation of sources of law into premises in practical reasoning, the undoing of all that the constitution purports to do." (Hereinafter Webber, *The Negotiable Constitution*.)

proportionality analysis must respect not only the moral priority of rights but also the nature of the *particular* rights the community has committed to protect. That is so, I will argue, because the decision to adopt a bill of rights is a decision to give heightened legal status to *particular* rights, rather than to rights in general. Whether a particular right is protected by a bill of rights, and what its protection entails, are questions prior to the authority of courts to engage in proportionality analysis.

In order to determine what rights a bill of rights protects, courts need to attend to the idiosyncrasies of bills of rights, and among other things this requires that they pay close attention to their text. In practice, however, courts committed to proportionality analysis are likely to interpret rights broadly, sometimes treating meaning as synonymous with the full range of semantic possibility.[7] This sort of approach to interpretation is sometimes said to be required by the way in which bills of rights are written. Bills of rights may include a general limitation clause that purports to authorize the establishment of limitations on all rights[8] or may set out limitations specific to particular rights,[9] and courts have often insisted that questions of definition and justification must be separated as a result. On this approach, evaluative considerations are deferred to the justificatory stage. The adoption of broad interpretations of rights at the definitional stage eases the burden on claimants to establish that their rights have been limited, while increasing the range of cases in which the state is required to justify its actions.

If rights are interpreted broadly, the real protection they afford turns out to be dependent on how difficult or easy the court makes it to justify the establishment of limits on the right. It can be misleading to speak in terms of "rights" as

[7] For example, the Supreme Court of Canada has held that freedom of expression protects any activity that conveys or attempts to convey meaning, provided only that it is neither violent nor threatens violence (*Irwin Toy Ltd. v. Quebec (Attorney General)*, [1989] 1 S.C.R. 927 and *R. v. Khawaja*, [2012] 3 S.C.R. 555); and that freedom of religion protects any activity undertaken in accordance with sincerely held religious beliefs, provided only that the interference is more than trivial or insubstantial (*Syndicat Northcrest v. Amselem*, [2004] 2 S.C.R. 551). That Court does not define every right so broadly, however; it has sought to limit the equality right by means of a purposive interpretation. Compare *Law v. Canada (Minister of Employment and Immigration)*, [1999] 1 S.C.R. 497 (emphasizing human dignity, focusing on comparator groups) with *Withler v. Canada (Attorney General)*, [2011] 1 S.C.R. 396 (emphasizing prejudice and stereotyping, abandoning comparator group analysis). Deep divisions on the Court are apparent in *Quebec (Attorney General) v. A*, 2013 SCC 5.
[8] See, e.g., the Canadian Charter of Rights and Freedoms (s. 1); the New Zealand Bill of Rights Act (s. 5); South African Bill of Rights (s. 36).
[9] See, e.g., the European Convention on Human Rights (arts. 8–11); the International Covenant on Civil and Political Rights (part III).

a result: although the Supreme Court of Canada has, like the U.S. Supreme Court, endorsed the idea of "content neutrality" in defining freedom of expression (speech), the freedom turns out to be not nearly as expansive in Canada, for the Court has justified all manner of limits on expression it considers to be unworthy – not despite the content of the expression but because of it. Thus, the adoption of broad interpretations of rights does not necessarily result in greater rights protection. There may be significant motivation for courts to adopt broad interpretations of rights, however, because rights have enormous symbolic appeal and courts are more likely to be lauded for generosity than restraint when it comes to interpreting them. Courts adopting expansive conceptions of rights are likely to speak in romantic terms about the importance of respecting rights even as they approve the establishment of significant limits on them.[10] The consequences of broad interpretations of rights – a broadening of the range of state action subject to judicial review and an increase in judicial power in the constitutional order – is seldom acknowledged, but there is no doubt that the judiciary is not a disinterested party when it comes to interpreting rights.

Now, interpretation is a difficult and often controversial exercise, and it is easy to see why courts might prefer to determine rights disputes using proportionality analysis: it offers a familiar analytical framework that purports to deliver objective results.[11] Inspired by German law, however, leading proponents of proportionality go further, advocating that interpretation should, in essence, be abandoned. The normative desirability of justification is all that matters, they argue, and rights should be interpreted as widely as possible so as to require justification for state action – established through proportionality analysis – to the greatest extent possible.

The "irrelevance of interpretation" thesis is, I will argue, fundamentally at odds with the commitments that underlie the decision to adopt a bill of rights. Bills of rights are best understood as effecting a "constitutional settlement" as to the place of rights in a legal order. They are finite rather than open-ended commitments to the protection of rights and their content has moral significance that must be respected. If proportionality analysis requires or leads courts to conclude otherwise, then it is not a good fit in a community that takes its constitutional commitments seriously.

[10] Freedom of expression, according to the New Zealand Court of Appeal, is "as wide as human thought and imagination". *Moonen v. Film and Literature Board of Review*, [2000] 2 N.Z.L.R. 9.
[11] The claim that proportionality analysis allows courts to avoid the difficulties inherent in moral reasoning is critiqued in Miller, "Proportionality's Blind Spot: 'Neutrality' and Political Philosophy," Chapter 16 in this volume.

II. THE ESSENTIAL AND PARTICULAR NATURE OF
BILLS OF RIGHTS

Let me begin by sketching the nature of bills of rights, in general and in particular. Democratic constitutional orders are marked by the authority of the elected branch of government to legislate – to make, amend, or repeal any law within its jurisdiction. Nothing follows from this in terms of the quality of lawmaking: no one supposes that every law passed pursuant to a democratic process is necessarily a good or just law. The point is simply that the elected branch has the authority to legislate subject to such constitutional constraints as may exist. Those constraints are typically, if not exclusively, found in bills of rights.

Bills of rights may be said to arise out of a community's commitments to liberty, equality, and dignity, but these commitments take different forms; bills of rights are products of their times and reflect the values and concerns of those who adopt them, along with their conception of the appropriate role of government. For example, the venerable U.S. Bill of Rights is a liberty-centric document that, among other things, includes a right to bear arms and a right not to have soldiers quartered in one's home.[12] These rights are not found in most bills of rights and look anachronistic to much of the world, but their inclusion in the U.S. Bill of Rights can be understood in the context of historical grievances from the revolutionary history of the United States. In contrast, the South African Bill of Rights was designed as a corrective to racial apartheid and is characterized by its commitment to the protection of equality and dignity. But it also includes a range of social and economic rights – rights of access to housing, health care, food, water, and social security[13] not included in other contemporary bills of rights.

Differences between bills of rights may be insignificant or profound, and may reflect different purposes behind the bill of rights enterprise. For example, a bill of rights grafted onto an extant constitutional order may be designed to confirm the existence of rights already assumed to be enjoyed. The Canadian Charter of Rights and Freedoms and the New Zealand Bill of Rights Act are examples here. Both Canada and New Zealand were well-functioning democratic constitutional orders committed to the rule of law and respect for rights prior to the adoption of their bills of rights, and the adoption of bills of rights in these countries was neither intended nor expected to cause radical

---

[12] Second and Third Amendments, respectively.

[13] Sections 26 and 27 of the South African Bill of Rights require the state to take "reasonable legislative and other measures, within its available resources, to achieve the progressive realization" of these rights.

change.[14] The opposite is true of South Africa. The South African Bill of Rights was designed to be transformative in nature – to establish, rather than confirm, the rights and freedoms it protects, and to do so as part of a new, democratic, constitutional order.

But regardless of the historical differences between them, all bills of rights can be understood as effecting a constitutional settlement: they settle not only the place of rights in the legal order of a political community, but also the place of *particular* rights. Bills of rights include a range of rights that may be more or less extensive and may include vague or specific conceptions of the particular rights they protect. It follows that interpretation is necessary in order to determine the nature of the settlement a bill of rights effects.

It is sometimes presumed that if something is important, it must be protected in the constitution; its protection simply must have been intended, so it is appropriate for courts to interpret vaguely worded provisions in a bill of rights as protecting it. This is a mistake, however, and it stems from the failure to attend to the distinction between moral and legal rights. Bills of rights are concerned primarily with civil and political rights – rights that establish limits on the exercise of state power. By no means do these sorts of rights exhaust the universe of rights. A larger set of moral rights lies beyond the bill of rights, and it is possible for legislation to be inconsistent with these rights (that is, legislation may be morally deficient) without being unconstitutional in the legal sense.

Inconsistency with moral rights is of no moment when it comes to judicial review under a bill of rights. The question in judicial review proceedings is not simply whether a right has been limited; it is whether a right *protected by the bill of rights* has been limited. This is an "is" rather than an "ought" question: courts must determine whether a particular right is protected by the bill of rights, not whether it ought to be. To adopt a bill of rights is to make only some rights enforceable in legal proceedings, and there are good reasons why a community may want to limit the number of rights it chooses to protect in this way. The community may have genuine concerns about the relative institutional competence of legislatures and courts to assess competing priorities, or about their relative legitimacy in doing so.

---

[14] Although the Canadian Charter came into force in 1982, the equality rights provision (s. 15) did not come into force until 1985. The suggestion is that the Charter equality right was assumed to require change in the Canadian legal order, and that time was required to allow legislation to be amended in accordance with the requirements of the right. As it happened, however, relatively little significant legislative change occurred prior to 1985, reflecting the modest conception of the right that prevailed in political circles.

Many important moral rights are not protected by bills of rights. Although commitments to liberty, equality, and dignity can be understood as underlying the decision to posit particular rights in a bill of rights, courts must be careful not to mistake the moral reasons supporting the protection of a particular right with the scope of the legal right that was actually posited. For example, although it is reasonable to conclude that a moral right to privacy underlies the freedom from unreasonable search and seizure protected by a bill of rights – it helps explain the decision to protect the freedom – the freedom from unreasonable search and seizure is not the same thing as a legal right to privacy, and the protection it affords is not coextensive with it.[15]

Thus, it is not incoherent to claim that one's rights have been infringed by the state simply because the right asserted is not included in a bill of rights. But a claim that a moral right has been infringed cannot be dealt with under the bill of rights. It must be addressed as a political rather than legal matter – raised in the political forum rather than in judicial review proceedings. Moral rights may prove to be less well protected as a result, but this result need not follow. For example, basic economic and social rights are secure in many jurisdictions, even though they are not protected in bills of rights, because they are sustained by a durable political consensus.

Proponents of the common law constitution offer an important objection to this account, arguing that bills of rights are simply *examples* of rights that are otherwise immanent in the common law. On this approach, far from being exclusive sources of constitutional rights, bills of rights are essentially superfluous. As T.R.S. Allan puts it in his contribution to this volume (Chapter 10), "bills or codes of rights are important, but inessential, approximations".[16] I will have more to say about this later. For present purposes, I am concerned only with bills of rights and the particular rights they protect. My claim is that there is an important interpretive task to be done in determining the scope of the rights protected by bills of rights before questions of justification for the establishment of limits on those rights can be considered.

The notion that bills of rights protect some, but not all, rights is encapsulated in the idea that bills of rights are *finite* in nature.[17] Finiteness means that there are limits to the nature and scope of the rights protection that bills of rights

---

[15] See, e.g., *Katz v. United States*, 389 U.S. 347 (1967); *Hunter et al. v. Southam Inc.*, [1984] 2 S.C.R. 145 (freedom from unreasonable search and seizure protecting "reasonable expectations of privacy").

[16] Allan, "Democracy, Legality, and Proportionality," Chapter 10 in this volume at 205.

[17] See Grant Huscroft, "Vagueness, Finiteness, and the Limits of Interpretation and Construction" in Grant Huscroft and Bradley W. Miller (eds.), *The Challenge of Originalism: Theories of Constitutional Interpretation* (2011) 203.

provide, and these limits reflect choices made by the community in adopting its bill of rights – what I described earlier as the constitutional settlement about the place of rights in the legal order. The choices made by the community in adopting its bill of rights are morally significant on this account. The finiteness of bills of rights is significant, too, because it implies the finiteness of judicial review. Legislation that establishes limits on the rights protected by a bill of rights must be justified in judicial review proceedings, but for our purposes it is the corollary that is important: legislation that does *not* establish limits on the protected rights need *not* be so justified. In such a case, proportionality analysis is neither mandated nor legitimate.

III. THE IMPORTANCE OF INTERPRETATION

To say that legislation does not limit rights protected by a bill of rights may mean that it is not in conflict with the right asserted. For example, a claim that legislation regulating or proscribing a particular activity establishes a limit on the freedom of association will fail if the activity in question does not constitute an act of association, as that concept is understood following interpretation. Some rights include definitional limitations that narrow their scope and hence make it more difficult to establish an infringement. A claim that the "freedom of peaceful assembly" is infringed will be defeated if the assembly in question is violent in nature.

Some definitional limitations subsume difficult moral appraisals. Consider a claim that legislation establishing a mandatory minimum sentence of imprisonment for a particular crime is inconsistent with the freedom from cruel or unusual treatment or punishment. The claim is coherent: the freedom necessarily limits the legislature's power to establish punishment to *some* extent, but that extent is uncertain because it depends on a judgment as to moral wrongfulness – what it is that makes something "cruel or unusual". Case law may do no more than establish that the freedom is to be understood in terms of discretionary moral evaluations,[18] and there will often be disagreement as to whether a particular punishment is so severe as to be morally wrongful. But whether or not the claim succeeds, there is no doubt that it must be resolved by determining the scope of the freedom – what the freedom means and what it requires – and applying it to the circumstances of the case. If the punishment is not considered cruel or unusual, no infringement of the freedom will be made out and that will be the end of the matter.

---

[18] E.g., "evolving standards of decency that mark the progress of a maturing society". See *Trop v. Dulles*, 356 U.S. 86 at 101 (1958).

In these cases, there is no doubt as to the existence of the right claimed; argument lies as to its nature and scope and, as a result, whether or not its protection extends to the activity in question. Sometimes, however, a claim may depend not on establishing the scope of a particular right, but rather its existence. That is, it may be necessary to establish the existence of a particular right before an argument claiming infringement of the right can be entertained. It may be claimed that legislation violates the right to privacy, for example, but if it is not established that a right to privacy is protected under a bill of rights, then the claim that the legislation violates the bill of rights must fail. This sort of case seems easy, in that the existence of a right appears to be a question that gives rise to a categorical answer: either the right is protected by a bill of rights or it is not. In many cases, however, rights are worded so vaguely that categorical answers are impossible.

The problem, in short, is that even accepting that bills of rights are finite, their parameters are uncertain. Bills of rights are cast in positive terms and do not specify the rights they do not include. Their finite character is implicit and can be established only on the basis of such inferences as are properly drawn from the text or, in some cases, its silence. If a particular right was not included in a bill of rights – if it was left out deliberately – its omission must be respected if the constitutional settlement is to be respected. But this may be a difficult conclusion to draw, even if a court were otherwise amenable to drawing it, for it depends on the cogency of evidence of drafting history and intention, not to mention arguments establishing the legitimacy of according primacy to this sort of evidence in interpreting a bill of rights.

The conclusion that a right is not protected by a bill of rights is especially difficult to draw for courts committed to a "living constitution". Courts that allow rights to grow and expand in accordance with changing societal circumstances – a common conception of living constitutionalism[19] – are likely to decide cases in a manner that preserves their interpretive discretion in future cases. Nevertheless, in some cases even courts committed to living constitutionalism may close the door to the protection of particular rights, and this conclusion may become so well accepted as to preclude the possibility of recognizing those rights in future.

Consider the example of property rights. Many bills of rights protect property rights, but it is considered uncontroversial to say that the Canadian Charter and the New Zealand Bill of Rights Act do not, even though neither bill of rights excludes the protection of property in explicit terms. From the outset it

---

[19] See W.J. Waluchow, *A Common Law Theory of Judicial Review: The Living Tree* (2006).

has been accepted that property rights were a deliberate omission from both bills of rights – a constitutional settlement that was to be respected – and as a result arguments that property rights are subsumed within the protection of one or another of the vaguely worded rights that are protected are considered hopeless.[20] It is widely accepted that amendments are required if property rights are to be protected by either of these bills of rights.

The example of property rights affirms the finite character of these bills of rights, and additional examples could be raised. Although it is uncontroversial that bills of rights are concerned primarily with the protection of civil and political rights, they are not necessarily exhaustive statements of even these sorts of rights. The decision to adopt a bill of rights is often said to flow from a community's desire to give effect to its commitment to the International Covenant on Civil and Political Rights,[21] but it is noteworthy that few states simply adopt the terms of the Covenant as their domestic bill of rights. Most states draft their bills of rights in their own terms, and these terms may or may not provide rights protection as extensive as that in the Covenant.[22]

We need not agree on exactly what a bill of rights includes to accept the larger point that no bill of rights provides protection for every conceivable right. A wide range of rights may not be included in a particular bill of rights, including the sorts of rights set out in the International Covenant Economic, Social, and Cultural Rights, as well as so-called third-generation rights such as environmental protection and sustainability. These sorts of rights enjoy significant support in the community and amongst political elites, and courts are likely to be petitioned to recognize some of them in interpreting vaguely worded provisions in bills of rights. Judges may be sorely tempted to do so in the face of legislative measures they consider unjust, rather than leaving it to the community to amend the legislation or the bill of rights.

---

[20] Peter Hogg explains the omission of property from the Canadian Charter on originalist grounds, even as he rejects originalism as an interpretive approach. See Hogg, *Constitutional Law of Canada* (1997, updated in looseleaf) ch. 47.7, 47.9.

[21] This is sometimes made explicit, as for example in the New Zealand Bill of Rights Act. The preamble to that bill of rights describes it as an Act: (a) "To affirm, protect, and promote human rights and fundamental freedoms in New Zealand"; and (b) "To affirm New Zealand's commitment to the International Covenant on Civil and Political Rights."

[22] Courts often assume that bills of rights whose passage was inspired by the Covenant necessarily provide at least as much protection as the Covenant. This is a mistake. The mere fact of a state's accession to the Covenant neither authorizes nor justifies a broad interpretation of vaguely worded rights in a bill of rights. In any case, the commitment established by acceding to the Covenant can be honored regardless of the content of a bill of rights or the way in which it operates. Indeed, the commitment can be honored without having a bill of rights at all, provided that ordinary legislation and common law give effect to Covenant obligations.

But even though vaguely worded rights are more or less "underdeterminate", in the sense that they allow a range of interpretive outcomes, they are not radically indeterminate: they cannot be made to mean absolutely anything an interpreter desires.[23] The range of legitimate interpretation is necessarily constrained to some extent.

Underdeterminate expressions of rights pose an important challenge to the idea of finiteness. Although the semantic possibility of a particular interpretation is necessarily relevant to determining the scope of a right, it cannot be determinative. The scope of particular rights must be constrained by the larger commitment – the constitutional settlement – the bill of rights entails.

IV. PROPORTIONALITY AND THE IRRELEVANCE OF INTERPRETATION

Proportionality theorists tend to have a very different conception of bills of rights than the one I have outlined. They are more concerned with justification for state action than they are with the idea of rights and the particular rights commitments a political community makes in its bill of rights.

Robert Alexy's account of rights is a starting point for many proportionality theorists. Alexy argues that a distinction between rules and principles is basic to constitutional rights theory. Rules apply absolutely and give rise to questions of validity: only one rule can apply, so in the event of conflicting rules either an exception must be made or one of the rules must be declared invalid. Vaguely worded rights operate as principles, applying to varying degrees in various contexts. They are, as he terms them, "optimization requirements",[24] and conflicts between competing principles – between rights and interests pursued by the state – must be resolved by comparisons of weight. On Alexy's account, rights are at once everything and nothing:[25] they are everything because their existence is a prerequisite to the possibility of proportionality analysis; they are nothing because the broad definitions ascribed to them necessarily deprive them of the moral force rights are supposed to have.

Following Alexy's lead, many proportionality proponents have sought to maximize the opportunities for courts to engage in proportionality analysis by advocating broad interpretations of the rights enumerated in bills of rights.

---

[23] Lawrence B. Solum, "On the Indeterminacy Crisis: Critiquing Critical Dogma," 54 *U. Chi. L. Rev.* 462 at 473 (1987); Timothy Endicott, *Vagueness in Law* (2000).
[24] Robert Alexy, *A Theory of Constitutional Rights* (Julian Rivers translation, 2002) at 47–48.
[25] Webber, *The Negotiable Constitution, supra* note 6 at 65, puts it this way: "What does one have by virtue of having a right? . . . both very much and, also, very little".

This approach has usually been grounded in normative arguments about the desirability of justification for state action, often described as developing a "culture of justification". The phrase was coined by South African scholar Etienne Mureinik in his discussion of the then-nascent South African Constitution:

> If the new Constitution is a bridge away from a culture of authority, it is clear what it must be a bridge to. It must lead to a culture of justification – a culture in which *every* exercise of power is expected to be justified; in which the leadership given by government rests on the cogency of the case offered in defence of its decisions, not the fear inspired by the force at its command. The new order must be a community built on persuasion, not coercion.[26]

Mureinik did not have any particular approach to justification in mind, and in particular did not equate justification with proportionality.[27] He conceived the culture of justification as an alternative to the culture of authority – of racist, authoritarian rule – that had obtained in apartheid South Africa, and hoped that the South African Bill of Rights would help bring about democratic rule.

Of course, the situation in well-developed constitutional democracies is quite different, and in these contexts the culture of justification idea is invoked by proponents in pursuit of a different purpose: the expansion of judicial review that proportionality analysis encourages, and according to some, entails.[28] The motivation, as Cohen-Eliya and Porat explain, is essentially a preference for decision making by judges:

> [T]he culture of justification is based on rationalism and elitism that are thought of as bulwarks against the prejudice and irrationality of unchecked popular democracy. In contrast to the culture of authority the culture of justification is not content with authority and legitimacy based on populism. It is suspicious of letting popular elected bodies decide for themselves, and

---

[26] Etienne Mureinik, "A Bridge to Where? Introducing the Interim Bill of Rights," (1994) 10 S. *Afr. J. Hum. Rts.* 31 at 32.

[27] In regard to administrative justice, for example, he stated that "[t]he courts will have to develop a theory of what makes a decision justifiable, and what makes it unjustifiable" and did no more than suggest that the focus should be on the soundness of the decision-making process, rather than the decision itself. Ibid. at 40–41.

[28] Enthusiastic proponents of the culture of justification and judicial review include David Dyzenhaus, "Law as Justification: Etienne Murenik's Conception of Legal Culture," (1998) 14 S. *Afr. J. Hum. Rts.* 11; "Dignity in Administrative Law: Judicial Deference in a Culture of Justification," SSRN 2029818; and "Proportionality and Deference in a Culture of Justification," Chapter 11 in this volume; and Murray Hunt, "Reshaping Constitutionalism" in J. Morison, K. McEvoy and G. Anthony (eds.), *Judges, Transition and Human Rights* (2007). The culture of justification is approved in passing by Aharon Barak, *Proportionality: Constitutional Rights and Their Limitations* (2011) at 459.

requires instead that they provide justification for their actions to external professional and elitist bodies, such as the courts.[29]

If the expansion of judicial review is motivated by elitist preferences, it is accomplished by relatively simple expedient of rendering questions of inter-pretation irrelevant, as Mattias Kumm and Kai Möller demonstrate.[30]

Kumm argues that the point of judicial review under bills of rights is to institutionalize what he terms a practice of "Socratic contestation" which he elaborates as a form of practical reason. According to Kumm:

> When using a proportionality test to assess whether an action infringing a rights are (sic) justified, it is misleading to say that Courts interpret rights. Instead of attempting to make sense of authoritative legal materials the focus of courts engaged in proportionality analysis is the assessment whether a public action can be demonstrably justified by reasons that are appropriate in a liberal democracy. Call this the *turn from legal interpretation to the public reason oriented justification*.[31]

This approach leads Kumm to diminish the idea of rights:

> [A] rights-holder does not have very much in virtue of his having a right. More specifically, the fact that a rights holder has a *prima facie* right does not imply that he holds a position that gives him any kind of priority over countervailing considerations of policy. An infringement of the scope of a right merely serves as a trigger to initiate an assessment of whether the infringement is justified.... The second characteristic feature of rights is the flip side of the first. Since comparatively little is decided by acknowledging that a measure infringes a right, the focus of rights adjudication is generally on the reasons that justify the infringement.[32]

On Kumm's account, rights are no more than triggers for justificatory evalua-tions; they are simply "positions" whose strength is determined by proportion-ality analysis, and as a result there are "no obvious reasons" for defining them

[29] Moshe Cohen-Eliya and Iddo Porat, "Proportionality and the Culture of Justification," 59 *Am. J. Comp. L.* 463 at 483 (2011) (hereinafter Cohen-Eliya and Porat, "Proportionality and the Culture of Justification").

[30] Stephen Gardbaum proposes an alternative normative justification he calls the "culture of democracy," which accommodates a more stringent approach to interpretation. But he does not argue that proportionality is the only or the best rights regime. See "Proportionality and Democratic Constitutionalism," Chapter 12 in this volume.

[31] Mattias Kumm, "The Idea of Socratic Contestation and the Right to Justification: The Point of Rights-Based Proportionality Review," (2010) 4 *Law & Ethics of Human Rights* 141 at 142 (emphasis in original) (hereinafter Kumm, "Socratic Contestation").

[32] Ibid. at 150. Kumm acknowledges the compatibility of Rawlsian public reason with proportion-ality reasoning, but denies that his argument depends on Rawls's conception of public reason (ibid. at note 46).

narrowly.[33] Text, history, precedent, and most of the other traditional tools of legal analysis – the very basics of the legal process when it comes to the practice of rights adjudication.[34] – do not matter. All that matters is justification. Kumm asks rhetorically: "Shouldn't all acts by public authorities affecting individuals meet the proportionality requirement? Does the proportionality test not provide a general purpose test for ensuring that public institutions take seriously individuals and their interests and act only for good reasons?"[35] For Kumm, it appears, the authority of legislation stems not from its democratic pedigree but, instead, from its justification.[36] From here it is a short step to concluding that the provisions of a bill of rights are essentially irrelevant.

Kumm is not alone in rejecting the normative force of rights. Kai Möller argues that the point of rights is not to single out certain especially important interests for heightened protection. "Rather, it is to show a particular form of respect for persons by insisting that each and every state measure that affects a person's ability to live her life according to her self-conception must take her autonomy interests adequately into account."[37]

Möller claims that there is a general right to personal autonomy, which he describes as "a right to everything which, judged from the perspective of the agent's self-conception, is in his interest".[38] From this, it follows that attempts to limit the scope of rights are necessarily arbitrary; rights should be interpreted sufficiently broadly so as to minimize what he describes as "gaps" in the protection of personal autonomy.[39] Möller terms this "rights inflation",[40] and it means that trivial activities such as feeding the birds in the park[41] will be protected as rights along with evil activities such as murder.[42]

Neither Möller's nor Kumm's approach can be reconciled with the conception of bills of rights I have outlined. If, as I have argued, bills of rights

---

[33] Ibid. at 151.   [34] Ibid. at 144.

[35] Ibid. at 151.

[36] "The question is not what justifies the 'countermajoritarian' imposition of outcomes by non-elected judges. The question is what justifies the authority of a legislative decision, when it can be established with sufficient certainty that it imposes burdens on individuals for which there is no reasonable justification." Ibid. at 170 (internal footnote omitted).

[37] Möller, "Proportionality and Rights Inflation," Chapter 7 in this volume at 166.

[38] Kai Möller, *The Global Model of Constitutional Rights* (2012) at 73 (hereinafter Möller, *The Global Model*).

[39] "The argument is that (1) all things being equal, an interpretation of the constitution should be adopted which is in line with the general point or purpose of the constitution as a whole; (2) the constitution as a whole is best explained by a commitment to a comprehensive protection of personal autonomy; (3) therefore a prima facie right which is open to a broader or narrower interpretation should be interpreted broadly so as to include the respective personal autonomy interest at stake." Ibid. at 87.

[40] Kai Möller, "Proportionality and Rights Inflation," Chapter 7 in this volume.

[41] Ibid., citing BVerfGE 54 at 143.   [42] Ibid.

are bills of *particular* rights, then an interpretation that treats any one of those rights as an all-encompassing right to liberty or autonomy must be rejected, for it renders all of the other rights in a bill of rights – the constitutional settlement itself – redundant. In effect, proportionality proponents assume a constitutional settlement in which the validity of all democratically enacted legislation is contingent on judicial approval, on a more or less exacting proportionality standard.[43]

Suffice it to say that this conception is belied by the constitutional history of every country in which a bill of rights has been adopted. It renders the negotiation, compromise, and agreement involved in the adoption of a bill of rights irrelevant and portends a massive shift in power in the constitutional order from the legislature to the judiciary that cannot plausibly be said to have been intended.[44]

V. CONCLUSION

I have considered the importance of interpretation in a democratic constitutional order in which the elected branches of government are understood as having the authority to legislate subject to such constitutional constraints as may exist. Those constraints, I argued, are found typically in bills of rights, and the courts must determine their extent through process of interpretation.

I noted earlier that common law constitutionalists pose a challenge to the concept of a constitutional settlement and the idea of finiteness this entails, for they insist that bills of rights are simply examples of rights that are otherwise immanent in the common law. This is a radical claim: it is one thing to insist that there is more to democracy than procedural majority rule – that democracy

---

[43] I say "more or less" because most (but not all) proportionality proponents assume that proportionality analysis will be applied deferentially. Mattias Kumm puts it this way: "The fact that a court engages in proportionality analysis does not imply anything about the degree of deference it should accord political actors. . . . A court can inquire more or less searchingly whether the relevant prongs of the test are satisfied." Kumm, "Socratic Contestation," *supra* note 31 at note 55. Elsewhere, Kumm has enumerated four relevant considerations for deference, but these are stated at a high level of generality and he declines to explore them in any detail. See Kumm, "Democracy is Not Enough: Rights, Proportionality, and the Point of Judicial Review," (2009) NYU Public Law and Legal Theory Working Papers, Paper 118. Kai Möller, emphasizes a concept of deference as reasonableness (as opposed to correctness) in reviewing answers reached at the *stricto sensu* stage of proportionality analysis. See Möller, *The Global Model, supra* note 38 at 200–203.

[44] "For framers of new constitutions," Möller writes, "the idea of a comprehensive right to personal autonomy calls into question the necessity of a set of distinct constitutional rights" (ibid. at 88). Nevertheless, Möller endorses the adoption of a "well designed list of rights", among other things, because it is easier for the public to understand.

involves richer, substantive commitments – but it is quite another to insist that judges may identify and elaborate those commitments, invest them with legal force, and purport to invalidate legislation on the basis that is inconsistent with them. For all of the academic[45] and extrajudicial[46] support common law constitutionalism has enjoyed, as Jeffrey Goldsworthy has noted, judges have never exercised the power common law constitutionalists insist that they have.[47] They may well speak romantically of the common law constitution, or even go so far as to assert the existence of rights underlying the constitution.[48] When asked to give effect to underlying constitutional rights – sometimes referred to as "unwritten rights" – however, courts are likely to accord primacy to the terms of the written constitution.[49] As the Supreme Court of Canada explained in rejecting the argument that the "rule of law" could be invoked to invalidate legislation, "[this] conception of the unwritten constitutional principle of the rule of law would render many of our written constitutional rights redundant and, in doing so, undermine the delimitation of *those rights chosen by our constitutional framers*."[50] That, it seems to me, is the correct result in any political community that adopts a bill of rights. But if courts are likely to reject the claims of the common law constitutionalists, they have failed to notice that in diminishing the importance of interpretation they risk reaching outcomes that they would otherwise consider illegitimate.

---

[45] T.R.S. Allan has written extensively on the subject. See, e.g., *Constitutional Justice: A Liberal Theory of the Rule of Law* (2001), and "Constitutional Justice and the Concept of Law" in Grant Huscroft (ed.), *Expounding the Constitution: Essays in Constitutional Theory* (2008) 219. See also Mark D. Walters, "Written Constitutions and Unwritten Constitutionalism" in *Expounding the Constitution* (ibid. at 245); David Dyzenhaus, "The Unwritten Constitution and the Rule of Law" in Grant Huscroft and Ian Brodie (eds.), *Constitutionalism in the Charter Era* (2004) 383.

[46] Hon. Beverley McLachlin, "Unwritten Constitutional Principles: What Is Going On?" (2006) 4 N.Z. J. Pub. and Int. Law 147. I criticize McLachlin's approach in Grant Huscroft, "Romance, Realism, and the Legitimacy of Implied Rights," (2011) 30 *U. Queensland L.J.* 1 (hereinafter Huscroft, "Romance, Realism").

[47] Jeffrey Goldsworthy, "Homogenizing Constitutions," (2003) 23 O.J.L.S. 483, reviewing Allan, *Constitutional Justice*, ibid. The power was championed by Lord Cooke, as President of the New Zealand Court of Appeal, in a series of dicta, famously in *Taylor v. New Zealand Poultry Board* [1984] 1 N.Z. L. Rev. 394 at 398. Cooke's position is criticized as heresy by Justice Michael Kirby in "Lord Cooke and Fundamental Rights" in Paul Rishworth (ed.), *The Struggle for Simplicity in the Law: Essays for Lord Cooke of Thorndon*) (1997) 331.

[48] The Supreme Court of Canada's oft-misunderstood implied bill of rights jurisprudence in the pre-Charter era is discussed in Huscroft, "Romance, Realism," *supra* note 46.

[49] The Supreme Court of Canada emphasized the "compelling reasons to insist upon the primacy of our written constitution" in *Reference re Secession of Quebec*, [1999] 2 S.C.R. 217 at para. 53.

[50] *British Columbia v. Imperial Tobacco Canada Ltd.*, [2005] 2 S.C.R. 473 at paras. 65–67 (emphasis added).

To focus on proportionality at the expense of interpretation is to expand the realm of protected rights in a manner that common law constitutionalists find congenial. It is, in effect, to recognize rights that may not be part of the constitutional settlement.

The merits of proportionality analysis are now considered so obvious that proponents feel free to invite courts to simply ignore questions of interpretation, and to focus on justification. Moshe Cohen-Eliya and Iddo Porat describe this development in bracing terms:

> The new focus of constitutional judges throughout the world on justification moves them away from the text and from interpretation. While it is true that the texts of new constitutions direct judges to assess whether the limitations are 'justified in a democratic society', *this amounts to an authorization by the text to downplay the text, i.e.,* to engage in the assessment of justification, rather than textual interpretation.[51]

But constitutions reflect choices and commitments of a political community that are morally significant, and these choices must command the respect of the judiciary.[52] A culture of justification is possible, in other words, only within the confines of the bill of rights that establishes it. Interpretation is not all that there is to rights-based constitutionalism, but it is far more than proportionality proponents would have it.

---

[51] "Proportionality and the Culture of Justification," *supra* note 29 at 489–490, emphasis added. In an earlier SSRN version of the paper, Cohen-Eliya and Porat went further, describing the requirement of justification as "authorization of the text to disregard the text, and thus go engage in the assessment of justification and not in interpretation."

[52] Proponents of living constitutions concede as much. W.J. Waluchow notes that bills of rights "entrench prior decisions about which rights deserve constitutional protection.... Reasonable people might wish, if we could start with a clean slate, for a slightly different collection of rights from those settled upon" (*A Common Law Theory of Judicial Review: The Living Tree* (2007) at 240).

PART III

PROPORTIONALITY AND JUSTIFICATION

10   Democracy, Legality, and Proportionality

T.R.S. Allan

I. INTRODUCTION

Contrasting conceptions of democracy are closely related to competing accounts of the concept of law. Our concepts of law and democracy are ultimately connected; and our view of the judicial role in constitutional adjudication is bound to reflect our understanding of these basic ideas. A positivist conception of law, emphasizing the authority of constitutional texts and formally enacted statutes (as principal *sources* of law) is a better fit with a majoritarian conception of democracy: the law ultimately obtains its sanction from the votes of the majority of elected representatives, whether to the constitutional convention or the legislative assembly. An alternative conception of law locates its authority in allegiance to an abstract idea of human dignity, to which bills or codes of rights are important, but inessential, approximations. It is companion to a conception of democracy as an open dialogue, among citizens of equal worth or status, about both the public good and the fundamental rights of individuals. Because that dialogue takes place in the context of a legal tradition, emphasizing individual autonomy and respect for persons, it seeks to understand and improve an existing order of justice. New rules and resolutions must be accommodated within a complex tapestry of law, maintaining a balance between stability and change, moral principle and political aspiration. The application of formally adopted rules must, in particular, be sensitive to potential injustice in particular instances: there is a moral dimension to adjudication that even the regimentation of values secured by a charter of rights cannot fully exhaust or accommodate.

Because justice consists in the correct regulation of affairs or resolution of disputes, according to the moral principles applicable, it invokes the notion of proportionality: there must be an appropriate weighting of relevant principles to reflect their proper balance in all the circumstances. Principles of justice are

always dependent on context in the sense that what they permit or require must
be determined by analysis of all the relevant facts; the balance of principles
will vary accordingly. It is implicit in this understanding, however, that the
relevant principles together compose a harmonious order of justice, so that
everyone is treated impartially: like cases are decided alike, where likeness is
determined according to consistent criteria, reflecting the overall scheme of
moral principle. The distinctions drawn between people, to justify different
treatment, must be rationally defensible; they must make reference to stable
features of the order or scheme of justice, showing that differential treatment
is not the result of personal bias or official whim. It need not be supposed
that the general scheme of principle is incapable of change or development,
as novel perceptions of justice arise to challenge traditional ideas; but a fresh
appraisal of one matter of justice will have implications for all such matters.
There is an implicit striving for coherence: the balance of principles, in any
particular case, is ultimately justified by reference to the order of justice as a
whole.[1]

The common law comes close to giving such a conception of justice a
practical, institutional form. Lacking any canonical linguistic form akin to an
enacted text, a common law rule is no more than a convenient, provisional
summary of the balance of principles applicable to a certain type or category of
case. It is the ideas rather than their specific verbal expression that possess the
relevant authority: the rule must be understood in the light of the principles of
justice that inform and justify it, making its application dependent on appraisal
of its *appropriateness* in all the circumstances. It follows that, although a
common law judge is to some extent bound by precedent, he treats it as a
guide to the correct balance of principles rather than an exclusionary rule of
the sort that precludes an examination of all the pertinent moral reasons. As
Stephen Perry has explained, a judge may depart from the reasoning of an
earlier case only when the collective weight of a new formulation of principles
appears to him to be "above a threshold of strength which is higher than what
would be required on the ordinary balance of reasons".[2] The weight of any
given proposition of law will depend on many factors, including the seniority
of the courts that have invoked it, the frequency of such reliance, and the age
of the relevant precedents. Nor is its weight fixed, independent of context:

---

[1] Cf. Ronald Dworkin, *Law's Empire* (1986) esp. ch. 6.
[2] Stephen R. Perry, "Judicial Obligation, Precedent and the Common Law," (1987) 7 O.J.L.S.
     215 at 240. Perry provides an effective critique of Joseph Raz's unsuccessful attempt (in Raz,
     The Authority of Law: Essays on Law and Morality (1979) [hereinafter Raz, The Authority of
     Law]) to apply the idea of exclusionary rules to common law precedent.

"its weight is also relative to the position in the judicial hierarchy of whatever court is contemplating modifying it, as well as to the extent of the modification which is proposed".[3]

We can see that proportionality is a principle that operates on two levels. It is implicit in the idea of the balance of first-order reasons, applicable to the facts of the particular case. It also plays a role in maintaining the balance between such first-order reasons and the constraints of precedent: such constraints give way when the weight of a new formulation of principle passes a certain threshold of strength. In practice, however, there is rarely such a clear distinction between distinct levels of reasoning. Previous cases are usually *distinguished* rather than overruled completely, whether by adding new conditions for the applicability of a common law rule or (extending the scope of the rule) abandoning previous ones. In the result, a balance is maintained between loyalty to the established order of justice and innovation designed to improve it, whether by adaptation to novel contexts or eradicating (what are now perceived to be) errors or deficiencies. Again, however, that distinction must not be exaggerated. The correction of error is always made on the basis of insights drawn from the existing order of justice, which at a fundamental level inspires and organizes our shared understandings and moral assumptions and commitments.[4]

A rule that prohibits the disclosure of information obtained in confidence, for example, may be applied to a context that differs from the usual commercial one: a former government minister may be restrained by injunction from revealing the secrets of the Cabinet room.[5] In the new context, however, the principle of confidentiality must be weighed against the principle of freedom of speech, which is of great importance in the political sphere. Because an injunction preventing the publication of relatively stale information would be disproportionate to the curtailment of free speech, the doctrine of breach of confidence must be qualified accordingly.[6] In the course of development, however, the requirement of an initial confidential relationship has itself disappeared: encompassing the disclosure of matters that should reasonably be

---

[3] Ibid. at 242.
[4] *Cf.* Gerald Postema, "Integrity: Justice in Workclothes," 82 *Iowa L. Rev.* 821 at 830 (1997); Scott Hershovitz, "Integrity and Stare Decisis" in Scott Hershovitz (ed.), *Exploring Law's Empire: The Jurisprudence of Ronald Dworkin* (2006) 103 at 113–116.
[5] *Attorney-General v. Jonathan Cape*, [1976] Q.B. 752.
[6] Lord Goff envisaged a balancing of the relevant principles (or public interests) in *Attorney-General v. Guardian Newspapers (No 2)*, [1990] 1 A.C. 109. Lord Griffiths also observed that any harm caused by disclosure "must be examined and weighed against the other countervailing public interest of freedom of speech and the right of the people in a democracy to be informed by a free press" (at 273).

treated as confidential, the tort is better described as the misuse of private information.[7] The common law has developed to meet the perceived deficiencies of its previous protection of personal privacy, and as the relevant cause of action has broadened in scope, the balance of principles has assumed a more important role. The common law now matches the balance of principles required under articles 8 and 10 of the European Convention on Human Rights. It is a question, in each case, of the extent to which it is *necessary* to qualify each right in order to protect the basic value protected by the other.[8]

When a bill of rights is treated as an affirmation of the fundamental values of an existing legal tradition, on the basis of appropriate conceptions of law and democracy, constitutional adjudication will reflect the cautious incremental approach of the common law. The content of individual rights will be heavily dependent on social and political context, allowing full scope for argument about the needs of the common good. The proportionality doctrine will be employed to secure a defensible accommodation of competing rights and interests, according to the circumstances of the particular case. Although a code of rights will necessarily distinguish between assertions of right on one hand, and grounds of limitation on the other, the scope and content of rights cannot in practice be separated from the moral and social considerations that may be urged against their application (or extension) in particular instances. Practical reasoning becomes distorted if bill of rights doctrine is too rigidly formulated, allowing text and structure to overwhelm more fundamental questions of substance.[9] Not only is it usually necessary to weigh competing rights and interests before concluding that a constitutional right has been infringed; but talk of "infringement" or "violation" can foster the impression that rights may be dispensed with when highly inconvenient, or when government or Parliament is sufficiently robust in its determination to override them.

The idea that the construction of statutes is a radically different exercise from ordinary common law reasoning is an implication of a deficient conception of the rule of law. Rather than being treated as the sovereign's command, substituting preemptive authority for moral principle, legislation should be conceived as influential guidance to the requirements of reason in a range of specific instances. The true meaning of the statutory text is a product of an interpretation sensitive not merely to the expectations generated by plain or ordinary meaning, but also to a broader constitutional context within which

---

[7] *Campbell v. M.G.N.* [2004] U.K.H.L. 22 at para. 14 (per Lord Nicholls).

[8] Ibid. at para. 55 (per Lord Hoffmann).

[9] See Bradley W. Miller, "Justification and Rights Limitations" in Grant Huscroft (ed.), *Expounding the Constitution* (2008) 93.

immediate public purposes must be reconciled with more enduring legal values. There must be an appraisal of the particular "mischief" to which a statute is primarily addressed and the nature of the remedy it provides.[10] Beyond the plain or standard case, where there is broad agreement about the applicability of a rule's classifying terms, its application to more doubtful or marginal instances must be a matter of judgment in which all relevant considerations must be fairly and wisely balanced.[11] An ordinary or literal reading will quickly give way to a construction more suited to a statement of *guidance*, framed by a legislature whose responsibility for the public good embraces the interests and well-being of every citizen. Restrictions of individual rights must be *proportionate* to the aims and benefits envisaged.[12]

A formal conception of the rule of law, providing only a formal equality before the law (whatever it permits or proscribes) is a reflection of law as the command of a sovereign ruler, whose function is to settle disagreement by authoritative decree.[13] The point of democracy, however, is to secure government not only by the people (or their representatives) but to secure it in their collective interest: there must be provision for advancement of a common good, in recognition of which everyone can, in principle, collaborate by obedience to a legitimate regime of law. For such a regime, only a more thorough-going and substantive equality can serve: each person's treatment must be capable of *justification* by reference to an explicitly articulated conception of the public good, open to uninhibited debate and criticism. If the citizen of a democratic state is entitled to the protection of a rule of law on the basis of equal dignity, particular laws may only discriminate between persons for good reasons: the relevant distinctions must be shown to relate to governmental objectives that all could acknowledge as legitimate, consistent with their self-respect as equal citizens. It is implicit in this conception of democracy, moreover, that the burdens borne by individuals must be proportionate to the advancement of the public interest.[14]

---

[10] See *Heydon's Case* (1584) 3 Co. Rep. 7a, 7b; 76 Eng. Rep. 637.

[11] *Cf.* H.L.A. Hart, *The Concept of Law*, 2nd ed. (1994) at 126–127 (hereinafter Hart, *The Concept of Law*).

[12] I have defended an approach to statutory interpretation analogous to common law reasoning in Allan, "Text, Context, and Constitution: The Common Law as Public Reason" in Douglas E. Edlin (ed.), *Common Law Theory* (2007) 185 (hereinafter Allan, "Text, Context, and Constitution"). See also, T.R.S. Allan, "Legislative Supremacy and Legislative Intention: Interpretation, Meaning, and Authority," (2004) 63 *C.L.J.* 685.

[13] *Cf.* Hart, *The Concept of Law, supra* note 11 chs. 2–4.

[14] See, generally, T.R.S. Allan, *Constitutional Justice: A Liberal Theory of the Rule of Law* (2001) (hereinafter Allan, *Constitutional Justice*); and T.R.S. Allan, "Constitutional Justice and the Concept of Law," in Grant Huscroft (ed.), *Expounding the Constitution* (2008) 219.

Although the judicial enforcement of constitutional rights imposes significant limits on the scope of legislative and governmental decision making, it
provides a necessary guarantee of individual autonomy. Freedoms of speech,
conscience, and association are basic ingredients of any liberal democratic
polity; judicial protection of their core requirements safeguards citizens' moral
independence, ensuring their continuing ability to challenge the exercise of
power. Nor could democracy flourish without freedom of movement, rights
against arbitrary detention and punishment, rights of fair trial, and the other
familiar civil and political liberties that together afford the individual citizen the security necessary to resist the arbitrary will of officials (elected or
otherwise). A true republic, which provides the framework for deliberative
democracy, is one in which freedom as independence, or non-domination, is
secured by legally enforceable constitutional safeguards; it must be an "empire
of laws", within whose shelter everyone is at liberty to defend his own conception of the public good and denounce and challenge what he considers
injustice or wrongdoing.[15]

Within a true democracy, the citizen's assent to the laws is not obtained
merely by his participation in the election of members of Parliament; it is
obtained, if possible, by the process of reasoned deliberation by which the law,
abstractly expounded or enacted, is made concrete in the course of application
to his own affairs. Positive law, in a liberal democracy, cannot be merely an
efficient instrument for attaining specific political ends, even if they serve a
defensible view of the public good; rather, it provides a structure for intelligent
deliberation about how such ends can best be secured without unnecessary
harm to the fundamental well-being of individuals.[16] It is precisely because the
general law is directed to legitimate public ends, to which all could assent in
principle, that its implications for particular cases require *judgment*, sensitive
to countervailing rights and interests.

When statutory interpretation is conceived as the integration of enacted rules
with basic moral standards, in the manner of common law construction, there
is normally little occasion for conflict between parliamentary initiative and the
judicial defense of constitutional rights. Potential conflict between fundamental rights or between such rights and general public interests is best resolved
according to context, allowing reasonable solutions to be found, respectful of

---

[15] See Philip Pettit, *Republicanism: A Theory of Freedom and Government* (1997).
[16] For a conception of the rule of law as the mark of efficiency, see Raz, *The Authority of Law*,
      supra note 2 ch. 11. For a helpful critique, see David Dyzenhaus, *The Constitution of Law:
      Legality in a Time of Emergency* (2006) at 220–233.

all the relevant considerations. The closer the dependence of judgment on all the circumstances of a particular case, the weaker the supposed "democratic" objection to judicial review. Because it is not the function of a legislature to determine particular cases – except insofar as they fall uncontroversially within the terms of a general rule – it cannot be usurped by adjudication, responsive to the specific weight of relevant legal principles. When the legislative responsibility for enacting general rules is properly distinguished from the judicial responsibility to determine the outcome of particular cases, parliamentary supremacy is reconciled with the rule of law. Enactments that violate any plausible view of equal citizenship, however benignly construed, forfeit the status of *law*; those that would infringe fundamental rights, if construed literally, must be read as authorizing only more modest encroachments, proportionate to legitimate public ends.

II. EQUALITY, RATIONALITY, PROPORTIONALITY

The traditional reluctance of English courts to apply a proportionality test to the acts of public authorities in the course of judicial review indicated an exaggerated deference to superior technical expertise or democratic credentials. There was resistance to proportionality as a ground of review because it was thought to substitute judicial for administrative discretion, abridging the distinction between review for legality and appeal on the merits.[17] The elastic and all-purpose *Wednesbury* doctrine, however, was capable of adaptation to protect the basic rights of individuals, even if the necessary element of weighing or balancing conflicting interests was often obscured or inarticulate.[18] At root, however, lay a reluctance to embrace the administrative state as part of the fabric of the common law; the exercise of governmental powers took place under statutory authority, which existed alongside, but not as an integral part of, the ordinary common law. The ultra vires doctrine symbolized this conception of judicial review: the enforcement of legality meant keeping the public agency within whatever limits and boundaries Parliament had stipulated, whether expressly or impliedly. Even the familiar common law grounds of review (such as *Wednesbury* unreasonableness) were applied in line with what was conceived as the intention of Parliament, and subject therefore to any contrary indications. The more recent repudiation of ultra vires by many

---

[17] See, e.g., *R. v. Secretary of State for the Home Dept, ex p Brind* [1991] 1 A.C. 696.
[18] *Cf.* Jeffrey Jowell and Anthony Lester, "Proportionality: Neither Novel nor Dangerous" in J. Jowell and D. Oliver (eds.), *New Directions in Judicial Review* (1988) 51.

administrative lawyers suggests a developing appreciation of the fundamental nature of judicial review as a safeguard of basic rights protected by the common law constitution.[19]

The failure to acknowledge the proportionality requirement as an intrinsic element of rationality or reasonableness contrasted with the courts' delineation and defense of common law constitutional rights. The "principle of legality" is applied by English courts to protect such basic rights against damage inflicted in the exercise of a statutory power. As a necessary adjunct of the fundamental right of access to the courts, for example, the right to confidential legal advice placed implicit constraints on the Home Secretary's powers, under the Prison Act 1952, to manage prisons and control prisoners.[20] In the absence, at any rate, of explicit statutory curtailment, the executive could impose no limitations without proving a "demonstrable need" for them. There was a power to intercept correspondence between a prisoner and his lawyer only if a "self-evident and pressing need" for it could be established.[21] Similarly, in *R (Daly) v. Secretary of State for the Home Department*,[22] a policy of routinely excluding prisoners from their cells during searches was held to be a disproportionate intrusion into the same right. The examination of privileged correspondence in a prisoner's absence would endanger its confidential status; it could be justified only in the case of "dangerous, disruptive and manipulative" prisoners whose presence might obstruct or intimidate prison officers.[23]

Lord Steyn's attempt, in *Daly*, to distinguish between reasonableness and proportionality, as contrasting grounds of review, is not persuasive.[24] His distinction between identifying the relevant considerations (under *Wednesbury*) and assessing their respective weights, via proportionality, is too formalistic; the scope of a public authority's discretion to attach a greater or lesser weight to a relevant matter must depend on all the circumstances. Whether or not a decision falls within the permissible "range of rational or reasonable decisions" depends on the extent of that range, and when a decision restricts a fundamental right, the range is necessarily curtailed. The failure to accord a proper weight to a factor of great importance is the hallmark of a wholly unreasonable decision, adopted in breach of the *Wednesbury* standard of legality. The constitutional context is always critical to any appraisal of rationality: the "more substantial the interference with human rights", the more the court should

---

[19] See, generally, Christopher Forsyth (ed.), *Judicial Review and the Constitution* (2000); T.R.S. Allan, "The Constitutional Foundations of Judicial Review: Conceptual Conundrum or Interpretative Inquiry?" (2002) 61 C.L.J. 87.

[20] *R. v. Secretary of State for the Home Dept, ex p Leech (No 2)*, [1993] 3 W.L.R. 1125.

[21] Ibid. at 1137.   [22] [2001] U.K.H.L. 26.

[23] Ibid. para 19 (per Lord Bingham of Cornhill).   [24] Ibid. para 27.

"require by way of justification before it is satisfied" that a decision is that of a reasonable decision maker.[25] A measure that has a wholly disproportionate effect on those affected adversely may be suspected of serving illegitimate ends, incompatible with respect for equal citizenship: we may well have good grounds for doubting the bona fides of the allegedly proper ends envisaged.[26]

The principle of legality is usually defended as an interpretative device that protects basic rights from unforeseen and unintended injury. Parliament must make any qualifications or restrictions unequivocally plain: "In the absence of express language or necessary implication to the contrary, the courts . . . presume that even the most general words were intended to be subject to the basic rights of the individual."[27] That presumption, however, has a constitutional basis that must be jealously guarded: legality cannot be reduced to explicit commands, literally interpreted. If it is a feature of basic rights that what they permit or require is always dependent, in detail, on all the circumstances, there cannot be any legislative "intention" (or instruction) to abrogate or *override* them, even by express provision. Legislative intent is only a metaphor, it signifies the importance of making the application of legislation responsive to the policies or purposes that best appear to animate and justify it. Whether or not a statutory discretion entails some qualification of rights, or affects the relevant individual interests, is a *conclusion* of the interpretative process, in which the respective public and private interests are appraised and balanced in the light of all the relevant facts.

Although a fundamental right, on the basis of what respect for human dignity requires, will make varying demands on government, according to all the circumstances, it cannot be *overridden* in favor of other interests. Justice Wilson was therefore right, in her concurring opinion in the *Motor Vehicle Act Reference*, to reject the notion that a provision offending the principles of "fundamental justice" (under section 7 of the Canadian Charter of Rights and Freedoms) might nonetheless be capable of rescue under section 1 of the Charter.[28] The right not to be deprived of life, liberty, or personal security

---

[25] *R. v. Ministry of Defence, ex p Smith* [1996], 1 All E.R. 257 at 263 (per Sir Thomas Bingham M.R.).

[26] *Smith and Grady* is discussed in the text below.

[27] *R. v. Secretary of State for the Home Dept, ex. p. Simms*, [1999] 3 All E.R. 400 at 412 (Lord Hoffmann) (hereinafter *Simms*).

[28] *Reference re B.C. Motor Vehicle Act (BC)* s 94(2), [1985] 2 SCR 486 at para. 104 [*Reference re B.C. Motor Vehicle Act*]. The majority judgment assumed that a breach of section 7 might be justified by reference to section 1. According to Lamer J., however, it would be only under "exceptional conditions" that rights under section 7 could properly be "sacrificed to administrative expediency" (para 85).

in a manner that infringes the principles of fundamental justice must be absolute: fundamental justice is a matter of what human dignity and equal citizenship in that context requires. It would, then, be a contradiction in terms to hold that a breach of section 7 of the Charter might nonetheless be "reasonable" or "demonstrably justified in a free and democratic society." A free and democratic society is one in which the rule of law is observed and human dignity upheld. Even the notion that government might "dispense with the requirements of fundamental justice" under section 33 is deeply problematic, amounting to the displacement of law by naked political power (just as Lord Hoffmann envisaged by his exaggerated homage to parliamentary sovereignty in *Simms*).[29]

In stipulating that it created "an absolute liability offence in which guilt is established by proof of driving", whether or not the defendant knew that he had been prohibited from driving or that his license had been suspended, the legislation plainly contradicted the ordinary presumption of the need for mens rea.[30] The specification of liability to a fine and minimum period of imprisonment also appeared to curtail the scope for leniency in the case of a blameless driver.[31] It would have been possible, nevertheless, to treat the provision as applicable only to cases in which a license was canceled automatically, pursuant to a provincial statute, so that any lack of knowledge was merely the result of ignorance of law.[32] The liability to imprisonment could have been deemed inapplicable to other cases falling within the literal scope of section 94. Literally interpreted, however, the statute clearly infringed the Charter, as a violation of the right not to be deprived of liberty except in accordance with the principles of fundamental justice.

If, as the Supreme Court of Canada appeared to accept, the imposition of absolute liability was sometimes legitimate, the question of proportionality must lie at the heart of the question of fundamental justice. The statutory prohibition had to be "measured against the offence being one of strict liability open to a defence of due diligence, the success of which does nothing

---

[29] See *Simms, supra* note 27. According to Wilson J., section 33 of the Charter could be invoked "to dispense with the requirements of fundamental justice" in an emergency: that would be "a policy decision for which the government concerned will be politically accountable to the people" (para. 119). There is, however, arguably a difference between an overriding of rights and the legislative veto of a judicial declaration of invalidity where (in the latter case) there has been insufficient deference to reasonable, prudential legislative judgment: see Alan Brudner, *Constitutional Goods* (2004) at 283–285.

[30] *Motor Vehicle Act*, R.S.B.C. 1979 (as amended) s. 94(2).

[31] Ibid. at s 94(1)(c),(d).

[32] For an example, see *R. v. MacDougall*, [1982] 2 S.C.R. 605.

more than let those few who did nothing wrong remain free".[33] Justice Wilson concluded that "the conscience of the court would be shocked and the administration of justice brought into disrepute by such an unreasonable and extravagant penalty", which was "totally disproportionate to the offence" and incompatible with any legitimate penal objective.[34] Although Justice Wilson observed that a punishment should be a "fit" sentence, proportionate to the seriousness of the offence, the underlying idea must be a fundamental equality between offenders. It is not that "there is an inherently appropriate relation between a particular offence and its punishment, but rather that there is a scale of offences and punishments into which the particular offence and punishment must fit".[35] In adhering to such a scale, judges maintain the state's impartiality, punishing the offence rather than the offender. Arbitrary breaches of that impartiality flout both the rule of law and democracy: they exclude the offender from the protection of the community's law, applicable in democratic principle to everyone.

Unfair punishments, disproportionate to the crime, strike at democratic equality not merely because they violate the formal principle of treating likes alike, but more especially because they do not match the moral blame properly attributable. An excessive penalty is one that is not *deserved*; it victimizes the offender by inflicting harm that cannot be justified by reference to culpability: "It is beyond anything required to satisfy the need for 'atonement.'"[36] Such victimization contravenes the basic principle of *responsibility* that is closely tied to the idea of independent moral agency, underpinning our commitment to democracy itself. Punishing those who are morally innocent, or inflicting excessive punishments out of all proportion to the crime, are no less violations of democracy than denying disfavored persons the vote; adherence to the rule of law runs in tandem with respect for democratic governance. Like fair and equal representation, compliance with the ordinary principles of criminal justice is demanded by the affirmation of persons' equal dignity, basic to the liberal democratic ideal.

If any right deserves recognition as the "right of rights" in a true democracy, it is the right not to be subjected to cruel or unusual or arbitrary punishment; for such a form of official victimization, by depriving a person of the ordinary protections of impartial criminal justice, in effect expels him from the political community. Arbitrary punishment, inconsistent with the general principles of law, is inherently irrational; it imposes burdens on the individual that cannot

---

[33] *Reference re B.C. Motor Vehicle Act, supra* note 28 at para. 94.
[34] Ibid. at para. 127.   [35] Ibid. at para. 128.
[36] Ibid. at para. 130.

be justified as necessary for the public good. As Justice Murphy recognized, in respect of (unwritten) Australian constitutional law, a right against the infliction of such punishment is implicit in the constitution of a "free society", on the basis of democratic principles and the rule of law.[37] For Jeremy Waldron, following William Cobbett, the right of rights is the right to participate in lawmaking;[38] but when lawmaking entails a departure from general principles, drawing indefensible distinctions between different groups contrary to basic justice, it loses its legitimacy. Our concepts of law and democracy are ultimately bound to our conception of equality or equal citizenship.

There may, of course, be legitimate and reasonable disagreement about the arbitrariness of a specific penalty, and to the extent of such disagreement, if no further, the courts should concede an appropriate sphere of political discretion. Lord Bingham acknowledged that, in the context of a challenge to the mandatory sentence of life imprisonment for murder, "a degree of deference is due to the judgment of a democratic assembly on how a particular social problem is best tackled".[39] The mandatory sentence survived unscathed because, as administered in practice, it allowed the release of a prisoner who posed no danger to the public once the punitive element of his sentence (or "tariff") had been completed. A convicted murderer did not, on correct analysis, forfeit "his liberty to the state for the rest of his days", wholly at the mercy of unfettered ministerial discretion.[40] Because the tariff reflected the judge's view of the gravity of the individual offence, the formal sentence could not be deemed so arbitrary or disproportionate as to constitute a breach of Article 3 or 5 of the European Convention. A qualified deference to Parliament was therefore justified: "It may be accepted that the mandatory life penalty for murder has a denunciatory value, expressing society's view of a crime which has long been regarded with peculiar abhorrence."[41]

A judgment of proportionality, fairly made, sustains democracy by preserving a defensible moral balance between individual and collective interests. No one is simply sacrificed for the general good as if his own welfare were of no account. The greater the burden a measure imposes on those affected, judged by reference to stable and widely accepted criteria, the more securely its contribution to the public good must be established: "The more severe the deleterious effects of a measure, the more important the objective must be if the measure is to be reasonable and demonstrably justified in a free and

---

[37] *Sillery v. R.* (1981) 35 A.L.R. 227 at 233–234.
[38] Jeremy Waldron, *Law and Disagreement* (1999) ch. 11.
[39] *R. v. Lichniak*, [2002] U.K.H.L. 47 at para. 14.
[40] Ibid. at para. 8.   [41] Ibid. at para. 14.

democratic society."[42] A greater public benefit justifies, in principle, a more serious limitation of (the extent or scope of) rights. The test of proportionality or necessity must not impede the exercise of legitimate discretion, whether in determining public objectives or choosing how strenuously to pursue those thought to be most urgent. There must be "judicial restraint" in the sense that it is not for the courts to select which of a potentially extensive set of proportionate decisions is best; the judicial role is "to secure legality, not correctness."[43]

In general, a measure is proportionate whenever an alternative, less restrictive of rights, would be significantly less effective. It is only *disproportionate* if a less-intrusive alternative would not be very much inferior as a means to a legitimate end. In *Smith and Grady v. United Kingdom*,[44] the European Court of Human Rights held that termination of the applicants' membership of the armed forces on the ground of their homosexual orientation had breached their right to respect for private life under Article 8 of the Convention. The Court acknowledged that a government policy intended to secure operational effectiveness was one that pursued the legitimate aim of maintaining national security. It also accepted that, in the light of the strength of entrenched attitudes within the forces, it was reasonable to anticipate that revocation of the policy would cause some difficulties. However, the British government had failed to show that such difficulties could not be substantially mitigated by adoption of a strict code of conduct to prevent inappropriate behavior. Only weighty reasons could justify such a serious intrusion into a person's private life, and the threatened dangers to morale were largely on the basis of antipathy and prejudice of the sort that any right of privacy must be intended to counteract. The government conceded that the policy was not based on any depreciation of the innate physical capability, courage, or other relevant qualities of homosexuals. In view of the very dubious basis in homophobic sentiment of the policy's justification, it was plainly right to insist on a clear demonstration of public need; the availability of alternative arrangements, unlikely to be very much less effective in ensuring good discipline and morale, pointed to the violation of fundamental rights of personhood closely tied to the value of human dignity.

In judging the relative effectiveness of alternative measures, there is usually scope for deference to governmental views – the court can rarely match the experience or expertise of the public agency. The appropriate degree of deference, however, depends on what is at stake:

---

[42] *R v Oakes*, [1986] 1 S.C.R. 103 at 140 (hereinafter *Oakes*).
[43] Julian Rivers, "Proportionality and Variable Intensity of Review," (2006) 65 *C.L.J.* 174 at 193 (hereinafter Rivers, "Proportionality and Variable Intensity").
[44] (1999) 29 E.H.R.R. 493 (hereinafter *Smith and Grady*).

This does not mean that the court increasingly displaces the executive and the legislature in matters of factual expertise and policy-choice. Rather, it means that the more serious a limitation of rights is, the more evidence the court will require that the factual basis of the limitation has been correctly established, and the more argument it will require that alternative, less intrusive, policy-choices are, all things considered, less desirable.[45]

In *Smith and Grady*, the Court was entitled to call attention to the use of disciplinary codes in ensuring the successful integration of women and members of racial minorities within the armed forces, as well as noting the satisfactory cooperation with allied foreign forces that included homosexuals. It was entitled to doubt the government's view that nothing could be learned from the experience of those other European countries that now admitted homosexuals to serve in their armed forces. A proper hesitation before rejecting a defense based on past experience or expert risk assessment should not be confused with a supine acceptance of unsubstantiated assertion or unconvincing argument.

III. THE BALANCE OF VALUES AND THE BOUNDARIES OF POLITICAL CHOICE

There can be no plausible "democratic" objection to judicial rejection (or limitation) of measures that undermine basic freedoms in the absence of any sufficient public benefit, at least where more modest measures, better tailored to legitimate ends, could achieve such ends without injury to established constitutional values. It does not follow, however, that any curtailment of fundamental rights is acceptable if there are no alternative means available to secure a governmental objective, let alone that such rights may be abrogated entirely. In some circumstances, the choice of a public policy bound to cause serious damage to basic rights (or the scope of their application and enjoyment) calls into question the sincerity of commitment to those rights, even when no less-intrusive alternative presents itself; their integrity is threatened by action wholly inconsistent with their rationale. Hence, the "fair balance" (*stricto sensu*) limb of the proportionality test: does a suitable and necessary restriction of rights (having regard to the objective in view) nonetheless impose an excessive burden? Governmental objectives are ordinarily a matter of legitimate political choice, but "sometimes the game is not worth the candle".[46] The detention without trial of all suspected terrorists (regardless of

---

[45] Rivers, "Proportionality and Variable Intensity," *supra* note 43 at 205.
[46] Ibid. at 190.

nationality or immigration status) might well be thought incompatible with the right to personal liberty, whatever the alleged gains in terms of national security.[47] The ban on homosexual service personnel is another good example: a marginal and speculative enhancement of national security was purchased at too great a cost to the dignity and self-respect of those excluded.

The same point can be seen from a different angle. Although it is not for courts to determine the needs of the public interest, they should not allow their role to be emasculated by the adoption of an artificially narrow specification of the legislative or governmental purpose. For the identification of a very specific aim, closely tied to the actual effect of a measure, can result in circumvention of the proportionality test: no other measure could attain the relevant aim, making it necessarily the least injurious to constitutional rights. A narrowly focused objective identifies the governmental purpose with the specific consequences of enforcement in particular instances. If the purpose of a government policy is to exclude homosexuals from the armed forces, whether for reasons of mere tradition, shared preference, or even moral disapproval, only an outright ban could achieve it. But it would then be open to serious question whether such underlying attitudes were really consonant with basic values of equal respect and human dignity, and whether a democratic government would be able or even willing to attempt the requisite justification.[48]

In such cases the curtailment of rights is implicit in the alleged objective: the elimination of the threat posed by a small group of identifiable suspects entails the abrogation of their right to liberty; or a group's exclusion from public office involves a denial of their rights to privacy or personhood. Such a measure, however, is akin to a bill of attainder, punishing a selected group on dubious grounds or in the absence of any proof of personal wrongdoing, fairly and impartially established.[49] It precludes any proper appraisal of relative

---

[47] Discrimination between suspects on the basis of nationality was held unlawful in *A. v. Secretary of State for the Home Dept*, [2004] U.K.H.L. 56. A substantial deprivation of liberty, imposed by a "control order" restricting freedom of movement and involving a curfew, was held unlawful in *Secretary of State for the Home Dept., ex p J.J.*, [2007] U.K.H.L. 45. Note Lord Brown's observation at para 107: "The borderline between deprivation of liberty and restriction of liberty of movement cannot vary according to the particular interests sought to be served by the restraints imposed. . . . Liberty is too precious a right to be discarded except in times of genuine national emergency."

[48] *Cf.* Matthias Kumm, "Political Liberalism and the Structure of Rights: On the Place and Limits of the Proportionality Requirement" in George Pavlakos (ed.), *Law, Rights and Discourse: The Legal Philosophy of Robert Alexy* (2007) at 142–148.

[49] The bill of attainder is the classic violation of generality, or equality, providing for the punishment of named (or readily identifiable) persons and depriving them of the benefit of a fair trial. See Allan, *Constitutional Justice, supra* note 14 at 148–160.

burdens and benefits, characteristic of constitutional equality, by making the relevant public purpose tantamount to the curtailment of rights. If, then, government chooses to defend a decision or policy by reference to a narrowly defined target, it cannot complain if the court questions the propriety of the target; the recognition of fundamental rights imposes limits on what can qualify as a legitimate public purpose. The "fair balance" test operates, in effect, to prevent the victimization of a vulnerable group or minority – it preserves their equal status as members of the political community.

There is an analogy with common law rights of natural justice or procedural fairness. The requirements of a fair hearing depend on a range of factors, including the nature of the relevant tribunal or inquiry and the consequences of its findings for those principally affected. The closer a hearing comes to a judicial determination of rights, or liability to penalties, the more closely it should approximate the style of a judicial trial; there should be analogous rights to notice of complaints or charges and appropriate opportunities to inspect and challenge adverse evidence.[50] It is also generally recognized that powerful considerations of public interest may properly qualify the procedural rights that would otherwise apply: reasons of national security, in particular, may justify restrictions on the disclosure of evidence or relevant sources. But such limitations or qualifications must not be so extensive as wholly to undermine procedural rights, making a trial or hearing unfair. Equal citizenship demands a basic minimum or core of procedural protection.

The British courts were obliged to confront a serious challenge to procedural rights in litigation arising under the Prevention of Terrorism Act 2005, which provided for control orders to be made against suspected terrorists, sharply curtailing their freedoms of movement and association. The Act provided for judicial supervision; the High Court was required to determine whether the minister's decision to make an order satisfied the statutory criteria. However, the court was required to permit the material giving rise to suspicion of terrorist activity or connections to be withheld from a suspect or his advisors when it considered that disclosure would be contrary to the public interest. In a number of cases, most or all of the relevant material was contained in closed evidence that the suspect was unaware of and so unable to controvert. Although a "special advocate", appointed on the suspect's behalf, could probe the evidence and challenge the necessity for nondisclosure, the special advocate could not take further instructions once having seen the closed material. The House of Lords was divided over whether or not it was possible to have a fair trial in such

---

[50] Ibid. ch. 5.

circumstances; but Lord Bingham held that "the concept of fairness imports a core, irreducible minimum of procedural protection", which required an effective opportunity to challenge adverse evidence.[51]

In *A v. United Kingdom*,[52] the Grand Chamber of the European Court of Human Rights considered the procedural requirements of Article 5(4) of the Convention in relation to the former detention of terrorist suspects under the Anti-terrorism, Crime and Security 2001 Act. It accepted that the special advocate procedure was a valuable safeguard when material had to be withheld from the detainee: the advocate's role could help to "counterbalance" the lack of full disclosure and the absence of a "full, open, adversarial hearing" before the Special Immigration Appeals Commission (SIAC). However, the special advocate could not perform his function effectively unless the detainee was provided with sufficient information about the allegations to enable the detainee to give useful instructions. When "the open material consisted purely of general assertions and SIAC's decision to uphold the certification and maintain the detention was based solely or to a decisive degree on closed material, the procedural requirements of article 5(4) would not be satisfied".[53]

In *A.F. (No 3)*, the House of Lords applied these conclusions to the control order cases, holding that where the case against a suspect is "based solely or to a decisive degree on closed materials" the requirements of a fair trial would not be satisfied, however cogent the case based on those materials might seem to be. Lord Scott considered that "the common law, without the aid of Strasbourg jurisprudence, would have led to the same conclusion".[54] Lord Hope held that if the rule of law were to mean anything in cases such as these, "the court must stand by principle", insisting that persons affected be told what is alleged against them.[55] Although Lord Phillips considered that a judge could sometimes be confident that an order was rightly made even when the suspect had not seen and addressed the relevant material, he held that "strong policy considerations" favored "a rule that a trial procedure can never be considered fair if a party to it is kept in ignorance of the case against him". In particular, feelings of resentment would inevitably be aroused; and public confidence in the system of justice might be undermined if justice were not seen to be done but instead had to be taken on trust.[56]

---

[51] *Secretary of State for the Home Dept. v. M.B.*, [2008] A.C. 44 at para. 43.
[52] European Convention on Human Rights, Article 5(4): "Everyone who is deprived of his liberty by arrest or detention shall be entitled to take proceedings by which the lawfulness of his detention shall be decided speedily by a court."
[53] *A. v. United Kingdom*, (2009) 49 E.H.R.R. 29 at paras. 219–220.
[54] *Secretary of State for the Home Dept v. A.F. (No 3)*, [2009] U.K.H.L. 28 at para 96.
[55] Ibid. at para. 84.   [56] Ibid. at para. 63

Whereas policy considerations of this sort may no doubt register in the general balance of public interests, it is easy to lose sight of the more fundamental fair balance test: the right to a basic minimum of procedural fairness must ultimately prevail regardless of the overall balance of interests. The right to a fair hearing is an absolute right in the sense that the outcome of an *unfair* trial, in which the suspects or defendants have no real opportunity to defend themselves against the charges, is illegitimate. Because the decision can make no claim to the affected party's respect, the natural resentment is not merely predictable but *justified*. It is central to the recognition of human dignity that a party be accorded the status of genuine participant; there must be a serious attempt to engage the suspect's critical judgment, so that he can at least understand the grounds of his treatment and recognize the good faith, if not the wisdom, of the court or tribunal.[57] Like other fundamental rights, procedural fairness has a conceptual core that cannot properly be ignored or overridden. Shorn of its irreducible core, the concept of procedural fairness is empty and the judicial (or quasi-judicial) hearing only a sham.

Admittedly, it is in regard to the "fair balance" limb of the proportionality test that questions about the commensurability of competing rights and interests become most urgent. It is likely to be only in a rare case that a court should repudiate a decision or enactment on the grounds that, although necessary to attain a legitimate objective, its consequences for the enjoyment of basic rights are not acceptable. Nevertheless, such a ruling does pit judicial against political appraisal of the limits of permissible state action. As I have argued, however, the fair balance test is implicit in any coherent proportionality standard. The greater the encroachment on a fundamental right, the more cogent must be the countervailing interests; when a right is curtailed nearly to the point of abrogation, threatening to deprive a person of protection extended in principle to everyone, the test of justification must be appropriately demanding.

It should not be supposed that the incommensurability of basic values threatens the rationality of balancing; incommensurability, even if we grant its existence, does not entail incomparability.[58] Rights, principles, and interests are weighed not in the abstract, but in relation to particular circumstances, as the common law exemplifies. It is perfectly rational to prefer a more trivial interference with one right or interest to a greater encroachment on another.

---

[57] See further, Allan, *Constitutional Justice, supra* note 14 at 77–87.

[58] See Virgilio Afonso da Silva, "Comparing the Incommensurable: Constitutional Principles, Balancing, and Rational Decision," (2011) 31 O.J.L.S. 273; and Timothy Endicott, "Proportionality and Incommensurability," Chapter 14 in this volume. For a powerful case in support of the unity of value, see Ronald Dworkin, *Justice for Hedgehogs* (2011), especially chapters 5 and 6.

According to Robert Alexy's "Law of Balancing," the greater the degree of harm to one principle, the greater the importance of satisfying the other: degrees of satisfaction and non-satisfaction can be compared, at least roughly.[59] The respective rights and interests can be weighed sufficiently to show whether or not a legislative or administrative solution falls within an acceptable range. Within that range, encompassing a variety of possible solutions consistent with a proper respect for each of the pertinent values, there is no basis for judicial intervention; the court should defer to the legitimate choices of Parliament or Government.

IV. STATUTORY INTERPRETATION AND CONSTITUTIONAL RIGHTS

I have argued that the meaning and scope of a general rule are given by a deliberative process, comparing the aims or purposes indicated by the statutory language with the harm to important constitutional values that would ensue from pressing those aims too far. The need for judgment, maintaining a fair balance between statutory objective and claims of individual right, is inherent in any effort of rational interpretation. No statutory formula, however clearly and skillfully framed, can apply itself to the infinite range of different instances that changing circumstances may produce. Judgments of proportionality are therefore intrinsic to the judicial process, with or without a bill of rights. An interpretation that would do disproportionate damage to a fundamental value is necessarily disqualified; it attributes irrational instructions to the legislature, careless of important moral imperatives that any conscientious legislator would be quick to acknowledge.

Even if the "ordinary meaning" of the words "to prove" suggests a persuasive burden,[60] it does not follow that the defendant necessarily bears such a burden when he is required, in a prosecution for possession of illegal drugs, "to prove that he neither knew of nor suspected nor had reason to suspect the existence of some fact alleged by the prosecution" relevant to guilt.[61] The

[59] Robert Alexy, *A Theory of Constitutional Rights* (translated by Julian Rivers) (2002) 100–109. Alexy's "Law of Competing Principles," whereby the competition between principles results in a conditional relation of precedence in the light of the circumstances of the case, bears a strong resemblance to common law reasoning; a rule is created, but subject to the recognition of new exceptions: ibid. at 50–61. For discussion of Alexy's theory of rights in the context of the common law constitution, see Allan, "Constitutional Rights and the Rule of Law" in Matthias Klatt (ed.), *Institutionalized Reason: The Jurisprudence of Robert Alexy* (2012) at 132.

[60] *R. v. Lambert*, [2001] U.K.H.L. 37 at para. 72 (per Lord Hope of Craighead) (hereinafter *Lambert*).

[61] Misuse of Drugs Act 1971, s. 28(2).

ordinary meaning would only be the *correct* meaning if a serious inroad on the presumption of innocence, which normally requires the prosecution to prove the guilt of the accused beyond reasonable doubt, would be necessary in the light of serious difficulties in establishing mens rea, peculiar to the crime in question. Yet the imposition on the defendant of an *evidential* burden, requiring him only to adduce sufficient evidence to raise doubts about his knowledge of the substance found in his possession, would in practice suffice to prevent frustration of the legislative purpose. In those circumstances, as the House of Lords held in *Lambert*, a reversal of the ordinary legal burden of proof would be a disproportionate curtailment of the rights of the accused. Correctly construed, the words "to prove" mean, in context, "to give sufficient evidence".[62]

The Court in *Lambert* treated its conclusion as dependent on section 3 of the Human Rights Act, which requires legislation to be read compatibly with the European Convention on Human Rights, so far as possible; but it is hard to see why a rational interpretation according to common law principle should not produce precisely the same outcome. The favored interpretation assimilates the enactment to the established position in the case of such common law offences as provocation and duress. Lord Steyn's conclusion that the statute's "transfer of the legal burden" did not "satisfy the criterion of proportionality", allowing him to invoke section 3 by way of remedy, contradicted his own appraisal of the balance of argument. It would, he observed, be wrong to ignore the possibility that a guilty verdict might be returned in respect of an offence punishable by life imprisonment even though the jury considered it possible that the accused had been duped.[63] Because such a possibility is relevant to the correct construction of the statute, consistent with constitutional principle, the invocation of section 3 is otiose; the question of proportionality, or fairness, is internal to the correct reading of the relevant provisions. Either a preferred reading is possible, having regard to the context in which the words appear, or it is not.[64] Lord Clyde acknowledged the strength of the case for a reading favorable to the defendant: "In the ordinary case, where the presumption of innocence has been recognized at common law long before its embodiment in the Convention, I should be slow to construe a criminal provision so as to impose a persuasive burden upon him."[65]

---

[62] *Lambert, supra* note 60 at para. 94 (per Lord Hope).
[63] Ibid. at paras. 38–41.
[64] The Human Rights Act 1998, s. 3 should be treated, accordingly, as a reaffirmation of existing (common law) principle rather than (as it is usually treated) as authorizing a different mode of construction.
[65] *Lambert* at para. 131.

Similarly, the quashing of section 8 of the Narcotic Control Act 1970, as an infringement of section 11(d) of the Canadian Charter, was the direct and unnecessary consequence of its being interpreted as a reverse onus provision, imposing a legal burden on the defendant.[66] This interpretation was dependent on a rather literal reading of a rule that required the defendant's conviction if he failed "to establish that he was not in possession of the [relevant] narcotic for the purpose of trafficking". Chief Justice Dickson's assertion that the phrase "to establish" meant "to prove" ignores the possibility that the correct, constitutional meaning was "to show by adduction of evidence", leaving the ultimate burden of proving guilt on the prosecution. The defendant was entitled to be "acquitted of the offence" if he established that he was not in possession for the purposes of trafficking in the sense of adducing evidence sufficient, in all the circumstances, to prevent the Crown meeting the requisite standard of proof. Courts in several Canadian jurisdictions had already affirmed that alternative reading, concluding that the presumption of innocence was not offended, and the Ontario Court of Appeal had held a similar provision, thus interpreted, consistent with the presumption of innocence guaranteed (in very similar terms) by the Canadian Bill of Rights.[67]

The Supreme Court in *Oakes* found the statutory "infringement" of section 11 disproportionate to its legitimate objective and hence unjustified for purposes of section 1. There was no rational connection between the fact of possession and the presumed fact of possession for the purpose of trafficking: one could not infer an intent to trade on the basis of the possession of a very small quantity of drugs. In the case of an evidential burden, however, the problem would substantially disappear; it would be sufficient for the defendant to deny any intent to traffic, leaving the Crown with the burden of proving otherwise. If, moreover, the Court's interpretation of the Charter "must be guided by the values and principles essential to a free and democratic society", including "respect for the inherent dignity of the human person" and "commitment to social justice and equality",[68] it is not clear why its interpretation of ordinary legislation should not be similarly informed. The requirement of proportionality between public purpose and curtailment of individual right, secured by appeal to the Charter, was actually inherent in any defensible view of the statute, consistent with basic constitutional values.

In both *Lambert* and *Oakes* the judges adopt an artificially literal construction of the statutory words before invoking the Human Rights Act or the Charter as a necessary remedy. In consequence, they set the legislative

---

[66] *Oakes*, *supra* note 42.
[68] *Oakes*, *supra* note 42 at 136.

[67] *R. v. Sharpe* (1961), 131 C.C.C. 75.

provision against the constitution – it is either rendered invalid or apparently amended to make it conform to legal principle. In the absence of clear instructions, however, making explicit reference to the distinction between legal and evidential burdens of proof, such a confrontation is unnecessary and disrespectful. It attributes to Parliament an ignorance of, or insensitivity to, basic legal values, which at least at an abstract level are hardly controversial. If the seriousness of the offence in question, carrying the possibility of imprisonment for life, confirmed the irrationality of a literal construction,[69] it strengthened the case for a superior reading, consonant with the presumption of innocence. In the absence of special considerations of reliance or certainty applying to the terms of a statutory prohibition, the "ordinary" meaning has no constitutional priority. When law is understood as serving an order of justice, appropriate to a community of equal citizens, the courts are charged with the administration of the law as a whole, viewed as a rational and defensible structure of rights, duties, and powers. The correct interpretation, accordingly, is the one that best reconciles the general statutory aims with established constitutional principle. In *Lambert*, Lord Clyde observed that although trafficking in controlled drugs was a notorious social evil, "if any error is to be made in the weighing of the scales of justice, it should be to the effect that the guilty should go free rather than that an innocent person should be wrongly convicted".[70] It is a safe assumption that any conscientious legislator, respectful of the settled tradition of criminal justice, would be inclined to agree.[71]

Admittedly, the court's assurance about the assent of the hypothetical conscientious legislator will vary according to the subject matter. Where either Parliament or executive agency has a significant level of expertise or experience lacked by the court, there is a need for caution. There will often be good reason, for example, to trust in the efficacy of parliamentary deliberations about a complex matter of social policy; judgments of proportionality can only be as sound as the reliability of their factual basis, or the plausibility of relevant assessments of likely outcomes. In deferring to the expertise of the political branches, the court does not relinquish its responsibility for the defense of

---

[69] Ibid. at 142.   [70] *Lambert, supra* note 60 at para. 156.

[71] See, generally, T.R.S. Allan, "Parliament's Will and the Justice of the Common Law: The Human Rights Act in Constitutional Perspective," (2006) 59 *C.L.P.* 27. Lord Hope drew attention to the fact that more recent legislation, such as the Terrorism Act, expressly placed the legal burden on the prosecution to counter a defense that the defendant was required to "prove" by adduction of evidence "sufficient to raise an issue with respect" to the relevant matter: Terrorism Act 2000, s. 118(2). It was "not unreasonable" to think that Parliament would now be content with a similar approach to the Misuse of Drugs Act: *Lambert, supra* note 60 at para. 93.

rights; it does not, or should not, withdraw from an area marked out as non-justiciable. A "political question" is merely a legal question on which, in all the circumstances, there is strong reason to trust the judgment of government or legislature in the absence of compelling argument to the contrary.[72]

In *Bell ExpressVu Limited Partnership v. Rex*, the Supreme Court of Canada expressly rejected the idea that a statute should be interpreted, initially at least, in the light of the constitutional values of the Charter.[73] Only in the case of a "genuine ambiguity" arising "between two or more plausible readings, *each equally in accordance with the intentions of the statute*" was it appropriate to look beyond the statute itself for guidance.[74] But why should the "intentions of the statute" be constructed without any regard for constitutional rights or general principles? If it is conceded (as Justice Iacobucci concedes) that the "entire context" of the statute must be considered to determine whether or not it is "reasonably capable of multiple interpretations", how can the constitutional background be excluded without artificially divorcing the statutory aims or purposes from the conditions in which they must be sought? The Court's approach is premised on the dubious assumption that Parliament may choose to flout fundamental legal values: in interpreting statutes, the courts must bow to the "sovereign intent of the legislator", however hostile to the rule of law such "intent" is supposed to be. Even if a statute, thus interpreted, is subsequently held to breach the Charter, a dialogue between Court and Parliament may culminate in an override under section 33. But this is a very formal and highly regimented version of constitutionalism, making Charter rights and values external to the ordinary interpretative process in which common law and statute are interwoven as a coherent and defensible structure of interrelated rights, duties, and powers.

The objection (rehearsed by the Supreme Court) that an interpretation of statute congruent with Charter rights has the consequence that the Charter is merely consulted rather than applied is false. It mistakenly assumes (or asserts) that the Charter can only be applied in the sense of determining validity,[75] but invalidity is (or should be) a counsel of despair; a statute is rejected as irredeemably in conflict with basic values – an assault on the rule of law of which any true democrat should be ashamed. The Charter is applied in determining the true meaning of the statute. And we should also challenge

---

[72] See *A. v. Secretary of State for the Home Dept*, [2004] U.K.H.L. 56 at para. 29 (per Lord Bingham).

[73] [2002] 2 S.C.R. 559.

[74] Ibid. at para 29, quoting Major J. in *Canadian Oxy Chemicals Ltd v. Canada (Attorney General)*, [1999] 1 S.C.R. 743, at para. 14.

[75] *Symes v. Canada*, [1993] 4 S.C.R. 695, at 752, cited in *Bell ExpressVu* at para. 64.

the further objection that "it would never be possible for the government to justify infringements as reasonable limits under section 1 of the Charter, since the interpretive process would preclude one from finding infringements in the first place".[76] When constitutional adjudication is properly conducted, such reasonable limits are recognized as constitutive, in context, of the rights in question. constitutional rights are "infringed" only when governmental action cannot be justified as a reasonable limitation or qualification, having due regard to legitimate public purposes and any pertinent countervailing rights of other persons.

A statute can be struck down as invalid, or implicitly amended by judicial reconstruction, only if it has first been held to violate constitutional principle, but the conclusion that Parliament has chosen to deny the constitution should be a last resort, akin to civil disobedience in the face of obdurate rule oblivious to basic rights. (The tone of Justice Wilson's judgment in the *Motor Vehicle Act Reference* strikes the right note.) In a constitutional democracy on the basis of respect for human dignity and the rule of law, the true meaning of legislation is as much a reflection of constitutional justice as of more local and immediate public aims or policies. The tension between governmental aims and constitutional rights should be resolved by interpretation, translating general purposes into more specific rights and duties that give due weight to the moral and conceptual demands of law and legal process. A construction of statute that might be appropriate to enforce the will of an autocrat, or even the party policy of an elected government, will generally be inimical to the reconciliation of law and policy central to competent constitutional adjudication. The correct construction is the one that best advances legitimate legislative aims within the constitutional constraints that respect for the citizen's autonomy and dignity requires.[77]

A rule is by its nature over-inclusive: it will apply in some circumstances where the overall balance of reasons dictates a different result. We tolerate these consequences for the sake of countervailing considerations of efficiency or simplicity or certainty; it is not always practicable, given limited resources, to determine every case in the light of the full panoply of applicable aims or principles. There is also the question of political authority. Parliament can only legislate in the form of general rules, even if these sometimes delegate discretionary power to public officials. If every such rule were dissolved into its underlying reasons, to be weighed against contrary considerations, legislative authority would in effect be ceded to courts or public agencies. It follows

---

[76] Ibid.
[77] See Allan, 'Text, Context, and Constitution," *supra* note 12.

that a rule affecting or abridging rights will sometimes cause disproportionate harm, having regard to its legitimate aims, in particular instances, but such harm may be a necessary consequence of adopting a clear and certain rule, possessing democratic legitimacy. It is no objection, then, that a statutory rule is sometimes capable of causing injury that is not strictly proportionate to the ends that explain its adoption.

Whether a statutory rule meets the standard of legality must depend on whether it strikes a reasonable balance, overall, between its aims or objectives and countervailing interests. Although it will generate outcomes that are less than ideal in many cases, it must be sufficiently flexible to safeguard basic rights when a single-minded pursuit of legislative aims would inflict serious damage. There must be judicial restraint, permitting some freedom of maneuver, but not too much, and inevitably context will be critical. The demands of clarity and certainty will be greater in some fields than others. Legislative expertise may also carry more weight in some areas than others, especially when public opinion is deeply divided about contentious moral or political issues. A certain rigidity, impervious to the circumstances of particular cases, may even be an intrinsic element of the law in question. The denunciatory value of the mandatory sentence of life imprisonment for murder was properly conceded on such grounds.[78]

An unqualified rule may sometimes be a necessary general safeguard of people's rights or freedoms, even if it diminishes the autonomy of particular individuals who would willingly forego the protection. In *R (Pretty) v. Director of Public Prosecutions*,[79] the blanket prohibition on assisted suicide under the Suicide Act 1961 was challenged as a breach of the claimant's rights of personal autonomy and self-determination. Being paralyzed, although mentally alert, the applicant was dependent on her husband's assistance in ending her life when she wished to do so; she had been denied an official undertaking that her husband would not be prosecuted for providing such assistance. The House of Lords held that Parliament was entitled to enact a law that protected vulnerable people who might feel pressure to choose a premature death, even if it would apply to those such as the claimant who were much less vulnerable. Lord Hope of Craighead held that the statute "struck the right balance between the interests of the individual and the public interest which seeks to protect the weak and vulnerable".[80] Given the importance of the state's interest in protecting the lives of its citizens, it was "a proportionate response

---

[78] See *R. v. Lichniak*, [2002] U.K.H.L. 47 (discussed in the text at note 39).
[79] [2001] U.K.H.L. 61 (hereinafter *Pretty*).   [80] Ibid. at para. 97.

for Parliament to conclude that that interest could only be met by a complete prohibition on assisted suicide".[81]

The justifiability of a blanket rule must be considered in the light of its means of enforcement. In *Pretty v. United Kingdom*, the European Court of Human Rights noted the requirement that the consent of the Director of Public Prosecutions must be obtained for any prosecution under the Suicide Act, allowing discretion to be exercised in the public interest, and observed that, although a maximum sentence was prescribed, lesser penalties could be imposed when appropriate.[82] Whether or not a general rule is disproportionate in its effect on individual rights depends, in part, on the manner of its application or enforcement. Questions of application or enforcement, however, are not wholly distinct from questions of *meaning*: what may be expressed in the form of an absolute rule may, in appropriate circumstances, be interpreted as permitting exceptions, necessary to protect fundamental values from disproportionate damage. If a provision does not contain an *express* exception sufficient to protect the threatened rights, an exception may be implied on the reasonable assumption that Parliament does not intend to violate fundamental rights. If, for example, the literal effect of a provision is that the accused is prevented from adducing evidence necessary to his defense against a serious criminal charge, the statute must be construed in a manner that departs from that literal reading: he must be able to adduce such evidence, despite its unwelcome consequences for the complainant, if his trial would otherwise be rendered unfair.[83]

It is, then, only very rarely that legislation need be struck down for infringement of constitutional rights, or (under the UK Human Rights Act, section 4) declared incompatible with the human rights protected by the European Convention. Compliance with basic rights is chiefly a matter of meaning or

---

[81] Similar conclusions were reached by a majority of the Supreme Court of Canada in *Rodriguez v. British Columbia (Attorney-General)*, [1993] 3 S.C.R. 519. Four out of nine judges, however, dissented: in their view it was possible to provide appropriate safeguards for the protection of the vulnerable, making a complete prohibition unconstitutional. In *Pretty v. United Kingdom* (2002), 35 E.H.R.R. 1 at para. 74, the European Court of Human Rights observed that although the condition of terminally ill individuals will vary, "many will be vulnerable and it is the vulnerability of the class which provides the rationale for the law in question."

[82] In *R. (Purdy) v. D.P.P.*, [2009] U.K.H.L. 45 the House of Lords held that to satisfy the requirements of legality it was necessary for the Director of Public Prosecutions to publish the guidelines he would use in exercising his discretion to prosecute in such cases. The guidelines would address the "obvious gulf between what section 2(1) says and the way that the subsection is being applied in practice in compassionate cases" of assisted suicide (per Lord Hope at para. 54).

[83] *R. v. A. (No 2)*, [2001] U.K.H.L. 25.

application, which necessarily lies in judicial hands. When the consequences of applying a rule are unacceptable – causing serious damage to individual interests out of all proportion to any real public benefit – it must be treated as subject to the necessary exception. Provided that sufficient weight is given to the legitimate reasons for adopting general rules, according to the context in point, the courts have a responsibility to interpret statutory provisions in a manner that safeguards fundamental rights. The search for a proper balance between the general rule and demands of the particular case – between legality and (perfect) justice – is intrinsic to adjudication when individual autonomy and dignity are treated as basic constitutional values.

It is only where any plausible legislative purpose *entails* the abrogation of rights, in the sense that the public interest is unfairly identified with their suppression, that judicial interpretation is frustrated. Any such enactment, however, is analogous to a bill of attainder, which by proclaiming its violation of fundamental equality – abandoning all pretence at fairness and generality – forfeits the status of law. A measure that provided for the detention without trial of foreign, but not British, suspected terrorists, even though the latter were conceded to pose a similar threat, was irrational and arbitrary unless it could be established that immigration status was relevant to the question of British national security.[84] The legality of derogation from European Convention rights depended on whether or not the measures taken were "strictly required" to meet the "public emergency".[85] If, however, nationality were irrelevant, the denial of rationality or equality undermined the enactment's status as law, entitled to judicial respect: "No one has the right to be an international terrorist. But substitute 'black', 'disabled', 'female', 'gay', or any other similar adjective for 'foreign' before 'suspected international terrorist' and ask whether it would be justifiable to take power to lock up that group but not the 'white', 'able-bodied', 'male' or 'straight' suspected international terrorists. The answer is clear."[86] In litigation over the procedural rights of suspected terrorists against whom the Secretary of State had made a control order under the Prevention

---

[84] See *A. v. Secretary of State for the Home Dept.*, [2004] U.K.H.L. 56 (hereinafter *A. v Secretary of State*). For the view that immigration status was relevant, and hence the statute susceptible of interpretation compatible with the Convention, see John Finnis, "Nationality, Alienage and Constitutional Principle," (2007) 123 *L.Q.R.* 417.

[85] European Convention on Human Rights, Art. 15(1).

[86] *A. v. Secretary of State, supra* note 84 at para. 238 (per Baroness Hale of Richmond). Admittedly, a declaration of incompatibility (under the Human Rights Act) did not formally challenge the validity of the statute; but its status as law – its ability to justify the continued imprisonment of those detained – was certainly put in issue by the finding of irrationality or arbitrariness. A measure that violates the rule of law cannot be "law" in a liberal democracy, which must treat that ideal as fundamental.

of Terrorism Act 2005, the House of Lords adopted an appropriately nuanced interpretative approach. The rule obliging the court to permit nondisclosure of material, when disclosure would be contrary to the public interest, was made subject to an implicit proviso: "except where to do so would be incompatible with the right of the controlled person to a fair trial".[87] If the Minister refused to disclose material in such circumstances, the court could direct that it must be disregarded. When passing the Act, Parliament must (it was reasoned) have thought that the relevant provisions were compatible with fundamental rights. In interpreting the Act compatibly with the Convention, the Court was doing its best to make it work, giving "the greatest possible incentive to *all* parties to the case . . . to conduct the proceedings in such a way as to afford a sufficient and substantial measure of procedural justice."[88]

In *A.F. (No 3)*, however, the House of Lords accepted that its earlier confidence that an unfair trial could normally be avoided, despite the use of closed material, had been exaggerated. Baroness Hale conceded that she had been "far too sanguine about the possibilities of conducting a fair hearing under the special advocate procedure."[89] New evidence showed that the scope for contesting the government's objections to disclosure was, in practice, very limited and that the great majority of such objections were upheld. There were bound to be many more cases than previously anticipated "where the judge is forced to conclude that there cannot be an effective challenge without further disclosure and the Secretary of State is left to decide whether she can agree to it."[90] There was, however, no governmental pressure to modify the previous interpretation of the relevant provisions; the "reading-down" adopted in *M.B.* was sustained. Therefore, despite the hesitation of several judges, the fundamental requirements of fairness were upheld as a matter of common law or Convention law; the judicial interpretation, suitably robust, acknowledged the fundamental status of fair procedure as an inalienable feature of the rule of law.

V. CONCLUSION

I have sought to defend a form of democratic constitutionalism modeled on common law reasoning, in which the court seeks an accommodation of competing principles on the facts of a particular case – maintaining a constructive

---

[87] *Secretary of State for the Home Dept. v. M.B.*, [2007] U.K.H.L. 46 at para. 72 (per Baroness Hale of Richmond) [hereinafter *M.B.*].

[88] Ibid. at para. 73 (emphasis in original).

[89] *Secretary of State for the Home Dept. v. A.F. (No 3)*, [2009] U.K.H.L. 28, para. 101.

[90] Ibid. at para. 106.

tension between the general rule and the necessary exception. Acts of Parliament should be interpreted in a manner that conforms to general principle, seeking to reconcile immediate policy aims with more enduring constitutional values. Executive or administrative decisions are valid only when they comply with constitutional rights, which protect basic individual liberties against unnecessary or disproportionate interference. When the requirements of rationality or proportionality are satisfied, a genuine democratic equality is secured; individual and collective interests are fairly balanced, as the specific context requires. Judicial intervention is usually warranted only when a governmental decision falls outside the permitted range; a greater public benefit will normally permit a more serious curtailment of rights (or, more accurately, of their scope or extent in all the circumstances). But the ultimate requirement of fairness – or fair balance – imposes a necessary limit to what might otherwise be action that overwhelms a right, undermining the integrity of the legal order. The courts, as guardians of the legal order, are the appropriate bodies to enforce that requirement of fairness, acting as impartial arbiters between public authorities and those adversely affected by their decisions.

The requirement of proportionality provides an important link between our related concepts of law and democracy. Law itself is conceptually egalitarian, imposing constraints of generality and rationality that resist disproportionate measures, which treat their victims' legitimate interests as of little or no account. And democracy consists of more than collective deliberation and decision about matters of public policy and social justice; it entails a more thoroughgoing equality, requiring collective decisions to be fairly applied to particular cases, having proper regard to the constitutional context. There must be appropriate allowance made for the necessarily over-inclusive element of enacted rules; there is an inescapable tension between legality and justice that courts can mitigate but not dissolve. And as well as judicial restraint, as regards the nature and urgency of the public interest, there must be judicial deference to superior expertise and experience; but the degree of such deference must depend on what is at stake in the particular case. The more important a constitutional right and the greater the curtailment envisaged, the greater must be the depth and rigor of judicial scrutiny. Moral judgment cannot be evaded by resort to the plain words of legislation or the expertise of public officials – legality and rationality are too much dependent on appraisal of the particular case, albeit in the light of its broader context. Proportionality is not only an implicit feature of constitutional rights, it also regulates the boundary between governmental discretion and judicial review.

11 Proportionality and Deference in a Culture of Justification

David Dyzenhaus[1]

I. INTRODUCTION

I will argue that proportionality is one of the main devices that maintains "congruence" on Lon L. Fuller's understanding of that term: that "actual administration" should be congruent with the "rules as announced".[2] Congruence, Fuller said, is the "most complex" of the eight rule of law desiderata he identified, both because it could be destroyed or impaired in various ways and because the "procedural devices designed to maintain it take, of necessity, a variety of forms".[3] In Fuller's view, judges have a role reviewing official action for congruence because adjudication is central to a mode of social ordering whose central feature is the presentation of "proofs and reasoned arguments".[4] Reasoned argument is not the sole preserve of the courts, but judicial review offers a "form of participating in a decision that is institutionally defined and assured": "Adjudication is . . . a device which gives formal and institutional

[1] A large part of this paper has been adapted from an earlier, unpublished paper, "Militant Democracy in the House of Lords?" For comments, I thank my colleagues at the Faculty of Law, University of Toronto; the New York University Law School Symposium on Hate Speech; the seminar on constitutional theory at the Faculty of Law, University of Western Ontario; the joint Cardozo/New York University Law School constitutional law colloquium; and the constitutional theory seminar in Oxford. I also thank Helena Gluzman for initial excellent research assistance, and Marcelo Rodriguez Ferrere for just as excellent final assistance. For written comments on various drafts, I thank Trevor Allan, Daniel Augenstein, Lisa Austin, John Finnis, Tom Hickman, Murray Hunt, Robert Leckey, Cheryl Misak, Tom Poole, Rayner Thwaites, and Sheila Wildeman. Finally, I thank the participants in the conference on proportionality at the Faculty of Law, University of Western Ontario, where this version of the paper was first presented.
[2] Lon L. Fuller, *The Morality of Law* (1969, revised edition) at 39, 46–91.
[3] Ibid. at 81.
[4] Lon L. Fuller, "The Forms and Limits of Adjudication" in Fuller, *The Principles of Social Order: Selected Essays of Lon L. Fuller*, Kenneth Winston ed. (2001) 101 at 106.

expression to the influence of reasoned argument in human affairs. As such it assumes a burden of argument not borne by any other form of social ordering. A decision which is the product of reasoned argument must be prepared itself to meet the test of reason."[5] A decision can meet the test of reasoned argument without itself being the product of such argument. But Fuller suggests that in certain forms of social order, a legitimate decision is one that is not only capable of meeting the test of reasoned argument, but also the product of such argument; and legal order is for him exemplary of this kind of order. Put differently, in his view, there is no sharp distinction between procedure and substance – between the process of reasoned justification and the justifi-ability of the actual decision. So when judges review the decisions of public officials, they should be concerned as much with the officials' justification of the decision as with its content.

I will argue that Fuller's view of the process/substance distinction is central to an understanding of legal order as a "culture of justification", in which a doctrine of proportionality is twinned with a doctrine of "due deference",[6] of judicial deference to appropriately reasoned administrative decisions. Propor-tionality, in this way, becomes integral to a culture of justification and the congruency principle. However, there is a considerable resistance to the idea that proportionality should be a part of administrative law, as I will now explain.

II. RESISTING PROPORTIONALITY

In constitutional law, the doctrine of proportionality sets out in a formal fashion the steps for a valid exercise of public authority when a constitutionally-protected right has been infringed.[7] Hence, proportionality analysis might seem apt only when such a right is violated and most decisions taken by public officials do not affect constitutionally protected rights, although they are still subject to the rule of law. In other words, the "rights" motor that ordinarily "propels" proportionality review is "missing" in much judicial review of administrative action.[8]

---

[5] Ibid. at 109.
[6] See Murray Hunt, "Sovereignty's Blight: Why Contemporary Public Law Needs the Concept of 'Due Deference'" in Nicholas Bamforth and Peter Leyland (eds.), *Public Law in a Multi-Layered Constitution* (2003) at 337.
[7] The onus is on the government to show that: (1) the governmental objective is a legitimate one; (2) there is a rational connection between the means chosen by government and that objective; (3) the government has chosen the least restrictive means to further that objective; and (4) the benefits of achieving that purpose are proportionate to the violation of the right.
[8] Michael Taggart, "Proportionality, Deference, *Wednesbury*," [2008] N.Z. L. Rev. 423 at 472 (hereinafter Taggart, "Proportionality, Deference, *Wednesbury*").

We should, however, recall that proportionality was developed as a specif-ically legal methodology by the Supreme Administrative Court of Prussia in the late nineteenth and early twentieth centuries in a context in which judges developed modes of ensuring that exercises of governmental power were respectful of individual rights. Although one should be careful not to romanticize this period,[9] it is significant that proportionality analysis has its roots in the area of public law we now call "administrative law" rather than in "constitutional law". But, it is important to see, the significance is ambiguous.

On the one hand, even though proportionality has its roots in administrative law, it is a methodology developed primarily in the second half of the twentieth century in the context of judicial enforcement of legally protected fundamental rights. The extension of that methodology into the area of administrative law might seem then to risk constitutionalizing the administrative state in ways that undermine its operation. Thus, that proportionality analysis has its roots in administrative law does not necessarily mean that bringing it back into administrative law is beneficial, especially if we think that the kind of embryonic rights protection it provided in Prussian administrative law are better protected in other areas of law.

On the other hand, one might think that it was a mistake to import that methodology from administrative law into constitutional law; the fact that proportionality analysis affords the state the opportunity to justify its limita-tion of rights might be taken to undermine the point of making judges the guardians of legally protected rights. We get not the constitutionalization of administrative law, but the administravization of constitutional law: rights are reduced to mere interests, too easily outweighed by considerations of admin-istrative efficiency. Proportionality talk then seems to be a rhetorical device to cover clashing estimates of the costs and benefits of administrative decisions, with the only honest solution to leave officials to their own devices because judges are ill-equipped to enter that fray.[10] Perhaps we get both: inappropriate

9 See Kenneth F. Ledford, "Formalizing the Rule of Law in Prussia: The Supreme Administrative Law Court, 1876–1914," (2004) 37 *Central European History* 203.
10 I believe this to be the conclusion to which Grant Huscroft's argument drives in Chapter 9 of this volume; see Huscroft, "Proportionality and the Relevance of Interpretation," although he would prefer to portray what we get as rule by parliament, whereas I think it is rule by public officials, in Carl Schmitt's terms, the administrative state in place of the legislative state. Perhaps Grégoire Webber's argument in this volume (Chapter 6) arrives at the same place; see Grégoire Webber, "On the Loss of Rights." It all depends on the extent to which there is the middle ground I argue for in the text between rights as trumps and cost-benefit calculations of interest, a ground on which rights frame inquiry into appropriate justifications for limiting rights in particular contexts.

rights analysis in administrative law and inappropriate rights limitations in constitutional law.

In my view, proportionality promises legitimate rights analysis in administrative law and legitimate rights limitations in constitutional law. Any inappropriate rights analysis in administrative law is tempered by the doctrine of deference; any inappropriate deference in constitutional law is tempered by the doctrine of proportionality. These complementary doctrines form the culture of justification. It is a mistake to have a "bifurcated" legal order in which one keeps proportionality analysis out of administrative law and deference doctrine out of constitutional law.[11] I will argue directly for only the second half of this claim: proportionality promises legitimate rights analysis in administrative law. But because either half helpfully blurs the distinction central to bifurcation, I take my argument to support the first: proportionality promises legitimate rights limitations in constitutional law.

III. THE CULTURE OF JUSTIFICATION

When South Africa's Interim Constitution was adopted in 1994, Etienne Mureinik, the country's leading public lawyer, had this to say about his hopes for the rule of law in the new legal order:

> If the new Constitution is a bridge away from a culture of authority, it is clear what it must be a bridge to. It must lead to a culture of justification – a culture in which every exercise of power is expected to be justified; in which the leadership given by government rests on the cogency of the case offered in defence of its decisions, not the fear inspired by the force at its command. The new order must be a community built on persuasion, not coercion.[12]

The shift Mureinik thought South Africa had to undertake from a culture of authority to a culture of justification has recently been argued by Moshe Cohen-Eliya and Iddo Porat to have occurred in recent years at a global level, manifested most strongly in the adoption of the doctrine of proportionality by constitutional courts as their "main pillar of adjudication".[13] Yet in another

---

[11] See Murray Hunt, "Against Bifurcation," in David Dyzenhaus, Murray Hunt, and Grant Huscroft eds. *A Simple Common Lawyer: Essays in Honour of Michael Taggart* (2009) at 108 (hereinafter Hunt, "Against Bifurcation").

[12] Etienne Mureinik, "A Bridge to Where? Introducing the Interim Bill of Rights," (1994) 10 *S.A.J.H.R.* 31 at 32; and David Dyzenhaus, "Law as Justification: Etienne Mureinik's Conception of Legal Culture," (1998) 14 *S.A.J.H.R.* 11.

[13] Moshe Cohen-Eliya and Iddo Porat, "Proportionality and the Culture of Justification," (2011) 59 *Am. J. Comp. L.* 463.

article, the same authors note the strong resistance to this doctrine in the United States of America,[14] and a powerful argument has been made by Michael Taggart, a leading administrative lawyer, against the spread of proportionality from the protection of fundamental rights to judicial review of administrative action in which fundamental rights are not engaged, a category that Taggart terms "public wrongs".[15]

Taggart articulates the growing disquiet among administrative lawyers in the common law world about the potential of a rights-protecting device such as proportionality to upset the delicate relationship between courts and the executive, because the intensity of proportionality review will cause courts to move from the appropriate standard of unreasonableness to a standard of correctness. They move from reviewing only if the applicant can show that the public official acted unreasonably to reviewing if the judges would have made a different decision on the merits. And whereas for many supporters of proportionality the device is important because it helps keep legislatures and public officials accountable to the rule of law, for Taggart it is as or even more important that judges be similarly accountable. The rule of law is meant to constrain judicial as well as official discretion, and the application of proportionality review across the board might, he feared, make the law "chaotic, unprincipled, and result-orientated."[16]

Support for these concerns comes from decisions by the House of Lords that held that the difference between cases involving fundamental rights and cases involving public wrongs is that, in the former, what matters is precisely whether the public official made the decision which the court deems correct, whereas in the latter a far less intensive form of judicial scrutiny is appropriate.[17] The House of Lords also held that when proportionality review is appropriate, the issue for the reviewing court is whether the decision was in fact proportional, and not whether the administration showed that it was so. To require the administration not only to get the conclusion right but also to get there in accordance with the methodology of proportionality would lead to the legalization, and even the judicialization, of the administrative process. As Taggart

---

[14] Moshe Cohen-Eliya and Iddo Porat, "American Balancing and German Proportionality: The Historical Origins," (2010) 8 *Int'l. J. Con. Law* 263.

[15] Taggart, "Proportionality, Deference, *Wednesbury*," *supra* note 8 at 425.

[16] Ibid. at 453.

[17] *R (on the application of Begum [by her litigation friend, Rahman]) (Respondent) v. Headteacher and Governors of Denbigh High School (Appellants)*, [2006] U.K.H.L. 15 [hereinafter *Begum* (HL)], overruling *R. (on the application of SB) v. Headteacher and Governors of Denbigh High School* [2005] E.W.C.A. Civ. 199 (hereinafter *Begum* [CA]); *Belfast City Council v. Miss Behavin' Ltd.*, [2007] 1 W.L.R. 1420 (hereinafter *Miss Behavin'*).

put it, "The reasoning process of the primary decision-maker and the reviewing court need not, and in many cases should not, be the same".[18]

However, there is an important difference between Taggart and the House of Lords: the latter reasoned that the process by which the public officials arrived at their decision is irrelevant because in the fundamental rights category all that matters is the correctness of the substantive decision. Of a piece with this reasoning is the House of Lord's across-the-board rejection in *Huang* of the kind of doctrine of deference that has been developed in the administrative law jurisprudence of the Canadian courts.[19]

According to that doctrine, courts should defer to administrative interpretations of the law when the reasons of the officials who made the decision provide a reasonable basis for the decision. Among the reasons for rejecting that doctrine, the House of Lords said, that "there has been a tendency, both in the arguments addressed to the courts and in the judgments of the courts, to complicate and mystify what is not, in principle, a hard task to define, however difficult the task is, in practice, to perform." This did not mean that courts should refrain from giving weight to factors, such as the judgment of those who have a "responsibility for a given subject matter and access to special sources of knowledge and advice."[20] But, the Law Lords added, the "giving of weight to factors such as these is not, in our opinion, aptly described as deference: it is performance of the ordinary judicial task of weighing up the competing considerations on each side. . . . That is how any rational judicial decision-maker is likely to proceed."[21]

Taggart, in contrast, claims that "proportionality and deference are complementary and counterbalance each other"[22] and so he vigorously criticizes *Huang*. He charts the development in administrative law from the time when English courts, and Commonwealth courts following them, would review only if an administrative decision displayed an error in terms of a limited set of specific grounds of review or, a residual category, for "*Wednesbury* unreasonableness". This restrictive attitude toward judicial review was also manifested in other ways, notably, that public officials rarely gave reasons for their decisions and were considered to be under a duty to do so only when such a duty was imposed by statute, and that the onus was on the applicant for judicial review to demonstrate the specific error or the unreasonableness of the decision. Naturally, the absence of reasons made this onus harder to

[18] Taggart, "Proportionality, Deference, *Wednesbury*," *supra* note 8 at 460–461.
[19] *Huang v Secretary of State for the Home Department*, [2007] 2 AC 167.
[20] Ibid. at para. 16.   [21] Ibid. at para. 16.
[22] Taggart, "Proportionality, Deference, *Wednesbury*," *supra* note 8 at 425.

discharge. This "classic model" of judicial review, says Taggart, "purported to keep judges' noses out of the tent of politics."[23]

This restrictive attitude relaxed as more grounds of review were added to the list, as judges began to appreciate that there was no sharp distinction between review of administrative interpretations of the law and review of exercises of discretion, as the latter also involved interpretation of the law, and as the idea took hold that at the basis of judicial review is a principle of "legality" anchored in common law fundamental rights.[24] The "traction" of this principle becomes even greater when the rule of law is invoked as an overarching principle of legal order, as in what Taggart calls the "classic statement" by Justice L'Heureux-Dubé in *Baker v. Canada (Minister of Citizenship and Immigration)*, where in the context of the control of discretionary power, she said: "discretion must be exercised in accordance with the boundaries imposed in the statute, the principles of the rule of law, the principles of administrative law, the fundamental values of Canadian society, and the principles of the Charter."[25] This decision also established a common law duty on public officials to give reasons for decisions that have an impact on important individual interests, and adopted the conception of due deference; that is, "deference as respect": judges should defer to administrative decisions not by submitting to them on the model of obedience to commands, but by displaying a "respectful attention to the reasons offered or which could be offered in support of . . . [the] decision, whether that decision be the statutory decision of the legislature, a judgment of another court, or the decision of an administrative agency."[26]

Taggart points out that the shift in administrative law from an exclusive concern with the content of the decision to include attention to the justification offered for the decision had already led British courts to a variegated approach within *Wednesbury* unreasonableness, so that the graver the impact of the decision on the individual affected by it the more substantial the justification required.[27] He suggests that the move to justification within the common law of judicial review resulted in a shared methodology with proportionality, because at the core of both is the idea that the legality of decision by a public authority depends on the justification – the quality of the

---

[23] Ibid. at 428–429.   [24] Ibid. at 429–432.
[25] [1999] 2 SCR 817 at para. 56; Taggart, "Proportionality, Deference, *Wednesbury*," *supra* note 8 at 432.
[26] Here the Court adopted my distinction between deference as respect and submissive deference, as well as the formulation of the former in Dyzenhaus, "The Politics of Deference: Judicial Review and Democracy" in Michael Taggart (ed.), *The Province of Administrative Law* (1997) at 286.
[27] Taggart, "Proportionality, Deference, *Wednesbury*," *supra* note 8 at 433.

reasons – offered by the public officials who made the decision.[28] Hence, he supposes that confining proportionality review to the fundamental rights side of the review rainbow will not cause the culture of justification to be "fractured".[29]

Taggart thus argues that the House of Lords in *Huang* made a "serious mistake" in rejecting deference. In particular, it was an "abdication of responsibility" to reject the Canadian approach, which weighs up relevant deference factors: the mere fact that primary responsibility has been delegated to the official (not the courts); the superior expertise of the official in the area; the modes of accountability that are prescribed for the official other than judicial review; the nature of the right in issue; whether the decision is highly individuated; and so on. Similarly, he rejects T.R.S. Allan's claim that such factors are "external" to the process of judicial review,[30] which implies that the court should simply consider whether, in the specific context, the official made the correct decision – that is, the decision the court would have rendered. Because, Taggart says, is it both "implausible" and "undesirable" that courts should adjudicate every challenge to check that the official has made a correct decision, Allan has to concede some "wiggle room" to the administrative state, which will inexorably take him back to the very factors he deems irredeemably external.[31] Thus, whereas some commentators have said that deference is nothing more than a symbol, Taggart emphasizes that it is "nothing less either": "The court responds to the reasoning and the context of the initial decision–maker. Justification by both the primary decision-maker and by the reviewing court is critically important for the legitimation of both."[32] It follows that even though the courts should not expect the administration to follow the exact methodology they adopt in proportionality analysis, they still have to be properly attentive to the reasons offered by the administration:

> The courts must ensure that the decision is reasonably rights-respecting, and so the court must deploy a methodology on substantive review to assure itself on that score. . . . [T]he court can [consequently] expect the public authority to explain what it is doing and why. If the public authority has not done so, then it can hardly complain if the court reaches a different result using the proportionality methodology. That is the link between reasons and deference (that Lord Hoffmann, for one, does not appear to appreciate).[33]

---

[28] Ibid. at 457. [29] Ibid. at 477.

[30] T.R.S. Allan, "Human Rights and Judicial Review: A Critique of 'Due Deference,'" (2006) 65 C. L.J. 671 (hereinafter Allan, "Human Rights").

[31] Taggart, "Proportionality, Deference, *Wednesbury*," *supra* note 8 at 456.

[32] Ibid. at 460. [33] Ibid. at 460–461.

Taggart's dig at Lord Hoffmann is aimed at that judge's remark in a decision prior to *Huang* that "deference" is inappropriate to describe "the relationship between the judicial and the other branches of government" because of its "overtones of servility, or perhaps gracious concession".[34] But, as I will now argue, if there is a link between reasons and deference, the case for bifurcation crumbles. Taggart underestimates here the strength of what he and I called, in an earlier essay, the "pull of justification": the pull of reason-giving as a necessary element in the justification of official decisions that affect important legal interests such that the very authority of such decisions depends in part on the reasons offered in their support.[35] And it is that underestimation that permits him to suppose that bifurcation is desirable.

I will make the argument against bifurcation on the basis of an analysis of the Court of Appeal's and House of Lords' decisions in *Begum v. Denbigh High School*, the latter of which Taggart cited as authority for the proposition quoted above "that the reasoning process of the primary decision-maker and the reviewing court need not, and in many cases should not, be the same".[36] I will suggest that there is more to the Court of Appeal's decision overruled by the House of Lords than he and others have supposed.[37] On its best interpretation, that decision tells us why the primary decision maker does not have to mimic a court's proportionality analysis, but has to offer a justification that complies with the informal logic of proportionality in order to earn the deference of a reviewing court.

IV. THE ARGUMENT AGAINST BIFURCATION

Begum *in the Court of Appeal*

Shabina Begum, a Muslim student of almost fourteen, attended Denbigh High School, a coeducational, community school in Luton, England, where almost 79 percent of the students (and many of the staff and administrators) were

[34] R. *(on the application of ProLife Alliance) v. British Broadcasting Corporation*, [2004] A.C. 185 (HL) at para. 75; Taggart, "Proportionality, Deference, *Wednesbury*," *supra* note 8 at 455.

[35] David Dyzenhaus and Michael Taggart, "Reasoned Decisions and Legal Theory" in Douglas E. Edlin, ed., *Common Law Theory* (2007) at 134.

[36] Taggart, "Proportionality, Deference, *Wednesbury*," *supra* note 8 at 460–461.

[37] For trenchant critique of the Court of Appeal, see Thomas Poole, "Of headscarves and heresies: the *Denbigh High School* case and public authority decision-making under the Human Rights Act," [2005] *Public Law* 685; Thomas Poole, "The Reformation of English Administrative Law," (2009) 68 *C.L.J.* 142 (hereinafter Poole, "The Reformation of English Administrative Law").

Muslim.[38] In compliance with the school's uniform policy, Begum had worn
a shalwar kameeze (a combination of tunic and trousers) to the school for two
years. On the first day of school in 2002, she announced to the assistant head
teacher that she wished to start wearing a jilbab (a plain dress covering the
arms and ankles), which was not in compliance with the policy. Begum had
entered puberty, and maintained that her religion's requirement of modest
dress meant that she had to wear the jilbab.

The school tried to persuade Begum to change her mind or to consider
being placed in another school in the area that would permit her to wear the
jilbab. It also consulted various Islamic authorities and obtained advice that the
uniform code did not offend against the requirements for modest dress. Begum
obtained contrary advice. In 2003, a committee of the governors gave a lengthy
decision upholding the school's position. It urged Begum to return to the
school wearing the prescribed uniform or to seek a place at another school.
She sought judicial review of the decision, although later began attending
another school that permitted her to wear the jilbab.

Begum's main claim was that the school had unjustifiably breached her
right to freedom of religious expression in terms of Article 9 of the European
Convention on Human Rights:[39]

> Everyone has the right to freedom of thought, conscience and religion; this
> right includes . . . freedom, either alone or in community with others and
> in public or private, to manifest his religion or belief, in worship, teaching,
> practice and observance.

> Freedom to manifest one's religion or beliefs shall be subject only to such
> limitations as are prescribed by law and are necessary in a democratic society
> in the interests of public safety, for the protection of public order, health or
> morals, or the protection of the rights and freedoms of others.[40]

Brooke LJ, writing for a unanimous Court of Appeal, found that Begum's
freedom to manifest her religion had been limited and that the limit was not
justified. By the time of the appeal, the only ground for justifying the limitation

---

[38] I rely here on the facts as reported in the Court of Appeal and the House of Lords, as well
as the account in Dominic McGoldrick, *Human Rights and Religion: The Islamic Headscarf
Debate in Europe* (2006) at 180–184.

[39] She also based this claim on section 6(1) of the Human Rights Act (1998). In addition, Begum
sought a declaration that she had been unlawfully "excluded" from the school and that she
had been denied access to suitable and appropriate education in breach of Article 2 of Protocol
1 to the European Convention on Human Rights and section 6(1) of the Human Rights Act.

[40] The European Convention on Human Rights, ROME November 4, 1950. Retrieved from
http://www.hri.org/docs/ECHR50.html.

that was still in play was the goal of protecting the rights and freedoms of other students.[41] One key reason for instituting the uniform policy had been to foster diversity and cooperation by reducing visible divisions between students along the lines of religion or race as expressed through clothing, and events following Begum's attempt to wear the jilbab to school had triggered fears among other Muslim students of social pressure to conform to that mode of dress.

Brooke LJ distinguished the matter before him from *Sahin v. Turkey*, where the European Court of Human Rights upheld a Turkish ban on all headscarves in Turkish universities on the basis of Turkey's adherence to a constitutionally entrenched principle of secularism.[42] England, he said, "is not a secular state, and although the Human Rights Act is now part of our law we have no written Constitution".[43] In *Begum*, the Court was hence concerned with the "more subtle" issue whether, "given that Muslim girls can already be identified in this way, it is necessary in a democratic society to place a particular restriction on those Muslim girls at this school who sincerely believe that when they arrive at the age of puberty they should cover themselves more comprehensively than is permitted by the school uniform policy."[44] In order to meet that test, Brooke LJ continued, the school had to follow a "decision-making structure" which involved answering six questions:

1. Has the claimant established that she has a relevant Convention right which qualifies for protection under Article 9(1)?
2. Subject to any justification that is established under Article 9(2), has that Convention right been violated?
3. Was the interference with her Convention right prescribed by law in the Convention sense of that expression?
4. Did the interference have a legitimate aim?
5. What are the considerations that need to be balanced against each other when determining whether the interference was necessary in a democratic society for the purpose of achieving that aim?
6. Was the interference justified under Article 9(2)?[45]

But, Brooke LJ said, the school did "not approach this matter in this way at all":

---

[41] No argument had been made with regard to the protection of public morals and an argument with regard to public safety had already been rejected at trial, based on evidence that other schools that had permitted girls to wear a jilbab experienced no problems with regard to health or safety.

[42] *Sahin v. Turkey* (2007), 44 E.H.R.R. 5 paras. 30–34.

[43] *Begum* (CA), *supra* note 17 at para. 73.

[44] Ibid. at para. 74.   [45] Ibid. at para. 75.

Nobody who considered the issues on its behalf started from the premise that the claimant had a right which is recognised by English law, and that the onus lay on the School to justify its interference with that right. Instead, it started from the premise that its uniform policy was there to be obeyed: if the claimant did not like it, she could go to a different school.[46]

Thus, the school "approached the issues in this case from an entirely wrong direction" by not "attributing to the claimant's beliefs the weight they deserved."[47]

In this light, it was not impossible for the school to justify its decision. To do so, the school would have to consider, among other factors, whether (a) it is appropriate to override the beliefs of "very strict Muslims" given the permission granted to liberal Muslims, and (b) the school could do more to reconcile its wish to retain "something resembling its current uniform policy" with the beliefs of those such as the claimant.[48]

Begum *in the House of Lords*

In overruling the Court of Appeal, the majority of the House of Lords held there was no limit at all on Begum's religious freedom. In the view of Lord Bingham for the majority, what constitutes a limit depends on all the circumstances of the case, including the extent to which an individual can reasonably expect to be at liberty to manifest his or her beliefs in practice.[49] Prohibiting the jilbab was a time and place regulation that did not interfere with her right to manifest her religion, as she could go to a school that permitted the jilbab.

But out of respect for his colleagues, Lord Nicholls and Baroness Hale, who both held there was a limit to Begum's religious freedom, Lord Bingham proceeded to the question of justification. On this, the Law Lords were unanimous in rejecting the procedural solution of the Court of Appeal. The issue, in their view, was not whether the school had followed the procedure prescribed by the Court of Appeal in making its decision, but whether its decision violated the substantive right protected by Article 9 of the European Convention. Lord Bingham offered three reasons in support of his conclusion. First, Strasbourg jurisprudence did not focus on the question whether the decision-making process was flawed, but only on the question whether there had been a violation

---

[46] Ibid. at para. 76. Instead, the Governors' Complaints Committee, in rejecting Begum's claim, had "observed that they did not purport to have the legal knowledge to interpret complex legislation" (ibid., at para. 58).
[47] Ibid. at para. 78.   [48] Ibid. at para. 81.
[49] *Begum* (HL), *supra* note 17 at para. 22.

of a protected right.[50] Secondly, proportionality review differed from domestic judicial review of administrative action because it required a greater intensity of review – an objective confrontation of the merits. Difficult as that might be, courts should not "retreat to procedure" to avoid the difficulties: "The school's action cannot properly be condemned as disproportionate, with an acknowledgment that on reconsideration the same action could be very well maintained and properly so."[51]

Thirdly, Lord Bingham said that the Court of Appeal's approach, although "admirable guidance to a lower court or legal tribunal", could not be required of a school. That would introduce "a new formalism" and be a "recipe for judicialisation on an unprecedented scale".[52] The school had taken great care to design its uniform policy and had achieved success with that policy. It had reconsidered the policy but also had feared the possible "significant adverse repercussions" if it did. Thus, it would be "irresponsible" of any court to interfere with a decision that had been given to the school "for the compelling reason that they are best placed to exercise it."[53]

However, the jurisprudence of the Strasbourg Court does in general require that the state has the onus of showing that a limit is necessary in that it meets a pressing social need (that is, a legitimate aim), it does so in a way that is rationally connected to that aim, and the means to achieve that aim do not impose an excessive burden on those whose rights were limited.[54] The only Law Lord who came close to confronting this issue was Baroness Hale. However, all that she said was that the school's policy was a "thoughtful and proportionate response to reconciling the complexities of the situation" given "the social conditions in that school, in that town, and at that time"; and that proportionality was "demonstrated by the fact that girls have subsequently expressed their concern that if the jilbab were to be allowed they would face pressure to adopt it even though they do not wish to do so."[55]

As John Finnis has pointed out, this last fact cannot supply a justification because it does not respond to the question whether the school's policy on uniforms was necessary "in the face of alternative policies which would have permitted the jilbab."[56] So what then is the argument for necessity in the

---

[50] Ibid. at para. 29.   [51] Ibid. at para. 30.
[52] Ibid. at para. 31. The quotations are taken by Lord Bingham from Poole, "Headscarves," *supra* note 36.
[53] Ibid. at para. 34.   [54] See ibid. at 169–170.
[55] *Begum* (HL), *supra* note 17 at para. 98.
[56] John Finnis, "Endorsing Discrimination Between Faiths: A Case of Extreme Speech?" in Ivan Hare and James Weinstein (eds.), *Extreme Speech and Democracy* (2009) at 433 (hereinafter Finnis, "Endorsing Discrimination").

English context? In Finnis's view, the argument lies in the political nature of Islam with its commitment to shariah, a commitment that is fundamentally incompatible with democracy and the rule of law.[57] He finds this argument buried in what he calls the House of Lords' "terse references" to the nature of Islam; for example, that the Law Lords clearly saw Shabina Begum as the pawn of her older brother, who had accompanied her to school on the day she made her initial demand, and also saw her brother as the adherent of, in Lord Hoffmann's words, an "extremist version of the Muslim religion".[58]

The main problem for the House of Lords is not, however, that they adopted such a view, but that their failure to deal with the issue of justification makes their reasoning incoherent, and that opens the door to the kind of attribution to them of the view of Islam advocated by Finnis. Finnis is closer to the mark when he claims that the flaws in their reasoning could be seen as evidence of the "conceptual slackness of human rights law in action."[59] But although he might regard this slackness as an inevitable feature of adjudication under human rights regimes, it is, as I will now argue, the product of the House of Lords' approach to review and not evidence of some inevitable slackness.

Reasons and Justification

There is some tension between the Law Lords' position that all that matters is checking substance – whether a right has been violated – and the fact that they do at times take seriously the process the school followed to reach its substantive judgments, both when the school established the uniform code in 1993 and when it responded to Begum's challenge. Indeed, no less than the Court of Appeal, the House of Lords deferred the substantive decision to the school at the same time as it insisted that the school's reasons were immaterial, thus adopting a kind of procedural solution.

Recall that one of the reasons advanced by Lord Bingham for rejecting the procedural approach of the Court of Appeal was that "[t]he school's action cannot properly be condemned as disproportionate, with an acknowledgment

---

[57] Ibid. at 435.

[58] *Begum* (HL), *supra* note 17 at para. 65. For Finnis, it follows from the position that we should consider "deliberating seriously" ways of dealing with a minority whose numbers are "increasing rapidly by immigration and a relatively high birth rate". That is, we have to contemplate not only prohibiting "any further migratory increase in that population" but also whether we should "accept the presence of immigrant, non-citizen Muslims", in turn leading us to deliberate seriously a "possible reversal" of the "inflow" of these Muslims, of course "humane and financially compensated for and incentivized"; Finnis, "Endorsing Discrimination" at 440. He does not elaborate how considerations of humanity are compatible with such policies.

[59] Finnis, ibid. at 433.

that on reconsideration the same action could be very well maintained and properly so." However, Beatson et al., the authors of *Human Rights Protection in the United Kingdom*, one of the leading texts on its topic, argue that this is not a sound reason.[60]

First, courts are generally better suited to assess matters of procedure and identify procedural defects in reasoning processes than to second-guess the primary decision maker on substantive findings. Second, when courts insist that decisions be made in the right way, they improve the standard of decision making in public authorities, thereby "more firmly embedding a human rights culture in public decision making." Third, an individual is arguably entitled to have a decision remade on the proper basis "where there is a prospect of a different result being reached" after the European Convention is properly considered. In this last regard, the authors suggest that such an approach accords better with the kind of deference properly owed by courts to those charged with primary responsibility for making the decision, a stance which is often justified because the court may not be best placed to assess proportionality. In such a case, a court acts appropriately when it remits the matter back to the primary decision maker for redetermination. If the court fails to do this, "judicial supervision risks falling between two stools: the court declines to look at the decision-making process, but only the result; and it declines to engage closely with the result on the basis of relative institutional competence".[61]

The authors also point out that a court is in a "particularly difficult position" when it does not have before it a properly considered exercise of primary judgment. For example, if the decision maker has not properly considered the question whether there is an alternative, less-intrusive measure, the court will likely not be satisfied that the measure is proportionate. However, it does not follow that the measure is disproportionate, and for this reason it is sensible for the court to remit the matter back for reconsideration.[62]

---

[60] Jack Beatson, Stephen Grosz, Tom Hickman, Rabinder Singh, with Stephanie Palmer, *Human Rights Protection in the United Kingdom* (2008) at 234–238. They also point out that the decision of the House of Lords is inconsistent both with some of its own jurisprudence, in which it was assumed that the decision maker had to have carried out a proper balancing exercise and asked himself the right questions, although a structured approach was not required, and with some Strasbourg jurisprudence.

[61] Ibid. at 236.

[62] Ibid. at 236–237. I reject, however, their further claim that such a decision is properly characterized as procedural rather than substantive, as it is a mistake to make a sharp distinction. The point of requiring a better process of justification rests entirely on the faith that appropriate justification produces better substance; that is, decisions that are in fact justified. Judges might be better equipped to inspect the process of justification than they are to second-guess the officials on substance, and it might also be right that the second role raises hard questions about institutional legitimacy that the first does not. But judges cannot avoid looking at substance in

These points together provide an effective riposte to the House of Lords. Consider Lord Hoffmann's much-quoted jibe at the Court of Appeal: "Head teachers and governors cannot be expected to make such decisions with text-books on human rights law at their elbows. The most that can be said is that the way in which the school approached the problem may help to persuade a judge that its answer fell within the area of judgment accorded to it by the law".[63] Lord Hoffmann is surely right that it would be absurd to require a school board or other administrative body to produce the equivalent of an appeal court's judgment on proportionality every time it had to decide a matter that affected fundamental rights. But if he and the rest of the Law Lords were also right that all that mattered is the result the body reached (whether that result is endorsed by the judges' proportionality analysis), then the way in which the school approached the problem should be wholly irrelevant to a court. The way the school went about things can, in other words, "help to persuade a judge that its answer fell within the area of judgment accorded to it by the law" if and only if it meets the following condition: the way in which the decision was reasoned demonstrates that any limit placed on the right in question is "necessary in a democratic society in the interests of public safety, for the protection of public order, health or morals, or the protection of the rights and freedoms of others."[64]

As Beatson et al. indicate, if all a court had before it were the result, it would also not be equipped to make any judgment about proportionality because the proportionality doctrine is contingent on analysis of the reasons that justify a limit on a right. Thus, there must exist some middle ground between, on the one hand, the simple announcement of a decision unsupported by justifying reasons and, on the other, a decision that is supported by the kind of proportionality analysis that proceeds in accordance with the formal criteria laid out by Brooke LJ. Only if the body that makes that decision properly occupies that middle ground is it equipped to make the case on judicial review that its decision was justified as necessary or reasonable in a democratic society. And judges should conclude that it is appropriate for them to defer to that body only if that is the case made.

What does it take to occupy that middle ground? Here, I think that Brooke LJ is correct that what went wrong in the school's decision process is that "[n]obody who considered the issues on its behalf started from the premise

these sorts of cases, as the issue is always whether the reasons were good enough to justify the result.

[63] *Begum* (HL), *supra* note 17 at para. 68.
[64] This is so even if the necessity test in the context of Article 9 is understood not to be as strict as that to be deployed for other Articles in that it does not require the least-intrusive means to achieve the objective, but only a reasonable means.

that the claimant had a right which is recognised by English law, and that the onus lay on the School to justify its interference with that right."[65] He is also right that what went wrong is that the "school started from the premise that its uniform policy was there to be obeyed: if the claimant did not like it, she could go to a different school".[66] Where he went wrong was in laying out the formulaic set of questions when a process that supplied reasons to justify the limit on the right would have sufficed.

There is a difference between the approaches to rights claims taken by two different kinds of school. On the one hand, there is a school intent on efficient management of its affairs that wishes its decisions to be as attentive as possible to the claims of those within its care. This institution may naturally wish to be especially sensitive to claims that are made in the language of rights, but will only accommodate those rights insofar as they are consistent with the overall objectives of the school. On the other hand, there is a school that regards its educational task as placed within a wider societal context constituted by commitments to fundamental human rights. In such a context, in pursuing a legitimate objective, the school must justify any limitation on a rights claim by a pupil as necessary to accomplish that objective. That justification has to go primarily to the rights claimant, but also has to be sufficient to meet a more general test of public acceptability, a test in which judicial review may play a role. This difference between the two schools is between a managerial culture and a culture of justification in which justification is on the basis of claims to fundamental, legally protected rights.

Of course, there is the problem whether the claim is genuinely one of right. We have seen that the majority of the House of Lords did not think there was any limit on a right because Begum could have gone to a school that permitted the jilbab. However, this fact can appear in two radically different lights. It may seem to sustain the conclusion that Begum's right had not been limited. Alternatively, if one starts from the premise that there had been a limit of her right, that fact casts into doubt arguments that prohibiting the jilbab is a proportional policy, especially in a school that, as Brooke LJ pointed out, already permitted girls to "wear a headscarf which is likely to identify them as Muslim."[67] Put differently, because other schools in the area permitted the jilbab, the school was faced with the question of why its prohibition was either the least intrusive way of reconciling Begum's right with the school's goal of protecting the rights and freedoms of other students or, if this test seems too strict, why the prohibition was a reasonable way of achieving that same goal.

---

[65] *Begum* (CA), *supra* note 17 at para. 76.   [66] Ibid. at para. 76.
[67] Ibid. at para. 74, read with paras. 72 and 73.

The school, as we have also seen, did not think that Begum's claim could simply be dismissed. But it was at best ambiguous about whether hers was a claim of right. The ambiguity arises because a managerial school that is sensitive to rights claims, perhaps because of its history and makeup, will conduct its enquiry into whether to accommodate any rights claim in a way that will start to shade into the kind of enquiry that the Court of Appeal thought was lacking. But it makes a qualitative difference when the enquiry starts in a culture of justification from the assumption that the onus is on the public body seeking to impose a limit on a legally protected right to justify that limit by showing that, in the circumstances, it has adopted proportionate means.

Such an enquiry can follow a kind of informal logic of proportionality without being legalistic in the judicializing way objected to by the House of Lords. Indeed, far from being designed to elicit complex legal arguments, or reams of facts, what should come out of any enquiry are the kinds of facts and characterizations and weightings of such facts that are crucial to any public process of justification. Only the front line or primary decision maker, with firsthand knowledge of the context and actors involved, is capable of eliciting and assigning initial weight to such facts. The appeal to facts should not, however, be mistaken for the claim that the enquiry is value neutral. It is shaped by the assumption that the public authority bears the onus of justifying the limit of the right asserted, and it requires that the authority regard persons as bearer of rights, not as individuals who may or may not be accorded a privilege. In this way, Brooke LJ's approach is best understood as procedural in a way that does not distinguish between process and substance.

Process and Substance

A reviewing court's inquiry is not into correctness, but into reasonableness, which includes checking to see whether the decision maker has framed the issue in the right way. It is this consideration that connects process and substance, as it has a significant effect not only on how facts are approached, but also on how they are characterized.

Consider, for example, how Baroness Hale in *Begum* found the demonstration of proportionality to reside in "the fact that girls have *subsequently* expressed their concern that if the jilbab were to be allowed they would face pressure to adopt it".[68] That is, the concern manifested itself after the school had decided not to change its policy, so it had to be unclear to the Court

---

[68] *Begum* (HL), *supra* note 17 at para. 98.

how that concern figured in the school's decision. In addition, claims about the intimidatory pressure that would follow permitting the jilbab require some inquiry into whether wearing the shalwar kameeze had put pressure on Muslim girls who wished to wear the secular school uniform. If that inquiry revealed, as Begum subsequently claimed it would, that there was this kind of pressure,[69] the school would have to explain why the jilbab would make things worse, given the experience of other schools in the area. In this context, it would have been a sufficient basis for the school's position that permitting the jilbab would result in the intimidation of other girls such that Begum's right to religious freedom was outweighed by the threat to the freedom of others.

As we can now see, the approach adopted by the House of Lords results, somewhat paradoxically, in a kind of abdication of the supervisory responsibility of a reviewing court.[70] In addition, the evaluative exercise the school would have to undertake is sensitive to the different rights claims in the context. It does not simply weigh, on the one hand, Begum's preference against, on the other hand, the interest of all in a secure environment and in securing their own preferences. As such, the exercise has to be alert to another consideration, stemming from the role of the school as a public body in a culture of justification, one well expressed in a Canadian Supreme Court decision on the right of a Sikh boy to wear a kirpan (ceremonial dagger) to school:

> Religious tolerance is a very important value of Canadian society. If some students consider it unfair that Gurbaj Singh may wear his kirpan to school while they are not allowed to have knives in their possession, it is incumbent on the schools to discharge their obligation to instil in their students this value that is . . . at the very foundation of our democracy.[71]

---

[69] See the interview with Shabina Begum in the *Sunday Times* after the House of Lord's decision, by Jasper Gerard, "Faith, the veil, shopping and me," March 26, 2006, retrieved from http://www.timesonline.co.uk/tol/news/article696181.ece.

[70] For an illuminating discussion, see Nicholas Gibson, "Faith in the Courts: Religious Dress and Human Rights," (2007) 66 C.L.J. 657; and Tom Lewis, "What not to Wear: Religious Rights, the European Court, and the Margin of Appreciation," (2007) I.C.L.Q. 395.

[71] *Multani v. Commission Scolaire Marguerite-Bourgeoys*, [2006] 1 S.C.R. 256 (hereinafter *Multani*). The minority (Deschamps and Abella JJ) held that in order to avoid legalizing the administrative process the case should be dealt with as an administrative law matter to be resolved by judicial review for unreasonableness. However, they also said (para. 99) that "in making its determinations, the school board must take all fundamental values into consideration, including not only security, but also freedom of religion and the right to equality. The prohibition on the wearing of a kirpan cannot be imposed without considering conditions that would interfere less with freedom of religion." That is, the non- or less-legalistic process still required framing the inquiry with the right, and so forth.

That is, the school would have to take into account not only the cost to Begum of failing to accommodate her choice as an expression of her religious freedom, but also the cost to the general climate of tolerance and respect in not permitting a girl who had spent two years at a school and who had chosen a new direction in her faith to continue as part of the school's community.[72]

We are now at the point at which the connection between process and substance can be properly made and so can appreciate why the link between reasons and deference helps to establish the validity of the premise that Begum's right had been limited. Consider Sheldon Leader's argument that the kind of approach adopted by the majority of the House of Lords in *Begum*, although not requiring of the individual a *"comprehensive* surrender of a basic right" does still "shrink the opportunities for exercising a right."[73] Such shrinkage does damage to a "dynamic" conception of personal integrity according to which people who "want to do their best to find, and sometimes to redraw, the most suitable relationship between" their conception of their religious duties, on the one hand, and the demands, on the other, of their professional life.[74] If the institutions in which their professional life is conducted demand the "right to fix their own combination of those elements", for example, by offering a less desirable job or school, they force the individuals to "confront a serious problem."[75]

Leader recognizes fully that individuals cannot expect to be provided with an "ethically frictionless environment."[76] But he suggests that the idea of fundamental rights offers the way forward. For this idea is hostile to the claim that institutions may "unilaterally set the terms of the compromise" the individuals must make. He criticizes Denbigh High School for just such a unilateral act, endorsed by the House of Lords, because the majority of the Law Lords thought that there was "no interference at all with the right because the individual could always exit."[77]

---

[72] See the majority opinion in *Multani*, ibid., where Charron J, in dealing with the last stage of proportionality, "Effects of the Measure," held (para. 79):

> A total prohibition against wearing a kirpan to school undermines the value of this religious symbol and sends students the message that some religious practices do not merit the same protection as others. On the other hand, accommodating Gurbaj Singh and allowing him to wear his kirpan under certain conditions demonstrates the importance that our society attaches to protecting freedom of religion and to showing respect for its minorities. The deleterious effects of a total prohibition thus outweigh its salutary effects.

[73] Sheldon Leader, "Freedoms and Futures: Personal Priorities, Institutional Demands and Freedom of Religion," (2007) 70 M.L.R. 713 at 716.

[74] Ibid. at 719.   [75] Ibid. at 719.

[76] Ibid. at 721.   [77] Ibid. at 725.

Leader argues that individuals have an obligation to themselves to shape and reshape the relationship between their priorities and that there is a corresponding obligation on schools and workplaces to "provide space for people to transform their deepest priorities from being a source of self-estrangement into elements of a sense of personal progress."[78] As he points out, a person's commitment to religion might vary in intensity over time. And if the majority of the House of Lords' position is adopted, a person might when she becomes more religious be "obliged to abandon . . . [an education of high quality] in favour of a less good – but minimally adequate – education. . . . She will have paid a heavy price in one important side of her life because of changes that she did not choose to happen in other important sides of her life."[79] In other words, the majority of the House of Lords adopted a morally controversial understanding of rights in order to find that there was no limit. That understanding in turn influenced the ease with which they found a justification.

The lesson here is not only that reasons have to justify a limit on a right, and so must be taken seriously by a reviewing court when an official attempts a justification. It is also that the justification, although essential to establishing the authority of a decision, does not run primarily to the reviewing court but to the person affected by the decision. The position taken by the majority of the House of Lords is antithetical to a culture of justification because in such a culture the authoritative institutions may not unilaterally set the terms of any compromise that an individual has to consider making when it comes to balancing her rights with competing considerations. While, as I have suggested, there is some ambiguity in the school's position on this issue, the majority of the House of Lords disambiguated that position with the unfortunate result that such institutions are relieved of the burden of justification.

V. REASONS IN THE CULTURE OF JUSTIFICATION

We can say more abstractly that what Taggart and I called the "pull of justification" – the requirement that official decisions must be justified by reasons when they affect legally protected, individual interests – is ultimately driven by a normative vision of political society. When the exercise of power interferes with a legally protected interest, the justification must be attuned to justifying that interference, whether the interest is protected by constitutional law or the common law of judicial review. There is, of course, the worry, as Taggart noted, that reason-giving in itself leads to excessive or unpredictable judicial

---

[78] Ibid. at 730.   [79] Ibid. at 728.

intervention because it "delivers up to the courts the power to evaluate that reasoning and the result reached." But the answer, he said, is not to turn the clock back but "to be aware of the propensity and to acknowledge that reason-giving itself is the start of deference-as-respect".[80]

As I and others have argued, far from giving more power to judges, the shift to a culture of justification empowers the administrative state. It does so because its decisions should survive review as long as they are shown by the reasons provided to be justifiable, rather than because the conclusion reached by the body happens to coincide with the conclusion that the judges would have considered correct without the benefit of engagement with the administrative body's reasons. The culture of justification delineates and enforces the separation of powers. By requiring the executive to justify the exercise of its power, and by requiring the judiciary to defer to reasonable justification, the roles each branch plays are made clearer.

Of course, that shift has profound consequences for the administrative state, as the officials who staff it have to adopt a mode of decision making that accords with a culture of a justification, a mode that requires them not only to think of each decision as one that has to be justified to those affected by it, but also to articulate that justification. The only way to avoid this extra burden on the administrative state is not by deeming irrelevant the process by which the body reached its conclusion, but through the total exclusion of the reasons that are the manifestation of that process.

The House of Lords' failure to appreciate this point led to incoherence in their reasoning in *Begum*. They made matters even worse when, in a subsequent decision, they continued to claim that process is irrelevant, all the while reasoning that the more carefully reasoned a decision is and the more carefully and exactly the competing interests have been balanced, the greater the weight that should be given to the assessment of the primary decision maker.[81]

I suspect that opposition to my argument will stem from the concern that judges will have to give up the idea that they have a monopoly on right answers

---

[80] Taggart, "Proportionality, Deference, *Wednesbury*," *supra* note 8 at 463.

[81] In *Miss Behavin'*, where the House of Lords, following *Begum*, found that the Court of Appeal in Northern Ireland had erred in holding that a city council's refusal of license to run a sex shop was invalid because the council had not expressly addressed Miss Behavin' Ltd.'s right to freedom of expression, under Article 10 of the Convention. However, three of the judges also found that where the public authority had properly addressed itself to the appropriate questions and balanced the competing considerations including Convention rights, the courts should be ready to defer. For cogent criticism, see Alison L. Young, "In Defence of Due Deference," (2009) 72 *M.L.R.* 554 at 569–570 (hereinafter Young, "Defence"); and Tom Hickman, *Public Law After the Human Rights Act* (2010), chapter 8, "The Forbidden Process Element in Human Rights Review."

when it comes to questions of fundamental rights. For in the culture of justification, administrative bodies participate as partners with other institutions
in the process of determining how fundamental rights commitments are to
be interpreted and implemented.[82] But, as we have seen, it is very difficult
for those in the opposition to avoid the kinds of problems encountered by the
House of Lords in *Begum*.

Consider, for example, the opposition to due deference and its requirement
of respect for administrative reasons on the basis that, if adopted, this will
distract judges from their proper task of deciding what the law requires. Those
who make this claim still want to say that what is right is context-dependent,
so that judges will have to be sensitive to the characteristics of the particular
context in which a decision is made. Moreover, the kinds of factors that are
listed by Canadian courts as the components of a doctrine of deference are
nothing more, but also nothing less, than a kind of catechism that disciplines
judicial review by requiring judges to be explicit about what they take the
context to be. Because one cannot individuate the context without relying on
such factors, it is inconsistent to say that judges should not be distracted by
them and yet must be attentive to context.[83] Similarly, one cannot say that
weight should be given to judgments of those with special expertise without
having some prior sense of what constitutes the kind of factor that will tell one
when to accord weight.

Nor can one say that weight should be given to expertise, but not to the
reasons offered by the expert. Expertise can be presumed, but not assumed;
the difference being that the presumption requires that the expert demonstrate expertise through the reasons offered in support of the decision. As Jerry
Mashaw has put it, the "progressive submission of power to reason" in administrative law requires that expertise be "no longer a protective shield to be worn
like a sacred vestment"; rather, it is to be "a competence to be demonstrated
by cogent reason-giving".[84]

[82] See, further, David Dyzenhaus, "Constituting the Rule of Law: Fundamental Values in Administrative Law," (2002) 27 *Queen's L.J.* 445.
[83] I take this inconsistency to mark Allan's argument in Allan, "Human Rights," *supra* note 30.
For relevant critique, see Young, "Defence," *supra* note 85 at 575–576; and Hunt, "Against
Bifurcation," *supra* note 11 at 115–116. Allan seems now to accept some of the force of this
critique; see T.R.S. Allan, "Deference, Defiance, and Doctrine: Defining the Limits of Judicial
Review," (2010) 55 *U.T.L.J.* 41 at 56. In addition, his contribution to this volume, "Democracy,
Legality and Proportionality," Chapter 10, makes his position and mine consistent in almost
every respect.
[84] Jerry L. Mashaw, "Small Things Like Reasons Are Put in a Jar: Reason and Legitimacy in the
Administrative State," (2001) 70 *Fordham L. Rev.* 17 at 26. At 35, Mashaw says that administrative
law is "reason's preeminent, legal home."

VI. CONCLUSION: REJECTING BIFURCATION

My final remarks are addressed to Taggart's claim that proportionality is best confined to the fundamental rights side of the review rainbow, the claim that results in the bifurcation of constitutional and administrative law. However, Taggart also thought that reason-giving itself is not only the start of due deference (deference as respect), but also "an important check on judges inappropriately positioning the case on the rainbow of review."[85] In this regard, I can understand how one might rationally try to design a legal order bifurcated between a constitutional sphere, in which judges review alleged infractions of entrenched constitutional rights on a correctness standard, and an administrative sphere in which judges will review only if the applicant can show that a discrete public wrong from a limited list of such wrongs was committed. But once reasonableness is added to the list within the administrative sphere as a residual category, the other items on the list are better seen as factors that name specific kinds of unreasonableness, so that underpinning the list is a foundational norm of a right to just administrative action, of the sort advocated by Mureinik and entrenched in the South African Constitution.

As Mureinik emphasized, the justness of such action is, in a culture of justification, a quality to be demonstrated by reason-giving. Among those reasons, the administrator will have to articulate, where appropriate, whether the decision limits a fundamental right or affects a legally protected interest, and, if it does, why the administrator supposes the limit or the effect to be justified.[86] And as Taggart and I noted in our essay on the common law duty to give reasons, "it is a short theoretical, if not historical, step from a commitment to a reason-based conception of authority to a constitutional requirement of a duty to give reasons, a step from presumed reasonableness to demonstrated or justified reasonableness."[87]

Once that step is taken, the differences between review of alleged public wrongs and review of alleged breaches of fundamental rights become highly nuanced, to the point where bifurcation seems highly artificial. And at the same time, it becomes clear that the logic of proportionality applies across

---

[85] Taggart, "Proportionality, Deference, *Wednesbury*," *supra* note 8 at 463.

[86] Tom Hickman points out that although the proportionality test imposes a burden on the official to justify conduct, "under traditional judicial review the burden is on the claimant to demonstrate that the decision was unfair or unreasonable, reflecting a presumption that public officials exercise their powers bona fide and reasonably"; "Problems for Proportionality," [2010] *NZ L. Rev.* 303. In the culture of justification, that presumption has, I recognize, to be rethought.

[87] Dyzenhaus and Taggart, "Reasoned Decisions and Legal Theory," *supra* note 35 at 152.

the public law legal order. Proportionality reasoning is simply the exercise of justifying to individuals an exercise of official authority that affects legally protected interests. It is true that the more fundamental the interest the more onerous is the burden of justification, but that marks differences in degrees of intensity, not differences in kinds of public law of the sort presupposed by the idea of bifurcation.

Taggart himself laid the groundwork for rejecting bifurcation in his argument that the move to justification within the common law of judicial review has the result that it now shares a methodology with proportionality, so that a court must ensure that official decisions are "reasonably rights-respecting", deploying "a methodology on substantive review to assure itself on that score".[88] My analysis of *Begum* serves to underline why he should have taken the further step and rejected bifurcation. For it shows that bifurcation depends on a distinction between process and substance that is incoherent in practice and that undermines the ideal of legal authority that animates a culture of justification.

---

[88] Taggart, "Proportionality, Deference, *Wednesbury*," *supra* note 8 at 461.

12 Proportionality and Democratic Constitutionalism

Stephen Gardbaum

As scholarship on proportionality has taken a welcome normative turn in the last few years, some of its proponents have portrayed it as an essential part of a broader "culture of justification".[1] Within this culture, as a condition of its legitimacy, all government action – and not only (in Rawlsean terms) the basic structure of society – must be justifiable in terms of public reason to the individuals burdened by it. Proportionality analysis provides the analytical framework for this required exercise in public justification. This account of proportionality tends to emphasize its strength as imposing a second set of constraints – substantive in nature – on government action in addition to the procedural requirement of political equality as manifested in democratically accountable decision making. In this way, these proponents argue that proportionality's burden of justification is a necessary "second pillar" of constitutional legitimacy; democracy is not enough.[2]

By contrast, critics of proportionality have emphasized its weakness rather than strength as a constraint on government action, particularly in the rights

---

[1] The term originated with Etienne Mureinik in 1994, who contrasted it to "a culture of authority," as a way of characterizing the aims of the new South African Constitution.

> If the new Constitution is a bridge away from a culture of authority, it is clear what it must be a bridge to. It must lead to a culture of justification – a culture in which every exercise of power is expected to be justified; in which the leadership given by government rests on the cogency of the case offered in defense of its decisions, not the fear inspired by the force at its command (Etienne Mureinik, "A Bridge to Where?: Introducing the Interim Bill of Rights," [1994] 10 S.A.J.H.R. 31 at 32 [hereinafter Mureinik, "A Bridge to Where?"].

> See also David Dyzenhaus, "Law as Justification: Etienne Mureinik's Conception of Legal Culture," (1998) 14 S.A.J.H.R. 11 (hereinafter Dyzenhaus, "Law as Justification").

[2] Mattias Kumm, "Democracy Is Not Enough: Rights, Proportionality and the Point of Judicial Review," NYU School of Law, Public Law Research Paper No 09–10 (2009) (hereinafter Kumm, "Democracy is not Enough").

context. By placing constitutional rights on a par with governmental interests, engaging in "rights inflation"[3] so that rights are ubiquitous but devalued, and reducing rights analysis to the purely quantitative and technical, critics claim that proportionality rejects the special normative force of constitutional rights and renders them inconsequential.[4] For the critics, protecting rights only against disproportionate infringements is not enough. One strand within this general position additionally incorporates a democratic critique of proportionality: in granting courts the power both to specify the meaning and scope of abstractly framed constitutional rights and evaluate the justifiability of legislative limits on them, the rise and triumph of proportionality has been a central factor in the juridification or judicialization of contemporary constitutionalism.[5]

In this chapter, I propose an alternative normative perspective to the influential culture of justification from which to understand and evaluate proportionality. From this perspective, proportionality should primarily be understood as enhancing, not constraining, democracy. Rather than the constitutionalist legitimacy of democracy, proportionality is centrally about the democratic legitimacy of a constitutionalized rights regime and an appropriate balance between judicial and legislative powers. It is part of a conception of constitutional rights and a rights regime that, in contrast with certain others, seeks to accommodate and temper enduring and legitimate democratic concerns. This conception is typically institutionalized through its characteristic textual vehicle of the limitations clause, which grants to legislatures significant power and leeway in the resolution of rights issues. Accordingly, this alternative normative perspective can be thought of as promoting a "culture of democracy". It also responds to the democratic critique of proportionality by showing how the very "weakness" its critics complain of forms the basis of a democratic justification for it. In short, I argue that the critics are mostly correct in their characterization of proportionality, but wrong that this undermines its normative appeal.

It will be clear that in presenting my culture of democracy analysis and case for proportionality, I am not attempting a fine-grained defense of the various prongs of the near-universal proportionality test. Nor am I defending any one specific version of proportionality over another, or even proportionality versus other similar modes of constitutional balancing. Rather, I am seeking

[3] See Kai Möller, "Proportionality and Rights Inflation," Chapter 7 in this volume.
[4] See text accompanying notes 14–19.
[5] Grégoire C.N. Webber, *The Negotiable Constitution: On the Limitation of Rights* (2009) at 201–212

to present a more broadly gauged conception and defense of a proportionality-like test for limiting rights (and of the conception of constitutional rights of which it is an inherent part) that is part and parcel of contemporary "strong-form judicial review".[6] In claiming that proportionality can and should be viewed through the lens of democratic constitutionalism, I am certainly not arguing that it is the only or best rights regime from this perspective. What I am suggesting is that a system of proportionality-based constitutional rights can be made less vulnerable to certain democratic critiques than alternative systems of strong-form judicial review, and that this should be taken into account in the normative debate about the merits of proportionality and, indeed, about institutional forms of constitutionalism more generally.

The first section of the chapter sets out the normative perspective of the culture of justification shared by certain recent proponents of proportionality, as well as the critique of it on the part of proportionality's opponents. The second section presents the alternative perspective of the culture of democracy from which to understand and assess proportionality, including the normative case for proportionality that derives from it and the implications of this case for the exercise of judicial review. If, as I argue, proportionality can properly be viewed as one version of democratic constitutionalism, the final section broadens the picture by outlining the other major versions and offering some preliminary and tentative thoughts on their comparison and respective merits.

I. PROPORTIONALITY AND THE CULTURE OF JUSTIFICATION

Recent scholarship sympathetic to proportionality analysis as a near-universal feature of contemporary constitutionalism has tended to embed it – for explanatory or normative purposes – in a broader culture of justification. This culture consists in a general requirement that in order to be legitimate, all government action must satisfy a burden of public justification. It therefore imposes substantive – not only procedural or jurisdictional – constraints on government action, prohibiting as illegitimate laws and other conduct that fail this test of justification. The function of proportionality analysis is to provide the analytical framework for much of this required burden of justification. This standard of political legitimacy is more onerous than the conventional one in

---

[6] That is, where courts have the final word and their decisions are unreviewable by ordinary majority vote, by contrast with the newer forms of "weak-form" judicial review discussed in Part IV. Mark Tushnet introduced the helpful terminology of strong and weak-form judicial review. See Mark V. Tushnet, "New Forms of Judicial Review and the Persistence of Rights- and Democracy-Based Worries," 38 *Wake Forest L. Rev.* 813 (2003); Mark V. Tushnet, "Weak-Form Judicial Review: Its Implications for Legislatures," (2004) 23 S.C.L.R. 213.

modern liberal political theory, because it applies a test of reasonable public justification not merely to the basic or constitutional structure of society, but to each and every action of government operating within that structure.

According to Moshe Cohen-Eliya and Iddo Porat,[7] proportionality is an inherent part of a broader culture of justification, and it has been the profound switch toward this general culture and away from the contrasting "culture of authority" that helps explain the spread and appeal of the proportionality principle. "At its core, a culture of justification requires that governments should provide substantive justification for all their actions, by which we mean justification in terms of the rationality and reasonableness of every action and the trade-offs that every action necessarily involves, i.e., in terms of proportionality."[8] By contrast, within the culture of authority that they argue characterizes the American constitutional model,[9] legitimacy derives from the fact that the actor is authorized to act, and constitutional law focuses on delimiting the borders of public action and making sure that decisions are made by those authorized to make them. Within the bounds of its authority, an institution is not regularly required to justify its actions, but merely to identify the legal source of its authority to act. For the culture of justification, however, authorization to act is a necessary but not sufficient condition for legitimacy and legality. In other words, this culture requires an additional or second stage of scrutiny for all government action, in which it must provide substantive justification in terms of public reason for what it has done. And this is the second way (the first being scope, or what needs to be justified) in which a culture of justification, of which proportionality is an inherent part, imposes stronger or more onerous constraints on government action.

Taking a more directly normative position on the issue, Mattias Kumm argues that proportionality is to be understood as part of a general require-ment of substantive or outcome-oriented justification that forms the "second leg" of constitutional legitimacy, in addition to the procedural commitment to political equality and majoritarian decision making that flows from it.[10] For Kumm, the point of judicial review is to institutionalize the practice of "Socratic contestation" that puts government action to the necessary test of

---

[7] Moshe Cohen-Eliya and Iddo Porat, "Proportionality and the Culture of Justification," 59 *Am. J. Comp. L.* 463 (2011) (hereinafter Cohen-Eliya and Porat, "Proportionality and the Culture of Justification"). See also, Porat's contribution to this volume, "Mapping the Debate over Balancing," Chapter 17.

[8] Ibid.

[9] This characterization of the contrasting culture of authority obviously departs from Mureinik's original one. See Murenik, "A Bridge to Where?" *supra* note 1.

[10] Kumm, "Democracy Is Not Enough," *supra* note 2.

public justification, so that its presence in a properly functioning constitutional democracy is essential. As he puts it: "Proportionality based judicial review institutionalizes a right to justification that is connected to a particular conception of legitimate legal authority: That law's claim to legitimate authority is plausible only if the law is demonstrably justifiable to those burdened by it in terms that free and equals can accept."[11] Once again, this second dimension of legitimacy, of which proportionality provides the analytical framework, functions to strengthen the constraints on government action and make them more onerous. They must satisfy not only the procedural requirements of democracy but also the substantive burden of demonstrable public justification.

On the other side of the debate there is, of course, a longstanding general conception of rights that rejects the notion that they are only presumptive or prima facie claims, potentially overridable by conflicting public policy objectives.[12] More specifically, there is an almost equally longstanding anti-balancing critique in the United States,[13] where constitutional balancing is generally perceived less favorably, at least among legal academics, than it is elsewhere as the final part of proportionality analysis – although in practice American constitutional law remains firmly in the age of balancing.[14] Within Europe, and Germany in particular, Jürgen Habermas has been a well-known critic of balancing and proportionality for its alleged irrationality and subjectivity, and has fought several rounds with perhaps its major proponent, Robert Alexy.[15]

---

[11] Mattias Kumm, "The Idea of Socratic Contestation and the Right to Justification: The Point of Rights-Based Proportionality Review," 4 *Law & Ethics of Human Rights* (2010) (hereinafter Kumm, "The Idea of Socratic Contestation").

[12] See, for example, Robert Nozick, *Anarchy, State and Utopia* (1974); Ronald Dworkin, *Taking Rights Seriously* (1977).

[13] See, e.g., T. Alexander Aleinikoff, "Constitutional Law in the Age of Balancing," 96 *Yale L.J.* 943 (1987).

[14] As one among many examples of balancing in contemporary American constitutional law, see *Hamdi v. Rumsfeld*, 542 U.S. 507 at 532 (2004) ("striking the proper constitutional balance here [between the individual right to liberty and the government's interests in ensuring that those who have in fact fought with the enemy during a war do not return to battle against the United States] is of great importance to the Nation during this period of ongoing combat").

[15] See Jürgen Habermas, *Between Facts and Norms: Contributions to a Discourse Theory of Law and Democracy* 254–259 (1996); "Reply to Symposium Participants," in Michel Rosenfeld and Andrew Arato (eds.), *Habermas on Law and Democracy* (1998) 429–430. Robert Alexy has responded to these criticisms of proportionality in Robert Alexy, *A Theory of Constitutional Rights* (Trans. Julian Rivers) (2002) 388–394 (hereinafter Alexy, *A Theory of Constitutional Rights*); and "Balancing, Constitutional Review, and Representation," (2005) 3 *Int'l J. Const. L.* 572–77.

But there has of late been a flurry of critiques by newer entrants to the debate as part of the recent general normative turn it has taken. The title of one of them, "Proportionality: An Assault on Human Rights?"[16] makes clear the main line of attack. The basic argument in this latest round of criticism is that far from imposing strong constraints on government action, proportionality is too permissive and takes rights insufficiently seriously. Proportionality analysis is too weak because rights are (1) equated with, rather than given any sort of normative priority over, the public policy objectives that conflict with them; (2) reduced to interests to be quantified and optimized, thus losing their distinctive moral content; and/or (3) subject to merely reasonable, publicly justifiable limitations. In short, the culture of justification in effect becomes a culture of justifying rights inconsequentialism.

According to Grégoire Webber,[17] there are three main counts in the indictment against proportionality. First, the attempt to depoliticize rights by purporting to turn the political and moral questions inherent in the process of rights reasoning into technical questions of weight and balance is futile, especially in the absence of a common criterion for evaluation. Second, by reducing constitutional rights to an interest or value to be optimized, proportionality does "violence to the idea of a constitution"[18] in providing no strict demarcation against unacceptable state action. Third, in addition to its denial of the special normative force of rights, the "received approach" is democratically illegitimate in that it empowers courts rather than legislatures to specify the meaning and scope of abstractly framed rights and evaluate the proportionality of legislative "infringements" of rights.[19] For Stavros Tsakyrakis, "The balancing approach, in the form of the principle of proportionality, appears . . . to pervert rather than elucidate human rights adjudication. With the balancing approach, we no longer ask what is right or wrong in a human rights case but instead, try to investigate whether something is appropriate, adequate, intensive or far-reaching."[20] Moreover, proportionality "erodes these [human] rights' distinctive meaning by transforming them into something seemingly quantifiable".[21]

---

[16] Stavros Tsakyrakis, "Proportionality: An Assault on Human Rights," 7 *Int'l. J. Const. L.* 468 (2009) (hereinafter Tsakyrakis, "An Assault on Human Rights?").

[17] Webber, *The Negotiable Constitution, supra* note 5 ch. 3; Grégoire Webber, "Proportionality, Balancing, and the Cult of Constitutional Rights Scholarship," (2010) 23 *Can. J. Law & Jur.* 179 (hereinafter Webber, "The Cult").

[18] Webber, "The Cult," ibid. at 198.

[19] Webber, *The Negotiable Constitution, supra* note 5 at 201–212.

[20] Tsakyrakis, "Proportionality: An Assault on Human Rights?" *supra* note 16 at 487.

[21] Ibid. at 488.

Now, to some extent this opposite evaluation of proportionality can be explained by different objects or framings of the proportionality inquiry on the part of each side. Proponents sometimes frame the issue as the general one of the legitimacy of governmental action – what are its criteria and how should they be institutionalized – and not the more specific one of whether and when rights should be limitable by legislatures. Moreover, they also insist that "'every' governmental action is in need of justification, since justification rather than authority, is the main source of legitimacy,"[22] and not only that subset of actions implication or limiting rights. Within this framing, proportionality is a principle that limits government action. As part of a culture of justification, it imposes the substantive constraint that government action must be publicly justifiable to those it burdens. This view has its historical and conceptual roots in the general principle of the rule of law, where government action is not otherwise limited by specific constitutional rights or higher law of any kind. In this context, proportionality provides an inherent limit and functions to rebut a prima facie case for what the government has done. The general concept of proportionality originated in eighteenth-century Prussian administrative law,[23] and the proponents' position is structurally connected to the context of providing the only limit to otherwise substantively unlimited government action. This is the conception that T.R.S. Allan successfully and skillfully employed in the pre-Human Rights Act United Kingdom as part of the inherent constitutional limits provided by the rule of law even absent an express set of limits in the form of a general bill of rights.[24]

By contrast, the critics focus squarely and uniformly on the more specific issue: what is being justified under proportionality analysis is government action that implicates constitutional rights. In this context, proportionality is a principle that limits constitutional rights and therefore empowers at least as much as it constrains governments. Their focus reflects the fact that proportionality changes its nature in the context of such a bill of rights. It now operates in the context of a prima facie case against, not for, the relevant government action – here of an infringement of rights. Once there are limits on government action in the form of constitutionalized rights, proportionality

---

[22] Cohen-Eliya and Porat, "Proportionality and the Culture of Justification," *supra* note 7 at 477.

[23] For a recent discussion of the origin of proportionality, see Moshe Cohen-Eliya and Iddo Porat, "American Balancing and German Proportionality: The Historical Origins," (2010) 8 *Int'l. J. Const. L.* 263.

[24] T.R.S. Allan, *Law, Liberty, and Justice: The Legal Foundations of British Constitutionalism* (1993); and developed in *Constitutional Justice: A Liberal Theory of the Rule of Law* (2001). See Allan's contribution in Chapter 10 of this volume, "Democracy, Legality, and Proportionality."

operates not only as a substantive limit on government action, but also on the limits to government action enshrined in such rights. This change in legal context also changes the object of proportionality analysis: what is being justified under proportionality analysis is not simply (any and all) government action, but specifically government action infringing rights. Accordingly, proportionality is transformed when it applies to a set of constitutional rights rather than operating as a residual rule of law constraint on general government action. The key normative issue becomes less why government should generally be required to act proportionately than why government should be empowered to limit constitutional rights proportionately.

Ultimately, however, I do not think the difference between the two sides can be explained away in this manner. For one thing, although perhaps for some it is not the focus of their more general analysis, no proponent would likely deny that proportionality analysis should apply in the constitutional rights context, where it exists. It would be a seemingly implausible lacuna in a general theory of the legitimacy of law within contemporary liberal democracies for it not to apply to rights.[25] Secondly, for those proponents who take German constitutional practice as the paradigm of proportionality analysis,[26] its very broad conception of liberty and equality rights in particular means that there is less of a gap between all government action and rights-infringing action than elsewhere. Indeed, one such proponent, Kai Möller, argues that "rights inflation" of this sort is not merely compatible with but necessitated by proportionality and its underlying conception of a constitutional right.[27] Just as there is no special normative distinction between constitutional rights and conflicting government interests, there is also none between (what in some other rights regimes are considered) an individual's constitutional liberty rights and other lesser liberty interests. All interferences with individual autonomy, no matter how seemingly small or unimportant, trigger the duty of justification and its proportionality inquiry. And it is precisely these features of proportionality that its critics react to most strongly. For them, rights are special in both respects.

[25] Even those who believe proportionality is an administrative law principle and not a constitutional law one would likely accept that it applies to constitutional rights claims against administrative action, only not against legislative acts.
[26] As seems to be the case with both Kumm – who uses German constitutional practice as an exemplar of what he refers to as the (European) "Rationalist Human Rights Paradigm (see Mattias Kumm, "The Rationalist Human Rights Paradigm, Legitimate Authority and the Point of Judicial Review," 1 E.J.L.S. 1 at 28 [2007]); and Kai Möller in "Proportionality and Rights Inflation," Chapter 7 in this volume.
[27] Möller, ibid.

II. PROPORTIONALITY AND THE CULTURE OF DEMOCRACY

Whereas the culture of justification perspective views proportionality through the lens of whether or not it enhances the constraints on government action in the name of constitutional legitimacy or respect for individual autonomy, the culture of democracy perspective views proportionality through the lens of whether or not it enhances the specifically democratic legitimacy of a constitutionalized rights regime. It is a culture that puts democratic, not justificatory, goals at its center. Within this framework, the point of proportionality is to accommodate and temper certain enduring democratic concerns with judicially enforced higher law rights.

From this perspective, proportionality is an inherent part of the dominant contemporary conception of constitutional rights as not only having limits (that is, their force or scope is not absolute), but as limitable by the political institutions. This feature is typically highlighted and given explicit textual form by the limitations clause or clauses in a bill of rights. In other words, the second of the two steps of rights analysis, the step in which proportionality review is undertaken, incorporates the proposition that the political institutions are empowered to place limits on and ultimately override constitutional rights (as authoritatively interpreted by the judiciary) in the face of conflicting public policy objectives when the substantive criteria provided by the relevant proportionality-like tests have been satisfied.[28] Accordingly, the dominant general conception of a constitutional right should be understood as granting the political institutions a limited power to override judicially interpreted rights, and the external limits on rights provided by the proportionality test as a whole specify the parameters of this power.[29]

Although this general conception of a constitutional right – of which balancing at the second stage is an inherent part – is very widely adopted among contemporary constitutional systems, it is not the only possible or available one. There are at least two alternative conceptions, both of which reject proportionality and balancing. The first, sometimes referred to as the immunity

---

[28] Here I am employing and analyzing what Webber refers to as the "received approach" to rights and their limits. Webber himself offers a critique and an alternative conception of limits and the function of limitations clauses that I will consider in Part III. Typically, although not always, this limited power is granted to both the legislature and the executive. However, because they generally represent more collective and participatory modes of decision making, the democratic justification for this power that I present in Part II applies more strongly to legislatures than the executive, as does the consequent standard of judicial review for its exercise

[29] For an extended analysis of external limits and the dominant conception of rights, see Stephen Gardbaum, "Limiting Constitutional Rights," 54 *U.C.L.A. L. Rev.* 789 (2007).

conception or "rights as trumps," holds that where properly at issue and implicated, constitutional rights cannot be limited or overridden by non-rights
claims at all.[30] It was in contrast to this conception, and in the context of
describing the structure of constitutional rights in the United States, that
Frederick Schauer referred to constitutional rights as "shields" rather than
"trumps",[31] and this helpfully captures the basic notion not just in the United
States but in contemporary constitutional law generally.

By contrast, the second alternative, usually termed the "structural" or
"excluded reasons" conception of constitutional rights, permits a right to be
limited or overridden not because (or where) it is outweighed by the competing
public policy claim, but because (or where) the state has acted for a permissible –
rather than an excluded – reason in the relevant sphere.[32] On this structural
view, rights are not essentially individualistic in function but are, rather, "the
tools constitutional law uses to maintain appropriate structural relationships of
authority,"[33] and rights adjudication becomes a categorical exercise that does
not require or permit balancing but turns on the nature or type (not the weight)
of the state's justification for acting. If the state "infringes"[34] or "qualifies"[35] a
right for a permissible reason, its action is automatically constitutional; if for
an excluded reason, it is automatically unconstitutional.[36] Although I believe

---

[30] This conception of a constitutional right is, in effect, accepted for those rights in various modern
constitutions that are deemed in principle non-overridable; for example, the right against cruel
and inhumane (or unusual) punishment. The slogan of rights as trumps is usually associated
with Ronald Dworkin, although there is some controversy as to whether, to what extent, or in
what sense Dworkin himself ever did or does endorse this first conception. See, for example,
the exchange between Jeremy Waldron and Richard Pildes in the *Journal of Legal Studies*:
Jeremy Waldron, "Pildes on Dworkin's Theory of Rights," 29 J. *Legal Stud.* 301 (2000); Richard
H. Pildes, "Dworkin's Two Conceptions of Rights," 29 J. *Legal Stud.* 309 (2000). Arguably,
Grégoire Webber makes this claim for constitutional rights, at least once they have been
specified. Webber, *The Negotiable Constitution, supra* note 5 at 101–104.
[31] See Frederick Schauer, "A Comment on the Structure of Rights," 27 Ga. L. Rev. 415 at 429–430
(1993).
[32] See Richard H. Pildes, "Avoiding Balancing: The Role of Exclusionary Reasons in Constitutional Law," 45 *Hastings L.J.* 711 (1994); Richard H. Pildes, "Why Rights Are Not Trumps:
Social Meanings, Expressive Harms, and Constitutionalism," 27 J. *Legal Stud.* 725 (1998)
(hereinafter Pildes, "Why Rights are not Trumps").
[33] See Pildes, ibid. at 734.
[34] Ibid. at 734: "Government can infringe on rights for reasons consistent with the norms that
characterize the common goods that those rights are meant to realize, but when government
infringes rights for reasons inconsistent with these common goods, it violates individual rights."
[35] Ibid. at 761: "Because rights are not trumps over the common good, they can be qualified
when the state acts on the basis of justifications consistent with the character of the relevant
common good in question. That is what makes a state interest compelling, not its 'weight.'"
[36] Ibid. at 735: "When government acts for reasons that are impermissible, its objectives are not
weighed in an all-things-considered balance against the interests individuals have in their own

that certain claimed differences between this excluded-reasons conception of rights and the more dominant general conception that affirms and highlights balancing are generally false,[37] this categorical nature of state authority does point to a real difference between them. Whereas for the excluded reasons conception, which focuses exclusively on the kind or type of purpose the state offers in justification for its action, acting for a permissible reason is sufficient for a valid limitation of a right, for the more dominant general conception it is necessary[38] but not sufficient; other factors must be taken into account, precisely those that require a weighing or balancing of the competing claims.

A third alternative, which may or may not be a variation on one or other of the first two, is the specificationist conception of rights, which holds that the typical abstract framing of constitutional rights requires further specification of their meaning, scope, and boundaries before they are capable of resolving rights issues, and that this process of rendering rights determinate is performed by setting limits to them. Accordingly, this conception rejects the standard two-step approach to rights analysis, for rights are constituted, and not burdened or restricted, by their limits. Once delimited in this way, constitutional rights provide exclusionary reasons with conclusory force.[39]

The critical point in the face of these alternatives is that the dominant general conception of a constitutional right, of which a proportionality-type

---

autonomy, or dignity, or liberty. Rather, government action that rests on an impermissible justification simply is unconstitutional."

[37] These are primarily: (1) that balancing presumes an atomistic or individualistic notion of rights as protecting and promoting the autonomous self, and (2) that balancing involves an exclusively quantitative weighing of such rights against competing state interests. As for the first, the rights to be balanced can certainly include the type of collective goods (such as the proper boundary lines between different spheres of political authority) or group rights that proponents of the excluded-reasons conception properly call attention to. As for the second, it is not true that the process of weighing rights against competing public policy objectives necessarily involves only quantitative reasoning to the exclusion of qualitative. If we say, for example, that there are strong or weighty reasons for (or a compelling interest in) protecting Holocaust survivors from the psychological harm caused by Holocaust denial or an American Nazi Party march or African-American families from the harms caused by the KKK burning crosses in their backyards, we are not necessarily saying that the strength or weight of these interests is purely quantitative; part of the weight may be qualitative, relating to the kind of harm involved.

[38] Necessary in that there is a threshold requirement of the reason or objective being either a specified or sufficiently important one before the proportionality test of means is triggered.

[39] See Webber, *The Negotiable Constitution, supra*, note 5; see also Webber's contribution to this volume, "On the Loss of Rights," Chapter 6; Bradley W. Miller, "Justification and Rights Limitations" in Grant Huscroft (ed.), *Expounding the Constitution: Essays in Constitutional Theory* (2008); John Oberdiek, "Lost in Moral Space: On the Infringing/Violating Distinction and Its Place in the Theory of Rights," (2004) 23 *Law and Philosophy* 325; John Oberdiek, "Specifying Rights Out of Necessity," (2008) 28 *O.J.L.S.* 127. This different conception of limiting a right than the dominant one will be discussed in Part III.

test for valid limits is an inherent part, is in need not only of identification and clarification but also of justification. That is, it must be explained why constitutional rights should be balanced against, and potentially overridden by, nonconstitutional rights claims. It may well be that (at least, absent a normative hierarchy) in conflicts between two constitutional rights claims balancing is unavoidable or inherent, but between a constitutional rights claim and a non-rights claim, it surely is not.[40] Accordingly, the existence of alternative conceptions of constitutional rights that do not – or rarely – permit such balancing renders justification imperative.[41] Within the culture of justification perspective, I am not certain what the position of proportionality's proponents is on this key threshold question, as they tend to focus on the subsequent one of the proper test or required burden of justification for an override, but let me try to express the answer from within the culture of democracy perspective.

I believe that David Dyzenhaus pointed us in the right direction by referring to this conception of constitutional rights (typified by the presence of a general limitations clause) as the "democratic model of constitutionalism".[42] In attempting to flesh out this insight in what follows, my claim is that a proportionality-type test provides as strong a set of constraints on government action as is consistent with legitimate and enduring democratic/Kelsenian concerns about constitutionalizing rights and institutionalizing judicial review to enforce them in the first place.

[40] Here, Dieter Grimm's observation, referring to the Federal Constitutional Court, that "the principle [of proportionality] was introduced as if it could be taken for granted" is apposite and, indeed, generalizable. Dieter Grimm, "Proportionality in Canadian and German Constitutional Jurisprudence," (2007) 57 *U.T.L.J.* 383 at 387. In this context, Robert Alexy's rational reconstruction of the structure of constitutional rights in Germany may perhaps be recharacterized as presenting a conditional justification of balancing: if constitutional rights are conceptualized as principles to be optimized, and if certain nonconstitutional rights claims are also granted this same status, then balancing is unavoidable or necessary. Of course, the task of justifying the conditions remains.

[41] I am, of course, referring to normative, not interpretive, justification. Accordingly, even where constitutions contain express limits on rights, the normative question of whether proportionality and balancing are justified still arises.

[42] David Dyzenhaus refers to the alternatives of a liberal model of constitutionalism (where a constitution "embodies a set of more or less absolute principles") and a democratic model of constitutionalism (where there is a general limitations clause). Dyzenhaus, "Law as Justification," *supra* note 1 at 32. In practice, the alternative, "liberal" model may exist more with respect to specific rights than to specific constitutions as a whole, as balancing is also a central feature of those constitutions without express limits on rights, such as the U.S. constitution. See also Dyzenhaus "Proportionality and Deference in a Culture of Justification," Chapter 11 in this volume. I have discussed at length the absence of American exceptionalism on this issue in Gardbaum, "The Myth and the Reality of American Constitutional Exceptionalism," 107 *Mich. L. Rev.* 391 at 416–431 (2008).

There are three arguments in support of this claim – three ways in which a proportionality-like test enhances democratic values within a system of constitutionalized rights. The first is that it provides an appropriate balance between the competing demands of (1) politically accountable legislative decision making as the normal implication of democracy's foundational principle of political equality; and (2) the limits on such decision making embodied in the legal form of constitutional rights. It is undoubtedly inherent in the concept of a constitutional (that is, constitutionalized) right that it places limits on ordinary politically accountable decision-making procedures, but what is not inherent is the type of limit involved. The conception of constitutional rights as trumps demands that such limits be peremptory or categorical; that in the face of a valid constitutional rights claim, politically accountable decision making is totally disabled. But the general concept does not necessarily require that the particular limit take this form. Analytically, there is space for different types of limits, and the argument from democracy supports a conception of constitutional rights that is less disabling of popular self-government.

This conception is constitutional rights: balancing, proportionality, and the limited override power, as the distinctive features of this conception, reflect such a less extreme limit on politically accountable decision making. In the face of a valid constitutional rights claim as determined by the courts, the political institutions are neither totally disabled nor totally empowered. Rather, they are put to a special burden of justification that constrains both the objectives pursued and means of pursuing them, and will never be satisfied by a mere majoritarian desire not to respect the right. This contrasts, of course, with the normal situation where no constitutional right is implicated, in which the political institutions are legally free to act for any reason or objective. Accordingly, the limited override power steers a middle course between the two polar positions of: (1) the absolute disabling of ordinary democratic majoritarian procedures in the face of a constitutional right; and (2) the absolute empowering of ordinary democratic majoritarian procedures when a constitutional right is not in play. By thus employing a special, non-ordinary constraint on majoritarian decision making, it satisfies the essential requirement of a constitutional right, but does not totally disable popular self-government.

A slightly different way of expressing this argument is that by rejecting the peremptory status of constitutional rights, the principle of proportionality acknowledges the democratic weight attaching to other competing claims asserted by the politically accountable institutions. This conception of constitutionalized rights, I suggest, better reflects democratic values than the absolute, disabling conception. To be sure, those specific things we believe governments should never lawfully be able to do regardless of the circumstances or conflicting objectives can be singled out for absolute protection without accepting that this inheres in all constitutional rights at all times – or that constitutional rights have no relevance to other situations. It is unnecessarily and unjustifiably restrictive of both democratic decision-making procedures and the role of constitutional rights for the latter to have such a totally disabling effect.

The second way in which proportionality enhances democratic values within a constitutionalized rights regime is by reducing the intertemporal tension between the set of entrenched rights established by a past majority and the consequent disabling of today's citizens from deciding how to resolve many of the most fundamental moral-political issues that they face. The limited override power grants the current citizenry a deliberative role, through consideration of whether they wish to and can invoke it, that provides an intermediate alternative in between the two options of either complete exclusion of the current citizenry and formally changing rights through the (typically cumbersome) amendment process.[43]

Finally, my argument so far applies equally to determinate and indeterminate (or underdeterminate) constitutional rights: (1) the limits that rights impose on democratic decision making need and should not be absolute; and (2) acknowledging this reduces the democratic tension between past and current citizenry. That is, up to this point the argument for proportionality does not depend on the existence of reasonable disagreement about what rights there are and what they include among and between judges, legislators, and citizens. Rather, it is about the power to limit or override a right as or however interpreted in the face of conflicting non-rights claims.

In reality, however, there is the well-known additional democratic problem posed by the fact that many constitutional rights in many constitutions are (and perhaps inevitably so) indeterminate in their meaning, scope, and application. In the face of such indeterminacy, the traditional argument that, in being given the final word on whether rights have been infringed, courts are simply subjecting the political institutions to the democratic will of the people as enshrined in the constitution is rendered additionally problematic.[44] As Michael Perry puts it: "Democracy requires that the reasonable judgment of electorally accountable government officials, about what an indeterminate

---

[43] Of course, (1) the more recent the constitution and (2) the easier the constitution is to amend – that is, the closer to ordinary democratic decision-making procedures the amendment is – the less important or relevant this argument becomes.

[44] This argument goes back at least to Alexander Hamilton in Federalist 78.

human rights forbids, trump the competing reasonable judgment of politically independent judges."[45] Under a traditional system of strong-form judicial review granting interpretive finality to the courts (as, for example, in Germany and the United States), if constitutional rights were the only relevant claim, the outcome of constitutional adjudication would necessarily turn exclusively on the meaning, scope, and application of the right to the situation. In this context, the consequence of indeterminacy is that many of the most fundamental, important, and divisive moral and political issues confronting a society are decided by courts to the exclusion of citizens and their representative institutions, even though the courts are often divided along the same lines as the citizenry about the existence and scope of many rights.[46]

Proportionality and the limited override provide an alternative solution to this democratic problem than that of rejecting judicial supremacy, or ultimacy, in interpreting constitutional rights.[47] It also, of course, provides an alternative to rejecting judicial review of constitutional rights altogether. They grant a role to the representative institutions in the decision-making process, not by challenging final judicial authority to determine the meaning and scope of an implicated constitutional right, but by introducing a second relevant claim: a discretionary and noninterpretive claim concerning the importance and weight of conflicting public objectives. The function of the limited override power is precisely to inject this essentially and inherently legislative role into the process of constitutional adjudication, even if the courts ultimately decide who wins the case. Constitutional adjudication is thus split into the two separate stages of (1) rights interpretation and application; and (2) assessment of competing public policy objectives. In short, balancing and the limited override power counter the judicial monopoly in constitutional decision making that typically occurs where rights conclusively determine constitutional outcomes within a system of judicial review – a finality that is rendered highly problematic by the indeterminate nature of many of the relevant rights. Because their indeterminacy raises the democratic problem

---

[45] Michael J. Perry, "Protecting Human Rights in a Democracy: What Role for the Courts?" 38 *Wake Forest L. Rev.* 635 at 661 (2003) (hereinafter Perry, "Protecting Human Rights").

[46] See Jeremy Waldron, "A Right-Based Critique of Constitutional Rights," 13 *O.J.L.S.* 18 at 28 (1993).

[47] This solution of rejecting judicial interpretive supremacy has been suggested by several people, including Perry, "Protecting Human Rights," *supra* note 45; and Larry Kramer, *The People Themselves: Popular Constitutionalism and Judicial Review* (2004), although in Kramer's case this is primarily on historical grounds rather than as a solution to the problem of indeterminacy.

in perhaps its most acute form, constitutional rights should not be the only relevant claim in a case in which they are implicated.

In sum, the case for a proportionality-like test in the rights context is that it seeks to accommodate standard concerns about both constitutional rights and unlimited legislative power by neither rendering the former an absolute bar to conflicting legislative action nor granting legislatures an absolute power to override rights. Rather, proportionality limits this power by imposing the substantive constraint of demonstrable justification in terms of public reason. We thus arrive at the same point as the culture of justification proponents, but do so as the result of a prior, threshold stage of normative inquiry that provides a broader, more comprehensive view in which the constraining and justificatory function of proportionality is seen as secondary to its primary point of enhancing the democratic part of constitutional democracy.

This understanding of proportionality has significant implications for how courts should exercise their judicial review function in the rights context. If at least part of the point of proportionality is to temper and accommodate democratic concerns that judicial enforcement of (often indeterminate) con-stitutionalized rights creates by permitting them to be limited or overridden subject to its substantive burden of justification, then those tensions should not be reproduced or aggravated by the way in which courts review exercises of this power. A standard of review that authorizes courts to substitute their own view on whether the burden is satisfied and power validly exercised for the reasonable one of the political institutions seems clearly counterproductive.[48] Moreover, review of the limited override power by the courts arguably increases the tensions because it adds a step to constitutional rights adjudication that raises special concerns about judicial legitimacy and integrity over and above the standard ones.[49] Accordingly, both the purpose and nature of the limited override power under proportionality-like tests strongly suggest that the ques-tion reviewing courts should ask is whether the legislative judgment that the substantive constitutional criteria for an override have been satisfied in the particular context is a reasonable one, and not whether the judges agree with it. Once again, we arrive at the same point as certain culture of justification proponents,[50] but do so from a more comprehensive and foundational view of the landscape.

[48] I have spelled out my view on the implications of this justification for the standard of review to be applied by the courts in detail elsewhere. See Gardbaum, "Limiting Constitutional Rights," 54 *U.C.L.A. L. Rev.* 789 at 829–851 (2007).
[49] See Adam Tomkins, "The Role of Courts in the Political Constitution," (2010) 60 *U.T.L.J.* 1.
[50] For example, Kumm, "Democracy Is Not Enough," *supra* note 2.

III. PROPORTIONALITY AND OTHER VERSIONS OF DEMOCRATIC CONSTITUTIONALISM

In the previous section, I set out the case from a culture of democracy perspective for the contemporary constitutional paradigm of rights and their limits, with its well-known two-step analysis. Within this paradigm, the second step incorporates a limited power granted to the political institutions to act inconsistently with the rights as judicially construed at the first step, the limit being specified by the substantive constraint of public justification as given by the various prongs of the proportionality test. Other proportionality-like tests for overriding rights, such as U.S.-style balancing, provide slightly different specifications of the limit. In the general debate about the merits of judicial review, it is primarily this system that ought to be the object of discussion, as it is increasingly the norm around the world. Such a system is different from – and, as I have attempted to establish, somewhat easier to justify than – a mostly hypothetical one without such a power.

I have not claimed, however, that this system is the only one that can plausibly be understood as democratic constitutionalist, in the sense of ensuring some greater balance of power between legislatures and courts than under traditional conceptions of judicial supremacy. Nor have I claimed that a proportionality-based system has a stronger democratic justification than these others. In this final section, I will briefly outline these other versions of democratic constitutionalism and offer some tentative thoughts on their comparison and relative merits.

These other versions consist of two alternative institutional forms of constitutionalism that currently exist in practice, and an alternative theoretical conception of constitutional rights and their limits to the dominant paradigm that does not. The institutional forms are (1) political constitutionalism or traditional legislative supremacy, in which, very roughly speaking, there are no higher law rights or judicial powers to review the substance of legislation; and (2) "weak-form judicial review" or "the new Commonwealth model of constitutionalism" as introduced by recent bills of rights in Canada, New Zealand, the United Kingdom, the Australian Capital Territory and state of Victoria.[51] The alternative conception of rights and their limits is "legislative specificationism". As outlined, this conception rejects the dominant paradigm's two-step approach, in which the meaning and scope of a right are determined prior

---

[51] In my view, weak-form judicial review is a key constituent part of the new Commonwealth model, but not the whole of it: the other key part is pre-enactment political rights review. See Stephen Gardbaum, *The New Commonwealth Model of Constitutionalism: Theory and Practice* (2013) (hereinafter Gardbaum, *The New Commonwealth Model of Constitutionalism*).

to the limitation analysis for justified infringements, in favor of the view that rights are constituted and rendered determinate by their limits as specified by the legislature.[52] In what follows, I will focus on these two latter versions, as political constitutionalism is a longstanding, very well-known and much-discussed option. It is also a more distant comparator of proportionality, as it is not a version of democratic constitutionalism that generally recognizes or accommodates higher law rights and judicial review, unlike the other two.

Increasingly, the real-world alternative to the limited override power that I have argued is a central feature of the dominant, proportionality-based paradigm of constitutional rights is not a system without an override power at all, but one with a substantively unlimited one. Thus, the recent innovation of weak-form judicial review as part of the new Commonwealth model of constitutionalism empowers the political institutions to override protected rights as interpreted by the judiciary without satisfying the burden of justification provided by the proportionality test.[53] In arguing that proportionality represents as strong a constraint as is consistent with legitimate democratic concerns about judicial review, this unlimited override power obviously represents a weaker (though not nonexistent) constraint. Accordingly, the respective normative and practical merits of these two alternatives are, I believe, a more interesting and pressing topic than the abstract merits of two polar systems – judicial review without a limited override power and no judicial review at all – that do not, or barely, exist in practice.

Under weak-form judicial review, the constraints on the political institutions in the rights context are a combination of the legal and political. Typically, courts will first employ proportionality analysis, as under standard contemporary strong-form review, to determine whether a right has been justifiably infringed. Only if the answer is no do the distinctive mechanisms of weak-form review come into play. In Canada, legislatures may exercise their substantively unlimited power under section 33 of the Charter to override most (but not all) rights by ordinary majority vote for a renewable period of five years.[54] In New Zealand, the UK, and the two Australian jurisdictions that have adopted

---

[52] Webber, *The Negotiable Constitution, supra* note 5 chs. 4–6.

[53] As we will see, typically in these systems, the proportionality test operates as it does in strong-form systems, but with the added feature that the political institutions may override a right that the courts have declared not justifiably limited.

[54] Section 33(1) of the Canadian Charter of Rights and Freedoms provides: "Parliament or the legislature of a province may expressly declare in an Act of Parliament or of the legislature, as the case may be that the Act or a provision thereof shall operate notwithstanding a provision included in section 2 or sections 7 to 15 of this Charter." Section 33 may be used preemptively, thereby immunizing a law from judicial review.

versions of the new Commonwealth model, courts then go on to ask whether the statutory provision in question can be interpreted consistently with the right, and if so, they have a duty to employ that interpretation.[55] As with statutory interpretation generally, legislatures have the legal power to respond by amending the statute if they believe the court is mistaken. If the statute cannot be interpreted consistently with the right, the courts must apply it to the case in hand, but may issue a declaration of incompatibility or inconsistent interpretation.[56] This has no direct legal effect, as legislatures have no legal duty to amend or repeal such a statute, but not doing so could potentially result in significant political costs for the government. In short, the substantive legal constraint of proportionality is superseded in certain cases by the political constraint of acting contrary to a judicial declaration of rights infringement. Similarly, the legal burden of justification under proportionality is superseded in these cases by the political burden of justifying the continuing judicially and publicly declared infringement.

Accordingly, the choice between proportionality's substantively limited override power and the new Commonwealth model's unlimited one is typically not an either-or one, but whether to have only the limited power or both. The best-known example of this is the Canadian Charter, in which section 1 specifies the limited override power and section 33 the unlimited. Indeed, to the extent that "dialogue" between courts and legislatures has been claimed as a benefit of weak-form review, it may not be a distinctive one, as section 1 has been presented as an alternative and more successful source of dialogue in practice.[57] Moreover, although the legal allocation of the final word is granted to courts under the limited power, in which its proportionality analysis is the second and final step of rights adjudication, and to legislatures under the unlimited power, this allocation may not reflect the reality in practice. Thus, it has been claimed that under section 1, the de facto final word is given to

---

[55] New Zealand Bill of Rights Act 1990, s. 6; UK Human Rights Act 1998, s. 3(1); ACT Human Rights Act 2004, s. 30; Victorian Charter of Human Rights and Responsibilities Act 2006, s. 32(1).

[56] UK Human Rights Act 1998, s. 4; ACT Human Rights Act 2004, s. 32; Victorian Charter of Human Rights and Responsibilities Act 2006, s. 36. This power was seemingly implied by the New Zealand Court of Appeal in its 1999 decision in *Moonen v. Film and Literature Board of Review* [2000] 1 N.Z.L.R. 9 (CA), although it has never clearly been used.

[57] Peter Hogg and Alison Bushell, "The Charter Dialogue between Courts and Legislatures (Or Perhaps The Charter of Rights Isn't Such a Bad Thing After All)," (1997) 35 *Osgoode Hall L.J.*; Kent Roach, "Dialogic Judicial Review and its Critics," (2004) 23 *Sup. Ct. L. Rev.* 49; Cf. Grant Huscroft, "Rationalizing Judicial Supremacy: The Mischief of Dialogue Theory" in James Kelly and Christopher Manfredi eds., *Contested Constitutionalism: Reflections on the Charter of Rights and Freedoms* (2009).

legislatures in their characteristic responses to judicial invalidation of statutes;[58] whereas under section 33 and the UK Human Rights Act, the de facto
final word is granted to courts.[59]

In thinking about the relative merits of proportionality and the new Commonwealth model as two versions of democratic constitutionalism, one question is whether the greater judicial power of strong-form review versus weak
form can be justified from this perspective. To address this question, let me
simply stipulate for current purposes that the normative case for the new model
is premised on reasonable disagreement with the courts on a rights issue.[60] In
one sense, therefore, if courts and legislatures both adhere to their normatively
assigned roles and courts only invalidate legislation for which there is no reasonable public justification under proportionality analysis, then legislatures
would never exercise their override power – which perhaps becomes redundant. But by the same token, under this scenario it cannot be said that strong-
form judicial review is necessary, for weak-form review would achieve exactly
the same result. More realistically, however, the risk that both will depart
from their normatively circumscribed powers must be taken into account: that
courts will invalidate reasonable legislative decisions in favor of the court's view
of the correct one and legislatures will exercise their override power in support
of unreasonable legislative decisions. In these circumstances, is strong-form
judicial review rather than weak justified? In current practice, the normative
standard I have proposed for judicial review under proportionality analysis is
not in fact the one that is generally understood to govern, and courts regularly
overturn legislative decisions which cannot be said to be unreasonable.[61] But
what if it were? Under strong-form review, there is little to counter the risk of
judicial overreaching on this issue – as by reason of their very independence,
courts face no direct political constraint – and the legislative override power
would be a useful institutional check in the absence of others as a form of separation of powers. Moreover, we are by hypothesis here – a court has invalidated
a reasonable legislative act – in the situation where the principle of a reasonable
legislative judgment trumping a reasonable judicial one applies, so that use

---

[58] Hogg and Bushell, ibid.

[59] Aileen Kavanagh, *Constitutional Review under the UK Human Rights Act* (2009) at 416–420.
      For my response to this claim and the one cited in the previous note, see Gardbaum, *The New
      Commonwealth Model of Constitutionalism, supra* note 51 chs. 5 and 7.

[60] For explanation and defence of this stipulation, see Gardbaum, ibid. ch. 4.

[61] That is, in applying the second and third prongs of the proportionality principle courts tend
      to ask whether the legislature's justification for limiting a right is in fact necessary (or the
      least-restrictive means) and proportionate in the strict sense, rather than reasonably necessary
      and proportionate.

of the override would be justified. By contrast, unlike the strong-form judicial power, this legislative power would be subject to a significant institutional or political constraint against the risk of misuse; namely, the fact that a court has issued a formal judgment finding there to be no reasonable public justification for the legislation violating individual rights. Finally, so far we have been discussing the situation in which there have been clear departures from the standard of reasonableness, but the limits of reasonable disagreement may also be subject to reasonable disagreement.[62] That is, courts and legislatures may reasonably disagree about whether a legislative act is within the bounds of the reasonable. For the same two reasons just noted – the checking function of the override and the default or tie-breaking nature of legislative power that democracy requires – weak-form review also seems the more justified solution here.

In some ways, it is easier to mask an override of rights under the limited power than the unlimited version. Where an override is given the "blessing" of the court under proportionality analysis, the visibility and political costs are likely to be far lower – the courts have played their role as the watchdog of rights and the reasonableness of government action has been demonstrated. It is a form of preemptive override within the legal system without the friction and publicity of the reactive override, which heightens political accountability. In both cases, however, rights are being overridden by the government within the bounds of its legal powers, and the issue is which mode is more consistent with our full range of normative commitments.

Finally, the argument that the fundamental point of judicial review is to institutionalize "Socratic contestation" – to put government action to an enforced test of public justification as a prerequisite of its legitimacy – is arguably fulfilled by weak-form review as well as strong. Because proportionality analysis is typically carried out in same way under both, the same process of putting the government to the burden of justification has been undertaken by the courts. The only difference is that it is legitimate for the political institutions to proceed even though they have not satisfied this burden according to the courts. Perhaps the function of Socratic contestation can then be said to move from the courts to citizens, from legal to political legitimacy; a slightly different test to be sure, but one that is not obviously inconsistent with the principles of democratic constitutionalism.

Turning now to the alternative conceptualization (rather than institutionalization) of rights, let us compare the legislative specificationist account of limitations on rights with the limited and unlimited override powers of the

---

[62] Kumm, "The Idea of Socratic Contestation," *supra* note 11 at 28, note 43.

proportionality paradigm and the new Commonwealth model, respectively. In his elegantly conceived and executed book, Grégoire Webber rejects the "received approach" to limiting rights with its two separate stages of first defining the scope of a right and assessing whether it has been interfered with, and then determining if the legislature has justifiably – that is, proportionately – acted inconsistently with the right as previously defined. Rather, limits on rights and limitations clauses should be understood as part of the single function of determining the meaning and scope of rights, which as typically framed in bills of rights are "underdeterminate" and require further specification in order to resolve the issues in which they are implicated. In this way, limits constitute rights rather than restrict them. The task of specification, of rendering underdeterminate rights determinate, belongs, he argues, to legislatures rather than courts for both democratic and textual (this is what limitations clauses, properly understood, prescribe) reasons. Once specified, rights provide exclusionary reasons and have conclusory force. Finally, judicial review is limited to invalidating legislative specifications for which no public reasons can be offered in support.[63]

Webber's overarching claim that limits on rights should properly be conceived as constitutive rather than restrictive has both descriptive/textual and normative components. The descriptive/textual component is that courts and scholars are misunderstanding or misinterpreting limitations clauses in a way that falsely equates the single expressly stated term "limits" on rights with infringements, restrictions, interferences, or overriding of rights – using them interchangeably.[64] Rather, such limits should be understood in the distinct and separate sense of setting the boundaries of, or delimiting, rights. To support this claim, Webber relies primarily on the text of the Canadian Charter's general limitations clause and the ones in New Zealand, South Africa, and Australia directly influenced by it, which indeed employ only the term "limits".[65] However, this is not true of the limitations clauses in other influential bills of rights, including the German and European Convention on Human Rights, from which the dominant proportionality paradigm emerged. Thus, in its several special limitations clauses attaching to particular rights, the German Basic Law variously employs the terms "limits",[66] "restrictions",[67] and

---

[63] Webber, *The Negotiable Constitution, supra* note 5.
[64] Ibid. at 123–125.
[65] Canadian Charter of Rights and Freedoms, section 1: "The Canadian Charter of Rights and Freedoms guarantees the rights and freedoms set out in it subject only to such reasonable limits prescribed by law as can be demonstrably justified in a free and democratic society."
[66] *Basic Law for the Federal Republic of Germany*, Article 5(2) (hereinafter *German Basic Law*).
[67] Articles 8(2); 10(2); 11(2); 13(7); 19(1).

"interferences"[68] in describing the relevant legislative empowerment. Similarly, limitations clauses in the European Convention on Human Rights use the terms "interferences,"[69] "limitations,"[70] and "restrictions"[71] on rights. By contrast, both the German Basic Law and the European Convention on Human Rights use the term "violation" to refer to an impermissible limitation of a right for which the individual is guaranteed a remedy.[72] Accordingly, the two-step approach and conceptualization is not simply a creation of judicial and scholarly minds, but has a more solid basis in the texts of limitations clauses than Webber suggests. Moreover, although he is undoubtedly correct that as a general semantic matter the word "limit" does have these two distinct meanings, so that "by understanding *limitation as specification*, one can read a limitation clause as calling for 'reasonable boundaries' or 'reasonable definitions' or 'reasonable perimeters' of rights",[73] as an intuitive matter this does not seem the most compelling or plausible reading of the term in this particular context, to the extent there is any clear or obvious difference between them here. If the government limits your rights, it sounds as if it is restricting or interfering with rather than defining them; redefining perhaps. In this context at least, limiting and delimiting rights do not seem synonymous.

The normative component of the claim is that even if enshrined in constitutional texts and "human rights law-in-action",[74] we should nonetheless reject the "received approach" and conceive of rights and their limits in this way because it better comports with both democracy – in that it transfers the power of specification from courts to legislatures – and the special normative force attaching to rights. But it is not obvious why, at least as viewed through the lens of the culture of democracy perspective, the two-step conceptualization needs to be rejected outright for these reasons rather than perhaps amended. There appears to be nothing inherent in the framework itself to prevent a more stringent approach to the first step, one that defines rights in a more circumscribed and less "inflationary" way, for example ruling out trivial liberty claims.[75] And to the extent that only more serious rights claims qualify under the first step, proportionality in the strict sense under the second step would correspondingly permit only more serious competing considerations to justify limiting or overriding them. This would generally bolster the normative force of rights claims.

---

[68] Art 2(2); 13(7).
[69] European Convention on Human Rights, Article 8(2).
[70] Ibid. Article 9(2).   [71] Ibid. Article 10(2).
[72] *German Basic Law*, Article 19(4); E.C.H.R., Article 13.
[73] Webber, *The Negotiable Constitution, supra* note 5 at 133.
[74] Webber, "On the Loss of Rights," Chapter 6 in this volume.
[75] *Cf.* Kai Möller, "Proportionality and Rights Inflation," Chapter 7 in this volume.

Moreover, as already mentioned, those specific rights that ought to have the strongest normative force can be given within the framework of the received approach either by categorical textual provision – as with the rights against "torture or inhuman or degrading treatment or punishment," slavery and forced labor, and the right to a fair and public hearing under Articles 3, 4, and 6 of the European Convention on Human Rights – or by refusing to deem any conflicting objective sufficiently important or proportionately pursued.

When all is said and done, there seems to be little clear practical or normative difference in the scope of legislative or judicial power between the culture of democracy perspective on proportionality and legislative specificationism. In both, a reasonable public justification for the legislative act is sufficient (and necessary) for it to survive judicial scrutiny. Indeed, even some culture of justification proponents of proportionality propose this lenient standard of judicial review.[76] So, for example, under proportionality analysis a valid statute prohibiting individuals from openly expressing racist political views in the public square that reject or deny equality of citizenship would be deemed a reasonable legislative limit in the sense of a reasonable restriction on, or infringement or override of, the right to free expression; whereas under specificationism, it would be deemed a reasonable legislative limit in the sense of a reasonable setting of the boundary of the right – as not encompassing such racist political expression. Both accounts grant legislatures greater powers over rights issues than under standard understandings, and for similar democratic reasons. The only difference is conceptual: whether legislatures should be understood as lawfully limiting judicially specified rights or specifying rights themselves. Even if the latter approach is analytically cleaner, there does not seem to be much of a normative difference between these two conceptualizations in terms of democracy or the special force of rights. Finally, although both proportionality as presented and legislative specificationism reduce the judicial role to reviewing for reasonable public justifications only, this still gives the legal power of the final word to the courts, unlike the case under the new Commonwealth model.

IV. CONCLUSION

From the perspective of democratic constitutionalism, the appeal of proportionality is that it creates a greater balance between judicial and legislative power than certain other models of rights analysis and conceptions of

[76] Kumm, "Democracy Is Not Enough," *supra* note 2.

constitutional rights, granting legislatures a greater role in the resolution of contentious and controversial rights issues. A conception of constitutional rights as putting government action to the burden of reasonable public justification tempers certain enduring democratic concerns about judicial review and a constitutionalized rights regime by providing a more proportionate accommodation of the respective values. From this perspective, proportionality is not about the power of judges to resolve indeterminate rights claims or issues of policy outside their formal areas of expertise, but about the power of legislatures to balance valid rights claims against other significant public policy objectives subject to the constraint of substantive reasonableness. The concern about proportionality is that, as with all normative constraints on an independent judiciary when their decisions are final within the parameters of the legal system, courts have the practical power to undermine this balance and tip it firmly in their direction.

13 The Rationalism of Proportionality's Culture of Justification

Mark Antaki*

I. INTRODUCTION

Proportionality and balancing[1] have quickly established themselves as essential to, if not also as the be-all and end-all of, the adjudication of constitutional rights disputes.[2] Their rise is thought to reflect a shift away from constitutional cultures of authority to constitutional cultures of justification, of the giving of reasons. Their rise also reveals an attendant realism and rationalism that, together or separately, aims to demystify and simplify the tasks of judgment and justification. This simplification involves turning them into an exercise of "blind" universal human reason and eliding their character as matters of belonging and attunement to a specific tradition and context.

Leaving much of the contested details of the method of proportionality to others, this chapter focuses on some of the modes of thought that make proportionality so appealing, including some of the habits we develop when

---

* I would like to thank Max Jarvie, Jessica Magonet, Zain Naqi, and Grégoire Webber, as well as the participants in the workshop on Proportionality in Human Rights Law at Western University's Faculty of Law for their helpful comments.
[1] Balancing being the cousin, sibling, or even identical twin of proportionality. Cf. Frederick Schauer, "Proportionality and the Question of Weight," Chapter 8 in this volume.
[2] On the spread of proportionality, see Alec Stone Sweet and Jud Matthews, "Proportionality Balancing and Global Constitutionalism," (2008) 47 *Colum. J. Transnat'l. L.* 73 (hereinafter Sweet and Matthews, "Proportionality"). They write that "over the past fifty years, proportionality analysis (PA) has widely diffused" (73).

> From German origins, PA has spread across Europe, including to the post-Communist states in Central and Eastern Europe, and into Israel. It has been absorbed into Commonwealth systems – Canada, South Africa, New Zealand, and via European law, the U.K. – and it is presently making inroads into Central and South America. By the end of the 1990s, virtually every effective system of constitutional justice in the world, with the partial exception of the United States, has embraced the main tenets of PA (74).

we practice and talk about proportionality. In other words, this chapter focuses on the culture, the *ethos*, or even the mood to which much proportionality-talk belongs. More specifically, it explores how this culture is deeply marked by its rationalism, its adherence to a cult of reason, or to be more specific, a cult of rationality.[3] A culture marked by rationalism reduces or tends to reduce *Logos*, reason or word at their richest and most polysemous, to *logismos*, reckoning or calculation.[4] This reduction leads to a forgetting that judgment is as much, if not more, a matter of "perception" as it is one of "cognition",[5] and that justification, understood as the provision of a ratio or ground, cannot be separated or purified from persuasion, understood as necessarily including the appeal to, and construction of, a shared world.

I am particularly interested in rationalism's tendency to worldlessness,[6] that is, its denial of our throwness into a world.[7] Proportionality's rationalism betrays an impatience with the world-revealing and world-maintaining "metaphorical and analogical" character of "natural language".[8] This point is close to Alexander Aleinikoff's earlier critique of balancing as threatening the "constitutive potential of constitutional law",[9] itself indebted to James Boyd White's understanding of the inescapably poetic and literary character of both judgment and justification[10] and close to Robert Cover's understanding of the primordial co-belonging of nomos (law in its rich and broad sense) and narrative.[11] What is more, the tendency to believe in the possibility of human beings gaining an "objective" set of scales with which to judge (an Archimedean standpoint from which to judge[12]) also leads to the too-easy dismissal of

[3] Note the title of Jon Elster, *Reason and Rationality* (2008); see Tran Van Doan, *Reason, Rationality and Reasonableness* (2001).

[4] The distinction between *Logos* and *logismos* is not so simple. Note the following words of Hobbes in *Leviathan*: "REASON, in this sense, is nothing but *reckoning* (that is, adding and subtracting) of the consequences of general names agreed upon for the *marking* and *signifying* of our thoughts" (1994) at 22–23.

[5] Jill Frank, *A Democracy of Distinction: Aristotle and the Work of Politics* (2005) (hereinafter Frank, *Democracy of Distinction*).

[6] See, e.g., Mark Antaki, "The World (lessness) of Human Rights," (2003) 49 *McGill L.J.* 203.

[7] On "throwness" (*Geworfenheit*), see Martin Heidegger, *Being and Time* (1962).

[8] Linda Meyer, *The Justice of Mercy* (2010) at 32.

[9] T. Alexander Aleinikoff, "Constitutional Law in the Age of Balancing," (1987) 96 *Yale L.J.* 943.

[10] There are too many relevant White pieces to cite. See, for example, James Boyd White, "Law as Rhetoric, Rhetoric as Law: The Arts of Cultural and Communal Life," (1985) 52 *U. Chicago L. Rev.* 684.

[11] Robert Cover, "Nomos and Narrative," (1983–84) 97 *Harv. L. Rev.* 4 (Hereinafter Cover, "Nomos and Narrative"). Cover sees nomos as a "normative universe." The connection between nomos and narrative means law "becomes not merely a system of rules to be observed, but a world in which we leave" (4–5).

[12] Note the title of Thomas Nagel, *The View from Nowhere* (1986).

authority – to a confounding of the authoritative and the authoritarian,[13] itself tied to an inability or unwillingness to see authority as "positive", as world-maintaining.

Because my interests in proportionality-talk are close to those of Aleinikoff, White, and Cover, I use Albie Sachs's *The Strange Alchemy of Life and Law* as a thread and a foil.[14] Sachs's own struggles with rationalism, his own "strange alchemy," shed light on the rationalism of proportionality-talk. On the one hand, Sachs swims in dominant currents when he embraces proportionality as the core or essence of constitutional rights adjudication. "[I]f I were to be stranded on a desert island and allowed to take only two constitutional elements with me, I would take human dignity and proportionality,"[15] writes Sachs. "Proportionality, proportionality, proportionality. I cannot repeat these words often enough,"[16] he adds. As his repetition of "proportionality" shows, the method of proportionality can easily become a mantra, perhaps even threatening to overshadow dignity. On the other hand, Sachs exhibits his poetic soul and sounds much more like a proponent of "law and literature" than a representative of the mainstream proportionality scholarship when he writes: "In the beginning and in the end is the word, at least as far as the life of the judge is concerned. We pronounce. We work with words, and become amongst the most influential story-tellers of our age."[17]

Sachs' reference to *Logos* in its rich sense – as evidenced both by his reference to storytellers (which we can also hear as myth-tellers as in *muthos*) as well as his echo of John 1:1 ("in the beginning was the Word") – combined with his however reluctant or playful[18] reference to "alchemy" serves as a caution regarding the reductiveness of the rationalism of proportionality-talk. To think through rationalism is to see it as issued from what Weber called "rationalization" and which he tied to the "disenchantment of the world".

---

[13] See Joseph Vining, *The Authoritative and the Authoritarian* (1986); and Hannah Arendt, "What Is Authority?" in *Between Past and Future: Eight Exercises in Political Thought* (1977) (hereinafter Arendt, "What is Authority").

[14] Among other things, Sachs was a judge on the Constitutional Court of South Africa from 1994 to 2009.

[15] Albie Sachs, *The Strange Alchemy of Life and Law* (2009) at 202 (hereinafter Sachs, *Strange Alchemy*). Although he does not fully elaborate on the relation between dignity and proportionality, in a chapter titled "Human Dignity and Proportionality," dignity appears as the ultimate goal of constitutional rights adjudication and proportionality as its core method. Precisely because the "what" of dignity and the "how" of proportionality go to the heart of constitutional adjudication, Sachs identifies them as indispensable. One might ask why "constitutional elements" would be necessary when stranded on a desert island.

[16] Ibid. at 206. As his repetition of "proportionality" shows, the method of proportionality itself can easily become a mantra, perhaps even threatening to overshadow dignity. This may be because proportionality appears as and promises calculation and mastery, something dignity cannot deliver.

[17] Ibid. at 270.   [18] Ibid. at 8.

The idea that "one can, in principle, master all things by calculation," wrote Weber, means "the world is disenchanted".[19]

This chapter focuses on some aspects of contemporary proportionality-talk that may lead one to mistake a desert island for the world, thus becoming quite satisfied to be stranded on one, abstracted, drawn away from the world, including much of the stuff of judgment, of justification, of constitutional adjudication. I proceed as follows: first, I paint a picture of the dominance of proportionality and, by way of the work of Mattias Kumm, begin to give an account of its rationalism. Second, by way of Sachs's attempt to distinguish reason and judgment, with which he tempers (if not resists) proportionality-talk's rationalistic tendencies, I consider Hannah Arendt's account of worldly judgment. Third, using Paul Kahn and Roberto Unger, two scholars who have taken seriously the idea of rationalism as a culture (but without being invested in this culture themselves), I outline how an understanding of judgment as worldly can lead to a rehabilitation of authority and analogy. Fourth, I revisit proportionality by (re)turning to Aristotle, whose *analogon* is translated and translatable both as "analogy" and "proportionality". Although we do not necessarily think through these two English words together, the Greek can serve to remind us of the dangers, perhaps even the futility, of separating the two in practical matters and thus, also, of separating the aesthetic from the mathematical, perception from cognition, the poetic from the propositional, world from reason.

The chapter as a whole focuses on proportionality-talk as it reflects a certain appeal or attractiveness or seduction of reason *qua* rationality and, it must be said, of "method" more generally.[20] I do not deny that instances of practical wisdom in judgment and justification can and do take place under the guise of proportionality. I simply wish to draw attention to the abstraction and objectification of human being-in-the-world that comes along with much contemporary proportionality-talk. In this respect, much proportionality-talk may be a symptom or reflection of an underlying rationalist culture, *ethos*, or mood that, no doubt, also finds expression in many other ways and places.

II. PROPORTIONALITY'S RATIONALISM

In Sachs's exposition, proportionality emerges as closely connected to the characterization of the "bridge" in the 1993 Interim Constitution of South Africa, as standing in for a journey from a "culture of authority" tied to parliamentary

---

[19] Max Weber, "Science as a Vocation" in *From Max Weber: Essays in Sociology*, eds. H. Gerth and C.W. Mills (1946), 129–156 at 139.

[20] See Hans-Georg Gadamer, *Truth and Method* (2nd rev. ed., 1989) (hereinafter Gadamer, *Truth and Method*).

supremacy to a "culture of justification" tied to constitutional supremacy.[21] With the prominence given to the pair of dignity and proportionality,[22] the South African constitution and South African constitutionalism both catch up to the rest of the world and lead the way forward. If "proportionality-based rights adjudication now constitutes one of the defining features of global constitutionalism",[23] it is precisely because of its "rationality".[24] Indeed, the progressive and inexorable movement from authority to justification is universalized such that "authority" constitutionalism is somehow backward and "justification" constitutionalism belongs on the right side of history – that of reason, of human rights. Even cultures of constitutional rights, which are usually tied to justification, are characterized by this division between authority and justification: there is an American exceptionalism that, to the extent it embraces categorical reasoning, refuses reason.

Sachs's words – the words of a former South African Constitutional Court judge – regarding the constitutional elements he would take with him if stranded on a desert island reflect a widespread tendency to reduce rights-adjudication to dignity and, especially, to proportionality. Practically all scholars agree that contemporary rights-protecting and-limiting legal instruments require something like proportionality analysis, or that proportionality is at the "heart of modern human rights and constitutional rights practice".[25] However,

---

[21] Sachs, *Strange Alchemy, supra* note 15 at 204. This characterization of the bridge originates with Etienne Mureinik, "A Bridge to Where? Introducing the Interim Bill of Rights," (1994) 10 S.A.J.H.R. 31. For a critical take on the bridge metaphor, see A.J. van der Walt, "Dancing with Codes – Protecting, Developing and Deconstructing Property Rights in a Constitutional State," (2001) 118 S.A.L.J. 258. See also Grant Huscroft, "Proportionality and the Relevance of Interpretation", Chapter 9 in this volume, and Mark Antaki, "The Bridge and the Book as Metaphors of Transformative Constitutionalism" (manuscript on file with author).

[22] Sachs's words reflect the text of the Constitution of the Republic of South Africa (1996). In that constitution, dignity appears as the first "value" on which the Republic of South Africa as a whole is founded (s. 1), as the first "democratic value" affirmed by the Bill of Rights (s. 7), and as a right itself (s. 10). Dignity also appears as the first constitutive element of "open and democratic society" that underlies both the limitation of rights (s. 36) and their interpretation (s. 39). Section 36 codifies the proportionality test that has swept through contemporary constitutionalism, albeit not by laying out a series of steps to be followed, but rather listing a set of factors to be taken into account.

[23] Sweet and Matthews, "Proportionality," *supra* note 2 at 74. They add: "if global constitutionalism can be said to exist at all."

[24] Cohen-Eliya and Porat characterize human rights and rationalism as "intrinsic" rather than "instrumental" explanations of the rise of proportionality. Moshe Cohen-Eliya and Iddo Porat, "Proportionality and the Culture of Justification," (2011) 59 *Am. J. Comp. L.* 463.

[25] Mattias Kumm, "Institutionalizing Socratic Contestation: The Rationalist Human Rights Paradigm, Legitimate Authority and the Point of Judicial Review," (2007) 1 *E.J.L.S.* 1 (hereinafter Kumm, "Institutionalizing Socratic Contestation").

the agreement tends to be about more than proportionality having a place. Put starkly, proportionality is the supreme principle in every constitution and judicial review of legislation or state action is "all and only about proportionality" as "proportionality is what basic rights . . . actually guarantee."[26]

The proportionality "test" that has become dominant in the adjudication of constitutionally protected rights is meant to focus on the grounds, or reasons, for the rights-limiting or -violating[27] governmental action. Its early steps are characterized by a kind of instrumental rationality, by way of which judges ask whether, for example, a legislative scheme could be designed better so as to infringe a right to a lesser extent. Its last step is characterized by a kind of axiological rationality oriented to the relative worth, in the specific context at issue, of (usually only two) competing values, interests, or principles.[28] In line with its particular axiological rationality, contemporary proportionality-talk systematically translates both constitutional rights and the legitimate or laudable purposes of legislation into values, interests, or principles.[29]

In part because practically all interests tend to be accorded some measure of constitutional protection, proportionality, as Grégoire Webber puts it, tends to "de-constitutionalize" rights.[30] This de-constitutionalization may also be a de-juridification as proportionality analysis is taken to be a less (traditionally) legal form of judgment, closer to practical reasoning more generally, in part because it is less beholden to constitutional texts, traditions, and precedents. Proportionality's broader commitment to reason appears to take Hobbes's side

---

[26] David M. Beatty, *The Ultimate Rule of Law* (2004) at 170 (hereinafter Beatty, *Ultimate Rule of Law*). Put more diplomatically, "[A] rights-holder does not have very much in virtue of his having a right." Kumm, "Institutionalizing Socratic Contestation," ibid. at 11.

[27] On the substitution of "infringing" or "violating" for "limiting," see Grégoire Webber *The Negotiable Constitution* (2009) at 118–119.

[28] The test, in its most popular construction, arises (or is implicated) once a prima facie rights violation has been found and involves four steps: first, determining whether the (legislative) goal is legitimate; second, suitability, determining whether the means chosen are rationally connected to the goal; third, necessity, determining whether the legislature has chosen the least rights-infringing means available; fourth, proportionality in the strict sense, weighing or balancing the concrete benefits of the (legislative) measures against the concrete damage done to the right in question.

[29] See Mark Antaki, "The Turn to 'Values' in Canadian Constitutional Law" in Luc B. Tremblay and Grégoire C.N. Webber, *La Limitation des Droits de la Charte: Essais Critiques sur l'Arrêt R. c. Oakes/The Limitation of Charter Rights: Critical Essays on R. v. Oakes* (2009) (hereinafter Antaki, "The Turn to 'Values'").

[30] Thereby, he adds, "undoing the constitution." Webber, *The Negotiable Constitution, supra* note 27 at 100, 101.Webber argues that in undoing the constitution, proportionality leads to the "loss of rights." See Webber, "On the Loss of Rights," Chapter 6 in this volume. Note, in particular, his criticism of Möller's willingness to speak of a prima facie right to murder as an example of the translation of practically all interests into the language of constitutional right(s).

290   *Mark Antaki*

against Coke in claiming that there is no "artificial reason of the law"[31] – but it no longer does so in the name of Hobbes's sovereign. This has led both proponents and critics of proportionality to wonder why we need judges at all (others query why we need authoritative legislatures at all), or why judges (or legislators) specifically ought to be entrusted with the responsibility of undertaking proportionality analysis.

These themes are all reflected in the recent work of Mattias Kumm. Kumm understands proportionality as close to "rational policy assessment".[32] Proportionality emerges as the core of a "rationalist human rights paradigm" that institutionalizes (at one and the same time!) Rawlsian political philosophy and "Socratic contestation" in the practice of judicial review. According to Kumm, proportionality reflects the displacement of sovereignty, and the "mythical monster called Leviathan",[33] as the "foundation of law", with the "no less mysterious" "idea of human dignity".[34] What follows from this displacement is the requirement of a culture of justification in which the judiciary's task is to scrutinize and expose legislative reasons (or the lack thereof), for which proportionality analysis becomes the proper or best or only tool. Kumm dismisses the American literature and its obsession with "We, the People", because it does not fit a European experience tied to a "rationalist human rights paradigm".[35]

Kumm invokes Socrates to highlight the essentially negative character of judicial review under proportionality (the judiciary is to scrutinize the reasons of the legislature but not to substitute its own) as well as the kind of "expertise" judges engaged in proportionality analysis are expected to have: knowing what questions to ask.[36] Kumm links Socrates to Rawls because not all reasons "count" as (public) reasons – for instance, tradition, convention, and prejudice do not count.[37] In this manner, it would seem, Kumm's Socrates can be said to subscribe to the contemporary liberal or Rawlsian separation of the right and the good. Kumm ultimately links proportionality to the importance of thoughtfulness for justice, and even gestures toward Arendt's counterposition of Socrates, an (if not the) exemplary figure of thoughtfulness, and Adolf Eichmann, whose extreme thoughtlessness led him to do great evil.[38] Proportionality emerges as the peak of enlightenment in dark times. In the words of another scholar, proportionality is "the ultimate rule of law".[39] It is

---

[31] Sir Edward Coke, *Prohibitions del Roy* (1658).
[32] Kumm, "Institutionalizing Socratic Contestation," *supra* note 25 at 12.
[33] Ibid. at 31.   [34] Ibid. at 32.
[35] Ibid. at 2, inter alia.   [36] Ibid. at 14.
[37] Ibid. at 19.
[38] Ibid. at 17, fn 32; see Hannah Arendt, *Eichmann in Jerusalem* (1964).
[39] Beatty, *Ultimate Rule of Law, supra* note 26.

the ultimate – that is, last – rule of reason. Have "we" arrived at the end of history? And, if so, where?

"Rationalist"[40] (as in Kumm's "rationalist human rights paradigm") is a telling adjective to describe a "paradigm" of judgment and justification. Rationalism is a tendency to embrace and celebrate a "cult of reason", or more precisely "a cult of rationality", wherein human beings are enamored with, perhaps carried away by, the promises of their own cognitive faculties.[41] Rationalism turns against tradition, against the past, because truth is not to be found in past practices, but in the voice of reason. Consequently, it tends to sever the "cognitive" from "the rest" of human being-in-the-world. For the moment, two aspects of rationalism – demystification and calculation – are worth further consideration.

The method and rhetoric of proportionality are usefully situated within broader understandings and commitments that combine realism and rationalism and find their common expression, at least in the Anglo-American tradition, in the movement to demystify the law,[42] itself closely related to what Marianne Constable has called the "social scientification"[43] of law. By realism, I refer not simply to legal realism and its legacy, but to the general desire to show the world "as it is" – and to the conceit that one has done so. The urge to demystify and rationalize is manifest in the confident way in which readers are told in judicial opinions and scholarly articles alike that rights *really* are interests and values, that what constitutions *really* do is enshrine value systems or compendia of values, and that what judges (and legislators) *really* do is balance interests and values.[44] The whole discussion usually proceeds as if "values", "interests", "balancing", "proportionality", and the associated lexicon are not themselves historically situated modes of speaking and being-in-the-world and,

---

[40] "Rationalist" appears in Kumm's title, but part I, which begins at page 5, is entitled "The 'Rational Human Rights Paradigm.'"

[41] Which means, to follow Oakeshott, the dominance of theoretical understandings of practice that lose sight of practice as practice. Michael Oakeshott, *Rationalism in Politics and Other Essays*, expanded ed. (1991).

[42] On demystification, see H.L.A. Hart, "Bentham and the Demystification of the Law," (1973) 36 M.L.R. 2. On demystification and disenchantment, see also Mark Antaki, "The Turn to Imagination in Legal Theory: The Re-Enchantment of the World?" (2012) 23 *Law and Critique* 1.

[43] Marianne Constable, "Genealogy and Jurisprudence: Nietzsche, Nihilism, and the Social Scientification of Law," (1994) 19 *Law & Soc. Inquiry* 551 (hereinafter Constable, "Genealogy and Jurisprudence").

[44] For "value structures," see La Forest J. in R. v. *Lyons*, [1987] 2 S.C.R. 309, at para. 21. See also Gonthier and McLachlin JJ. in their dissent in R. v. *Hess; R. v. Nguyen*, [1990] 2 S.C.R. 906, at para. 113: "What is really at stake in determining the scope and priority of constitutional rights are conflicting values and interests."

therefore, perhaps themselves deserving of a little Socratic contestation. For example, is talk of "values" consistent with a belief in "human dignity"? Is the "balancing of interests" a proper way to speak of "justice," the "good"? And what are "values"[45] and "interests",[46] anyhow? Too often, the authority of the obvious, including rather recent shorthand very closely tied to social science thinking, seems to lie at the heart of the contemporary discourse of justification. The casting-off of legal formalism and categorical straitjackets does not necessarily deliver reason or "reality".[47]

The belief that the translation of rights into values and interests and of judgment and justification into weighing and balancing brings us (closer) to what is *really* going on also reflects the transformation of judicial reasoning into, supposedly, general moral or practical reasoning. But it also reflects a specific (historically and culturally situated) conception of practical reasoning, rooted in the technical or the calculative, and tied to the objectification of human-being-in-the-world that comes along with demystification. As Oliver Wendell Holmes famously wrote: "For the rational study of law the black-letter man may be the man of the present, but the man of the future is the man of statistics and the master of economics."[48] (The man of the future is the man who has successfully killed the dragon that is law or tamed it and made it a useful animal, having counted its teeth.[49])

At its extremes, proportionality-talk, if not proportionality analysis itself, looks and feels like naked human reason parachuted into specific contexts and "facts" that speak for themselves[50] – particularly when the importance of text, tradition,

---

[45] On "values," see, e.g., Antaki, "The Turn to 'Values,'" *supra* note 29; and Edward G. Andrew, *The Genealogy of Values: the Aesthetic Economy of Nietzsche and Proust* (1995).

[46] On "interests," see, e.g., Albert O. Hirshman, *The Passions and the Interests: Political Arguments for Capitalism Before Its Triumph* (1977). Arendt hears interest as "inter-esse" and, more specifically, "inter homines esse". See Hannah Arendt, *The Human Condition* (1958) at 51.

[47] Indeed, it may lead to the loss of both. See Constable, "Genealogy and Jurisprudence," *supra* note 43; and, of course, Friedrich Nietzsche, "How the Real World Became a Fable" in *Twilight of the Idols and the Anti-Christ*, trans. R.J. Hollingdale (1990) at 50–51. Nietzsche's German title reads *wahre Welt*, so "true world" is a better translation than "real world."

[48] O.W. Holmes, "The Path of the Law", (1897) 10 *Harv. L. Rev.* 457 at 469 (hereinafter Holmes, "Paths of the Law"). Constable writes, "[i]t appears that the dragon has been tamed and transformed into a spouse by the forces of social science," Constable, "Genealogy and Jurisprudence," *supra* note 43 at 553.

[49] Holmes, "Paths of the Law," ibid. at 469.

[50] Although Beatty insists on the contextual nature of proportionality analysis, his account, and the "objectivity" he thinks it delivers, rely greatly on "facts" being more or less self-evident because they are bound up with the perspective of the parties. As he says, "Judgments are based on findings of fact about the parties' own evaluation of the significance of whatever government initiative or decision is before the court. Applied in this way, proportionality offers judges a clear and objective test to distinguish coercive state action by the state that is legitimate from

precedent, and analogical reasoning is minimized or even dismissed.[51] Proportionality sometimes appears as a kind of superhero or Hercules[52] coming from nowhere to rescue us when we are faced with a difficult problem that does not lend itself to any obvious answer.[53] In line with its attraction to naked human reason, much proportionality-talk (indeed, much talk about objectivity in general) reflects the transformation of ethics and morality in our day-to-day and philosophical vocabulary: we no longer understand ethics and morality in their older sense of *ethos* and *mores* as dwelling-place, habit, and custom – as necessarily tied to tradition and the world into which we are thrown, and therefore, unavoidably tied to our prejudices – prejudgments from which we necessarily begin, but with which we need not necessarily end.

Precisely because we no longer hear *ethos* and *mores* in ethics and morality, our search for objectivity leads to objectification, to adopting a jargon of "values" and of "weighing all the objective considerations" that George Orwell, among others, would certainly have decried.[54] Moreover, the rise of the technical or calculative can be seen in how even questions of so-called axiological-rationality are sought to be reduced to calculative or instrumental questions by way of such devices as intensity or weight.[55] Proportionality

that which is not." Beatty, *Ultimate Rule of Law, supra* note 26 at 166. According to Beatty, proportionality turns "conflicts about people's most important interests and ideas into matters of fact, rather than matters of interpretation or matters of moral principle", thus allowing "the judiciary to supervise a discourse in which each person's perception of a state's course of action is valued equally and for which there is a correct resolution that can be verified empirically." Ibid. at 171; see also, 182.

[51] Kumm, "Institutionalizing Socratic Contestation," *supra* note 25 at 5.

[52] Ibid. at 22. Kumm writes, "[T]he Socratic commitment to reason has something heroic about it, whereas the institutionalisation of Socratic contestation does not generally require judges to be the hero that Socrates was."

[53] The proponents of proportionality will respond that the method is designed merely to eliminate the more unreasonable legislative schemes and not to identify the most reasonable scheme.

[54] In "Politics and the English Language," Orwell contrasts a verse from Ecclesiastes with its "equivalent" in bad modern English prose. Ecclesiastes: "I returned and saw under the sun, that the race is not to the swift, nor the battle to the strong, neither yet bread to the wise, nor yet riches to men of understanding, nor yet favour to men of skill; but time and chance happeneth to them all." Modern prose (his parody): "Objective consideration of contemporary phenomena compels the conclusion that success or failure in competitive activities exhibits no tendency to be commensurate with innate capacity, but that a considerable element of the unpredictable must invariably be taken into account." See George Orwell, "Politics and the English Language" in *A Collection of Essays* (1981) at 163.

[55] If Beatty turns to the actual viewpoint of the parties to translate all problems, including moral ones, into factual ones (see *supra* note 50), Alexy turns to a constitutional point of view to avoid the problem of incommensurability. Robert Alexy, "On Balancing and Subsumption: A Structural Comparison," (2003) 16 *Ratio Juris* 433 (hereinafter Alexy, "On Balancing and

assumes, or fantasizes, that all considerations can be "weighed" on the "same" scale. Proportionality, balancing, and weighing can and do metaphorically seduce human beings who, once seduced, seek to translate the qualitative into the quantitative without worrying too much about what might be lost in this translation. The price of objectivity is an objectification (not very Kantian or dignifying?) of human-being-in-the-world.

Although one can surely approve of Kumm's invocation of Arendt to underline the importance of thoughtfulness, as well as its primordial relation to justice, one must not forget that Arendt was also extremely (and rightly) critical of the "social scientification" of thought, itself a form of thoughtlessness. She made a tremendous effort to understand, situate, and refuse much social scientific jargon. Indeed, she tied the rise of the social sciences to a massive and radical transformation in who and how we are.[56] For instance, whether or not we believe rights-talk is secondary, problematic, or even nonsensical, values-talk is not obviously truer, closer to what is *really* going on than rights-talk. What Kumm seems to neglect is that Arendt's understanding of thinking and its importance to our common world cannot so easily be reduced to a neo-Kantianism or neo-Rawlsian public reason.

III. REASON AND JUDGMENT: PUTTING THE WORLD BACK INTO JUDGMENT

If rationalization is about demystification, which Sachs presumably embraces, "[h]aving grown up in the tradition of the enlightenment,"[57] his turn to alchemy and storytelling emerges as a remedy for, or response to, rationalism, as an important reminder that *logismos* is grounded in and inseparable from *Logos*. Although Sachs's book has its fair share of proportionality- and balancing-talk, including values-talk and appeals to objectivity, it also includes a tempering of all of these modes of talk and thought. He tempers these by drawing attention to the irreducible element of judgment in judging (even in the metaphor of balancing), which proportionality-talk tends to minimize, and which scholars and judges hint at when they write of "attaching" weight to various considerations, facts, values, or interests. Because facts do not speak for themselves – recall that a *factum* is made (or done, as in a feat)[58] and a

---

Subsumption") at 442. Intensity presupposes commensurability: see Webber, *The Negotiable Constitution*, supra note 27 at 89–100.

[56] E.g., Arendt, *Human Condition*, supra note 46 at 38 and ff.

[57] Sachs, *Strange Alchemy*, supra note 15 at 8.

[58] For an account of the genesis of "fact," see Barbara J. Shapiro, *A Culture of Fact: England, 1550–1720* (2000).

datum is given – judges must bear the burden not only of articulating facts, but also of attaching weight to them. To put the matter differently, judges do not "have" scales; they *are* the scales, and how they calibrate themselves determines the weight of things. This is a big point for Sachs. Although certainly not reducing his capacity as judge to his biography, much of the book, and the strange alchemy to which it refers, is about his own (judicial) attunement to the world.

Moreover, it turns out, if one sticks with the metaphor of balancing and to proportionality, one's articulation of the "facts" cannot be dissociated from the weight one attaches to them (or to the "interests" they implicate). Richard Posner draws attention to this in his review of Beatty's book. For example, he refers to Beatty's approval of a German Constitutional Court decision allowing voluntary prayers but rejection of Bavaria's decision to place crucifixes in the classroom. He notes Beatty's use of the term "glare" to refer to the experience of the crucifix in the classroom and writes: "Without more detail concerning the court's analysis, which Beatty does not give, this sounds like a pretty arbitrary judgment, with much of its force carried by the odd choice of the word 'glare' to describe the appearance of a crucifix."[59] In this criticism, Posner draws attention to how Beatty's "calculation" is bound up with a choice of words that provides texture and invites a certain experience of resonance or dissonance. Indeed, he underlines the inseparability of persuasion from justification. As Sachs puts it, "We [judges] work with words."[60]

Sachs picks up on these themes throughout his book and, in particular, in a chapter entitled "Reason and Judgment" (which plays on the double sense of judgment: judgment as in the act of judging and judgment as justification, as exemplified in the judicial opinion). In this chapter, Sachs recalls a conversation he had with a Canadian law professor. The conversation concerned Arendt's work on Kant and, in particular, the distinction between reason and judgment. Sachs writes that, unlike reason, judgment is not "compelling" and so is not a "purely logical exercise". On the other hand, "[i]t is not dependent on personal taste".[61] Rather, judgment is somewhere in between, as it presupposes membership in a community. Accordingly, judgments "woo" more than they "compel acceptance".[62] And persuasion, rather than being a "gratuitous add-on"[63] to justification, is inseparable from it.

---

[59] Richard A. Posner, "Constitutional Law from a Pragmatic Perspective," (2005) 55 *U.T.L.J.* 299 at 303.

[60] Sachs, *Strange Alchemy*, *supra* note 15 at 270.   [61] Ibid. at 141.

[62] Ibid. at 142. Arendt also uses "woo": Hannah Arendt, *Lectures on Kant's Political Philosophy* (1982) at 72 (hereinafter Arendt, *Lectures*).

[63] Sachs, *Strange Alchemy*, *supra* note 15 at 142.

It is worth dwelling on Sachs's appeal to Arendt, as it is a direct response to rationalism's tendency to worldlessness. When Arendt famously turned to Kant's *Critique of Judgment* to articulate Kant's (unwritten) political philosophy, she did so precisely to escape what she took to be his rationalism in the *Critique of Practical Reason*. The crucial point, for Arendt, is that the *Critique of Practical Reason* concerns all rational beings, whereas the *Critique of Judgment* concerns human beings more specifically; that is, sensible beings who share a world. In other words, only the *Critique of Judgment* truly takes into account the fundamental human condition of plurality: "that men, not Man, live on the earth and inhabit the world."[64] Because it concerns human beings who are sensible – who "have" experiences – the *Critique of Judgment* concerns particulars (actually singulars): this or that being or action. Beings and actions arise in a shared world that is always already "there". And, as Arendt writes, "[j]udging is one, if not the most, important activity, in which this sharing-the-world-with-others comes to pass."[65]

Judgment's worldliness is most manifest in "reflective" as opposed to "determinant" judgments. In determinant judgments, the universal is given and the so-called operation of judgment is one of subsumption. In reflective judgments, the universal is not given and must somehow be generated from the particular (the singular).[66] Sachs does not make this distinction but relies on it when he uses Kant's example of a judgment that *this* rose is beautiful, a reflective judgment. No preexisting and articulable rule or universal – that is, no articulable major premise, such as "All roses are beautiful", – can "ground" this judgment. The judgment can only be grounded in the shared experience of a world.

Arendt's (and, albeit less robustly, Sachs's) rejection of rationalism amounts to a rejection of the primacy of rules and an appreciation of the impossibility of judgment as mere rule application and of justification as intellectual arm-twisting driven by the rules of logic, geometry, or mathematics. The rejection of the primacy of rules accords with contemporary proportionality-talk. However, proportionality-talk is less willing to let go of justification as intellectual arm-twisting. It does not recognize just how "unruly" judgment can be.[67]

---

[64] Arendt, *Human Condition, supra* note 46 at 7.
[65] Hannah Arendt, "The Crisis in Culture" in *Between Past and Future: Eight Exercises in Political Thought* (1977) at 221.
[66] Arendt, *Lectures, supra* note 62 at 83.
[67] See, e.g., Philippe Nonet, "Judgment," (1995) 48 *Vanderbilt L. Rev.* 987. At 988: "There are, and there can be, no rules regarding the application of rules. If Kant is right, a sizable part of what we take to be 'law', and almost all jurisprudence, are nothing but a futile striving to overcome this essential unruliness of judgment."

Proportionality-talk's rationalism is manifest in the attempt to make proportionality as rational as the application of rules.[68] To the contrary, Arendt turns to the *Critique of Judgment* precisely to show that the nub of judgment, whatever kind of judgment is involved, resides in one's appreciation of singulars, for example, the minor premise of a syllogism in so-called rule-based judgment. Proportionality-talk tends to avoid this topic; it tries to render rational and calculative the appreciation of singulars, or appeals to the obviousness of a certain appreciation.

Because facts do not speak for themselves, the appreciation of singulars is possible only thanks to common sense, a cultivated taste, and, ultimately, imagination.[69] In other words, Arendt turns to the *Critique of Judgment* in large measure because it is concerned with what we today call aesthetics. Recall that *aesthesis* first and foremost means "sensibility". To some extent, Arendt uses Kant against Kant to overcome the separation of cognition and aesthetics that he inaugurated and is partially constitutive of modern rationalism.[70] It is no surprise then that Arendt also follows Kant in making the example, indeed the exemplary, rather than the rule central to human judgment. The example presupposes and refers to (or within) a shared world. Indeed, "[t]he judgment has exemplary validity to the extent that the example is rightly chosen."[71] To put it differently, examples resonate, or fail to resonate, to the extent that they draw on, or fail to draw on, a shared past and world. And this is the case, it must be said, even if they are put forth to make us question our way of dwelling in the world or our mode of inheritance of that past, and thereby invite a new way of dwelling in the world or of inheriting or appropriating the past. Not all turns away from the primacy of rules are rationalist.

Sachs's "strange alchemy" and Arendt's reflections on Kant evoke Cover's famous words:

> No set of legal institutions or prescriptions exists apart from the narratives that locate it and give it meaning. For every constitution there is an epic, for each Decalogue a scripture. Once understood in the context of the narratives that give it meaning, law becomes not merely a system of rules to be observed,

---

[68] See, e.g., Robert Alexy, "Constitutional Rights, Balancing, and Rationality," (2003) 16 *Ratio Juris*. 131 (hereinafter Alexy, "Constitutional Rights").

[69] Arendt, *Lectures, supra* note 62 at 62 and ff. and at 79–85.

[70] See Gadamer, *Truth and Method, supra* note 20 at part I. Ronald Beiner draws attention to Gadamer in his interpretive essay accompanying Arendt's lectures on Kant's political philosophy. Ronald Beiner, "Interpretive Essay" in Arendt, *Lectures, supra* note 62 at 136. Beiner writes: "From Gadamer's Aristotelian standpoint, Kant 'intellectualizes' the *sensus communis* and 'aestheticizes' the faculty of taste."

[71] Arendt, *Lectures, supra* note 62 at 84.

but a world in which we live. In this normative world, law and narrative are inseparably related. Every prescription is insistent in its demand to be located in discourse – to be supplied with history and destiny, beginning and end, explanation and purpose.[72]

This quotation reveals how the rationalism of contemporary proportionality-talk is analogous, even tied, to a problem recently identified with Habermas' critical theory, his attempt to recuperate reason as communicative. Habermas' almost single-minded focus on justification and validity reflects an attempt to separate what cannot be separated: the communicative or "problem-solving" capacities of language and its "world-disclosing" or world-constituting capacities.[73] Although Kumm may be right to refer to Arendt, her work ought not to be assimilated to the rationalism of neo-Rawlsians or neo-Habermasians (whatever Habermas' views on proportionality[74]). Whatever her attachment to, and insight regarding, human dignity, Arendt is much closer to Nietzsche, Heidegger, and the "world-disclosers" than Kumm. To judge is not simply to weigh, but to locate oneself in and tell a story. Moral (and legal) reasoning is not simply reasoning about what is "right"; it is reasoning about a way of life, about what is fitting for "us" (however conceived) here and now. Moreover, part of what we learn from Cover, Nikolas Kompridis, Aleinikoff, and White is that there is no avoiding this appeal to and construction of a shared world and hence of an "us". We cannot escape world for reason. We cannot move from the *Critique of Judgment* to the *Critique of Pure Reason* or the *Critique of Practical Reason*, from human, situated beings to simply rational beings. We must recognize the limits of pure reason, give up on its cult, give up on rationalism (but not necessarily on reason).

Some contemporary critics of proportionality recognize some of these points, but not all of them, when they follow Aleinikoff in criticizing proportionality for being too technical and for the threat it poses to the constitutive character of constitutional law. For instance, Webber argues that proportionality, particularly the last stage of the dominant test, aims to make incommensurables commensurable by seeking to reduce moral questions into technical ones – but fails to do so. Although he does not say this, his criticism, in part, seems to be that the calculative or instrumental rationalism of the previous stages carries over into this last one.[75]

---

[72] Cover, "Nomos and Narrative," *supra* note 11.

[73] Nikolas Kompridis, *Critique and Disclosure: Critical Theory between Past and Future* (2006) at 135 and 139.

[74] See Jürgen Habermas, *Between Facts and Norms*. Trans. W. Rehg (1996). For Robert Alexy's response, see Alexy, "Constitutional Rights," *supra* note 68.

[75] Paradoxically, to echo Webber, each idealized exercise of balancing is so attached to the specific context of its specific facts that it abstracts completely from the broader context that

Proportionality and balancing, says Webber, also threaten the rule of law because standards take the place of rules and continuity with the past (and future) seems to disappear.[76] However, to the extent that Webber is enamored with rules, with legislative prescription, with delimiting rights in advance, he may be displaying a measure of hostility to the common law, as well as some measure of rationalism. Law does not reside in rules but rather examples. And the continuity of past and future, including perhaps even the rule of law, is assured by rules only in a limited way – and only to the extent that rules hearken back to the exemplary and to the world. In other words, in practice, working with rules is derivative of an experience of "fit" rather than a calculation. Webber's criticisms may only partially escape the allure of rationalism. As I have tried to suggest, a fuller account of contemporary proportionality-talk must attend even more to its rationalism.

IV. TAKING A CULTURE OF RATIONALISM SERIOUSLY: RECUPERATING AUTHORITY AND ANALOGY?

In different but interesting, and perhaps complementary, ways, Unger and Kahn invite us to think about rationalism as a culture, an *ethos*, even a mood. For example, in viewing comparative constitutionalism "culturally", Kahn invites his readers to shift some of their focus from doctrine and institutions to culture. This shift in focus requires giving up one's investment in reform (in making the law, as one has received it, the best it can be)[77] and, instead, thinking of the purpose of comparison as a deeper self-understanding. He writes: "To understand the meaning of judicial review [note the word "meaning" rather than function or efficacy] . . . "[w]e have to look instead at the rituals and myths of law – the content of the faith in laws rule."[78] In other words, we must let go of the belief that "we have arrived," of the conceit that our rationalism is, somehow, free of rituals and myths. Unger echoes Kahn when he invites us to confront what is at stake in our rationalism, writing that "[w]e cannot separate the practical and the spiritual shape of our civilization."[79]

---

includes constitutional commitments and precedent. Either naked human reason is thrust into a specific context and must "smuggle" in all that balancing has banished in its rationalism or, alternatively, proportionality covers up decision under the guise of calculation.

[76] See Grégoire Webber, "Legal Reasoning and Bills of Rights" in R. Ekins (ed.) *Modern Challenges to the Rule of Law* (2011).

[77] Paul W. Kahn, "Comparative Constitutionalism in a New Key," (2002–2003) 101 *Michigan L. Rev.* 2677 [Kahn, "Comparative Constitutionalism"].

[78] Ibid. at 2692.

[79] Roberto Unger, *What Should Legal Analysis Become?* (1996) at 9 (hereinafter Unger, *What Should Legal Analysis Become?*).

By taking seriously the idea of a culture of justification, of proportionality, of rationalism, both Kahn and Unger help us call into question an all-
too-human and all-too-hasty celebration of an actual or eventual world-wide
(so-called global) convergence of constitutional method. Turning to Unger,
proportionality-talk may be a form of "rationalizing legal analysis", a pragmatism that does not go far enough, one that reflects an institutional fetishism and
an implicit or explicit belief in convergence "toward a single set of best available practices throughout the world."[80] Kahn echoes Unger when he writes: "It
would be too much to say of comparative constitutionalists that their ambition
is to find the hidden science of constitutionalism that should unite all liberal
constitutions as variations on a common theme", but, he adds, "it would not
be exaggerating all that much."[81] In refusing to be swept away by the cult of
rationality, by the march toward an end of constitutional history, Kahn and
Unger also help us reconsider two of the actual or potential casualties of this
march forward: authority and analogy.[82]

Rehabilitating Authority?

Kahn explains that the "structure of belief that characterizes a court engaged
in judicial review" is *will* (popular sovereignty) in the United States and
reason in many other places. Paradoxically, "the most important source of
the expression of the transtemporal will of the popular sovereign in the United
States is to be found in the Supreme Court," and not electoral politics.[83] Kahn
explains:

> This distinction of reason and will marks a fundamental difference in answer-
> ing the question of what a constitution does. On one view, the constitution is
> the expression of reason within what would otherwise be a continuous con-
> flict of interests among the individuals, parties, and institutions that constitute
> the state. The problem it addresses is not the construction of a nation, but the
> just organization of interests and interest groups. Its aim is not to make one
> out of many, but rather to impose order on disorder. The foundational act
> is not the analogue of God's speaking the world into existence, but rather a

---

[80] He continues: "According to this idea the institutional evolution of the modern world is
best understood as an approach, by trial and error, toward the only political and economic
institutions that have proved capable of reconciling economic prosperity with a decent regard
to political freedom and social security." Ibid. at 8.
[81] Kahn, "Comparative Constitutionalism," *supra* note 77 at 2684.
[82] Kahn is clear to specify the aim of his inquiry (self-understanding). His "refusal to be swept"
away, then, is not the same as Unger's refusal.
[83] Kahn, "Comparative Constitutionalism," *supra* note 77 at 2696.

kind of Rawlsian inquiry into the reasonable structure of a common political project.[84]

In distinguishing will and reason, Kahn distinguishes "existential" and "experimental" constitutions or understandings of constitutions. Experimental constitutions "are subject to external norms – whether justice or efficiency – rather than constitutive of the meaning of the political".[85] In line with both Beatty and Aleinikoff, he explains that the constitutional text loses its importance in a "culture of justification" (not his words) because "[t]o say that something is unconstitutional is to say that it is unreasonable."[86] Abstract reason comes prior to a specific constitutional text. Sachs's text reflects much of Kahn's experimental constitution, but his echo of John 1:1 and reference to storytelling or myth-making highlights an inescapable existential element. Dwelling on this existential element can help one appreciate or even rehabilitate authority.

Although he does not reference her, Kahn's thinking evokes that of Arendt. In *On Revolution*, a work dedicated in large measure to the possibility of foundational acts in modern politics, Arendt writes that the Roman concept of authority, with some modifications, was carried over into the American republic. In Rome, she explains, "the function of authority was political, and it consisted in giving advice, while in the American republic the function of authority is legal and it consists in interpretation."[87] Hence, the aptness of Kahn's characterization of the Supreme Court as the truly authoritative institution, being the ultimate interpreter of the law. The relation of authority to foundation is primordial, emphasizes Arendt, as authority means "augmentation of foundations". The etymological root of *auctoritas*, says Arendt, is *augere*, "augment".[88] As an authoritative institution, the United States Supreme Court is meant to augment the founding and, thereby, stabilize and anchor the political world the founding made possible. The Court does not simply exercise universal reason or make abstract calculations but, rather, augments a singular – not universal – founding moment.[89] Elsewhere, in her essay on authority,

---

[84] Ibid. at 2697.   [85] Ibid. at 2697.

[86] Ibid. at 2697.

[87] Hannah Arendt, *On Revolution* (1963) at 201 (hereinafter Arendt, *On Revolution*).

[88] Hannah Arendt, "What is Authority?" *supra* note 13 at 121–122. Although she would not agree with Kahn about the "will of the popular sovereign," she would agree with him that the Supreme Court – and not electoral politics – has a privileged relation to the founding and the Founding Fathers.

[89] In *On Revolution*, Arendt writes that the United States Senate and Supreme Court were the "lasting institutions" for opinion and judgment, respectively. Opinion and judgment are both worldly faculties free from the coercion of pure reason and indicative of the fundamental condition of human plurality (recall the importance of world to judgment and judgment to

Arendt writes that "the loss of worldly permanence and reliability" is "politically . . . identical with the loss of authority."[90] It is significant that the loss of authority does not mean the loss of the world, but, rather, makes the world that much more precarious and fragile, and difficult to maintain.

The shift from authority to justification then risks, in Arendt's terms, jeopardizing worldly permanence and reliability. However, Arendt's response to the decline of authority in modern times is not necessarily to recuperate authority but, rather, to show the increased burden judgment must bear. In other words, to return to Sachs, the decline of authority need not lead to more justification – in terms of more reason, more rationalism – but, rather, to more worldly judgment. As opposed to rationalism, but like authority, situated, worldly judgment must rely on the past and its resources for examples.[91]

Kahn points specifically to the spread of proportionality as a reflection of a constitutional culture of reason, of reasonableness. He writes:

> Proportionality review is often criticized as a practical judgment that lacks the indicia of legal principle and instead involves the courts in making policy. This criticism, however, fails to understand the genealogy of proportionality review, which lies in the belief that the rule of law is the internalization of reason itself as a regulative ideal within the political order. Proportionality is the form that reason will take when there is no longer a faith in formalism – i.e., when reason must be sensitive to circumstance – and there is no longer a belief in a single coherent order among what are otherwise conflicting interests.[92]

As the widespread embrace of the move from authority to justification shows, Kahn is likely right about the genealogy of proportionality review. He surely is right, too, that the role of reason in proportionality's genealogy reveals the way in which it is "principled". However, Kahn goes further when he specifies that "[t]he model of judicial reasoning [of proportionality] is the situated

world). *On Revolution, supra* note 87 at 231. About opinion and judgment, she writes, "these two, politically most important, rational faculties had been almost entirely neglected by the tradition of political as well as philosophic thought."

[90] Hannah Arendt, "What is Authority?" *supra* note 13 at 95. Arendt distinguishes authority from both persuasion, "which presupposes equality and works through a process of argumentation," and violence, which involves "external means of coercion" (93). (In this sense, South Africa's apartheid culture was not one of authority. Mureinik clearly points to authority as involving coercion in his account of the bridge.)

[91] See, e.g., Mark Antaki, "The Critical Modernism of Hannah Arendt," (2007) 8 *Theoretical Inquiries in Law* 251.

[92] Kahn, "Comparative Constitutionalism," *supra* note 77 at 2698. At 2699, he adds: "If we move from national to transnational courts, the appeal of reason appears even stronger precisely because there is no counterpart to the sovereign will."

judgment of 'equity' – a form of reason already identified by Aristotle."[93] "When reasonableness replaces science," he continues, "the work of a court looks like little more than prudence".[94] (Recall that prudence is one translation of one of Aristotle's keywords: *phronesis*.) Here, Kahn equates proportionality with reasonableness, even with equitable judgment, which is a variation on Aristotelian practical wisdom. This is where he may be going too far.

Kahn's "defence" of proportionality here sounds a lot like contemporary proportionality-talk, and appears to emphasize proportionality's realism. However, Kahn may be hasty in assimilating proportionality to equity, precisely on account of proportionality's rationalism. Equity is a corrective to rules that are necessarily over- and under-inclusive. Moreover, it presupposes a shared world and seeks "what is fitting". Proportionality analysis may not be a model of situated judgment as much as a model of judgment about situations – and it aims not at what is "fitting", but at an optimal balance of interests.[95] The shift in language is important, as it reflects a much greater degree of abstraction (even if one is meant to plunge right back into a context) and the objectification of human being-in-the-world.

Rehabilitating Analogy?

Unger's work suggests that it is too quick to say that proportionality is a model of situated judgment, particularly to the extent that much proportionality-talk reflects what he calls the prejudice against analogical reasoning.[96] He suggests that the "decline of the project of nineteenth-century legal science may leave a vacuum that undisciplined analogy can once again occupy."[97] However, from a rationalist point of view, he adds: "An unreconstructed practice of analogical judgement turns out, in retrospect, to be the first, confused step toward reasoning from policy and principle. It stands to rationalizing legal analysis as crawling stands to walking."[98] From a rationalist point of view, analogical judgment is merely crawling because, in the language of this chapter, analogical judgment does not go far enough in demystifying judgment and making calculation possible. However, from a more worldly and less rationalist perspective, analogical judgment's crawling is its virtue: analogical judgment

---

[93] Ibid. at 2698.   [94] Ibid. at 2698–2699.

[95] Kahn appears to "romanticize" pre-proportionality legal reasoning by suggesting there was once a belief in "a single coherent order." But the sharing of a world does not mean otherwise conflicting "interests" are somehow all reconciled or reconcilable.

[96] Unger, *What Should Legal Analysis Become? supra* note 79 at 51.

[97] Ibid. at 59.   [98] Ibid.

stays close to the ground and does not get carried away by the promises of demystification and calculation.

Unger identifies three attributes of analogical reasoning that reflect its staying close to the ground. First, he notes "the recurrent dialectic between ascription of purpose and classification of circumstance", which means that "the minor premise of the syllogism — tricycles are (or are not) vehicles — is the whole work of analogy".[99] Second:

> [T]he guiding interests or purposes on which the analogist draws are open-ended. They do not make up a closed list, nor are they hierarchically ordered in a system of higher- and lower-order propositions, the former trumping the latter. They reflect the variety, renewal, and disorder of real human concerns. Analogical reasoning is not just some purist practice imposed upon these concerns from the vantage point of higher insight or authority; it is an integral part of their ordinary articulation in everyday life.[100]

Third, Unger adds: "Analogical reasoning is noncumulative: its repeated practice over time does not turn it, little by little, into a system of hierarchically ordered, more abstract and more concrete propositions, because the guiding interests or purposes themselves do not move toward a system of axioms and inferences."[101] To some extent, Unger's observations are reminiscent of proportionality's refusal of an abstract and context-independent ordering of the relative worth of so-called values and interests. In this respect, proportionality analysis also appears to be noncumulative. However, Unger's observations do not fit proportionality-talk in one crucial way: the analogist does not believe she can represent to herself the whole of what is at stake in a rights-dispute, perhaps by naming all the implicated interests, and then herself weigh so as to arrive at an answer or a list of unreasonable legislative answers. The following words of Unger could be said about proportionality: "The analogist wears his uncertainties on his sleeve, exhibiting them as part of his business. The rationalizing legal analyst must deny his brand of arbitrariness."[102]

The brand of arbitrariness of the analogist reflects human, finite, situated judgment struggling with what is "fitting" in a specific case. Precisely because it is finite and situated, this kind of judgment engages with the past and is not an ad hoc case-by-case method of proceeding: a succession of calculations or balances of pre-given and frozen interests are not the same as a succession of interconnected narratives that can constitute or destabilize interests in

---

[99] Ibid. at 60.   [100] Ibid. at 60.

[101] Ibid. at 61.

[102] Ibid. at 78. At 114, Unger writes: "The heart of most legal analysis in an adjudicative setting should and must be the context-oriented practice of analogical reasoning in the interpretation of statutes and past judicial decisions."

the search for what is fitting. The analogist cannot be accused of thrusting naked human reason into the various contexts to which he or she is sensitive. Proportionality analysis abstracts greatly before returning to context. To some extent, the rhetoric of proportionality analysis – values, interests, balancing – reflects this abstraction and objectification of human being in the world. Despite its claims to be pragmatic, proportionality-talk reflects a desire to turn what is a form of practical reason or wisdom into a form of theoretical reason. Note how "wisdom" just does not sound right for a model of judgment as calculation.

V. REVISITING ANALOGY AND PROPORTIONALITY

Probably unbeknownst to many contemporary jurists and judges, proportionality and analogy have common roots. Returning to these common roots can help explain the tendencies to make judgment technical or mathematical and defend proportionality by saying it is "as rational" as subsumption.[103] Returning to these common roots can also counter such tendencies. Proportionality's turn away from categorical reasoning, from deductive reasoning, is not necessarily the problem here, however. The problem is its turn away from world, its turn to abstraction and objectification.

If the aim of law is to render justice, then proportionality may be not only the last, the ultimate, rule of law,[104] but even one of the oldest rules of law, if not the oldest. In the *Nicomachean Ethics*, justice appears as proportion,[105] of which corrective, distributive, and reciprocal justice appear as different kinds. And so, the doing of corrective, distributive, and reciprocal justice are exercises in proportionality. Aristotle even models these kinds of justice and justice-doing using mathematics and geometry – pointing to an ancient link to the modern rationalism of proportionality-talk. However, this is only half the story, and we find an opportunity for insight and another key link when we look at the Greek word for "proportion". When Aristotle says that justice is a kind of proportion, the Greek word translated as "proportion" is *analogon*. He uses the same word in the *Poetics*, but to describe what we understand as analogy. There, he gives the name "analogy" to cases "where *b* is to *a* as *c* is to *d*." He gives as an example: "The wine bowl is to Dionysus as the shield to Ares."[106] If Aristotle's use of analogon in the *Ethics* appears rationalistic, his use of analogon in the *Poetics* is eminently worldly.

[103] Alexy, "On Balancing and Subsumption," *supra* note 55.
[104] Beatty, *Ultimate Rule of Law*, *supra* note 26.   [105] Aristotle, *Ethics*, Book V, iii 2–8.
[106] Aristotle, *Poetics* 1457b15 and ff as found in Jill Frank, *A Democracy of Distinction: Aristotle and the Work of Politics* (2005) at 95 (hereinafter Frank, *Democracy of Distinction*).

In an extremely thoughtful and painstaking reconstruction of Aristotle on justice, Jill Frank reads these passages in the *Ethics* and the *Poetics* together, suggesting that proportionality is grounded in, or even a variant of, analogy. As "Aristotle's formulations [in the *Ethics*] are not meant to imply mathematical rigor or deductive logic in determining justice.... the proportional equality characteristic of reciprocal and distributive justice, taking the form A:B::C:D (though somewhat differently for each), represents an analogy."[107] Indeed, "Aristotle's formulae for justice model the mode of thinking appropriate to a practice of judging that is not theoretical but practical and not deductive but generative."[108] Frank's emphasis on the practical and generative nature of the practice of judging point, in Arendtian fashion, to judgment's primordial significance in world-maintaining and world-constituting. It is no surprise, then, that Frank writes that "[d]oing justice involves producing felicitous analogies, which is to say, practicing the virtue of good judgment."[109]

The production of "felicitous analogies" is the work of practical wisdom or *phronesis*. Producing felicitous analogies involves finding the "right words" that hearken to a shared world in the "right way". Finding these words help one and others "see" the specificity of a singular situation while allowing us to relate it to other situations. These right words, however, are not simply "there" to be found just like the "sight" of the specificity of the singular situation is not "there" to be seen. Hence, the generative character of judgment. Maintaining *this* world necessarily involves its constitution as a different one.

Although Aristotle "is sometimes treated as the authority for the syllogistic account of judging", Frank notes how "in Aristotle's hands, the syllogism, when applied to practical matters, is not driven by the general rule or major premise".[110] Because the minor premise is key, "perception does the primary work of judgment". Analogical thinking, however, is also "cognitive, involving some universalization and abstraction.... It appreciates particulars in their differences and it compares these differences under a common term. But it finds the common term without rendering the particulars general."[111] To put the matter somewhat differently, thoughtful perception is indispensable to judgment (and justification), which is essentially about seeing (or making visible). This seeing (analogy) grounds any "calculation" (proportionality) and is, therefore, prior to it.

---

[107] Ibid. at 97. She adds: "The same can be true of corrective justice, which can be understood in terms of proportional equality as well, when A:B = 1." Ibid. at 97–98.
[108] Ibid. at 98.   [109] Ibid. at 98.
[110] Ibid. at 95.   [111] Ibid. at 95.

To return to Arendt and Kant and Sachs' reminder that judges work with words, the "common term" is not gained from an objectifying, theoretical point of view but from worldly, situated judgment involving what Frank calls "discursive exchange". Indeed, Frank's understanding of Aristotle on judgment and analogical thinking is tied to her interpretation of reciprocal justice, or the exchange of goods. As she explains, "[L]ike the use that allows for reciprocal exchange of goods and services, the felicitous use of analogies arises in and depends on a context of discursive exchange."[112] In her reconstruction of Aristotle, two goods exchanged in barter are treated "*as if* they were the same."[113] There is no theoretical commensurability, only practical, situated, contingent acts of commensuration grounded in use.

The appeal of theoretical commensurability, so prominent in contemporary proportionality-talk, is reminiscent of the rise of money. As Frank writes, "[T]he rise of money . . . encourages people to focus on exchange value rather than on use."[114] When money takes on a life of its own, so to speak, particulars – that is, singulars – are no longer so easily perceived as such; they are more easily objectified. Not unlike the objectification of exchange that comes along with the rise of money, the rise of proportionality risks us becoming divorced from practical, situated, contingent acts of commensuration grounded in use and that demand worldliness and practical wisdom. Such commensuration grounded in use becomes theoretical commensurability grounded in exchange, abstracted and pulled away from the world. Indeed, when the conventional ground of money (*nomisma* is grounded in *nomos*) is forgotten, situated judgment can give way to quantitative judgment about objectified situations.

Frank's work on Aristotle shows how futile and dangerous it is to attempt to disentangle *logismos* from *Logos*, and proportionality from analogy, in practical matters. Proportionality-talk's rationalism is manifest in its desire to disentangle these, in its impatience at the messiness of their entanglement.[115] As Linda Meyer, echoing Frank, explains in a section on common law reasoning in her book *The Justice of Mercy*, deciding which factors are relevant or not when making analogies is "a complex judgment of pattern finding, more perception than deduction."[116] Seeing the perception at work in judgment, reading the *analogon* of the *Ethics* together with the *analogon* of the *Poetics*, allows Frank to put the world back into judgment or, as Meyer puts it in a chapter fittingly

---

[112] Ibid. at 97.   [113] Ibid. at 89.
[114] Ibid. at 90.
[115] However, the entangling of *logismos* and *Logos*, of counting and recounting, is both age-old and inescapable. For example, Miller invites us to think of the bank-"teller" or the accountant and what it is to give an account. William Ian Miller, *Eye for an Eye* (2006) at 226.
[116] Meyer, *Justice of Mercy, supra* note 8 at 31.

entitled "Before Reason", to highlight the "being in the world of judgment and legal reasoning".[117] Although Sachs repeats the mantra of proportionality, his worldliness is manifest through his book, and particularly in his insistence that, for judges, "[i]n the beginning and in the end is the word."[118] Sachs's insistence on the word reveals the worldly burden of both judgment and justification as one of "discursive felicity". Paradoxically, a good calculation requires that one find the right words.

[117] Ibid. at 30.
[118] Sachs, *Strange Alchemy, supra* note 15 at 270.

PART IV

PROPORTIONALITY
AND REASONING

14 Proportionality and Incommensurability

Timothy Endicott

The judges of the European Court of Human Rights govern certain important aspects of life in forty-seven countries across Europe. The European Convention on Human Rights guarantees a right to respect for private and family life.[1] The judges have interpreted that right to prohibit an otherwise lawful deportation of an illegal immigrant, if the impact on his or her family life (or on the family life of his or her partner or child) outweighs the public purpose in deportation. And they have held that it is their responsibility to decide whether one outweighs the other. The cases on immigration deportation are salient instances of the newly dramatic effect that the European Convention is having in this century, particularly because of the judges' doctrine of proportionality.

The proportionality doctrine requires the judges to reconcile incommensurable interests. The judges and many commentators call the reconciliation "balancing", but the interests at stake cannot actually be weighed with each other on any sort of scales. If the judges are purporting to balance things that cannot actually be balanced, it may seem that the European Convention involves a departure from the rule of law, in favor of arbitrary rule by judges. I will argue that the judicial resolution of disputes over incommensurabilities is not in itself a departure from the rule of law; the rule of law demands a system in which judges reconcile incommensurable interests. But some theorists have seen a potential in proportionality for rationality, transparency, objectivity, and legitimacy, which the doctrine cannot actually deliver. And proportionality reasoning involves potential and actual pathologies, by which I mean structured tendencies toward misconceived decisions.

---

[1] European Convention for the Protection of Human Rights and Fundamental Freedoms, 4 November 1950, ETS 5, Article 8 (hereinafter "European Convention").

I conclude by commenting on some of these dangers, to illustrate the claim that they all depend on particular mistakes and do not arise automatically from the judges' role in resolving conflicts among incommensurable interests.

I. BALANCING THE UNBALANCEABLE: DEPORTATION AND FAMILY LIFE

The right to respect for family life in Article 8 of the European Convention has become a very common recourse for people who have no right to stay in the United Kingdom under that country's immigration rules. Whether seeking asylum, or entering the country irregularly, or entering on a visa and then applying for ordinary immigration, or overstaying illegally, would-be immigrants are often in the country long enough to develop family ties. And then, an eventual refusal of permission to remain in the country will most likely be detrimental to their family life. The courts have held that respect for family life requires the state not to do something that is detrimental to a person's family life, if the detriment is disproportionate to the value of the public goal that is being pursued. The House of Lords decided in *R (Huang) v. Home Secretary* that the question is "whether the refusal of leave to enter or remain . . . taking full account of all considerations weighing in favour of the refusal, prejudices the family life of the applicant in a manner sufficiently serious to amount to a breach of the fundamental right protected by Article 8."[2] Initially, some decisions had suggested that a deportation would only be held to violate Article 8 if it had an exceptionally detrimental impact on family life,[3] or that the role of the courts was only to decide whether other authorities had done a fair job of assessing the proportionality of the action.[4] But the courts have turned away from these restrained approaches, and have assumed responsibility to decide what would be proportionate.[5] Since *Huang*, it is up

---

[2] *R (Huang) v. Home Secretary*, (hereinafter *Huang*) [2007] U.K.H.L. 11 at para. 20.
[3] *R (Razgar) v. Home Secretary*, [2004] U.K.H.L. 27: "Decisions taken pursuant to the lawful operation of immigration control will be proportionate in all save a small minority of exceptional cases, identifiable only on a case by case basis", at para. 20 per Lord Bingham.
[4] "[A] breach will only occur where the decision is outwith the range of reasonable responses to the question as to where a fair balance lies between the conflicting interests. Once it is accepted that the balance could be struck fairly either way, the Secretary of State cannot be regarded as having infringed the claimant's Article 8 rights by concluding that he should be removed.": *Edore v. Secretary of State for the Home Department*, [2003] E.W.C.A. Civ. 716 at para. 44, Lord Justice Simon Brown; the decision was overruled in *Huang*. On Lord Brown's approach to the courts' role in proportionality reasoning, see also his dissenting reasons in *Quila*, *infra* note 19.
[5] See *Huang*, *supra* note 2 at para. 20.

to judges to decide whether the impact on a claimant's family life is *too serious* in light of legitimate public purposes.[6] The question is not just whether the burden on the complainant is necessary to achieve a legitimate purpose; if it is necessary for the purpose, then the government must not pursue that purpose if the detriment to an interest protected by the European Convention outweighs the public benefit of a deportation.

II. WHAT GOES INTO THE SCALES?

The word "proportionality" is often used as a term for a set of criteria for assessment of public decisions, in which the judge asks whether: (1) a public authority interfering with a freedom or (under Article 8) with family life is pursuing a legitimate purpose; (2) there is a rational connection between that purpose and the measure that interferes with freedom or family life; and (3) another measure (not involving such an interference) could have been used instead to achieve the purpose. Finally, the judge asks, if the answer to the first two questions is "yes" and the answer to the third question is "no", (4) whether the measure should still be found to violate the right in question, on the ground that its impact on the protected interest is too great in comparison with the benefit of pursuing the public purpose in the way that the impugned measure would pursue it. This last issue is sometimes called the issue of "proportionality *stricto sensu*."[7] I will use the word "proportionality" as a term for proportionality *stricto sensu*. The other criteria do not involve the question of whether the pursuit of a public purpose is proportionate to some detriment to private interests; that question presupposes those other criteria.

Proportionality involves a balance between public interests and the claimant's private interests (or between the claimant's interests and other

---

[6] Or at least, it is up to judges unless children are involved; if the illegal immigrant has a child who is a United Kingdom citizen, neither the government nor the judges have much choice: "[T]he best interests of the child must be a primary consideration": *ZH (Tanzania) v. Secretary of State for the Home Department*, [2011] U.K.S.C. 4 at para. 33. That consideration may conceivably be outweighed by other considerations, but not by considerations as to the parent's misconduct (such as immigration fraud), or by considerations such as the parent's knowledge that he or she had no right to start a family in the country, because children "are not to be blamed for that" (para. 33). So the immigrant wins, if there is a child in the country who would benefit from the immigrant's presence in the country, unless there is some extraordinary circumstance.

Otherwise, the decision is up to the judge, and attempting to compare one case with another would be "entirely inappropriate" as all such cases are "highly fact sensitive": *RS (Uganda) v. Secretary of State for the Home Department*, [2011] E.W.C.A. Civ. 1749 at para. 1 (LJ Patten).

[7] E.g., Aharon Barak, "Proportionality and Principled Balancing," (2010) 4 *Law & Ethics of Human Rights* 1 at 6.

private interests). In our example of the refusal of permission to stay in the United Kingdom, the immigrant's interest in staying with family in the UK, and also their family members' interests in her staying with them, go into one pan of the scales. Detriment to that interest counts against a refusal. What public purpose could outweigh the detriment? The European Convention recognizes that an interference with family life may be justifiable "in the interests of national security, public safety or the economic well-being of the country, for the prevention of disorder or crime, for the protection of health or morals, or for the protection of the rights and freedoms of others".[8] We can imagine ways in which immigration controls may possibly serve those interests. But the British government has never actually said whether its purpose in prohibiting free entry to the UK is to pursue any of these good purposes. Limiting immigration to a country is not necessarily unprincipled, but the British law and practice will not tell you what the principles are.

By an interpretation of the abstract right to respect for family life, the judges have taken on the role of weighing the immeasurable (that is, the gravity of the impact of deportation on a family) against the unspecified (that is, whatever benefit might be secured for legitimate state purposes through immigration control). They assess the value of pursuing public purposes in the way that the legislature or the government has done or proposes to do. Or to be more exact (as none of the deportation cases explain what the public interest is), you might say that the judges have *not* assessed the public interest in the proposed deportation, but have simply allowed that there is some public purpose in immigration control, and decided that the private interest outweighs it in the particular case.[9]

The consequence has been a series of decisions in which the Court of Appeal and the Supreme Court have had to decide whether family ties in the UK make it unlawful[10] to deport a person with no regular immigration status, or to deport a noncitizen who has committed crimes. The court simply asks the open-ended question whether, in light of the public interests at stake, the

---

[8] Article 8(2).

[9] In *Huang, supra* note 2, the House of Lords listed four considerations in favor of refusal of permission to remain in the UK, such as making immigration control "workable, predictable, consistent and fair as between one applicant and another" (at para. 16). But the purposes – if it has any – *of immigration control* are not on the list of considerations. Yet reasons for immigration control, if there are any (and not just reasons for consistency) are the considerations that conflict with the personal interests at stake in the case.

[10] Under the Human Rights Act 1998, s. 6, which makes it unlawful for a public authority such as the Home Office to act in a way that is incompatible with the rights in the European Convention, unless primary legislation requires it.

proposed action would have *too serious* an impact on the claimant's family life.

There has been a parallel development – with two important differences – in the law of extradition. No one is extradited from the UK today without first getting a hearing in court on their claim that the resulting disruption to their family life would outweigh the public purpose. The first difference between the role of Article 8 in extradition and in immigration deportation is that the extradition claimants generally lose. As Lady Hale put it in *HH v. Italy*, "[T]he balancing exercise is the same" in extradition as in immigration deportation, but "the nature and weight of the interests to be put into each side of the scale" may differ.[11] The immigration claimants win if they have serious family connections in the United Kingdom; the extradition claimants ordinarily lose. The second, related, difference is that in their extradition decisions, the judges *do* state the public benefit of extradition (which, of course, is a purpose that is more readily cognizable to judges in their role as judges, than are the purposes of immigration control).[12] The judges do not state the public benefit of a deportation, if there is any, in the immigration cases.

Is the state's decision-making process distorted by a pretense: that judges can weigh the unweighable? In the immigration deportation cases in particular, the scales of justice become a poor symbol for the judges' role, when judges take over the open-ended task not merely of weighing up the unweighable personal considerations, but also of deciding how serious any countervailing public interest is. To make these decisions, they have to throw the scales out the window and just choose.

III. THE INCOMMENSURABILITY PROBLEM

The public interest in a deportation cannot be weighed in a common set of scales against the personal interests in continuing family life in the United

---

[11] [2012] U.K.S.C. 25 at para. 30. *HH* itself is the only case I am aware of in which the courts have prohibited an extradition on the ground of the impact on the alleged offender's children. The case was described as exceptional, but the law imposes no criterion of exceptionality; the court is simply meant to "weigh the nature and gravity of the interference [with the family life of the offender and of his or her children] against the importance of the aims pursued" (at para. 30). See also *Norris v. United States (No. 2)*, [2010] U.K.S.C. 9 (hereinafter *Norris*) at para. 54: "[W]e have been referred to no reported case, whether at Strasbourg or in this jurisdiction, where extradition has been refused because of the interference that it would cause to family life."

[12] See *Norris* ibid. at paras. 82 (Lord Phillips), 105 (Lord Mance).

Kingdom. The interests on each side are incommensurable.[13] In fact, the personal considerations cannot be *weighed*: there is no scale of measurement for the gravity of the impact of a deportation on a family. The immeasurability of an interest or set of interests entails incommensurability between that interest and conflicting interests.[14] And also, the public interest is incommensurable with the private interests because the public interest, assuming that there is one – and if it were fully specified – would involve the achievement of complex goods that are deeply different in kind from the complex goods that may be involved in a family's uninterrupted life in the UK. How good is it for the UK if a particular irregular migrant is deported? How good is it for that migrant and his family if he is able to stay with his family in the UK? Even if these two questions were answered *well* in a particular case, there is no reason to expect that the answers would offer the court a ground for saying that one good is greater than the other.

It is, needless to say, possible for a public interest to be critically important or somewhat serious or minor or trivial, and of course private interests, too, can be more or less serious in a variety of ways. But the magnitude of the interests at stake on each side in the deportation cases cannot be measured in equivalent units of gravity. For any given articulation of the public purpose (but there is none in these cases), there would be no rational basis for deciding *just how serious* the effect must be on the person's family life before it would outweigh the public benefit of the deportation.

The metaphor of the scales of justice is inapt in human rights adjudication, where the decision involves a choice between incommensurables. In a particular case, because of that incommensurability, there may be no rational basis for saying that the impact on family life would be disproportionate

---

[13] On the role and importance in general of incommensurability in practical reasoning, see Joseph Raz, *The Morality of Freedom* (1988) chapter 13; John Finnis, "Commensuration and Public Reason" in Ruth Chang (ed.), *Incommensurability, Incomparability, and Practical Reason* (1997), and "Natural Law and Legal Reasoning" in Robert P. George (ed.), *Natural Law Theory* (1992); Timothy Endicott, *Vagueness in Law* (2000), chapters 3.5 and 7.3.

[14] See Endicott, *Vagueness in Law*, ibid. chapter 3.5. Immeasurability also entails the failure of an ingenious attempt to use social choice theory to "justify proportionality analysis by demonstrating that the weighing of competing rights and values is not necessarily mere judicial hand-waving": Paul-Erik Veel, "Incommensurability, Proportionality, and Rational Legal Decision-Making," (2010) 4 *Law & Ethics of Human Rights* 177 at 180. Veel's "choice rule" depends on a significant cardinal measurement of the values at stake, and he has to adopt an arbitrary rule ("a conceptual device to create numerical scales of cardinal significance for the realizations of values") to construct such a measurement (at 200–201).

or would not be disproportionate. There seems to be a general objection to proportionality reasoning by judges:

> **The incommensurability problem:** if there is no rational basis for deciding one way rather than the other, then the result seems to represent a departure from the rule of law, in favour of arbitrary rule by judges.

One obviously attractive response to the incommensurability problem is to argue that there is actually one criterion at stake, after all. Aharon Barak has given the best articulation of this defence of proportionality reasoning: "My answer [to critics of proportionality reasoning in human rights adjudication who "claim that it attempts to balance incommensurable items"] is that a common base for comparison exists, namely the social marginal importance."[15] Barak's solution to the incommensurability problem is to say that instead of balancing two things against each other that cannot be compared in light of conflicting values, the judge applies a *single* criterion: social importance (or, as Barak also calls it, "relative social importance"[16]). The social importance of deportation is not incommensurable with the social importance of letting the person stay with his or her family in the country, he argues, because social importance is the same thing on both sides of the scales; the judge can decide which way the scales swing in light of a single criterion.

It might seem objectionable to suggest that the single criterion is the *social* importance of the interests on each side, as if the court were not deciding on the rights of the person in question but on whether some restriction on freedom, or some interference with privacy or family life, is important enough to society. But bias in favor of the majority and against the individual is not at all what Barak is recommending, as can be seen from his own work as a judge. He wrote, "Our democracy is characterized by the fact that it imposes limits on the ability to violate human rights; that it is based on the recognition that surrounding the individual there is a wall protecting his rights, which cannot be breached even by the majority."[17] In cases such as the British deportation

---

[15] Aharon Barak, "Proportionality and Principled Balancing," *supra* note 7, at 15–16. For a more general argument that there is virtually no incommensurability in value judgments and normative judgments – and none at all when the law requires an answer to a dispute – see Ronald Dworkin, "On Gaps in the Law" in Neil MacCormick and Paul Amselek (eds.), *Controversies about Law's Ontology* (1991) 84, and "Objectivity and Truth: You'd Better Believe It," (1996) 25 *Philosophy & Public Affairs* 87.

[16] Barak, ibid. at 7.

[17] *Beit Sourik Village Council v. Government of Israel* [2004] Isr. S.C. 58(5) 807, quoted in Barak, ibid. at 17 (hereinafter *Beit Sourik*).

cases, Barak has in mind the social importance of respecting the interests protected in a bill of rights (and in particular, the importance of respecting privacy and family life), as well as the importance of pursuing public purposes by proceeding with, for example, a deportation. As Barak puts it, "[T]here must be a proportionate balance between the social benefit of realizing the appropriate goal, and the harm caused to the right."[18]

This approach does not ignore private interests, because it recognizes the importance of respecting those interests; but this very aspect of Barak's approach means that the incommensurability problem remains. In fact, the problem is undiminished. It is quite true that respect for family life is important, and that immigration control is also important (or *may* be important, for all we can tell from the British cases). That does not mean that the importance of a person's family life is commensurable with the importance of immigration control.

Identifying a single criterion does not eliminate incommensurability if the application of the criterion depends on considerations that are themselves incommensurable. If we are trying to decide whether to go to a restaurant with excellent food that is expensive, or a restaurant with less-than-excellent food that is cheaper, you would be right to say that there is a common base for comparison (we could call it "preferability"); and you would be right to insist that there *may* be rational ground for judging that one restaurant is preferable to another (because, for example, there can be definite reason to choose a much-less-expensive restaurant where the food is almost as good). But you would have no reason to claim that the considerations that determine which restaurant is preferable are commensurable, and no reason to think that, for every pair of alternatives, there is determinate reason in favor of one choice between the two.

[18] Barak, ibid. at 6. Although, for the reasons explained here, Barak cannot be accused of subordinating human rights to the interests of the majority, there is a suggestion in his work that the force of a human right depends on the "conceptions" of the society in question: "The social importance of a right – and by extension its weight in relation to conflicting principles – is derived from its underlying rationale and its importance within the framework of society's fundamental conceptions" (ibid. at 9). And he asserts, without explanation, that "the concept of a 'right' derives from the concept of society; without society, rights have no meaning" (ibid. at 3). For an argument that the concept of a right – and, in fact, the concept of a human right – do not at all depend on the concept of society, see Timothy Endicott, "The Infant in the Snow" in Timothy Endicott, Joshusa Getzler, and Edwin Peel (eds.), *Properties of Law* (2006) 348. But I do not think that this arbitrary restriction on the concept of a right affects Barak's defence of proportionality reasoning by judges in human rights cases; he assumes that human rights are important to whatever society we are talking about.

In human rights cases, the availability of the covering value, "importance", does not give us any reason to think that the grounds on which judgments are to be made are commensurable. Major incommensurabilities need to be resolved in order to make the judgment that Barak recommends as to whether it is more socially important to interfere with family life (or freedom of speech or of religion) in a particular way, or more socially important not to do so.

IV. RADICAL INCOMMENSURABILITY AND VAGUE INCOMMENSURABILITY

Perhaps the motivation for denying incommensurability arises from the danger of confusion between different kinds of incommensurability. Let's call one "vague incommensurability" and the other "radical incommensurability." Incommensurability is radical when there is no rational basis for comparing *any two objects* in a given domain, in respect of some property or properties. The sky can be blue, and a person's mood can be blue, but they cannot be compared as to their blueness. Even when the sky is *very* blue and your mood is not particularly blue, it makes no sense (or only a figurative sort of sense) to say that the sky is bluer than your mood. The two items in each pair (when one item in the pair is your mood, and the other item is the sky) are *incomparable*. Note the crucial difference between incomparability and incommensurability: if two things are incommensurable, they cannot be measured against each other; if they are incomparable, they cannot be compared with each other. If your mood and the sky are incomparable as to color, there is no reason for saying that one is bluer or less blue or that the two are equally blue. The incommensurability is radical.

The urge to deny incommensurability may spring from the assumption that incommensurability must be radical, combined with the sound insight that for some pairs of alternatives (for example, for some pairs of conflicting interests in human rights cases), a comparison is possible.

Instead of being radical, incommensurability is a source of vagueness when some pairs can be compared in respect of some property or properties, and some cannot. Colors are vaguely incommensurable because of their complex components. A patch of turquoise may be neither bluer than a patch of navy nor less blue nor equally blue. If the turquoise becomes gradually more green, or if the navy becomes darker, one will eventually be less blue than the other. The two may never be precisely as blue as each other. The property of blueness involves hue and saturation and brightness, and these properties are vaguely incommensurable.

Radical Incommensurability – A blue sky, a blue mood	*All* pairs are incomparable (that is, your mood is never bluer than the sky or less blue or equally blue).	The comparative term ("bluer than") has no literal sense.
Vague Incommensurability – Two-colored objects	*Some* pairs are incomparable (that is, sometimes one is bluer than the other or they are equally blue, and sometimes it is indeterminate whether either is bluer, and they are not equally blue).	The comparative term ("bluer than") makes sense, and is vague (so that for some pairs, one item is determinately bluer than the other, and for other pairs, it is indeterminate whether one is bluer than the other).

The color blue is affected by vague incommensurability, because there is no answer to the question, "What hue is required for an object of *this* saturation to be precisely as blue as an object of *that* saturation?" Sometimes the sky is determinately bluer than the water in the background of the *Mona Lisa*, and sometimes the water in the background of the *Mona Lisa* is determinately bluer than the sky, and sometimes it is indeterminate which is bluer.

V. VAGUE INCOMMENSURABILITY IN HUMAN RIGHTS CASES

Incommensurabilities between public and private interests in human rights cases need not be radical. But they are dramatically more significant than incommensurabilities among the components of colors. It makes sense to say that the impact of some public action on a protected interest is less important than the attainment of the purpose of the action. It may be definitely true or definitely false in some cases, and neither definitely true nor definitely false in others. Some public actions have a detrimental impact on family life that is clearly less important than the pursuit of some public purposes, and some public actions have a detrimental impact on family life that is clearly more important than the pursuit of some public purposes. These facts are quite consistent with the view that there are significant incommensurabilities in the considerations at stake, because not all incommensurability is radical.

Consider *R (Quila) v. Secretary of State for the Home Department*.[19] The immigration rules provided that a marriage visa (permitting the spouse of a

[19] [2011] U.K.S.C. 45.

person settled in the United Kingdom to enter or to remain in the country) would not ordinarily be issued unless both partners were at least twenty-one years old. The government had raised the age from eighteen. The purpose was to deter forced marriage, by protecting young women from family pressure, motivated by the prospect of getting a marriage visa for a would-be immigrant. This is a classic case in which proportionality was the right question – first for the minister to ask herself in formulating the rules, and then for the courts to ask (given their interpretation of their role) in considering a challenge to the rules on the basis of Article 8. The purpose was legitimate (as the Supreme Court unanimously accepted). The technique used to pursue the purpose had the effect of interfering with the family life of eighteen to twenty year olds who were not forced into marriage, by imposing a delay on the entry of one partner to the UK. The Court set out to decide whether that effect outweighed the value in pursuing a public purpose by imposing the increase in the age for marriage visas.

The *Quila* problem illustrates vague incommensurability: it might conceivably be the case that the delay would have a massive impact on the practice of forced marriage or virtually no impact, and that the delay would affect very many voluntary couples or very few. If the delay would have a massive dampening impact on forced marriage and little impact on voluntary couples, the conclusion would be irresistible that the interference with the family life of voluntary spouses is not disproportionate to the step taken to protect the rights of others. If the delay would have only a trivial impact on forced marriage and a serious impact on very many young couples, the conclusion would be irresistible that the interference is disproportionate. But if we knew all the extremely complex social facts, there might be no conclusive rational grounds for deciding that the good effect would or would not be greater than the detrimental impact. The value of deterring forced migration through this step is vaguely incommensurable with the detriment to the family life of young voluntary spouses whose entry to the UK is delayed. Depending on the magnitude of each value, one may be clearly greater than the other. But even where all the facts are known, there may be no conclusive reason for deciding that either is greater than the other.

In fact, in the *Quila* case, little information was available to the Home Secretary or the Court. The government could not quantify the usefulness of the measure in fighting forced marriage. Faced with a number of young couples who were inconvenienced by the delay in starting their married life together in the place where they wanted to live, and faced with a nebulous prospect that the measure might deter some forced marriages, the United Kingdom Supreme Court held that the measure was disproportionate in its impact on voluntary spouses (and therefore unlawful under the UK Human Rights Act).[20]

The *Quila* situation is a reminder that vague incommensurabilities can be very significant (so that the incommensurability problem is a significant problem), even when they are not radical.

VI. RADICAL INCOMMENSURABILITY IN HUMAN RIGHTS CASES

When two considerations are vaguely incommensurable, a substantial change in one consideration is relevant (it may or may not be decisive), even where there are multiple, incommensurable considerations. Radical incommensurability arises in human rights cases, in which a substantial change in the public interest can make no difference to an overall decision.

A minor benefit to a public interest does not justify torturing someone; and if the benefit to the public interest increases, we are still not even *moving in the direction* of a justification for torturing a person. In human rights cases, the prohibition on torture is the paradigm of radical incommensurability between protected private interests and public purposes. There are no provisos to the prohibition on torture in Article 3 of the European Convention. Article 15 provides that there can be no derogation from Article 3. This right is absolute. The United Nations Convention against Torture provides that "No exceptional circumstances whatsoever, whether a state of war or a threat of war, internal political instability or any other public emergency, may be invoked as a justification of torture."[21]

It may seem that the public interest (in, for example, public security) is *necessarily less important* than that interest, and therefore that it is *not* incommensurable with the person's interest in not being tortured. But pointing out the necessity of the comparison is simply another way of describing a form of incommensurability. This is a reminder of the difference between incommensurability (the impossibility of measuring two considerations in the same

---

[20] Lord Brown, dissenting, wrote:

> What value . . . is to be attached to preventing a single forced marriage? What cost should each disappointed couple be regarded as paying? Really these questions are questions of policy and should be for government rather than us. . . . Article 8 is a difficult provision which has already led to some highly contentious, not to say debateable, decisions. Upon that I am sure we would all agree. In a sensitive context such as that of forced marriages it would seem to me not merely impermissible but positively unwise for the courts yet again to frustrate government policy except in the clearest of cases (*Quila, supra* note 19 at paras. 91, 97).

[21] Convention against Torture and Other Cruel, Inhuman or Degrading Treatment or Punishment, 1984, U.N.T.S., vol. 1465, p. 85, Article 2.2.

scales) and incomparability (the impossibility of finding rational grounds for choosing between two alternatives). Incomparability may or may not result from incommensurability. When incommensurability is vague, incomparability arises in some cases and not in others; when incommensurability is radical, comparisons may be senseless or may hold by necessity. Whenever two considerations are incommensurable, assessment of some action in respect of those considerations cannot depend on finding a common measure for the conflicting considerations.

Of course, another way of expressing the radical incommensurability between considerations of private interest and public interest under Article 3 is to say that the public interest is irrelevant.

VII. THE SOLUTION TO THE INCOMMENSURABILITY PROBLEM

The problem, remember, is that if courts are "balancing" things that *cannot* be balanced, then their decision seems to represent a departure from the rule of law, in favor of arbitrary rule by judges. It is true that the metaphor of the scales is misleading. The vague incommensurabilities involved in the proportionality judgments in *Quila* and the deportation cases mean that there are bound to be wide ranges of cases in these fields, in which there is no rational ground for decision one way rather than the other.

To solve the problem, we need to remind ourselves that courts often have to pull off such impossible feats. If you cause me loss by your tort, the law gives me a right to compensation that is aimed "to put the injured parties into the same position as far as money will allow as if they had not sustained the wrong for which they are being compensated".[22] Suppose that by your negligence you cause me a chronic, serious backache. In such a circumstance, it is actually impossible to identify a sum of money that will put me in the same position as if I did not have a backache.[23] And there is, of course, no sum of money that will put a child in the same position as if her mother or father had not

---

[22] *Rees v. Darlington Memorial Hospital NHS Trust*, [2003] U.K.H.L. 52, [2004] 1 A.C. 309 (House of Lords), at para. 73, citing Lord Blackburn in *Livingstone v. The Rawyards Coal Company* (1879–80) L.R. 5 App. Cas. 25 at 39 (House of Lords): "... that sum of money which will put the party who has been injured, or who has suffered, in the same position as he would have been in if he had not sustained the wrong for which he is now getting his compensation".

[23] Damages for pain and suffering are the most obvious and poignant example of incommensurabilities in general damages, but I think that the same problem regularly arises in general damages, where (for example) the court must identify a sum of money that will put you in the same position as if your reputation had not been tarnished, or as if the heating in your home had been installed by the contractual date rather than delayed for months.

been killed in an accident. There is no rational basis for saying that the just amount of compensation is *this* rather than *that*. Yet for such injuries, the court will quite rightly award compensation; it will award substantial damages, but not an infinite amount. It will try to do something decent in balancing the unbalanceable.

Similarly, although every civilized legal system is committed to proportionate sentencing in criminal cases, there is no precise period of incarceration that is equal in its penal seriousness to the seriousness of the criminality of a rape or a serious assault. A uniform fixed penalty for all serious assaults would be arbitrary. There is no practical alternative to a judicial power and responsibility to balance the unbalanceable – the seriousness of the crime with the severity of the sentence.[24]

The incommensurabilities in civil damages and in criminal sentencing are only particularly dramatic instances of this essential judicial role. Legal systems justifiably – and, in fact, necessarily – authorize judges to reconcile incommensurable considerations. Very many instances arise from the needs of legal systems, for example:

- the need to give courts general interpretive responsibility in many areas of the law (instead of requiring them, for example, to refer questions of statutory interpretation to the legislature, or to refuse to give effect to contracts when the parties disagree as to their interpretation, or to hold a will to be ineffective when there are incommensurable considerations in favour of interpreting it in different ways);
- the need for courts that control their own procedure, with discretion to resolve disputes as to process where there are incommensurable considerations on either side;
- the need for courts to resolve questions of fact (in civil cases, "on a balance of probabilities") when witnesses who are persuasive in very different ways give conflicting evidence;
- the need for discretion as to costs in the light of conflicting and incommensurable considerations;
- the need for courts to make judgments of probability in remedies; and so on.[25]

---

[24] See Morris J Fish, "An Eye for an Eye: Proportionality as a Moral Principle of Punishment," (2008) 28 O.J.L.S. 57.
[25] Paul Craig gives further instances in "The Nature of Rationality Review," (2013) *Current Legal Problems* 1.

Some of these judicial roles in resolving incommensurabilities are necessary features of a legal system (such as some form of general interpretive responsibility on the part of independent tribunals), and some arise from techniques of ordering adopted in a particular system (such as discretion in schemes of litigation funding). We actually need a system that authorizes judges to balance the unbalanceable. Perhaps we can say that the judges' power to balance the unbalanceable is not arbitrary (in the pejorative sense of arbitrariness that is relevant to the rule of law), where it is necessary, for good legal purposes, that judges should have that power. No system of compensation for civil wrongs could provide precise rules of compensation for personal injuries (or for the loss of the life of a relative), unless those rules themselves were arbitrary. It might actually be useful to have a fixed rate of compensation for the loss of an eye, for example. But that itself is an arbitrary measure, and if that approach were taken far enough to remove the judges' role in balancing the unbalanceable, the arbitrariness would become extreme and unjust. Leaving the matter of compensation to the discretion of judges is less arbitrary than trying to take away the discretion. So the extraordinary indeterminacies in the law of remedies for civil damages do not mean that the resultant judicial discretion is a departure from the rule of law.

That is so, I think, even if the incommensurabilities in those cases are *radical*. And some of them are. It is not just that there is no period of imprisonment that is precisely equal to the criminality of a rape; increasing the sentence would not even *move in the direction* of equating the seriousness of the sanction with the criminality of the conduct of the defendant. And increasing the damages awarded to a child whose parent has been killed by a tortious action does not even move in the direction of putting the child in the same position as if the loss had not been suffered. And yet, still we need a system in which courts, in a rule-governed order, will respond to the tort or the crime with some substantial (but not infinite) measure of redress. And even if the incommensurabilities in the relevant considerations are radical, it will have to be a precise measure, so that the prison authorities will know on which day the prisoner has a right to freedom, and so that the tortfeasor will know how much he must pay and the court will know whether the order has been fulfilled. The scales of justice are not a good representation of the judges' role in deciding the amount of general damages, or in criminal sentencing, or in deciding whether the age for marriage visas can lawfully be raised from eighteen to twenty-one in an attempt to fight forced marriage.

The judges' role in resolving the extraordinary incommensurabilities in human rights law is not an arbitrary power, just because the considerations at stake are incommensurable. Or at least, it is not arbitrary if it is necessary for good legal purposes that the judges should have power to impose their reconciliation of the considerations on other branches of government.

Is it necessary? The fact that human rights are fundamental and inviolable does not entail that judges must have that power. In the constitution of every state, and in all of the state's law and practice, it ought to be presupposed that there are human interests that must be respected and that need protection against abuse. Respect for human rights is a responsibility in justice of every agency of government, and not a special judicial responsibility. Why should anyone be ruled by the judges' assessment of human rights? To justify judicial review of other public authorities' decisions on human rights grounds, a further premise is needed besides the moral force of human rights. I take the following further premise to be a presupposition of the Canadian Charter of Rights and Freedoms, and of the European Convention, and of the John Marshall doctrine on the justiciability of the United States Bill of Rights. If it does not hold, then those arrangements give judges an unwarranted role in governance.

> **The institutional premise:** the respect that all public authorities must have for certain human interests can best be secured by a power in an independent tribunal of the state (or even, in Europe, by an international court) to pass judgment on the justice of pursuing public purposes in ways that affect those interests.

The institutional premise implies that the relevant judicial institutions can do well enough at identifying fundamental human rights, and that the relevant executive and legislative decision makers may have contempt for those rights, or, at best, cannot be relied on to identify them in a way that is undistorted by their pursuit of public purposes.

People (reasonable people who are committed to respect for human rights) deeply disagree about these cases, and there may be no rational ground for decision one way or the other.[26] These facts do not in themselves mean that judges should not be resolving the incommensurabilities. But we will see that

---

[26] Note that these two phenomena – deep disagreement and absence of rational grounds for decision – are different! It is a common mistake to suppose that if people disagree, then there is automatically no rational ground for decision. But as Ronald Dworkin has shown, the phenomenon of disagreement (even disagreement among reasonable people) has no such consequence, and in fact you could not rationally disagree with me if you could not offer some argument or reason against the view I take, and in favour of taking a different view. See, e.g., Ronald Dworkin, *Law's Empire* (1986), chapter 2. But of course, the fact that people deeply disagree does not mean that there is conclusive reason in favor of one side or the other, either. And incommensurabilities guarantee that in some cases there will be no such reason.

the proportionality doctrine creates a serious, ongoing set of issues for the legitimacy of human rights adjudication.

VIII. PATHOLOGIES OF PROPORTIONALITY

Solving the incommensurability problem merely clears away a general objection to proportionality reasoning. The solution does not mean that the proportionality doctrine brings reason and legitimacy to the judicial role. Incommensurabilities undermine certain advantages that many judges and commentators have seen in proportionality reasoning.

The putative advantages of balancing have been put most clearly by Aharon Barak:

> The advantages of proportionality *stricto sensu* with its three levels of abstraction are several. It stresses the need to always look for a justification of a limit on human rights; it structures the mind of the balancer; it is transparent; it creates a proper dialog between the political branches and the judiciary, and it adds to the objectivity of judicial discretion.[27]

Among serious theorists, Barak's is not the only eloquent articulation of the attraction. Here are the ABCs:

Alexy:

> [C]ontestability does not imply irrationality. If this were the case, not only balancing, but legal reasoning as such would be for the most part irrational. Precisely the opposite, however, is the case. Justifiability, despite the fact that it cannot be identified with provability, implies rationality, and, with it, objectivity, understood as lying between certainty and arbitrariness.

> The end is attained. Balancing turns out to be an argument form of rational legal discourse.[28]

Beatty:

> Building a theory of judicial review around a principle of proportionality, it turns out, satisfies all the major criteria that must be met for it to establish its integrity.

---

[27] Aharon Barak, "Proportionality and Principled Balancing," *supra* note 7, Abstract.
[28] Robert Alexy, "The Construction of Constitutional Rights," (2010) 4 *Law & Ethics of Human Rights* 20 at 32. Alexy defends proportionality specifically against the charge that incommensurability leads to arbitrary balancing judgments; for a critique of this aspect of Alexy's argument, see Grégoire Webber "Proportionality, Balancing, and the Cult of Constitutional Rights Scholarship," (2010) 23 *Can. J.L. & Jur.* 179 at 194–198.

It serves as an optimizing principle that makes each constitution the best it can possibly be.

[P]roportionality offers judges a clear and objective test to distinguish coercive action by the state that is legitimate from that which is not.[29]

Craig:

The proportionality test provides a *structured form of inquiry*. The three-part proportionality inquiry focuses the attention of both the agency being reviewed, and the court undertaking the review.[30]

The structural attraction is that judicial review on a basis of proportionality encourages the initial decision maker to seek a justification for public action, in which account can be given of: (1) whether the purpose could have been attained by a less burdensome means, (2) the ways in which the means chosen will actually promote the intended objective, and finally, (3) the ways in which the action may "impose an excessive burden".[31] And the putative second-order structural attraction, articulated by Barak, is that proportionality reasoning will enhance the objectivity of judicial review and help secure the right relationship between the judges and the other branches of government.

But the crunch point is the final, crucial node in the structure, where the judge decides whether the impact on the claimant is *too much*. The attractive structure of the judicial role crumbles at that point into an unstructured, opaque choice, when the task involves balancing the unbalanceable. The solution to the incommensurability problem does not at all guarantee the legitimacy of the choices of any court. The court goes through the structure – deciding, for example, that the government was pursuing a legitimate purpose in opposing forced marriage, and that the delay in marriage visas might be expected to achieve something, but noting that the action has an adverse impact on some people's family life. And then, at the crunch point, if the impact on voluntary couples cannot actually be balanced against the interest in deterring forced marriage, *the court just chooses* whether the delay is to be imposed.

Proportionality reasoning does not bring objectivity or transparency to human rights adjudication.[32] It cannot do that any more than we can make

[29] David Beatty, *The Ultimate Rule of Law* (2004) at 160, 163, 166; chapter 5 in general is a panegyric on proportionality.
[30] Paul Craig, *Administrative Law* (6th ed. 2008) at 637.
[31] Ibid.
[32] *Cf.* the view of Michael Taggart, that proportionality has a "determinate-looking" structure without "the reality of determinacy", Taggart, "Proportionality, Deference, *Wednesbury*," [2008] N.Z. L. Rev. 423 at 477.

liability to general damages in tort objective and transparent by asking judges to put the claimant in the same position as if the wrong had not been suffered. The only viable argument in favor of proportionality reasoning in human rights adjudication is an argument of necessity; that it is necessary, in light of the institutional premise, even though it does not bring objectivity or transparency to governance.

The incommensurabilities in human rights cases (like the incommensurabilities in so many issues in litigation) do not necessarily lead to arbitrary decision making (given the above argument, and the institutional premise). So proportionality reasoning is not generally pathological. If the institutional premise holds, then there is good reason for a justiciable bill of rights. And then, the pathologies of proportionality that might affect the system are particular, and depend on particular mistakes. The incommensurabilities and the pathologies are not unrelated, because the incommensurabilities result in a dramatically creative judicial role. And because the creativity is substantial, the pathologies are potentially serious. Let me illustrate the potential pathologies (but some are actual) by mentioning three pairs.

They come in pairs, because in each of three respects we can imagine courts distorting the relevant considerations in favour of the claimant, or in favour of the public authority. But the pathologies are asymmetric. The odd-numbered pathologies (in which the courts err on the side of upholding the public decision under challenge) are – assuming that the institutional premise holds – worse. On the other hand, they are (in Europe) largely potential; the lesser, even-numbered pathologies are actual.

Pathologies One and Two: Proportionality Spillover

One distinctive danger of judicial protection of human rights is overextending proportionality reasoning, to balance things that should not be balanced. This danger is built into the enthusiasm of theorists for proportionality as a general technique. And it is embraced wholeheartedly by the English courts' doctrine on proportionality: "[T]he need to balance the interests of society with those of individuals and groups . . . should never be overlooked or discounted" (Lord Bingham for the unanimous House of Lords in *Huang*).[33] Given the vivid profile of proportionality and its vogue as a judicial technique and given the judges' distinctively impartial role of deciding between the arguments of counsel for a complainant and counsel for a public authority, the risk is that

---

[33] *Supra* note 2 at para. 19.

judges will try to balance society's interests against private interests when the interests on one side or the other do not belong in the balance.[34]

The dramatically worse possibility – Pathology Number One – is that decision makers, including courts, might try to balance public interests against private interests when public interests do not belong in the so-called scales. As Denise Réaume has put it, "If limitation clauses allow the possibility . . . that a smidgen more public utility can turn an unacceptable rights violation into a justified infringement, they become a backdoor means of negating the protection that constitutionally entrenched rights are often thought to provide."[35] The absolute prohibition on torture is an example of a rule in the European Convention that is a protection against Pathology Number One. But there are other possible ways of illegitimately putting public interests in the balance. It is an implication of the Strasbourg Court's consequentialist approach to Article 8 that any interference with your family life or mine would be compatible with the right, if it accomplished something for the public that is worth more than the cost to you or to me of the "interference". The Court's generalizing approach to proportionality is flawed because the reason (for example) why the government should not install surveillance cameras in everyone's home is *not* that the government would not get enough useful information to outweigh the interference with privacy. The reason has nothing to do with the amount of public benefit that would accrue; the reason is that the invasion of people's homes would be an outrage. Sometimes, public interests do not belong in the balance. The Strasbourg judges *talk* as if any outrage could legitimately be perpetrated on your privacy or your family if society would gain enough; but the judges' instincts will presumably never allow them to hold that the scales come down in favor of an outrage.

The lesser risk of proportionality spillover is the unwarranted weighing of private interests in the balance. This lesser pathology, however, is actual, not potential. In balancing the public purpose in deportation against the impact of a deportation on family life, the courts treat people with no lawful immigration status as if they were unlucky victims of a policy not addressed to them, and not as persons who are answerable to the country's immigration law or who have responsibility for their own family life. Suppose that the

---

[34] For an argument that proportionality reasoning risks putting second-order considerations (which can be reasons for *excluding* some first-order considerations) into the "balance" with first-order considerations, see Alon Harel, "Skeptical Reflections on Justice Aharon Barak's Optimism" (a book review of *The Judge in Democratic Society* by Aharon Barak, 2006), (2006) 39 *Israel L. Rev.* 261.

[35] Denise Réaume, "Limitations on Constitutional Rights: The Logic of Proportionality," (hereinafter "Limitations on Rights") Oxford Legal Studies Research Paper No. 26/2009, SSRN 1463853 at 3.

immigration controls are legitimate (and the judges have never contested that).[36] Suppose in addition (as is actually the case in the leading judicial decisions on deportation and Article 8) that an irregular migrant knows his immigration status, and is capable of making decisions about his family life, and is responsible for his movements. Suppose, that is, that he developed family ties in the United Kingdom knowing that he was subject to deportation, and knowing the impact that deportation would have on him, and on his loved ones. In that case – in all of the deportation cases discussed here – it would show no disrespect for his family life to say that he cannot remain in Britain, even if deportation is a *disaster* for his family life. In fact, it would show no disrespect for the family life of his son or daughter. The impact of applying the immigration rules, however disastrous, is the father's responsibility.

The person's interest in staying with family in the country does not actually belong in the scales. Yet in all these cases, the judges have held that deportation violates Article 8, if the impact on the family outweighs the benefit to the unspecified public purpose.

Here is a vivid expression of proportionality spillover, in the leading decision of the Strasbourg Court on proportionality in eviction of a person from his or her home:

> The loss of one's home is a most extreme form of interference with the right to respect for the home. Any person at risk of an interference of this magnitude should in principle be able to have the proportionality of the measure determined by an independent tribunal in the light of the relevant principles under Article 8 of the Convention, notwithstanding that, under domestic law, his right of occupation has come to an end.[37]

The mistake lies in saying that the loss of one's home is an extreme form of "interference with the right to respect". It certainly is an extreme interference with the person's *home life*. But taking a person away from his home does not necessarily show disrespect for his or her home life. Disrespect for the home, or for family life, depends not just on whether an action causes a detriment, but on the nature and the purposes of the action. There need be no lack of respect for the home (or privacy or family life) if, for example, a murderer is

---

[36] It is beyond the scope of this paper to assess the supposition. Suppose, instead, that the immigration controls are not legitimate. Then can the doctrine on deportation and family life be justified as a judicial initiative to restrict the effect of unjust restrictions on migration? No such injustice could be remedied by a measure that prefers people who develop family ties over other candidates. The judges have no effective techniques for imposing a sound immigration policy on the state, and there is no lawful ground for them to do so.

[37] *McCann v. United Kingdom* (Application No.19009/04) (2008) 47 E.H.R.R. 40 at para. 50. I do not mean to imply that proportionality reasoning is out of place in tenancy cases (see note 42); the explanation of it in *McCann* shows the approach that overextends proportionality.

taken out of his home and imprisoned on a lawful sentence after a fair trial. The impact is drastic, but the action is compatible with respect for privacy, for family, and for the home.

The proportionality decisions in the deportation cases imply that no person with a family should ever be imprisoned after conviction without a court first balancing the detriment to his home life and to his family life (and/or the detriment to his partner's or child's family life) against any public benefit that will accrue in pursuing the purpose of imprisonment. But in *Norris*, Lord Phillips commented obiter as follows, in reasons with which all the Justices of the Supreme Court agreed:

> [D]etention will necessarily interfere drastically with family and private life. In theory a question of proportionality could arise under article 8(2). In practice it is only in the most exceptional circumstances that a defendant would consider even asserting his article 8 rights by way of challenge to remand in custody or imprisonment. . . . Normally it is treated as axiomatic that the interference with article 8 rights consequent upon detention is proportionate.[38]

It would have been simpler, and compatible with the human rights of offenders, to say that imprisonment after lawful conviction is not an "interference with article 8 rights".

Perhaps the drafting of Article 8 has encouraged judges to think that the right is violated if an official action has a consequence for a person's family that is disproportionate to the public purpose. It started as a borrowing of the well-drafted right in Article 12 of the Universal Declaration of Human Rights ("No one shall be subjected to arbitrary interference with his privacy, family, home or correspondence. . . . Everyone has the right to the protection of the law against such interference or attacks."). In the drafting process, it was mangled into an ungrammatical shambles, using the same format as the articles that protect fundamental freedoms. It reads as follows:

(1) Everyone has the right to respect for his private and family life, his home and his correspondence.

(2) There shall be no interference by a public authority with the exercise of this right except such as is in accordance with the law and is necessary in a democratic society in the interests of national security, public safety or the economic well-being of the country, for the prevention of disorder or crime, for the protection of health or morals, or for the protection of the rights and freedoms of others.

---

[38] *Norris, supra* note 11 at para. 52.

The state should *always* respect family life and privacy. The right to respect is not a right that anyone exercises. Legitimate actions taken in the interests listed in Article 8(2) are not "interferences" with the "exercise" of the right to respect, but actions that are compatible with respect for privacy and family life and the home. But an early Strasbourg decision held that the courts must first decide whether there was a lack of respect for family life, and then (if there was a lack of respect) decide whether the lack of respect was or was not justified under Article 8(2).[39] Nowadays, the courts deal with the flaw, instead, by treating Article 8(1) *not* as enshrining a right to respect, but as if it had enshrined a right not to suffer any interference with privacy or the home or any detriment to family life. And they treat Article 8(2) as if it were a proviso that such interference or detriment can be justified if it is necessary in the listed interests. Baroness Hale, for example, has said, "The language of 'fair balance' is much more compatible with a search for justification under article 8(2) than with identifying a 'lack of respect' under article 8(1)."[40] The result is that the courts treat the Convention right to respect for family life as if it were a right to something more than respect for family life – but also to something less than respect, if there is a great public interest in some violation of privacy or family life.

If extradition would be justified in the case of a person with no family, it implies no disrespect for family to extradite a person with a family.[41] Likewise with deportation: it implies no disrespect for the importance to a person's home or family life. In the deportation cases, the courts would have been respecting the right enshrined in Article 8 if they had held that a deportation does not show disrespect for family life simply in virtue of enforcing lawful controls on immigration (although some aspect of the government's conduct in a case might show some particular contempt for family); instead, they have turned the right into a balancing of the claimant's interests against the public interest.

---

[39] *Abdulaziz v. U.K.* (Application no. 9214/80; 9473/81; 9474/81)

[40] *Quila supra* note 19 at para. 69, and see her discussion of the Strasbourg cases.

[41] Note that extradition is different from deportation, insofar as the measure may subject a person to a very adverse impact for which he or she has no responsibility (if, e.g., he or she is not guilty of the alleged offence). But an extradition does not show disrespect for family life of a person with family (or for the family life of his or her children), any more than it shows disrespect for the freedom of the person extradited; the need for international cooperation in responding to crime can be a reason to cooperate, regardless of the impact on the family (assuming, crucially, that the same requirements of just extradition are met, as would be essential in the case of a person with no family). Imprisonment on remand is the same: the person imprisoned may not be guilty of any offence, and detention may affect a family very badly, and yet it does not show disrespect for family life as long as it meets the same criteria of justice that are needed to justify the detention on remand of persons with no family.

There *is* a place for proportionality reasoning under Article 8. In *Quila* (unlike in the deportation and eviction cases) the claimants really were mere victims of a policy aimed at someone else; they were voluntary spouses, whose settlement in the UK was delayed by a measure aimed against forced marriage. Here, the proportionality question is the right question because the impact on voluntary spouses was collateral to the purpose of the measure, and needed to be taken into account: if the government were to delay their entry for the extraneous purpose of deterring forced marriages, without securing any benefit that is worth securing, it would be acting without due respect for their family life.[42]

But in the deportation and extradition cases, Pathology Number Two is actual, because of the proportionality overspill. It cannot hurt to reiterate that we should *cherish* this pathology, if the alternative is Pathology Number One, which would involve supine courts that wrongly put public interests in the so-called scales and allow persons to be abused. But the actuality of Pathology Number Two shows that proportionality reasoning ought to be kept in its place. Enthusiasm for proportionality reasoning should be tailored to the particular function it can rightly play, in cases such as *Quila*, where good governance demands that an interest of the claimant should be protected against disproportionate detriment.[43]

Paul Craig has argued that "proportionality should be a general principle of judicial review that can be used both in cases concerned with rights and in non-rights based cases".[44] He deals persuasively with various objections to the idea, arguing in particular that proportionality review can be carried out with different levels of intensity (this approach is capable of dealing with the further potential pathologies discussed shortly). But courts should only be asking (at any level of intensity) about the proportionality of the impact of a decision on a complainant's interests where there is some legal reason to protect the interests in question. That is, of course, true of the European

[42] I think that there is a place for proportionality reasoning, too, in the cases on eviction from a home. Those cases are massively more complex than the cases of deportation, extradition, or imprisonment on remand or after conviction. I do not have room here to discuss the justifiability of protection for a family's tenancy in their home even in the face of breach of a tenancy agreement (and, in particular, in the face of misconduct by one or more family members in a family that has serious problems), and the reasonableness of the view that respect for family life requires such protection, and the potential for courts to use Article 8 to secure justice for tenants. It should be obvious that there is also scope for courts to use Article 8 to let tenants get away with abusing their tenancy.

[43] See Martin Luterán, "The Lost Meaning of Proportionality," Chapter 2 in this volume.

[44] Paul Craig, "Proportionality, Rationality and Review," [2010] N.Z. L. Rev. 265 at 265. See also Paul Craig, "The Nature of Rationality Review," *supra* note 25.

Union (EU) cases on which Craig builds part of his argument, as the EU project involves giving persons legally protected interests in (among other things, but most notably) free trade and free movement across borders within Europe. Likewise, in certain areas of administrative law in England in which proportionality has been used, even before the Human Rights Act, there is legal reason to protect certain interests: most notable are the cases asserting the "principle of legality", under which the courts protect a rather ill-defined category of interests (notably, interests in access to justice).[45] Signing the European Convention and passing the Human Rights Act in the UK were acts to create legal protections for the interests enshrined in the rights.

But administrative review would suffer from proportionality overspill, and in particular from Pathology Number Two, if it required public authorities generally to justify an action that, according to the complainant, has too much impact on the complainant's interests. So, for example, a disappointed applicant who has a very pressing interest in securing a job with a public authority should not be able to challenge a decision to hire someone else instead, on the ground that the decision has a disproportionate impact on his or her interests. Even if hiring the claimant would not hurt the public interest (or even the interests of the preferred candidate) very much, the claimant has no right to the legal protection of the urgent interest that he or she has. A company should not be able to challenge a public authority's decision to stop purchasing its goods or services on the ground that the result will have a disproportionate impact on the company's interests. And so on. Perhaps the need to identify interests of a kind that call for legal protection is implicit in Professor Craig's view. In any case, it is true of common law judicial review of administrative action, as of cases under the European Convention, that not all interests of a complainant belong in the scales. Proportionality review cannot legitimately be general in the sense that it is to be applied to private interests in general – or to public interests in general.

Pathologies Three and Four: Uncertainty[46]

In *Quila*,[47] the impact on voluntary spouses of a delay in the age for a marriage visa was fairly clear: they would have to wait until they were both twenty-one

---

[45] See Timothy Endicott, *Administrative Law*, (2nd ed. 2011) at 270.
[46] I am grateful to Robert Leckey for pointing out to me the importance of these problems. For a discussion of the implications of empirical uncertainty for proportionality reasoning, see Denise Réaume, "Limitations on Rights," *supra* note 35.
[47] *Supra* note 19.

(rather than eighteen) before the non-British spouse would be able to live in the UK.[48] But it was not at all clear what impact the delay would have, if any, on the practice of forced marriage. This was not a mere gap in the evidence presented by the government. The sophistication of the empirical social sciences has not reached the point at which we could expect an accurate and verifiable assessment of the relevance of entry to the UK between ages eighteen and twenty-one in the thinking that motivates those who force young people into a marriage. And that assessment would not be nearly enough; if social psychologists achieved unheard-of access and insight into all that criminal thinking, they would be unable to give the government or the court any definite indication as to how the people in question would respond in future to the constraint of the delay to age twenty-one (to what extent, for example, they would give up on forcing a marriage, or would find a way of forcing a marriage later, or would go ahead with the forced marriage and cope with the visa delay). The criminals themselves might not know.

When proportionality really is the right question (that is, when proportionality reasoning does not involve Pathologies Number One or Two), it is very common for the considerations that are meant to go into one side of the scales (or for considerations on *both* sides) to involve just such dramatic uncertainties as to the massively complex social facts and future contingencies that may emerge from massively complex and unpredictable social responses to policy choices.

An executive or legislative policy choice – or *the judges'* policy choice in human rights litigation – will suffer from Pathology Number Three if the decision maker in question deals with the uncertainty by (1) exaggerating the capacity of the choice in question to achieve the prospective public benefits, or (2) underestimating the risks to the private interests at stake because they are uncertain. And a policy choice (executive, legislative, or judicial) will suffer from Pathology Number Four if the decision maker deals with the uncertainty by (1) exaggerating the risks to private interests, or (2) underestimating the capacity of the choice in question to achieve the prospective public benefit because the benefits are uncertain. The potential for mistakes is huge, and they probably happen regularly. These pathologies involve a dilemma, which I will call the "dilemma of uncertainty".

Consider *Quila*. The Home Secretary's decision was affected by Pathology Number Three if she was merely taking a measure (at some significant cost to the claimants) that had no genuine prospect of securing real public benefit,

---

[48] Yet note that the impact is still immeasurable. Even if we know how many such couples there are, and how old they are, the issue depends on how bad the delays are for each couple's family life.

and was treating the deep uncertainties about the success of the measure as a reason for trying it on as a gesture. On the other hand, the United Kingdom Supreme Court's decision was affected by Pathology Number Four if the judges treated radical uncertainties as meaning that the government could not succeed on the issue of proportionality.

It may seem that the burden of proof resolves the matter. The claimants must show that the delay in marriage visas would affect their family life. Once they showed that, it was up to the government to prove facts that would justify the measure as necessary for the protection of the rights and freedoms of others (so that it would be compatible with Article 8(2)). The uncertainty as to the impact on forced marriage, you might say, meant that the government had to lose, because they could not prove that anything of great weight should be put into the public interest side of the scales. But then, no public effort to protect people's rights and freedoms would ever be justifiable, unless there were proof (and, in fact, justiciable proof) that the effort would succeed sufficiently to outweigh any impact on protected private interests.

If the burden of proof means that the complainants must prove on a balance of probabilities that they will suffer detriment outweighing any public benefit that the government proves, then the court's decision will suffer from Pathology Number Three. If the burden of proof is used to mean that the government must prove on a balance of probabilities that the measure will result in public benefit that outweighs any detriment proven by the claimant, then the court's decision will suffer from Pathology Number Four. The reason is that the facts of public benefit and private detriment are not like the facts in a tort case, as to whether it was the defendant who drove the car that injured the claimant. The need for public decision in circumstances of radical uncertainty means that a public authority needs to be ready in principle to seek a significant public benefit without proof that *any* public benefit will be secured. This should be obvious from the mere fact that sometimes it is worth incurring some cost in order to pursue an uncertain possibility of achieving something worthwhile. By the same token, a public authority should be concerned about the potential for private detriment (when it is relevant to the decision), without proof that any will come about.

Here is the dilemma of uncertainty: on the one hand, it would be a fallacy to think that only proven gains can legitimately be pursued where there is a proven detriment to a person's family life.[49] On the other hand, *some* speculative

---

[49] Think of public financial and monetary policy decisions, which may affect people's families very acutely and, in fact, measurably, and which must be taken in conditions of radical uncertainty; if some detriment is reliably predictable, and the potential gain cannot be proven, that does not entail that a decision is wrong.

measures to pursue uncertain gains are bad mistakes. How can the courts resolve the dilemma of uncertainty? One way (recommended by Lord Brown in his dissent in the *Quila* case) would be to leave it to the initial decision maker, who – although having no evidence that would prove anything to a court – may well have a sense of (for example) whether a delay in marriage visas will really have a prospect of making a worthwhile dent in the practice of forced marriage. The difficulty is that such a strategy would incur the risk that instead of acting with a sound sense of the realities, the initial decision maker is engaged in a doomed gesture (not necessarily through any sort of bad faith, but conceivably through a determination to do or to appear to be doing *something* – anything – to make a stand against the practice of forced marriage).

There is no very definite way of deciding what approach the courts should take to this dilemma of uncertainty. There is no way to determine whether the Home Secretary's policy decision in *Quila* suffered from Pathology Number Three, or whether the Supreme Court's decision suffered from Pathology Number Four, without considering the issues (and the scanty information about, for example, the opinions of persons and groups consulted by the Home Secretary) for yourself and siding with the instincts of the Home Secretary or of the judges.

Lord Wilson put it well in *Quila* when he said that "[t]he burden is upon the Secretary of State to establish that [the impact on voluntary couples of the delay in marriage visas], *was justified*" under Article 8(2). That is, the burden should not be thought of as a burden of proving that the resulting benefit would outweigh the detriment, but that the measure was one that could be taken with respect for the family life of the voluntary couples.

Pathologies Five and Six: The Pathologies of Deference

The first four pathologies can arise not only in adjudication, but also *in the initial proportionality decision* by, for example, the government in deciding whether to delay marriage visas in an attempt to fight forced marriage. An executive official or a legislature or a court might put interests in the scales that do not belong there, and might do a poor job of coping with uncertainty. Pathologies Number Five and Six, by contrast, are distinctive failures of courts. They relate to a challenge that courts face in *any* review of executive or legislative action: the challenge of taking an appropriate attitude to the judgments of the authorities whose decisions they are reviewing. If the courts defer excessively to the initial decision maker, then the point of judicial protection of human rights will be lost and the system will suffer from Pathology Number Five. If courts do not defer to the judgment of others where there is good reason, the system will suffer from Pathology Number Six.

Is there *ever* good reason for deference? The doctrine of the judges under the European Convention makes them into a ruling council for government decisions that affect certain aspects of the privacy and family life of persons.[50] In that role, if they were to defer excessively to the legislature or the executive, the system would suffer from Pathology Number Five, and they would be standing idly by in the face of abuses. But if the courts do not defer to those other bodies at all, the system will suffer from Pathology Number Six, to the extent that authorities other than the courts are better able to assess the relevant considerations (through their expertise, or because of their processes and the information available to them, or on account of their democratic or other forms of political responsibility).

Meanwhile, the English judges do not even want to use "deference" as a word for their attitude to the judgment of other authorities, perhaps because they think that deference means leaving matters *entirely* to another authority. They prefer to put this, too, in terms of "weight". Lord Bingham said this in the *Huang* decision, concerning factors that the Home Secretary relied on in her deportation decision:

> The giving of weight to factors such as these is not, in our opinion, aptly described as deference: it is performance of the ordinary judicial task of weighing up the competing considerations on each side and according appropriate weight to the judgment of a person with responsibility for a given subject matter and access to special sources of knowledge and advice. That is how any rational judicial decision-maker is likely to proceed.[51]

It is easy to see why judges should be wary of deference, as it could land them in Pathology Number Five. But if the Home Secretary is better placed than they are to decide some fact or assess its significance (because of expertise in the Home Office, or because of the fact that she makes a decision with sensitive attention to the political context, or because of useful sources of information

---

[50] The courts have carefully avoided *some* questions of respect for personal and family life. For example, they have largely avoided turning Article 8 into a right to welfare even though, ironically, a state really does display disrespect for family life if it provides inadequate social security to families when it could provide adequate social security. But the judges have rightly stepped back from taking over the control of expenditure that would be needed to impose justice in social security. See Timothy Endicott, *Administrative Law* (2nd ed.) (2011) at 92. This does not mean that the European Convention has no impact on social security; it affects the complex system in a variety of ways: see Jo Kenny, "European Convention on Human Rights and Social Welfare" (2010) 5 *Eur. H.R.L. Rev.* 495.

[51] *Huang, supra* note 2 at para. 16; see also *Quila, supra* note 19, at paras. 46 and 91.

that are unavailable to judges, or because of the deliberative process in which she is involved within a government department or within Cabinet . . .), then they would do well to defer to some extent – in a sense that the English judges describe, instead, as giving weight to the consideration that appealed to the Home Secretary. But in making some assessments, her judgment might be distorted by the very features that enable her to make other assessments very well. And the judges' techniques and experience equip them to assess some considerations better than she can.

If judges are better at some things and executive and legislative authorities are better at other things, can we generalize about their respective strengths and weaknesses? Aharon Barak suggested the following, in the Israeli Supreme Court's landmark proportionality case on the construction of a separation fence in the West Bank:

> The military commander is the expert on the military aspects of the Fence's route. We are the experts of the humanitarian aspects of the route. The military commander can determine the geographical placement of the Fence – across mountain or plain. This is his expertise. We review whether the military commander's route inflicts disproportionate injury upon the local inhabitants. This is our expertise.[52]

There is an obvious puzzle: if the military commander is expert at assessing the considerations on one side of the scales (in that case, the "military aspects of the Fence's route"), and the judges are expert at assessing the considerations on the other side (its "humanitarian aspects"), how can it be the judges' expertise to decide whether one is proportionate to the other? Why should *they* hold the scales? By calling it "our expertise" to make the proportionality decision, President Barak was presupposing the institutional premise discussed previously: that the essential respect for certain human interests can best be secured by a power in an independent tribunal to pass judgment on the justice of pursuing public purposes in ways that affect those interests. Without that premise, judges cannot claim expertise in answering the proportionality question, and it would be a mistake to have judicial review on the ground of proportionality.

IX. CONCLUSION: ARBITRARINESS AND THE RULE OF LAW

We lose the rule of law to the extent that matters such as deportation are decided arbitrarily. If those matters are decided arbitrarily by the Home Secretary, we have the rule of the Home Secretary instead of the rule of

---

[52] *Beit Sourik, supra* note 17 at para. 48.

law. If they are decided arbitrarily by judges, we have the rule of judges instead of the rule of law. Judicial decision making is capable of being arbitrary. The resolution of conflicts between vaguely incommensurable values leads to very significant indeterminacies, so that there is often no reason to adopt one resolution rather than another. It may seem that judicial decision making becomes arbitrary when there is no reason for decision one way rather than the other. It would be a mistake to think that. Judicial decision making does not become arbitrary in the sense that is relevant to the rule of law merely because judges are reconciling conflicts among incommensurable values. On the contrary, the rule of law demands a system in which independent tribunals can reconcile (or "balance" – as they call it in a misleading figure of speech[53]) considerations that cannot be balanced.

Justiciable charters of human rights are not necessarily a departure from the rule of law just because they involve judges in reconciling incommensurable values under a proportionality doctrine. The pathologies of proportionality are particular, and do not arise generally from the very significant problem of incommensurability.

And yet, incommensurabilities undermine the putative attractions of objectivity, transparency, and judicial legitimacy that many have sought in proportionality reasoning. If the institutional premise is true, then we can expect courts to make some judgments of proportionality better than other public authorities. Even if that is the case, judicial judgments of proportionality may be systematically distorted by one of the six pathologies discussed (or presumably by others).

Is a justiciable bill of rights a good idea? The pressing moral force of human rights does not itself answer this question, and a further, institutional, premise is needed to justify human rights adjudication: that there are human interests that need protection against abuse and misjudgments by executive and legislative agencies of government in a form that can best be provided by an independent institution authorized to pass judgment on the justice of pursuing public purposes in ways that affect those interests.

If the institutional premise is true, then the potential pathologies are particular, but they are serious. I would expect that actual pathologies can be found in every human rights regime (as, I have argued, they can be found under the European Convention). That is to be expected because of the complexities of the issues, the ingenuity of advocates, and the commitment of every decent judge in every human rights decision to hear both sides.

---

[53] See Frederick Schauer, "Proportionality and the Question of Weight," Chapter 8 in this volume.

And the odd-numbered pathologies are worse, you may say. That is, as I have suggested, it might be worse if judges put public interests into the scales when they do not belong there, or if judges err in favour of the state in cases of radical uncertainty, or if judges defer excessively to other authorities. For if they do those things, judges will be failing to protect human beings from abuse. The danger of violation of human rights is more serious than the danger of excess litigation over extradition, or the danger of instituting a preference for immigration candidates who have developed family ties in the country, or the general danger of overenthusiastic judicial elaboration of abstract rights.

Yet the danger of violation of human rights is not actually the same thing as the danger of leaving it to public authorities other than judges to determine what human rights require. The question ought to be whether the potential benefits (through judicial interference with distorted legislative and executive judgments) are worth pursuing, at the cost of the distorted judgments that judicial decision making may introduce into the formation and implementation of public policy. It is quite likely to be impossible to come up with an exact balance sheet even for a particular system; the advantages are themselves incommensurable with the drawbacks of the arrangement. There is no way to establish a court with independent judges, and to give them power to interfere with the non-controversial cases of human rights violations, without giving them power to develop new, creative, highly controversial interpretations of the rights at stake.

Even when the institutional premise holds, the propriety of the answer that the judges give to a proportionality question will be in question in virtually every particular case, because of their creative role in reconciling incommensurable considerations. The political tensions over their roles in Canada, Europe, India, Israel, South Africa, the United States., and many other countries are permanent features of that role. The judges can, of course, do better or worse in each particular case (and the institutional premise is a broad generalization). And insofar as the initial decision maker has expertise in assessing public interests, they can benefit from that expertise, whether they call it deference or not.

What they cannot expect to do (partly because of deep disagreements in their communities) is to make decisions that consistently attract widespread assent to the institutional premise. It is worth concluding with one principle concerning that essential premise for the legitimacy of human rights adjudication: it may conceivably be made out, even in spite of serious, actual pathologies of proportionality.

15 Legislating Proportionately

Richard Ekins

I. INTRODUCTION

Many scholarly treatments of proportionality concern constitutional adjudication and hence the reasoning and authoritative choice of judicial institutions. This chapter instead considers the place of proportionality within legislative reasoning. That is, I aim to explain what it is to legislate proportionately. This study may have implications for how one conceives of, and evaluates, various modes of judicial review of legislation. However, my primary aim is to outline this aspect of what it is to legislate well and to suggest the ways in which this outline may depart from common understandings of the proportionality doctrine. My method is to adopt the internal point of view of the legislator and reflect on how he or she should reason, on the shape and objects of his or her reasonable action. I argue that the virtue of proportionality consists in the adoption of fit means to sound ends. I go on to consider the relationship between legality and proportionality and the ways in which one acts rationally, qua legislator, in the face of incommensurables. I then outline how legislators should conceive of, and deliberate about, rights, and finally, suggest some ways in which talk of proportionality may distort this deliberation.

II. THE AMBIGUITIES OF PROPORTIONALITY

Why legislate proportionately? The answer may seem obvious. In constitutional rights adjudication, the court applies the doctrine of proportionality to determine the constitutionality of legislation that is the subject of review. The court asks whether the legislation has a legitimate objective, it adopts suitable and necessary means to such an objective, and the objective is proportionate to the rights impairment. This final stage is often thought the most significant and is termed proportionality *stricto sensu*. Legislation is upheld, is constitutionally licit, if it adopts suitable and necessary means to a legitimate objective, which is proportionate to the right impaired. That is, legislation is valid, within power, if it is a proportionate limitation on the applicant's right. Conversely, legislation is invalid, ultra vires, if the limitation is disproportionate; that is, if the objective is illegitimate, the means adopted are either unsuitable (irrational) or unnecessary, or if the right impaired is disproportionate to the objective.

If the validity of the legislature's lawmaking act turns on its proportionality, this would seem to entail that the legislature *should* act proportionately and should take the doctrine to frame how it reasons and chooses. That is, the legislature should evaluate legislative proposals by asking itself these questions. However, this conclusion may be too hasty. The relevant body of scholarship displays two related ambiguities. The first is whether the point of the doctrine is to frame the reasoning and choice of all public officials, including legislators and ministers, or only of judges. That is, when the court applies the doctrine, is it repeating the reasoning process that the legislature and minister should have (and perhaps already have) undertaken in making the decision that is now before the court? In the alternative, is the court in applying the doctrine reviewing the impugned decision in a specifically judicial way, such that its reasoning is in principle different to the reasoning and choice of the legislature or minister?

The difference matters. And the difference relates to another ambiguity, concerning whether the doctrine is at most a (perhaps) helpful way of enjoining judges (and all others) to consider all that is morally relevant; to license open, fully substantive practical reasoning;[1] or whether it is alternatively a technical, strictly legal process that is neutral or agnostic and may be applied without licensing such open reasoning.[2] One can see that the idea that the doctrine of proportionality is for courts, not legislatures, has some affinity with the proposal that it is technical rather than substantive. Still, this is no necessary connection. One might think that legislatures such as courts should employ a technical measure in making law, commensurating public benefits and private burdens. Or one might think that the doctrine, which is open to the full range of practical reasoning, is primarily for the courts precisely because the legislature is generally incapable of (or perhaps even *should* be incapable of)

---

[1] Mattias Kumm, "The Idea of Socratic Contestation and the Right to Justification: The Point of Rights Based Proportionality Review," (2010) 4(2) *Law and Ethics of Human Rights* 1 at 2, 11–12; Kai Möller, "Proportionality and Rights Inflation," Chapter 7 in this volume.

[2] See, for example, the material quoted by Timothy Endicott, "Proportionality and Incommensurability," Chapter 14 in this volume, text at notes 27–30 (hereinafter Endicott, "Proportionality and Incommensurability").

such reasoning, acting instead in response to the force of popular preferences.[3] These alternatives plainly turn on different conceptions of the separation of powers.

These ambiguities make the discussion of proportionality and its relevance to legislative and judicial reasoning rather difficult to pin down, for the discussion may readily shift. The criticism that the doctrine of proportionality is too technical, too reductive, or stultifying is met with the reply that in truth it is open to all possible considerations, whereas the criticism that it is too open or empty, unfit for judges, is met with the reply that it disciplines reasoning and is hence especially suitable for judicial consideration and application. For this reason, my account of what it is to legislate proportionately begins by thinking about legislating quite apart from rights or constitutional adjudication. I return in the later part of the chapter to rights and the significance of the ambiguities, suggesting that some understandings of proportionality are liable to misconceive – namely, to fail to recognize – reasonable legislative action.

III. LEGISLATING WELL: AN OUTLINE

How does one legislate well?[4] The reason to authorize some person or body to legislate is to make it possible for the law to be changed, by deliberate action to this end, when there is good reason for change. This lawmaking capacity is one of the central ways in which a legal system helps realize the common good. I argue elsewhere that authorizing an assembly (a representative and democratically legitimate body) to legislate changes who legislates, not what it is to legislate. Hence, I outline what it is to legislate well by exploring how one person, authorized to change the law by deliberate action to this end, should reason and choose.

The legislator acts to change the law for the common good. The legislator should determine the extent to which the existing law supports or realizes the valuable states of affairs that constitute the common good and, if need be, should act to amend the law so that it better secures the common good. This reflection on the common good may provide reasons for the legislator to develop a proposal to change the law in some way, which proposal is a complex means to the ends that constitute the relevant aspect(s) of the common good. This proposal the legislator will develop and evaluate, revising it to avoid some

---

[3] Ronald Dworkin sees legislative capacity in this (skeptical, reductive) way; see further my *The Nature of Legislative Intent* (2012), chapter 4, sections I–III.

[4] See further my *The Nature of Legislative Intent*, ibid. at 118–142.

(not all) foreseen but unintended consequences and make it a means capable of securing some other intelligible end(s). The legislator develops this proposal and may choose it if he or she concludes that it is fit to be chosen, such that there is good reason for the legal changes it introduces.

The legislator's lawmaking act is a moral choice made in response to reasons. One cannot legislate well without sound moral judgment. However, sound moral reflection does not reveal an ideal legal code, which the legislator may transcribe or translate. Rather, the reasonable legislator will perceive that there are many goods, which do not reduce to any one master-value and may be realized in the lives of the many persons for whose common good he should act. The legislator will also recognize that, although there are sound intermediary principles and some absolute prohibitions that structure how persons should live, moral norms alone are insufficient. The legislator's action is framed by general moral truths, but his duty is very often to "specify" these truths, choosing in what particular forms they shall be given effect in the law of his community.

Legislative deliberation is informed by empirical reasoning, in which the legislator aims to discern the relevant facts about the state of the world, such that he may change the law in a way that introduces the patterns of social life (say, an absence of strife or fair and thriving commerce), for which he acts. Legislating well (or indeed even at all) also requires technical reasoning – about the existing law and about how one's proposed lawmaking act is to work to change the law and the world. The craft of legislating involves developing proposals in a form fit to change the law and the life of the community as intended. The elaboration of a set of legal rules, which is intended to capture the moral conclusion that a problem ought to be addressed in a certain type of way, may suggest alternative ends for which the legislator should act or may even warrant revising or abandoning that prior moral conclusion.

Part of the craft of legislating is attending to how and why the persons one aims to coordinate are likely to act. The law the legislator enacts will appeal to the reasonable, while often compelling the unreasonable to comply. The legislator may foresee that many persons are likely to fail to comply with the legal rules he introduces and yet rightly refrain from choosing some alternative, more effective means of compliance if, for example, that means is too harsh or too costly. Here, the legislator chooses some particular (complex) means to the end(s) for which he acts, not on the limited grounds of instrumental rationality but rather by considering the range of valuable goods in play.

The legislator's reasoning is an extended reflection on the position of his community, its common good and the opportunities he has to act for that good. His deliberation involves the formation, refinement, and scrutiny of proposals for how to change the law in ways that are supported by good reasons; that is, which support, protect, or instantiate some aspect of the common good. The legislator may begin with relatively abstract ends, such as maintaining a clean environment or a social order free from violence, but his reflection on those ends involves their specification, identifying more particular states of affairs that are attractive elaborations of the more abstract ends and which are fit to be chosen.[5] The formation of means to those states of affairs may in turn develop further ends that warrant the legislator's response (or at least his intelligent consideration), and particular means to further ends may constitute partial ends in their own right. The final proposal for legislative action in which deliberation culminates is a complex scheme of means-end relations, which the legislator may choose, in which case he acts intending the means and the ends.

IV. THE VIRTUE OF PROPORTIONALITY

My aim is to consider the relevance of proportionality to sound legislative reason. For this reason, I now outline what seems to me the virtue of proportionate lawmaking. One legislates to bring about, to instantiate, certain states of affairs that constitute an aspect of the common good. These intelligible ends of legislative action justify the adoption, the choice, of means that are fit to realize these ends. The fitness of the means chosen will determine whether one legislates proportionately or *dis*proportionately. The latter is a vice and the former a virtue, such that legislators should discipline their lawmaking choices to be proportionate, setting aside that which is disproportionate. For a legislative act to be disproportionate is for it to change the law in ways that are not warranted by reason. However, not all modes of unreasonable lawmaking are unreasonable in the sense that they are disproportionate. They might simply be misconceived in their perception of the common good – of the objects of sound legislative action – and of sound means to its realization, or they might be (intentionally) vicious, undermining the common good in some respect. The specific vice of the disproportionate legislative act, I suggest, is that it acts in excess of sound reasons that otherwise justify the legislative act. That is, to legislate disproportionately is to adopt a means to the legislative end that is excessive (unnecessary), and which by reason of that excess undermines the common good in some way to the extent of the excess. Thus, the law in question is arbitrary, failing to be supported by the reasons for which the legislature

---

[5] On specification, see Henry S. Richardson, *Democratic Autonomy: Public Reasoning about the Ends of Policy* (2002), especially 104, 108–110, 127.

acted (or perhaps should have acted), which are the intelligible ends of the legislative act.

So disproportionality is a form of arbitrariness, which legislators should avoid, striving instead to act to change the law for good reasons. The question the legislator should ask of any legislative proposal is this – what is required, no more but also no less, to realize the states of affairs, the intelligible ends, for which it is proposed we act? It would be odd to say that doing less than is required to secure the ends for which one acts is to act disproportionately. Better, I say, to think of proportionality as the mean between two alternatives – the adoption of disproportionate (excessive) means on the one hand and ineffectual, insufficient means on the other. This finds an echo in Paul Yowell's argument that the virtue of clarity, which is one desideratum of the rule of law, is the mean between vagueness and over-specificity.[6]

Proportionate lawmaking turns on efficiency in the choice of means, on the adoption of some plan of action that is capable of securing the ends for which one acts. One should consider alternative plans of action and choose whichever, if any, has all the advantages of the other without its attendant disadvantages. This prescription for legislative reason does not enjoin commensuration of incommensurables. For efficiency in the choice of means has its rightful, but limited, place in practical deliberation.[7] One should reject some plan if it involves willing some state of affairs that has disadvantages that might have been avoided by adopting some other plan, which plan is as good a means to the ends for which one acts. Here there is no room for reasonable choice: reason demands the adoption of the one plan over the other. So, too, with the foreseen but unintended side effects of alternative plans (assuming there is reason to avoid such): one should adopt the plan that is a means to the ends in question but which lacks the side effects in question.

More generally, the foreseen but unintended side effects of some plan may provide a good reason against choosing that plan, suggesting that one should instead adopt some other means, even if less effective, to the ends in question. Here, what is to be done is less clear-cut because there may be reason to choose the more effective means notwithstanding the unwelcome side effects. Still, one may say that some plan is disproportionate if, even though it secures the intended end, it has side effects that should, if considered or foreseen, provide sufficient reason to reject the plan. Again then, to act proportionality calls for

[6] Paul Yowell, "Legislation, Common Law and the Virtue of Clarity" in Richard Ekins (ed.), *Modern Challenges to the Rule of Law* (2011) 101 at 116–121.

[7] John Finnis, *Natural Law and Natural Rights* (1980) at 111–118 (hereinafter Finnis, *Natural Law and Natural Rights*).

an evaluation of the chosen means. And a proportionate legislative act is one in which the means is fit to secure the intended end(s) without unintended side effects that warrant rejecting the means.

Evaluating the available, conceivable means to some end may call into question the wisdom of aiming for this end, perhaps by any (foreseeable) means. This need not rule the end out as an intelligible object of continued deliberation, but of course one may not rightfully choose the end if there is no reasonable means to it.

The proportionate legislative act is an intelligent means to intelligible ends, in which the legislature does not intend (choose) propositions or states of affairs that are not supported by the ends for which it acts and in which the chosen means does not have unintended side effects that warrant rejecting the means. Whereas one may sometimes act proportionately by adopting the uniquely efficient means, often the legislature faces a choice amongst various attractive proposals. The reason for this is that the legislature very often aims for a set of nested *ends*, which entails that the adequacy of the means turns on its relation to more than one intelligible object of choice, with the particular form and detail of the means itself often constituting some state of affairs that warrants instantiation, apart from its capacity to serve as a way of achieving some further end. This is not to say that the means would be fit for choice apart from that further end but rather that given the intelligible appeal of that end there is good reason to aim to secure it in this particular way.

Legislative deliberation involves working up proposals for action, which consist in complex means to various ends, setting aside the inefficient, and then choosing amongst the alternatives that remain, which realize different ends by way of different means, with their different (unintended) side effects. The legislative choice is of this particular means-end package, the wisdom of which turns on the reasons there are to act in this way; that is, to act for these ends in the proposed way. In the sections that follow, I extend this brief sketch of proportionate lawmaking to consider the importance of the rule of law, legality, and the relevance of incommensurability, and to understand the ways in which rights feature in legislative deliberation.

V. THE RELEVANCE OF LEGALITY

The rule of law should bear on the legislator's deliberation about whether some proposed legislative act is a proportionate means to some intelligible end(s). This section explains how the rule of law informs this deliberation.

In an insightful article, Philip Sales and Ben Hooper consider when the European Court of Human Rights is willing to hold general, clear statutory rules to be proportionate.[8] The authors' interest is in how to square the generality of law with the doctrine of proportionality's concern with how rules apply in a range of particular cases. They discern that so-called fact-sensitive laws, the application of which is highly responsive to the detail of particular cases, are more likely than "fact-insensitive" laws to be held to be proportionate. Laws may be fact sensitive in two ways: first, by being more detailed than an otherwise-general rule, such that they respond in a fine-grained way to a wide range of particulars; or second, by increasing the discretion of the rule-applier.[9] Thus, a limitation rule might be made more fact-sensitive by including an exception in the case of fraud or by authorizing the court to extend the limit when justice requires. The problem with the latter is that it seems to move away from the ideal of the rule of law and its focus on clear, general rules. Is there then a tension between proportionality and legality?

T.R.S. Allan thinks not, and argues that they are unified in a sound theory of the rule of law.[10] His argument is that the nature of law and related separation of authority between judiciary and legislature require and make possible proportionality. The judiciary's responsibility to adjudicate particular cases, he says, calls for it to settle how the legislature's general purposes should apply in the context of each particular case.[11] This context includes, centrally, the burden that the pursuit of the public benefit imposes on the individual. The court seeks a proportionate weighing, a balance, of that benefit and burden.[12] This balancing exercise, Allan continues, settles the true meaning of the statute, which contra positivist dogma does not follow, from legislative intent or (literal) linguistic meaning of the statutory text.[13]

I agree with Allan that there is no reason to think that proportionate legislation undercuts the rule of law. However, my reasons for this conclusion depart sharply from Allan's own and indeed involve a rejection of his reconciliation, which sacrifices the rule of law to an unsound account of proportionality (I cannot quite say "an account of proportionate lawmaking" for part of the problem is that Allan takes the legislature not to make law but instead to initiate the process of lawmaking, which is completed, in relevant part, only when the court adjudicates the particular case).

---

[8] Philip Sales and Ben Hooper, "Proportionality and the Form of Law," (2003) 119 *L.Q.R.* 426 (hereinafter Sales and Hooper, "Proportionality").

[9] Ibid. at 428–429.

[10] T.R.S. Allan, "Democracy, Legality and Proportionality," Chapter 10 in this volume (hereinafter Allan, "Democracy, Legality and Proportionality").

[11] Ibid. at 7–8, 26–27.   [12] Ibid. at 9–10.

[13] Ibid. at 5, 26–27. My argument here does not address interpretation directly but grounds, and is consistent with an account quite different to Allan's in which interpreters rightly respond to the plans of action that the legislature, which is a complex reasoning agent, likely chose; see further, my *The Nature of Legislative Intent*, chapter 9.

It is true that the legislature does not exercise adjudicative authority, which means that it is not responsible for determining the application of the law, including the law it enacts, in any particular dispute. However, this does not at all entail that the legislature does not consider the (type of) particular cases yet to arise. The legislature acts to change the law in respect of classes of future cases, intending its general rules to apply to such. Like any practical agent, the legislature does not foresee the full set of cases to which its rules will apply, but its choice is of some rule or other, which will capture some class of case because it judges that there is good reason for members of this class to be dealt with in this way. The difficulties in classification that arise in relation to some particular case in no way entail that the legislature acts only to outline a general – in the sense of abstract or incomplete – scheme, which the courts may rightly adjust to avoid what they conclude would be disproportionate or otherwise unreasonable outcomes. That the courts settle whether a rule applies in a particular case does not entail the freewheeling power to consider the justice of its application and amend the rule to suit. The legislature enacts rules that are general in the sense that they are addressed to classes of case (the instances of which may be very few) fully intending to settle how we are to act in such cases.

The duty of the legislature is to choose how (and if) to change the law, which calls for the introduction of clear, general legal rules that constitute a complex means to intelligible ends. It would be an abdication of legislative responsibility for the legislature to act at the level of abstraction that Allan enjoins, leaving to courts, after persons have acted no less, the messy business of specifying incomplete legislative acts. The exception of course is that the legislature may, and often does, choose to delegate legislative authority or to enact an imprecise standard, the full detail of which remains to be settled. The legislature's limited foresight and the uncertainty of the means in question might well warrant its choice of general, vague standards or its delegation of rulemaking authority. But this is a particular mode of exercise of legislative authority, which takes its place within the general truth that the legislature should change the law as clearly as it may, with an eye to introducing into the law, and thence into the life of the community, the changes that it thinks reasonable.

Legislators respond to reasons (centrally) with the choice of general rules. It is possible of course that the choice of a somewhat different (or more elaborate, particular) rule, or the introduction of exceptions to the chosen rule, would more closely limit the reach of the chosen legal propositions to the end(s) for which the legislature acted. This would seem to suggest that for a statutory rule to be proportionate it must avoid any gap between means and end. However, this suggestion requires qualification. The standing demands of the rule of law, as well as the legislature's institutional position, call for the legislature to respond to reasons with the choice of general rules. This generality in legal form serves to instantiate the rule of law and its attendant recognition of the equality of persons, which are themselves ends for which the legislature rightly acts. Thus, one's analysis of the ends for which the legislature acts must attend to the very good reasons there are for the legislature to choose in a certain way; in other words, adopting general rules the application of which one may reasonably foresee will not in every case serve the primary end for which the legislature acts.

The limits of legislative foresight and uncertainty of fact and aim, to which Hart points,[14] may well warrant the adoption of a vague standard or the delegation of legislative authority. However, there are often compelling reasons for choosing clear, general rules, notwithstanding one's foresight of (at least the possibility or likelihood of) a mismatch between means and ends.[15] (I set aside an important class of case in which the general rule is a good means to the legislature's chosen ends precisely because this mismatch is absent, with the application of the rule to this general class in each case serving the primary ends for which the legislature acted.) The use of general rules is very often efficient, enabling a much more effective use of limited resources than would either more elaborate, fine-grained rules or, especially, official discretion. The prospect of costly litigation about the scope and application of the rules is a related, relevant consideration.

The choice of a general rule, rather than discretion or a more opaque standard, may also best guarantee sound action in a majority of cases, notwithstanding the likelihood (or possibility, the future being somewhat unknown) of its mismatch in some. This is related to a further reason for general rules, which is that their use may help ensure consistency in application, which is often very valuable in its own right quite apart from the question of mismatch of means and ends. Further, the choice of general rules may follow from a judgment about the competence (or probity) of the officials who might otherwise exercise discretion. It is very often sound for the legislature to choose directly what should be done, rather than leaving the lawmaking function to later, inferior officials (including judges).

The relationship between proportionality and legality was in question in *Purdy*,[16] which Allan takes to be an example of the courts insisting on legality

---

[14] H.L.A. Hart, *The Concept of Law* (2nd ed., 1994) 128.
[15] See further, Sales and Hooper, "Proportionality" *supra* note 8 at 442–450.
[16] R *(on the application of Purdy) v. Director of Public Prosecutions (Society for the Protection of Unborn Children intervening)* [2009] U.K.H.L. 45, [2010] 1 A.C. 345.

and in this way helping make legislation proportionate.[17] The Suicide Act 1961 introduced an absolute proscription on assisting suicide, but provided that no prosecution was to proceed without the consent of the Director of Public Prosecutions (DPP). The House of Lords insisted that legality, which was itself a condition of proportionality (no limitation of the right to private life save "according to law"[18]), required the DPP to promulgate an offence-specific policy, so as to provide guidance to Ms. Purdy as to whether her husband would likely be prosecuted for assisting her suicide. The judgment does violence to the rule of law.[19] In effect, the court attempted to carve out an exception to the substantive criminal law by way of a de facto immunity to prosecution, rationalized on the perverse ground that would-be criminals are entitled to guidance as to the odds of their prosecution.

This judicial attempt to realize proportionality flouted the rule of law, which Parliament acted in part to secure in the Suicide Act. That Act was proportionate, in the sense I have outlined, introducing a blanket ban on assisting suicide in large part because of the importance of maintaining an exceptionless moral norm. Parliament acted to secure the sanctity of human life, including the lives of persons who might otherwise be assisted to commit suicide. The chosen means was an absolute proscription and the DPP's supervisory control over which cases should be prosecuted. The latter choice was a reasonable change to the standing proposition that any person may initiate a prosecution but in no way undercut the force or good sense of the absolute proscription. Parliament adopted a proportionate means to its chosen ends, and it is the Court that failed to understand the interplay between relevant means and ends, including the rule of law.

VI. LEGISLATING AMIDST INCOMMENSURABLES

George Pavlakos notes that the papers in this collection are divided into two camps by their attitude toward reason.[20] I doubt his division,[21] but discern a wide variation in relation to incommensurability. Contrast Allan's

---

[17] Allan, "Democracy, Legality and Proportionality" *supra* note 10 at note 78.

[18] Per Art. 8(2) of the European Convention on Human Rights.

[19] John Finnis, "Invoking the Principle of Legality against the Rule of Law" in Richard Ekins (ed.), *Modern Challenges to the Rule of Law* (2011) at 129–142.

[20] George Pavlakos, "Between Reason and Strategy: Some Reflections on the Normativity of Proportionality," Chapter 5 in this volume at note 4: "It would appear that contributions to this volume are divided in two camps according to their stance on the significance of reason and rationality."

[21] At least insofar as the division is taken to entail that skepticism of (much, some) proportionality-talk turns on, or is a concealed form of, skepticism about reason.

dismissal – relying on Alexy as authority – with Endicott and Luterán's careful treatment.[22] The latter have the better of the argument. Incommensurability rules out any technical or aggregative conception of legislative reason (which is not to say there is no technical element within legislating). For, it would be senseless to attempt to weigh intended ends against unintended side effects if "weigh" were, as in some theories, to mean "commensurate". There is no single master value to which the many basic goods that constitute human well-being reduce. It follows that acting proportionately cannot intelligibly involve commensurating, trading off, balancing, or optimizing in any technical sense the considerations at play, if they are incommensurable. One may rightly "balance" only in the metaphorical sense that one takes into account the relevant reasons and then chooses amongst reasonable alternatives.

The incommensurability of goods rules out certain modes of reasoning. It does not paralyze deliberation and action, even if it makes possible and significant the exercise of free choice. In the face of incommensurables, there may be and often is only one reasonable course of action open to the agent, by reason of intermediary principles that frame practical reason, such as the proposition – rejected by consequentialists everywhere – that one should not will evil that good may come.[23] Likewise, one's commitments, including especially the life-changing commitment of religious conversion or marriage,[24] limit the way in which it is reasonable for one to respond to otherwise incommensurable alternatives. And often, reasonable choice in the midst of incommensurables turns on one's emotions, as when one follows the golden rule, for example, the content of which turns on what one would have another do to you. The strategic role of commitment and emotion in the deliberation and choice of natural persons has its analogue, or equivalent, in the reasoning of groups and political communities and their responsible authorities.

Endicott's careful discussion of incommensurability and proportionality points to:[25]

The incommensurability problem: if there is no rational basis for deciding one way rather than the other, then the result seems to represent a departure from the rule of law, in favour of arbitrary rule by judges.

[22] Allan, "Democracy, Legality and Proportionality," *supra* note 10, text at note 59; Timothy Endicott, Chapter 14, "Proportionality and Incommensurability"; and Martin Luterán, Chapter 2, "The Lost Meaning of Proportionality" (hereinafter Luterán, "The Lost Meaning"), both in this volume.
[23] John Finnis, "Commensuration and Public Reason" essay 15 in *Collected Essays of John Finnis: Volume I*, 233 at 246–247.
[24] John Finnis, "Personal Identity in Aquinas and Shakespeare" essay 2 in *Collected Essays of John Finnis: Volume II*, 36 at 53–54.
[25] Endicott, "Proportionality and Incommensurability," *supra* note 2 at 317.

This is an interesting formulation. To my mind, it shifts focus too quickly toward adjudication and its consistency with the rule of law, and away from the prior question of what authorities should do in the face of incommensurability. This is not to say that Endicott has no answer on point: he is clear that one must choose, without reason settling what is to be done.[26] And his discussion at various points suggests that proportionality is a discipline that applies to legislators and ministers no less than judges.[27] Still, Endicott's way of framing the problem obscures its reach and his focus on the rule of law seems to presuppose a parallel with his work on vagueness.[28] He goes on to argue that it is necessary that judges perform this impossible task and therefore it is not arbitrary.[29] The air of paradox is deliberate. I have my doubts about the adequacy of his answer to the charge that such adjudication flouts the rule of law.[30] But my interest here is in the relationship between incommensurability, arbitrariness, and (proportionate) legislative choice.

Endicott's argument is that although incommensurability may seem to entail judicial arbitrariness, free judicial choice is reasonable and indeed legislative (or other) attempts to limit that choice constitute the greater risk of arbitrariness. He says, inter alia:

> Similarly, whereas every civilized legal system is committed to proportionate sentencing in criminal cases, there is no precise period of incarceration that is equal in its penal seriousness to the seriousness of the criminality of a rape or a serious assault. A uniform fixed penalty for all serious assaults would be arbitrary. There is no practical alternative to a judicial power and responsibility to balance the unbalanceable – the seriousness of the crime with the severity of the sentence.[31]
>
> ... It is not just that there is no period of imprisonment that is precisely equal to the criminality of a rape; increasing the sentence would not even *move in the direction* of equating the seriousness of the sanction with the criminality of the conduct of the defendant.[32]

Is this argument contradictory? The assertion that a uniform penalty would be arbitrary seems at odds with the assertion that a longer period of imprisonment is no more capable than a shorter period of equating to the offender's wrong.

[26] Ibid.   [27] Ibid.
[28] Ibid.; see further his *Vagueness in Law* (2000).
[29] Ibid.
[30] Grégoire Webber, "Legal Reasoning and Bills of Rights" in Richard Ekins (ed.), *Modern Challenges to the Rule of Law* (2011) 143.
[31] "Proportionality and Incommensurability," *supra* note 2 at 14; the passage ends with a footnote to Morris J. Fish, "An Eye for an Eye: Proportionality as a Moral Principle of Punishment," (2008) 28 O.J.L.S. 57.
[32] Ibid. at 15–16.

However, it is true that some (any) term of imprisonment, or any other sanction for that matter, is incommensurable with the wrong of rape (or theft or murder or blackmail). It seems mysterious then how *any* sentence may be rational that includes both the uniform penalty and penalty freely chosen by the judge.

Let me now attempt, somewhat rashly, to outline the rationality of sentencing. My aim is to clarify how the legislature is able to reason and choose in the face of incommensurables and also to contest the proposition, which Endicott maintains by implication, that the prospect of incommensurables warrants judicial discretion.[33] Proportionate legislative action, I argue, requires one to attend to that which is relevant and to choose specifications of propositions that are otherwise incomplete or unsettled. What the legislature chooses may and sometimes should be general rules that sharply confine judicial discretion.

Why would a uniform fixed penalty (say, five years imprisonment) be arbitrary? The reason is that it fails to be proportionate in the sense I outlined above, being both (in relation to different cases) *dis*proportionate and ineffectual. The uniform penalty regime would not be a sound means to the ends for which the reasonable legislature acts in this domain. Those ends include first retribution,[34] which is the restoration of the just order disrupted by the offender's wrongful choice, and second the maintenance of that just order by deterring would-be offenders, who see that their wrongful choices are likely to elicit just punishment. The former is valuable in its own right, but of course its realization constitutes in part a means to the latter (one may not rightly seek to realize the latter apart from realization of the former; proportionality is a master principle in sentencing for it limits how one may seek other ends). The uniform-penalty regime does not secure the end of retribution for it fails to respond to – it is strictly indifferent to – the particular wrongs that are committed. This failure of differentiation treats as irrelevant to an assessment of wrongfulness the many features of the wrong in question apart from its mere categorization as a "serious assault". Yet these features (premeditation, sadism, remorse) are relevant. The murder of a child is a graver wrong than injuring another in a bar fight. Realizing retribution requires consistency in response to the various wrongs offenders may commit, which entails some ranking of wrongs.

The lack of rational connection between sentence and wrong is overstated. A more severe sentence (imprisonment over fine, lengthier term over shorter

---

[33] He reiterates the point in relation to civil remedies. Ibid.
[34] On which, see John Finnis, "Retribution: Punishment's Formative Aim," 44 *Am. J. Juris.* 91 (1999).

term) does move in the direction of equating the seriousness of the sanction with the offender's wrongful choice. This is only possible because the point of imposing *any* sanction is to answer the offender's exercise of will, which is his unreasonable departure from the just order that should obtain amongst persons, with the imposition of corresponding limits on his will, on the exercise of his freedom (of which limits, imprisonment is but one form[35]). For this reason, it is intelligible to impose a relatively more severe punishment (a longer term of imprisonment) to answer the relatively graver wrong in question, and of course vice versa.

The premise of intelligible punishment is that imposing limits on the offender's exercise of his will is a meaningful response to his wrong. Deny that premise and punishment is indeed irrational. I take Endicott to mean not that punishment is irrational but that any particular sentence is incommensurable with any particular wrong. Again, there is plainly a truth here. We have reason to punish but seemingly no reason for any particular, precise punishment. The answer, I think, is that we should impose whatever sanction seems (feels) capable of realizing retribution, which choice is framed by secondary ends that include protecting the public and rehabilitating the offender (whatever the merits of imprisonment as a response to crime, it is adopted in part for these reasons). However, the legal authorities confront a series of wrongs, and conceivable wrongs, and the realization of retribution requires some consistency in how they are addressed, else no particular sentence will be understood (by the community or offender) to answer this wrongful choice, to address the features that make this choice grave or minor. My point is that there is good reason to impose punishments; the detail and severity of punishment may rightly vary by time and place, but there is good reason for all communities to impose relatively more severe punishments on graver wrongs and vice versa. There is reason, in other words, for authorities to artificially commensurate wrongs and sentences, to make judgments about the relative wrongfulness of this and that murder or rape, of this theft and that assault, and to equate this judgment of gravity with a correspondingly more or less severe sanction.

The commensuration is framed by the ends of the regime, which entail further a focus on relative gravity of the wrongfulness of the choice. The latter turns on multiple incommensurables but is not for that reason unintelligible, unlike "relative social importance",[36] which is a conclusion rather than a criterion. Although there is no common measure that permits ready comparison

---

[35] Note the artificial hierarchy of forms of punishment in the Sentencing Act 2002 (NZ).
[36] Aharon Barak, "Proportionality and Principled Balancing," (2010) 4 *Law & Ethics of Human Rights* 1 at 7.

of many wrongs, it remains intelligible to rank (roughly) particular wrongs. The golden rule assists.

The scheme of artificial commensuration must be responsive to at least much of what is relevant. But in its particular resolutions it will be underdetermined by reason. The design and choice of some sentencing regime is the complex business of *determinatio*. It involves that balance between abstract principle, existing commitments, and free choice that characterizes the move from the moral conclusion that there should be some law for this or that domain and the concrete conclusion that this set of propositions shall be that law. The legislature has first responsibility for the design and choice of this regime, enacting particular criminal proscriptions and making provision for their punishment. It would be quite wrong of the legislature simply to authorize the courts to impose just punishments for crimes, without limiting or confining that discretion, especially if there was good reason to foresee that the courts themselves would not immediately discipline and corral their discretion. The legislature should instead frame, limit, and sometimes even replace the judicial discretion to impose a particular sentence on a particular offender. For this reason, the legislature should limit the type of sentences that may be imposed in general and the sentence that may be imposed for any type of wrong in particular. The legislature should also specify considerations that must and must not be taken into account, as well as the ends for which sentencing judges should act in selecting within the open range. This process of legislative specification is consistent also with a more thorough-going rejection of judicial discretion, authorizing some body to specify guidelines that frame sharply, and even settle decisively, how some type of wrong is to be sentenced. This may, but need not, be arbitrary; it all turns on how carefully the body in question frames what is or is not relevant and how much discretion it is reasonable to leave to particular sentencing judges (who may be erratic, unprincipled, or simply inconsistent).

Proportionality is a central principle of just sentencing, an entailment of the retributive end.[37] The legislature acts proportionately in making provision for sentencing when it chooses a regime that is capable of artificially commensurating the types, and particular instances, of criminal wrongs and their corresponding sentences. This choice of regime and the commensuration it

---

[37] The virtue of mercy consists in setting proportionality aside and in choosing, in exercise of charity and for love of the offender, to punish the offender less than he otherwise deserves. There is no corresponding virtue in imposing an excessive, undeserved punishment. The law and practice of a sound polity recognizes this asymmetry in making provision (perhaps uncertain) for mercy, but forbidding disproportionate punishment.

involves and authorizes (on the part of sentencing guideline bodies or appellate courts or even first-instance sentencing judges) is an instance of *determinatio*, in which the sound ends of legislative action underdetermine the detail of what should be done.[38] The legislature progressively specifies the means to these ends, taking into account that which should be taken into account, which includes the detail of the relevant community in this time and place and including, moreover, the existing body of law on point. It follows that when one introduces a new criminal offence, one's choice of sanction is rightly and sharply constrained by the existing criminal law, which is a commitment of the political community that makes it rational to select this sanction (or range of sanctions) from amongst all the alternatives that would otherwise be rationally open. In this way, the legislature aims to legislate proportionately (and to achieve proportionality in sentencing), notwithstanding the reality and significance of incommensurability. And this does not require the strong conclusion that there is no practical alternative to open judicial discretion.

VII. RIGHTS IN LEGISLATIVE REASONING

Proportionality, suitably understood, is a general virtue of legislative deliberation and action. The legislature acts for the common good by changing the law when there is good reason for change. The legislature should not balance the common good *against* the rights of any member of the community. Any such attempt at balance would be incoherent. The reason for this is not that rights do not place moral limits on the legislator (and all authorities), but rather because rights are constitutive elements in the common good, such that reasonable reflection on the common good will involve – very often centrally – judgment about what persons are entitled to. The common good, which is the set of conditions under which members of the community are able to flourish, consists in large part of securing to each person that to which each is entitled from all other persons. What each person is entitled to is that person's rights, which take various forms: a liberty to act or refrain from acting in some way (free from a duty of the countervailing form), a claim right that some person or body perform or refrain from some act, a power to change some person's legal position, or an immunity from one's legal position being changed in some way.

The reasonable legislature does not set out to secure some public benefit, the pursuit of which involves intentional or incidental interference with people's rights, the infringement of which (or worse, violation) is justified

---

[38] John Finnis, *Aquinas: Moral, Political and Legal Theory* (1998) at 267–271.

if proportionate. Rather, the legislature deliberates about what rights citizens have, which is to say to what each should be entitled. (The legislature may also speculate about how the courts are likely to review their legislation, but this is of secondary interest.) This deliberation is moral reasoning informed and framed by empirical and technical reasoning and often calls for the exercise of free choice amongst reasonable alternatives. That is, legislative reasoning about rights is central to legislative reason in general. The reasonable legislator, like any other person, will discern that there are some absolute human rights, including the right not to be intentionally killed or tortured, which impose duties on all other persons, for example not to intentionally kill or torture others. Like any other authority, the legislature should not authorize or enjoin such acts. Indeed, the legislature has very good reason to proscribe, punish, and deter them. Thus, the legislature may act to affirm in law, to give legal support and effect to, the absolute rights that are central to sound morality.

This recognition of absolute human rights turns on recognition of the intelligible human goods that are the objects of reasonable action and insight into the principles that frame how one should realize these goods in one's life and the lives of others. More generally, this course of reflection, which is fundamental to practical reasoning and choice, informs all legislative choice, including in relation to rights. The legislature's reasoning culminates in the choice of some legal propositions, which very often specify some pattern of claim rights, duties, liberties, and powers and thus jointly constitute a series of defined relationship amongst persons. This set of relationships, which are three-term rights (some action and two persons), constitutes the legal rights of the persons in question.[39] True, the set may be voidable in part on judicial review, but subject to that qualifier, rights are legislated: they are given form and content in legislation.[40] We commonly speak of two-term rights, one's right to some subject matter, whether life or free speech or equality. These rights unify, loosely, some set (perhaps an inchoate, incomplete, yet to be fully specified set) of three-term rights, in which form they must be extended to be legally significant (that is, apart from their significance as a standing source of such extension, including invalidation of some other institution's purported extension).

The point of two-term rights, and the reason they should be recognized in legislative deliberation, is to capture some continuing aspect of human well-being and perhaps some mode of action that is consistent with, or well suited to,

---

[39] Grégoire Webber, *The Negotiable Constitution* (2009).
[40] And in rules of the common law, although very often displaced by statute.

supporting or realizing some such aspect. This general aspect the legislature should consider and take into account in its reasoning and choice of legal change. It follows that rights feature in legislative reasoning in a number of ways. The legislature aims to identify and give effect to the rights that citizens have, which requires in part reasoning about the general aspect of human well-being and/or the general normative proposition affirmed as a standing means to some such aspect. Thus, the legislature may both act to realize – introduce, support – the right in question, which means that it is an end for which it acts, and also to act consistently with the right, which disciplines the means one may choose to other ends.

Affirming the right makes salient the importance of some interest, and measures that may tend to support it, which in turn enables right-holders to call attention to their interests and to ground argument about what should be done. However, determining precisely how this under-determined aspect of human well-being is to be given legal effect requires specification. That is, the incomplete affirmation of the right is made complete by specifying the particular states of affairs to which it generally refers that are in truth valuable and to be protected, and also to specify the types of action that are to be prohibited, permitted, or enabled to that end. This specification requires the lawmaker to make more concrete the distinctions on which the general affirmation is silent; for example, between worthwhile, protected speech and false, pernicious speech. This process of specification involves focusing in detail on how the abstract value affirmed in the general right is or is not valuable in particular contexts and less abstract instantiations. It also involves careful attention to whether some particular type or action, which might be a possible concrete specification, is truly reasonable, which turns on whether it would remain the object of the reasonable person's choice when the detail of this specification and its impact on the lives of others is known. (The reasonable person in all his or her deliberations and choices is open to, and actively wills, the flourishing of all persons.)

Consider this analogy with practical reasoning in general. Some states of affairs are goods and so in principle warrant choice – they constitute the final ends of intelligent human action and are thus sufficient reasons for action. The states of affairs may be captured by referring to an abstract good, say truth or friendship or beauty. Each such abstract good captures part of that for which persons may intelligently act, reasonable participation in these goods constituting human flourishing. Identifying the abstract good in general terms is helpful for practical reasoning, not least to avoid reductive error. However, many possible states of affairs fall within, or seem to, the abstract good. The reasoning person must proceed carefully to distinguish that which is truly good and choice worthy from that which merely resembles the good. Further, identifying worthwhile states of affairs does not settle what one should do. The plurality of goods and the ways in which they may be realized or harmed in the lives of others ground norms that shape how one should reasonably act for that which is good. Thus, one must specify the abstract good, perceiving that particular states of affairs are truly worthwhile, and reflect on the norms that should restrain how one acts for those states of affairs, norms that follow from the good of intelligent self-direction and the basic equality of all persons.

When one deliberates about the common good, one should be aiming to pick out worthwhile states of affairs, realized in the lives of individual members of the community and in their interaction as members of one community. More precisely, the states of affairs constitute the set of conditions that make possible human flourishing, in which each person may live well. Hence, the good of each person and the opportunities for each person to flourish are constitutive of the common good. There is no space on this account to exploit some few (or many), deliberately harming them for some greater good or collective interest. All collective interests, properly understood, are goods for individual persons and should be sought in ways that keep the good of each person in view. That is, the neglect, through ignorance or contempt, of the good of some is unreasonable. Rights affirmed in general terms, which pick out and make salient some aspect of the well-being of each person, may help authorities to avoid acting either against the good of some for the good of others or neglecting the good of some. Thus, rights certainly express a constraint on how authority may be exercised, for rights point out particular aspects of the well-being of persons whose opportunities to flourish constitute part of the common good. However, the rights that constrain and constitute the common good, and so warrant choice, protection, and support, are not the general, incomplete rights but the rights duly specified, picking out particular states of affairs and types of action.

There is no general formula for specifying general rights to particular states of affairs and actions. The task is to choose how to secure the conditions that make possible the flourishing of members of the community. Finnis frames the task well when he argues that one should have in one's mind's eye some attractive pattern of social life and action, in which persons may live well, and then choose those particular rights that favor and support this pattern.[41] This process, which involves specification and confronts multiple irreducible goods is framed by reason but not settled by reason. Once reason has framed

---

[41] Finnis, *Natural Law and Natural Rights*, 219.

the options for choice, ruling out the many unreasonable options, what is required is choice, led by imagination, empathy, and insight and made by one whose character is sound.

Specifying rights requires – indeed *is*, in large part – reflection on the objects of a well-lived life. This requires careful attention to the ways in which the good of other persons constitutes a reason to choose, or not to choose, certain actions and the ways in which the side effects of an action may warrant its rejection. That is, what is specified may bear differently on intentional actions as opposed to unintended (even if foreseen) side effects.[42] The European Court of Human Rights obscures this central distinction in its jurisprudence on torture, wrongly extending an absolute right (proscribing intentional acts of torture) beyond its reach.[43] The sense of the distinction is also clearly relevant in relation to rights to be secure in one's property holdings. This set of rights, specified in the law of property and the public law of eminent domain, should and (notwithstanding the protestations of economists everywhere) does recognize a distinction between expropriation and regulatory impairment. The former consists in the state's intentional seizure or other use of some person's property. The latter is a side effect; in other words, a reduction in the value of one's holdings, of a state action the object of which (the means, the ends) is not such seizure or use of another's property. The economic cost may be indistinguishable but the state action is different in kind and the corresponding norms, which specify the right to property, are justly different. To be clear, that regulatory impairment is a side effect does not exclude it from moral consideration. The legislature (and other authorities) should consider the likely, foreseeable consequences of its action on the value of some citizen's property and should reject certain legislative proposals by reference to these. However, the norms that the legislature should recognize, and give effect to in the relevant bodies of law, are specified in relation to the legislative (and other official) action in question, in which the distinction between intended and unintended consequences is key.

VIII. AN EXAMPLE: RAPE SHIELD AND FAIR TRIAL

Let me outline further, by way of an example, this sketch of the relationship between rights and legislation. Consider the right to a fair trial. This captures, loosely, an important aspect of human well-being and articulates, in

---

[42] Luterán, "The Lost Meaning," *supra* note 22.
[43] *Chahal v. United Kingdom* (1996) 23 E.H.R.R. 413, on which, see John Finnis, "Nationality, Alienage and Constitutional Principle," (2007) 123 *L.Q.R.* 417, note 58.

incomplete form, a sound normative proposition. The legislature should specify the right. The rape-shield legislation in question in *R v. A (No 2)* attempted
some such, sharply limiting the circumstances in which rape defendants (and
their counsel) could cross-examine complainants on their sexual history.[44]
The legislature aimed to change the law of evidence in a way that would make
it possible for defendants to contest the charges against them, without putting
in question that which the legislature judged irrelevant, namely the sexual
history of the complainant, a focus on which might often compromise the
integrity of the trial. Further, the legislature aimed to protect complainants
from, and would-be complainants from the prospect of, intrusive, degrading
questions about their sexual history. That is, the legislature acted to give effect
to its judgment of what constitutes a fair rape trial, in which the trial does not,
save in exceptional circumstances, extend to the complainant's sexual history.

Perhaps the complainant's sexual history is often relevant evidence. Still, the
decision that some evidence that is in principle relevant should be excluded
is not novel. The right to a fair trial need not entail an absolute rule that all
relevant evidence should be admissible (or compellable). The various limits
on the introduction of evidence (say, the immunity to compulsion of priests or
doctors or lawyers who have relevant information) are not limits on the right to
a fair trial but are rather particular specifications of that right, which constitute
part of what it is to have a fair trial; specifically, that one may introduce any
evidence that is relevant that there is not otherwise a good reason to exclude.
There is more than one form of fair trial. The length and thoroughness of
criminal trials turns in part on the resources made available. Any modern
legal system should make provision for defendants to be legally represented,
but this turns on the premise that this is affordable, which entails further (alas)
that the quality of representation is limited also.

The legislature acts to protect complainants from brutal cross-examination
in part because it perceives that it is wrong, again absent exceptional circumstances (where there are reasons why the complainant's character should be
put in issue), to permit (likely) victims to be treated thus. The legislature also,
quite reasonably, has its eye on the consequences of the status quo, in which
many victims of serious sexual crime fail to report or to proceed to trial because
of their (justified!) fear of what they may endure in the witness box. This state
of affairs the legislature has good reason to address, for the sake of the just order
that is an absence of sexual crime and for the vindication of the integrity of
the rights of the particular victims in questions (to be free from sexual assault).

---

[44] *R v. A (No 2)* [2002] 1 A.C. 45; Youth Justice and Criminal Evidence Act 1999 (UK), s 41.

Thus, the pitiful figures of rape reporting and conviction rightly inform the legislature's deliberation about what constitutes a fair trial. True, a narrow focus
on this consideration alone would derail that deliberation, for the legislature
might lose sight of the importance of the open, truth-telling process that a trial
should be or, that which is related, of the prospect of unsound convictions
being entered. The legislature might act wrongly in its specification in this
domain. Still, it is not trading away the right to a fair trial against other interests
when it undertakes this deliberation and chooses as it does. Its choice is of
what is a fair trial, to which the considerations outlined here (and doubtless
many others) are relevant.

Enacting a rape-shield law may be a proportionate legislative act and a
reasonable specification of the right to a fair trial. The act is proportionate
if it is a reasonable – neither excessive nor ineffective – means to the set of
related ends for which the legislature acts: finding the truth relevant to the
charges against the defendant, protecting (likely) rape victims from unfair
treatment in the witness box, encouraging victims to come forward, avoiding
excessive costs, and maintaining the charity toward defendants that grounds
the presumption of innocence. These ends all warrant consideration and
are incommensurable. The legislature develops and evaluates proposals to
change the law by reference to these ends. The discipline of proportionality
may filter out various proposals, which are cavalier about some consideration
or ineffective means to one or other end. Still, the proportionate legislative
specification of abstract right, although informed by careful thought about the
relevant facts and possibilities (uncertainties), centrally involves the choice to
act for some state of affairs because it is judged valuable.

A postscript: it might be that the court in *R v. A (No 2)* was right and that
Parliament should have made provision for the type of case in question there
(sexual history between complainant and defendant). The court's interpretation, which it thought a more proportionate means to the legislative ends, is that
the courts have discretion to permit cross-examination whenever necessary for
a fair trial. This is telling. The court's interpretation shatters the legislative specification, reintroducing the standing prospect of unjustified cross-examination
and ignoring the significance of the truths that the courts might exercise their
discretion badly and/or that the prospect of possible cross-examination, on
uncertain grounds, might deter many complainants.

IX. PROPORTIONALITY AND RIGHTS-TALK: SOME PROBLEMS

I have set out an account of proportionate lawmaking. But imagine now that
the doctrine of proportionality is adopted as a schema for legislative reason,

at least in relation to rights. The doctrine may mislead. Perhaps legislators (and courts) often reason well under the auspices of the doctrine. Still, the doctrine does not do justice to the complexity of sound legislative reason, which I have attempted to outline, and its tenor departs from sound reason in some ways. The most obvious is the suggestion that legislation involves a conflict between rights and the common good (or public benefit or general welfare), one of which is to take precedence. The language of balancing and the often related talk of the costs and benefits of legislation suggest a disposition to collapse to an aggregative mode of reasoning, in which what should be done is thought to be a function of commensurable options. Hence, the right is contrasted with the (common) good, but the two are thought commensurable, capable of being traded off against each other and thus optimized, maximized. This perception of the relationship between right and (common) good is unsound and will stultify legislative reasoning, which should aim to specify that to which each is entitled, consistent with the disposition to be open to the flourishing of all persons. The doctrine and the corresponding scholarly discourse imply that technical reasoning, whether legal or economic, should be paramount in legislative deliberation. Forming and adopting legislative proposals requires technical competence, but the evaluation of such proposals is not at all exhausted by technical considerations. Rather, the merits of some legislative acts turn on the extent to which it is an intelligent choice of means to attractive ends. Efficiency and proportionality in the narrow sense outlined in Section IV are relevant, as are questions about legislative craft, but this does not at all mean that legislating is a technical, aggregative act.

One might say that the proportionality doctrine need not entail this unsound focus on the technical. Instead, the doctrine just draws one's attention to the ends for which the legislature acts, the means it adopts, and the other considerations relevant to whether one should adopt this means to those ends. The openness of the doctrine to collapse to the technical seems to me significant. However, let me consider this alternative understanding. Kai Möller and Mattias Kumm argue for such, and also defend the widely noted phenomenon of rights inflation.[45] Indeed, in this volume in Chapter 7, Möller explains its rationale, namely, that demanding state action constitutes a proportionate interference with the right to X (any conceivable action, or, I imagine, inaction) secures the point of proportionality, which is that limits on autonomy are justified.[46] Whereas rights inflation is, I think, no necessary entailment

---

[45] Kumm, *supra* note 1 at 12–13.
[46] Möller, *supra* note 1 at 163. Grant Huscroft criticizes rights inflation in his contribution to this volume, "Proportionality and the Relevance of Interpretation," Chapter 9, on the basis that it fails to respect the constitutional settlement that underlies the adoption of bills of rights.

of the doctrine, it is perhaps unsurprising that it occurs or is defended, for it is consistent with the technical, aggregative modes of understanding and the aspiration to question the justification of legislation. That is, when seen in these ways, rather than as a full, complete scheme for legislative deliberation and choice, the doctrine's focus on autonomy at large is understandable. This it seems to me is the ambiguities coming back to bite. For the ostensibly open, complete account is itself informed by the technical, secondary[47] conceptions.

Why object to rights inflation and the collapse to autonomy? The reasonable legislator would not adopt this focus in his deliberation, I suggest, because it obscures the multiple dimensions of what is valuable. Even autonomy loses its distinct place in this exercise, for one fails to see the point and value of intelligent self-direction, which consists in the opportunity to participate in the many alternative reasonable ways of living. One's freedom as to whom (or if) to marry or which church (if any) to attend are radically different from one's freedom as to whom (or if) to rape and torture. The latter is an action, true, but warrants no special concern in legislative reasoning save as the object of proscription and denunciation. The exclusive focus on autonomy (with other interests arising only insofar as they are called in aid to warrant limiting autonomy) follows, I think, from the self-refuting thesis of (at least some iterations of) political liberalism that the state should be neutral amongst conceptions of the good. Hence, the argument that the various stages of the proportionality doctrine serve to filter out choices that fall afoul of liberalism.[48] The defender of the doctrine might well argue that rival conceptions of the doctrine are informed by different theories of political morality. Perhaps, but then one should concede that the doctrine is not a helpful intermediary principle. One should also worry that controversial (unsound!) propositions of practical reason will be smuggled in on the sly, trading on the apparent rationality of proportionality analysis and hence receiving greater prestige in legislative deliberation than is warranted. Again, the ambiguities of proportionality are significant.

My concern that the doctrine may be reductive, obscuring the aspects of the common good and the life well led that should be the concern of the legislature, is echoed by Endicott's "overspill" pathologies.[49] What he terms "overspill" is the consideration of interests that do not warrant a place in the deliberative process. This seems to me, even if not framed as such, a perception

---

[47] That is, it is primarily directed to judges reviewing the acts of others, rather than to all who aim to act well.

[48] Mattias Kumm, "Political Liberalism and the Structure of Rights: On the Place And Limits of the Proportionality Requirement" in S. Paulson and George Pavlakos (eds.), *Law, Rights, Discourse: Themes from the Legal Philosophy of Robert Alexy* (2007) 131.

[49] Endicott, "Proportionality and Incommensurability," *supra* note 2 at 329–335.

of the way in which proportionality analysis is disposed to be reductive, to be instrumental, to fail to attend to each value or interest in its own right and also without considering the ways in which that value or interest are implicated by the state action in question. That is, one loses sight of the significance of the state action intentionally limiting an aspect of some person's well-being or merely limiting it as an unintended side effect of the pursuit of some end. I find compelling Endicott's extended example of the way in which the proposition that the state should "respect family life" has collapsed to an undiscerning exercise in balancing family life against some state objective.[50] (However, I note in passing that I doubt his asymmetry thesis:[51] first because he gives no grounds to substantiate it and second because it seems to presuppose some version of the disjuncture between common good and individual rights that I critiqued above.)

Finnis argues that notwithstanding its many opportunities for distortion and misunderstanding, there are three advantages to rights-talk: it affirms the equality of all persons, it eschews consequentialism, and it draws attention to various aspects of (and supports for) human flourishing.[52] All three of these advantages are put in question by some of the ways in which the doctrine is understood. The collapse to the technical gives comfort to consequentialism, and the collapse to autonomy obscures the breadth and depth of human well-being, or at least arbitrarily privileges one such aspect, shorn from context and supporting structure, over all others.

Quite apart from the likelihood that the doctrine, as embellished and elaborated by its scholarly proponents, may distort one's perception of the objects of intelligible human action, the doctrine misdirects legislative reasoning in another way. It encourages salience bias and a loss of perspective in which the question at hand is the resolution of this case and this case only. This means that the other cases that fall under the rule in question do not receive the attention they deserve and that the other ends for which the legislature should act, including the rule of law, may slip out of focus. This is part and parcel of a more general reduction of legislative reasoning to a kind of instrumental rationality, in which the question is the efficiency of means to some single end, which is an objective to be attained by skillful execution rather than a state of affairs consisting in a range of complex ends, the breadth and depth of which bears on the evaluation of suitable means. The doctrine may be taken

---

[50] Ibid. (whole chapter).

[51] The thesis is that one should "positively cherish" judges erring in favor of the individual if the alternative is that they err in favor of the state. Ibid. at 25.

[52] Finnis, *Natural Law and Natural Rights, supra* note 7 at 221.

also to give legislators reason to focus on some particular case only, rather than attending to the range of cases that fall within their chosen rules, and also to authorize judicial or other official discretions rather than to make law in the form of rules.

There is a connection here to Endicott's second pathology:[53] by virtue of the salience of this particular case and the pseudo-logic of the burden of proof in constitutional litigation, the interests (or claims) of the applicant in question, who contests some general rule, are granted too much sway in the inquiry into what should be done. What each person is entitled to – no more and no less – is the upshot of deliberation that holds in mind the good of all and culminates in reasonable choice. This secures, inter alia, some absolute rights. It does not warrant particular exceptions, or provision to be made for such, to each and every general rule.

X. CONCLUSION

One legislates proportionately by working up and choosing proposals to change the law, which are fit to serve as means to the intelligible ends for which one acts. That is, the legislature should choose proposals that are effective (or at least not ineffective) but not excessive means to the ends of its action, which are the states of affairs that constitute the common good. These ends are complex, multiple, and incommensurable. Their realization calls for specification, which often involves choices under-determined by reason, informed by the standing rational force of the rule of law. The proportionality of legislative action, as I have explained it, is an irreducible aspect of sound legislative reason. But it does not exhaust legislative deliberation and warrants being kept in due proportion in its turn. When taken for the whole, and thus understood to extend to all that is relevant in determining the relationship between legislation and rights, proportionality is liable to reduce or obscure much that is important. The legislature should discipline itself to act proportionately, but this is not to say that it would be wise to adopt the doctrine of proportionality as a guide to its deliberation and choice. The doctrine, especially as elaborated by some of its judicial and scholarly advocates, is disposed to confuse elements of sound legislative reason. Hence, for the legislature to act proportionately, as it should, it may need to set aside the doctrine itself.

---

[53] Which is: "the unwarranted weighing of private interests in the 'balance,'" Endicott, "Proportionality and Incommensurability," *supra* note 2 at 330.

16 Proportionality's Blind Spot: "Neutrality" and Political Philosophy

Bradley W. Miller*

I. INTRODUCTION

The promise of proportionality analysis is to structure legal and moral reasoning, directing decision makers to consider relevant interests that tend to be overlooked, and to expose irrelevant or inappropriate considerations that might deflect reasonable decision making. In the context of judicial review under a bill of rights, proportionality analysis is said to constrain judicial discretion and promote objectivity and transparency in judicial reasoning.[1] Several scholars, however, argue that there are problems inherent to proportionality analysis that necessarily prevents it from delivering the promised goods.[2] Other critics, although sharing these pragmatic concerns, raise a fundamental objection of political principle: that proportionality analysis undermines constitutional settlements and constitutes an illegitimate, judicially sponsored transfer of power.[3] This chapter pursues a third line of criticism, which investigates how

* A draft of this chapter was first presented at a faculty seminar at Princeton University organized by the James Madison Program in American Ideals and Institutions. I would like to acknowledge the support of the James Madison Program, provided through the Ann and Herbert W. Vaughan Visiting Fellowship. For helpful comments on earlier drafts of this chapter, I would like to acknowledge Grant Huscroft, Grégoire Webber, Iain Benson, Martin Loughlin, Adam McLeod, Bradford Wilson, and Paul Carrese.

[1] Aharon Barak, *Proportionality: Constitutional Rights and Their Limitations* (2012), at 131–33, 457–67 (hereinafter Barak, *Proportionality*). See also, contributions to this volume by Kai Möller (Chapter 7), Georgios Pavlakos (Chapter 5), T.R.S. Allan (Chapter 10), and David Dyzenhaus (Chapter 11).

[2] See Martin Luterán, "The Lost Meaning of Proportionality," Chapter 2 in this volume; and Grégoire Webber, "On the Loss of Rights," Chapter 6 in this volume. Also Grégoire C.N. Webber, *The Negotiable Constitution: On the Limitation of Rights* (2009) at 87–115 (hereinafter Webber, *The Negotiable Constitution*).

[3] On proportionality's expansion of judicial discretion and inability to provide guide decision making, see Grant Huscroft, "Proportionality and the Relevance of Interpretation" (Chapter 9); and Luterán, "The Lost Meaning of Proportionality" (Chapter 2), in this volume.

the dominant judicial practice of reasoning with a proportionality test tends to result in judges excluding – without justification – entire classes of interests from their deliberations.

The practice of proportionality is not best understood as a simple transfer of decision-making authority from legislators to judges, or as a means of ensuring that legislative acts are justified. The adoption of proportionality reasoning in fact alters the nature of legal reasoning, and does so in ways that are easily overlooked.[4] Timothy Endicott's perceptive exploration of what he terms "the pathologies of proportionality" maps out some of these problems.[5] But there is a significant pathology – identified in passing by Richard Ekins[6] – that Endicott leaves unexplored: the judicial propensity when reasoning through a proportionality doctrine to discount, or exclude a priori, many aspects of the public good that are commonly the concern of the legislator. This chapter advances the argument that this structure of reasoning, one that is intended to promote objectivity and transparency, has unfortunately come to serve as ready cover for the judicial adoption of undefended (and sometimes unarticulated) commitments of political philosophy, most notably the assumption of the commitments of political liberalism, particularly the thesis that the political community must remain neutral about what constitutes a good life. This tendency within the practice of proportionality reasoning can be judged to be pathological not only by those who disagree with the principles of political philosophy that are now declared to be axiomatic, but by anyone who believes that legitimacy of judicial review requires that controversial principles of political philosophy not be pressed into law either covertly or accidentally.

The course of this chapter is to first to identify a few conceptual problems that tend to accompany the discourse of proportionality reasoning, before proceeding to investigate the relationship between proportionality reasoning and transparency in the adoption of commitments of political philosophy.

II. PROPORTIONALITY AND LEGAL REASONING – SOME PITFALLS

The rapid proliferation of proportionality analysis in human rights adjudication makes it hazardous to talk of proportionality analysis simpliciter, rather than the commitments of particular proportionality theorists, or the doctrines and

---

[4] On the way in which proportionality distorts reasoning by adopting an unsound conception of rights, see Webber, "On the Loss of Rights," Chapter 6 in this volume; and Bradley W. Miller, "Justification and Rights Limitations" in Grant Huscroft (ed.) *Expounding the Constitution* (2008) at 93 (hereinafter Miller, "Justification and Rights Limitations"). See also, Webber, *The Negotiable Constitution, supra* note 2 at chapter 4.

[5] Timothy Endicott, "Proportionality and Incommensurability," Chapter 14 in this volume.

[6] Richard Ekins, "Legislating Proportionately," Chapter 15 in this volume at 367.

practices of particular courts. Like most interesting constitutional concepts, proportionality does not have a generally accepted canonical formulation[7] or theoretical basis. The critic who endeavors to addresses proportionality analysis "writ large" risks skating over many differences in theory and practice, and drawing the objection that, as Grégoire Webber notes, the critic is either attacking a straw man or a noncentral, idiosyncratic version of proportionality.[8] Criticism of judicial practice is especially troublesome, as the weakly reasoned decisions of a court in one jurisdiction may well be a local and contingent problem, rather than a problem immanent in proportionality doctrine. Like the pathologies identified by Endicott, proportionality's inclination toward "neutral" liberalism is a particular and not general pathology; it is neither conceptually necessary nor invariably practiced. That said, where courts in unrelated jurisdictions converge on a pattern of reasoning such as the adoption of the commitments of political liberalism, and are supported in doing so by a substantial body of academic opinion, that convergence warrants some attention. The fact that a dominant practice is neither logically entailed by proportionality nor conceptually necessary is not a reason to withhold critique. If proportionality analysis, in its dominant use by judges and exposition by scholars, can be shown to suffer from a characteristic and observable flaw, this is a reason to reform the dominant practice.

As a preliminary to addressing the question of the relationship between proportionality reasoning and political philosophy, it will be useful to first address two common obstacles to clear thinking about proportionality analysis and legal reasoning: (1) the alleged distinction between policy and principle, and (2) confusion about the simultaneously moral and technical dimensions of legal reasoning.

The Problem of the Principle/Policy Distinction

In evaluating the practice of proportionality, it is important to distinguish between its use in the service of legislation and its use in judicial review, because the nature of the reasoning involved in legislating is often significantly

---

[7] Aharon Barak's formulation, however, is serviceable: "Proportionality . . . can be defined as the set of rules determining the necessary and sufficient conditions for a limitation of a constitutionally protected right by a law to be constitutionally permissible." A limitation is permissible if "(i) it is designated for a proper purpose; (ii) the measures . . . are rationally connected to the fulfillment of that purpose; (iii) . . . there are no alternative measures that may similarly achieve the same purpose with a lesser degree of limitation"; and (iv) balancing between the achievement of the purpose and the importance of preventing the limitation of the right. Barak, *Proportionality*, supra note 1 at 3.

[8] Webber, "On the Loss of Rights," Chapter 6 in this volume at 123–124.

different from the nature of the reasoning involved in judicial review.[9] Contrary to an influential and enduring misconception, however, this is not because of a supposed division of labor between legislatures as the forum of policy, and courts as the forum of principle.[10] It is necessary to get clear of this proposed division, because if left untreated it can badly distort one's understanding of not only proportionality analysis, but judicial review in general. The misconception, most often associated with the early work of Ronald Dworkin, is that the legislature is predominantly concerned with matters of *policy*, conceived as the pursuit of collective goals and projects whose realization are important for economic, political, or social reasons.[11] A decision to build a bridge, for example, (including the ancillary decisions of where to locate it, and with what budget) would be considered, on this conception, to be a matter of policy. On this view, legislative reasoning is consequentialist, and legislative proposals are evaluated on the basis of their expected economic, political, or social results. Questions of principle might arise (would it be fair to build the bridge so close to the Smiths' house that the value of their property – and their enjoyment of it – will be sharply diminished?) and the legislature would not be precluded from attending to them. On Dworkin's model, however, no one should expect the legislature to look out for the best interests of any individual, or to be responsive to anyone's assertions of right or complaints of unfair treatment. That task falls to the courts, the "forum of principle", which is understood to have been assigned the responsibility of making principled determinations as to whether an individual before it has been treated unjustly according to standards posited in the constitutional law.[12]

Dworkin's principle/policy dichotomy has been severely criticized, not only because of its bleak view of legislatures, but also because of the aggregative, utilitarian conception of public good that the dichotomy depends on.[13] On

---

[9] Ekins, "Legislating Proportionately," Chapter 15 in this volume; and see further, Ekins, *The Nature of Legislative Intent* (2012). On the nature of legal reasoning, see John Finnis, "Legal Reasoning as Practical Reasoning" in *The Collected Essays of John Finnis*, I.14 (2011) (hereinafter *C.E.J.F*) (hereinafter Finnis, "Practical Reasoning"), and "Commensuration and Public Reasons," (hereinafter Finnis, "Commensuration") in *The Collected Essays of John Finnis*, I.15 (2011). On the difference between legislative reasoning and judicial reasoning, see Jeremy Waldron, "Do Judges Reason Morally?" in Huscroft (ed.), *Expounding the Constitution* (2008) 38 (hereinafter Waldron, "Do Judges Reason Morally?").

[10] This is a position most commonly associated with Ronald Dworkin. See Ronald Dworkin, *Taking Rights Seriously* (1977) at 22, 90–94 (hereinafter Dworkin, *Taking Rights Seriously*), and *A Matter of Principle* (1985) at 359 and 387 (hereinafter Dworkin, *A Matter of Principle*).

[11] *Taking Rights Seriously*, ibid. at 22.   [12] Ibid. at 90.

[13] D.N. MacCormick, *Legal Reasoning and Legal Theory* (1978) at 259–264 (hereinafter MacCormick, *Legal Reasoning*); John Finnis, "Human Rights and Their Enforcement," in

the aggregative account, legislatures make decisions on the basis of what benefits the majority (and, not coincidentally, what contributes to the legislative members' reelection), so that the Smiths' interest in their house could be outweighed by the convenience of a thousand commuters. On a non-aggregative conception of the public interest – or public good – the legislature has an obligation to consider impartially the needs and well-being of all persons (including the Smiths), such that any decision to expropriate property, for example, must not be a manifestation of favoritism, or undertaken as a means to punish, or made without reasonable compensation.[14] If the legislature's motivation for pursuing so-called policy goals is to promote (impartially) the well-being of all persons, it is plausible to describe most policy decisions made by the legislature as a function of principle: of furthering the well-being of those persons for whom they are responsible.[15] The central case of legislation,[16] like the central case of judicial review, involves principled decision making; that is, acting for *reasons* that are ordered to the pursuit of the public good. And in this context, the pursuit of the public good must not be caricatured as the sheer imposition of majoritarian will or part of a utilitarian cost-benefit analysis, but should be understood as a conscientious consideration of what course of action is in the best interests of a community made up of persons, each of whom is entitled to have their well-being taken into account.[17]

If one follows Dworkin into the principle/policy error, it will hamper one's conception of proportionality reasoning in the following manner. On the two-stage model of analysis adopted by many courts, such as the Israeli Supreme Court and the Supreme Court of Canada, the onus is on the individual complainant to establish a limitation on the complainant's constitutional rights. Thereafter, the onus shifts to the government to establish that the limit placed

---

C.E.J.F., III.1 (2011) 19 at 31–37 (hereinafter Finnis, "Human Rights"); Jeremy Waldron, "Rights and Majorities: Rousseau Revisited" in Waldron, *Liberal Rights* (1993) at 392; Robert P. George, *Making Men Moral* (1993) at 85–93; Miller, "Justification and Rights Limitations," *supra* note 4 at 100–105; Aileen Kavanagh, *Constitutional Review under the UK Human Rights Act* (2009).

[14] See Martin Luterán's discussion of moral reasoning in the context of expropriation in "The Lost Meaning of Proportionality" Chapter 2 in this volume at 33.

[15] Miller, "Justification and Rights Limitations," *supra* note 4 at 105; John Finnis, "Human Rights," *supra* note 13; Finnis, *Natural Law and Natural Rights* (2nd ed. 2011) at 168, 210–218 (hereinafter Finnis, *Natural Law*); George, *Making Men Moral* at 90–93; Webber, *The Negotiable Constitution*, supra note 2 c. 5.

[16] On the central case, see H.L.A. Hart, *The Concept of Law* (1961) at 15–16, Finnis, *Natural Law*, ibid. c. 1; N.W. Barber, *The Constitutional State* (2010) at 8–12.

[17] None of this is to deny that it is possible for legislators to shirk their obligations and subordinate their reasoning to crass and ignoble purposes (e.g., to pander to the demands of a majority or a minority for reasons of reelection), or that judges face parallel temptations to willfully ignore binding precedent and manipulate their reasoning to serve careerist or ideological ends.

on the complainant's right was nevertheless justified and not, all things considered, a violation of anyone's rights.[18] If the policy/principle distinction is not resisted, it will lead to conceiving of the government's role, at the second stage, as arguing that legislation ought to prevail over the rights of the individual simply because it is the will of the majority imposed by pure legislative *fiat*. It misconceives of legislation as centrally a matter of the imposition of power. This is a bad conceptualization of both legislating and legal reasoning. Typically, the submissions of Attorneys General are not best understood as voluntarist or as presupposing utilitarianism; that is, they are not arguments that although there has been a violation of rights, that violation is nevertheless justified *because* the majority will it, or because a greater net good will result from the deprivation of the complainant's rights. Instead, a court is typically asked by an attorney general to conclude that the legislature's decision to adopt a statute, in view of the totality of the circumstances, is in no way a violation of anyone's rights. The arguments made by both the complainant and the government should be understood as arguments of principle.[19]

Judicial Reasoning: Not Merely Technical, Not Purely Moral

Proportionality reasoning is sometimes presented as being in the order[20] of technical reasoning rather than moral reasoning.[21] This is an error. Although proportionality analysis is, in part, a matter of technique, it also (often) requires moral evaluation. A brief reflection on the differences between judicial

---

[18] For the conceptual problems caused by the two-stage bill of rights, see Finnis, "Human Rights," *supra* note 13; Miller, "Justification and Rights Limitations," *supra* note 4; and Webber, *The Negotiable Constitution, supra* note 2 chapter 3. For a sound account of the conception of rights from which I am working, see Webber, "On the Loss of Rights," Chapter 6 in this volume.

[19] Miller, "Justification and Rights Limitations," *supra* note 4 at 101–105.

[20] On the four kinds of order, including the moral and technical/cultural and their significance in legal reasoning, see Finnis, "Practical Reasoning," *supra* note 9 at 216 220; also John Finnis, *Aquinas* (1998), c. 2.

[21] This questionable position is elaborated by David Beatty in *The Ultimate Rule of Law* (2004) (generally, and at 166–176). Beatty's defense of proportionality is premised on the belief that evaluation in the moral order can be avoided by recasting moral questions as questions about logic or facts: "[P]roportionality turns the review process into a relatively straightforward exercise of logical or syllogistic reasoning" (169), and "Turning conflicts about people's most important interests and ideas into matters of fact, rather than matters of interpretation or matters of moral principle, allows the judiciary to supervise a discourse in which each person's perception of a state's course of action is valued equally and for which there is a correct resolution that can be verified empirically" (171, footnotes omitted). For a critique of this position, see Webber, *The Negotiable Constitution, supra* note 2 at 104–110 and Richard A. Posner, *How Judges Think* (2008) at 353–362.

reasoning and legislative reasoning can bring into relief the role of moral reasoning in judicial application of a proportionality doctrine.

Although it is most often addressed in the context of judicial reasoning, proportionality analysis, as Richard Ekins demonstrates, has a life outside of judicial reasoning that is not merely the legislators' predictions or anticipations of how a judge reviewing the legislation would conduct proportionality analysis.[22] The nature of the differences between the reasoning proper to judicial review and the reasoning proper to legislating is well-traveled ground.[23] It is sufficient to note, for present purposes, that the decision to adopt a legislative proposal more closely resembles open-ended, free-ranging moral reasoning. By contrast, judicial reasoning (at least in so-called hard cases) is well described as moral reasoning that is artificially constrained.[24] Although moral reasoning can emerge close to the surface of judicial reasoning (particularly in interpreting concepts such as "equality", "reasonableness," and "fundamental justice"), judicial reasoning is never coterminous with moral reasoning. Prior commitments posited through legislation and acts of adjudication, as well as common law doctrines including precedent and the more or less technical rules of statutory interpretation, all serve to constrain and direct the moral reasoning of judges.

That said, judges overstate the nature of the difference between moral and legal reasoning to the extent that they claim that resolving a constitutional challenge to legislation can be a matter of settling a *purely* legal question, implying that it is entirely a matter of value-free *technical* reasoning, with no room whatsoever for moral reasoning. There is, of course, an incentive for judges to downplay the degree to which they are engaging in moral reasoning. Judges, trained in the techniques of reasoning with the law, can be expected to have comparative expertise in resolving the technical questions of law. But in circumstances where questions of law draw close to unbounded moral reasoning, that comparative expertise disappears. Where the moral evaluation in question will be particularly controversial (for example, should we as a society permit euthanasia or abortion? which social arrangements should we recognize as marriages?), courts risk push-back from dissatisfied legislators (and members of the public) who understand themselves to have been second-guessed on matters not solidly within either judges' or lawyers' expertise.

---

[22] Ekins, "Legislating Proportionately," Chapter 15 in this volume.
[23] See, for example, Jeremy Waldron, "Do Judges Reason Morally?" *supra* note 9 at 38.
[24] Finnis, "Practical Reasoning," and Finnis, "Commensuration" *supra* note 9 at 233; MacCormick, *Legal Reasoning, supra* note 13.

The judicial pull toward characterizing proportionality analysis as technical is in part explained by the recent history of proportionality as a doctrine of constitutional law.[25] In many jurisdictions, such as Germany, Canada, and Israel, the introduction of proportionality into constitutional law was an initiative of the judiciary. There is nothing in the text of the Canadian Charter of Rights and Freedoms, to take one example, that compels the use of a proportionality test.[26] Instead, the limitations clause in the Charter of Rights and Freedoms simply states that the posited rights are "guaranteed only to such reasonable limits prescribed by law as can be demonstrably justified in a free and democratic society".[27] The text raises large interpretive questions. Does the text incorporate – as it appears to – the entire political morality of a free and democratic society? This is not only a question about what constitutes a reasonable limit, but about what the nature of a *society* is and its relationship with its individual members. What constitutes a society (specifically a democratic society) and its common good, and what sorts of restrictions on persons can be justified by that common good, are large, perennially contested questions of political philosophy. These are not questions that have been historically understood to be questions of *law*, to be answered by judges. Nevertheless, that it is what these texts seem to contemplate.

It is not surprising that a judge confronted with the task of interpreting such a text from a standing start would look for a means to turn it into something more familiar, more closely related to legal learning, more technical. A proportionality test is thought to serve the purpose. Instead of having to dispute contested questions of political philosophy, judges could instead focus on a discrete set of technically worded inquiries. And in the very specific circumstances articulated by Martin Luterán, proportionality reasoning can be largely technical reasoning. In many instances, a proportionality inquiry can be resolved using the criterion of "necessity" or "minimal impairment," rather than the more controversial "balancing". That is, if the objectives of the impugned legislation could have been achieved more *efficiently* (that is, with the [more or less] same results achieved by some less-restrictive means),

---

[25] A much richer history is chronicled by Luterán in "The Lost Meaning of Proportionality," Chapter 2 in this volume.

[26] This is in contrast with the much more detailed Article 36 of the Constitution of the Republic of South Africa, which posits the same grounds of limitation as those articulated judicially in Canada in *R. v. Oakes*, [1986] 1 S.C.R. 103.

[27] The New Zealand language is almost identical: "subject only to such reasonable limits prescribed by law as can be demonstrably justified in a free and democratic society." New Zealand Bill of Rights Act 1990. See Paul Rishworth, Grant Huscroft, Scott Optican, and Richard Mahoney, *The New Zealand Bill of Rights* (2003).

then the legislation could be disposed of without having to delve into the even more wide-ranging evaluation of the legislative purpose and the restricted act required by balancing.[28] But the point should not be overstated. Even minimal impairment/necessity tests cannot do entirely without evaluation. The criteria for establishing whether other means will allow for a legislative proposal's purposes to be achieved *sufficiently*, or whether a limitation on a right can be considered to be minimal, will be, in part, moral criteria. Likewise, the question of the importance of the legislation itself is not a question that can be answered empirically or through the ordinary techniques of legal reasoning.

As judges grapple with constitutional texts that require moral reasoning, the moral reasoning often occurs off-stage. Either they: (1) genuinely err in mistranslating moral questions into technical/factual questions, or (2) take up Mattias Kumm's invitation to turn from *interpretation* – which is concerned with what the text of a bill of rights means and which legal doctrines ought be constructed from it – and toward *justification*,[29] which is more or less a matter of unconstrained practical reasoning.[30] Kumm, although advocating for unconstrained practical reasoning in proportionality reasoning, nevertheless understands the imperative that judges appear to be engaged in purely technical reasoning. He views proportionality's shadow-play as a key to its success; in order to maintain popular support for judicial review, it is essential that controversial moral reasoning be disguised as nonevaluative and technical.[31]

Aside from the question of whether, as Kumm argues, the "noble lie" can be justified, two problems now emerge. The first, which will be surveyed only briefly, relates to judicial review generally. The second is specific to proportionality and will occupy the balance of this chapter. First, we must confront the difficulties of judges engaging in full-blown moral reasoning on behalf of an entire society, choosing the commitments that will define national character and authoritatively settle how persons and communities will live together. This raises questions both about judges' ability to reason

---

[28] Luterán, "The Lost Meaning of Proportionality," Chapter 2 in this volume.

[29] Mattias Kumm, "The Idea of Socratic Contestation and the Right to Justification: The Point of Rights-Based Proportionality Review," 4 *Law & Ethics of Human Rights* (2010) at 142 (hereinafter Kumm, "Socratic Contestation").

[30] See Kumm and Walen, "Human Dignity and Proportionality: Deontic Pluralism in Balancing," Chapter 4; as well as T.R.S. Allan, "Democracy, Legality, and Proportionality," Chapter 10; David Dyzenhaus, "Proportionality and Deference in a Culture of Justification," Chapter 11; and Kai Möller, "Proportionality and Rights Inflation," Chapter 7, all in this volume.

[31] "Perhaps the secret of the success of rights-based proportionality review is directly connected to its technocratic camouflage (a multi-pronged legalistic sounding test) and its embeddedness in legal institutions that work together to obscure its true nature." Kumm, "Socratic Contestation," *supra* note 29 at 174.

well to these sorts of conclusions, as well as the legitimacy of their doing so.[32] Briefly, with respect to ability, judges face a host of institutional infirmities related to the exigencies of the court room: (1) the limits on who has standing to make submissions and produce evidence (further restricted by a plaintiff's objection to interveners on the basis that the larger issues they raise will distract from the plaintiff's particular complaint); (2) the plaintiff's timing of the suit (and perhaps pursuit of an expedited hearing) so as to prejudice the government's ability to secure expert witnesses and present a complete record; and (3) the limited number of days that are available for a hearing, compared to the more open-ended schedules available to government committees and royal commissions. All of these restrictions – necessary in civil and criminal trials so as to prevent a legal system from completely bogging down – serve to ensure that the information available to a judge is a fraction of that to which a legislator would have access. Added to these systemic epistemological problems are problems personal to judges: for the most part, judges have no significant training in moral reasoning. But even if they had all received remedial continuing legal education by, say, Ronald Dworkin, it would hardly answer the objection. Practical reasoning is, by its nature, deeply controversial. Disagreement about how best to resolve the sorts of issues that end up before constitutional courts is endemic.[33] There is no obvious reason why the moral reasoning of judges – which may be deeply idiosyncratic or may track the predilections of the community from which they were selected or (more likely) to which they now belong – should prevail over the moral reasoning of legislative bodies.[34]

The second – and larger question, for the purpose of this chapter – is whether the remedy (of adopting proportionality analysis as a means of coping with a greatly expanded judicial function under a bill of rights) is cost free? The adoption of proportionality analysis under a bill of rights is not merely a matter of facilitating a transfer of power from one political institution to another. Several hidden costs and distortions of proportionality reasoning are

---

[32] I will not investigate a further problem related to whether judges have in fact been entrusted with this task. That is a question of positive law and, as such, is jurisdiction specific. For a defense of the proposition that the power of judicial review under a constitution is a question of positive law rather than natural law, see Robert P. George, "Natural Law, the Constitution, and the Theory and Practice of Judicial Review," 69 *Fordham L. Rev.* (2001) at 2269–2283.

[33] See Jeremy Waldron, *Law and Disagreement* (1999); Cass Sunstein, *Legal Reasoning and Political Conflict* (1996).

[34] Jeremy Waldron, "The Core of the Case Judicial Review," (2006) 115 *Yale L.J* 1346. But see W.J. Waluchow, *A Common Law Theory of Judicial Review: The Living Tree* (2007) (hereinafter Waluchow, *A Common Law Theory*), for the argument that judicial independence from electors makes judges better able to rise above the biases of the majority and make decisions on a more principled basis than legislators.

documented in this volume by Endicott (Chapter 14), Webber (Chapter 6), and Ekins (Chapter 15). The remainder of this chapter explores how a further distortion in reasoning is caused by proportionality proponents' casual assumption of the commitments of anti-perfectionist liberalism.

III. PROPORTIONALITY'S PERMEABILITY TO PRACTICAL REASONING

Proportionality reasoning cannot proceed without moral evaluation. This is most obviously the case when balancing the value of achieving a legislative goal against the loss experienced by persons who are denied some liberty or benefit that they claim as a matter of right. But moral evaluation is also significant to other stages of the analysis, often in ways that go unnoticed. This is not to suggest that proportionality reasoning is purely moral reasoning. Particularly when assessing necessity (or minimal impairment), technical evaluations and factual assessments are required. For example, the question of whether a requirement that cigarette manufacturers provide health warnings that are attributed to a government agency will be equally effective to a requirement that cigarette manufacturers provide unattributed health warnings is a factual and technical question.[35] But determining what constitutes *adequate* or *substantial* fulfillment of a governmental objective (will it be a 10 percent reduction in smoking, a 50 percent reduction, achieving a completely smoke-free society?), or whether the political community ought to be willing to accept a 20 percent reduction in efficacy (instead of a 50 percent reduction) in exchange for less-burdensome legislation is not a factual or technical matter.

Outside of balancing *stricto sensu*, moral evaluation is also often required in ascertaining the purpose of legislation, and assessing whether that purpose is sufficiently important to justify the limitation of right. Ascertaining legislative purpose is a matter of moral evaluation because it is a matter of both describing and interpreting a social institution – legislation.[36] This point is easy to overlook because in many jurisdictions, little analytical work appears to take place at this stage. "Proper purpose" typically presents a low hurdle, and very few cases are decided on the basis that the purpose of the impugned legislation is constitutionally infirm.[37] However, to fully appreciate the nature of this stage

---

[35] *RJR MacDonald Inc. v. Canada (AG)*, [1995] 3 S.C.R. 199.

[36] John Finnis, *Natural Law, supra* note 15, ch. 1.

[37] A rare example is *R. v. Big M Drug Mart Ltd.*, [1985] 1 S.C.R. 295, where the Lord's Day Act, which mandated shop-closing on the Christian Sabbath, was characterized as having the improper purpose of compelling religious practice. In effect, the legislation was understood to have as its purpose the violation of a person's s. 2(a) right to freedom of religion.

of proportionality reasoning, one has to attend not only to those rare cases in which courts conclude that a statute does not have a proper purpose, but to the many cases in which courts decide that it does. Of greater significance than the straightforward judicial statements evaluating the purpose of a statute are the characterizations or descriptions of the purpose. Significant evaluations of legislative purpose sometimes occur off-stage, in that legislative purposes are either perceived and dismissed out of hand, or simply never cross the judge's field of vision. For example, in reviewing the decision of the Canadian government not to grant a safe-injection site an exemption from the criminal prohibition of possession and trafficking in narcotics,[38] the Supreme Court of Canada never considered, or even addressed, the arguable purpose that the government had refused to grant the license in question so as not to be complicit in the use of illegal, intravenous drugs by members of the state.[39] This is a purpose that was not raised by the courts because, presumably, it did not fall within the range of legislative purposes that the court would be willing to accept.

Now conclusions as to the reasons why courts do not raise – even to dismiss – certain legislative purposes must be speculative. A less speculative and more complex example of moral evaluation in ascertaining legislative purpose involves the positive misdescription by reviewing courts of the moral evaluations underlying the enactment of legislation.

Consider how Victorian legislators (and their successors up to the mid-twentieth century) who criminalized acts of indecency or obscenity are often portrayed as acting for the purpose of preserving conventional morality per se. That is, they are understood as acting for the trivial purpose of preventing the offence that results from flouting social conventions. The conventions themselves are understood to be mere matters of taste – matters that are indifferent in themselves – such that there can be no genuine, free-standing wrong in breaching them. In contrast, contemporary criminal prohibitions are usually characterized in terms of combating "harm" (usually understood thinly, in the sense of empirically observable acts of violence, theft, fraud, and the like) rather than as preserving "morality" (understood as individualistic, subjective, and incapable of being true or false).[40] The result is that the purpose of "vintage" legislation is often badly mischaracterized by contemporary reviewing

---

[38] *Canada (AG) v. PHS Community Services Society*, [2011] 3 S.C.R. 134 [*Insite*].

[39] This point was raised in the factum of the Attorney General of Canada in *Insite* (retrieved from http://www.scc-csc.gc.ca/factums-memoires/33556/FM010_Appellants_Attorney-General-of-Canada-and-Minister-of-Health-for-Canada.pdf) at paras. 21 and 90–91, 97–102, 118–23).

[40] See, for example, *R. v. Butler*, [1992] 1 S.C.R. 452, and the discussion of that case in Bradley W. Miller, "Morals Laws in an Age of Rights: Hart and Devlin at the Supreme Court of Canada," 55 *Am. J. Juris.* 79 (2010) (hereinafter Miller, "Morals Laws").

courts, in a way that seriously and unreasonably hampers the legislation when assessed in a proportionality analysis.

This sort of mischaracterization of legislative purpose is illustrated in a recent decision striking down a criminal prohibition relating to prostitution. In *Canada (Attorney General) v. Bedford* (2013),[41] the Supreme Court of Canada came to the surprising conclusion that none of the various criminal prohibitions related to prostitution (such as maintaining a bawdy house, living off the avails of prostitution, and communicating for the purposes of prostitution) could be characterized, either separately or taken as a suite of provisions, as directed toward the eradication of prostitution itself.[42] Parliament's attitude toward prostitution, as reflected in the criminal prohibitions, was said to be no different than its attitude toward any other legal commercial enterprise: prostitution was not to be discouraged, but to be tolerated.[43] The objectives of the bawdy-house provisions were characterized by the Ontario Court of Appeal in *Bedford* as "safeguarding the public peace and protecting against corruption of morals".[44] This latter purpose, however, was condemned on the basis that it constitutes "imposing certain standards of public and sexual morality"[45] for no greater reason than these happen to be the mores of the community.[46]

There is wide agreement (across many competing schools of political philosophy) that prohibiting acts for no better reason than to maintain social solidarity, and without regard to whether the acts in question were truly immoral (as Patrick Devlin famously championed)[47] would indeed be an improper purpose.[48] But it is not at all clear that the bawdy-house provision is well described in these terms. It seems implausible that the purpose of legislation such as the prohibition of bawdy houses and related offences was simply to preserve conventional standards of morality *qua* conventional. It would be reasonable to conclude that legislators then, as now, were motivated by the moral judgment that certain acts are seriously wrong (in the sense that they both constitute and lead to further serious *harms*), including the moral judgment that persons (particularly children) are treated unjustly if they are not

---

[41] *Canada (Attorney General) v. Bedford*, 2013 SCC 72 (hereinafter *Bedford*).

[42] Ibid., paras. 131–132, 137–138, 146–147.

[43] The Supreme Court of Canada compares prostitution with "riding a bike", ibid., at para. 87. The Court of Appeal for Ontario characterizes it as indistinguishable from "any other lawful commercial activity" (2012) 109 O.R.(3d) 1, at para. 123 (hereinafter *Bedford (CA)*).

[44] *Bedford (CA)*, para. 189.   [45] Ibid.

[46] The Court also held that a prohibition of bawdy-houses could be maintained if the purpose was instead advancing "modern objectives of dignity and equality". *Bedford (CA)*, para. [190].

[47] Patrick Devlin, *The Enforcement of Morals* (1965) at 89–91 (hereinafter Devlin, *The Enforcement of Morals*).

[48] I have made this argument at greater length in "Morals Laws," *supra* note 40.

protected from observing the occurrence of these acts, and from the inference that their toleration shows that they are accepted by the political community as an acceptable kind of conduct. That is, Parliament can be taken to have believed: (1) that there is a need to protect the public from a genuine threat, and (2) that it would be an injustice to the people for whom they are responsible (both actors and third parties) if they fail to act legislatively against that threat. The legislation in *Bedford* would have flowed, not from a concern to prevent offence, but precisely from those sorts of considerations that the Ontario Court of Appeal accepted as properly grounding legislation: concerns about the harms to persons that flow from a denial of their dignity and equality. Legislatures then as now were motivated to prevent genuine harms to persons. The judgment that an act is immoral typically flows from the judgment that it causes some harm (either to the actor or to a third party). Contemporary courts risk misunderstanding (and devaluing) legislation (old and new) to the extent that they manifest the misunderstanding that legislators then were concerned only with morals (understood without reference to harm, equality, or dignity), that criminal legislation may only be enacted to prevent harm (understood in some thin sense of harm that prescinds from any evaluation of what is good for persons), and that contemporary legislators are not manifesting moral judgments, but merely judgments about what is harmful (understood without reference to the moral nature of the harm).

So proportionality analysis, as this brief meditation on the judicial characterization of legislative purpose illustrates, affords multiple points of entry for practical reasoning. And the most analytically significant moments of practical reasoning in proportionality analysis will not necessarily occur at the balancing stage.[49] How the legislative purpose is characterized may be far more significant, feeding not only the overall balancing analysis, but also the assessment of the importance of the legislative purpose, and – crucially – the assessment of necessity or minimal impairment.

IV. PROPORTIONALITY'S SOURCES OF MORAL AND POLITICAL PHILOSOPHY

The practical reasoning that is a mainstay of proportionality reasoning includes not only moral philosophy but political philosophy as well. Whether

---

[49] Indeed, in Canada, in more than twenty-five years of proportionality review, only a single case before the Supreme Court of Canada has been resolved on the basis of overall balancing: *Alberta v. Hutterian Brethren of Wilson Colony*, [2009] 2 S.C.R. 567. I am grateful to Adam McLeod for pressing this point.

purchasing sex, to keep with the *Bedford* example, is merely wrong or is also a matter of injustice or is neither is a question of moral philosophy. Whether the state, through its governments and laws, ought to discourage prostitution or even prohibit the selling of sex is a question of political philosophy. One of the perennial questions of political philosophy that is relevant to proportionality analysis is "what are the principles that are to establish the limits of legitimate governmental authority?" There are, of course, many competing schools of political philosophy, with vastly different conceptions of what the proper function of government is. If proportionality is adopted as a forum where practical questions of political philosophy are to be resolved, we should investigate to what extent that forum is neutral among the commitments of competing schools of political philosophy, and whether it tends to skew the pitch.

Proportionality analysis, according to Aharon Barak, is broadly ecumenical. Although it is not compatible with every conceivable political philosophy, Barak argues that it can be a "vessel" for many competing theories, because it is simply a legal tool that is "fed by extrinsic data" that is supplied by each legal system that adopts it.[50] The evaluations that are the product of proportionality reasoning are thus contingent on whatever principles of political morality are fed into the test.[51] So it should be expected that different polities constituted by different commitments and legal histories can adopt this same structure of reasoning but nevertheless generate different conclusions. This will not simply be because jurisdictions such as Canada, Israel, and South Africa have profoundly different social and legislative histories and social priorities, or that common law and civil law jurisdictions (such as New Zealand and Germany, respectively) do not share the doctrine of precedent. More importantly, there is no reason to assume that differences in the moral and political philosophies that are dominant in the different jurisdictions will be insignificant.

Barak's argument that polities are free to input into proportionality analysis whatever political morality they choose raises an important question that he does not address: how is it that commitments of political morality – the "extrinsic data" – are fed into proportionality analysis? The promise of proportionality analysis is, in part, to decrease judicial subjectivity. So we should

---

[50] Barak, *Proportionality, supra* note 1 at 467.
[51] Ibid. at 247–248, 460, 467–472. Mattias Kumm and Alec Walen carry the argument further in "Human Dignity and Proportionality," Chapter 4 in this volume, bringing an argument that proportionality analysis is compatible with deontological reasoning – a category of moral philosophy outside of what Barak would allow.

expect an account of proportionality reasoning that identifies sources of political morality external to the judge. Bear in mind that in most jurisdictions, the use of proportionality doctrine in constitutional adjudication was not legislatively mandated, but was instituted through judicial choice. More importantly, the content of a proportionality test – even one that is established through legislation – is entirely within the hands of the judiciary. It is a closed system, with no opportunity for inputs by legislators or the polity. Legislators could, theoretically, bring legislation to bear on the question of how judges are to reason within the proportionality test, although in many polities such legislation would be constitutionally infirm for violating judicial independence. The members of the political community, who have some formal avenues for bringing matters to the attention of legislators, have no automatic standing before courts. One can of course quibble about the ability of ordinary persons to influence government. But in most polities, institutions do exist for the express purpose of providing individuals with an avenue of input into governmental decision making. No comparable channels exist for individuals to be heard by courts, save in the extraordinary circumstance of being a plaintiff or defendant. Even in jurisdictions where public interest intervention is permitted, the terms of intervention will be limited and will not necessarily extend to addressing fundamental constitutional doctrine. The decision of which commitments of political morality to feed into the proportionality test rests with the judiciary.

Of course, most members of the political community would not appreciate the degree to which moral and political philosophy plays a role in constitutional adjudication. Nor would they appreciate that judges are in a position to adopt some principles of political morality from among other possibilities, rather than simply working from the fixed points of a constitutional settlement. Accordingly, it would never occur to anyone to object. Their ignorance is assured, as Kumm concedes without embarrassment, by the judicial use of a grammar of proportionality that appears to translate moral commitments into technical language.[52] If the public believes that legal judgments are the inevitable and objective conclusion of meticulous, technical reasoning, they will not understand themselves (or their representatives in the legislature) to be qualified to object to the results. Governments (particularly those that have a power to refer constitutional questions to the judiciary) have much to gain from passing morally controversial questions to the judiciary to be resolved as though they were pure questions of law.[53]

---

[52] Kumm, "Socratic Contestation," *supra* note 29.
[53] I am grateful to Iain Benson for pressing this point.

A proponent of proportionality might object that the foregoing mischarac-
terizes the process by which a political morality becomes ensconced in a legal
system. A proponent could harness the arguments of scholars of constitutional
interpretation such as Dworkin or Wil Waluchow, who argue that constitutional interpretation is not a matter of individual judges imposing their personal
and idiosyncratic morality, but is rather a matter of judges looking to the totality of the materials of the legal system and discerning within it more general
constitutional principles[54] or the community's constitutional morality,[55] and
reasoning from these more general principles to specific determinations. The
proponent of proportionality could argue that the turn from interpretation
hailed by Kumm is not complete – the judge must still interpret, if not a text,
then the commitments generated by a body of previous statutes and judicial
decisions. I have argued elsewhere that this approach to constitutional interpretation is too indeterminate to provide any real guidance to judges in hard
cases.[56] But there is a further problem in adapting it to a defense of proportionality reasoning. Waluchow's theory does not presuppose that a community's
constitutional morality will be all of a single piece. Instead, in working from
legal sources, a judge is to work back and forth between "specific rules and
maxims" and "the opinions and judgments about particular cases and types of
cases" to establish a reflective equilibrium.[57] In effect, Waluchow's judge is
looking for an overlapping consensus – common ground – "in the absence of
an *articulated consensus* and in the presence of radical disagreement about all
sorts of questions, both particular and abstract".[58] Waluchow's methodology
does not presuppose that a political community has committed to a single
political philosophy. In fact, his theory is a proposal for judicial decision making in circumstances where such agreement is elusive. Waluchow's judge
must be frank in acknowledging that some judgments, statutes, and other
relevant institutions may be consistent (for example) with perfectionist political philosophy and others may be consistent with anti-perfectionism.[59] There

---

[54] Dworkin, "Introduction: The Moral Reading and the Majoritarian Premise" in *Freedom's Law:
The Moral Reading of the American Constitution* (1997) 1–38.

[55] Waluchow, *A Common Law Theory, supra* note 34; "Constitutional Morality and Bills of
Rights" in Grant Huscroft (ed.) *Expounding the Constitution*, (2008) 65; "On the Neutrality of
Charter Reasoning" in Ferrer Beltrán et al. (eds.), *Neutrality and Theory of Law* (2013).

[56] Miller, "Review of W.J. Waluchow, *A Common Law Theory of Judicial Review*" (2007) 52 *Am.
J. Juris.* 297. In reply to Dworkin, see John Finnis, "Reason and Authority in Law's Empire"
(1987) in *C.E.J.F.* vol. IV.12 at 290–295 (hereinafter Finnis, "Reason and Authority"), and
"Introduction" *C.E.J.F.* vol IV at 14–16.

[57] Waluchow, *A Common Law Theory, supra* note 34 at 224–226.

[58] Ibid. at 228 (emphasis in the original).

[59] The contours of perfectionism and anti-perfectionism are explored at 388–394 in this chapter.

will be many principles that pull in opposite directions, and the judge will have to decide the relative weight to be attached to each in the circumstances. Waluchow's judge (like Dworkin's Hercules) has to sort out the contradictory (or at least competing) strands of a community's constitutional morality and, crucially for Waluchow, must do so without resort to the judge's own moral convictions. It is in this latter requirement that I have argued that Waluchow is asking the impossible.

Neither can the necessity of moral reasoning be "bootstrapped" away through the effluxion of time and accumulation of precedent. Where, for example, a court strikes down a statute (say, prohibiting polygamous marriage) on the basis that it fails to comport with principle of autonomy discerned by a judge, that judgment will thenceforth count as evidence of the significance (or weight) of the principle of autonomy within that legal system. Autonomy will thus have been elevated against other competing principles, particularly against the principles that inspired the statute in question (perhaps pertaining to the needs of children for stability in family life). Once the choice is made (and however it was made), it will appear settled by operation of the doctrine of precedent.[60] Judges deliberating in future cases will be able to appeal to this decision as objective evidence of the relative priorities of moral and legal principles on the constitutional plane. A moral judgment from the pen of one judge thus becomes empirical evidence in the hands of her colleagues. But despite the appearance of dealing with facts (the fact of a previous court's judgment) instead of evaluation, judicial reasoning with precedent can never escape the necessity of moral reasoning. This is not simply because the nature of proportionality is such that no settlement can have much precedential value, because the inputs (both the facts of the case and the evaluations) that are placed into the balance will never be exactly the same. Any appellate court must consider whether it will be bound by existing precedent, and whether there is sufficient justification not to choose an outcome that perhaps has better "fit" with the totality of precedent.[61]

The judge reasoning with proportionality – such as Waluchow's and Dworkin's constitutional interpreter – will be called on to choose from among competing principles of moral and political philosophy that can plausibly claim a foundation in the law. But particularly in the realm of political

---

[60] On proportionality and precedent, see Giovanni Sartor, "Doing Justice to Rights and Values: Teleological Reasoning and Proportionality," (2010) 18 *Artificial Intelligence Law* 175.

[61] On fit and justification in Dworkin's theory of adjudication, see Ronald Dworkin, *Law's Empire* (1987); and Finnis, "Reason and Authority," *supra* note 55 at 280, and "Commensuration," *supra* note 9 at 233, 251–253.

philosophy, judges seldom demonstrate much awareness that there were alternatives to choose from, that there were any choices to be made. Proponents of proportionality abet in this, to the extent that they write as though a community commits itself to political liberalism once its judiciary adopts a proportionality doctrine.

This subject demands a more extensive treatment than I can provide here. But even the cursory treatment that I have provided is sufficient to call into question Barak's reassurance that it is the political community that imports into the proportionality test whatever commitments of political philosophy that it chooses. That decision rests in the hands of the judiciary, and it is a judiciary that is not keenly aware that it has any decision to make.

V. PROPORTIONALITY AND ANTI-PERFECTIONISM

Nevertheless, Barak is right to insist that proportionality "is not neutral" in the sense that it is not equally suitable to all theories of political morality.[62] But is proportionality somehow more congenial to the anti-perfectionist strain of liberalism that maintains the state must be "neutral" as to what constitutes a good life?

There are many schools of political philosophy that are consistent with liberal democracy and not all of them are typically associated with the label of "liberal"; we can begin the list with communitarian[63] and natural law theories.[64] And within liberalism itself is a vibrant range of competing schools,[65] including the twentieth-century anti-perfectionist strains associated with Ronald Dworkin[66] and John Rawls,[67] and the perfectionist variants articulated by Joseph Raz[68] and William Galston.[69] Despite this diversity of thought, to the extent that proportionality scholars address political morality, they tend to preload proportionality with the commitments of anti-perfectionist

---

[62] Barak, *Proportionality*, *supra* note 1 at 467–468.

[63] Alisdair MacIntyre, *Whose Justice? Which Rationality?* (1988); Michael Sandel, *Liberalism and the Limits of Justice* (2nd ed. 1998); Charles Taylor, *Sources of the Self* (1989).

[64] John Finnis, *Natural Law, supra* note 15, and "Human Rights," *supra* note 13; Robert P. George, *Making Men Moral* (1993), and *In Defence of Natural Law* (1999).

[65] Christopher Wolfe suggests that there are six schools of liberal thought: i) anti-perfectionist liberalism, ii) libertarianism, iii) radical or postmodern liberalism, iv) communitarian liberalism, v) classical liberalism, and vi) perfectionist liberalism ("Issues Facing Contemporary American Public Philosophy" in Boxx and Quinlivan (eds.) *Public Morality, Civic Virtue* (2000). I am grateful to Iain Benson for bringing Wolfe's taxonomy to my attention.

[66] Dworkin, *Taking Rights Seriously*, and *A Matter of Principle*, *supra* note 10.

[67] John Rawls, *A Theory of Justice* (1971), *Political Liberalism* (1993).

[68] Joseph Raz, *The Morality of Freedom* (1986) (hereinafter Raz, *The Morality of Freedom*).

[69] William Galston, *Liberal Purposes* (1991).

liberalism. Even scholars such as Mattias Kumm, who carefully maintain that proportionality can be consistent with non-liberal political morality, never-theless give pride of place to political liberalism and anti-perfectionism when addressing political morality.[70]

In fact, anti-perfectionist liberalism is the only theory of political moral-ity that Barak takes seriously (notwithstanding a passing hat-tip to communi-tarianism).[71] Although he poses the question of whether liberalism *can* actually be compatible with proportionality reasoning,[72] the result is never in doubt; the question is merely a setting for his meditation on *how well* the commitments of anti-perfectionist liberalism map onto the analytical structure of proportion-ality. Barak's account of the concepts used within proportionality analysis – from "proper purpose" to "public interest" – all assume the commitments of anti-perfectionist liberalism. Whether proportionality is, in fact, a vehicle equally suitable for other theories of political morality is not a question that Barak genuinely pursues.

The anti-perfectionist principle is well articulated by Joseph Raz; it is the claim "that implementation and promotion of ideals of the good life, though worthy in themselves, are not a legitimate matter for governmental action".[73] That is, government must be neutral as to what constitutes the good life. On this model, government can base its action on judgments about what is right and wrong (understood as a matter of interpersonal justice, usually relying on a thin version of the harm principle), but not on the basis that some actions are conducive to achieving the good life and others are not.[74] As far as what is morally good and what is not, government is to take no position whatsoever.[75]

The anti-perfectionist principle is central to Kumm's account of political liberalism (an account endorsed by Barak[76] and Robert Alexy[77]),[78] which he explores in the following passage:

---

[70] E.g., Mattias Kumm, "Socratic Contestation," *supra* note 29 and "Political Liberalism and the Structure of Rights: On the Place and Limits of the Proportionality Requirement" in George Pavlakos (ed.) *Law, Rights and Discourse* (2007) 131 at 141–148 (hereinafter Kumm, "Political Liberalism").

[71] Barak, *Proportionality, supra* note 1 at 467.   [72] Ibid. at 468.

[73] Joseph Raz, *The Morality of Freedom, supra* note 68 at 110.

[74] Ibid. at 136.

[75] Note that "morally good" is used here in the sense of the full range of the objects practical reasoning, and not in the popular understanding which restricts "moral" to an evaluation of sexual behavior.

[76] Barak, *Proportionality, supra* note 1 at 468–472.

[77] Robert Alexy, "13 Replies" in George Pavlakos (ed.) *Law, Rights and Discourse* (2007) 333 at 340.

[78] Kumm, "Political Liberalism," *supra* note 70 at 142.

Here the basic liberal idea is that rights protect individuals from strong paternalist impositions relating to how they should live their lives, in particular with
regard to dominant religious practices. Questions relating to what it means
to aspire to be the best person you can – to instantiate an example of human
perfection – is not the proper subject matter of political decision-making and
legal coercion.[79]

This statement by Kumm can serve as a platform to explore the differences
between paternalist and anti-paternalist political philosophies. Kumm's target
is "strong paternalist impositions", which is usually understood to relate to
paternalism about a person's chosen ends. Presumably, he would accept that
anti-perfectionist liberalism can be compatible with a weak paternalism that
would, for example, allow for interference with a person's autonomy to assist
them in achieving ends they have set for themselves.[80] A stock example here
is a law that would require motor vehicle passengers – who are presumed to
value safety – to wear seatbelts in order to best achieve motor vehicle safety.

Kumm's reference to governments seeking to make persons the best persons
they can be – "to instantiate an example of human perfection" – seems to target
a very distinct species of perfectionism, one which would have few, if any,
contemporary defenders in the proportionality jurisdictions. The example of
perfectionism that Kumm supplies is of a state that uses its coercive powers to
force students in a public school to make a Christian doctrinal confession of
faith.[81] Kumm's example, I fear, could lend itself to the misinterpretation that a
perfectionist state is one which claims jurisdiction over that sphere of concern
that is particular to religious communities.[82] Bear in mind that a religious
body is concerned not only with the limited domain of exterior conformance
to rules (and to the development of those personal habits and dispositions
that are coincidentally conducive to such exterior conformance), but with the
promotion of full, unrestricted virtue in its members. And the virtue that is
properly the jurisdiction of the religious body is not simply ordered toward
"human perfection" in the current life, but for the attainment of salvation in
the life to come. So a possible (but I think mistaken) interpretation of Kumm's
example is a picture of a state whose claims to jurisdiction extend not only

---

[79] Ibid. at 142.
[80] This is a distinction accepted by Ronald Dworkin, *Sovereign Virtue* (2001) at 216–218.
[81] Kumm, "Political Liberalism," *supra* note 70 at 143.
[82] Kumm explores several other reasons why a state might adopt such a requirement (other than
a direct concern for the salvation of students) including the conventionalist reason that it is
simply a matter of enforcing cultural conformity as a good in itself, and the perfectionist reason
that the state has a responsibility to support those parents who endeavor to raise their children
in their religious faith.

over the promotion of the all-round virtue of its members, but also over their salvation.

Such a reading would obscure the genuine differences between anti-perfectionists and perfectionists (liberal or otherwise). None of the competing schools of political philosophy that are familiar to the world of proportionality would endorse such an unrestricted jurisdiction of the state.[83] Furthermore, few perfectionists – perhaps no contemporary exponents – would subscribe to the proposition that Kumm attributes to them: that legal coercion and political decision making should be used to inform and guide persons to "instantiate an example of human perfection". Perfectionists (including liberal perfectionists such as Raz, or natural lawyers such as John Finnis or Robert P. George) do not make the claim that there is a single, highest way of life, much less that persons should be coerced into it by the state. Typically, they hold that there is a *range* of morally valuable choices and a *range* of morally valueless choices, and an individual's autonomy is not threatened but advanced by state action that rightly identifies, discourages, and (in a limited class of cases) prohibits the morally valueless; in Joseph Raz's formulation, "The goal of all political action is to enable individuals to pursue valid conceptions of the good and to discourage evil or empty ones."[84]

So where the differences emerge between perfectionists and anti-perfectionists is not over matters pertaining to salvation. It starts with the imprecise question posed by H.L.A. Hart: "Is it morally permissible to enforce morality as such?"[85] Assuming that "morality" here refers to a morality that critically and correctly judges certain acts to be immoral,[86] the perfectionist tradition, as noted by Finnis, divides into two streams.[87] The paternalistic

---

[83] We can include among these the theory of state jurisdiction explored by Aquinas: see John Finnis, "Public Good: The Specifically Political Common Good in Aquinas" in Robert P. George (ed.) *Natural Law and Moral Inquiry: Ethics, Metaphysics and Politics in the Work of Germain Grisez* (1998) 174.

[84] Raz, *The Morality of Freedom, supra* note 67 at 133. Cited by Gonthier J. (dissenting) in *Sauvé v. Canada (Chief Electoral Officer)*, [2002] 3 S.C.R. 519 at para. 20.

[85] Hart, *Law, Liberty, and Morality* (1963) at 10–11.

[86] Rather than (merely) conventional mores, which Supreme Court of Canada rightly rejected as suitable for grounding a criminal prohibition (*R. v. Butler* [1992]). See Miller, "Morals Laws," *supra* note 40. Unlike the social-cohesion conservatism articulated by Patrick Devlin (*The Enforcement of Morals, supra* note 47), perfectionism does not support criminalization of acts simply because they transgress a conventional morality that happens to be widely held in a community. Such "morality" may in fact be profoundly immoral, and the soundness of a moral judgment is a precondition to a state having legitimate authority to prohibit an act because it is judged to be immoral.

[87] Finnis, "H.L.A. Hart as Political Philosopher" in *C.E.J.F.* vol. IV.11 (2011) at 270 (hereinafter Finnis, "Hart as Political Philosopher").

stream – associated with Plato and Aristotle – "authorizes penalizing immoral acts for the sake of the character of those who do or would otherwise engage in them".[88] The non-paternalistic stream – associated with Aquinas – authorizes "penalization only when the act has a public character and jeopardizes public order or public morality or the rights of others".[89] The difference is in the attitude toward genuinely private immoralities.

The Thomist stream has provided the structure for the contemporary legal approach to combating many significant social problems, an approach that is currently under attack in several jurisdictions. In many jurisdictions, prostitution (for example), when conducted in private, is viewed as a private immorality and accordingly is not subject to criminal sanction.[90] This is not to say that the state is (or must therefore be) neutral as to whether prostitution is a valuable way of life. On the contrary, on the standard Western model, prostitution is viewed as both harmful and destructive. A state that determines that a principled political morality prevents it from criminalizing private acts of prostitution is not therefore required to prescind either from moral evaluation of acts of prostitution or from taking other steps intended to eradicate prostitution. The question remains, what should be the policy of the law, and of society's other governing institutions (for example, public education) in relation to the *public promotion or facilitating* of such acts?[91] This tradition of perfectionism would allow for a policy to discourage prostitution through noncoercive means, such as public information campaigns intended to highlight the often predatory and damaging nature of prostitution (for those who engage in acts of prostitution, their spouses, their children). But, crucially, it also allows (and provides the principled case) for the coercive measures commonly used to make prostitution more difficult and costly: including the criminalization of acts ancillary to prostitution (such as those in issue in *Bedford*: soliciting, living off the avails of prostitution, and maintaining a bawdy house). Whether these *particular* prohibitions are effective or wise in any particular community is of course debatable, but they are rooted in a principle that the state can indirectly discourage (through even coercive measures) that which it ought not to prohibit directly.

---

[88] Ibid. This is the stream that Barak rejects when he declares that "liberal approaches to human rights are based on the notion that no individual should be forced to adopt a certain way, directed by the government, to pursue his or her own happiness (the 'good life')", (Barak, *Proportionality, supra* note 1 at 469).

[89] Finnis, "Hart as Political Philosopher," *supra* note 87 at 270.

[90] Other examples, such as the lawfulness of acts of suicide, coupled with prohibitions on assisting in acts of suicide, follow this structure.

[91] Finnis, "Hart as Political Philosopher," *supra* note 87 at 268.

The structure of this set of distinctions was missed entirely by the Supreme Court of Canada in *Bedford*,[92] leading it to the surprising conclusion that none of the various criminal prohibitions related to prostitution (such as maintaining a bawdy house, living off the avails of prostitution, and communicating for the purposes of prostitution) could be characterized, either separately or taken as a suite of provisions, as directed toward the eradication of prostitution itself. On the Court's interpretation of the statutory provisions, Parliament's decision not to criminalize prostitution was the product of the judgment that prostitution and all other commercial enterprises are morally equivalent.[93] This characterization of the statute was largely driven by the Court's choice of political philosophy: either an ignorance or off-stage rejection of the political philosophy that supplied the structure for the legislation, coupled with an inclination (also unexpressed) toward anti-perfectionism. These commitments of political philosophy prevented the Court from perceiving any rationality in the indirect prohibition, such that the conclusion that the provisions were arbitrary and therefore disproportionate became irresistible.

So legislation that is crafted using the assumptions and commitments of one school of political philosophy (such as non-paternalist perfectionism) can be literally incomprehensible when read through the filter of anti-perfectionist or neutral liberalism. I have raised the likelihood (I have not claimed to prove) that in many legal jurisdictions, the law as a whole is not uniformly a product of (and not consistent with) a single political philosophy. Neither is it the case that in most jurisdictions that have adopted a bill of rights in the post–World War II era, the adoption of a bill of rights was unambiguously a matter of overthrowing

---

[92] *Bedford, supra* note 41.

[93] The Ontario Court of Appeal is particularly clear on this point, *Bedford (CA)*, para. 123: "In the eyes of the criminal law, prostitution is as legal as any other non-prohibited commercial activity." In the Court's characterization of the prostitution offences, however, the veil slips occasionally and a normative judgment drops into the line of sight. Thus, the Court lists the harms "associated" with street prostitution as including "noise, impeding traffic, *children witnessing acts of prostitution*, harassment of residents, problems associated with drug use by prostitutes, unsanitary acts, violence, unwelcome solicitation of women and children by customers, and unwelcome solicitation of male residents by prostitutes" (at para. 289 [emphasis added]). One can ask what it is about a child witnessing an "act of prostitution" that warrants greater concern (and the intervention of the criminal justice system) than merely witnessing any other "act of sex" not already prohibited by the law of indecency and obscenity. Coming, as it does, in a discussion of the anti-communication provision, it is reasonable to read the "acts of prostitution" with which the law is here concerned as primarily transactional, rather than sexual. That is, there is something about witnessing a commercial transaction for sex that is thought to be harmful to children. That harm, it is reasonable to conclude, results from an interference with an interest that children have in developing an understanding of sex as something mutual and noncommercial.

a disfavored political morality and replacing it with something else.[94] The text of contemporary bills of rights – containing terms such as "free and democratic society", "public morality", and "fundamental justice" – can be given readings consistent with a number of political philosophies, including anti-perfectionist liberalism and paternalist and non-paternalist forms of perfectionism. And I have demonstrated that in some instances at least, the judicial selection of political philosophy will bear on, and perhaps drive the results of, proportionality analysis. Much turns then on commitments of political philosophy. Legislation should not be judged to be unconstitutional on the basis of a constitutional settlement that was, in fact, never made. If legislation is to be invalidated on the basis that it is inconsistent with anti-perfectionism, it is necessary that a commitment to the interpretive priority of anti-perfectionism be located in the relevant constitutional text.

VI. CONCLUSION

Questions about the appropriate limits of government in a free and democratic society are fiercely debated in political philosophy. Yet they are strangely absent in the academic and judicial discourse of proportionality.[95] Instead, much

---

94 South Africa is an important, and partial, counterexample. But other jurisdictions that have recently adopted bills of rights, such as New Zealand, UK, and Canada, did not do so in order to overturn an existing legal or cultural tradition, notwithstanding the uses to which these bills of rights have been put. If the drafters and ratifiers of the Canadian Charter, for example, believed that enactment entailed a rejection of the existing legal tradition, one would have expected that the legislatures would have been afforded time to review (and repeal or amend) legislation as needed to bring the legal system into conformity with the new order. Instead, when the Charter was introduced in 1982, it took effect immediately, except for a single section – s.15, the antidiscrimination provision – which was delayed for two years in order to allow legislatures to adopt the new standard and make legislation compliant. The implication is that the drafters and ratifiers of the Charter did not believe that any other provision of the Charter posed a serious problem for existing law. (And this belief in the basic continuity of the Charter with the pre-Charter legal system finds expression in reasons for judgment: e.g. "The promulgation of the Charter was marked more by continuity than discontinuity in our political and constitutional culture." *R v. Demers*, [2004] 2 S.C.R. 489 at para. 84, LeBel J [dissenting]; "I disagree with those who argue that the Charter requires that we emulate American society and discard the unique balance of fundamental values which existed in this country prior to 1982. . . . The impact of the *Charter* will be minimal in areas where the common law is an expression of, rather than a derogation from, fundamental values." *Dagenais v. Canadian Broadcasting Corporation*, [1994] 3 S.C.R. 835 per Gonthier J [dissenting], at 928–929, supported by L'Heureux-Dubé J. [dissenting] at 915–916.)

95 For a rare counterexample, see the dissent of Gonthier J. in *Sauvé v. Canada (Chief Electoral Officer)*, [2002] 3 S.C.R. 519 at para. 67:

   [S.] 1 of the *Charter* requires that this Court look to the fact that there may be different social or political philosophies upon which justifications for or against the limitations of

contemporary constitutional litigation proceeds on the basis that legislation that is premised on a rejection of the proposition that some acts are choice-worthy (whether that legislation directly prohibits the conduct in question or seeks to discourage it indirectly through coercive or noncoercive means), fail in principle because of the often hidden (and always undefended) proposition that proportionality requires states to be neutral to the goodness or badness of those acts.

The structure of proportionality reasoning facilitates the undefended assumption of commitments of political philosophy generally, and to date anti-perfectionism has been the chief beneficiary. The drift of proportionality reasoning has been to shuffle out of view controversial moral evaluations, often, as we have seen, rebranding them as technical matters.[96]

But the "supreme law of the land", as developed through the doctrine of proportionality, makes engagement with the "debate about morality, equality, personal autonomy"[97] simply unavoidable. The judgments have to be made. The only question is whether these decisions will be made by artificially (and non-transparently) excluding reasons through doctrinal machinations. In fact, judges have no qualms about being seen to engage in morally reasoning so when the stakes are sufficiently low; when what is at issue is a matter of widespread consensus (such as the wrongs of child pornography[98] or permitting

rights may be based. In such a context, where this Court is presented with competing social or political philosophies relating to the right to vote, it is not by merely approving or preferring one that the other is necessarily disproved or shown not to survive *Charter* scrutiny.

See also paras. 109–121.

[96] Compare the overt moral evaluation of Lamer J. is characterize of prostitution as "at its most basic level a form of slavery" (*Reference re ss. 193 and 195.1(1)(c) of the Criminal Code*, [1990] 1 S.C.R. 1123 at 1193 (Lamer J.) [the *Prostitution Reference*] with the standard disclaimer recited by the Ontario Court of Appeal in *Bedford*: "Prostitution is a controversial topic, one that provokes heated and heartfelt debate about morality, equality, personal autonomy and public safety. It is not the court's role to engage in that debate. Our role is to decide whether or not the challenged laws accord with the Constitution, which is the supreme law of the land." *Bedford* (*CA*), para 9. Similarly, in cases concerning the permissibility of abortion, the Supreme Court of Canada concluded both that "ascribing personhood to a foetus in law is a fundamentally normative task", and that it was "not required to enter the philosophical and theological debates about whether or not a foetus is a person." *Tremblay v. Daigle*, [1989] 2 S.C.R. 530, at 552–553. Again in *Morgentaler*, "[T]he task of the Court in this case is not to solve nor seek to solve what might be called the abortion issue, but simply to measure the content of s. 251 against the *Charter*" *R. v. Morgentaler*, [1988] 1 S.C.R. 30 at 138 (McIntyre J. [dissenting]). With respect to euthanasia, "[T]he court should answer this question without reference to the philosophical and theological considerations fuelling the debate on the morality of suicide or euthanasia. It should consider the question before it from a legal perspective". *Rodriguez v. British Columbia (Attorney General)*, [1993] 3 S.C.R. 519 at 553 (Lamer J. dissenting).

[97] *Bedford*, ibid.   [98] *R v. Sharpe*, [2001] 1 S.C.R. 45.

tobacco advertising[99]). But when the stakes are high, the anti-perfectionist assumptions are simply asserted or assumed, as though no other position was constitutionally possible. The result is that the authority for making fundamental commitments of political philosophy has been removed from the legislative and executive branches of government on a basic misunderstanding that these matters were settled by the aspirational terms of bills of rights. Courts, which exercise the de facto power over these questions, have illegitimately used the tools of proportionality reasoning to maneuver discreetly made commitments of political philosophy into a blind spot, where they are barely noticeable, and wholly immune to challenge.

[99] *RJR-Macdonald Inc. v. Canada (Attorney General)*, [1995] 3 S.C.R. 199; *Canada (Attorney General) v. JTI-Macdonald Corp.*, [2007] 2 S.C.R. 610.

17 Mapping the American Debate over Balancing

Iddo Porat

Balancing is a decision-making process in which considerations for and against a certain course of action are identified and pitted against one another according to their perceived weight. Under this description, balancing can be employed in any decision-making process, personal or public, moral or practical. In the context of constitutional judicial review, balancing is resorted to when a court balances conflicting considerations in deciding whether to strike down a statute or nullify governmental action for being unconstitutional. In particular, it is resorted to when governmental action infringes rights, and the court balances governmental objectives and individual rights in deciding whether to strike down governmental action.[1]

What is the role of a constitution in this type of process? There is no easy answer to this question.[2] There is, however, a conventional response: the outcome of judicial balancing is determined by the constitution itself, for it establishes a certain balance between competing considerations, which the court then imposes on the state. Each constitutional right is interpreted as a

---

[1] As David Dyzenhaus, following Lon Fuller, shows in "Proportionality and Deference in a Culture of Justification", Chapter 11 of this volume, balancing could be viewed as a prescription for governmental decision-making processes, as well as a standard for the court's review process. Although one might view the first to be the logical conclusion of the second, that is not necessarily the case. As Dyzenhaus notes, a governmental decision might conform to the standard required by the proper balance, but not be the conclusion of a balancing process itself. This distinction is increasingly blurred as we get closer to an administrative model: see Moshe Cohen-Eliya and Iddo Porat, "Proportionality and the Culture of Justification," 59 *Am. J. Comp. L.* 463 (2011) (discussing the administrisation of constitutional law). In this chapter, I discuss balancing only as a standard for the court's review process.

[2] See, e.g., T.R.S. Allan's contribution to this volume, "Democracy, Legality and Proportionality" (Chapter 10), maintaining that the answer to this question may depend on our conception of democracy and the rule of law. See also Cohen-Eliya and Porat "Culture of Justification" ibid. at 479, arguing that a constitutional culture based on proportionality and balancing, termed a "culture of justification", downplays the importance of constitutional text.

strong consideration in government decision making, and courts ensure that the government takes this consideration into account and accords it the weight mandated by the constitution.

Some constitutions do not provide for any balancing mechanism. In such cases, the balancing process comes into play only through judicial interpretation. For example, the free speech provision in the American Constitution declares simply that "Congress shall make no law . . . abridging the freedom of speech, or of the press."[3] It does not state that "Congress shall balance free speech with other considerations when enacting a law." Balancing enters American constitutional law by way of judicial interpretation. By contrast, most modern constitutions set out some sort of balancing mechanism, either explicitly or implicitly. This is usually by way of one or more limitation clauses, which add to the declaration "Congress shall make no law" some form of restriction, such as "unless there are compelling reasons for doing so."[4] This implies seeking a balance between those "compelling reasons" and the protected right.

Balancing also enters constitutional analysis in the framework of the proportionality doctrine, which is either implicitly required by a limitation clause or specifically provided for in the constitutional text. Proportionality requires that all limitations on the given constitutional right be proportionate to the importance of achieving the governmental goal. This entails weighing the government goal against the need to protect the right as evaluated by the following: first, the means adopted to advance the governmental end must be appropriate for furthering that goal (suitability); second, the means adopted must be those that least infringe on the right of the individual (necessity); and third, the loss to the individual resulting from the infringement of the right must be proportional to the governmental gain in terms of furthering the governmental goal (proportionality in the strict sense or balancing).

Whether balancing is applied only through judicial interpretation or implicitly provided for in the constitutional text, the question remains whether balancing is a good model for constitutional judicial review. In other words, is it a good idea for courts to decide whether to invalidate statutes as unconstitutional by balancing conflicting considerations? This question is especially important in systems where balancing is not mentioned explicitly in the constitutional text, as in the United States, but it is also of practical importance in systems where balancing is explicitly provided for in the constitutional text: here the

---

[3] Constitution of the United States (1787), First Amendment.
[4] See, e.g., Canadian Charter of Rights and Freedoms, s. 1: "The *Canadian Charter of Rights and Freedoms* guarantees the rights and freedoms set out in it subject only to such reasonable limits prescribed by law as can be demonstrably justified in a free and democratic society."

need arises to justify the extent of its use and its centrality relative to other constitutional doctrines.

Balancing has been at the center of heated debates wherever it has been introduced: debates that touch on the core of our conceptions of constitutionalism, democracy and, law. Notwithstanding widespread debate, it is not always clear what is being argued. The aim of this chapter is to differentiate between different positions on balancing and to distinguish between different levels in which the debate over balancing takes place. To this end, I rely on the distinction drawn by Joseph Raz between first-order and second-order considerations, and argue that it is important to grasp two separate questions: (1) are constitutional rights balanceable?; that is, should rights be interpreted as first-order or second-order (exclusionary) considerations; and (2) should courts use balancing in adjudicating rights?

I apply this question to American constitutional law and identify different combinations of answers to these questions over its history. American constitutional law provides an especially rich reservoir of positions in this debate, as balancing has been at the center of disputes both in judicial opinions and academic writing since the early part of the twentieth century.[5] Finally, I aim to show that only those that support affirmative answers to both of the questions support what I term the "strong" position on balancing. Other combinations result in weaker positions. By and large, the weaker positions reflect current and historical positions in American constitutional systems, whereas the stronger position reflects the current position over balancing in European-based constitutional systems, in particular in Germany.

I. THE DUAL MODEL OF BALANCING – FIRST-ORDER VERSUS SECOND-ORDER CONSIDERATIONS

In one of his earliest books, Joseph Raz argued that practical considerations of any kind can be divided between first-order and second-order considerations.[6] *First-order* considerations are considerations for or against a certain course of action. When they conflict, they are balanced against each other. *Second-order* considerations apply to first-order considerations and not to the course of action itself. They exclude some or all first-order considerations from being

---

[5] See T. Alexander Aleinikoff, "Constitutional Law in the Age of Balancing," 96 *Yale L.J.* 943 at 949–952 (1987) (hereinafter Aleinikoff "Age of Balancing"); Moshe Cohen-Eliya and Iddo Porat "American Balancing and German Proportionality: The Historical Origins," 8 *Int'l J. Con. Law* 263 at 276–283 (2010).

[6] Joseph Raz, *Practical Reason and Norms* (1999) at 35–36. (I use the term "considerations" here as interchangeable with the term "reasons" used by Raz.)

considered in the decision-making process. For example, the consideration "it is costly" functions as a first-order consideration in the decision whether to buy a Cartier watch for a friend. It can be balanced with another first-order consideration, such as, "it is very accurate." On the other hand, the consideration "I promised my friend to buy him a Cartier watch" functions (mainly) as a second-order consideration in that decision. It excludes the first-order consideration that it is costly and the first-order consideration that it is accurate from the decision-making process regarding whether to buy a Cartier watch for my friend. These considerations might have motivated whether to make the promise to my friend in the first place, but once the promise is made and so long as it is valid, I have a (second-order) consideration – the promise – to regard such (first-order) considerations as no longer valid for the decision.[7]

One of the important implications of this distinction, and one of Raz's achievements in his analysis, is the realization that only first-order considerations can be balanced with other first-order considerations. A second-order consideration cannot be balanced with a first-order consideration. In my example, I cannot balance the consideration "I promised" with the consideration "it is costly." Rather, the consideration "I promised" should exclude the consideration "it is costly" altogether from the decision-making process. To put it otherwise, the two considerations are considerations of different orders, or different levels, and therefore cannot be balanced against each other.

Raz's framework has been the subject of criticism in both philosophy and law, focusing mainly on whether all types of considerations can be explained as first-order considerations of varying weight.[8] Second-order considerations, according to critics, are simply weighty first-order considerations. I doubt this debate can be decided by any "knock-down" argument: both Raz and his critics present workable and coherent explanatory systems. That said, Raz's account has advantages over explanations based on weight alone, as it provides a more sophisticated and nuanced set of tools to capture our understanding of practices and concepts of practical reason. In particular, his explanation provides us with the ability to argue against balancing certain considerations without arguing that they are absolute or paramount over all other considerations. In Raz's framework, non-balanceablity derives from the function of certain considerations, and not from their weight; their function is to exclude certain other considerations from being weighed in the balance.

---

[7] The only valid consideration now is the (first-order) consideration that I promised (the promise in this case is therefore both a first-order and a second-order consideration).

[8] See, e.g., Chaim Gans, "Mandatory Rules and Exclusionary Reasons," (1986) 15 *Philosophia* 373.

Raz's framework has been applied to constitutional law and to constitutional rights mainly to show that rights should be viewed as second-order (exclusionary) considerations.[9] In previous work, I have tried to contribute to this discourse by showing that we can use Raz's framework to understand both first-order and second-order uses of rights.[10] I there sought to show that constitutional provisions in general and those that deal with individual rights in particular can be interpreted either (a) as providing a consideration for government to do something or refrain from doing something (first-order considerations), or (b) as providing government with a consideration to exclude other considerations from its decision-making process (second-order, exclusionary considerations). For example, the First Amendment's free speech clause can be interpreted either as giving government reason to refrain from interfering with speech (this consideration would then be balanced against government's other valid considerations) or as prescribing that certain considerations must be excluded from government's decision-making process when enacting legislation or taking action. Under this second interpretation, government would be prohibited from weighing the consideration that it objects to certain points of view against the consideration of protecting free speech, as free speech excludes the first type of consideration.[11] I have termed this scheme, the "dual model of balancing". In this chapter, I apply the dual model to the debate over balancing itself with the aim of better understanding the different claims made and positions taken in this debate.

II. ARE CONSTITUTIONAL RIGHTS BALANCEABLE? RIGHTS AS FIRST-ORDER OR SECOND-ORDER CONSIDERATIONS

Two Historical Debates

Two historical debates concerning balancing in American constitutional law can be framed as revolving around the question whether rights should be interpreted as first-order or second-order considerations.

---

[9] See, e.g., Richard H. Pildes, "Avoiding Balancing: The Role of Exclusionary Reasons in Constitutional Law," 45 *Hastings L.J.* 707 (1994).

[10] See Iddo Porat, "The Dual Model of Balancing," 27 *Cardozo L. Rev.* 1393 (2006). See also, Iddo Porat, "On the Jehovah Witnesses Cases, Balancing Tests, Indirect Infringement of Rights and Multiculturalism: A Proposed Model for Three Kinds of Multicultural Claims," (2007) 1 *Law and Ethics of Human Rights* 429.

[11] This does not mean that free speech is absolute, as there could be many other first-order considerations not excluded by the second-order consideration of free speech. On this simplified view, one need only maintain, at a minimum, that speech cannot be restricted based on government's objection to a particular message.

The first debate concerns the interpretation of the Fourteenth Amendment's requirement of "due process" in the deprivation of "liberty". The application of the dual model to this debate frames it as a debate whether the due process clause establishes a second-order (exclusionary) consideration (a due process *right*) or only a first-order consideration to be balanced with other valid first-order considerations (a due process *interest*).

Nineteenth-century jurisprudence and the *Lochner* Court interpreted the due process clause as establishing a second-order (exclusionary) consideration. The due process clause was interpreted as excluding certain considerations from governmental interference with individual liberty and, consequently, as invalidating laws based on such motives: no balancing was involved.[12] In *Lochner v. New York*,[13] the due process clause was interpreted by the majority as excluding any governmental interference with liberty of contract on the basis of the wish to regulate the labor market or to protect workers from exploitation by employers. The Court interpreted the due process clause as excluding any such "redistributive" considerations from animating government decision making, rather than calling for a balance between redistributive considerations and the consideration of individual liberty.[14]

On the other hand, critics of the *Lochner* Court argued that the due process clause did not create such second-order considerations, but only a first-order consideration to be balanced with other first-order considerations. Consider the words of one of the foremost critics of the Court at the time, Roscoe Pound:

[The Fourteenth Amendment is] imposed [as] a standard on the legislator. It sa[ys] to him that if he trenched upon these individual interests he must not do so arbitrarily. His action must have some basis in reason. It is submitted that that basis must be the one upon which common law has always sought to proceed, the one implied in the very term "due process of law," namely, a weighing or balancing of the various interests which overlap or come in conflict and a rational reconciling or adjustment.[15]

---

[12] For the claim that late nineteenth-century and early twentieth-century due process jurisprudence did not involve balancing, see Aleinikoff, "Age of Balancing", *supra* note 5 at 949–952.

[13] 198 U.S. 45 (1905).

[14] The only valid bases of governmental interference, allowed by the Due Process Clause, according to the *Lochner* Court, were those concerned with the promotion of "safety, health . . . and the general welfare of the public." The Court argued that these were not the real purposes behind the law in question: "[M]any laws of this character while passed under what is claimed to be the police power for the purpose of protecting the public health or welfare are in reality passed from other motives." Ibid. at 53.

[15] Roscoe Pound, "A Survey of Social Interests," 57 *Harv. L. Rev.* 1 at 4 (1943).

Consider further Pound's critique of the Court's exclusionary interpretation of the due process clause:

> The "rights" of which Mr. Justice McKenna spoke [the right to "liberty" protected by the Fourteenth Amendment] were not legal rights in the same sense as my legal right to the integrity of my physical person or my legal right to ownership in my watch. They were individual wants, individual claims, individual interests, which it was felt ought to be secured through legal rights or through some other legal machinery. . . . Thus, the public policy of which Mr. Justice McKenna spoke is seen to be something at least on no lower plane than the so-called rights.[16]

Pound's endorsement of balancing should be interpreted as a claim that the Fourteenth Amendment's due process clause is a first-order consideration or, as he puts it, a consideration of "public policy." As a first-order consideration, it stands at "no lower plane" than other first-order considerations of public policy. It is a claim for the furtherance of a certain social good (individual liberty) to be balanced with claims for the furtherance of other social goods, such as the regulation of the labor market and protection of workers from exploitation.

The Court eventually endorsed the critics' view of the due process clause. This famous shift in the Court's jurisprudence is understood by the dual model as a shift in the interpretation of the due process clause from the status of second-order (exclusionary) consideration to that of a first-order consideration.[17]

A similar historical move occurred in the area of free speech in the 1950s and 1960s. The right to free speech, protected by the First Amendment, has shifted in the Court's jurisprudence from the status of a second-order (exclusionary) consideration (a free speech *right*) to the status of a first-order consideration to be balanced with other first-order considerations (a free speech *interest*). The promoters of this shift were Justices Frankfurter and Harlan of the American Supreme Court and Judge Learned Hand of the American Court of Appeals for the Second Circuit. Justice Black, on the other hand, strongly objected to this shift in the Court's jurisprudence and the use of balancing in free speech jurisprudence.

---

[16] Ibid. at 4 (emphasis added).

[17] Duncan Kennedy describes this shift in private law jurisprudence in similar terms: "One of the most striking developments of the 1940s was the transformation of the 'formalist' requirements of the will theory . . . into mere policies to be balanced within the larger analysis." Duncan Kennedy, "The Disenchantment of Logically Formal Legal Rationality, or, Max Weber's Sociology in the Genealogy of the Contemporary Mode of Western Legal Thought," 55 *Hastings L.J.* 1031 at 1073 (2004).

Consider Justice Black's interpretation of the First Amendment in *Dennis v. United States*[18] as securing a regime of complete "unfettered communication of ideas": "Undoubtedly, a governmental policy of unfettered communication of ideas does entail dangers. To the Founders of this Nation, however, the benefits derived from free expression were worth the risk. They embodied this philosophy in the First Amendment's command that 'Congress shall make no law . . . abridging the freedom of speech, or of the press.'"[19] This interpretation of the First Amendment presents free speech as an exclusionary consideration (a free speech right) that excludes governmental action designed to regulate public opinion; as such, it rejects balancing. The following by Black further clarifies this point: "[T]he idea of 'balancing away' First Amendment freedoms appears to me to be wholly inconsistent with the view strongly espoused by Justice Holmes and Brandeis, that the best test of truth is the power of the thought to get itself accepted in the competition of the market."[20]

On the other hand, Justices Frankfurter and Harlan, regularly on the Court's majority in these cases, interpreted the First Amendment as a first-order consideration (a free speech interest) to be balanced with other considerations. The clearest example of this view is captured by Hand's dictum that the First Amendment is "too uncommunicative – too lacking in guidelines – to be treated as law."[21] Hand argued that the First Amendment, as with other provisions of the American Bill of Rights, should be interpreted as "[a] merely hortatory suggestion, as it were, to those officials to whom the Constitution has entrusted power and competence that here is a goal – among others – which these officials should respect in the exercise of their prudential, managerial functions."[22] The First Amendment, according to this interpretation, does not establish an exclusionary principle but rather outlines a first-order goal that should be considered, amongst other goals, in the exercise of governmental powers. It calls for a balance between the interest of speech and other valid interests of government.

Harlan and Frankfurter's views, although not as blunt as Hand's, similarly interpreted free speech as establishing a first-order consideration. Consider Harlan's view in *Konigsberg v. State Bar*: "Throughout its history this Court has

[18] 341 U.S. 494 (1951) (hereinafter *Dennis*).   [19] Ibid. at 580.
[20] *Konigsberg v. State Bar*, 366 US 36 (1961) at 62 (hereinafter *Konigsberg*).
[21] "The Spirit of Liberty" 177–178 (1952), quoted in Wallace Mendelson, "On the Meaning of the First Amendment: Absolutes in the Balance," 50 *Colum. L. Rev.* at 826 (1963) (hereinafter Mendelson, "Meaning").
[22] Learned Hand, *The Bill of Rights* (1958) at chapters II, III as rephrased by Charles Fried in Charles Fried, "Two Concepts of Interests: Some Reflections on the Supreme Court's Balancing Test," 76 *Harv. L. Rev.* 755 at 722 (1963) (hereinafter Fried, "Two Concepts").

consistently recognized . . . [that] constitutionally protected freedom of speech
is narrower than an unlimited license to talk." Harlan continues: "[When]
constitutional protections are asserted against the exercise of valid governmental powers a reconciliation must be affected and that perforce requires an
appropriate weighing of the respective interests involved."[23]

Harlan interpreted the First Amendment as protecting a first-order "license
to talk". As such, for Harlan, this interest is necessarily limited and subject to
balancing with other valid governmental interests.

Mainly or Solely First- or Second-Order Considerations? Further Analysis of Normative Debates

The previous section interpreted normative debates on balancing as debates
concerning the question whether certain constitutional provisions should be
interpreted as first- or second-order considerations. Even within each of these
views, there can be different levels of stringency regarding the interpretation
of the constitutional provision and the role of balancing, either at the level of
a specific right or at the level of all constitutional rights generally.

The application of the dual model to Black's rejection of balancing, for
example, would require that we ask whether he meant to say that the First
Amendment should be interpreted *solely* as a second-order (exclusionary)
consideration or only *principally* as such. The first interpretation would reject
balancing altogether in the interpretation of the right; the second would allow
some balancing. Black was not clear on this point. His jurisprudence, however,
seems to favor the second interpretation. It seems that Black held the view that
the First Amendment not only acts as a second-order consideration to exclude
a number of first-order considerations, but also that it protects the first-order
interest of speech and thus allows balancing in some cases.[24] This view is
shared by several modern constitutional writers, who, like Black, regard the
First Amendment as principally, but not solely, an exclusionary principle.[25]

---

[23] *Konigsberg, supra* note 19 at 49–51.
[24] Kalven refers to cases in which Black did indeed balance as proof to the fact that Black accepted
balancing, but only in cases where he believed that the government "attempted no regulation
of the content of speech and [was] *neither openly nor surreptitiously aimed at speech.*" Harry
Kalven, Jr., "Upon Rereading Mr. Justice Black on the First Amendment," 14 *U.C.L.A. L. Rev.*
428 at 444 (1963) (hereinafter Kalven, "Rereading").
[25] See Richard H. Pildes, "Avoiding Balancing: The Role of Exclusionary Reasons in Constitutional Law," 45 *Hastings L.J.* 711 (1994) (hereinafter Pildes, "Avoiding Balancing"): "A focus on
defining 'excluded reasons' will not completely eliminate balancing"; Elena Kagan, "Private
Speech, Public Purpose: The Role of Governmental Motive in First Amendment Doctrine,"
63 *U. Chi. L. Rev.* 413 at 415 (1996) (hereinafter Kagan, "Private Speech"): "Some aspects of

Harlan's interpretation of the First Amendment as a first-order consideration must be similarly qualified. Although Harlan regarded the First Amendment to be principally about the interest in free speech (a first-order consideration), he seems to have allowed for its interpretation as a second-order (exclusionary) consideration invalidating direct regulation of opinion.[26] The debate between Harlan and Black can therefore be interpreted as a debate considering the centrality of cases of regulation of speech that involve free speech as a second-order consideration (second-order, exclusionary cases). For Black, such cases were the main concern of the First Amendment; for Harlan there were relatively few and far between.

Other constitutional writers propose a more stringent interpretation of the First Amendment. Some argue that the First Amendment protects *only* the second-order consideration against the suppression of opinion and not the first-order consideration of more speech. Consider the following by Edwin Baker:

> The right [of free speech] would not be a right to speak but a right to have the government not aim at suppressing speech. . . . [Therefore] the government's use of a time, place or manner regulation [of speech] should not in itself be taken as a limitation on the right of speech. Rather, an abridgment or limitation occurs only if the restriction of expressive conduct is the government's purpose.[27]

According to this view, some burdens on the first-order consideration (the interest of more speech) raise no constitutional concern at all. This view would therefore regard cases of indirect regulation of speech, such as restrictions of time, place, and manner of speech (first-order free speech cases) not as marginal to free speech law, but as outside its scope.[28]

First Amendment law resist explanation in terms of motive." Both Kagan and Pildes stress the centrality of motive review and exclusionary invalidation of illegitimate motives in First Amendment law. However, both writers allow some room for the first-order interpretation of the First Amendment and balancing. Robert Post seems similarly to hold the view that whereas the invalidation of content-based regulation is the norm, cases such as *Schneider* should allow for balancing. Robert Post, "Recuperating First Amendment Doctrine," 47 *Stan. L. Rev.* 1249 at 1256 (1995) (hereinafter Post, "Recuperating").

[26] See Harlan's opinion in *Konigsberg, supra* note 19 at 50: "[Balancing is applicable only to] general regulatory statues, not intended to control the content of speech but incidentally limiting its unfettered exercise."

[27] C. Edwin Baker, "Limitations on Basic Human Rights – A View from the United States," in Armand de Mestral et al. (eds.), *The Limitation of Human Rights in Comparative Constitutional Law* (1986) at 75, 80, 87 (hereinafter Baker, "Limitations").

[28] For a similar view, see Jed Rubenfeld, "The First Amendment's Purpose," 53 *Stan. L. Rev.* 767 (2001) (hereinafter Rubenfeld, "The First Amendment").

A similar view can be found in the interpretation of the commerce clause. Donald Regan has argued that the commerce clause should be interpreted as protecting *only* the (second-order) right against protectionist governmental motives. Infringements of the (first-order) interest of free interstate commerce are therefore not protected at all by the commerce clause, and raise no constitutional concern: "When we say every producer ought to have access to all the country's markets, what we mean is just that he should not be shut out of any market by preferential trade regulations directed against him as a foreigner.... If [a] law incidentally diverts some business to local producers, that is a matter of no constitutional significance."[29] The same debate can be detected at a more general level. Several constitutional writers have argued that the entire Bill of Rights should be interpreted as guaranteeing only first-order considerations or only second-order (exclusionary) considerations. Thus, Hand's view of the Bill of Rights, reviewed earlier, can be described as the view that *all* rights included in the Bill of Rights should be regarded only as first-order "hortatory suggestions" for the legislator. A similar view is promoted by Justice Stone, writing that "the great constitutional guarantees of personal liberty and of property . . . are but statements of standards. . . . They do not prescribe formulas to which governmental action must conform."[30]

Wallace Mendelson held a similar view, and argued that Madison also viewed the Bill of Rights in this way.[31] On the other hand, Laurent Frantz,[32] Charles Fried,[33] as well as several more recent constitutional writers (such as Baker[34] and Richard Pildes[35]) argue that the entire Bill of Rights should be interpreted (at least mainly) as establishing exclusionary considerations on the work of government. Pildes, for example, argues that the constitutional rights generally are "about defining the kinds of considerations that are impermissible justifications for state action in different spheres."[36]

---

[29] Donald H. Regan, "The Supreme Court and State Protectionism. Making Sense of the Dormant Commerce Clause," 84 *Mich. L. Rev.* 1091 (1986) (hereinafter Regan, "The Supreme Court").

[30] Harlan F. Stone, "The Common Law in the United States," 50 *Harv. L. Rev.* 4 at 23 (1936).

[31] Mendelson, "Meaning", *supra* note 20, at 827 (quoting Madison as saying that he has "never thought the omission [of a bill of rights from the original Constitution] a material defect").

[32] Laurent B. Frantz, "The First Amendment in the Balance" 71 *Yale L.J.* 1424 (1962).

[33] Fried, "Two Concepts", *supra* note 22 at 773: "The adjudication, therefore, must proceed on the basis of an inquiry into the role allocated by the Constitution to both parties and this inquiry in turn can only be discharged by the formulation of rules defining the limits of the respective competences."

[34] Baker, "Limitations," *supra* note 27.

[35] Pildes, "Avoiding Balancing," *supra* note 25.   [36] Ibid. at 712.

III. SHOULD THE COURT BALANCE?

The question whether rights generally or a specific right should be interpreted as first-order or second-order considerations can be analytically separated from the question whether *courts* should use balancing. Thus, certain normative claims on balancing can be interpreted as follows: (i) notwithstanding that the constitutional rights provision is interpreted as a first-order consideration to be balanced with other valid considerations, courts should not balance because they should leave balancing to the legislator; (ii) notwithstanding that the constitutional rights provision is interpreted as a second-order consideration that excludes illegitimate governmental motives, courts should balance because balancing can "smoke out" illegitimate governmental motives. This section reviews both these options, and shows examples of their use.

Should the Court Balance in First-Order Cases? Judicial Deference in the Use of Balancing

Some of the early endorsements of the idea of balancing rights were coupled with the view that courts should not balance. This was the view taken by the proponents of balancing such as Holmes, Pound, Hand, and Frankfurter, all of whom were associated with the legal pragmatism and progressivism movements. Although they conceded that rights, such as due process (Pound and Holmes) and freedom of speech (Hand and Frankfurter) were balanceable, they regarded this as a reason for the Supreme Court to exercise judicial restraint and leave the balancing process to the legislature. Indeed, they saw the *very fact of the balanceability* of rights as a reason for the court to leave balancing to the legislature. Frankfurter, for example, singled out free speech cases as entailing balancing, but argued that "[i]t is not our province to choose among competing considerations"[37] and that the "[p]rimary responsibility for adjusting the interests which compete in the situation before us of necessity belongs to the Congress."[38] In turn, Holmes argued that only when the Constitution is absolutely clear should courts exercise judicial review, indicating that in cases of balancing the Constitution leaves the matter open to legislative determination.[39] Indeed, for some time, the entire doctrine of balancing was

---

[37] *Minersville School Dist. v. Gobitis*, 310 U.S. 586 at 598 (1940).

[38] *Dennis, supra* note 18 at 525.

[39] "I think that the word liberty in the Fourteenth Amendment is perverted when it is held to prevent the natural outcome of a dominant opinion, unless it can be said that a rational and fair man necessarily would admit that the statute proposed would infringe fundamental principles as they have been understood by the traditions of our people and our law." Holmes J., dissenting, *Lochner v. New York*, 198 U.S. 45 at 76 (1906).

associated in American constitutional law with the notion of judicial restraint and not with activist judicial review.[40]

Pragmatist thinkers were motivated on the one hand by anti-conceptualism and anti-formalism, which brought them to reject absolutes and adopt balancing in the interpretation of rights, and on the other hand by a deep suspicion the ability of "grand" theories to answer logically or once and for all deep moral disagreements and to arbitrate between different conceptions of the good. The second of these motivations brought pragmatists to adopt the view that it is best to leave balancing to "the People" through their political representatives, rather than to entrust the exercise to the judiciary.

Today, the conception of balancing espousing judicial restraint has all but disappeared, and any claim for balancing is almost always presumed to place the task in the hands of the courts.[41] However, echoes of the former view can be detected in the modern phenomenon of judicial minimalism.

Judicial minimalism, advocated by American constitutional scholar Cass Sunstein,[42] draws on the heritage of the legal pragmatists and promotes minimalist judicial decision making whereby judgments resolve only what is necessary in order to answer the dispute, leaving the "big" questions to be decided by the democratic process or the incremental evolution of precedent. Minimalism, in this way, rejects absolutes in law and prefers balancing grounded in the specific facts of the case. But in addition, minimalism also advocates judicial restraint and leaving matters to be decided by organs others than the courts. In a recent case, Chief Justice Roberts rejected the majority's categorical and rule-based interpretation of the Eighth Amendment. He argued that the rule created by the majority was "applicable well beyond the particular facts" of the case and preferred instead a balancing approach limited to the circumstances before the Court.[43] The outcome of his balancing was that the

---

[40] See, e.g., Craig R. Ducat, *Modes of Constitutional Interpretation* (1978) at 130–136 (discussing balancing as a necessary result of the judicial restraint theory).

[41] The earliest case to move to the current interpretation, equating the first-order interpretation of rights, with judicial balancing is *Schneider v. State* 308 U.S. 147 (1939) at 161: "And so, as cases arise, the delicate and difficult task falls upon the courts to weigh the circumstances and to appraise the substantiality of the reasons advanced in support of the regulation of the free enjoyment of the rights."

[42] Cass R. Sunstein, "Incompletely Theorized Agreements," 103 *Harv. L. Rev.* 1733 (1995); Cass R. Sunstein, "Foreword: Leaving Things Undecided," 10 *Harv. L. Rev.* 6 (1996); Cass Sunstein, *One Case at a Time: Judicial Minimalism on the Supreme Court* (1999); Cass R. Sunstein, "Minimalism at War," [2004] *Sup. Ct. Rev.* 47.

[43] *Graham v. Florida*, 560 U.S. __ (2010), Chief Justice Roberts criticized the Court for using the *Graham*'s case "as a vehicle to proclaim a new constitutional rule – applicable well beyond the particular facts of *Graham*'s case" and argued that such a categorical approach "is unnecessary as it is unwise". Ibid. at 9–10.

Supreme Court should not intervene with decisions taken by state legislatures and state courts: the federal courts should adopt a "highly deferential 'narrow proportionality' approach" that, inter alia, "emphasize[s] the primacy of the legislature in setting sentences." "Such an approach," continued Roberts, "does not grant [federal] judges blanket authority to second-guess decisions made by legislatures or sentencing courts."[44] The Court should exercise judicial restraint, as the law should evolve from the "bottom up" rather than be imposed from above by the Supreme Court.

Should the Court Balance in Second-Order Cases? Balancing as a Method for Smoking-Out Illegitimate Motives

Constitutional writers who interpret rights as solely second-order considerations regularly also argue that the Court should never balance such rights. To account for the use of balancing by the Court, they often argue that the Court's balancing should be interpreted in such cases as a tool for smoking out or finding evidence of invalid governmental objectives that are excluded under the particular right.

Consider the following claim by Burt Neuborne: "I suspect that any judge, lacking hard evidence of motive, uses the relative insignificance of the government interests, the existence of alternatives, and the weakness of the causal nexus between speech and harm as an evidentiary shorthand that generates a degree of doubt as to the censures' true motive."[45] The argument presented by Neuborne can be reframed as follows: if we take free speech to be a second-order consideration, then it excludes any censorship of speech that is motivated by opposition to the message delivered. Yet, such motives can be concealed by the government by arguing that the injury to free speech is incidental to another proclaimed purpose. But if the government's true aim differs from its proclaimed purpose, the means it uses will usually not be well suited to the latter, the proposed measure might be over-inclusive or under-inclusive in relation to the objectives sought, and the importance of the declared aim could be relatively trivial in comparison to the harm to free speech. The balancing process can effectively uncover the pursuit of an illegitimate purpose by the government.[46]

---

[44] Ibid. at 2.
[45] Burt Neuborne, "Notes for a Theory of Constrained Balancing in First Amendment Cases: An Essay in Honor of Tome Emerson," 38 *Case West. Res. L. Rev.* 576 at 582 (1988).
[46] Compare with Laurence Tribe: "[O]ver-breadth and vagueness analyses [often associated with balancing tests] serve as quick and easy substitutes for the examination of improper legislative and administrative motive," Laurence H. Tribe, *American Constitutional Law* (1978) at 572–585.

Several constitutional writers argue that most of the cases in which the Court has used balancing in free speech law are actually about the smoking-out of illegitimate purposes, rather than real balancing.[47] In such cases, the Court *says* it is balancing. It *says* that the interest of free speech outweighs the government's interest, or that the government's interest is not important enough to justify the infringement of speech. Thus, the Court appears to be interpreting the case as a balancing case. It appears to be balancing between speech as a first-order consideration and the government's first-order consideration. But what the Court actually *means* is that the government aimed at a purpose other than its proclaimed purpose, and that this other purpose is excluded by the second-order right of free speech. It is only because the Court finds it hard to prove that the government's real motive is illegitimate that it frames the case as a first-order balancing case. Consider the following interpretation of Black's jurisprudence by Kalven: "He may, however, be saying merely that in cases where the regulation has an impact on speech content but an ostensible purpose not keyed to speech, he simply does not believe the ostensible purpose and read the measure as one designed to limit freedom of speech."[48] A similar analysis has been offered in other areas of constitutional law, as well. Under the commerce clause jurisprudence, Regan has argued that "we might engage in … balancing … simply as a means of smoking out protectionist purposes."[49] In the Equal Protection Clause context, Jed Rubenfeld asserts that balancing has been "applied to racial classifications in order to 'smoke out' those classifications that were 'in fact motivated by illegitimate notions of racial inferiority' or 'prejudice'".[50] Both are claiming that the respective constitutional provisions are second-order considerations excluding illegitimate motives. Both allow balancing only as a means for smoking-out such purposes.

IV. MAPPING THE DIFFERENT POSITIONS

The application of the dual model to normative debates concerning the role of balancing suggests that claims respecting balancing can be categorized into

---

[47] See Kagan, "Private Speech" *supra* note 25 at 453–456; Rubenfeld, "The First Amendment," *supra* note 28 at 786; Post, "Recuperating," *supra* note 25 at 1256.

[48] Kalven, "Rereading" *supra* note 24 at 444.

[49] Regan, "The Supreme Court," *supra* note 29 at 1105. See also, the following by Regan: "Less restrictive alternative analysis can itself be part of an indirect approach to the question of legislative purpose." Ibid. at 1107.

[50] Rubenfeld, "The First Amendment," *supra* note 25 at 786, quoting from *City of Richmond v. J.A. Croson Co.*, 488 U.S. 469 at 493 (1989) (plurality opinion). See also Jed Rubenfeld, "Affirmative Action," 107 *Yale L.J.* 427 at 436–443 (1997).

four major claims: (1) rights are first-order considerations and courts *should* balance; (2) rights are first-order considerations and courts *should not* balance; (3) rights are second-order considerations and courts *should not* balance; and (4) rights are second-order considerations and courts *should* balance to smoke out illegitimate purposes.

Only the first of these four claims (claim 1) could be termed a *strong* position on balancing, in the sense that it not only supports balancing but views it as the most central doctrine within rights adjudication. The other three claims either reject balancing or assign it a limited role. In addition, as described earlier,[51] there could be middle positions that do not view *all* rights or *all* instances of a particular right as falling under a first-order or a second-order interpretation. In such cases, the question whether the position is strong or weak would depend on the centrality of first-order or second-order cases in constitutional law. Thus, even the first position would not be as strong if it were combined with the view that only some rights or only some instances of rights should be interpreted as first-order considerations. It would be a stronger position if it viewed all rights and all instances of rights as first-order considerations and held the view that courts should always balance.

Note also that this categorization finds surprising coalitions between seeming opponents on the issue of balancing. Such a coalition can be found between proponents of a literalist or stringent interpretation of rights, such as Black, Frantz, and modern-day Justice Scalia (claim 3), and proponents of indeterminacy or vagueness in the interpretation of rights such as Frankfurter, Hand, and Harlan and modern-day minimalist judges (claim 2). Although the members of the first group of jurists (Black et al.) are known as rule-based interpreters and, correspondingly, opponents of balancing, and the second (Frankfurter et al.) as standard-based interpreters and, therefore, as proponents of balancing, both groups argue for a similar result: courts should not balance. The first group of jurists arrives at this conclusion by arguing that constitutional rights are second-order considerations; the second group argues that rights are first-order considerations but that courts should leave the balancing to the legislator. Both groups also hold a similar jurisprudential view of the role of the courts: courts should not balance in first-order cases because balancing involves questions of policy that should be left to the legislator. Because the second group (Frankfurter et al.) argues that all rights are first-order considerations, it would support judicial deference. In turn, because the first group (Black et al.) views all rights as second-order considerations, it would

---

[51] See 405–407 in this chapter.

support a stance of judicial activism, but by means of rules and exclusionary considerations and not balancing.

However, the view that balancing can be used as a smoking-out device, even in exclusionary-type cases (claim 4: Neuborne, Rubenfeld), is very different in its practical implications from the view that courts should be mainly concerned with first-order cases (claim 1). For although the first view allows for some balancing, it substantially limits its scope. It would allow balancing only if there is doubt respecting the legitimacy of the government's motive. Cases that raise no such doubts would not call for balancing. Rubenfeld, for example, argues that "as a smoking-out device, [balancing is] triggered only upon strong suspicion of an impermissible, speech-suppressing purpose."[52] Furthermore, balancing changes its nature under such interpretation. It does not stand on its own, but functions only as an evidentiary tool, subordinate to another principle: the second-order consideration excluding illegitimate motives.[53]

V. WEAKER AND STRONGER POSITIONS ON BALANCING

The main objective of this chapter has been to identify the different positions on balancing that have played out in American constitutional law. I would now like to use this typology to differentiate between the ways balancing is perceived and used in American and European (especially German) constitutional systems.

The stronger position on balancing reflects its role in European-based systems; in American constitutional law, uses of balancing consist mainly of different combinations of the weaker positions. Moshe Cohen-Eliya and I identified this difference in the role of balancing in an earlier article, and termed it a difference between *inherent* balancing and *bounded* balancing.[54] We argued that the different political and legal cultures in the United States and Germany shaped different functions and roles for balancing and proportionality within these two countries.

German political theory emphasizes the embeddedness of the person in a community that shares common values and expresses solidarity toward all members. This organic and communitarian conception of the state, which views the relationship between the state and citizen as based on trust and cooperation, and the purpose of the state as the realization of common shared

---

[52] Rubenfeld, "The First Amendment," *supra* note 25 at 786.

[53] See *infra* note 54 and accompanying text.

[54] Moshe Cohen-Eliya and Iddo Porat, "The Hidden Foreign Law Debate in Heller: Proportionality Approach in American Constitutional Law," 46 *San Diego L. Rev.* 367 (2009).

values, creates a central and inherent role for balancing (and proportionality).[55] Balancing under this conception is an essential, basic, and indispensable legal tool, as it is the means by which society, through its courts, achieves harmony between its different values.[56] The German Federal Constitutional Court has gone as far as stating that proportionality emerges "basically from the nature of constitutional rights themselves."[57] The judiciary, furthermore, is assigned the role of deciding these conflicts, and this assignment is relatively unproblematic: the judiciary, like the other organs of the state, is not viewed with suspicion and balancing is perceived to be objective and formalized.[58]

It is in such legal and political culture that balancing appears in its strong sense. In European constitutional systems such as Germany, it is both the case that rights generally (that is, all rights in principle) are perceived as first-order considerations and that the courts, rather than the legislator, are assigned with performing the balancing.

Robert Alexy's writings, which are amongst the most representative accounts of the conception of balancing in German constitutional law, and arguably in European constitutional systems more generally, represent this position on balancing. According to Alexy, rights are principles; they are requirements for optimization.[59] They never exclude one another or the realization of other

---

[55] The German fundamental concept of the *Rechtsstaat* – "a state governed by law" – differs from the common law concept of rule of law, in that it is tied to an organic conception of the state that seeks to integrate state and society. See Donald Kommers, *The Constitutional Jurisprudence of the Federal Republic of Germany* (2nd ed., 1997) at 36. The ideas go back to the Weimar republic and even earlier. In his influential writings, Rudolf Smend argued that the role of the constitution and constitutional interpretation is to integrate society around shared values. On Smend's influential integration theory, see Stefan Korioth, "Rudolph Smend: Introduction," in *Weimar: A Jurisprudence of Crisis* (Arthur J. Jacobson & Bernhard Schlink eds., Belinda Cooper et al. trans., 2000) at 207. See also, Mathias Reimann, "Nineteenth Century German Legal Science," (1990) 31 *B.C. L. Rev.* (discussing the influence of Hegelian and communitarian ideas on nineteenth-century German legal science).

[56] As first stated by Konrad Hesse, the late Constitutional Court justice: "The principle of the constitution's unity requires the optimization of [values in conflict]: Both legal values need to be limited so that each can attain its optimal effect. In each concrete case, therefore, the limitations must satisfy the principle of proportionality; that is, they may not go any further than necessary to produce a concordance of both legal values." Konrad Hesse, *Grundzuge Des Verfassungsrechts Der Bundesrepublik Deutschland* (1988) 27, English translation from Kommers, Ibid. at 36.

[57] 19 BVerfGE 342 at 348 (1965).

[58] See Jacco Bomhoff, "Luth's 50th Anniversary: Some Comparative Observations on the German Foundations of Judicial Balancing," (2008) 9 *German L.J.* 121 at 124.

[59] "[P]rinciples are norms requiring that something be realized to the greatest extent possible, given the factual and legal possibilities at hand. Thus, principles are *optimization* requirements. As such, they are characterized by the fact that they can be satisfied to varying degrees, and that the appropriate degree of satisfaction depends not only on what is factually possible but

values or interests and are never realized in their entirety because they have to be balanced with other rights-as-principles that also require optimization. Alexy's view on rights is therefore very close to the idea of first-order considerations. Alexy's scheme is a clear example of the strong position on balancing in that he claims that *all* rights are principles – indeed, their nature as principles (that is, as first-order considerations) is what distinguishes rights from other legal considerations. According to Alexy, balancing "logically follows from the nature of [rights as] principles; it can be deduced from them."[60]

In American constitutional law, on the other hand, the different uses of balancing reflect the weaker positions. In contrast to the German organic conception of the state, the American conception of the state is characterized by a well-known distrust of government, deriving from the idea of individual autonomy and self-rule.[61] This distrust extends to all branches of government, including the judiciary, and lies at the base of the particularly American emphasis on the separation of powers: because no institution can be trusted not to overstep its legitimate bounds, power must be decentralized by clearly defining the limits of each branch of government and clearly separating them.[62] Consequently, American constitutional culture focuses on setting limits to all (including judicial) power and distinguishing the judicial role from the roles of the other branches of government.[63] Rights are accordingly framed as categorical constraints on governmental power or as rules of the democratic game, not as substantive values. As rules of the game, rights must be couched in terms of clear guidelines, lest the judiciary impose its own conception of the good on the polity. Unlike the German organic and communitarian conception of the state as aimed at furthering shared goals, the American model portrays the state as a neutral framework for individualistic conceptions of the good that compete with each other through the democratic game. The Constitution supplies the infrastructure for democratic play to take place, but ideas and ideologies must not be governed or imposed through the Constitution; they must be hashed out through the democratic process.

---

also on what is legally possible. Rules aside, the legal possibilities are determined essentially by opposing principles. For this reason, principles, each taken alone, always comprise a merely prima facie requirement." Robert Alexy, "The Construction of Constitutional Rights," (2010) 4 *L. & Ethics Human Rights* 21.

[60] Robert Alexy, *A Theory of Constitutional Rights* (2002) at 66.

[61] The most distinct exposition on the centrality of distrust in American political culture can be found in John Hart Ely, *Democracy and Distrust* (1980).

[62] See, e.g., Cass Sunstein, *The Partial Constitution* (1993) at 21, explaining the intention of the framers that "in a large republic, the various factions would offset each other".

[63] See, e.g., Alexander M. Bickel, *The Least Dangerous Branch* (1962).

Such conception of the polity and rights is basically antithetical to balancing. Balancing is not excluded from American constitutional law, but it is usually assigned a marginal role as manifested in the weaker positions on balancing. The basic American conception of rights remains alien to the idea of optimization and is instead based on a categorical conception of rights as trumps, as deontological constraints, or as exclusionary considerations.[64]

To conclude: the strong position and combinations of the weaker positions entail different justifications of balancing in a democracy. Weaker versions of balancing can be justified within a framework that aims at a strong separation between politics and law, and a clear demarcation between the reasoning modes of the judiciary and the political branches. By departing from this framework, balancing cannot be the paradigmatic tool for constitutional law. The stronger position on balancing must find its justification in views that do not separate so starkly between legal and political decision making and that allows for courts to be major players in deciding society's conflicts.

---

[64] Robert Post, "Constitutional Scholarship in the United States," 7 *Int'l. J. Con. Law* 416 (2009).

Index

Printed in Great Britain
by Amazon